PRAISE FOR

THE POPE AND MUSSOLINI

"A book whose narrative strength is as impressive as its moral subtlety . . . [David] Kertzer has uncovered a fascinating tale of two irascible—and often irrational—potentates, and gives us an account of some murky intellectual finagling, and an often startling investigation of the exercise of power."   —*The Guardian*

"Vividly recounted . . . Kertzer had access to recently opened Vatican archives regarding Pius XI, and his thorough research goes a long way in overturning conventional notions about Catholic Church resistance to Mussolini."   —*USA Today*

"Stunning . . . remarkable . . . Kertzer authoritatively banishes decades of denial and uncertainty about the Vatican's relationship with Italy's fascist state."   —*The Christian Science Monitor*

"At once sweeping and nuanced . . . required reading for anyone with an interest in the Roman Catholic Church and early twentieth-century European history."   —*St. Louis Post-Dispatch*

"The papacy of Pius XI [has been remembered as] a foil for discussing his successor. Kertzer's excellent volume will change [that]. . . . From the outset of his new book, Kertzer deftly reconstructs the parallel lives of Achille Ratti, who became Pius XI, and of Benito Mussolini, both men whose beginnings do not point to the historic role that they began to play in 1922. The narration unfolds along the separate political, ideological, and institutional backgrounds of the Pope's and Duce's careers and brings up in fascinating detail the issues on which their interests converged and clashed. . . . Kertzer's essential book reveals a window on this sordid history—a window that for a long time was shuttered, but will not be obscured anymore." —*The New Republic*

"[Kertzer has made] a remarkable achievement in bringing to light, through researches wide in scope and profound in depth, a previously hidden history." —*Commentary*

"Captivating . . . The pomp and shadowy intrigue of *The Pope and Mussolini* [is] a grim update on Machiavelli. . . . [The] real *Da Vinci Code*—only it's rigorously documented and far less implausible." —*San Francisco Chronicle*

"Compelling . . . Kertzer charts his own course not only by virtue of the depth of his archival research and analysis, but also by virtue of his engaging prose." —*America: The National Catholic Review*

"[Kertzer] reconstructs, as if in an historical docudrama, the paths taken by these two men who had such a great impact on the course of the twentieth century. . . . Brilliant . . . [with] pages that are enthralling for their narrative skill." —MARCO RONCALLI, *Avvenire*

"Makes a compelling case that the Catholic Church should pay greater penance for its support of Mussolini and the rise of fascism—and what they got in return. . . . Kertzer has advanced John Paul's call for 'purification of the historical memory' in a manner that the pope could probably have not imagined." —The Daily Beast

"A seedy, disturbing tale, passionately told by Kertzer, and based on new papers released by the Vatican's own archive." —*The Sunday Times* (UK)

"Fast-paced and well-written . . . This book is a readable popular history, with well-drawn characters and interesting incidental detail. It is also a serious study that incorporates the most recent scholarship made possible by the 2006 opening of the Vatican archives for the reign of Pius XI."

—*The Irish Times*

"A capstone on David Kertzer's already crucial work, *The Pope and Mussolini* carefully and eloquently advances the painful but necessary truth of Vatican failure to meet its greatest moral test. This is history for the sake of justice."

—JAMES CARROLL, National Book Award–winning author of *Constantine's Sword*

"*The Pope and Mussolini* is a riveting story from start to finish, full of startling, documented detail, and nobody is better prepared to tell it than David Kertzer."

—JACK MILES, Pulitzer Prize–winning author of *God: A Biography*

"Wholly deserving—even demanding—the adjectives 'groundbreaking,' 'courageous,' and 'captivating,' *The Pope and Mussolini* decisively challenges the received narrative about Pius XI and the Fascist leader. The relationship, in short, was one not of hostility but of mutual dependence. David Kertzer's conclusions are unflinchingly and conclusively proven, thanks to his profound and thorough research, scholarly authority, and narrative panache. This is a meticulously researched and crafted book, exquisitely written, fresh, mesmerizing, and enlightening."

—KEVIN MADIGAN, Winn Professor of Ecclesiastical History, Harvard University

"*The Pope and Mussolini* tells the story of two remarkable men, Achille Ratti, Pope Pius XI, and Benito Mussolini, Duce of Fascism. Both demanded absolute obedience. Those who knew the pope called him 'a block of granite' and 'cold as marble.' The highest prelates trembled in his presence. Mussolini, swollen with his success, became 'a statue' who listened to no one. David Kertzer tells their stories in counterpoint as they could never have been told before. The opening of the Vatican archives in 2006 and the discovery of a vast archive of Mussolini's spies in the hierarchy of the Vatican provide Kertzer staggering new evidence, and his wonderful portraits of everybody involved give this book the fascination of a great novel."

—JONATHAN STEINBERG, Walter H. Annenberg Professor of
Modern European History, University of Pennsylvania,
and New York Times bestselling author of Bismarck

"David Kertzer, who pored through the recently opened Vatican secret files, gives us a ghastly history of the poisonous alliance between a weakened Vatican and an ambitious Mussolini. The Pope's blessing gave *Il Duce* the needed credibility to take Italy and the Italian people where he wanted them to go. In exchange for that approval, the Fascists provided the Church with its only perceived bulwark against the forces of Communism and the modern age. Enter Hitler. I can imagine Machiavelli overseeing the manipulations on both sides and saying either 'Well played' or 'You go too far' or 'Beware.' David Kertzer has written a harrowing portrait of a ghastly union whose only by-product was the nightmare of World War II."

—JOHN GUARE, award-winning playwright and author of
Six Degrees of Separation

"A thoroughly engrossing story with an ever-changing cast of fascinating characters . . . Like a couple in a loveless marriage, entered into for all the wrong reasons, Pius XI and Mussolini could not get free of each other. Mussolini hated priests. Pius XI swallowed his scruples about the Duce's growing megalomania. Each reckoned that he had much to gain from the other. Beneath their endless squabbling about precedence, their continual posturing, Pius and Mussolini undermined and ultimately squandered the happiness of the millions who trusted them. Kertzer has written the definitive book on this tragic history."

—RICHARD S. LEVY, professor of history, the University of Illinois
at Chicago, and co-editor of Antisemitism: A History

"A study in selfishness and opportunism, mapping a parallel rise and fall as Fascism and Catholicism banded together . . . *The Pope and Mussolini* adds a disturbing wrinkle to one of the most influential periods in modern history."

—San Francisco Book Review

BY DAVID I. KERTZER

The Pope and Mussolini: The Secret History of
Pius XI and the Rise of Fascism in Europe

Amalia's Tale: A Poor Peasant,
an Ambitious Attorney, and a Fight for Justice

Prisoner of the Vatican: The Popes' Secret Plot to
Capture Rome from the New Italian State

The Popes Against the Jews: The Vatican's Role
in the Rise of Modern Anti-Semitism

The Kidnapping of Edgardo Mortara

Politics and Symbols: The Italian Communist
Party and the Fall of Communism

Sacrificed for Honor: Italian Infant
Abandonment and the Politics of
Reproductive Control

Ritual, Politics, and Power

Comrades and Christians: Religion and
Political Struggle in Communist Italy

THE POPE AND MUSSOLINI

THE POPE AND MUSSOLINI

THE SECRET HISTORY OF PIUS XI

AND THE RISE OF FASCISM IN EUROPE

DAVID I. KERTZER

RANDOM HOUSE TRADE PAPERBACKS · NEW YORK

2014 Random House Trade Paperback Edition

Copyright © 2014 by David I. Kertzer

Maps copyright © 2014 by Laura Hartman Maestro

Published in the United States by Random House Trade Paperbacks,
an imprint of Random House, a division of Random House LLC,
a Penguin Random House Company, New York.

RANDOM HOUSE and the HOUSE colophon are
registered trademarks of Random House LLC.

Originally published in hardcover in the United States by Random House,
an imprint and division of Random House LLC, in 2014.

LIBRARY OF CONGRESS CATALOGING-IN-PUBLICATION DATA
Kertzer, David I.
The Pope and Mussolini : the secret history of Pius XI and
the rise of Fascism in Europe / David I. Kertzer.
pages cm
Includes bibliographical references and index.
ISBN 978-0-8129-8367-8
eBook ISBN 978-0-679-64553-5
1. Pius XI, Pope, 1857–1939. 2. Mussolini, Benito, 1883–1945.
3. Fascism and the Catholic Church—Italy I. Title.
BX1377.K47 2014 322'.1094509042—dc23 2013019402

Printed in the United States of America on acid-free paper

www.atrandom.com

Book design by Barbara M. Bachman

For the three Bears
Sam, Jack, and Charlie
nipotini straordinari
From their Zaide

CONTENTS

PART THREE

MUSSOLINI, HITLER, AND THE JEWS

MAPS *of*
CENTRAL ROME *and*
VATICAN CITY

———

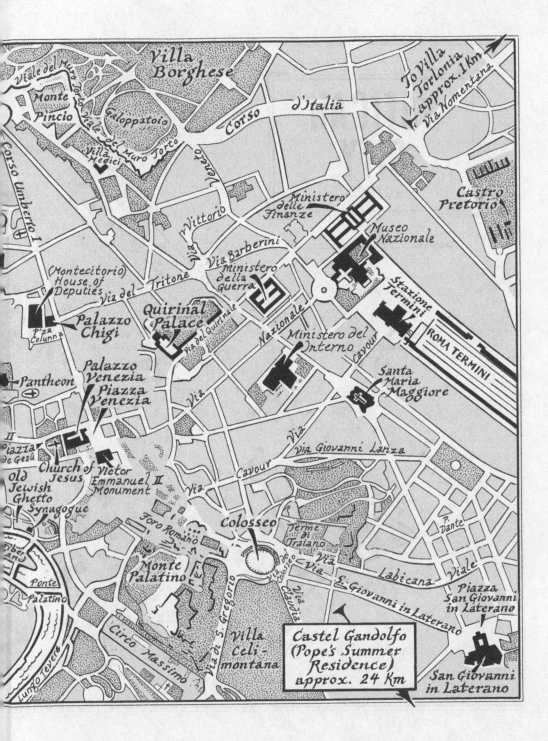

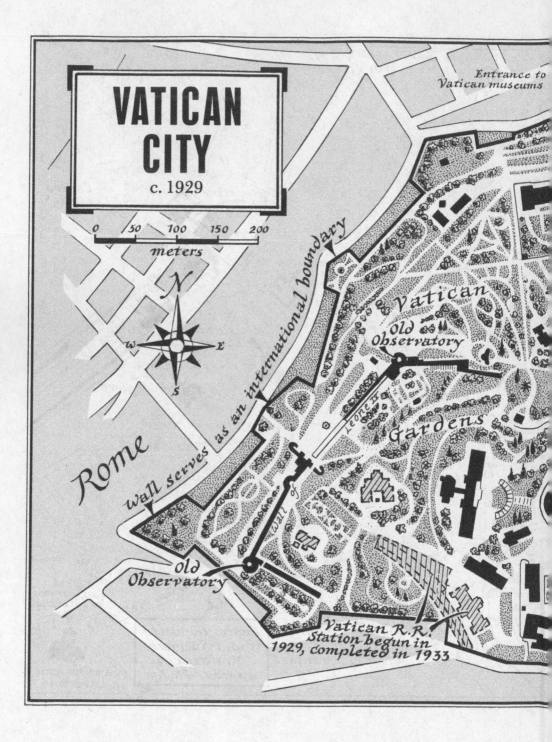

VATICAN CITY

c. 1929

0 50 100 150 200

meters

N
W — E
S

Entrance to
Vatican museums

Rome

Wall serves as an international boundary

Vatican

old
Observatory

Leone IV

Gardens

old
Observatory

Vatican R.R.
Station begun in
1929, completed in 1933

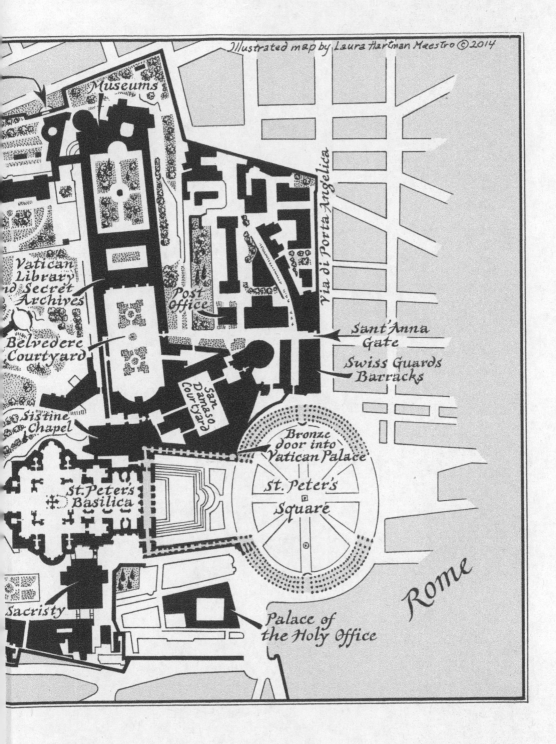

Illustrated map by Laura Hartman Maestro ©2014

Museums

Vatican
Library
and Secret
Archives

Belvedere
Courtyard

Post
Office

Via di Porta Angelica

Sant'Anna
Gate

Swiss Guards
Barracks

San
Damaso
Courtyard

Sistine
Chapel

Bronze
door into
Vatican Palace

St. Peter's
Basilica

St. Peter's
Square

Rome

Sacristy

Palace of
the Holy Office

CAST OF CHARACTERS

BALBO, ITALO (1896–1940) The swashbuckling Fascist boss of the city of Ferrara, Balbo was one of the leaders of the 1922 March on Rome. President Roosevelt awarded Balbo a Distinguished Flying Cross in 1933 when he led an expedition of twenty-four seaplanes to the United States. While his aerial heroics won him great popularity on both sides of the Atlantic, they sparked Mussolini's jealousy.

POPE BENEDICT XV (GIACOMO DELLA CHIESA) (1854–1922) Born to an aristocratic family in Genoa, Giacomo Della Chiesa rose to become archbishop of Bologna in 1913. Despite his nonpapal appearance, he was elected to succeed Pius X in 1914. He dismantled his predecessor's fierce antimodernist crusade and clerical spy force but failed in his efforts to play an effective role as peacemaker during and after the Great War.

BAUDRILLART, ALFRED (1859–1942) Catholic scholar and longtime head of the Catholic University of Paris, Baudrillart was named a bishop in 1921 and a cardinal in 1935. Keeper of a precious diary, Baudrillart worried over the intrigue surrounding the ailing Pope Pius XI as Mussolini solidified his alliance with Hitler.

BORGONGINI-DUCA, FRANCESCO (1884–1954) Born in Rome, Borgongini was appointed in 1921 to be secretary of the Congregation of Extraordinary Ecclesiastical Affairs, one of two key positions under the Vatican secretary of state. There he dealt with international affairs despite never having lived outside Rome. In 1929 Pius XI named him the Vatican's first nuncio or ambassador to Italy, a position he would occupy for over two decades. Devout and unworldly, Borgongini was an irresistible target for Mussolini's teasing.

BUFFARINI GUIDI, GUIDO (1895–1945) Elected Fascist mayor of Pisa in 1923 at age twenty-eight, Buffarini became Mussolini's undersecretary for internal affairs ten years later, responsible for the national police. A corrupt, fat bully, he took on ever greater power in the late 1930s, freeing Mussolini to focus on expanding his newly acquired Italian empire.

CACCIA DOMINIONI, CAMILLO (1877–1946) Appointed prefect of the papal household by Benedict XV in 1921, Caccia had known Achille Ratti when he and the future pope were in Milan earlier in the century. Kept on by Pius XI, charged with organizing his daily schedule and determining who would get to see him, he stood at the pope's side every day. Caccia had a terrible secret, widely known in the Vatican and among the Fascist police, that threatened him with disgrace.

CERRETTI, BONAVENTURA (1872–1933) One of the Vatican's leading diplomats, Cerretti was papal nuncio to France when Pius XI appointed him cardinal in 1926. A critic of the pope's partnership with Mussolini, he was further angered when Pius XI passed him over and named a rival as secretary of state in 1930.

CIANO, GALEAZZO (1903–1944) Son of a government minister, Ciano married Mussolini's eldest daughter, Edda, in 1930. A self-styled ladies' man, intensely disliked by Mussolini's wife, he quickly became his father-in-law's heir apparent, much to the dismay of the other Fascist leaders. After Ciano served a brief stint as minister of press and propaganda, Mussolini shocked the diplomatic world by appointing him minister of foreign affairs in 1936.

COUGHLIN, CHARLES (1891–1979) Born and ordained a Catholic priest in Canada, Coughlin used his parish in Detroit to broadcast a radio program that reached tens of millions of Americans in the 1930s. Initially a supporter of Franklin Roosevelt and social reform, he turned sharply rightward, accusing the president of being a Communist agent. An apologist for Hitler's crusade against the Jews, Coughlin was also eager to be of service to the Italian dictator.

DE VECCHI, CESARE (1884–1959) A monarchist from Turin, De Vecchi was one of the four leaders of the March on Rome. He served as Italy's first ambassador to the Holy See from 1929 to 1935. Arrogant, petty, thick-headed, and easily recognizable by his outlandish mustache, he was the object of much ridicule, not least by Mussolini. Although De Vecchi suffered through many of Pius XI's table-pounding tantrums, the pope ended up viewing him with some affection.

GASPARRI, PIETRO (1852–1934) Child of a poor family of mountain shepherds in central Italy, Gasparri became a scholar of canon law and one of the Vatican's most influential diplomats. As secretary of state first under Pope Benedict XV and then under Pius XI, the short, rotund Gasparri disguised his sharp political sense beneath a show of gregarious good humor.

GÖRING, HERMANN (1893–1946) One of the Nazi leaders closest to Hitler, he founded the Gestapo and held many top government positions in Nazi Germany. Mussolini at first dismissed him as a lunatic.

GRANDI, DINO (1895–1988) Undersecretary of the interior and then, from 1929 to 1932, Mussolini's minister of foreign affairs. The goateed Grandi was initially among the most radical of the Fascists. But the life of Italian ambassador in London (1932–39) agreed with him and would affect his view of Mussolini's increasing embrace of Nazi Germany.

HITLER, ADOLF (1889–1945) For years Hitler kept a huge bust of his hero, Benito Mussolini, in his Munich office. After becoming German chancellor in January 1933, he reached out to the Vatican in an effort to get Catholic support. Although suspicious of him, the pope was initially encouraged by his strong anti-Communist stance.

LEDÓCHOWSKI, WŁODZIMIERZ (1866–1942) Son of a Polish count and nephew of a cardinal, Ledóchowski was elected superior general—world head—of the Society of Jesus in 1915, a position he would retain until his death twenty-seven years later. A virulent anti-Semite, kindly disposed toward Fascism, he was a man Mussolini looked to for help.

MONTINI, GIOVANNI (1897–1978) As a priest in 1922, he joined the Vatican secretary of state office, where he remained for many years. In 1933 Pius XI dismissed him from his additional position as national chaplain of Italy's Catholic Action university organization but brought him back in 1937 to be one of his undersecretaries of state. In 1963 Montini would ascend to St. Peter's throne as Pope Paul VI.

MUNDELEIN, GEORGE (1872–1939) Named archbishop of Chicago in 1915 and appointed cardinal in 1924, Mundelein presided over an expanding Catholic Church and became a friend and political supporter of Franklin Roosevelt. His verbal assault on Adolf Hitler in 1937 provoked the Führer's rage.

MUSSOLINI, ARNALDO (1885–1931) Growing up sharing a corn-husk bed with Benito, Arnaldo became editor of his older brother's newspaper, *Il Popolo d'Italia*, in 1922, when Mussolini became prime minister. Every night Mussolini would phone him to discuss the next day's paper and whatever else was on his mind. Arnaldo—who unlike his brother thought of himself as a devout Catholic—was the one person Mussolini trusted fully.

MUSSOLINI, BENITO (1883–1945) Born to a modest family in a small town in Romagna, the center of Italian anarchism and socialism, Mussolini became one of the country's most prominent radical socialists in the early years of the twentieth century. In 1912 he was named national editor of the Socialist Party newspaper *Avanti!*, based in Milan. The Great War led him to break from the Socialists, establishing the Fascist movement in 1919. Formerly a fierce opponent of the Catholic Church, he recognized the benefit that a deal with the Vatican would have for his political ambitions.

MUSSOLINI, EDDA (1910–95) Edda was Mussolini's eldest, and favorite, child. Willful, impetuous, temperamental, and fond of riding horses and driving fast cars, she was much like her father. She settled down a bit in 1930 when she married Galeazzo Ciano.

MUSSOLINI, RACHELE (1890–1979) Born to a poor peasant family that lived not far from the Mussolinis, she dropped out of school at age eight and went to work as a maid. Benito became attracted to the blond, blue-eyed Rachele, whose mother was his father's mistress. Described by her daughter Edda as "the true dictator in the family," the strong-willed, semiliterate

Rachele never felt comfortable among the rich and well-connected. She would also never give up her deep aversion to the Church and the priests.

ORSENIGO, CESARE (1873–1946) A man of limited intelligence and even more limited worldview, Orsenigo was a priest in Milan when Pius XI appointed him nuncio to the Netherlands in 1922 and then to Hungary in 1925. In naming him to replace Eugenio Pacelli as nuncio to Germany in 1930, he bypassed many more qualified men of the Vatican diplomatic corps.

PACELLI, EUGENIO (1876–1958) The frail but highly intelligent child of a Roman family closely linked to the popes for generations, Pacelli joined the Vatican secretary of state office shortly after his ordination. Sent in 1917 to be papal nuncio to Munich, and from there to Berlin, he lived in Germany for a dozen years. Pius XI called him to Rome in 1929 to become cardinal and, in early 1930, to replace Pietro Gasparri as secretary of state. The cautious, soft-spoken Pacelli and the authoritarian, temperamental Pius XI developed a curious relationship. On the pope's death in 1939, he would be elected pope himself, taking the name Pius XII.

PACELLI, FRANCESCO (1872–1935) Older brother of Eugenio, Francesco Pacelli followed in their father's footsteps, becoming one of the Vatican's most prominent lawyers. Pius XI turned to him in 1926 to conduct secret negotiations with the Fascist government, aimed at ending the state of hostility that had existed between the Holy See and Italy since the nation's founding in 1861.

PETACCI, CLARA (1912–45) Daughter of a Vatican physician, the attractive, green-eyed, curly-haired Clara was twenty-four when she began her affair with the then fifty-three-year-old Mussolini. She lived for the call each day that would beckon her to their love nest at his office in Palazzo Venezia in central Rome. Her thousands of pages of diaries offer priceless insight into Mussolini.

PIGNATTI, BONIFACIO (1877–1957) Son of a count and a well-regarded career diplomat, Pignatti was Italy's ambassador to France when in 1935 he replaced Cesare De Vecchi as ambassador to the Holy See. Like most members of the pre-Fascist Italian diplomatic corps, Pignatti made the transition to serving the Fascist dictatorship without missing a beat.

POPE PIUS XI (ACHILLE RATTI) (1857–1939) The son of a silk factory supervisor from a small town north of Milan, Ratti decided as a child to become a priest. Appointed professor at Milan's Grand Seminary at age twenty-five, he soon took a position at Milan's famous Ambrosiana Library, ultimately becoming its director. In 1914 Ratti was appointed prefect of the Vatican Library, a position he assumed would be his last. But in 1918 Benedict XV unexpectedly chose him to be his envoy to Poland, where he experienced the invasion of the Red Army in the wake of the Russian revolution and developed a lifelong loathing of Communism. Recalled to Rome in 1921, he was appointed cardinal and archbishop of Milan. He had barely taken his new office when, following Benedict's death, his fellow cardinals elected him pope on their fourteenth ballot in February 1922.

POPE PIUS XII (see Eugenio Pacelli)

PIZZARDO, GIUSEPPE (1877–1970) Born near Genoa, Pizzardo joined the Vatican secretary of state office shortly after ordination. He left Rome for only three years (1909–12) to serve in the Vatican's nunciature (embassy) in Munich. Named substitute secretary of state in 1921, he replaced Borgongini as secretary of ecclesiastical affairs in 1929, a position he held until his appointment as cardinal in 1937. From 1923 until the new pope, Pius XII, replaced him in 1939, he was also the national chaplain of Italian Catholic Action, which often drew him into the crosshairs of the anticlerical wing of the Fascist movement. Pizzardo was a favorite of Pius XI but unpopular with many in the Vatican who linked his influence to his access to American Catholic money.

RATTI, ACHILLE (see Pope Pius XI)

ROSA, ENRICO, S.J. (1870–1938) A member since 1905 of the editorial group that put out the twice-monthly Jesuit journal *La Civiltà cattolica*, widely viewed as the unofficial voice of the Vatican, Rosa became its director in 1915. A close adviser of Pius XI, he was called upon by the pope to explain the Church's position on the Jews. Although initially hostile to Fascism, Rosa, on instructions from the Vatican, ended up using the pages of his journal to warn Catholics against abandoning the dictator.

SARFATTI, MARGHERITA (1880–1961) Born to a wealthy Jewish family in Venice, she developed a passion for literature and the arts. Married at eighteen to a Jewish lawyer, she and her husband moved to Milan, where she became involved in the socialist movement and met Mussolini soon after he arrived there. By the time Mussolini returned from the war in 1917, they were inseparable. Not only were they lovers, but for a decade Mussolini turned to her for advice. By the later 1920s her allure would begin to wear off.

SPELLMAN, FRANCIS (1889–1967) The son of Irish immigrants to Massachusetts, in 1925 he became the first American priest to serve in the Vatican secretary of state office. There he became close to Francesco Borgongini and later became a friend of Eugenio Pacelli. He was appointed archbishop of New York in 1939.

STARACE, ACHILLE (1889–1945) One of the few southerners among Fascism's leaders, Starace became national head of the Italian Fascist Party in 1931. A master of bad taste, lacking in intelligence, and without the faintest trace of sophistication, the sycophantic Starace would take Mussolini's cult of personality to a frightening new level.

TACCHI VENTURI, PIETRO, S.J. (1861–1956) Born to a prosperous central Italian family, Tacchi Venturi studied for the priesthood in Rome, where he joined the Jesuit order. When Pius XI and Mussolini decided they needed a secret go-between in early 1923, they chose him, and over the next sixteen years he met privately more than a hundred times with Mussolini, carrying the pope's requests.

TARDINI, DOMENICO (1881–1961) Part of the Roman clergy, he would spend much of his adult life in the Vatican secretary of state office, which he joined in 1921. Named undersecretary of ecclesiastical affairs there in 1929 under Pizzardo, be became substitute secretary of state in 1935, before taking the position of secretary for ecclesiastical affairs in 1937. A middle-of-the-roader, he blamed frictions with the Fascist regime not on Mussolini but on the anticlerics who surrounded him.

VICTOR EMMANUEL III (1869–1947) Made king of Italy at age thirty in 1900, when his father was assassinated, Victor Emmanuel III never felt secure as monarch. The object of much ridicule for his pint-size stature, he was intelligent and well informed but weak. Twice each week Mussolini put on his top hat to meet the king at Rome's Quirinal Palace to get the necessary royal signature on all new laws. Victor Emmanuel always obliged him. Although theirs was a marriage of convenience, the roughhouse Mussolini and the diminutive monarch found common ground. Not least, they shared a dim view of humanity and a visceral dislike of the clergy.

LIST OF PUBLICATIONS
AND ORGANIZATIONS

Publications

L'AVVENIRE D'ITALIA Founded in the late nineteenth century in Bologna with Pope Leo XIII's blessing, *L'Avvenire d'Italia* became the only truly national Catholic newspaper in Italy during Fascism.

LA CIVILTÀ CATTOLICA Edited by a collective of Italian Jesuits, the journal was founded in 1850 on the request of Pope Pius IX shortly after he returned to power in Rome following the revolution of 1848–49. The journal's director is appointed by the pope. Before each issue can be published—it comes out twice monthly—its proofs are reviewed and approved by the Vatican secretary of state office. In the Catholic world, the journal was read as the expression of the pope's views on the issues of the day.

L'OSSERVATORE ROMANO The daily newspaper of the Vatican, *L'Osservatore romano* was first published in 1861 as part of the effort to defend the pope's remaining territories from the newly formed Kingdom of Italy. Although it was closely overseen by the pope, a fig leaf of deniability was afforded by the formal stance that *L'Osservatore romano* was not the official organ of the Vatican. Once Mussolini solidified his dictatorship in the mid-1920s, it remained the only newspaper in Italy not subject to Fascist censorship, although when it published articles that Mussolini objected to, copies placed on sale outside the Vatican's walls were subject to seizure. *L'Osservatore romano* fulfilled its mission as the semiofficial newspaper of the Vatican by reporting on the pope's more notable meetings and remarks each day and offering news on Church activities worldwide. *La Civiltà cattolica,* by contrast, combined much longer analyses of the political issues of the day with regular book reviews and a digest of the major Italian and international political events of interest to the Church.

IL POPOLO D'ITALIA Benito Mussolini founded the daily newspaper in Milan shortly after being expelled from the Socialist Party in 1914. *Il Popolo d'Italia* became his vehicle for launching the Fascist movement five years later. When he became prime minister in 1922, he turned the editorship over to his brother Arnaldo. On Arnaldo's death in 1931, Arnaldo's son, Vito, became editor.

Organizations

CATHOLIC ACTION Created by Pius X in 1905 to provide a framework for organizing the Catholic laity, by the 1920s the organization had separate groups in Italy for men and women, boys and girls, and university students. With a national lay director appointed by the pope and an ecclesiastical overseer in the Vatican, Italian Catholic Action was organized at both the diocesan and the parish level. Mussolini remained suspicious of the organization, the only mass membership group in the country that he did not control. Pius XI, known as the "pope of Catholic Action," thought the organization essential to his efforts to Christianize Italian society.

FASCIST PARTY Launched in 1921, the Partito Nazionale Fascista (PNF) was the brainchild of Benito Mussolini. In the act of transforming what had been a looser political movement and collection of violent squads into a formal political party, Mussolini abandoned the anti-Church and antimonarchical roots of the earlier Fascist movement and turned decidedly rightward. In his early years in power, he would struggle to keep the local Fascist bosses in line. In 1928 the PNF became the only legal political party in Italy.

HOLY OFFICE Also known as the Roman Inquisition, it had its origin in 1542 as the Congregation of the Holy Roman, Universal Inquisition, founded by Pope Paul III and aimed initially at combating the Protestant Reformation. Its name was changed in 1908 to the Holy Office (Sant'Uffizio). Headed by the pope, it consisted of a group of cardinals aided by an assortment of other prelates. Its secretary, a cardinal, met regularly with the pope to discuss the cases before it. The mission of the Holy Office was to enforce doctrinal orthodoxy and stamp out heresy.

OPERA NAZIONALE BALILLA The ONB, or National Youth Organization, was founded in 1926 to socialize Italy's youth into the new Fascist ideology. It was divided into two age groups, separated by gender. The younger boys (8–13 years old) were known as *Balilla,* the older boys (14–18) *Avanguardisti.* The comparable female groups were called the Little Italian Girls and the Italian Female Youths. The Fascist youth groups threatened to undermine the Catholic youth organizations; upon their founding, the government disbanded the Catholic Boy Scouts. However, a vast network of priests was established so that all local ONB groups would have their own Catholic chaplain to lead them in religious worship alongside their Fascist indoctrination and paramilitary training.

POPULAR PARTY The Partito Popolare Italiano (PPI) was founded in 1919 as a national Catholic political party by a Sicilian priest, Luigi Sturzo, with Pope Benedict XV's approval. In the 1921 parliamentary elections, the PPI elected over 20 percent of the deputies. One of the main obstacles to the imposition of a Fascist dictatorship, the party was undermined when Pius XI made clear he was throwing his support to Mussolini. The party was disbanded in November 1926, although Mussolini would long suspect that elements of the PPI were secretly trying to reorganize in Catholic Action.

SOCIALIST PARTY Founded in 1892, the Italian Socialist Party came to dominate the left in Italy, with special strength in the north and center of the country. Divided into a reformist branch and one championing revolution—Benito Mussolini was among the leaders of the latter—the party split in 1912 in a purge of reformists. The party reached its high point in the 1919 parliamentary elections, getting almost a third of the vote and winning control of many cities and towns. In 1921 a dissident faction walked out and formed the Communist Party. The following year the party suffered another split, as the reformist wing splintered off to form the United Socialist Party. In 1924 its leader, Giacomo Matteotti, would be murdered by Fascist thugs led by an Italian American. In 1926 Mussolini outlawed the Socialist Party and its various progeny.

PROLOGUE

ROME, 1939

AILING, ELDERLY, AND HAVING BARELY SURVIVED CIRCULATORY FAILURE the previous year, Pope Pius XI begged God to grant him a few more days. He sat at his desk in his third-floor Vatican office in his white robe, a cane resting against the wall nearby. The rusted compass and barometer from his climbs to Italy's highest Alpine peaks lay on one side, a reminder of days long past. An old tuning fork remained in a drawer. It had been years since he had last taken it out. Proud of his singing voice and eager that his sense of pitch not desert him, he had practiced when he could, but only when he was sure no one was listening. Now, knowing the end was near, he went through each drawer, making sure his papers were in order.

For years the pope had enjoyed good health, and observers had marveled at his punishing schedule. He had insisted on knowing every detail of Vatican affairs and deciding everything of any significance. Now every day was a challenge, every step caused pain. At night, unable to sleep, he lay awake, his legs throbbing from varicose veins, his asthma making breathing a struggle, and worst of all, plagued by the feeling that something had gone terribly wrong.

In the daytime, light streamed into his office through the three windows that overlooked St. Peter's Square. But now it was night, and his small desk lamp cast a yellow glow over the sheets in front of him. The Lord, he thought, had kept him alive for a reason. He was God's vicar on earth. He could not die before saying what had to be said.

The pope had summoned all of Italy's bishops to Rome to hear his final message. The gathering was to be held in a week and a half in St. Peter's Basilica, on February 11, 1939. It would mark the tenth anniversary of the Lateran Accords, the historic agreement that Pius XI had struck with Italy's dictator, Mussolini, ending decades of hostility between Italy and the Roman Catholic Church. With that agreement, the separation of church and state that had marked modern Italy from its founding sixty-eight years earlier came to an end. A new era began, the Church a willing partner of Mussolini's Fascist government.

Seventeen years earlier, in 1922, Achille Ratti, freshly appointed cardinal, had been the surprising choice to succeed Pope Benedict XV. He took the name Pius XI. Later that same year, amid widespread violence, Benito Mussolini, the thirty-nine-year-old Fascist leader, became Italy's prime minister. Since then the two men had come to depend on each other. The dictator relied on the pope to ensure Catholic support for his regime, providing much-needed moral legitimacy. The pope counted on Mussolini to help him restore the Church's power in Italy. Now, with pen in hand, thinking back over these years, Pius felt a deep regret. He had allowed himself to be led astray. Mussolini seemed to think he was a god himself, and he had embraced Hitler, a man the pope despised for undermining the Church in Germany and championing a pagan religion of his own. The painful scene Rome had witnessed the previous spring haunted him: a sea of red and black Nazi flags had blanketed the city, as the German Führer passed through its historic streets in triumphal procession.

Two months after Hitler's visit, Mussolini shocked the world by proclaiming that Italians were a pure, superior race. Although Jews had lived in Rome since before the time of Jesus, they were now officially deemed a noxious foreign people. The pope was horrified. Why, he asked in a public audience, was Italy's leader so eager to imitate the Führer? The question enraged Mussolini, for nothing upset him more than being called Hitler's stooge. The men of the pope's inner circle rushed to repair the damage. More comfortable with authoritarian regimes than with democracies, and fearful of losing the many privileges that Mussolini had granted the Church, they thought the pope was getting reckless in his old age. He had already alienated the Nazi leaders; now, they worried, he was putting the Vatican's ties to Mussolini's Fascist regime at risk.

At his headquarters on the other side of Rome's Tiber River, Mussolini raged against the pope. If Italians still went to mass, it was only because he had told them to. If it weren't for him, anticlerics would be running wild through Italy's streets, sacking churches and forcing castor oil down the throats of cowering priests. If every classroom and courtroom had a crucifix on its wall, if priests taught religion in all of Italy's public schools, it was because Mussolini had ordered it. If generous state funds were being used to support the Church, it was because he had willed it, all in an effort to craft a mutually beneficial understanding between his Fascist government and the Vatican.

Pius stayed up late on the night of January 31, as he had the previous night, drafting his remarks for the gathering of bishops. The once-hearty, barrel-chested "mountaineer" pope was emaciated, his formerly full face deeply wrinkled and shrunken. But it was clear to all who saw him how determined he was to give that speech. He did not want to die before warning the bishops that Fascist spies were everywhere, including the halls of the Church. It would be his last chance to denounce Mussolini's embrace of Nazi racism.

In the week remaining before the speech, however, the pope's remaining reserve of strength began to fail him. Unable to stand, he took to bed. Cardinal Eugenio Pacelli, who as secretary of state was second-in-command at the Vatican, begged him to postpone the gathering. The pope would not hear of it and ordered the Vatican daily newspaper to report that he was in good health. On February 8, worried that he might not be strong enough to give the speech in three days' time, he ordered the Vatican printing office to make a copy of it for each bishop. The following night his condition worsened, and in the early morning hours of February 10, his breathing became more labored. Attendants, careful not to disturb the white skullcap on his head, fastened an oxygen mask over his mouth. At four A.M. they roused Cardinal Pacelli. The cardinal rushed to the pope's bedside, then fell to his knees to pray. His eyes reddened with tears.

Lying on his simple iron bed, rapidly fading, Pius XI soon took his last feeble breath. God had not granted his final request. The bishops would see him next not in St. Peter's Basilica but in the nearby Sistine Chapel where, on the afternoon of February 10, his ruined body was placed on a raised platform. To those who had known him in his prime, he was barely recognizable. It was as if someone else lay there, under Michelangelo's frescoed ceiling, wearing the pope's white silk cassock and red-ermine-lined cap.

Across the Tiber, Mussolini greeted news of the pope's death with a grunt of relief, eager that the papal wake not interfere with his next coupling with Clara Petacci, his green-eyed young mistress. But one last concern remained. Over the years, he had put in place an extensive network of spies in the Vatican and read their reports eagerly. In recent days, they had warned him that the pope planned to give an inflammatory anniversary speech denouncing Mussolini's anti-Semitic campaign and his ever-tightening ties to the German Führer. If the text got out now, he worried, it might yet do damage, a prophetic papal plea from the grave.

There was one man, thought the dictator, in a position to help. He contacted Cardinal Pacelli, who in his role as chamberlain was now in charge of everything Pius had left behind, including the handwritten pages piled on his desk and the stacks of freshly printed booklets ready for distribution to the bishops. Mussolini wanted all copies of the speech destroyed.

He had reason to think that Pacelli would oblige him. Hailing from a prominent Roman family closely linked to popes for generations, Pacelli had for the last months lived in fear that the pope would antagonize Mussolini. Too much, he thought, was at stake. Yes, he owed a great deal to the pope who had made him secretary of state and had promoted him in so many ways. But he felt he had an even greater responsibility to protect the Church. He ordered the pope's desk cleared, the printed copies of his speech seized.

Three weeks later a large crowd waited impatiently in St. Peter's Square as the cardinals met in conclave. At the appearance of the telltale ribbon of white smoke wafting from the Apostolic Palace, a cheer went up. "*Habemus papam,*" announced the cardinal deacon from the balcony perched above the main entrance of St. Peter's. Soon a tall, thin, bespectacled figure, newly clothed in white papal robe and bejeweled tiara, strode out to give his blessing. Eugenio Pacelli would take the name Pius XII, honoring the man at whose bedside he had recently wept.

PART ONE

THE POPE AND THE DICTATOR

CHAPTER
ONE

A NEW POPE

O UTSIDE THE VATICAN GATE, A SMALL CROWD GATHERED, APPLAUDING the black sedans as they slowly made their way inside the medieval wall. In recognition or appreciation, or simply from habit, each arriving cardinal waved a hand in ecclesiastical benediction from his backseat. Standing on either side of the gate was a harlequin-clad Swiss Guard, his white-gloved hand raised to his gleaming helmet in salute. A little later, once the last cardinal had found his room in the Apostolic Palace, six officials scurried through the long, cold halls, each swinging a bell. A voice shouted "*Extra omnes!*" as the last of the outsiders exited. Clutching a massive antique key chain, a Chigi prince, the conclave's ceremonial marshal, locked the heavy door from the outside. Cardinal Pietro Gasparri, the chamberlain, locked it from within. The windows were sealed. It was Thursday, February 2, 1922. The doors would not open again until there was a new pope.

ONLY TWO WEEKS EARLIER a persistent cough had begun to bother Pope Benedict XV. Although he was a small, frail man who since childhood had walked with a limp—the Vatican gossips called him the "little one"—he was not old and had enjoyed good health during his seven years on St. Peter's throne. But what began as bronchitis quickly turned into pneumonia, and the sixty-eight-year-old Benedict took last rites. The next afternoon, lying on his simple iron bed, he lost consciousness. The following morning, January 22, he was dead.[1]

Giacomo Della Chiesa had been an unusual choice when the genial but repressive Pius X died in 1914, just as the Great War began. When the fifty-two cardinals assembled in late August that year to elect a successor, Della Chiesa had been a cardinal for only three months. Born to an aristocratic but far-from-wealthy family, respected for his intelligence and good judgment, he did not look the part of a pontiff. Although dignified in bearing, and courtly in manners, he was undersized, with a sallow complexion, an impenetrable mat of black hair, and prominent teeth. Everything about him seemed slightly crooked, from his nose, mouth, and eyes to his shoulders.[2]

As a young priest, Della Chiesa worked in the Vatican Secretariat of State, which deals with the Holy See's relations with governments around the world. There he made his way through the ranks until 1913, when he was sent to Bologna to become its archbishop.

Some believed that Della Chiesa's departure from the Vatican was the work of Cardinal Rafael Merry del Val, Pope Pius X's secretary of state and his main partner in the crusade to stamp out any sign of "modernism" in the clergy. Pius X worried that modern ideas were replacing the Church's centuries-old teachings. Particularly noxious, in the pope's view, were beliefs in individual rights and religious freedom, along with the heretical notions that church and state should be separated, and that faith should come to terms with the lessons of science. Believing Della Chiesa to be too moderate, Merry del Val wanted him far from the seat of Church power.[3]

On the tenth ballot, Della Chiesa reached—just barely—the two-thirds vote required. One of Merry del Val's fellow hard-liners, Cardinal Gaetano De Lai, humiliated the new pope by demanding that his ballot be examined to ensure that he had not voted for himself.

Pius X had died at a frightening time for Italians, but his successor's death, in 1922, came amid even greater unrest. Many feared that revolution could erupt at any moment, although they differed on whether it was more likely to be sparked by the socialists or the fascists. The Great War, which the elite had hoped would help unify the hopelessly divided Italians and rally the population around the government, had done neither. Over half a million Italians had died, and even more had returned wounded. A demobilized army came home to find few jobs. The country's political leaders seemed incapable of finding a way out of the crisis.

The Socialists—whose numbers had been growing for decades—had hoped to ride the tide of popular anger to power. Workers occupied factories in Turin, Milan, and Genoa. Agricultural laborers struck, threatening the old rural landowner class. Only two years earlier, in 1917, a communist revolution had brought the Bolsheviks to power in Russia and destroyed the old tsarist order. Energized by their example, Italian protesters dreamed of a future when workers and peasants would rule.[4]

But the Socialists had to face a violent threat of their own. Shortly after the war, Benito Mussolini, thirty-five years old and formerly one of the country's most prominent Socialists, founded a new fascist movement. It drew heavily on disaffected war veterans. Fascist bands soon sprang up in cities throughout much of the country. Its first recruits came, like Mussolini, from the left and shared his hatred of the Church and the priests. But Mussolini quickly turned from vilifying priests and capitalist war profiteers to denouncing Socialists, guilty of opposing Italy's entrance into the war. Recruits began streaming in from the extreme right.

From their headquarters in the cities of northern and central Italy, black-shirted fascists crowded into cars and rampaged through the countryside, burning down union halls, Socialist meeting rooms, and the offices of left-wing newspapers. Mussolini had little direct control over these *squadristi*, who were led by local fascist bosses dubbed *ras*. Beginning in 1919 and with increasing frequency and size over the next three years, the bands attacked Socialist officials and activists, beating them and forcing castor oil down their throats. The *squadristi* took sadistic delight in using the oil, which produced not only nausea but humiliating, uncontrollable diarrhea. Panicked Socialist mayors and town councilors fled, leaving a large swath of Italy under the control of fascist thugs.[5]

These "punitive expeditions" also took aim at members of Italy's Catholic political party. The Popular Party was a new attempt by Italy's Catholics to compete for political influence. That the Vatican looked kindly on the establishment of a Catholic party in Italy was a new development. In 1861 Victor Emmanuel II, king of the Savoyard state based in Turin in the northwest, had proclaimed a new Kingdom of Italy, having annexed much of the Italian peninsula. Among the territories he acquired by a combination of rebellion and conquest were most of the lands long ruled by the popes. Only Rome and its hinterland remained as part of the Papal States. Then in 1870 the Italian army seized Rome as well, declaring it the new nation's capital. Pope Pius IX retreated to the Vatican, vowing not to leave its walls until the Papal States were restored.

The pope excommunicated the king and forbade Catholics to vote in national elections or run as candidates for parliament; he was hoping to gain international support to return Rome to papal rule. But as the nineteenth century wore on, this prospect seemed ever more remote. A new threat meanwhile arose with the rapid growth of the socialist movement. Popes from the time of Pius IX, in the mid-nineteenth century, had regularly condemned socialism. In 1891, in his famous encyclical *Rerum novarum*, Pope Leo XIII had charged socialists with "working on the poor man's envy of the rich." He blasted their proposal to abolish private property. By the dawn of the new century, the Vatican had made clear that socialism was one of the Church's most formidable enemies.

With the expansion of the right to vote in Italy in the early twentieth century, the Vatican's voting ban became untenable. Unless the Church did something, the socialists would likely come to power. In November 1918 Luigi Sturzo, a Sicilian priest, met with Vatican secretary of state,

Cardinal Pietro Gasparri, to discuss his plans for a Catholic party, to be called the Italian Popular Party. It would offer a progressive platform intended to lure peasants and workers away from the socialists. It was formally launched early the following year with Benedict XV's blessing. By 1922 it was among the country's largest.[6]

THE CONCLAVE THAT YEAR turned into a showdown between two factions. On one side were those cardinals dubbed the *zelanti,* the intransigents. They looked back nostalgically to the days of Pius X, eager to resume the Church's crusade against the evils of modern times. On the other side, the moderates, dubbed the "politicians," hoped to continue Benedict XV's more middle-of-the-road and outward-looking policies. Pius X's secretary of state, Rafael Merry del Val, led the *zelanti.* Pietro Gasparri, Benedict's secretary of state, was the champion of the moderates. The conclave was shaping up as an epic battle over the direction the Catholic Church would take in the twentieth century, made all the more dramatic by the uncertainty of its outcome. It seemed doubtful that either faction could obtain the two-thirds vote required for election, and there was no obvious compromise candidate.[7]

If Cardinal Gasparri was sometimes called the *pecoraio,* the shepherd, it was not in the pastoral sense. Sixty-nine years old at the time of the conclave, he came from a peasant family in a small sheep-raising village in the Apennine Mountains of central Italy. The nickname—which he delighted in himself—came with the Italian connotations of being a country hick, a parvenu amid the sophisticates of the Vatican hierarchy. When he was a child, his family followed its herd into the mountains each spring, returning each fall to the valley, where they sent Pietro to the local parish priest for school lessons. A bright child, he entered Church seminaries for his later education, but unlike many in the high Vatican diplomatic service, he did not attend Rome's prestigious Pontifical Academy of Noble Ecclesiastics, which traditionally drew on sons of the aristocracy.

Gasparri grew into a short, rotund adult, a priest who seemed to move without his feet ever leaving the ground. His dress "showed an unusual indifference to neatness." But he was popular with the diplomatic corps, making up in bonhomie what he lacked in polish. Gesticulating broadly, eyes sparkling, and laughing often, he was constantly pushing his red skullcap back into place. Gasparri saw himself—and was seen by others—as having a mountain peasant's shrewdness, intuition, tenacity, and capacity for hard work. "His black, intelligent eyes," one observer noted, "betrayed his finesse."[8]

On the evening of February 2, the conclave began in the Sistine Chapel; each of the fifty-three cardinals was provided with a seat at his own small table. Among those absent were the two cardinals from the United States, still on a ship somewhere in the Atlantic. The thirty-one Italians constituted a majority, and only with strong Italian support could anyone be elected. At the altar at the front of the chapel stood a large crucifix and six burning candles. Every time a vote was called, the cardinals approached the altar one at a time, in order of seniority. At the foot of the altar, each got down on his knees, spent a moment in prayer, and recited a Latin vow pledging to choose the man whom he believed God would want elected. He deposited his folded paper ballot and then bowed before the cross before returning to his seat.

Two votes were held each morning and two in the afternoon. Three cardinals, chosen by lot, counted the ballots. Over the next days, the solemn rite was repeated fourteen times, marred only once when, as he rose from his chair, a Dominican cardinal bumped into his table, draining an ink bottle over his white cassock.[9]

Twelve cardinals received votes. On the second day, Merry del Val reached what would be his high of seventeen. Gasparri received twenty-four votes by the sixth ballot but remained stuck at that number for the seventh and eighth as well. Outside the Vatican, a large crowd of Romans—both the curious and the devout—waited anxiously. "Only one thing is certain," the French paper *Le Figaro* reported, "no one knows anything."[10] Cardinal Gasparri spent the night after the eighth ballot lying awake in bed, aware that he would never become pope. The following morning, before the third day of voting began, he went to see the conclave's most junior member, Achille Ratti. He told the surprised Ratti, who had been made a cardinal only a few months earlier, that he would urge his supporters to switch their votes to him.

RATTI WAS BORN IN 1857 in the small town of Desio, in the deeply Catholic Brianza region just north of Milan, where his father managed a silk factory. His mother, a devout Catholic, was the kind of organized and intimidating woman who seemed born to run something much bigger than a household. In later years Ratti often spoke of her with deep affection and respect, but he never talked about his father. At the time of his birth, Desio and Milan were part of the Austro-Hungarian Empire, and Ratti's earliest memory was of his father telling him at age two that French and Savoyard forces were battling the Austrian army nearby.[11] Within weeks the patchwork of duchies and kingdoms that had long composed the Italian peninsula dissolved, and a new unified Italian nation took shape.

There being no school in Desio, at age ten Achille was sent to live with his uncle, a parish priest in the tiny town of Asso, near Lake Como. The frequent presence of neighboring priests, a gregarious lot, warmed his uncle's household. Achille decided that he too wanted to be a priest and soon went off to a seminary. He returned each summer, not to his parents but to his uncle. The seminary enforced a ferocious discipline. Priests were to be obeyed without question, and rules were to be followed to the letter. None of this bothered the studious boy.[12] His classmates called him "the little old man," for Achille would rather be left alone to his meditations than play with the other children.[13]

In 1875 Ratti entered Milan's seminary to prepare for the priesthood. He read voraciously, not only the Italian classics such as Dante, but also English and American literature. He expressed such concern for the challenges faced by Mark Twain's Jim, Huckleberry Finn's enslaved sidekick, that his classmates dubbed him *l'africano*. Although the nickname would not stick, Achille pronounced himself pleased with it, telling his classmates he would one day serve as a missionary in

Africa. Ratti's favorite author was the great Milanese writer Alessandro Manzoni. One day many years later, when he was pope, his master of ceremonies entered his study and, as was the custom, got on his knees to await instructions. The pope was pacing the room, absorbed in reading aloud a passage from Manzoni's novel *The Betrothed*. Twenty minutes passed before he stopped and took note of the kneeling cleric. The pope apologized for the delay but added with a smile: "These are pages that are worth listening to on one's knees, Monsignor!"[14]

After four years in Milan, Ratti moved to Rome to continue his studies at the recently opened Lombard College. Rome had been ruled by popes for over a millennium, but nine years earlier it had been conquered and was now the capital of the newly unified Italian nation.

Five foot eight, barrel-chested, with thinning blond hair, Ratti was already wearing the round spectacles that would become his trademark, giving him the appearance of a young scholar. Ordained at Rome's massive St. John in Lateran Basilica in December 1879, he stayed in the Eternal City for another three years, studying at the Gregorian University, where the Jesuit faculty lectured in Latin.

By 1882 Ratti was back in Milan, soon to be appointed professor of sacred eloquence and theology at the city's Grand Seminary. Despite his title, he was not terribly eloquent. He was so intent on being perfectly clear that he spoke at a painfully slow pace, struggling to find the right words, then constantly correcting himself when he thought what he had said wasn't quite right.[15] Never gregarious, Ratti was in some ways more comfortable around books than people. After six years as professor, he became an assistant at Milan's Ambrosiana Library, whose unparalleled collections of old manuscripts include such treasures as Leonardo da Vinci's *Codice atlantico*. He knew not only Latin but also Greek, French, and German.

But Ratti was not simply a bookworm. As a young man in Milan, he developed a passion for mountain climbing and joined the local chapter of the Italian Alpine Club. Each winter, along with his climbing companion, a fellow priest, he would study all the material he could find on approaches to the mountains they would scale the next summer. Success, he was convinced, was all a matter of careful planning. From 1885 to 1911 he went on a hundred Alpine climbs, each over eight thousand feet.[16] The shock of the cold air, the power of the Alpine cliffs, and the landscape stretching below all showed him the glory of God's creation.[17]

WHEN THE PREFECT of the Ambrosiana Library died in 1907, the fifty-year-old Ratti took his place. Four years later the head of the Vatican Library decided it was time to find a successor. As director of a library that was second in reputation only to the Vatican's own, Achille Ratti was hardly a surprising choice. Milan's newspaper announced news of the appointment accompanied by a photograph. It showed a balding prelate, but Ratti's most memorable physical trait remained his little round glasses. Along with his serious—some would say melancholy—demeanor, they gave him the look of a dour Church intellectual. But he took a paternal interest in the library staff. To help them feed their families during the Great War, he got permission from Benedict XV to turn the Vatican Library courtyard into a vegetable garden for their use. When one of them got sick, he would personally deliver a gift of sweets or a bottle of good wine.[18]

Had Ratti remained as Vatican librarian, as he assumed he would, he would never have been in a position to become pope in 1922. But in March 1918 he received a surprising request: Benedict XV wanted him to go immediately to Warsaw as his personal emissary. It is still not clear how the pope came to choose him for the delicate assignment. He had no experience in diplomacy and no special knowledge of Poland, although strangely, when his nomination was discussed by the cardinals of the Congregation of Extraordinary Ecclesiastical Affairs, they mistakenly thought he spoke Polish.[19] At sixty-one, Ratti was nervous about his new assignment, but he obediently set off in May. He had been led to believe he would be away only a few months, charged with preparing a report for the pope on the Polish situation.

The carnage of the Great War had barely ended when Ratti arrived in Warsaw. The Poles were preparing for the rebirth of their independent nation, most of which had been under Russian rule for a century, the rest under German or Austrian control. Ratti's task was delicate, for the borders of the new Polish state were not yet set, and tensions were great.

As he traveled around the country, one of the sentiments the Vatican librarian most often heard from the clergy was their hatred of the Jews, seen as enemies of Catholic Poland. While Italy's Jewish population was tiny, just one in a thousand, in Poland a tenth of the population was Jewish. A decade earlier Ratti had taken Hebrew lessons from the chief rabbi of Milan, and the city's largely assimilated Jewish population had not caused him any concern.[20] But while his own relations with Milan's small Jewish community had been cordial, he was aware that the Vatican had a much darker view of the Jews.

The history of Church demonization of the Jews is an old one, going back to shortly after Christianity's origins as a Jewish sect. In 1555 Pope Paul IV issued a papal bull, *Cum nimis absurdum,* ordering all Jews in the lands under his control to live in ghettoes. The Jews' contacts with Christians were to be severely limited, and they would be confined to the most menial occupations. The Jews, the pope argued, had been condemned by God to "eternal slavery," for their sin of murdering Jesus and refusing his teachings. Only in 1870, with the Italian conquest of Rome, were Jews fully liberated from the city's ghetto.[21]

In the last two decades of the nineteenth century, *La Civiltà cattolica,* the twice-a-month Jesuit journal closely overseen by the Vatican, had attacked the Jews mercilessly. The journal was read not by the Catholic masses, for it was pitched well above their heads; rather it offered Catholic opinion leaders, newspaper editors, and upper-echelon clergy a window into the Vatican's perspective on the issues of the day. A man in Achille Ratti's position at the Ambrosiana Library would have read each issue as it appeared.

"The Jews," one of scores of such denunciations in the journal warned, "eternal insolent children, obstinate, dirty, thieves, liars, ignoramuses, pests and the scourge of those near and far . . . managed to lay their hands on . . . all public wealth . . . and virtually alone they took control not only of all the money . . . but of the law itself in those countries where they have been allowed to hold public offices." The Church had long taught, the Vatican-supervised journal insisted, that Jews should be kept separate from Christians, or they would reduce Christians to their slaves: "Oh how wrong and deluded are those who think that Judaism is just a religion . . . and not in fact a race, a people, and a nation!" As a noxious foreign body, the journal charged, Jews could never be loyal to the country in which they lived, as they schemed to exploit the generosity of those who foolishly accorded them equal rights.[22] It was a campaign that the journal would take up again within months of Ratti's election as pope, in a series of articles blaming the Jews for the Russian revolution and sounding the alarm against a vast Jewish conspiracy aimed at ruling the world.[23]

Steeped in a Church in which such views of Jews were deeply engrained, Ratti could not help being affected by the deep anti-Semitism he encountered in Poland. The various written reports he received from members of the Polish Catholic elite told him how preoccupied they were with the Jewish threat. Jews were accused of having sided with the German invaders in the recent war and of serving as rapacious moneylenders in towns and villages throughout the country. Ratti was especially struck by their charge that the spreading Bolshevik movement was the work of the Jews.[24] In October 1918 he attributed the latest unrest in Poland to "the extremist parties bent on disorder: the socialist-anarchists, the Bolsheviks . . . and the Jews."[25] A wave of pogroms in Poland led to the murder of many Jews and the torching of their homes. Asked by Benedict XV—less sympathetic to anti-Semitic conspiracy theories than his predecessors—to verify whether the stories of these pogroms were true, Ratti responded that it was difficult to tell. But he insisted that the Jews were a dangerous element: although the people of Poland were good and loyal Catholics, he feared "that they may fall into the clutches of the evil influences that are laying a trap for them and threatening them." Ratti left no doubt as to who these enemies were, adding: "One of the most evil and strongest influences that is felt here, perhaps the strongest and the most evil, is that of the Jews."[26]

In the fall of 1919 the Vatican officially recognized the new Polish state. Ratti's mission was extended, and he was appointed papal nuncio. The following summer the Red Army, after a series of battles with Polish forces in the Baltic and in Ukraine, advanced into Poland and approached Warsaw itself. Men, women, and children armed themselves, ready to defend their city. While many foreigners fled, Ratti stood his ground. On August 15, as the armed inhabitants waited nervously, a Polish counteroffensive drove off the Bolshevik troops. For Ratti, the experience was traumatic. The conviction that the Western democracies failed to understand the Communist threat would stay with him the rest of his life.[27]

In 1921 Benedict XV recalled Ratti to Italy, naming him archbishop of Milan. Having little pastoral experience, a librarian most of his life, Ratti was a surprising choice, but Benedict had been impressed by his competence, his devotion to the Church, and his selflessness.[28] The fact that Ratti had lived most of his life in Milan undoubtedly played a role. With the appointment came the cardinal's hat that was traditionally due to the head of Italy's largest and wealthiest archdiocese.[29]

IN THE MIDDLE OF THE CONCLAVE, when the *zelanti* realized that neither Merry del Val nor any other of their candidates would prevail, they too decided to meet secretly with Achille Ratti. They seem to have thought that, as someone not identified with either of the two factions, he could be a successful compromise candidate. They also thought they could more easily influence someone with so little experience in the Church hierarchy, especially if he were to attribute his election to their support. Cardinal De Lai, head of the Vatican congregation in charge of choosing bishops, approached Ratti with an offer, speaking on behalf of the dozen cardinals in his group.

"We will vote for Your Eminence," De Lai told him, "if Your Emi-

Achille Ratti, archbishop of Milan, 1921

nence will promise that you will not choose Cardinal Gasparri as your secretary of state."

"I hope and pray," responded Ratti, "that among so many highly deserving cardinals the Holy Spirit selects someone else." But, he added, "if I am chosen, it is indeed Cardinal Gasparri whom I will take to be my secretary of state."[30] Whether Ratti had already promised as much to Gasparri is not clear, although it seems likely. Inexperienced in

Vatican affairs, he may in any case have wanted to have the experienced diplomat alongside him. Or he may have been savvier than they thought and recognized the value of a secretary of state who would help shield him from the demands of the *zelanti*.

"Your Eminence would be making a serious mistake," Cardinal De Lai warned.

"I am afraid that it would likely not be the only mistake I would make should I sit on Saint Peter's throne, but it certainly would be the first."

By the twelfth ballot, the last on the third day of voting, twenty-seven cardinals gave their support to Milan's archbishop.[31] Early the next day the cardinals again assembled in the Sistine Chapel. At ten A.M. they began depositing their thirteenth ballot, which was again inconclusive. It was on their next vote that Achille Ratti passed the two-thirds mark.

Fifty-two cardinals formed concentric circles around the stunned cardinal as he sat straight in his chair, head tilted down as if his shoulders bore a new weight. The cardinal deacon asked the obligatory question in a voice that even the most hard-of-hearing could make out: "Do you accept the election that selects you canonically to be the supreme pontiff?" Ratti did not respond immediately, and some of the cardinals grew nervous. After a full two minutes, he raised his head and replied in Latin. His voice trembled with emotion. "While deeply aware of my unworthiness," he began. The cardinals knew that they had a new pope.[32]

As all this was going on, a train from Naples pulled into Rome's station on the other side of the Tiber. Out stepped the two American cardinals, William O'Connell of Boston and Dennis Dougherty of Philadelphia. Having made the long ocean crossing aboard the *Woodrow Wilson,* then rushed from Naples to Rome, the men were unhappy to discover they had arrived too late. O'Connell had special reason to be displeased, as he owed his career in good part to the patronage of Cardinal Merry del Val. Had he been there to give him his support and that of Dougherty, perhaps things might have gone differently. Even more infuriating was the fact that the same thing had happened when Pius X had died seven and a half years earlier: no provision had been made to allow time for the Americans to get to Rome. Then too O'Connell had gotten to Rome only after the new pope had been elected.[33]

From the Sistine Chapel, Ratti was escorted to the nearby sacristy, where for the first time he put on the white papal robes. Three gowns had been readied, prepared for any eventuality, one small, one medium, and one large. The middle size fit him perfectly. He wore a white cassock, white silk stockings, and red silk slippers along with a red velvet cape, its border lined with ermine. On his head, over a white skullcap, he wore a red camauro, a papal cap with white ermine trim, pulled down to his ears. As he returned to the Sistine Chapel and walked to the throne placed in front of the altar, the cardinals got down on their knees. Each then approached him, in turn, kissing his foot and asking for his blessing. The man who had delighted in trekking through the mountains would now—if he followed the practice of his four predecessors—never leave the claustrophobic confines of the Vatican palaces.[34]

The world had been looking on eagerly to see who would emerge from the conclave. Italians, whose 40 million people were 99 percent Catholic, showed the most interest, but the 260 million Roman Catholics outside Italy eagerly awaited word as well.[35]

Crowds had been waiting in St. Peter's Square since the conclave began, their eyes drawn to the chimney, where the smoke produced by the burning of the paper ballots following each round would tell them when a pope had been elected.[36] Thirteen times over four days black smoke had belched from the chimney, but near noon on the fourth day, as the damp crowd stood under rainy skies, arms began pointing to the ribbon of white smoke wafting from the Apostolic Palace. Forty-five minutes later a cardinal emerged on the central balcony of St. Peter's church, facing the square, and slowly raised his right arm. "*Habemus papam* . . . we have a pope." Achille Ratti had chosen the name Pius XI, explaining that Pius IX had been the pope of his youth and Pius X had called him to Rome to head the Vatican Library.[37] The man who until a few years earlier had presided over a small staff of librarians was now responsible for the world's 300 million Catholics.

The cheering throngs began pushing toward the doors of St. Peter's Basilica. Ever since 1870, when Italian troops had seized Rome and the popes had proclaimed themselves "prisoners of the Vatican," no pope would show his face outside, even from one of the windows facing St. Peter's Square. Each of the three popes chosen since Pius IX's death had blessed the faithful inside the basilica.

Something surprising caught people's eye. Members of the noble papal guard appeared on the balcony just above the central massive door of St. Peter's, facing the square, and hung from its rail a red tapestry bearing the papal coat of arms. As the white-robed pontiff emerged onto the balcony to bless them, a hush spread through the vast piazza, and people fell to their knees. No one would forget the sight of Italian soldiers, stationed in the piazza to keep order, presenting their arms alongside the papal Swiss Guard. Together they saluted the new pope.[38] It was a rare moment of peace in a city in the grip of growing panic. Violence and chaos were spreading through the country, and the government was paralyzed. Before the year was out, the new pope would find himself facing a decision of enormous importance.

THE MARCH ON ROME

P REDAPPIO, THE SMALL TOWN IN ROMAGNA WHERE BENITO MUSSOLINI
was born, is no more than two hundred miles from Achille Ratti's
birthplace in Lombardy, yet their childhood experiences could hardly
have been more different. It was not so much the Rattis' greater wealth
but the difference between a conservative, religious family and one im-
mersed in the insurrectionary enthusiasms of Romagna. The Rattis'
heroes were saints and popes; the Mussolinis' were rabble-rousers and
revolutionaries.

Achille Ratti was already a twenty-six-year-old priest when Mussolini was born in 1883. Romagna was then the epicenter of Italy's anarchist and socialist movements, and Benito's father, Alessandro, a
bigmouthed blacksmith, eagerly preached his revolutionary faith to
any who would listen. He named his son after Benito Juárez, an impoverished Indian who became Mexico's president, scourge of Europe's
colonial powers, and enemy of the Church. He named Benito's younger
brother, Arnaldo, after Arnaldo of Brescia, a priest who had led an uprising that drove the pope from Rome in 1146 and was later hanged.
The boys' long-suffering mother, Rosa, did not share her husband's
revolutionary ardor. A regular churchgoer, she taught in the local ele-

mentary school. Each night, as her children lay sleeping, she made the sign of the cross over their heads.[1]

The family lived in a third-floor, two-room apartment. Benito and Arnaldo slept in the kitchen atop a big sack of corn husks on an iron bed their father had forged. Their parents shared the other room with their sister, Edvige. To enter the apartment, they had to walk through their mother's schoolroom, which occupied the rest of the floor.

Alessandro and Rosa had a stormy marriage. Not only did Alessandro have lovers, but he often returned drunk at night from local pubs and picked fights with his wife. Somehow she won one argument, and they sent Benito, age ten, to board at a nearby school run by Salesian monks. He did not last long. During a squabble with a classmate, he pulled a knife from his pocket and stabbed the boy in the hand. The Salesians expelled him. Benito continued his roughhouse ways, but, a bright boy, he somehow made it through secondary school. He began work as a substitute schoolteacher in 1901, losing one of his first jobs when his affair with a married woman came to light.

Unable to find a new post, Benito headed for Switzerland in search of work. There he joined the local world of socialists and anarchists, drawn by their excited talk of revolution. Swiss police soon produced a report on him, leaving us a description of him as a young man: five and a half feet tall, stocky, with brown hair and beard, he had a long, pale face, dark eyes, an aquiline nose, and a large mouth.[2]

In Lausanne in 1904, Mussolini agreed to debate a local Protestant pastor on the existence of God. After trying to impress his audience with citations ranging from Galileo to Robespierre, he climbed onto a table, took out a pocket watch, and bellowed that if there really was a God, He should strike him dead in the next five minutes. Benito's first publication, titled "God Does Not Exist," came the same year. He kept up his attacks on the Church, branding priests "black microbes, as disastrous to humanity as tuberculosis microbes."[3]

Mussolini's passion was for polemics and politics, and he would soon devote himself full time to both. By 1910 he was back in Forlì, near his family home in Romagna, editor of the local socialist weekly and secretary of the town's Socialist Party. That same year he tried his hand at fiction, publishing a steamy novel, *The Cardinal's Mistress*.[4]

In these first years of his political career, Mussolini cut a striking figure, part left-wing wild man and part Don Juan. Sporting a mustache that he would keep for the next decade, he always seemed to know how to become the center of attention. A transgressive roughhouser, more than a little bit of a provocateur, he was someone you would rather have on your side than against you. One of his most memorable traits was already on display: his steely stare. At once both intimidating and mesmerizing, Mussolini's gaze transfixed his listeners. His eyes seemed to bulge out. In 1910 a local union organizer described the experience: "He looked me over with one of those raisings of the eyebrows that reveals all the white of the eye, as if he wanted to take in some distant fleeting sight, giving his eyes and his face the pensive look of an apostle."[5]

In 1912, while still in his twenties, Mussolini was named to one of the Socialist Party's most influential posts, editor of the national party newspaper, *Avanti!*, based in Milan. He moved from the modest provincial outpost of Forlì to Italy's bustling financial and cultural capital.

As editor of *Avanti!*, Mussolini took aim at the Socialist Party's reform faction. Only revolutionary action, not parliamentary politics, he insisted, would bring about a new order. In 1913, when police south of Rome killed seven farmworkers during a protest, he called for revenge: "Death to those who massacre the people! Long live the Revolution!" he told a rally in Milan. In his newspaper he wrote, "Ours is a war cry. Those who massacre know that they can be, in their turn, massacred."[6]

When war broke out in Europe in August 1914, Socialists denounced it as the work of warmongering imperialists and capitalists happy to use the proletariat as their cannon fodder. The workers of the world were to unite, not to butcher one another in the name of God or country. But to his comrades' surprise, two months after the war began, Mussolini published an article questioning the wisdom of Italian neutrality. Pacifism was not in his character, and he chafed at the thought of Italy standing by and simply watching as the rest of Europe waged war.

Whether he thought he could persuade his fellow Socialists to follow his lead is unclear. If he did, he soon found out how mistaken he was: within a month he was not only forced out of *Avanti!* but expelled from the party.

Over the next years, in what his erstwhile comrades considered an inexplicable and traitorous transformation, the Socialist leader became the Socialists' worst enemy. He kept the revolutionary's disdain for parliamentary democracy and fascination with the possibilities of violent action. But he jettisoned much of the rest of Marxist ideology. The chaos surrounding the end of the Great War, he realized, had created a void, and he meant to fill it. He had always been committed, above all, to himself and to a belief in his own ability to rise to the top. Now he began to see a new path that could allow him to realize those dreams.

Four years earlier, in 1910, Mussolini had had a child, Edda, with his hometown lover, Rachele Guidi, who would later become his wife. They lived at the time in a two-room, literally flea-ridden apartment in Forlì. Such, however, was Benito's love life that for decades rumors spread that Edda's mother was not Rachele. Edda would later write with some irritation of the widespread gossip that her mother was really Angelica Balabanoff, a Russian Jewish socialist (and later secretary of the Third Communist International) who had settled in Italy and become one of Mussolini's more significant lovers and political mentors. "Knowing my mother," wrote Edda in her memoirs, "I know very well that she wouldn't have kept me for five minutes if I had been Balabanoff's daughter."[7]

Born to a poor peasant family, Rachele first met Benito when she was seven and he was substituting for his mother in the local elementary school. Rachele was not much of a student, and in any case her father died when she was only eight and she was sent to work as a maid in Forlì. Although she would later grow rather matronly, as a youth she was attractive, blond, short, slender, and blue-eyed.

Rachele thought Edda was Benito's first child. But a few months before Edda's birth, a coffeehouse waitress gave birth to a boy she named Benito. This little Benito died at a young age, but there would be other illegitimate children, including at least one other Benito.[8] One might be forgiven for wondering how Mussolini had any time for his journalistic and political career as he juggled several love affairs. His women could hardly have been more different. In 1913 he had a baby with another Russian Jew whom he had met a few years earlier, although he never recognized the child.[9] That same year he became enchanted by the unlikely Leda Rafanelli, thirty-two years old and one of the better-known anarchist authors in Milan, distinctive for having embraced Islam some years earlier after spending a few months in Egypt. Benito began sneaking from his office to pay visits to Rafanelli's incense-filled apartment, where guests sat on the floor. Their tryst lasted until the fall of 1914. Many decades later, as an old woman, Rafanelli published forty letters that the young Mussolini had written to her in those torrid months.[10]

In November 1915 a second Benito was born, this to another of Mussolini's lovers, Ida Dalser, a woman who worshipped him. Perhaps in an attempt to ward off Dalser's increasingly insistent claims that she was his true wife, Mussolini married Rachele. The hurried civil ceremony took place a month after Benito's birth, despite the fact that Mussolini was a patient in a typhoid ward at the time. When he failed to answer her letters, Dalser got a court order to have his furniture seized. In a spiteful rage, she gathered up his modest collection of tables and chairs in her hotel room and set it all ablaze.[11]

Back in November 1914, fresh from his ejection as editor of *Avanti!*, Mussolini announced he was starting his own newspaper, *Il Popolo d'Italia* (The Italian People).[12] Begun with support from Italian industrialists who would benefit from Italy's entrance into the war, it would remain his paper for the next three decades.[13]

Around the same time he started his newspaper, he organized the *Fasci d'azione rivoluzionaria,* revolutionary cells or, as he would describe them, "a free association of subversives," who supported Italy's entrance into the war and called for an end to the monarchy.[14] They held their first meeting in January 1915, four months before Italy entered the war on the side of Britain and France. Soon Mussolini was drafted and sent to the front in the mountains of northeastern Italy. On February 23, 1917, his military service was cut short when a mortar he was trying to fire exploded in its tube, killing five of his own soldiers and puncturing his body with shrapnel. Despite surgery, or perhaps because of it, infection set in and a fever raged. But he survived and returned to Milan, where his most important lover and political confidante awaited him.

Born in 1880 to a wealthy Venetian Jewish family, Margherita Sarfatti had studied at home with private tutors. By fourteen, she had learned French, German, and English. She read philosophy, memorized verses from Shelley, studied art criticism, and developed a passion for literature. Attractive and green-eyed, with auburn red hair, at eighteen she married a Jewish lawyer fourteen years her senior.

The newlyweds soon moved to Milan, where Margherita gravitated toward the Socialist Party and began writing cultural articles for its newspaper. She met Mussolini when he arrived in late 1912. What immediately struck her was his eyes. Bright and large, they seemed to move feverishly as he spoke. When she later got to see him in action at a Socialist rally, she marveled at his ability to capture a crowd with pithy eloquence. He was like a legendary hero of old, she thought, who, clad in rusty, dented armor, succeeded time after time in unhorsing the gleaming knights in royal tournaments. He also brought to her mind the fifteenth-century Dominican Savonarola. Mussolini shared with the fiery friar the same "strange fanatical gleam in his eyes and the imperious curve of his nose."[15]

They began their affair in 1913. When Mussolini returned from the war in 1917, the two became inseparable.[16] In November 1918 Benito's sister, Edvige, in Milan for the armistice celebrations, was surprised to see he had shaved off his mustache. He wore a good suit with a spotless white high collar and even had a flower in his lapel. He looked, she thought, remarkably clean cut. She guessed he was in love.[17]

Set against Mussolini's love life were the brutal upheavals of postwar Italy. In many northern cities, industrial workers seized factories.

The recent Russian revolution was on everyone's mind, and calls for an end to "bourgeois" democracy and the installation of a workers' state were bandied about. In the Italian countryside, left-wing peasant leagues struck. Landowners, accustomed to dictating terms to the peasants, now found themselves on the defensive. Hundreds of thousands of veterans were unable to find work. The government was out of funds and paralyzed by political bickering and personal feuds. Socialists were creating something of a state within a state, taking over municipal governments and building labor cooperatives throughout a vast northern swath of the country, from the feet of the Alps in the northwest to the Adriatic Sea in the east.

Mussolini found his natural constituency in the returning veterans, playing on their nationalism, their sense that the country owed them something, and their unwillingness to abandon the kind of camaraderie under arms that they had recently enjoyed. Attacks on war profiteers, defeatists, inept generals, and corrupt politicians proved a heady mix. On March 23, 1919, he convened the first meeting of his fascist movement.

Along with the rest of the establishment, the Church was one of the fascists' early targets. Mussolini called for seizing the property of religious congregations and ending state subsidies for the Church. In a November 1919 article in *Il Popolo d'Italia*, he invited the pope to leave Rome, and a month later he expressed his hatred for all forms of Christianity.[18]

The fascists got their first chance to run candidates for parliament that same month, but it proved a great embarrassment.[19] In Milan they received under two percent of the vote and failed to elect anyone. Nationally, they elected only one deputy.[20]

Although his movement was not yet getting many votes, Mussolini was attracting a great deal of police attention. Shortly before the election, the authorities prepared a confidential profile. It portrayed him as physically imposing but syphilitic. The claim that he had contracted syphilis, a common disease at the time, should not be surprising given his many sexual partners. People would whisper about it to the end of his life, and some would blame it for his later presumed mental decline. But his autopsy would find no sign of the disease.

Mussolini got up late each morning and left for his newspaper office around noon, but he did not return until long after midnight. Emotional and impulsive, the police reported, he also had a sentimental side, which helped explain why so many people found him attractive. Intelligent and astute, he had a knack for sizing up people's strengths and taking advantage of their weaknesses. A good organizer, able to make quick decisions, he stuck by his friends but long nursed grudges against those who slighted him. Uncommitted to any particular set of convictions, he readily abandoned old ones and took up the new. Most of all he was extremely ambitious, convinced that it was his destiny to shape Italy's future.[21]

By early 1920 Mussolini had jettisoned much of the socialist ideology that he had up to that point so loudly declaimed. Realizing that his path to success lay in taking advantage of the chaos in the country, he cast himself as the champion of law and order and national pride.

In the spring of 1920, in the Po Valley, socialist leagues organized an agricultural strike. When the government did nothing to intervene, the local landowners turned to the *fasci*. By autumn, armed fascist bands—wearing their trademark black shirts and black fezzes—were sacking socialist chambers of labor and other left-wing targets. Modern Italy had never known anything like it. While Mussolini presided in a loose way over the network of these fascist marauders, he did not directly organize them, relying on local fascist bosses to do his dirty work. On November 21 one such band invaded Bologna's city hall, where a newly elected Socialist administration was being sworn in. Ten people died in the resulting battle, and the government suspended the new city administration. The violence spread, as fascist bands attacked left-wing city governments, Socialist headquarters, and union halls.

Presiding over a new movement with little structure, Mussolini struggled to maintain control over his pugnacious political progeny, as the local fascist bosses established strongholds of their own, one to a city. His battle to turn a fractious, locally based series of violent fiefdoms into a national, top-down, smoothly functioning political organization would consume him for the next years.[22]

WITH THE GOVERNMENT PARALYZED, the king dissolved parliament and set new elections for May 15, 1921, only a year and a half after the last round. The resulting campaign took place amid an orgy of fascist violence that engulfed the country's northern and central regions, along with scattered areas of the South. The bands—furnished with trucks by the agricultural landowners—burned down Socialist clubs and union halls and attacked their leaders.[23]

In the five weeks preceding the 1921 election, a hundred people were killed and hundreds more injured. But the Socialists kept most of their seats, electing 122, to which could be added the 16 elected by the Communist Party, a Socialist Party faction that had split off earlier that year. The Catholic Popular Party, another object of Fascist attack, gained seats, electing 107 deputies. Mussolini and the Fascists had run in coalition with members of the old conservative elite, most notably with the then prime minister, Giovanni Giolitti, who saw the Fascists as the bludgeon he needed to bring the Socialists under control. Together they won a majority, with 275 deputies, including 35 Fascists, led by Mussolini.[24]

Shortly after the new parliament convened, Mussolini rose to give his first speech. It would prove memorable. Hundreds of millions of Catholics throughout the world looked to Rome as their spiritual home, he said. This was a source of strength that Italy could not ignore. Fascism, he pledged, to the shock of many who knew him, would help bring about the restoration of Christian society. It would build a Catholic state befitting a Catholic nation.[25]

Mussolini's surprising embrace of the Church came without any previous consultation with Vatican authorities. The Catholic Popular Party stood in the way of his efforts to portray himself as the country's best hope for stopping the Socialists. To get the pope to abandon it, he would have to convince him that he could help the Church more than the Popular Party could. In November the fascist movement formally became the Fascist political party and adopted a new program. Gone was all mention of expropriating Church property and separating church and state.[26]

In trying to enlist Vatican support, Mussolini had his carrot—ending the liberal democratic regime and imposing an authoritarian Catholic state—and his stick. Indeed, he literally did have a stick, the dreaded *manganello,* the wooden truncheon proudly wielded by the Blackshirts. From the Fascists' perspective, the Popular Party was part of a larger network of Catholic institutions in the countryside that stood in their way. At the local level, this obstruction included Catholic Action groups—groups of Catholic laymen and women engaged in religious activity under ecclesiastical supervision—and various Catholic cooperatives. The *squadristi* saw all as fair game for their bloody nighttime raids.

In March 1922 priests from the northern region of Mantua sent a letter to government authorities protesting the Fascist beatings of local priests and Catholic activists. The next month Fascists in Bologna assaulted two Popular Party city councilors. Ratti, who had become pope only a couple of months earlier, was especially incensed to learn that Fascist thugs had sacked the Catholic Action headquarters in his home area of Brianza.[27] And in May, in one of many such stories describing Fascist violence, *La Civiltà cattolica,* Rome's Jesuit journal, reported that, as a group of boys were leaving a Catholic youth club meeting one evening in Arezzo, a squad of Fascists set upon them with clubs and whips. In the months that followed, the daily Vatican newspaper, *L'Osservatore romano,* carried a steady stream of similar stories of attacks on Popular Party activists, local Catholic clubs, and priests. No mention was made of Mussolini, who kept a studied public distance from the raids.[28]

No one better served the role of Fascist stick in dealing with the Church than Roberto Farinacci, boss of Cremona, in northern Italy, another young veteran and former Socialist of the lower middle classes who dominated the early fascist movement. The most fascist of the

Fascists—a title he proudly embraced—Farinacci carried a pistol nestled in a garter strapped under his pants. He embodied not only the
exuberance, violence, intolerance, and authoritarianism of the movement but also its anticlerical roots. Later, when Mussolini would need
to keep the Vatican in line, he could count on Farinacci. Meanwhile
Mussolini's message was clear: he was the only one in the country who
could keep violent anticlerics like Farinacci under control.[29]

Watching the police stand by as marauding Fascist bands torched
their local centers and beat up their leaders, the Socialists decided to
act. On July 29 they called a national strike, threatening not to return to
work until the government stopped the violence. But the strike boo-
meranged. Fascist bands burned down union halls and forced strikers
back to work. On August 3 the *squadristi* took over Milan's city hall.
Only the Fascists, Mussolini proclaimed, could prevent Italy from following Russia's path.[30]

With the country in tumult, the government paralyzed, and the police and military showing their sympathies for the Fascists, the new
pope and his closest advisers began to question the wisdom of opposing Mussolini's crusade. Pius XI had never embraced the Popular
Party; although it had been founded with the blessing of Benedict, it
proudly professed independence from the Vatican. Nor was Pius XI by
ideology or temperament enthusiastic about parliamentary government. He believed that Italy needed a strong man to lead it, free from
the cacophony of multiparty bickering. If he could be sure Mussolini
would work to restore Church influence in Italy, he was not inclined to
hold his anticlerical past against him. Along with this cautious hope,
however, the pope also harbored a fear: if he were to oppose the Fascists and throw Church support to the Popular Party, might Mussolini
unleash the anticlerics of Fascism in a reign of terror against the
Church? Behind Mussolini, worried the pope, stood many Farinaccis.
Never under any illusion that Mussolini personally embraced Catholic
values or cared for anything other than his own aggrandizement, the
pope would be willing to consider a pragmatic deal if he could be convinced that Mussolini would deliver on his promises.[31]

On October 2, 1922, Cardinal Gasparri, the Vatican secretary of state, sent a circular to all Italian bishops telling them that priests were not to align themselves with any political party. As the Fascists plotted their path to power, the pope began to distance the Church from the Catholic party.

Matters came to a head later that month. On October 16 Mussolini convened a meeting of heads of the Fascist militias to finalize plans for an insurrection. Fascist squads would occupy government buildings in the major cities of the country while other Fascist forces would gather in different locations for a march on Rome, aimed at seizing the central government ministries.

Mussolini and the Fascist Quadrumvirate at Naples,
October 24, 1922. Front, left to right: Emilio De Bono, Michele Bianchi,
Italo Balbo, Benito Mussolini, Cesare De Vecchi.

As the man who was to head the new government, Mussolini was to remain in a safe place, able to follow reports from throughout the country and make a dramatic entry to Rome when it had fallen. Four Fascist leaders, Cesare De Vecchi, Italo Balbo, Michele Bianchi, and Emilio De Bono—destined to become the "Quadrumvirate" of Fascist myth—

were to lead the march on the capital. The other Fascist bosses would return to their cities and orchestrate the seizure of local government buildings.

What Mussolini did and where he was in the hours leading up to the uprising remain matters of dispute. In the standard version, which the Fascist regime promulgated, he spent the night of October 27 attending the Milan opera with his wife, trying to lull the government authorities into a false sense of security. In a slight variant of this story, Margherita Sarfatti, not Rachele, accompanied Mussolini to the opera. In a less flattering account, Mussolini holed up in Sarfatti's summer villa at Lake Como, ready to cross the nearby Swiss border to safety should the insurrection fail.[32]

Mussolini could be forgiven if he was a bit distracted at the time, for only a week earlier he had had a new daughter, Elena. He had begun his relationship with her mother, Angela Curti Cucciati, a year earlier, in the midst of his affair with Margherita Sarfatti. Elena would be unusual among his illegitimate children in gaining his deep affection. Years later she would be with him as he awaited his sordid end.[33]

Whether or not he was thinking of his new daughter, Mussolini did have last-minute doubts about the assault on Rome, realizing that if the army were ordered to stop his ragtag ruffians, it could easily destroy them. Just a few weeks earlier, one of Italy's top generals had confidently predicted that at the first shot from the army, "all of fascism will crumble."[34]

Margherita Sarfatti may have talked Mussolini out of his doubts. "Either march or die," she is rumored to have told him. In any case, it was too late to back down. Fascist squads were already beginning to move in cities throughout northern and central Italy.[35]

While the October 28 March on Rome would later become the product of an elaborate Fascist mythology, more significant were the attacks on local government offices that had begun the previous night. In Perugia, the prefect surrendered to the Fascist squads. In Cremona, Farinacci's squads cut off all electricity to the city and then seized the police station, the prefecture, and other strategic points.[36] Elsewhere

Fascist *squadristi* took up their positions surrounding police head-quarters, train stations, and telephone centers. Italian soldiers faced off against them but held their fire, awaiting orders from Rome.

No more than 26,000 men armed with old army rifles, and many carrying no more than a bludgeon, arrived on the outskirts of Rome, their enthusiasm literally dampened by heavy rain. Fascist legend would later claim they numbered 300,000. Facing the disorganized Fascist rowdies were 28,000 Italian troops, their machine guns and ar-mored cars at the ready.

Prime Minister Luigi Facta, realizing that only military action could stop the Fascist mob, drafted a proclamation of a state of emergency. Troops throughout the country would be ordered to disperse the *squadristi* and arrest the Fascist leaders. At six A.M. on the twenty-eighth, Facta presented the order to a hastily called cabinet meeting. Following the ministers' unanimous approval, at 7:50 A.M. prefects throughout the country were notified that a state of emergency was about to be announced. At 8:30 A.M. posters proclaiming the state of emergency began to be pasted onto the walls of Rome. Arriving at the royal Quirinal Palace just before nine, Facta placed the order in front of the king for his signature. But Victor Emmanuel III refused to sign. Facta was stunned. They had discussed the measure the previous day, and the king had seemed determined to defend Rome from the Fascist assault.[37]

The king was a curious character. His grandfather and namesake, Victor Emmanuel II, was the celebrated founder of modern Italy. His Savoyard troops had helped defeat the Austrians in the north and the forces defending the Papal States in the center of the peninsula. For depriving the pope of his lands, Italy's founding king had been excom-municated. His son, King Umberto I, was assassinated in 1900 by an Italian American anarchist from New Jersey, making Victor Emmanuel III king at age thirty. The object of ridicule for his small stature—the mustachioed monarch barely cleared five feet—he never felt secure as king. Intelligent and well informed, he disliked having to deal with po-litical parties and parliament. Nor did he have any love for the pope or the Vatican. Priests, he thought, served appropriately as chaplains to the king. He found sharing his capital with another man who claimed authority over it to be distasteful.

As the American journalist Anne McCormick observed, no one in Italy made less trouble than the king, who shunned all publicity, avoided interfering with the government, and appeared in public only when he had no choice. One of the few occasions he showed himself in Rome was for the opening of parliament, which required his presence. McCormick got to see him at one such an occasion in 1921. He arrived in a crystal chariot drawn by white horses with jeweled harnesses, a bevy of buglers leading the way. When he entered the chamber and sat down, he seemed "dwarfed by the size of the throne . . . and when he kicked away the red velvet footstool . . . he looked not unlike an unhappy small boy dangling his legs in a chair too big for him."[38]

The king had a strong sense of duty, but he was cautious and fearful. As he pondered his options on the morning of October 28, he worried that battling the Fascists might lead to even greater bloodshed. He knew he could not count on his own popularity, for he entirely lacked either the imperious confidence that might have inspired awe in his subjects or the warmth that might have promoted their goodwill. An inveterate pessimist, he worried that he could not count on the army's loyalty. He also thought it might be more prudent to have Mussolini in the government rather than fighting it from outside. After years of social unrest, many among the military brass and the heads of industry thought Mussolini was their best bet for putting an end to the Socialist threat and restoring order.[39]

Humiliated, Facta resigned. The king first tried to name a conservative former prime minister to head the new government and give Mussolini and a few of his Fascist colleagues positions in the cabinet. But with Fascist squads occupying strategic sites in much of central and northern Italy and the king having decided not to send the army into action, Mussolini was in a position to reject the proposal out of hand. Left with little choice, the king capitulated. He invited the Fascist leader to return to Rome and form a government.

Mussolini came down by train from Milan, emerging from his sleeping car in the capital on the morning of the thirtieth. Presenting himself in his black shirt at the royal palace, he is said to have told the king, "Majesty, I come from the battlefield—fortunately bloodless." Only on their leader's arrival in Rome were the wet and weary Blackshirts finally allowed to enter the city. They pranced through the streets, singing, chanting, celebrating, and sacking the occasional local Socialist headquarters.

Over the next days, Mussolini put together his cabinet, reserving the two most important positions—minister of internal affairs, in charge of the prefects and the police, and minister of foreign affairs—for himself. The cabinet included two members of the Popular Party, along with three Fascists and an assortment of others from the old Liberal elite. In presenting the king with his slate, he began a complex relationship that was to last over two decades. The urbane monarch would seem to share little with the champion of thuggery and violence, a man who bragged about being "unsocialized."[40] Nor could the king feel comfortable with the rabble-rousing blacksmith's son who had for years called for ending the monarchy. But he came to respect Mussolini's drive, his ability to end the country's chaos, his lack of personal venality, and his dream of restoring Italy's greatness.[41]

In one of his first acts as prime minister, Mussolini led his cabinet to a mass at the altar of the Unknown Soldier at the Vittoriano Monument in Rome. There he ordered the men to kneel in prayer for a minute. For many of them, Vatican secretary of state Gasparri quipped, this "must have seemed an exceedingly long time." Mussolini was eager to convince the pope that he would act aggressively to restore Church prerogatives. "Mussolini let us know that he was a good Catholic," Cardinal Gasparri explained to the Belgian ambassador.[42]

In mid-November, Mussolini stood in the Chamber of Deputies for a vote of confidence. Although there were only 35 Fascist deputies at the time, 316 members voted in his favor. Former prime minister Giovanni Giolitti and other members of the political establishment still believed they could use Mussolini to destroy the Socialists while retaining ultimate control themselves. Members of the Popular Party went along, many grudgingly. So it was that Mussolini first came to power, through a legal vote in a freely elected parliament.

He cut a rather odd figure, exuding an intense energy. He had not yet acquired the thick chest that he would later delight in baring for the cameras, preferably while standing atop a platform, straddling a horse, or grasping a hoe. His hairline had receded, giving him an imposing forehead, his thinning hair combed straight back; his mustache was long gone, and lacking sideburns, his hair was cut in a straight line from his temples to above his ears. But what most impressed those who saw him were his extraordinary vitality and his sharp, piercing eyes.

Benito Mussolini, the new Italian prime minister, November 1922

In his first months as head of the government, Mussolini wore a short black suit jacket and tight pants marred by a deep crease just below the knees. "He must be a poor devil," observed one of the ushers in Palazzo Chigi, the prime minister's headquarters. "He hasn't anyone to iron his pants for him." The contrast with previous government heads, drawn from the Liberal elite—older, gray-bearded men in tailored dark suits, accustomed to the finer things in life—could scarcely have been greater. "Mussolini was an unusual minister," his longtime assistant Quinto Navarra recalled; "you thought you were standing in front of a homeless man, a journalist with his sleeves stained by ink and worn heels on his shoes."[43]

A former prime minister, Antonio Salandra, described the enigmatic figure that Mussolini cut: an odd mixture of geniality and vulgarity, sincere expression of noble sentiments followed by base instincts for reprisal and vendetta, bluntness and theatricality, tenacious assertions followed by instant changes of course, striking and effective eloquence sprinkled with cultured references, and presumptuous ignorance expressed in lower-class slang. But what most struck the former prime minister and what most, he thought, drove Mussolini, was his devotion to the cult of his own personality. He showed exceptional energy and an iron will, and he tried to make up in intuition for his lack of any real training for running a government. He was "a force of nature."[44]

Shortly after becoming prime minister, Mussolini had to attend an official reception for the Spanish royal family, the kind of occasion he hated. When he arrived with his customary two days of stubble on his face, Queen Helen, Victor Emmanuel's very proper wife, glared at him. It would not be the only occasion she would have to note his failings in the way of personal hygiene. Nor could Mussolini ever get used to the bourgeois habit of taking a bath every day, (over)compensating by frequent splashings of cheap cologne.

Preparing for one of his first diplomatic dinners, held at the British embassy, Mussolini took advantage of the advice of Baron Russo, an aide to the prime minister who was left over from the previous administration.

"It is very simple, Excellency," explained the baron. "You will sit next to the British Ambassadress. Watch every move she makes. Use the same spoon, the same knife, the same fork that she does. Everything she does, you do."

Arriving at the grand hall of the embassy, Mussolini was the center of attention, but he felt ill at ease. His scowls and his bulging eyes worked well at his rallies, but they met a less enthusiastic reception among the tuxedoed diplomats. His host for the dinner, Sir Ronald Graham, the British ambassador, had himself earlier noted Mussolini's posturing. Reporting his first impressions of the new Italian prime minister to London, Graham admitted that he had been put off by the fact that in his public appearances, Mussolini "adopted an unnecessary degree of pose and manners which can only be described as Napoleonic." He elaborated, "He has stalked about with his hand across his breast and thrust in the lapel of his coat; his gaze was fixed; he never smiled and appeared wrapt in fierce gloom."[45]

At Graham's reception, Mussolini made his way through the eight-course dinner by watching Lady Sybil, the ambassador's wife. She soon realized what he was doing, as he followed her with every move of his fork and knife. Although he was momentarily taken aback when she brought her little soup cup to her mouth rather than use one of the innumerable spoons to drink it, he followed her lead.

As he finally got ready to leave, he thanked her, and she made oblique reference to the help she had provided.

"Only once was I confused," said Mussolini.

"And when was that?" she asked.

"I did not know that the English drank their soup like beer."[46]

LITTLE MORE THAN A YEAR after he had first been elected to parliament, and eight years since he had been expelled from the Socialist Party, the thirty-nine-year-old blacksmith's son had become the most powerful man in Italy. The previous years had been marked by gut-wrenching violence and frightening uncertainty. For some, the Fascist leader promised the possibility of a return to normality. For others, he threatened a new kind of social warfare. Where he would lead them, no one could then imagine.

THE FATAL EMBRACE

I F EITHER CARDINAL GASPARRI OR CARDINAL DE LAI WAS HOPING THAT the new pope would prove putty in their hands, they were to be disappointed. Pius XI would be no weak pope. His love of order and deep sense of obedience to authority quickly set the tone for his reign. "He wears his tiara even when he goes to bed," joked one of the priests in the Vatican. His commands were to be followed "not immediately, but sooner than immediately," the pope was fond of saying. For those clergymen who asked to be relieved from one of the many prohibitions found in canon law, he had no sympathy. "Laws are made to be obeyed," he told them. The French prelate Eugène Tisserant, who knew Ratti from the time he had been librarian in Milan, noted a striking change. They had been close, and Tisserant had seen Ratti's lighter side. In 1918, when Tisserant, on leave from the French army, had visited him at the Vatican Library, Ratti had introduced him to Benedict XV by saying, "Holy Father, here is my military attaché." But now he no longer seemed the same man. He was "so strongly overwhelmed by the grandeur of his new charge," observed Tisserant, "that he seemed extraordinarily distant to us."[1]

The new pontiff's commitment to proper protocol was on display at the first audience he called for the diplomatic corps, two weeks after his election. When the ambassadors and delegates to the Holy See arrived, along with their numerous assistants, they found that the papal throne stood at one end of the vast hall, with only six seats placed in front of it. Only the ambassadors having full diplomatic status would be permitted to sit down; all the rest were to stand.[2]

Ratti's sense of the dignity of the papal throne was so developed that he kept his own family members at a distance. On becoming pope in 1903, the unassuming Pius X had brought his two unmarried sisters to Rome, installing them in a small apartment above a shop near St. Peter's Square. They visited him often, chatting, sipping wine, and reciting the rosary together. Ratti had once been close to his siblings, but now that he was pope, he would see them only if they made an appointment with his secretary and awaited their turn in the waiting room. On these occasions, he insisted that his brother address him as "Holy Father" and "Your Holiness." He let it be known he did not want these visits to occur too often, for he was Father to a much larger family that required his attention. Years later, when the pope lay in bed mortally ill, his elderly sister begged to be allowed to come to his side to comfort him. She was turned away.[3]

Although the new pope angered the *zelanti* by remaining true to his promise to appoint Gasparri secretary of state, the Church's modernist wing was unenthusiastic as well. The fact that, in choosing his name, he had decided to honor Pius IX and Pius X seemed an ominous sign. At a moment of such great international tensions, wrote one commentator in Rome, what was needed was something much more than "the narrow-mindedness of a life-long paleographer, closed for decades in the dusty reading rooms of the Ambrosiana and the Vatican." The British envoy to the Vatican was similarly unimpressed. The new pope left the impression in those who met him, he wrote, of a pedantic teacher: "Change his skull-cap and soutane for the M.A.'s mortar-board and gown—and there is your Headmaster as depicted in Victorian schoolboy stories." True, the envoy added, the new pope was cordial, but he seemed to view all laymen as children who needed to be taught rather than as people from whom he might learn something. With Europe convulsed by threats of revolution and Italy's old order in shambles, was this the man who could deal with the challenges that lay ahead?[4]

The new pontiff surrounded himself with staff he could trust, bringing many of his Milan assistants to Rome. To care for his rooms and kitchen, he appointed Teodolinda Banfi, known simply as Linda: she had already been with him for thirty-six years and had worked for his mother for fourteen years before that.[5] He also brought the young Milanese priest Carlo Confalonieri to serve as his private secretary, along with his other Milanese assistant, Diego Venini, and the curiously named Giovanni Malvestiti (Malvestiti literally meaning "poorly dressed") to take charge of his wardrobe.[6] Although Ratti's tastes were simple, he was partial to Linda's cooking. In 1926, when he decided she should retire, he told the German Franciscans who were to replace her: "I don't want to have to remind you: German precision, German silence, but not German cuisine."[7]

Each morning at six his alarm clock woke him, and after saying his first prayers, he celebrated mass in his private chapel, followed by a light breakfast. His apartment, consisting of three rooms on the fourth floor,[8] was in the left wing of the U-shaped Apostolic Palace that enveloped the San Damaso Courtyard. Perched over Bernini's colonnade, it looked directly onto St. Peter's Square. His bedroom was simple, no different from that of a village priest, with a brass-frame bed and an old-fashioned chest of drawers covered with a white tablecloth. On the walls he hung photographs of his parents and his brother, as well as religious paintings.

After breakfast, the pope went down a floor to his office—or as he called it, his "library"—where he began the day reading his mail and the Italian, German, French, British, and American newspapers. It was a large room, with little furniture and only one small rug, placed under his desk. A few old paintings hung on the walls. The pope sat in an ornate Louis XV chair, his desk covered with piles of books and a large crucifix, along with a compass and barometer that told of his nostalgia for his Alpine expeditions. Three windows, their curtains opened during the day to let in the sun, faced St. Peter's Square behind him. As visitors entered, they saw a white figure silhouetted against the sunlight seated behind the desk. Three chairs faced him in front of the desk. One of the few personal touches the pope allowed himself was a book stand, where he always kept one of his favorite books open.[9]

Pius XI began his daily round of appointments at nine A.M., often by meeting his secretary of state. When visitors entered, they sank to a knee, which for many was already trembling, for given the pope's authoritarian nature, his brusque manner, and his insistence that his or-

Pius XI at his desk, 1922

ders be obeyed to the letter, his visitors were rarely at ease. They then stood up, took a couple of steps, and bowed again before taking a final two steps and genuflecting a third time. Given the confined space and their nervousness, some stumbled. Luigi Sincero, one of the highest-ranking cardinals, remarked that preparing to see the pope was like preparing for an exam as a schoolboy. Other high prelates admitted to nervously reciting a prayer as they crossed the pope's threshold. In departing, visitors again dropped to a knee and repeated the same three bows in reverse as they backed out.[10]

When the last morning visitor left, often not until two P.M., the pope took his lunch. He was fond of eating risotto, Milanese style, with saffron, or a thick Italian vegetable soup and a piece of meat with cooked vegetables, followed by fruit. He drank a half glass of wine along with several glasses of water. There was perhaps no more telling reflection of his view of the pontiff's dignity than his insistence on dining alone. While both Pius X and Benedict XV had eaten with their assistants or invited special guests to join them for a meal, Pius XI would not allow anyone to eat in his presence, although he did have his aides stand beside him to go over reports and write down his orders. One day, some weeks after his election, his weary assistants, not looking forward to years of standing as he ate but afraid to say anything, surreptitiously brought in little stools, which they placed against the wall. When they completed their reports, they sat down. Taken aback, the pope looked up from his plate but said nothing. The stools remained.[11]

After a brief nap, at four P.M. the pope walked out to the courtyard, where Swiss Guards, awaiting him, dropped to their knees, their right hands on their berets and their left clutching their long ax-topped poles.[12] In those first weeks, an elderly coachman sat with his long whip raised in his right hand, perched over two beautiful black horses. Within a few months, the carriage would be replaced by the pope's first automobile. After a short ride, the pontiff began his hour-long walk through the Vatican gardens, hands often clasped behind his back, a black fedora perched over the white skullcap on his head. In cooler weather, he wore a white double-breasted coat that reached his feet.

These were not leisurely strolls but purposive strides befitting the "mountaineer pope," as he repeatedly circumnavigated the gardens. An aide in long black gown, a clerical collar around his neck, struggled to keep up with him, several paces behind.

Pius XI during his walk in the Vatican gardens, accompanied by Monsignor Carlo Confalonieri

Following his walk, the pope devoted an hour to private prayer before returning to his office. At six or seven he began a new series of appointments, primarily with members of the Curia, the Holy See's central administration. After the last of them, he recited the rosary with his secretaries and at ten P.M. ate supper. The last thing he did each night was return to his office and take out a massive bound register.

There he recorded all the gifts he had received that day and all the expenses he had incurred. At midnight he went to bed.[13]

ROME IN THESE YEARS was a study in contrasts, as the ancient, the medieval, and the early modern rubbed up against the new. Since Italian troops had seized the city in 1870, the social landscape had been transformed. Monasteries had been converted into government buildings and schools. Men from the north streamed into the city to take up government jobs in Italy's new capital, and impoverished peasants from the center and south arrived in wooden-wheeled oxcarts with all their belongings, the booming population of civil servants and construction industry creating new jobs.

Although the Church no longer ran the city, Rome still seemed to have a church on every block. Priests in their black cassocks, nuns in their habits, tonsure-headed Dominicans in their white robes, maroon-gowned Franciscans, Greek Catholic seminarians in their blue cassocks and red sashes, and a kaleidoscope of other monks and seminarians clogged the city's roads. Carabinieri in their Napoleonic hats and red-striped trousers mixed with an assortment of soldiers and municipal police. Wet nurses, to whom the middle classes entrusted their infants, did their best to make their way through the crowded streets with their little wards.

While many Romans were impressed with all that was new—not least the electric tram, whose tracks crisscrossed the cobblestone streets, and the ever-growing number of automobiles on the impossibly narrow, winding, bumpy roads—signs abounded of a country that was still largely composed of semiliterate peasants. Horse-drawn wine carts descended from the countryside to deliver goods to the city's many *osterie*. Signs outside the fancier of these eateries promised *vini scelti* and *ottima cucina*. Alongside them, more modest shops simply advertised *pane e pasta*. Small produce shops, a riot of colors thanks to their stocks of fruits and vegetables, lined the roads, the tiny premises serving as the shopkeeper's living quarters as well. In early spring, small grapelike tomatoes arrived from the south. Greengrocers artfully arranged carrots, turnips, and broccoli around their doors. Romans also shopped at the small markets that sprang up each morning in the city's little piazzas. There grocers constructed impressive pyramids of oranges, apples, and white figs. Pasta vendors piled up mounds of freshly made macaroni and spaghetti. Plucked chickens hung by their feet from stall awnings. Gleaming, tightly packed rows of fish attracted those who could afford it.

The larger outdoor markets, their stalls protected from sun and rain by broad umbrellas, attracted a wide range of customers. Princes' fur-coated majordomos jostled alongside poor women in knitted peasant shawls. After haggling over price, women placed their modest purchases in large checkered handkerchiefs. Flower vendors balanced huge baskets brimming with daffodils, mimosa, carnations, and violets on their heads. Other hawkers sang the praises of their motley mix of clothes, folding knives, and onions, their wares swung over their shoulders or carried on trays hung from their necks.

Occasionally a distinctive, well-dressed figure could be seen sitting at a table in the middle of a small piazza. On benches arranged around him, his patrons—mainly old men and women—sat awaiting their turn. On his table lay an inkwell, some sheets of paper, and a blotting pad. He penned letters and filled out forms for the illiterate. Priests knew which streets had shops that sold clerical garb. Seminarians knew where to find secondhand bookstalls. Tourists consulted their guidebooks to locate the stalls that sold antiques and jewelry, not all of it fake. Old women stopped occasionally at a modest streetside shrine, saying a prayer to the fading image of the Madonna and Christ child that graced the stucco wall.

Mules and donkeys carried bricks and barrels, scarlet tassels hanging from their harnesses and scarlet cloths on their backs. Laundry hung from clotheslines that stretched across the narrow streets. Cobblers pounded their shoes, and stonecutters chipped their stones in tiny, dark shops. Women shouted down from their windows to bargain with peddlers on the street below. They put their payment in a basket and lowered it down by rope. The vendor replaced the coins with goods for the return trip. When the scorching sunlight gave way to clouds and rain, Rome burst out in umbrellas, from the tattered green ones of the scavengers to the shiny black ones that liveried servants held over the heads of the city's elite. Other than the automobiles, which had no need of them, practically every vehicle sprouted an umbrella as well. "There are few more grotesque silhouettes in Rome," wrote one observer earlier in the century, "than her cabmen, with their weary, ewe-necked horses and their ramshackle open victorias, shrinking under umbrellas which look like old mushrooms."[14]

The pope got to see none of this, for he refused to venture beyond the Vatican walls. For decades, every pope had suffered the ignominy of living on a tiny plot of land surrounded by the very state that had seized the Church's territories and drastically reduced its political power. The neighborhood outside, squeezed into the land between the Vatican palaces and the Tiber, retained something of the scent, sound, and feel of the old regime, a shabby, overpopulated jumble of small streets and alleys. Only when visitors made their way west through the narrow streets, filled with vendors of sacred memorabilia, did the magnificence of St. Peter's Basilica and Bernini's colonnade suddenly appear.[15]

THE POPE'S DECISION TO consider supporting Mussolini surprised many in the Church. None was more embarrassed than Father Enrico Rosa, editor of *La Civiltà cattolica,* who up to the time Mussolini came to power had used the journal's pages to denounce Fascism as one of the Church's worst enemies. Days before the March on Rome, Rosa had warned that the Fascist movement was "violent and anti-Christian, headed by sinister men . . . the failed effort of the old liberalism, of Masons, rural landowners, rich industrialists, journalists, tinhorn politicians and the like."[16]

La Civiltà cattolica had been founded in 1850, shortly after Pope Pius IX returned to Rome following the 1848 uprising that had driven him into exile. Twice a month the editor took the proofs of the upcom-

ing issue to the Vatican secretary of state office for approval before publication.[17]

The fifty-two-year-old Rosa had joined the Jesuit editorial collective seventeen years earlier and been appointed its head by Pope Benedict XV in 1915. Despite his experience, he had somehow missed the
signs of the pope's change of course. Reading Rosa's latest anti-Fascist
tirade, the superior general of the Society of Jesus, a man for whom Fascism would prove particularly congenial, was furious. He instructed
Rosa to change his tune.[18] Even worse, Rosa learned that Pius XI too
had had a change of heart. The pope had seen something in Mussolini
he liked. Despite all their differences, the two men shared some important values. Neither had any sympathy for parliamentary democracy.
Neither believed in freedom of speech or freedom of association. Both
saw Communism as a grave threat.[19] Both thought Italy was mired in
crisis and that the current political system was beyond salvation.

A conversation the pope had with Father Agostino Gemelli—recent
founder of the Catholic University of Milan and a man close to the
pontiff—offers a glimpse of Pius XI's attitude toward Mussolini in the
first weeks of the new government. "Praise, no," the pope told him. But
"openly organizing opposition is not a good idea, for we have many
interests to protect." Caution was needed. "Eyes open!" he advised.[20]

The pope instructed Rosa to throw out the critical piece on Fascism
that he had drafted for the upcoming issue of his journal and publish a
friendlier editorial in its place.[21] "When a form of government is legiti-
mately constituted," Rosa now wrote, "even though it may initially have
been defective or even questionable in various ways . . . it is one's duty
to support it, for public order or the common good requires it. Nor is it
permitted to either individuals or to parties to plot to defeat it or sup-
plant it or change it with unjust means."[22]

While *La Civiltà cattolica* would continue to denounce episodes of
Fascist violence aimed at Catholic organizations, it would never again
denounce Mussolini or Fascism. Quite the opposite: the journal would
work on the Vatican's behalf to legitimate Fascism in the eyes of all
good Catholics, in Italy and beyond.[23]

——

THE POPE'S NEWFOUND HOPES for Mussolini got a further lift when the prime minister concluded his first address to parliament by asking for God's help; no Italian government head since the founding of modern Italy had ever let the word *God* out of his mouth. Secretary of State Gasparri also saw grounds for hope. "Providence makes use of strange instruments to bring good fortune to Italy," he told the Belgian ambassador: Mussolini was not only a "remarkable organizer" but a "great character." Admittedly, the new prime minister knew nothing of religion, Gasparri added with a chuckle: Mussolini thought all Catholic holidays fell on Sundays.[24]

Pius XI set out the goals for his papacy in his first encyclical, *Ubi arcano*, in December 1922.[25] He lamented attempts to take Jesus Christ out of the schools and out of the halls of government. He bewailed women's lack of propriety in "the increasing immodesty of their dress and conversation and by their participation in shameful dances." The notion that, in turning away from the Church, society was advancing, he warned, was mistaken: "In the face of our much praised progress, we behold with sorrow society lapsing back slowly but surely into a state of barbarism." He stressed the importance of obedience to proper authority and took up Pius X's program of battling "modernism." He belittled the new League of Nations, on which so many in Europe were pinning their hopes for peace: "No merely human institution of today can be as successful in devising a set of international laws which will be in harmony with world conditions as the Middle Ages were in the possession of that true League of Nations, Christianity." The pope's plan was to bring about the Kingdom of Christ on earth. At heart, it was a medieval vision.[26]

Mussolini was meanwhile sketching out his own authoritarian plan. "I affirm that the revolution has its rights," he said in his opening speech to parliament. "I am here to defend the blackshirts' revolution and to empower it to the maximum degree. . . . With three hundred thousand armed young men throughout the country, ready for anything and almost mystically ready to carry out my orders, I could have punished all those who have defamed and tried to sully the name of Fascism."[27]

In late December, Mussolini convened the first meeting of the Grand Council of Fascism, which was responsible for addressing the most important issues of government policy and party organization. The following month the council approved the transformation of the sundry Fascist militias into the Voluntary Militia for National Security. These units had previously been the creatures of the local Fascist bosses; now Mussolini was eager to wrest control from them. Unlike the regular military, which swore allegiance to the king, members of the militia swore allegiance to Mussolini.[28]

He moved quickly to make good on his promises to the Vatican, eager to show that he could do what the Popular Party had been incapable of doing. He would restore the privileges that the Church enjoyed before Italian unification. He ordered crucifixes to be placed on the wall of every classroom in the country, then in all courtrooms and hospital rooms. He made it a crime to insult a priest or to speak disparagingly of the Catholic religion. He restored Catholic chaplains to military units; he offered priests and bishops more generous state allowances; and to the special delight of the Vatican, he required that the Catholic religion be taught in the elementary schools. He showered the Church with money, including three million lire to restore churches damaged during the war and subsidies for Church-run Italian schools abroad. In cities and towns throughout the country, in the course of Mussolini's many triumphal visits, bishops and local parish priests were encouraged to approach him to ask for funds for church repair. To further burnish his Catholic credentials, later in 1923 he had his wife Rachele and their three children—Edda and two sons, Vittorio and Bruno—baptized. Rachele, more principled in her anticlerical faith than her husband, went only reluctantly. Raised in the heart of red rural Romagna, she had learned early to despise priests and the wealth and power of the Church.[29]

Because many Italians and foreign observers were uncertain what to make of Italy's new leader and his violent Fascist movement, Vatican approval played a major role in legitimizing the new regime. In widely quoted remarks, Cardinal Vincenzo Vannutelli, dean of the College of Cardinals, praised Mussolini as the man "already acclaimed by all Italy as the rebuilder of the fate of the nation according to its religious and civil traditions."[30]

Mussolini was eager to cement his growing bond with the Vatican by meeting with its secretary of state, Cardinal Gasparri. Like him, Gasparri came from a humble background. "I was born May 5, 1852 in Capovallazza, one of the hamlets that form the Town of Ussita," Gasparri recalled in his typed memoir, "in the middle of the Sibillini mountains, about 750 meters above sea level. Clean air, enchanting view, healthy, hard-working, honest people, with large families, and the Gasparri families were most prolific of all." His parents had had ten children, of whom he, the last, was naturally the favorite. While his nine siblings were "especially robust and lively," he reflected, "I was frail, rather sickly, so that some predicted, and perhaps augured, that my life would be short, much to Mamma's displeasure." While his father spent many nights sleeping with the sheep in the pastures, little Pietro provided the family entertainment. As they huddled by the warmth of the fireplace, he read them stories of the saints. They all cried together as he recounted the terrible trials faced by the Church's martyrs. "Mother had the gift of tears, transmitted to all the children, especially to me."[31]

Gasparri's rendezvous with Mussolini had to be arranged with great care, for the Vatican secretary of state could not be seen meeting with the government's head—the Holy See still did not recognize Italy's legitimacy. The secret meeting was arranged by Gasparri's old friend Carlo Santucci. Part of an aristocratic family close to the popes, he had been one of the first members of the Popular Party to break off to support the Fascists. His home had a valuable feature: it was in a corner building that had entrances on two different streets.

On January 19 Mussolini arrived in a car with his chief of staff, who would wait outside the building while the prime minister went in. Mussolini entered through one door, where he was greeted by Santucci's

Cardinal Pietro Gasparri, Vatican secretary of state, 1914–30

father; the cardinal entered through the other, where Santucci's mother welcomed him.

The key issue on Cardinal Gasparri's mind that day was not whether the Vatican would be willing to help end Italy's democracy, for the Vatican had no particular fondness for democratic government. Rather, the question was whether Mussolini could be trusted to honor his promise to restore the Church's influence in Italy and how likely it was that, with Church support, he could succeed.[32]

For Mussolini, the former *mangiaprete*, or priest-eater, as he had been known in his earlier years, the stakes were high. If he could be the man to restore harmony between church and state, if he could win the pope's blessing for his government and bring the conflict between them to an end, he would succeed where his predecessors had all failed. He would be a hero throughout the Catholic world.

For an hour and a half, the two men met alone. When Gasparri left, he paused to tell Santucci how pleased he was with the meeting, calling Mussolini "a man of the first order." Mussolini rushed out the other door without saying a word. In the car, his chief of staff was eager to hear what had happened. "We must be extremely careful," Mussolini told him, "for these most eminent men are very shrewd. Before entering very far into even preliminary discussions, they want to be sure our government is stable."[33]

The two men did make one decision that day: they agreed on a confidential go-between, a person whom both the pope and Mussolini would trust to convey their messages on the most sensitive matters.

It is not entirely clear how the sixty-one-year old Jesuit Pietro Tacchi Venturi came to be the choice.[34] He was born in 1861 to a prosperous family in central Italy; his father, a lawyer, proudly kept the rifle he had used in 1849 in helping defeat Garibaldi's forces and retake Rome for the pope. Pietro went at an early age to study for the priesthood in Rome, then newly annexed to the Italian kingdom. In 1896 he began writing the official history of the Jesuit order and spent much of the next two decades in research that took him to libraries, archives, and monasteries across Europe. He published the first volume in 1910. During the Great War, Włodzimierz Ledóchowski, the Jesuit superior general, a Pole from the Austrian Empire, was forced out of Italy as an enemy alien. Tacchi Venturi, who had been appointed secretary general of the order in 1914, was left in charge of the Jesuits' activities in Rome.[35]

"Lean and severe," as one of Tacchi Venturi's colleagues described his appearance, he looked the part of the austere Jesuit. His baldness produced the effect of an oval face; his pointed ears set off against the fringe of gray hair on the back of his head. Clad in black clerical gown and white collar, he exuded seriousness and intensity.[36]

Achille Ratti first met the Jesuit scholar in 1899, when one of Tacchi Venturi's research trips brought him to the Ambrosiana Library.[37] Mussolini had apparently first heard of him from his brother, Arnaldo, who became friendly with the Jesuit during the months he spent in

Pietro Tacchi Venturi, S.J.

Rome during the war.[38] Then shortly before his secret meeting with Gasparri, Mussolini had met Tacchi Venturi. Within weeks of coming to power, Mussolini realized that one of the easier things he could do to ingratiate himself with the pope was to give the Chigi library to the Vatican. The government had purchased Palazzo Chigi—then as today the Italian prime minister's headquarters—in 1918. With the building came its private library, begun by the seventeenth-century pope Alexander VII, which included three thousand old manuscripts and thirty thousand books. Achille Ratti, then Vatican librarian, had heard that the government was purchasing the building and tried unsuccessfully to acquire the library. In response to Mussolini's offer to donate it, the Vatican sent Tacchi Venturi to evaluate the collection. Hearing one day that the Jesuit was in the building and perhaps recalling that his brother had spoken well of him, Mussolini sent word that he should come to his office to meet him. As it turned out, that encounter in late 1922 would be the first of many, many meetings between the Jesuit and Mussolini over the next two decades.[39]

THE EARLY DISCUSSIONS DID little to stop Fascist violence against priests and Catholic activists suspected of Popular Party sympathies. Three weeks after Mussolini became prime minister, the bishop of the northeastern city of Vicenza publicly denounced the latest attacks on local priests and proclaimed that perpetrators would be excommunicated.[40] In Ascoli Piceno, in the mountains east of Rome, a Fascist squad accosted a priest who edited a local paper and forced him to drink a liter of castor oil.[41]

In December forty club-wielding Fascists broke into a Catholic youth group meeting on church grounds in the northwestern town of Aosta, smashed the doors and windows, tore up the billiard table, and took their cudgels to the crucifix and the sacred images on the walls. When an outraged bystander tried to stop them, they beat him.[42] That same week in Padua, Fascist thugs ordered a teenager to remove his Catholic youth group badge. When he bravely refused, one of them put a gun to his head, while another ripped the badge off.[43] And on a December evening near Vicenza, a car pulled up outside a local Catholic youth club headquarters. Seven Blackshirts got out, carrying rifles. While their comrades stayed outside, three barged into the room. The men waved their rifles menacingly at the twenty terrified youths gathered there and ordered them to be quiet. They then directed their rifles at the two priests who were conducting the meeting, forcing them to drink bottles of castor oil.[44] Throughout 1923 such attacks continued, duly noted and lamented in the Vatican daily newspaper. But as the violence erupted periodically over the next years, the Catholic press adopted a common refrain: the attacks were the work of isolated extremists outside Mussolini's control.[45]

Local Catholic Action groups, created by Pius X in 1905 to provide a framework for organizing the Catholic laity, were among the most frequent targets of these attacks.[46] No group was dearer to Pius XI, who earned a reputation as "the Pope of Catholic Action." Men and women, boys and girls each had their own groups. The university students had a unit of their own, divided into separate chapters by university. Catholic Action activities were to be religious and educational but in fact went far beyond, for the pope thought of its members as ground troops for re-Christianizing Italian society, and this would require much more than simply prayer and lessons. To keep a close eye on the organization, he appointed Monsignor Giuseppe Pizzardo, the substitute secretary of state and one of Gasparri's two undersecretaries, to be its chaplain. The Church hierarchy was to be in charge. "You have only to follow the advice and the instructions that come from above," the pope once explained to a group of the Catholic Action lay leaders.[47]

The pope was unhappy and indignant about the attacks on local parish priests and Catholic Action clubs. But Mussolini proved adept at using the violence to his benefit, convincing the pope that he was the only man in Italy who could keep the rowdies under control. The *L'Osservatore romano* articles reporting the episodes of bludgeoning and castor-oil-guzzling almost all ended with respectful pleas to Mussolini to see that those responsible be punished. Occasionally, when local sentiments ran particularly high, Mussolini had a few people arrested, but it was rare that the culprits were ever brought to trial, much less convicted.

By early 1923 Mussolini had good reason to think that his strategy was paying off. A deal with the pope was taking shape. While he would not abandon the violence that had proven so effective in intimidating his opponents, he did not want to unduly anger the pope. He would continue to restore privileges that the Church had not enjoyed for many decades. In exchange, he needed the pope to eliminate the remaining Catholic opposition to his rule.

BORN TO COMMAND

I N THE SPRING OF 1923, THE POPULAR PARTY FOUND ITSELF IN AN untenable position. It depended above all on Church support, but the pope had decided to end it. In April, at the pope's direction, the Vatican daily told its readers that, given Mussolini's efforts on behalf of the Church, there was no longer any need for a Catholic party. Later in the month *La Civiltà cattolica* took up the pope's new line, singing the praises of the Fascist government. "The shouts of Mussolini's squads, 'down with Bolshevism!'"—the journal enthused—"are attracting supporters and sympathy from one end of Italy to the other. . . . In its thought, sentiment, action, all of fascism consists simply of a protest and revolt against socialism." It praised Mussolini for his efforts to restore order, hierarchy, and discipline. "Fascism," the journal proclaimed, "seeks to place spiritual values once again in the place of honor they once occupied, especially as required by the battle against liberalism, to restore the most conspicuous of these, religious upbringing and the nation's Catholic inspiration."[1] Heartened by these signs that the pope thought the Popular Party dispensable, Mussolini issued an ultimatum: unless the party gave him its unqualified support, he would dismiss its two government ministers and cast it out of his coalition. When party founder Don Luigi Sturzo and his colleagues refused, the ministers were forced out.[2]

The pope now found it intolerable that Don Sturzo should continue to serve as Popular Party head. Rome's Catholic newspaper, *Corriere d'Italia,* carried a plea by a domestic prelate of the pope urging the priest to resign. Readers assumed that the request came from the pope himself.[3]

Behind the scenes, Pius was indeed demanding that Sturzo resign, but the priest was slow to comply. Impatient with the foot dragging, the pope sent Tacchi Venturi, his special envoy to Mussolini, to see him.[4] Sturzo complained that in forcing him to step down, the pope was undermining the one party "that is truly inspired by Christian principles of civil life and ... today serves to limit ... the arbitrary rule of the dictatorship." This plea made no impression on Pius XI.[5]

Reluctantly, Don Sturzo agreed to obey the papal command. The pope sent Tacchi Venturi to work out the timing of the public announcement with Mussolini and to get him to play down the news in the press. In no case, said the pope, should the government "boast about a victory."[6] Over the next twenty-four hours, the Jesuit worked closely with Mussolini to orchestrate Sturzo's removal.[7]

Pius had hoped that mollifying Mussolini in this way would help end the ongoing violence against Popular Party activists and priests, but his action had the opposite effect. Once it became clear that the pope was pulling Church support from the Catholic party, members found themselves increasingly isolated and subject to the depredations of local *squadristi*. In late August a Fascist newspaper proclaimed that the regime's greatest enemy was no longer socialism but the Popular Party. Fascist squads were soon on the prowl.

Giovanni Minzoni was the young parish priest of a small town outside Ferrara, about thirty miles northeast of Bologna. He was known for his courage as a military chaplain at the front during the war, and his popularity with local youth and devotion to the Popular Party were getting in the way of local Fascist Party recruitment. One night, as he walked down a dark alley on his way to the parish recreation room, the priest realized he was being followed. Before he could turn around, two men jumped him, smashed his head with clubs, and fled. With blood pouring from his wounds, the priest struggled to his knees, then fell again. Somehow he lifted himself up and staggered toward his church, but he did not quite make it, collapsing, unconscious, nearby. Horrified parishioners found him sprawled there, his skull crushed, but still alive, and carried him in. By midnight he was dead.

As was his custom, Mussolini blamed the attack on unknown "assassins" who would be mercilessly tracked down and brought to justice. But although the assailants were found, they were never punished.[8] Ferrara's archbishop chose not to attend Minzoni's funeral, sending a Fascist priest in his place. The Vatican newspaper published a brief note on the murder, commenting that the news had saddened Mussolini.[9] Pius said nothing about it, accepting Mussolini's claim that the violence was the work of "idiots" and "undisciplined comrades."[10]

In mid-August, in the midst of the latest wave of violence, the Belgian ambassador to the Holy See, Eugène Beyens, met with the pope, who, he discovered, was more concerned about the danger of Communism than with any threat from Fascist violence. "Nothing is more fatal to civilization," Pius told him, "than communism. In the course of a few days, it destroys the work of several centuries." Only if France, Belgium, and Germany formed an alliance—despite their recent past as bitter enemies—could the Communist advance be stopped. "Mussolini is no Napoleon, nor even perhaps a Cavour," the pope remarked, "but he alone understood what was required to free his country from the anarchy that a powerless parliamentary system and three years of war had reduced it to." He added, "You see how he has gotten the nation to follow him. May he revive Italy! It is such men predestined for greatness who can bring about peace who are lacking today. May God soon give us some such beacons, so that they guide and enlighten humanity!"[11]

EVEN IN THESE EARLY YEARS, when formally he was simply the prime minister of a coalition government, Mussolini sought to build a personal cult. He began to appear more frequently in his uniform as leader of the Fascist militia, with black shirt and cavalry boots.[12] Growing up as he did, he had thought sports were a pastime for the elite, not for people like him. But now he took up skiing, fencing, race car driving, boating, horseback riding, and tennis. His flying lessons had suffered a setback in 1920 when he crashed his plane; he had been lucky to escape with only minor injuries. He was not bad as a fencer, but he never became much of a tennis player, despite having a world champion as his private tutor. Many of the photos of him on the ski slopes showed him gripping poles but lacking not only a shirt but also skis, offering some idea of how confident he felt in that sport.[13]

As his family ran to fat, Mussolini worried about putting on weight. He ate little meat, drank no alcohol, and weighed himself daily. Alarmed by his sister's increasing girth, he tried to use his rough charm to get her to diet, apparently to little effect. "I saw the latest photographs," he wrote her in 1925. "You have gotten terribly fat. You terribly need to lose weight instead. Reduce yourself to the essentials as I have, because fat not only does bad things, it kills."[14] Fretting about his own thinning hair and receding hairline, he began rubbing a variety of lotions onto his scalp, each morning nervously checking to see if they had done any good. Years later this was one battle he gave up, shaving his head in an effort to resemble a Roman emperor.[15]

When Rachele teased him about his habit of splashing great quantities of eau de cologne on his face and body each morning, he replied that a man who was not attractive to women was worthless.[16] Rachele and their three children—Edda, Vittorio, and Bruno—had not come to Rome with him, and he was not eager to have them there. He had initially stayed in the Hotel Savoia, then at the Grand Hotel, while Margherita Sarfatti took up residence in the Hotel Continental, not far away. When Mussolini first sneaked out of his hotel to visit Sarfatti, his driver alerted the security squad. Before long, bellboys suspiciously resembling undercover policemen were prowling the Continental's halls, on the lookout for Mussolini's furtive visits.[17]

"Dearly beloved, my beloved!" began the letter on hotel stationery

that Sarfatti wrote on New Year's Day 1923, two months after he became head of the government. "I want to begin the year by writing your
name on a piece of paper: Benito, my love, my lover, my beloved. I am,
I shout to the rooftops, I glory in being, passionately, entirely, devot-
edly, hopelessly yours." Whenever Mussolini could get away, he joined
Sarfatti at her summer house in the hills near Lake Como, north of
Milan. There they went for long walks and horseback rides, followed at
a discreet distance by his bodyguard. More difficult for his police escort were the times when Mussolini, who loved to drive at high speeds,
took Margherita and her fourteen-year-old daughter for a ride in his
Alfa Romeo.[18]

Margherita soon found Mussolini an apartment in Rome, where
they could have more privacy, and she also found him a housekeeper,
Cesira Carocci. A tough, short-haired woman, tall, thin, and lacking in
all social graces, she soon came to be referred to as *la ruffiana,* the pro-
curess. Fiercely devoted to Mussolini, she helped arrange not only
Margherita's visits but those of other women as well.

Mussolini had no use for luxury, and his dingy apartment lacked
even a kitchen. The sitting room, which visitors described as perme-
ated by the sickly sweet scent of cheap eau de cologne, featured a table
covered with Mussolini's violins. Back when Edda was a baby, he used
to stand by her crib and play until she fell asleep. In later years, while
awaiting the car that would take him to the office, he sometimes cranked
up his player piano and played a violin accompaniment.[19]

Given the number of long-term affairs Mussolini maintained,
together with the parade of one-night—or more accurately, one-
afternoon—stands, it is amazing that he not only found time to run the
government but insisted on reviewing even the most trivial details. He
trusted no one other than his brother, Arnaldo, who was now in charge
of *Il Popolo d'Italia,* with whom he spoke every night by phone, and to
a lesser extent Sarfatti. Each day he worked through an enormous stack
of police and political reports, met with a large number of people, and
read a pile of newspapers. "I am in the habit," he told a deputy, "of reading all the Italian newspapers, including those that don't deserve it."[20]

Drawn from the aristocratic or, more commonly, professional elite, previous prime ministers had had no mass base, no real political party behind them, and showed little if any interest in popularity. The idea of traveling around the country holding public rallies was something they would have found distasteful, had it even been conceivable.

Onto this scene came the former Socialist rabble-rouser from Milan, the blacksmith's son who boasted of his humble origins, a man exuding a virile popular appeal. Soon Mussolini was traveling from town to town—to places that had never seen a head of government—exhorting the curious crowds with his mesmerizing staccato harangues. He was becoming a master at mass hypnosis. What he understood, in a way that none of his predecessors had, was that people were ruled most of all by emotion, and that their reality had less to do with the external world than with the symbolic one he could fashion for them.

In Cremona he used what would become one of his most potent rhetorical gambits, a ritualized call for crowd response.

"Whose is the victory?" he bellowed.

"Ours!" they shouted back.

"Whose is the glory?"

"Ours!"

"Whose Italy is it?"

"Ours!"[21]

From May to October 1923, Mussolini visited towns and cities from Venice, Lombardy, and Piedmont in the north, through Emilia, Tuscany, and Abruzzo in the center, to Naples in the south, and both of Italy's major islands: Sicily and Sardinia. No prime minister had gone to Sardinia for an official visit in the six decades since it became part of Italy. The next year he repeated the round. People were hungry for a strong leader, a savior who would bring stability, order, and a brighter future. The better off saw him as the man who had stopped the Communist threat. For the rest, he was the *figlio del popolo,* the common man, one of their own.[22]

The foreign diplomatic community in Rome considered Mussolini an intriguing but enigmatic figure. The Belgian ambassador to the

Holy See recorded his observations of him at a diplomatic reception: his feet planted in the middle of the floor, his chin thrust out, Mussolini would say no more than a few words to those who came to greet him. "His serious, haughty face, his taciturn bearing, were impenetrable. One only read on his bronze mask, in his hard eyes, a rare energy." He made an indelible impression, recalled the ambassador: "I've kept from that evening the chilling vision of a man who seems utterly immune to any fear nor subject to any emotion."[23]

In dealing with the pope, Mussolini continued his well-calibrated mix of pressure and reward. As Fascist bands continued to attack local Popular Party leaders and headquarters, Mussolini cast himself as the only person able to control these overzealous Fascists. At the same time, he showered the Church with cash and privileges. He pushed through a new law allowing police to fire any editor whose newspaper belittled either the pope or the Catholic Church. He bowed to the Vatican's request that only books approved by the Church be used to teach religion in the schools. He agreed to close down gambling halls. He provided state recognition to the Catholic University of Milan, announced his opposition to divorce, and moved to save the Bank of Rome, closely tied to the Vatican, which was on the verge of bankruptcy. Crucifixes were back in the country's classrooms, and Church holidays were added to the civil calendar. He came up with generous funds to rebuild churches that had been damaged during the war. The list went on and on.[24]

As the pope was well aware, the support Mussolini was getting from the Church in return was priceless. In September 1923, the Vatican spelled this out in a "Program of Collaboration of the Catholics with the Mussolini Government." Mussolini had come to realize, the document reported, that he would be better off if he were not so dependent on the Fascists who had brought him to power. They were an undisciplined lot whom he could not fully control. He needed "a new mass" of support, and this could best be provided by Catholics, for they were accustomed to top-down rule. True, some in the Church hierarchy had initially been skeptical about him, but they now had to confess they had been wrong: "They have had to admit that no Italian Government, and perhaps no government in the world, would have in a single year alone been able to do so much in favor of the Catholic Religion."

Nor was this the only reason for the Vatican to support Mussolini: "Catholics could only think with terror of what might happen in Italy if the Honorable Mussolini's government were to fall perhaps to an insurrection by subversive forces and so they have every interest in supporting it." In short, the Vatican briefing concluded, "In every respect the constitution by Catholics of a mass of support for the Honorable Mussolini's government seems to be the most dependable and reassuring combination imaginable in Italy."[25]

IN NOVEMBER, AT MUSSOLINI'S DIRECTION, Fascists sacked the home of former prime minister Francesco Nitti, in the center of Rome. The police did nothing to intervene, and the marauders paraded triumphantly through the city streets. One morning the next month Giovanni Amendola, former cabinet minister and widely respected head of the Liberal opposition in parliament, was attacked near his home in downtown Rome. Four Fascists used clubs to smash his neck and face, then jumped into a waiting car and sped off. In reporting the attack, Mussolini's newspaper, *Il Popolo d'Italia,* argued that Amendola had only got what he deserved. Whether Mussolini himself had ordered the attack is not known, but it was part of the larger campaign of intimidation that he very much encouraged.[26]

North of Italy, in Bavaria's capital of Munich, the Fascist revolution was inspiring other Mussolini acolytes to violence. On November 8 the mustachioed thirty-four-year-old rabble-rouser Adolf Hitler, in an effort to imitate Mussolini's March on Rome of the previous year, announced a revolution in a large local beer hall. The Nazi movement had already adopted the Italian Fascists' straight-armed Roman salute. Hitler's followers, shouting "Sieg Heil!" until they were hoarse, succeeded in occupying the local police headquarters but failed to take over the Bavarian War Ministry. Ten people were killed, and Hitler was arrested.

He would spend a year in jail, but he put it to good use, writing his call to arms, *Mein Kampf.* At the time, Mussolini had no idea that his own fate would one day be tied to that of the imprisoned German wild man.

In April 1924 Italy prepared for a new national election, the first since Mussolini came to power. Fascist violence exploded. While directing beatings and worse at his enemies, Mussolini continued to introduce measures to benefit the Church. A new list of official holidays included several Catholic holidays that the state had never before recognized. Mussolini also took his first steps against Protestant organizations, which he knew would please the pope: he denied Methodists permission to construct a big church in Rome and rejected the YMCA's proposals to build centers in Italy. Catholic seminarians were exempted from the draft, and three weeks before the vote, he dramatically increased the government's payments to Italy's bishops and priests, much to their delight.[27]

In early April *La Civiltà cattolica,* the Vatican's unofficial voice, published its final issue before the election, explaining that the misbehavior of some anticlerical members of the Fascist Party should not obscure the fact that Mussolini was working tirelessly to improve relations between the government and the Church. The journal reminded readers of all the benefits that the Fascists had already produced for the Church compared with how little the Popular Party had accomplished.[28]

Election Day came on April 6. In his home base of Ferrara, Italo Balbo, one of the Quadrumvirate from the March on Rome, gave his Blackshirts their instructions. At each polling place, they were to grab the first voter to emerge and beat him up, while shouting "Bastard, you voted for the Socialists." True, the poor devil might well have voted for the Fascists, but if so, "too bad for him," said Balbo.[29]

In the wake of the beatings of opposition candidates, the torching of opposition newspapers, and the destruction of opposition ballots, the Fascist list—which included sympathetic non-Fascists—won two-thirds of the vote; the Fascists alone won 275 seats, giving them an absolute majority even without their allies. Of the opposition parties, the

Popular Party held on to 39 seats, the Socialists 46, and the Communists 19. A smattering of other seats went to republicans, liberals, and various other small groups. Mussolini was triumphant. "This is the last time that there'll be an election like this. The next time I will vote on behalf of everyone."[30]

The following day Fascist bands attacked Popular Party activists and local priests in places where the party had done well. In a small town outside Venice, armed Fascists arrived at night at the home of one such parish priest. Finding only the priest's sister at home, they beat her and then for good measure beat up the assistant priest as well.

Angered by scores of such attacks on clergy and Catholic organizations, someone in the Vatican secretary of state office prepared a circular, to be sent to all of Italy's bishops, telling them not to participate in the planned Fascist victory celebrations and especially forbidding them from performing special masses of thanksgiving for the Fascists. But although the circular was printed, it never left the Vatican. Written on the margin of the draft document (now found in the archives) is the note: "This should no longer be sent. By order of Monsignor Secretary." Gasparri—undoubtedly after discussing the matter with the pope—had decided it best not to do anything that might offend Mussolini.[31]

PIUS XI HAD BY NOW settled into a routine. His underlings lived in nervous fear of his reproach. He was curt with those who displeased him and was not intimidated by even the most exalted heads of state. When the king of Spain, Alfonso XIII, visited him at the Vatican, he made the mistake of asking the pope to nominate more South American cardinals; there was only one for the whole continent. Angered by what he saw as an inappropriate attempt to influence him, Pius decided to cancel his planned elevation of his majordomo, Monsignor Ricardo Sanz de Samper, who was from Colombia. He did not want to appear to be bowing to the king.[32]

But an occasional visitor could bring back flashes of his earlier enthusiasms. Pius invited the French intellectual Jean Carrère for a private audience and asked his views of various French and Italian literary figures. While he responded, the pope—as Carrère described it—looked upon him with a grave expression of "courteous superiority." But then Carrère mentioned Manzoni and called *The Betrothed* one of the world's masterpieces. As he uttered these words, "it seemed to me," recalled the Frenchman, "that my august interlocutor became transformed. From courteous benevolence that he had shown up to that point, he became all smiles and affable." Manzoni, the pope told him, was not only a great novelist but a great poet, and to Carrère's delight, the white-robed pontiff began reciting verses of a Manzoni poem from memory in a soft, musical cadence.[33]

Where Benedict XV had seemed overwhelmed by the weight of his office, Pius XI projected the vigor of a mountain climber. "He seemed born to command," said Confalonieri, the priest whom he had brought with him from Milan to serve as his private secretary. He radiated authority, the French ambassador later observed.[34] The pope was also a stickler for following proper procedure. One afternoon while strolling through the Vatican gardens, he saw an envelope, marked with large capital letters For His Holiness, lying on his path. With him that day was the archbishop of Bologna. Without thinking, the archbishop bent down and picked it up. He turned to hand it to the pope.

"Put it back where you found it," snapped Pius XI. "It is not the proper way to send mail."

The archbishop placed the envelope back on the path, and they continued on their walk.[35]

Although the pope had spent many years in libraries, he had, thought Monsignor Confalonieri, the personality not of a librarian but of a small businessman. The young priest attributed this to the pope's roots, for the industrial region of his birth was known for just such men. Pius XI thought in concrete terms and was uncomfortable with improvisation. He insisted on reasoning everything through and carefully studied all the reports that came to him. Once he did make a decision, he stuck to it. Criticism only made him dig in. The pope, complained the former secretary of state Cardinal Merry del Val, was "stubborn as a mule."[36]

For all their obvious differences, the pope and Mussolini were alike in many ways. Both could have no real friends, for friendship implied equality. Both insisted on being obeyed, and those around them quaked at the thought of saying anything that would displease them. They made an odd couple, but the pope had quickly come to recognize the benefits of casting his lot with the former priest-eater. As a result, within a year of the March on Rome, the Fascist revolution had become a clerico-Fascist revolution. A new partnership had begun. But it would soon face an unexpected threat, for something was about to happen that would very nearly bring Mussolini down.

CHAPTER FIVE

RISING FROM THE TOMB

————

O N MAY 30, 1924, THE THIRD DAY OF THE NEW PARLIAMENT, GIA-
como Matteotti strode to the podium in the Chamber of Deputies amid jeers and threats from the Fascist benches. Ejected from the
Socialist Party two years earlier in a purge of moderates, he had founded
a reformist Unitary Socialist Party. Today he had a message to deliver:
the recent election, marked by violence, should be annulled. As he detailed cases of voter intimidation from around the country, Fascist deputies kept interrupting him. "Lies!" they shouted. "Go back to Russia!"
One member yelled: "Enough already! What are we doing here? Do we
have to tolerate these insults?" An enraged phalanx of Fascist deputies
moved menacingly toward the front of the hall. "You shouldn't be in
parliament!" one screamed, "You should be under house arrest!"[1]
When, having been interrupted dozens of times, he finally finished,
Fascist catcalls drowned out the opposition's applause. "Now you'd
better prepare to write my obituary," Matteotti remarked to one of his
colleagues as he made his way out of the building.

Mussolini, who was present for that session, was enraged. He turned
to his press secretary, Cesare Rossi. "That man," he muttered,
"shouldn't be allowed to remain in circulation."

Giacomo Matteotti

On June 10 Matteotti was scheduled to speak again in parliament, this time to denounce Mussolini's government for corruption. After lunch, as he walked from his home near Piazza del Popolo toward the Chamber of Deputies, two men grabbed him and tried to drag him into a waiting sedan. Although he was neither big nor especially muscular, the thirty-nine-year-old Matteotti was both courageous and quick. He threw one of his attackers to the ground and was about to break away from the second when a third man set upon him, punching him in the face with brass knuckles. The men dragged the semiconscious deputy into the car. As he struggled, smashing the glass partition that divided the driver from the backseat, his abductors beat him savagely.

The car raced through Rome's streets, the driver pressing the horn in one constant blast to cover Matteotti's cries for help. The screams soon stopped. Matteotti was dead. Whether they had been ordered to kill him remains a matter of debate, but now that they had his cadaver in their laps, the men searched for a place to dump it. About fifteen miles from Rome, they made a shallow burial in woods not far from the road.[2]

When Matteotti did not return home for dinner, his wife learned he had never made it to parliament. The alarm went out. By the next evening, witness reports began to come in describing the scene of the Socialist's bloody abduction and the frenetic flight of the speeding car.

That a prominent member of parliament could criticize the Fascists one day and be violently abducted practically the next was shocking to all but the most hardened *fascisti*. Amid the furor, Mussolini tried to distance himself from the murder. By June 14 he had fired both the police head and the undersecretary for internal affairs. Suspicion fell on Cesare Rossi, who in addition to serving as Mussolini's press secretary headed a secret Fascist goon squad. Rossi went into hiding. Soon others high in the Fascist regime were caught in the investigation's web.

Evidence from the car that had been used in the abduction allowed the police to identify the men who had murdered the Socialist deputy. Their leader, Amerigo Dumini, had boasted to his comrades that he had already killed a dozen men on the orders from the highest ranks of the regime. Dumini was an American, born in 1894 in St. Louis, his father an Italian immigrant, his mother English. He had moved to Italy as a teenager, joined the Italian army during the war, and later became one of Mussolini's trusted henchmen, working under Rossi.

Five months earlier Mussolini had met with Rossi and several Fascist bigwigs to create a small, secret squad capable of carrying out violent missions. Dumini was entrusted with putting the group together. In June he received orders, most likely from Rossi, to go after Matteotti.[3]

The country was in an uproar. The occasional beating and castor oil guzzling meted out to socialist rabble-rousers was one thing, but the murder of the leader of one of the main opposition parties in parliament, to all appearances ordered by the highest levels of the Fascist regime, was another. That it was done in the middle of Rome in the middle of the day only added to the outrage. In the previous year and a half, Mussolini had risen from the head of a violent movement best known for its thugs, to the increasingly respected head of government. Many of his supporters had thought—or at least hoped—that he had put his brutal past behind him, but the Matteotti murder suggested otherwise. Over the next days and weeks, the whole network of support that Mussolini had so carefully put together—the old nationalists and Liberals, the large industrialists and the small shop owners—began to unravel.[4]

By the end of June, with Matteotti's body still not found, opposition deputies met and vowed that they would not participate in another session of the Chamber until Mussolini dissolved the Fascist militia and the other secret organizations that he had created to terrorize the opposition.

Conservative newspapers turned against him. *Il Giornale d'Italia*, which had until then offered support, demanded that full light be shed on those responsible for the murder. The middle classes that had largely embraced Mussolini began to turn from him as well: they had wanted a conservative, nationalist government, not a bloody tyrant. People began ripping up their Fascist Party membership cards, while opposition members of parliament found themselves applauded by passersby as they walked down the streets of Rome. In some areas, Fascist militiamen, who had so recently paraded haughtily through the streets, were now afraid to appear in public in their uniforms.[5] The regime teetered. Little stood in the way of its fall.

A stream of successes had boosted Mussolini's ego. But now, unnerved, he became unapproachable. So black was his humor that even his closest aides were too frightened to meet with him. "Inside Palazzo Chigi"—where Mussolini then had his office—"one breathed the air of the tomb," said Quinto Navarra, his assistant.[6]

The quiet was all the more remarkable because the blustery tyrant's shouts had regularly penetrated his door, as he lectured and hectored his underlings. Now not a sound made its way out. One day at the height of the crisis, Navarra found the prime minister in his office: "To say that Mussolini, when I surprised him opening the door a bit that morning, was just upset, would be far short of the mark." The disconsolate man sat shaking his head from side to side, knocking it against the gilded wood frame of his tall chair first on one side and then the other, with his eyes wide open, snorting and grumbling.[7]

A wiretap—for he had apparently ordered the police to tap his lover's phone—caught Mussolini's plaintive phone conversation with Margherita Sarfatti:

"How are you?" she asked.

"How do you expect me to be?"

"Anything new?"

"Nothing . . . by now, I'm not surprised at anything. . . . The thing that upsets me the most is that I don't know what my so-called friends are thinking—they who've betrayed me."

Margherita cautioned him not to let his temper color his judgment.

"It's not a question of temper," Mussolini replied. "Unfortunately fate has dealt its card in favor of my enemies, and if I lose the game, which is almost certain, there's not even the possibility of saving face!"[8]

Mussolini's attempts to distance himself from the murder foundered on the identity of those deemed responsible, for they included some of those closest to him. The end of the regime seemed near.

The Senate—a body whose members were chosen by the king, not elected—reopened two weeks after the murder. Mussolini got up to speak. He said he was as eager to get to the bottom of what had happened as anyone, pointing to the arrest of the presumed murderers and his dismissal of top government officials as evidence of his sincerity.[9]

While most judged his remarks woefully inadequate, one man rushed to compliment him. In a flowery, handwritten letter, Father Tacchi Venturi, the pope's secret emissary, told Mussolini how impressed he was with the speech. He gushed with praise for all of Mussolini's good work and called on God to ensure his future success.[10]

As word got out that their leader was in a state of shock, worried Fascist bosses from the provinces visited Rome to rouse him from his stupor. To their horror, they found him dazed. Leandro Arpinati, the Fascist boss of Bologna, was horrified to find Mussolini appearing feverish, his eyes red, as if he had been weeping. He looked, remarked Arpinati, like a businessman about to declare bankruptcy.[11]

For the pope, the Matteotti murder was a disaster. In Mussolini the Vatican finally had found an Italian leader with whom it could work. Now, with the opposition forces uniting to boycott parliament and call for the return of constitutional rights, Mussolini's hold on power was in danger. The pope decided to do all he could to save him, taking aim at the Popular Party's decision to join the coalition calling for a new government. While the party did not formally depend on the Church hierarchy, it could hardly continue to claim to be Italy's Catholic party if the pope were to openly renounce it.[12]

In late June, with Italians disoriented and Mussolini's fate in doubt, the Vatican's daily newspaper, *L'Osservatore romano,* published an editorial on the crisis, reminding Catholics of the Church's teaching to obey civil authorities and warning them against any "leap in the dark." *La Civiltà cattolica,* the Vatican-overseen Jesuit journal, followed up with an article written by its editor, Father Rosa, reminding readers of the Church's admonition to obey government authority. Any attempt to undermine the current government, he argued, risked anarchy. He took special aim at the Popular Party's supporters, warning that good Catholics could not cooperate with Socialists.[13]

The Vatican made it clear to the Catholic party's leaders that their efforts to bring down the Fascist regime were not welcome. Yet they continued to work with other opposition groups to steer Italy back to a parliamentary democracy.[14]

Pius tried to buck up Mussolini's sagging spirits. On Sunday morning, July 20, the pope told Tacchi Venturi to let the despondent leader know he still had his support. That afternoon the Jesuit sent Mussolini a note: "Excellence, This morning it pleased His Holiness to speak to me of Your Excellency in such terms that I am certain that they will succeed in being especially welcome and comforting." He underlined these last words and, telling Mussolini that it would be best if he could communicate the pope's thoughts in person, asked to meet with him soon. When two days later the embattled government head opened the note, he wrote across it in his colored pencil, "Thursday morning at 12." So it was that in the midst of Mussolini's darkest days, the pope's emissary came to convey the pope's support.[15]

But Pius XI did not confine himself to offering words of comfort. He again turned to Father Rosa for help. Meeting with the Jesuit editor in his library, the pope instructed him to prepare a new piece on the crisis. Two days later, at the end of July, Cardinal Gasparri himself arrived at the *Civiltà cattolica* headquarters in Rome to pick up Rosa's draft. Over the next days, drafts went back and forth between the Vatican and the journal office, now bearing Pius XI's black pencil markings. After getting the pope's final approval, the unsigned article went to press.[16]

After praising Mussolini for all he had done for the Church, and implying that he had nothing to do with the Matteotti murder, the *Civiltà cattolica* article warned that violent action against the government could never be justified. Even the use of legitimate means to bring it down, as through new elections, should be avoided, for it would bring "serious misfortune." Most important, the Popular Party could never be justified in entering into an alliance with the Socialists.[17]

The pope faced more embarrassment when Matteotti's wife and mother repeatedly asked to meet with him. Suspecting that their request was aimed at further weakening Mussolini, the pope refused. But he did not want to appear coldhearted and instructed Gasparri to receive the two women and give them each a rosary he had blessed.[18]

If there was any doubt about the pope's continuing support for

Mussolini, it ended in early September when he addressed a group of university students. Italian Catholics, Pius told them, could never cooperate with Socialists.[19]

MUSSOLINI KNEW HOW CRUCIAL the pope's support was in his fight for survival. In the midst of the crisis, he arranged for his children to take religious lessons. Edda, aged twelve, Vittorio, eight, and Bruno, six, all celebrated first communion and confirmation on the same day.[20]

At the time the pope heard this welcome news, he found himself confronted with another problem. Although Don Sturzo had resigned as head of the Popular Party, he was still writing articles critical of the regime. This was an irritant for Mussolini, and it meant that Sturzo remained a visible figure of the opposition. Pius XI ordered Sturzo to stop his attacks.[21]

In response, the Sicilian priest offered to leave the country, a suggestion that pleased the pope. Not only would it remove Sturzo from the Italian political scene, it would prevent what could be a huge embarrassment. As long as he was in Italy, the risk remained that some Fascist band would add him to the list of murder victims, making it all the more difficult for the pope to continue his support for the government. In late October Sturzo departed for what he hoped would be a short period abroad; it would turn into a twenty-two-year exile.[22]

Mussolini was meanwhile facing new headaches, as the Fascist bosses in the provinces increasingly questioned his resolve. At the end of 1924, an article titled "Fascism Against Mussolini" appeared, arguing that the leader's only true support lay in the provincial Fascist squads and denouncing his decision to arrest Matteotti's killers. Making matters worse, three days later an account of the murder prepared by Cesare Rossi was published in France—implicating Mussolini directly in the killing. The editor of Italy's most prestigious paper, Milan's *Corriere della Sera,* suggested that Mussolini might best resign. Rumors of a possible military coup d'état mixed with speculation that the king was about to appoint a new prime minister.[23]

If Mussolini was not deposed as a result of the Matteotti crisis, it was because the opposition—not least due to the pope's constant efforts to undermine any possible alliance to put an end to Fascist rule—failed to offer a credible alternative. Lacking this alternative, neither the king nor the army was willing to act.[24]

Sensing this reality, Mussolini regained his self-confidence. The moment when it looked certain to him that Fascism would fall had passed. On January 3, 1925, not quite seven months since Fascist goons had murdered Matteotti, he rose to speak in parliament. It would be the most dramatic speech of his career.

"I declare here, in front of the Assembly and all the Italian people," said Mussolini, "that I and I alone assume full political, moral, and historical responsibility for everything that has happened."

"We are all with you!" shouted the Fascist deputies.

"If Fascism has been a criminal organization, I am the head of this criminal association!"

"We are all with you!" The applause kept building.

"If all the violence was the result of a particular historical, political, and moral climate," said Mussolini, "then I take responsibility for it, because I created this historical, political, and moral climate.

"Sirs! You have deluded yourselves! You believed that Fascism was finished . . . but you will see. . . . Italy, sirs, wants peace, wants tranquility, wants calm. We will give it this tranquility, this calm through love if possible, and with force, if it becomes necessary."

With these words, the Fascist assault on the last vestiges of democracy in Italy began.

THE DICTATORSHIP

T HE SAME DAY MUSSOLINI SPOKE TO PARLIAMENT, FASCIST MILITIA units seized the headquarters of the remaining anti-Fascist parties and newspapers.[1] Opposition leaders were rounded up and jailed.[2] The beatings of opposition leaders resumed. The most prominent came in the summer with the Fascist assault on Giovanni Amendola, leader of the Liberals in parliament, who had already suffered a Fascist beating. He died of his injuries several months later.[3]

Recognizing the value of continued strong Vatican support, Mussolini looked for ways to nurture his alliance with the pope. Having had his children and wife baptized, then having arranged for his children's first communion and confirmation, he was running out of rites to show his Catholic credentials. But he did have one left. In July he told Tacchi Venturi that he wanted to celebrate a religious wedding with Rachele, most likely in September.

The Jesuit was delighted, knowing the news would please Pius XI. But when half of September passed and he had heard nothing more, he wrote to ask what had happened. "It is not because I doubt your good will in the least," Tacchi Venturi explained in his note to Mussolini, but if the wedding could be arranged within the next few weeks, he advised, "it will succeed in offering special consolation to the Holy Father and to not a few eminent personages who are sincerely devoted to Your Excellency."

The delay may well have been caused by Rachele, whose antipathy to the Church ran deep. When Mussolini had insisted a few years earlier that Rachele be baptized, he practically had to drag her to the ceremony. Master everywhere but his own house, Mussolini decided he would have to catch his wife by surprise. On December 29, 1925, Rachele was in her kitchen in Milan cooking tagliatelle when her maid told her that her husband had arrived with his brother, Arnaldo, and a priest. They wanted her to join them in the drawing room. Her antennae raised by her husband's uncharacteristic appearance with a man of the cloth, Rachele said she would come when she was finished. After waiting impatiently, Mussolini finally barged into the kitchen. "Off we go, Rachele. That's enough now. Don't make me insist." Rachele, not one to be easily pushed around, did her best to ignore him. Undaunted, he stepped behind her, undid her apron, and walked her to the sink to wash her hands. He then steered her to the drawing room, where the priest performed the wedding ceremony before she could escape.[4]

Things were once more going Mussolini's way. As he resumed traveling through the country, enthusiastic crowds greeted him everywhere. Always ready with a punchy phrase or a potent military metaphor, Mussolini spoke with emotion of sacrifice and faith.[5] He had an uncanny knack for increasing his volume at just the right time, with a voice that, as one observer put it, ranged from "the hiss of a python to the roar of the lion."[6]

But he soon found himself dealing with a problem within his own ranks. Once again Roberto Farinacci, the most fascist of the Fascists, was causing trouble. The previous year, shortly after announcing the dictatorship, Mussolini had made a calculated gamble. In an effort to keep an eye on Farinacci, he had appointed him head of the Fascist Party.

Farinacci was not so easily tamed. Tension between the two men came to a climax in March 1926, when he insisted on playing a high-profile role at the trial of Matteotti's murderers. It was now almost two years since the killing, and the last thing Mussolini wanted was to remind people of what had happened. In hopes of minimizing news coverage, he had moved the trial to Chieti, a remote town northeast of Rome. "During the court sessions," Mussolini wrote in a handwritten memo a few days before the trial, "we must avoid any and all elements of drama, which might arouse public opinion, domestically and abroad. Therefore no noisy incidents or political excursions."

To Mussolini's dismay, Farinacci decided to join the defendants' legal team and instructed Chieti's Fascist Party head to organize a big rally for his arrival. Angered by his grandstanding, Mussolini sent him a sharply worded letter: "I see that not one of your promises has been kept, and the trial . . . has become political. I judge all this with extreme severity, and great uneasiness is spreading within the party. . . . I warn you that I will not tolerate any rallies or celebrations at the end of trial."[7]

With the help of a Fascist prosecutor, a Fascist judge, and the national head of the Fascist Party as their defense attorney, two of the five defendants were acquitted. Dumini—Mussolini's American-born henchman—and two of his comrades were found guilty of involuntary homicide and freed less than two months later. While satisfied with the verdict, Mussolini was furious with Farinacci and promptly dumped him as party head.[8]

Seeking to strengthen his public image, Mussolini increasingly cast himself as the new Caesar, the man who would return Italy to its ancient grandeur. In this effort he had an important partner in his lover, Margherita Sarfatti. Her 1926 quasi-official biography bore the revealing Latin title *Dux*.[9] An Italian version of the term, *Duce*, meaning "leader," was becoming ever more common in references to Mussolini in the press and on public occasions.[10]

Mussolini also began to be cast as a Christ-like figure, in a fusion of Fascist and Catholic images. In Italian schools in Tunisia, a French colony, students recited a prayer that in one form or another would increasingly be heard on the Italian peninsula as well:

"I believe in the high Duce—maker of the Black Shirts—And in

Jesus Christ his only protector—Our Savior was conceived by a good teacher and an industrious blacksmith.... He came down to Rome....."[11]

Mussolini basked in the adulation but remained vigilant. Giuseppe Bottai, longtime member of the Fascist Grand Council, spoke of two different Mussolinis. One was expansive and spontaneous, guided by his instincts; the other was "small, petty, with the little envies and jealousies of common men, quick to lie, to use deception and fraud, dispenser of promises that he had no intention of keeping, disloyal, treacherous, mean, lacking in affect, incapable of loyalty or love, quick to dump his most faithful followers."[12] In fact, Bottai was one of the few major figures in the regime whom Mussolini did not replace. Even in these early years, Mussolini could abide no competition, and any hint that one of his top ministers was getting too much favorable public attention was likely to lead to reassignment to Africa or the Balkans.

IF 1925 WAS THE YEAR of Mussolini's triumph, it was also a proud time for the pope. In an effort to strengthen Catholics' bonds with their Church, he had proclaimed 1925 a Holy Year, the twenty-third to be held since Pope Boniface VIII announced the first in 1300. These were years when Catholics were urged to make a pilgrimage to the holy places of Rome, and prelates from parish priests to bishops, from the Americas to central Europe, led visits to the Vatican and the basilicas of the Eternal City. Pius XI was so pleased with the result that he would later promote two special Holy Years: in 1929, to celebrate the fiftieth anniversary of his priestly ordination, and in 1933–34, to mark the nineteen hundredth anniversary of Jesus's resurrection.

On Christmas Eve 1924 the pope appeared in St. Peter's Square and symbolically removed the seal from the Holy Door, to be left open for the duration of the year. Over the course of the following twelve months, he gave 380 speeches, as more than a million pilgrims streamed in from all over the Catholic world. Often he spoke without notes; other times he jotted down themes; but he rarely wrote out what he was going to say. His speech remained distinctively slow and deliberate, with pauses as he looked downward and to the left. After considering what to say, he lifted his head upward and slightly to the right and resumed speaking, often by repeating his last word, as if to confirm that it had been the right choice after all.[13]

Pius XI, 1925

The demanding schedule took its toll. A few weeks into the Holy Year, Rome's police chief received a confidential report. Although the pope was in reasonably good health, it said, he found papal life stifling. A man who reveled in the outdoors and relished physical activity was now confined to the tiny precincts of the Vatican and burdened with constant meetings, audiences, and ceremonies. Most of all the pope missed the fresh mountain air and even in winter insisted on leaving his bedroom window open. The pope's aide, Father Venini, thought the pope looked tired. Perhaps he was not getting a good night's sleep, for he kept telling Venini to do something about the mice that scurried across his bedroom floor at night.[14]

The pilgrimage to Rome, Pius believed, was one of the most sacred acts a Catholic could perform.[15] Hundreds each day waited on their knees in the grand halls of the Apostolic Palace, hoping to kiss the pope's ring as he walked by and, if they were especially lucky, receive a commemorative medal from his hands.[16] It was hard not to be awed by the spectacle of the white-robed pope surrounded by scarlet-gowned cardinals, assorted chamberlains, and gendarmes with cape and sword, dressed in high stiff ruffs and knee breeches.[17] The enormous rooms, with beautifully painted ceilings and walls covered with Renaissance art, combined with the quaintly dressed papal attendants, gave visitors the impression that they had traveled centuries back in time.

In a typical audience, Pius received hundreds of pilgrims, both clergy and lay. The men wore formal dress, although those who lacked such attire got by with a plain dark suit. Women wore black dresses, with sleeves. A black mantilla or black lace scarf covered their heads. The pope entered the hall surrounded by an escort of Noble Guards and chamberlains, along with the master chamberlain, Monsignor Caccia Dominioni. Pius made his way to a raised throne, where he sat facing the crowd. The pilgrims' leader spoke first, offering words of devotion and praise. The pontiff replied in his slow, deliberate, precise way, typically by referring to the beauty of the country the pilgrims came from and the piety of its Catholic population. He then directed praise at the senior cleric leading the group. As he offered his concluding benediction, the pilgrims got down on their knees.

Something of the emotional impact of the Holy Year comes across in an account recorded by the popular English writer Edward Lucas, a Quaker who was in St. Peter's for the closing ceremonies on Christmas Eve 1925. There was nothing like Vatican ritual, he wrote, anywhere in the world. Most impressive of all was the papal procession. The pope's Noble escorts, acting as ushers, scurried about, in their medieval outfits, with dazzling sword-hilts. Lucas felt transported back to the Middle Ages not only by the costumes but by the faces of the princes, prelates, priests, and monks. These, he observed, seemed not to change.

"Some of the clerics are in purple, some in black, some in cowls; one or two are bearded; some austerely robed in white. . . . Many are incredibly old; almost none look happy, care-free; many are lined and marked with anxiety. And then the cardinals . . . and then, carried high above all the rest, by servitors in red, and accompanied by two bearers of lofty feather fans, the Holy Father himself seated in his chair, with a great yellow mitre on his venerable head, and softly waving his hand from right to left in blessing."[18]

Pius XI brought the Holy Year to a close by issuing an encyclical, *Quas primas*. Humanity could be saved, he said, only if all embraced the one true religion, Roman Catholicism. Like popes before him, he denounced the French Revolution as the origin of much evil, spreading harmful notions of the "rights of man."[19] He concluded by warning that "rulers and princes are bound to give public honor and obedience to Christ." Those who failed to heed these words faced a terrible end, for Christ "will most severely avenge these insults."[20]

The pope used the encyclical to announce a new Church holiday, Christ the King, designed to combat what he saw as the great plague of modern times: the spread of secularism. While Catholics greeted the encyclical, and the new holiday it announced, with enthusiasm, the same could not be said of Protestants. In the United States, the National Lutheran Council blasted the encyclical as "sectarian in the worst sense" and "hostile to very large groups of Christians." It called on Protestants everywhere to boycott the pope's new holy day.[21]

GIVEN HIS VIEW of the dignity of the papal office, Pius XI refused to talk on the telephone or be photographed with guests. He kept a heavy schedule of public audiences but was not always eager to honor requests for private meetings. Once, when his secretary of state told him of an important personage requesting an audience, he expressed his reluctance. "But there is one excuse you cannot offer him," added the pope in one of his more lighthearted moments. "You cannot say I am not at home."[22]

Rome's clergy found Pius XI, compared to his recent predecessors Pius X and Benedict XV, cold and curt.[23] During one of the pope's daily walks, an elderly Vatican gardener nearby crumpled to the ground, felled by a heart attack. As other gardeners, along with a guard who had been accompanying the pope, rushed to help him, someone told Pius what had happened. He continued on his way. The incident became fodder for the gossip that swirled around the Vatican.[24]

Precious insights into the infighting around the pope come from the voluminous secret police informant reports sent from the Vatican. Since coming to power, Mussolini had set up a vast network of informants. Although their observations have to be read with care, given the various axes that the informants had to grind, they provide unmatched insight into what was going on in the Vatican in these years.[25]

Pius XI's bursts of anger were becoming more frequent. One monsignor confided to an informant that when he had to see the pope, he trembled, "so great were the mortifications he had to suffer," forced to remain on his knees. The pope treated Gasparri badly as well, this informant wrote, but fortunately the cardinal "has a thick skin, and pretends that he doesn't notice anything."[26]

The Belgian ambassador captured the view of the pope that was then common among the Vatican's foreign diplomats. Pius XI was a learned man and certainly less obsessed with questions of dogma and religious discipline than Pius X, who had his infamous spy service. But he was just as stubborn as his namesake and lacked any hint of diplomatic skills: "He marches straight to the end. He is a character committed to the most noble and generous ideals, but not open to those who counsel patience." Pius XI's most salient personality trait, noted the ambassador, was his insistence that he be obeyed.[27]

A recently discovered letter, reported in the Vatican's own newspaper, offers surprising, not to say flabbergasting, testimony of just how tough Pius XI was. In 1919, while he was in Warsaw as Benedict XV's envoy, Achille Ratti had written to his assistant at the Vatican Library, asking that someone bring him papers he had left in his desk, "along with the little revolver and ammunition" that he had left there. Amid the chaos and threats of revolution in Milan, Ratti had acquired a gun and kept it in his desk at the Ambrosiana Library. When he moved to the Vatican Library, he brought the revolver with him. Finding himself in Warsaw, under threat of a Red Army invasion, he did not want to remain unarmed.[28]

HAVING OFFERED A WELCOME to an international surgeons' convention, Mussolini emerged into Rome's sunshine. Seeing their Duce appear unexpectedly, an excited group of Fascists outside raised their arms in the Fascist salute. Without thinking, Mussolini raised his arm in response. As he tilted his head back, a shot rang out. Violet Gibson, a mentally unstable middle-aged Irish woman, had fired her pistol at his head. Thanks to his salute, rather than piercing his temple, the bullet only grazed his nose, producing copious blood.

Mussolini insisted on going ahead with his scheduled address to a Fascist Party gathering later in the day, April 7, 1926, appearing with a large white bandage stretched over the bridge of his nose. His concluding remarks there—with their oblique reference to the assassination attempt—became legendary: "If I advance, follow me; if I turn back, kill me; if I die, avenge me."[29] The next day he flew to Italy's African colonies. As he left, he is said to have joked that he was going with his nose already pierced.[30]

Around the country, the clergy led their flocks in prayers of thanksgiving, assuring the faithful that God was watching out for their leader. Just a few days before the attempted assassination, Pius X's elderly sister had presented the Duce with her brother's papal skullcap as a gift. Many believed that the former pope—who would one day be pronounced a saint—had produced yet another miracle.[31]

Mussolini would need more miracles that year, for as he solidified his dictatorship, disheartened anti-Fascists saw their only hope in his death. In September a twenty-six-year-old Italian anarchist hurled a homemade bomb at Mussolini's car. Again, the Duce seemed to be leading a charmed life—bouncing off the right side door, the bomb exploded, wounding several people but leaving its intended victim unharmed.[32]

The most dramatic assassination attempt came on October 31, when Mussolini was in Bologna to inaugurate a new sports stadium. As he drove through the city's crowd-lined streets, a shot was fired. It did not miss its target by much, tearing through the ceremonial sash that the Duce wore across his chest. Several men from the crowd jumped on a sixteen-year-old boy, the presumed shooter, and killed him on the spot. Throughout Italy, outraged Fascists burned down what was left of the opposition press and beat those suspected of anti-Fascist sympathies.[33]

Relieved that Mussolini had escaped harm, the pope let him know of his "immense joy" in learning that he was "safe and sound thanks to Jesus Christ's special protection."[34] The climate was now ripe for the Duce to secure his dictatorship. On November 5 a new law provided for internal exile for critics of the regime. Many would be sent from their urban homes to remote island and mountain villages, to be kept under police surveillance. Four days after the new law was announced, the remaining opposition deputies were ejected from parliament. Only members of the Fascist Party would be allowed to continue in office. By the end of 1926, Fascist unions alone were permitted, and strikes were banned. Mayors were no longer elected but appointed by the central government. Press censorship was tightened; a special tribunal was created to root out the remaining opposition, and capital punishment was reinstated.[35] It had not been known in Rome since the pope had last ruled the city, more than a half century before. [36]

CHAPTER

SEVEN

ASSASSINS, PEDERASTS, AND SPIES

F EW MEN HAD MORE INFLUENCE IN ROME THAN FATHER TACCHI
Venturi, the pope's emissary to Mussolini. A common sight in the
halls of government, he hurried from one ministerial office to another,
power broker extraordinaire. Over the years, he would make hundreds
of visits to government ministers and their staff, seeking help not only
on behalf of the pope but for many others who knew that the best path
to winning favors from the Fascist regime was to gain his ear.[1]

The Jesuit was discreet, but his bond with Mussolini did not go
unobserved. Romans dubbed him "Mussolini's confessor," the "éminence grise" who was said to meet with him every day.[2] A German
newspaper called him Mussolini's Rasputin.[3]

While Pius XI saw Tacchi Venturi's role as relaying his requests and
concerns to Mussolini, the Jesuit had a broader view of his own mission. Like others around the Vatican, he thought the pope was insufficiently exercised about the danger that Italy's Jews posed. He took it

upon himself to alert Mussolini to this supposed threat, as he would repeatedly do over the years.

In a document he drafted in the summer of 1926, Tacchi Venturi identified "the worldwide Jewish-Masonic plutocracy" as the greatest enemy the Church faced.[4] He called for strong government measures, including a special "secret police" to monitor Italy's Jewish bankers. The government should also abolish the stock exchange, which he dubbed "the most potent means of the occult empire." And because the world's press was almost entirely in the hands of the Jews and the Masons, governments needed to limit freedom of the press in all matters dealing with business and finance. They had to recognize the fact that the Jewish-Masonic plutocracy lay at the root of all the world's economic and political problems.[5]

Although the pope shared in the general Vatican view that the large numbers of Jews in central and eastern Europe posed a threat to Christian society, he had always excepted Italy's tiny Jewish community. But his Jesuit envoy made no such distinction. In September 1926 Tacchi Venturi gave the Duce a recently published fifteen-page pamphlet, *Zionism and Catholicism,* which had been dedicated to the Jesuit himself. The pamphlet, after recalling that God condemned the Jews to wander the earth and cursed them for rejecting Jesus, turned to the more immediate dangers the Jews posed. "No one can doubt," its author warned, "the Jewish sect's formidable, diabolical, fatal activity throughout the world." The Jews sought revolution, Bolshevism, "to destroy current society and dominate the world by themselves, as their Talmud prescribes."[6] Mussolini took the booklet, although whether he ever read it we do not know.

The fact that Tacchi Venturi got to have a private meeting with the Duce practically every month could not fail to arouse envy, even hatred. One Saturday in 1927 he entered Rome's Church of Jesus, where he was in the habit of taking confession each week. The massive sixteenth-century baroque building, Rome's most important Jesuit church, stood in the city center. As he walked through the dimly illuminated church and stepped into his confessional that day, he was startled to see a large sign. He read its block letters:

> *Venturi, Venturi, Venturi—*
> *if they bump off your Benito—*
> *your empire too will be* finito
> *So pray to God that they're in no hurry.*[7]

Such anonymous warnings were nothing new to the Jesuit priest, who was not one to be easily intimidated. But as it turned out, it was not Mussolini but Tacchi Venturi who would be the next target of the assassin's blade.

THE NEWS SPREAD QUICKLY. Sixty-seven-year-old Father Pietro Tacchi Venturi, confidant of both the pope and the Duce, had narrowly escaped death. As he would later tell the story, he had been working at his desk in the building adjacent to the Church of Jesus when he heard that a young man wanted to see him. He told the doorman to let him in. As the young man entered, he pulled a knife from his coat and, without saying a word, plunged it into the Jesuit's neck. Only the priest's reflexes saved him, as he instinctively recoiled; the wound narrowly missed his jugular. The assailant ran from the building. Stunned, the bloodied Jesuit staggered to the hallway, where his colleagues rushed to his aid, the knife still lodged in his neck.

The next day, February 29, 1928, *The New York Times* carried the news: "The Jesuit scholar, Father Tacchi Venturi, intermediary in the negotiations between the Pope and Premier Mussolini for a solution of the 'Roman question,' has been injured by a mysterious attempt on his life by a youth who, for no apparent reason, penetrated into his apartment and stabbed him in the neck with a paper-knife." The paper added, "there is extreme reluctance in Vatican spheres to discuss the case."[8]

Who tried to murder Tacchi Venturi, and for what reason? Milan's

Corriere della Sera speculated that the conspirators wanted to strike at the Fascist wing of the Jesuit order, of which Tacchi Venturi, the order's former secretary general, was reportedly the leader. Others were sure that behind the violence were Jesuit dissidents, unhappy with Tacchi Venturi's role in cementing the Vatican-Fascist alliance.

Over the next weeks, Tacchi Venturi did everything he could to convince the police that he had been the target of an international assassination attempt. When they expressed skepticism, he produced his own evidence, quickly picked up by the press. A March 1 *Washington Post* story, headlined "Anti-Mussolini Plot Seen in Rome Stabbing," reported the existence of a "black list" of planned assassination victims on which the Jesuit's name figured prominently.[9]

Tacchi Venturi told the police he had recently received a confidential report from a highly informed and trustworthy source. It revealed that the prominent anti-Fascist Gaetano Salvemini, in exile in Paris, had prepared a list of the leaders of the Fascist regime to be targeted for murder. Second on the list, right after Mussolini himself, Tacchi Venturi had found his own name. The identity of the man he accused could not fail to capture police attention, as Salvemini was one of Mussolini's most influential critics abroad. An esteemed scholar, professor of history at the University of Florence, Salvemini had entered parliament as a Socialist deputy after the war. Author of numerous works denouncing the dictatorship and briefly imprisoned in 1925, he had fled the country.[10]

The police were suspicious of Tacchi Venturi's claim that an internationally acclaimed intellectual like Gaetano Salvemini was organizing a series of assassinations. It was hard to believe. It seemed similarly far-fetched that such a conspiracy, if it existed, would identify Tacchi Venturi as the most important target after Mussolini.

Unnerved that the police seemed not to be taking his story seriously, and desperately wanting to stop their investigation from turning to his personal life, Tacchi Venturi tried to get Mussolini to intervene. On March 19 he went to see the Duce, eager to convince him that he had been the target of a dangerous anti-Fascist conspiracy. He handed

Mussolini the typed pages recounting the tale that his informant had told.

As Rome's police chief noted in his later report, even at first glance the mysterious informant's story was hard to believe. The source claimed he had arranged a meeting in Paris with Salvemini by telling the exiled professor he wanted to help him. The fifty-four-year-old scholar not only agreed to meet—although he had no idea who the man was—but immediately confided to him all the details of his secret assassination plot.[11] It was hard to imagine, the police chief observed, how someone as intelligent and politically sophisticated as Tacchi Venturi could have believed any of it, let alone think he could get others to believe it. For the police chief, the only issue was whether someone else had prepared it for him or he had concocted it himself.[12]

The police repeatedly urged the Jesuit to reveal who the report's author was, but Tacchi Venturi refused. Eventually the police did discover the author's identity: he was a notorious schemer who had previously run afoul of the law for trying to peddle preposterous stories.[13]

Tacchi Venturi, thought the police chief, was trying to throw off the investigation. On March 20 a police informant offered support for his suspicion. "We have confirmation from the Vatican," wrote the informant, "that it was Tacchi Venturi who did not want his attackers (whom he knows well, as he knows the reasons for the attack) to be identified."[14]

Ten days later the director of the political police, in a confidential memo, reported that the latest information on the case would explain Tacchi Venturi's strange behavior. It would also explain the silence of the Jesuits at the Church of Jesus, for they were not cooperating: the young man who had attacked the priest had done so because the two had had "illicit relations."[15] This was the secret that Tacchi Venturi wanted so desperately to conceal.

In June the police chief sent in his final report, bringing the investigation to an end. Tacchi Venturi's account of what had happened did not add up. If he really had been assailed by an assassin, why had he not shouted out for help but instead allowed his assailant to escape? Why had none of the Jesuits notified the police of the attack? The authorities had learned of it from the hospital, where the injured priest had gone to get stitched up.

The young man who had assaulted Tacchi Venturi had been sitting in the waiting room long enough to be seen by others. A little later, according to a priest in the room next to the attack, angry shouts had come from Tacchi Venturi's room. But according to Tacchi Venturi, the unknown visitor had barely entered when he attacked without saying a word.

And then there were questions about the assassin's weapon. It was a heavy letter opener of distinctive design, with a black wooden handle and a sharp metal blade. Examining the unusual weapon, the police were surprised to discover that it was identical to the letter openers used by Tacchi Venturi himself, although according to the Jesuit the man had brought it with him. It was odd, the police thought, that the weapon of choice of a team of international political assassins would be a letter opener, no matter how heavy or sharp.

The nature of the wound raised further questions. According to Tacchi Venturi, the would-be assassin had clutched the knife like a dagger and tried to plunge it into his neck. Although it missed his jugular, it had ended up lodged in his neck and produced a great deal of blood. But the medical reports recorded no deep stab wound, but rather a relatively superficial, if long, cut. Such a wound could not have resulted from a stabbing motion, much less one that resulted in a knife being lodged in the neck. An examination of the Jesuit's clothes similarly showed that while they were bloodied, there was not much blood. And while Tacchi Venturi reported that his fellow Jesuits had found the knife stuck in his neck, none of them had confirmed this account.

What really happened on that February day? The police chief was certain that the attack had had nothing to do with an anti-Fascist plot. The priest had been wounded as a result of an altercation with someone he knew well; the assailant, in a moment of fury, had picked up a letter opener on Tacchi Venturi's desk and thrown it at him. The motive had been personal, not political, and for this reason the Jesuit was doing everything he could to prevent the police from finding the assailant.[16]

There was an avenue of investigation that the police chief would not pursue in this case. In his final report, he acknowledged that he had not looked into the possibility that the priest had had illicit relations with the young man.[17] The police were not eager to delve into the personal life of the Jesuit who was so close to both Mussolini and the pope, much less look into his possible relations with boys or young men. Once they could rule out a political assassination plot, they were content to bring the investigation to an end. The attacker was never found.[18]

The pope, according to police informants, knew that Tacchi Venturi was trying to throw the authorities off the trail. But it did not diminish his belief or Mussolini's in the Jesuit's value, and he was soon once again meeting with the Duce on the pope's behalf. Perhaps the suspicions generated by the incident led Tacchi Venturi to overcompensate a bit, eager as he was to win back the Duce's trust. In a letter to Mussolini in May, he assured the Duce that he was both "a good Jesuit and a good fascist."[19]

THE STREAM OF POLICE INFORMANT reports from the Vatican makes clear that the pope was dealing with a number of pederasty accusations at the time, aimed at some of the clerics nearest to him.[20] Monsignor Caccia Dominioni had known the pope from his youth in Milan and now served as the pope's master of ceremonies, constantly at his side. Several accounts from the top government informer in the Vatican detailed the monsignor's alleged relations with both boys and young men.

The pope, the informer reported in 1926, had ordered a secret inquiry into the most recent allegations. A young man, interviewed by Vatican investigators, reported that Caccia had lured him to his Vatican rooms for sex. When the story became the subject of Vatican gossip, the pope ordered that no one speak of it. This was not the pope's first experience with such allegations. Monsignor Ricardo Sanz de Samper, the majordomo and prefect of the papal household, had also been charged with having sexual relations with young boys. Behind the pope's back, Vatican insiders joked that when Pius XI showed himself in public, he was "worthily surrounded, having at his sides two pederasts, Caccia and Samper." And in fact, at public audiences Caccia and Samper did stand on either side of the pope.[21]

But the fate of the two accused men would be very different. Unlike the Milanese Caccia, the South American Samper had no preexisting ties to the pope. In the end he could not survive the scandal. Not only did Pius XI not give him the cardinal's hat that he thought was owed him, he abruptly dismissed him in late 1928 with no public explanation. Thereupon Samper, hitherto one of the most visible presences in the Vatican, vanished from sight.[22]

For years to come, Caccia would face rumors about his penchant for bringing boys into his Vatican bedroom. A stream of secret reports, from several different police informants, chronicled the sordid details.[23]

Without Mussolini's network of spies, such Vatican secrets would never have been known. Even today, when the Holy See makes available its historical files to scholars at the Vatican Secret Archives, Church officials remove those that deal with such sensitive "personnel" matters. But Mussolini's spy network within the Vatican was robust. It included not only three or four well-placed clerics but also lay Vatican employees and Catholics with high-level Vatican sources, such as Emanuele Brunatto, an industrialist with close ties to Cardinal Gasparri. Brunatto was one of several informants who reported on Caccia's exploits.[24]

Following the attempts on his life in 1926, Mussolini fired the national police chief and replaced him with forty-six-year-old Arturo Bocchini. A career civil servant, from the ranks of the country's prefects, Bocchini was no Fascist zealot. Like many, he had simply switched his loyalty with the advent of the new government. But over the next years, no one would be more valuable to Mussolini, as Bocchini quietly but masterfully devised a vast network of surveillance designed to inform the police, and Mussolini, of any opposition to the regime.

Bocchini met with Mussolini every morning, showing him the secret informant reports that he thought would be of most interest. Intelligent, efficient, and dedicated to his task, he was not personally sadistic,
just thorough.[25] By the end of 1927, he had centralized all police surveillance under his control and had produced active files on more than
one hundred thousand people. His job was not only to keep an eye on
particular individuals but to keep a finger on the pulse of the population. His reports allowed the Duce—otherwise surrounded by sycophants—to get some sense of the public mood.[26]

Bocchini put his spy network together by recruiting people to serve
as the center of their own subnetworks of informants, and these subnet-
work chiefs were constantly on the lookout for recruits. Heading one of
the most important of these nodes was Bocchini's own tall, attractive,
mistress, Bice Pupeschi, a married but separated woman fourteen years
younger than he. Bocchini installed her in a Rome apartment that
served not only as their love nest but as the rendezvous for some of her
top informants.[27]

Few of them were more valuable to the police chief than Monsignor
Enrico Pucci, recruited in October 1927.[28] Pucci had first served in the
Vatican under Pius X; he then became priest of Santa Maria in Trastevere, a church not far from the Vatican. In 1919 he returned to the
Vatican as domestic prelate of the pope and editor of Rome's Catholic
newspaper, *Il Corriere d'Italia*. It was Pucci's 1923 article there that
had made public the pope's wish that Don Sturzo resign as Popular
Party head. Pucci put out a regular newsletter covering Vatican news.
Nurturing a vast range of personal contacts, by the mid-1920s he was
widely viewed as the Vatican's chief press officer. Pucci regularly met
with Cardinal Gasparri, although not with the pope, and he was a common sight in Rome's cafés and restaurants, sharing a drink or dining
with cardinals and bishops.[29]

It was thanks to this network of informants that Mussolini came to
know of Caccia's travails. A 1928 inquiry focused on two boys who
had been spotted coming out of the monsignor's rooms. When caught
and questioned, they detailed their illicit relations with him, down to a

description of his bedroom. Mussolini first learned of this from an informant identified in the police files simply as the "noted Vatican informer." The identity of this informer, who clearly was deep in the Vatican, remains obscure. Between 1925 and 1934 he filed scores of confidential reports. Many were sent on to Mussolini's private secretary, and the Duce read them avidly.[30]

In reporting the latest news of Caccia's exploits in 1928, the "noted Vatican informer," added that the police chief of Borgo, the Roman police district responsible for the Vatican, was collaborating with Vatican officials to keep the allegations from getting out.[31] This would not be the last time Rome's police would help the Vatican conceal embarrassing accounts of Monsignor Caccia's relations with young boys.

THE PACT

T HE "ROMAN QUESTION" HAD BEDEVILED THE COUNTRY'S LEADERS ever since the Kingdom of Italy, formed on the ashes of the Papal States in 1861, gobbled up Rome nine years later. For a millennium, popes had ruled a large swath of the Italian peninsula, stretching at the time of Italian unification from Rome northward through Umbria and into Ferrara and Bologna. In 1860, as the Papal States were crumbling, Pius IX had excommunicated Italy's king and announced that no Catholic could recognize his government.

For the next three decades, Pius IX and his successor, Leo XIII, had cast about for ways to retake the Eternal City. But by the end of the century, even the pope's most fervent supporters realized that the effort was futile. The continuing conflict created international complications for the new Italian state, for leaders of Catholic countries were loath to visit its capital. The pope would not see them if they met with Italian government leaders, yet to visit Rome and fail to pay homage to the pope risked incurring unpleasant consequences back home.

At the turn of the century, things finally began to change. Alarmed by the rapidly growing socialist movement, Pius X lifted the ban on

Catholics voting and running for national office. But the Holy See still refused to recognize the Italian government, and the Vatican's legal status remained murky.[1]

In the summer of 1924, in the midst of the crisis sparked by Matteotti's murder, Mussolini set up a special commission to review the laws affecting the Church. Its aim was to reduce the sources of friction between church and state. Because the Holy See still formally did not recognize Italy, the pope could not be seen collaborating with its government. But behind the scenes, working through Tacchi Venturi, he placed three prelates on the commission.[2]

The group met thirty-five times in 1925. In February 1926, as it prepared to announce new draft laws, the pope wrote a long handwritten letter offering his opinion of its work. Addressed to his secretary of state, the letter was published in the Vatican newspaper.

The Church, the pope wrote, could not approve any agreement on the Church's rights that was produced simply by a vote of parliament. Only direct negotiations between the government and the Holy See could bring about a new understanding.[3]

Mussolini was excited. The pope's letter, he told his minister of justice and religion, was "of capital importance." Having disposed of "the prejudices of liberalism," the Duce explained, the Fascist regime "has repudiated both the principle of the state's religious agnosticism, and the principle of separation of church and state." His government had worked hard "to restore the character of being a Catholic State and a Catholic Nation." It was time for negotiations to begin. As Mussolini was so quick to grasp, Pius XI was offering him the possibility of a historic agreement that would solidify support for his regime in a way that was otherwise unimaginable.[4]

Some diplomats doubted that the pope would ever end the Vatican's formal state of enmity with Italy. By portraying itself as implacably opposed to the Italian government, the Vatican avoided awkward questions about why it was entirely in Italian hands. Should the pope—an Italian surrounded almost entirely by other Italians—make peace with the Italian state, observed America's ambassador to Italy, he risked being seen as the king's chaplain. What was supposed to be a universal institution would appear as essentially Italian. "The Church is convinced," the ambassador advised Washington, "that its influence would be diminished rather than increased by a formal reconciliation with the Quirinal [the royal palace], and I should be surprised if this were to come about for years, if not indeed for centuries."[5]

Undaunted by the skeptics, Mussolini did all he could to identify the Italian state with the Catholic Church.[6] Declaring Saint Francis of Assisi "the most saintly of Italians, the most Italian of the saints," he declared October 4 a national holiday in the saint's honor. He provided Cardinal Merry del Val, the pope's representative to the inaugural rites in Assisi, with a special train, offering military honors along the way; this would have been inconceivable before the March on Rome. The cardinal returned the favor: Mussolini, he told the crowd at Assisi, was "visibly protected by God."[7] The dictator also decided that the country should be self-sufficient not only in agriculture but in miracles as well. Unhappy that so many Italians were attracted to the French pilgrimage site of Lourdes, he built up worship of the Madonna of Loreto, to no little effect.[8]

When, in August 1926, the pope launched the negotiations, he chose a layman, Francesco Pacelli, to serve as his personal representative. If he avoided relying on his secretary of state—or even on a clergyman—for this purpose, it was in good part because the Vatican still did not formally recognize the Italian state. Born in 1872—four years before his better-known brother, Eugenio, the future pope Pius XII—Francesco Pacelli came from a Roman family that had served the popes for generations. When Rome fell to Italian troops in 1870, the city's elite had divided into two factions. Those who embraced the new state were dubbed the white aristocracy, those loyal to the pope the black. The Pacelli family belonged to this *aristocrazia nera*.[9] Following in his father's footsteps, Francesco became a prominent Vatican lawyer.

Mussolini appointed Domenico Barone, a government lawyer, to represent him in the talks. Although both the pope and Mussolini were eager to keep them secret, there was no lack of gossip. Word reached as far as Chicago, where a news account told of the Duce's purported eagerness to create "a city of the Pope." Sensitive to the rumors, Romans began scrutinizing real estate sales, as a story was making the rounds that the pope was quietly buying up property, with the goal of creating a papal state that would stretch from St. Peter's to the sea.[10]

The course of negotiations was anything but smooth. What most frequently proved a stumbling block was the pope's fiercely protective attitude toward Catholic Action. Mussolini could never be comfortable with a group that he did not control. As a mass-membership organization over which he had no authority, Catholic Action constantly aroused his suspicion. He was certain that remnants of the Popular Party were finding a home there. But Pius viewed the organization as his main vehicle for spreading Catholic gospel to the Italian masses.

Reports of Fascist violence against Catholic Action groups had often provoked the pope's anger. In June 1925, in one such case, *squadristi* sacked the Catholic Action headquarters in Padua; the pope had dispatched Tacchi Venturi to do something about it. The resulting police investigation detailed the tight links in that city between Catholic Action and the Popular Party.[11] In this case and others, the pope's Jesuit emissary did all he could to calm him. Catholic Action leaders had been repeatedly warned to keep their activities separate from the Popular Party, he reminded the pontiff. The Catholic Action groups were bringing the trouble on themselves. How, he asked, could the Vatican permit a Church organization to criticize the Fascist government that was "so well disposed to the Catholic religion"?[12]

Early in 1926, upset by the latest reports of violence against a Catholic Action headquarters, this time in the northern city of Brescia, the pope again told Tacchi Venturi to lodge a complaint. After meeting with government officials, the Jesuit again tried to get the pope and Gasparri to see things from Mussolini's perspective. Many of the most active members of Catholic Action in Brescia, Tacchi Venturi reported, were also well-known Popular Party activists: "From this comes the confusion and almost identification of the one with the other." He continued, "The government does not lack clear proof that the [Brescia] Catholic Action, along with its semi-official paper, *Il Cittadino,* is often nothing but the disguise used by the anti-government political party."[13]

While local Fascists often took aim at adult Catholic Action groups, Mussolini was more exercised by the role played by the youth groups. As he solidified his dictatorship, he recognized how important it would be to mold children into loyal Fascists. A few months before the negotiations with the Vatican began, he announced the founding of his own national youth organization, the Opera Nazionale Balilla. It had four sections. The Balilla was for boys eight to fourteen, and the Avanguardisti for those fourteen to eighteen; they had their female counterparts in the Piccole italiane (Little Italian Girls) and the Giovani italiane (Female Italian Youth). Members wore quasi-military uniforms.[14]

For Mussolini, the Church's national network of youth groups—ranging from the Catholic Boy Scouts through various Catholic Action organizations for older youths—offered unwanted competition. Gaining control of the youth was important enough to him to risk angering the pope. He began by outlawing the Boy Scout groups. Angered by the news, the pope sent Tacchi Venturi to warn him to back off.

In early 1927, upset not only by the dissolution of the Catholic Boy Scouts but by signs that the ban would soon extend to the Catholic Action youth groups, the pope ordered the talks suspended. He demanded that Catholic Action be specifically excluded from regulations that would allow only those non-Fascist youth groups whose activities were "predominantly religious." Much of what drew youngsters to the Catholic groups was their recreational activities. Pius worried that if the groups offered only prayer and religious instruction, membership would dwindle. He sent Tacchi Venturi to give Mussolini an ultimatum: unless he relented, he could forget about reaching a deal on the Roman question. Realizing that he was in danger of overplaying his hand, in late February 1927 Mussolini sent word to his prefects to leave the Catholic Action youth groups alone. Pleased, the pope had Francesco Pacelli resume the talks.[15]

Over the next months, as the negotiations continued, the pope met with Pacelli several times a week. Fresh reports of Fascist violence against local Catholic groups would come in from time to time, and the pope would again threaten to break off the talks. But by now he had invested too much in the negotiations, and too much in his support for Mussolini and the Fascist regime, to risk having them fail. He blamed the violence on anticlerics surrounding Mussolini who were trying to thwart the dictator's will. Other points of conflict arose as well. In April 1928 the pope complained about the recent creation of the Fascist girls' organizations. He was especially pained by their practice of marching with muskets on their shoulders. But again, the fault was not Mussolini's. "There are many things that are going on that Mussolini does not know about," said the pope.[16]

The pontiff had earlier told the cardinals of the Curia that negotiations with the government were under way. But fearing that opposition might form, he decided against convening them until an agreement was reached. He worried in particular about Cardinal Bonaventura Cerretti, an influential voice on international affairs known to be hostile to the Fascist regime. In order to remove Cerretti from Rome during the crucial months of the negotiations in 1928, he sent him to Sydney, Australia, as his legate to the International Eucharistic Congress. The cardinal would return only after the agreement was completed.[17]

In October 1928, just as an agreement seemed near, the pope got unwelcome news: the king was having second thoughts and might not sign it. Victor Emmanuel III—named after the man who had robbed the pope of his territories—was, the pope knew, no friend of the papacy. Two years earlier Pius XI had further antagonized the king when his mother, known for her Catholic devotion and good works, had died. The king had wanted the pope to preside over her funeral or at least offer a public tribute, but the pope would do neither. Count Dalla Torre, editor of the Vatican daily, had prepared a flattering obituary of the queen mother, but it was never published—the pope had forbidden it.[18]

Pius now worried that the years of difficult negotiations might all be for naught. Desperate to find a way to win the king's approval, he focused on what he knew most bothered the monarch: the possible expansion of the lands under the pope's control. He decided to abandon his earlier demand that the vast gardens of the Villa Doria Pamphili, on the Janiculum Hill above the Vatican, be added to Vatican territory.[19]

"If they don't accept under these conditions," Domenico Barone, Mussolini's negotiator, told Pacelli, on hearing the news, "they are idiots."[20]

MUSSOLINI AND THE KING, so different in personality and background, had by the late 1920s settled into a stable if peculiar relationship. At one point Mussolini said that it was as if the two shared a bedroom but had separate beds. But they did have a number of traits in common, not least their discomfort around priests. Both, too, made casually cutting remarks about those around them. The king once, characteristically, described Italy's chief general, Pietro Badoglio (whom he would years later choose to replace Mussolini as prime minister) as having "the brains of a sparrow and the hide of an elephant." Mussolini, for his part, frequently ridiculed the king in private. The pint-size monarch made a poor impression, he complained, unworthy of a great nation. He was a "sour, treacherous little man." At various times he dubbed Victor Emmanuel "an empty carriage," a "dead tree," and an "old hen whose feathers should be plucked." But he did not tolerate ridicule of the king by others, including his wife. Coming from the same antimonarchical background as her husband, Rachele, ill at ease among the wealthy and the well bred, was never comfortable anywhere near the royal family. Mussolini undoubtedly understood this, but whenever she began telling her favorite joke about the king needing a ladder to mount his horse, he told her to be quiet.[21]

Every Monday and Thursday morning at ten, the Duce, in frock coat and top hat, went to meet Victor Emmanuel III in the vast and majestic Quirinal Palace, where the king would sign a raft of government decrees and personnel appointments. On those mornings, observed Quinto Navarra, he was like a different Mussolini. For the rest of the week, the imperial, dictatorial Duce who intimidated his ministers appeared frequently in his Fascist militia uniform, in a never-ending series of parades and rallies, the supreme leader in the regime's complex choreography of power. But during his mornings at the royal palace, Mussolini played the part of the respectful prime minister, mindful of the king's prerogatives in what was still formally a constitutional monarchy.[22]

ON FEBRUARY 7, 1929, Cardinal Gasparri called in the ambassadors to the Holy See and told them that a historic agreement was soon to be announced, ending the decades-long dispute between the Church and the Italian government. The cardinal was about to become the public face of a treaty that would be hailed by churchmen around the world. But it was a bittersweet moment for him. In recent years he had been getting clear signals that the pope no longer valued his services. Although down-to-earth, Gasparri had his pride. He had been stung in 1929 when the pope, on the occasion of the fiftieth anniversary of his ordination, snubbed him. His staff had made plans for a gala festival, a mass to be held in his honor in the Sistine Chapel, presided over by the pope; the cardinals of the Curia would all be there, along with the whole foreign diplomatic corps. But the pope did not attend, and the dignitaries who did gossiped about his surprising absence.[23]

By early 1928, Gasparri was no longer young. Suffering from diabetes and heart disease, he slept poorly. The once-jovial secretary of state increasingly appeared depressed and was quick to get misty-eyed. When others remarked on his pallor and the fact that his hands had begun to shake, he assured them that he felt fine. The pope urged him to take some time off to rest, but Gasparri, fearing that the pope would take advantage of his absence to replace him, insisted there was no need.[24] He did not know how long he could hold on, but he wanted to be present to bask in the glory of ending the seventy years of hostility between Italy and the Holy See.

The day after Gasparri assembled the diplomats in the Vatican to tell them the news, Mussolini sent a telegram to all of Italy's ambassadors with the same message. Word of the imminent signing ceremony was published in foreign newspapers, but the Italian press was silent, and few in Italy realized what was about to happen.[25]

"These are wonderful days!" Monsignor Francis Spellman—the only American in the secretary of state office—wrote to his mother in Boston from Rome on February 8. "Wonderful days to be alive and still more wonderful to be alive in Rome!" He added, "Everyone here is radiantly happy and well they might be. This Holy Father, Cardinal Gasparri and Monsignor Borgongini are assured of places in history and of course also Mussolini."[26]

The final details of the Vatican-Italian or Lateran Accords were ironed out by Mussolini and Pacelli on Saturday evening, February 9, 1929.[27] The first article specified that the Catholic religion was "the only religion of the State." The accords had three parts. The first, the treaty proper, established Vatican City as a sovereign territory under papal rule, in which the Italian government had no right to interfere. (Previously the Vatican palaces and gardens, and St. Peter's Basilica, had been under the pope's control, but the Italian government had always regarded them as lying on Italian soil, and their legal status had been ambiguous.)[28] The boundaries of Vatican City were largely to coincide with the existing medieval walls; St. Peter's Square, which was not circumscribed by the walls, was to be considered part of the new city-state but would be open to the public and under Italian police supervision. In all, the territory comprised 109 acres. Offending the dignity of the pope would be regarded as a crime equal to offending the king. Ambassadors to the Holy See were to enjoy the same immunities and privileges as ambassadors to Italy. In addition to its sovereignty over Vatican City, the Holy See was granted special rights to Rome's basilicas and to the papal summer palace in Castel Gandolfo, in the nearby Alban Hills. All cardinals in Rome would be regarded as citizens of the new state.[29]

The second part of the Lateran Accords, the concordat, governed relations between the Holy See and Italy. The Italian government would not allow anything to take place in Rome that would interfere with the Vatican's character as the sacred center of the Catholic world. The concordat recognized a series of Catholic feast days as public holidays, and for the first time the Italian state would recognize religious marriages. (Until then, couples who wed only in church were not considered legally married.) The concordat also specified that Catholic religious instruction, which the regime had already made mandatory in elementary schools, be extended to all secondary schools. Although no more than one in five Italian children made it beyond elementary school at the time, those who did would form the elite of the next generation, and their religious education was precious to the Church.[30] In another provision dear to the pope, the Italian state accepted the right of Catholic Action groups to operate freely.

The third and final part of the accords consisted of a financial agreement. Italy would pay 750 million lire, plus one billion lire in Italian bonds (totaling roughly one billion 2013 U.S. dollars), in exchange for the Holy See's agreement to give up all claims for the loss of its Papal States.[31]

At nine A.M. on Monday, February 11, Dino Grandi, undersecretary of foreign affairs, arrived at Mussolini's home. The Duce was in an unusually upbeat mood. In the car on the way to the signing, he sang an old Romagna folk song. While the Duce was happy, Grandi was nervous.

"Should I kiss the cardinal's ring?" he asked.

Cardinal Gasparri would likely expect it, replied Mussolini. Giddy, he told Grandi he knew the best way to decide the question. He reached into his pocket, pulled out a coin, and flipped it. The dictator glanced at the result and announced, "We'll kiss the ring!"[32]

At the Vatican early that morning, Gasparri and his undersecretary, Monsignor Borgongini, met in the pope's private library, where they assured the pontiff that everything was ready for the signing. They handed him the text of the treaty, fresh from the Vatican printer, along with a map that reflected the last-minute changes. After carefully examining the documents, the pope nodded his approval. Gasparri and Borgongini had to get going, but before leaving they knelt and asked for the pope's blessing. They all felt the enormity of what was about to take place. Tears clouded Cardinal Gasparri's eyes as he left the room.[33]

The ceremony was held in the Hall of the Popes in the Lateran Palace, on the other side of the city from the Vatican. The pope's seat as bishop of Rome was not St. Peter's Basilica but the Archbasilica of St. John Lateran. For a thousand years, from the fourth century (when the Emperor Constantine had given the popes his own palace on that site) to the fourteenth (when the popes went into exile in Avignon), popes had lived in St. John Lateran.[34] Vandals had devastated it in the fifth century, and it had been partly destroyed by fires in the fourteenth, but it was always rebuilt, ever grander. As "prisoners of the Vatican," however, no pope had set foot there since Italian troops took Rome in 1870.

Gasparri and Borgongini had already arrived—in a new Chrysler donated by a wealthy American—when Mussolini's car pulled up. A light rain fell.[35] The Duce emerged from his car, clutching white gloves in his left hand. He wore a morning suit, complete with tails and top hat.[36] The cardinal greeted Mussolini and Grandi, who were joined by Minister of Justice Alfredo Rocco and Mussolini's undersecretary, Francesco Giunta, and invited them to climb the imposing stairway with him. They walked slowly through what Grandi described as an "interminable" number of ornate rooms of the museum dedicated to the Church's missions around the world. The ebullient Gasparri waved his arms as he identified all the countries whose exhibits they were passing, from New Guinea and the Fiji Islands to Mongolia, India, and Nicaragua. "Names of strange and distant lands," recalled Grandi, "that the Prince of the Church pronounced with a smile, as if wanting to emphasize for us how vast was the power and the reach of the Catholic Church in the world."

Finally they reached their destination. At one end of the large room

Signing the Lateran Accords, February 11, 1929. Left to right:
Monsignor Francesco Borgongini-Duca, Cardinal Pietro Gasparri,
Francesco Pacelli, Benito Mussolini, Dino Grandi

Following the signing of the accords, Lateran Palace, February 11, 1929.
Cardinal Gasparri and Mussolini, front center; Monsignor Pizzardo on far left;
Francesco Pacelli in top hat on Gasparri's right; Monsignor Borgongini
on Mussolini's left, with Dino Grandi to his left.

stood a sixteen-by-four-foot rose-colored table; eight heavily carved black armchairs were arranged in a row along the far side.[37] At the center, Mussolini and Gasparri took their seats. As they prepared to sign the document, the dictator, who had earlier been so relaxed, looked pale and ill at ease, while the cardinal, feeling at home, kept smiling.[38]

When Mussolini and Gasparri emerged from the Lateran Palace, the rapidly growing crowd erupted in applause. No advance notice of the ceremony had been given, but the presence of so many police and militiamen outside the cathedral, and then the arrival of the Duce, had triggered rumors, and journalists and photographers had rushed over. Despite the light rain, the mood was bright. Priests and seminarians sang prayers of thanksgiving in chorus, interspersed with shouts of "Long live Pius, our Pope and King!" while others, gathering in the piazza in front of the historic church, cried "Viva Mussolini! Viva Italy!," intermingled with Fascist shouts of "alalà!" As he was being driven away, Monsignor Pizzardo got so carried away that he responded to the crowd's shouts by raising his arm in Fascist salute.[39]

Mussolini, in a more subdued mood, remained silent for the drive back to his office. Although this would be his greatest triumph, he would never feel comfortable around priests or in churches.[40]

It would be difficult to exaggerate the importance the pope gave to the accords. Renato Moro, one of Italy's foremost Church historians, observes that despite the establishment of the Italian government in the nineteenth century, with its commitments to separation of church and state and to liberal democracy, the popes had never abandoned their belief in a hierarchical, authoritarian Italian society run according to Church principles. After years in which these dreams for a return to the Church's former authority seemed unrealistic, the appearance of Fascism offered new grounds for hope.[41]

Until the signing, Catholics unhappy with the dictatorship could argue that the pope was not enthusiastic about the Fascist regime. Now this was no longer possible. Italian Catholics could have no doubt that in supporting Mussolini, they were following the pope's wishes. The pope himself, speaking to a group of university students two days after the signing, explained how the historic agreement had finally been made possible. Perhaps, he told them, it helped that one side was headed by a librarian, expert in combing through historical documents; and "perhaps too what was needed was a man such as the one that Providence had us encounter, a man who did not share the concerns of the liberal school." The pope's reference to Mussolini as the man sent by Providence would be repeated by bishops, priests, and lay Catholics thousands of times in the years to follow.[42]

In Bologna, special editions of local dailies sold out in a flash. The archbishop announced a special mass of thanksgiving for the next day, to which both government and military officials were invited. The archbishop of Chieti did not wait another day—an excited crowd packed into the cathedral for a special mass of thanksgiving on the very evening of the signing. The local Fascist authorities proudly took part in the ceremonies, carrying their flags and pennants, undaunted by the snowstorm outside.[43] Newspapers throughout the country, including the Vatican daily, hammered on the theme that the historic event could never have happened if Italy had still been under democratic rule. Only Mussolini, and Fascism, had made it possible.[44]

In Rome, government buildings and private homes were covered by a previously unthinkable combination: yellow and white papal banners alongside tricolored Italian flags. As it happened, it was the seventh anniversary of the pope's coronation, and he was scheduled to preside over a celebratory mass in St. Peter's. Twelve footmen in red uniforms, six on a side, carried the pope in his *sedia gestatoria,* his red-silk-covered throne, into the immense basilica. Tens of thousands of the faithful, having waited shoulder to shoulder for hours, finally got a glimpse of the pontiff. Rome's Fascist Federation had called on Fascists to show their enthusiasm by gathering in St. Peter's Square. Two hundred thousand people stood outside in the pouring rain. When later the pope stepped out onto the balcony to bless them, they roared in joy. Below him stood representatives of each of Rome's Fascist militia units, holding their banners aloft, as the endless crowd of the faithful and the curious stretched far beyond the piazza. Later that afternoon, summoned by Fascist Party and militia officials, swarms of other celebrants gathered outside the Quirinal Palace, where the king appeared on a balcony, with the queen at his right and the national head of the Fascist Party on his left.[45]

Throughout the world, the Duce was being hailed as a great statesman.[46] In the Vatican, a top aide described the thrill. Not even the celebrations of victory in the Great War could compare with the delirium in Italy that day: "The joy was complete, without a single cloud. Everyone felt that new heights of greatness and glory were on Italy's horizon." Throughout the country, from Turin to Sicily, bishops and priests ordered their church bells rung in celebration, honoring the man who had finally brought harmony between church and state.[47] For most Italians, the end of the decades-long hostility came as a huge relief. There was no longer any conflict between being a loyal Italian and being a good Catholic.

The agreement, as the American chargé d'affaires in Rome told the U.S. secretary of state, was "a triumph for Mussolini in ending the controversy and in winning over the clergy to Fascism." In his diary entry for that day, General Enrico Caviglia, hero of the First World War and confidant of the king, offered a different perspective: "These men who come to power through coup d'états need to legitimize themselves through the Vatican." But in twenty years, he asked, what would happen when people came to resent the dictatorship that had robbed them of their freedom? "How would they judge the Vatican," he wondered, "which had given the regime its moral support?"[48]

Mussolini heard only one sour note from his national network of spies. The February 13 report, based on informants in Rome, began warmly: "The news of the Conciliation produced joy and unspeakable enthusiasm in virtually all the population. . . . People say that the historical event represents an unparalleled success produced by the genius of the Duce . . . that the prestige and strength of Fascism have been increased enormously." But there were some malcontents, "a scattering of old and bitter liberals, what remained of the Masons, and the Jews."

For Italy's Jews, the Lateran Accords prompted nervousness and fear. Little more than a half century earlier, the demise of the Papal States had liberated them from the pope's ghettoes. Italian unification and the separation of church and state had been their salvation. Now they worried what the future might bring.[49]

PART TWO

ENEMIES IN COMMON

THE SAVIOR

TELEGRAMS POURED IN, CONGRATULATING PIUS XI ON THE HISTORIC accord. An American journalist who met with the pope shortly after the signing found him smiling and rejuvenated, "as fresh and dynamic as the day on which he was elected."[1] On February 17 the pope's Noble Guards held a lavish reception inside the Vatican, where Rome's black aristocracy fraternized with high prelates of the Curia. Lights were dimmed as they gathered around a movie screen to watch a news film commemorating the signing ceremony. When the Duce's image appeared, applause and cheers swept the room.[2]

The dictator had been eager to conclude the deal, for he had an important vote coming up. Since Italy now had only one political party, it needed a new way to elect parliament. Mussolini's casual comment at the time of the last vote in 1924 turned out to be prophetic: that would be the last time he would suffer the indignity of running against an opposition. In the new system, it would be up to the Grand Council of Fascism to select the candidates for the four hundred seats in the Chamber of Deputies. Voters would get to vote yes or no on the slate as a whole. Mussolini himself referred to it not as an election but a plebiscite on the regime.[3]

The Vatican threw its full weight behind Mussolini's campaign. On March 17, a week before Election Day 1929, *L'Osservatore romano* published an appeal urging all Catholics to vote yes. This was no small matter for Mussolini, for 99 percent of Italians were Catholic. The rest of the Catholic press, and priests throughout the country, eagerly joined the campaign.[4]

To most observers, it seemed that a grateful pope had simply mobilized the Church to support Mussolini's list of faithful Fascists. But behind the scenes, something else was going on. The pope was not willing to simply rubber-stamp Mussolini's choices.[5] Of the thousand names presented to the Grand Council from various Fascist and state organizations, from which it was to choose the four hundred candidates, the pope deemed three-quarters insufficiently Catholic. With the signing of the concordat, the pope argued, Italy was now "a confessional state." The membership of parliament should reflect that new reality.

The pope wanted the Duce to scrap his list and substitute one composed of those "free from any tie with Freemasonry, with Judaism and, in short, with any of the anticlerical parties." "In this way," the letter conveying the pope's wishes concluded, "the Duce will place . . . the most beautiful and necessary crown atop the great work of the treaty and the concordat. He will show one more time that he is (in conformity with what His Holiness recently called him) the Man sent by Providence."[6]

A few days later Tacchi Venturi brought Mussolini a list of the men the pope considered "worthy representatives of a confessional State."[7] The popes had long condemned Freemasonry, and one of the first things Mussolini had done to please the Vatican after coming to power was to declare Freemasons ineligible for membership in the Fascist Party.[8] Now the pope demanded that Jews and Masons be purged from the candidate list, and that Fascists of sure Catholic faith be added. Only after Mussolini made the changes did the Vatican organize a massive Church mobilization for a yes vote.[9] On Election Day, a Sunday, parish priests throughout Italy literally led their parishioners to the ballot box.[10] Mussolini's triumph was complete, winning 98.3 percent of the vote.[11]

The day after the plebiscite, one of the pope's old protégés came to see him. Stefano Jacini was one of the boys of Milan's nobility for whom Ratti had, years earlier, served as spiritual mentor. Entering the bronze door along the Bernini colonnade, to the right of St. Peter's, Jacini was greeted by Swiss Guards in their brightly striped uniforms. They checked his invitation and let him ascend the long stairway into the Vatican palaces. Jacini was then escorted through the vast, splendiferous halls by men from the pope's Noble Guard, Italians from aristocratic families. It was as if he had walked into a Renaissance costume drama. As he passed through the richly decorated halls, clusters of Papal Gendarmes—Italians dressed in exact replicas of the uniforms worn by Napoleon's grenadiers—stood watch. A domestic prelate of the pope came to walk the forty-two-year-old Jacini to the office of the man he had once known as a simple priest.

Pius XI smiled as he entered. In their seventy-minute conversation, the pope often slipped into the first person singular "I" rather than his customary "We." They spent a good deal of their time discussing the Lateran Accords.

"Situation resolved!" the pope told him happily. "Yes, I am pleased, but now comes the hard part, seeing that the provisions are applied. We have never had greater need to pray than we do now, but the future is in God's hands. I can't be expected to predict the future." He reminded Jacini of verses by Metastasio, an eighteenth-century Italian poet. " 'There is no past, memory paints it,' " the pope recited. " 'There is no future, for hope shapes it. There is only the present, but it is always escaping us.' "[12]

Knowing that Jacini had been a Popular Party leader, the pope was eager to justify his deal with the Duce. He could not have let the opportunity pass, he argued, for if he had, history might well judge him harshly. "The Lord helped me in all this." He complained of those who had criticized him for coming to terms with the Fascist regime. "It was like saying that you should stop breathing because you are in a room where the air is polluted." He explained, "For the Church, there is revolution and there is revolution, that which destroys authority, destroys the existing order, and that which transforms it. The Italian one is a revolution made with the king's and the monarchy's approval. We couldn't ask for more than that.

"It was not a real revolution," continued the pope, still trying to justify himself to the young nobleman. "An upheaval, yes. We need to see what comes of it." Words of his beloved Manzoni came to his mind: "'The twilight hour is neither light, nor dark. What will come of it? Day or night? Wait a bit and then you will see.'"

As the pope spoke, he grew more animated, shifting position in his chair, putting his elbows on his desk, using his hand to push his white *zucchetto* back into place on his head. "Hair still blonde, smiling behind his gold spectacles," recalled Jacini, "his face animated, a brief chuckle punctuating his remarks, he seemed for a time to become once again the Don Achille of olden times."[13]

ALTHOUGH THE DEAL WITH THE POPE had been a great public relations success for Mussolini, it was not without its downside. Nothing angered him more than being called the pope's patsy, and some were now accusing him of being just that. A proud, arrogant man whose ego was growing ever larger, Mussolini was sensitive to whisperings that he was selling out his principles and creating a state run not by Fascists but by priests. The fact that *La Civiltà cattolica* praised Mussolini's plebiscite victory as ushering in a "Christian restoration of society" did not help.

It was a delicate moment for Mussolini. There were those in and out of parliament who were unhappy. Fascists of the first hour—those who had been with the movement from its earliest days—saw the agreement as a betrayal of true Fascism, ceding unwanted influence to the pope. And some of the old liberal elite were upset that the Duce had abandoned the separation of church and state.

On May 13 Mussolini rose in the Chamber of Deputies to conclude its debate over the ratification of the accords. It would be one of his most famous speeches.

"Honorable comrades," he began, before a packed gallery. Much confusion was being spread about the recent agreement. In the Italian state, he assured them, "the Church is not sovereign nor is it even free." It remained subject to the laws of the land. Italy had the great advantage of being the home of a universal religion. But the Catholic Church's success owed much to Italy itself: "This religion was born in Palestine, but it became Catholic in Rome." He then added, in a remark destined to infuriate the pope, that if the early Christian community had remained in Palestine, "very probably it would have simply been one of the many sects that flourished in that overheated environment . . . and very likely it would have died out, without leaving a trace."[14] The Italian state, he concluded, "is Catholic but also Fascist, indeed before all else exclusively and essentially Fascist."[15]

The next day Pius dispatched the lawyer Francesco Pacelli to see the dictator. He carried a threat: the pope was irate and might suspend the talks on implementing the accords. Mussolini tried to calm the pope down. He would use his upcoming Senate speech, he said, to clear up any misunderstanding.

Three days later, as the Senate took up the motion to confirm the accords, Pacelli sat in the gallery to listen to Mussolini's speech. But what he heard was little different from what he had heard in the Chamber. "I have the impression," he wrote in his diary, "that [the speech] will not succeed in wholly pleasing the Holy Father."

Although few were aware of it, over the next two weeks both Mussolini and the pope in turn threatened to bring down the whole carefully constructed Lateran Accords. Pacelli shuttled back and forth in a desperate effort to avoid disaster. In the end, both sides realized they had too much to lose. On June 7 Mussolini went to the Vatican, and in Cardinal Gasparri's rooms, the two men sat down for the final signing.[16]

With the Lateran Accords, the pope and the Duce entered into a peculiar partnership. Each saw himself as heading a "totalitarian" orga-

Mussolini and Gasparri following ratification of the Lateran Accords at
the Vatican, June 7, 1929. Cardinal Gasparri and Mussolini seated;
Monsignor Borgongini standing between them, with, to his left,
Francesco Pacelli and Monsignor Pizzardo.

nization, a term they both embraced. It could have only one head and
demanded total loyalty. The pope was eager to use the Fascists' power
to resurrect a Catholic state, although he was not so foolish as to think
he could ever "Christianize" Mussolini. The Duce was eager to use the
power of the Church to solidify his own rule, but in his view the Catholic clergy were to be the handmaidens of the Fascist government, tools
to ensure popular support for the regime.

Each side had much to gain by the deal, but neither Mussolini nor
the pope would ever be entirely comfortable with it. The pope would
not be happy unless he could get Mussolini to respect what he regarded as the Church's divinely ordained prerogatives. Mussolini was
willing to give the pope what he wanted as long as it did not conflict
with his dictatorship and his own dreams of glory. As the pope would
discover, Mussolini could be pushed only so far. Both men jealously
guarded the rights they thought were theirs. Both were prone to bursts

of temper. There was ample reason to suspect that the partnership might not last.

WITH THE ESTABLISHMENT OF diplomatic relations, Mussolini appointed forty-four-year-old Cesare De Vecchi to be Italy's first ambassador to the Holy See. Trained as a lawyer, from a middle-class family in Piedmont, De Vecchi had commanded a shock troop unit during the war. He later became leader of the *squadristi* in Turin. One of the Fascist Party deputies elected in 1921, his moment of greatest triumph had come as one of the Quadrumvirate who led the March on Rome.

Why the Duce chose De Vecchi for the delicate diplomatic mission is a bit of a mystery. Mussolini regularly made fun of his pomposity and thickheadedness and complained that he had no political sense. In May 1923 he fired De Vecchi from his position as undersecretary of the Treasury, saying he was unfit for anything but a soldier's life.[17] He sent him to Italian Somalia to serve as governor, where he stayed for five years. But De Vecchi had some qualities that recommended him. A devout Catholic, he had ties both with the royal family and with the upper reaches of the military, two spheres that had largely resisted Fascist control. In appreciation for his devotion to the monarchy, the king gave De Vecchi the title of Count of Val Cismon, which he proudly bore. According to Dino Grandi, whenever anyone mentioned the king's name to De Vecchi, an involuntary tremor flashed through his body, as though a soldier were being called to attention.[18] But his arrogance, poor judgment, booming voice, shaved head, small eyes, big nose, and outlandish mustache—vaguely resembling a small squirrel—made him one of the regime's most frequent targets of popular ridicule.[19]

On the morning of June 25, the new ambassador arrived at the Vatican in a royal coach drawn by two gaily festooned horses. The coachman and three outriders standing on the back of the coach were dressed as if for the court of Louis XIV. Wearing a diplomatic uniform reminiscent of the admiral in H.M.S. *Pinafore,* De Vecchi presented his credentials to the pope. He was ushered into the small throne room, where

Cesare De Vecchi, Italian ambassador to the Holy See, 1929–35

the pope sat surrounded by his court. The new ambassador bowed three times, as was the custom, and after the formal exchange of greetings, Pius XI invited him to his library for a private conversation. De Vecchi got to say little, while the pope—perhaps prompted by the new ambassador's roots in the north—reminisced with pleasure about his past Alpine exploits. In then recalling his years as a young priest in the Eternal City, his mood momentarily darkened. He told De Vecchi of the time when jeering youths had chased him down the streets of Rome, throwing stones and shouting "Cockroach!"

Those days, De Vecchi assured him, were past. Since Fascism had come to power, priests were treated with respect.[20]

A month later De Vecchi again met with the pope, but this time their encounter was far less pleasant. He stepped into the pontiff's library with some trepidation, knowing how angry the pope was about the recent publication of Mussolini's parliamentary speeches. As he entered, a trick of the sunlight shining through the window made it look as if fire were flaring from the pope's eyeglasses. The pope tore into De Vecchi in terms the ambassador described as "harsh, resentful, often crude and cutting." "Things can't go on this way," he warned, shaking his head, "they absolutely cannot go on this way. Your behavior," said the pope, referring to the government's publication of the speeches, "offends the Church and its head. I went out to meet Italy with an open heart and in payment for our loyalty Signor Mussolini has shot us in the back with a machine gun." Riffling through papers on his desk, the pope pulled out reports of recent mistreatment of local Catholic Action chapters. In some areas, officers had been roughed up, and people had been told that good Italians did not join Catholic Action.

De Vecchi tried to defend the government. It could hardly be expected to stand by, he said, while anti-Fascists hid behind the Catholic groups.

The pope reacted as if he had been stung by a wasp and banged the table with his palm. "I don't want to hear this!" He had given explicit orders that Catholic Action not engage in politics, and the government had no right to harass its members.

That was all well and good, replied De Vecchi, but it was one thing to give orders and another to have them obeyed.

Darkness fell during their two-and-a-half-hour meeting. As De Vecchi prepared to leave, the pope, calmer now, said, "Tell Signor Mussolini, in my name, not to confuse his friends with his enemies and vice versa, for confusion of that kind would limit the place that he will have in history. . . . And," added the pope, "tell him that every day, in my prayers, I ask the Lord to bless him."[21]

In mid-September the pope addressed a huge group of young Italian Catholics. Still upset about the treatment of Catholic Action, he bewailed the "martyrdom" they faced. Soon afterward, De Vecchi told the pope how upset Mussolini had been to hear of his remarks. It would be best, he suggested, for the pope to remain silent about his Catholic Action complaints so that De Vecchi and others could work through diplomatic channels to resolve them.

The ambassador should have known better. The pope slammed his hand on the desk and asked indignantly, "So you don't want me to speak, you don't want me to say that which it is my duty to say?"

"That's not exactly what I mean, Holiness," responded De Vecchi. "I know the person on the other side and my advice is meant only to aid the common good."

"For the common good," Pius repeated. "Let me tell you how I will proceed from now on to satisfy you on certain occasions. I will open this window"—here the pope, his voice rising, pointed with his finger to the window behind his desk—"and I will shout so that everyone in Saint Peter's Square can hear me!"

De Vecchi was momentarily speechless. "That's what I will do," the pope repeated, "whether you like it or not, Mr. Ambassador!"[22]

Later in the fall, the hapless De Vecchi suffered through another bout of papal temper. Prince Umberto, the king's son and heir, was eager to be married in one of Rome's major churches, either in St. John in Lateran or in the monumental Basilica of Santa Maria Maggiore. But the pope turned down the request. Since the Savoyard kings had so long kept the popes a prisoner of the Vatican, he said, he himself had not yet visited either church, and it would not be appropriate for the great-grandson of the king who had deprived the popes of their lands to be married there.[23]

De Vecchi came to ask the pope to reconsider. "He is in a foul mood," Gasparri warned the ambassador, before he entered.[24] But under pressure from the royal family, the mustachioed monarchist nonetheless pressed the case.

In response, the pope "flew into a rage, sharply raising his voice, and often interrupting when I tried to speak," De Vecchi recalled. Unable to get a word in, he sat straight, immobile, in an effort to wait out the tirade. He tried his best to be expressionless but found it difficult to keep a nervous smile from his face.

The pope gesticulated dramatically. "I am offended, mortally offended," he kept repeating, shaking his head and twisting in his seat. "Open your mouth, and your breath offends the Pope; you move, and you humiliate me; you get your sinister brain in motion and you do it to plot things that insult the Church. . . . Enough! Enough!"

Then the pope returned to complaining about how Catholic Action members were being treated. The overmatched ambassador again tried to defend his leader, but the pope got so angry, he jumped to his feet. The muscles in his face pulsed, his mouth clenched. The heavy marble statue of Christ on his desk swayed as the pope pounded his fist. "Lies! Lies!" he shouted.

Pius paced the room, talking angrily as if to himself. He stopped periodically to bang his fist again on his desk. "This is what you have done," he exclaimed, regaining volume. "You have deceived the Pope! Everyone is saying so, everyone knows it, they are writing about it everywhere, inside Italy and abroad!"

De Vecchi endured it all, but when the pope went on to say, "Rome is mine," the ambassador could not contain himself.

"Rome," he sputtered, "is the capital of Italy, home of His Majesty the king and the government."

"Rome," replied the pontiff, "is my diocese."

"Certainly," agreed the ambassador, "in matters of religion—"

"Yes," the pope interrupted, "all the rest is just a matter of keeping the streets clean."[25]

THE CARDINALS OF THE CURIA were murmuring about the pope, tired of his angry outbursts and unhappy not to be consulted on important Church matters. They were particularly upset that during the two and a half years of negotiations with Mussolini, he had not thought it necessary to consult them.[26] In late 1928, at the pope's instruction, Gasparri had convened all of Rome's cardinals in his quarters to let them know that an agreement was near. Bombarded by requests for more details, he replied that the pope would tell them in due course. As it turned out, they would get to read the text of the Lateran Accords only on February 11, 1929, the day it was signed and made public. Cardinal Cerretti, on a ship returning from Australia at the time, did not hide his anger. Mussolini, he quipped, had the pope eating out of his hand.[27]

Among the cardinals unhappy with the pope's deal with Mussolini, none was more vocal than Basilio Pompili, cardinal vicar of Rome since 1916. Like a number of cardinals in Rome, the seventy-year-old Pompili saw Mussolini as no more trustworthy than the previous prime ministers, and no more Catholic. Ever since Italian armies seized Rome in 1870, the Church had insisted that the Eternal City could have no ruler but the pope. For Pius XI to abandon this claim and receive, in the cardinal's eyes, so little in return, was a scandal, a sentiment he shared not only with his inner circle but with a larger group of acquaintances. What especially grated on him was the fact that the pope had never consulted him, the cardinal vicar of Rome.[28] "They gave away Rome, its prestige, its historical importance, its monuments, its churches," he complained, "as if they were dealing with an Abyssinian village."[29] The pope was "incompetent, weak, the scourge and the ruin of the Church that he has betrayed by placing himself at the mercy of a government that doesn't remotely deserve the name of Catholic."

The pope repeatedly urged Pompili to show more respect for the papacy. But when reports of his fulminations kept coming in, he lost patience and asked him to resign.[30] The cardinal vicar, part of one of Rome's most prominent noble families, was not intimidated. "Holiness," responded Pompili, "you have the power to remove me from my post, and go ahead and do it if you please. But until the day I die, I will never willingly leave this position that I have held now for so much time, and of which I have never shown myself unworthy."[31]

A few months later, when the pope appealed once more for him to step down, Pompili again dug in his heels. "I am going to keep shouting the same thing until you can't stand it anymore: 'I will not move, I will not move, I will not move!'"[32] As it happened, natural causes solved the pope's problem. In 1931 Pompili died.[33]

JUST AS MUSSOLINI NAMED De Vecchi to be Italy's first ambassador to the Vatican, Pius XI appointed Francesco Borgongini-Duca, Gasparri's protégé, to be the Holy See's first nuncio to Italy. As the secretary of the Congregation of Extraordinary Ecclesiastical Affairs, Borgongini had served as one of Gasparri's two undersecretaries of state.

On Borgongini's appointment, the pope moved the other undersec-

Monsignor Giuseppe Pizzardo

retary, fifty-one-year-old Giuseppe Pizzardo, the substitute secretary of state, to the newly vacated position. Pizzardo came from a modest family near Genoa but had somehow made his way to the Pontifical Academy of Noble Ecclesiastics in Rome, the traditional training ground for the upper reaches of Vatican diplomacy. He had joined the Vatican secretary of state office shortly after his ordination. In 1909 he was sent to Germany as secretary to the papal envoy in Munich but found himself out of his element there and managed to return to the Vatican three years later. His own friends, reported a police informant, saw his desperate desire to return so quickly as the product of his "morbid and elephantine psychosis for power and bureaucratic office."[34]

By the time of the Lateran Accords, Pizzardo was the member of the secretary of state office enjoying the closest relationship with the pope. A police informant in the summer of 1929 described him as the leading candidate to replace Gasparri. According to the report, Pizzardo, small and slender, his dark eyes darting with nervous energy, was "the true arbiter of the pope's heart and the one to dominate every Vatican situation." Many in the Vatican resented his influence. His adversaries called him a chameleon, a man lacking in character and dignity, a bully with those below him and a coward in the face of those above. Suspected of intrigue and of feathering his own nest, he was little loved, least of all by those who worked for him.[35] According to these accounts, what especially recommended Pizzardo to the pope was his eager subservience, "cowering like a little dog" at the pope's frequent scoldings.[36]

As chaplain of the Knights of Columbus, Pizzardo had access to American money. In 1924, recognizing the growing importance of the Church in the United States, Pius XI had doubled the number of American cardinals, elevating Patrick Joseph Hayes, archbishop of New York, and George Mundelein, archbishop of Chicago. "American gold had something to do with the promotion of the two archbishops," Odo Russell, Britain's envoy to the Holy See, remarked at the time.[37]

Once they were made cardinals, the two American archbishops did little to change Russell's opinion. In 1927, in a spectacle that was breathtaking in its lavishness, even for those who lived amid the splendor of the Vatican, Mundelein hosted an International Eucharistic Congress in Chicago. To transport the cardinals who had crossed the Atlantic for the gathering, he commissioned a special train from New York City, which he had painted cardinal red and named for the pope. On June 11 the train arrived at the Chicago station, carrying ten cardinals, along with assorted bishops, archbishops, and the benefactor who paid for it all. Neither of America's two senior cardinals had been willing to make the journey in Mundelein's "Pius XI Express." Cardinal Dougherty of Philadelphia arrived in his own private railroad car, and Cardinal O'Connell of Boston landed with five hundred pilgrims in a private yacht. To cap the ceremonies off, Cardinal Mundelein sent the pope a gift of one million dollars.[38]

Pizzardo became the pope's main conduit for these American funds. When he helped arrange the gift of a luxurious automobile to the pope, rumor had it that the American car dealer paid him fifty thousand lire for his efforts. Pizzardo's two sisters lived with him in the Vatican and rode through Rome's streets in their own Cadillac, another American gift. "The car," a less-than-gallant informant reported, "carries two ugly unmarried women, their tinted faces smeared with cosmetics, on the hunt for a husband."[39]

In the forty-five-year-old Borgongini, who had lived his entire life in Rome, Cesare De Vecchi had an appropriate counterpart, for both were men of limited understanding of the world. The pope presumably appointed him because he liked his orthodoxy and valued obedience over sophistication. To handle more delicate matters, the pope would continue to use his own personal intermediary, Tacchi Venturi, who had survived the previous year's scandal of his stabbing.[40] Foreign ambassadors appreciated Borgongini's courtesy and eagerness to be helpful, but he was not well suited for the social world of the diplomatic corps. He refused to attend diplomatic dinners, explaining that they would keep him up past his bedtime.[41] The rather large, devout, doughty Borgongini and the small, dapper Fascist former artillery commander made a strange pair, although they would develop some affection for each other. "At bottom," the nuncio said of De Vecchi, "he is a good man. As long as he's allowed to go around wearing his plumes and his big medal, he's fine!"[42]

The new nuncio's first meeting with Mussolini came in early August, shortly after the publication of the parliamentary speeches that had so upset the pope. Mussolini greeted him with a smile and politely asked him how he was doing.

"So-so," he replied, explaining that the pope was upset with the Duce and had hinted that he might have to "do something very serious."

"What can he do?" asked Mussolini.

"If the situation doesn't change, we could end up having a rupture, which would be a very serious thing, only a couple of weeks after the beginning of diplomatic relations and at such a brief distance from the ratification."

Mussolini was not amused: "Good God! In a country where you have just had religious marriages recognized, religious instruction introduced, legal recognition of the religious orders . . ."

Everything had been going smoothly, Borgongini explained, until the Duce gave his address to the Chamber of Deputies: "Everyone was

**Mussolini visits the new nuncio,
Monsignor Francesco Borgongini-Duca, August 1929**

astonished. The Holy Father asked who had provoked such a speech. Nobody understood why Your Excellency spoke as you did." The pope was so upset, said the nuncio, that he had nearly convened the Sacred College of Cardinals to announce that he would not ratify the accords. And then just when the unpleasant memory of the Duce's parliamentary speeches was beginning to fade, the pope learned that Mussolini was having them published. He was furious.

"Ah, but the pope," responded Mussolini, "does not know how much difficulty I have found myself in." Critics were complaining that the bodies of Cavour, Mazzini, and Garibaldi—heroes of Italian unification and champions of separation of church and state—were rolling in their graves. He had had no choice, he told Borgongini, but to show that he was not placing the state at the mercy of the Church.

It was natural, he added, that after the exhilarating first days following the signing of the pact, some disagreements would crop up. "It's like the first quarrels of newlyweds after returning from their honeymoon."[43]

EATING AN ARTICHOKE

TALY HAD NO MORE IMPORTANT PATRIOTIC HOLIDAY THAN SEPTEM-
ber 20, the date when, in 1870, Italian troops conquered Rome. But while patriots celebrated the day, Vatican loyalists held special masses of mourning. In early September 1929 the pope sent his nuncio to see Mussolini. He wanted the holiday ended, to be replaced with one on February 11 commemorating the signing of the Lateran Accords.[1]

Mussolini was not sympathetic. "In all frankness," he replied, "I must tell you that Italians cannot renounce the celebration of September 20." The concordat said nothing about abolishing it. The event it marked had proven good for all, including the Church. It was all part of God's design.[2]

Annoyed by Mussolini's presumption in lecturing him on God's wishes, Pius XI responded through his nuncio a few days later: if the concordat made no explicit mention of abolishing the holiday, it was only because it was "so obvious."[3]

Negotiations continued up to the last minute, but the holiday was observed that year, albeit with little hoopla. Still, the pope had something to show for his efforts. In an effort to placate him, the Duce had given his promise that it would never be celebrated again.

FOR SEVEN YEARS MUSSOLINI had discouraged Rachele and the children from coming to Rome, but in November 1929 his wife arrived with all five children, including Anna Maria, born two months earlier. They moved into the magnificent Villa Torlonia, an early nineteenth-century palace with extensive grounds that lay just outside the old city walls.[4]

Mussolini's family life was complicated by his continuing tie to Margherita Sarfatti, whose home in Rome had become a salon where artists and writers mingled with Fascist grandees. In Margherita's eyes, Rachele was a barely literate peasant. She wore no lipstick or rouge and frequented no beauty salon. She had only two modest coats, which she alternated: a short sealskin and a silver fox that, one observer noted, was "the highest she has ventured in feminine extravagance." She insisted on washing the dishes after their meals and refused to attend state functions, no doubt a relief to her husband. In a corner of the estate's elegant gardens, she had an oven built so she could bake bread, along with a chicken coop and a pen where she kept two pigs.

Although Rachele was domestic, she was far from retiring when it came to her husband and children. "The true dictator in the family," observed Edda, "was my mother." When she did something wrong as a child, it was her mother she hid from, fearing the back of her hand. She counted on her father's arrival to save her. Edda idolized her father, thinking him poetic, indulgent, and affectionate, unlike her mother. But it was Rachele who gave the family its sense of stability. "Even in my earliest memories," recalled Edda, "I see her as tenacious and unmovable." Nor was Rachele one to let go of a grudge. For many decades she refused to speak to her sister, who had tried to take advantage of her connection to the dictator. None of Mussolini's children dared mention their aunt's name in their mother's presence.

In his elder daughter's only half-joking account, the reason Mussolini had gone into politics was to be able to spend as little time as possible around his wife. As a young man he had "preferred the blows from the policemen's clubs and the clubs of his adversaries to his wife's bitter recriminations." Mussolini kept his own rooms in a separate wing of Villa Torlonia. While he occasionally met a lover there, he generally found it safer to use his office for his trysts.[5]

IN DECEMBER 1929, amid great pomp, King Victor Emmanuel III and Queen Helen came to the Vatican to pay the pontiff their respects. Sixty-eight years after the Italian kingdom was founded, a pope would finally greet its monarch. Soldiers lined the streets to keep the crowds back. Swiss Guards wearing ornate medieval body armor and high-crested silver helmets formed two lines for the royal couple to pass through. As the entourage made its way into the heart of Vatican City, the Palatine Guard band struck up the royal march. The king in military uniform, the queen at his side in a white lace dress with white veil and white royal cloak, were escorted up the papal stairway into the Apostolic Palace. They passed through several lavishly decorated reception halls to the small throne room, where Pius XI awaited them, seated under a velvet canopy.

After a twenty-minute conversation and an exchange of presents,

King Victor Emmanuel III and Queen Helen visit the pope, December 1929

the king and queen went to greet Cardinal Gasparri at his quarters. There group pictures were taken. Pius XI thought it undignified to be photographed with visitors, royal or not; nor would he bow to Italian government pressure to reciprocate by visiting the Quirinal Palace. Rulers came to him. After the photographs, the secretary of state escorted the royal couple to St. Peter's, where they knelt at the Tomb of the Apostles.[6] That the day was a trying one for the anticlerical king was noted by Mussolini's sister, Edvige, not one of his admirers; throughout his visit to the Vatican, she remarked, he bore "an expression even grimmer and more malicious than usual."[7]

It was an eventful time for Pius XI, who later that month traveled beyond St. Peter's Square for the first time since becoming pope almost eight years earlier. Shortly after six A.M. on December 20, without any public announcement, a line of cars set out from the Vatican to St. John Lateran, on the other side of Rome. The pope was eager to say a mass at the church where, fifty years earlier, he had been ordained. It was the first time a bishop of Rome had entered his see since Pius IX proclaimed himself a prisoner of the Vatican in 1870.[8]

Pius XI, observed a French bishop, is "the most mysterious of men. He confides in no one, not even his closest advisors. He is very sensitive and even emotional, but he controls himself by his strong will and yields to no one. It is impossible to predict what he will decide to do."[9]

A FEW MONTHS LATER Mussolini's favorite child, Edda, got married. He hoped this might bring him some relief. Although he adored her, she seemed to delight in tormenting him. Of all his children, she was by far the most like him: willful, impetuous, temperamental, adventurous, high-strung, and opinionated, ever ready with a cutting remark and a withering look, with a passion for riding horses and swimming. Flaunting convention, she wore slacks, drove fast cars, and smoked. With her sharp, chiseled features and athletic figure, she presented quite a contrast to her chubby younger brothers, who more resembled their mother.[10]

Mussolini with Rachele and the children, 1930

Although only nineteen years old, Edda had already had a series of romantic flings—which had infuriated her father. In July 1929 she horrified him by declaring that she was in love with a Jew. To have a daughter marry a Jew, only months after he had won the applause of the Catholic world for bringing about conciliation with the Church, was too terrible to contemplate. Seeing that his wife's tirades against the match did no good, Mussolini asked his sister, Edvige, to try to talk sense into her. Edda later said her father's decision to punish her by taking her car away was the measure that most got her attention. But he needn't have worried, for flighty, headstrong Edda soon abandoned her Jewish boyfriend and took up with a dissolute, syphilitic young cocaine addict, the son of a rich industrialist.[11] Months later "the crazy little filly," as her family called her behind her back, finally headed in the right direction and announced her engagement to twenty-seven-year-old Galeazzo Ciano.[12]

Galeazzo's father, Costanzo, was a member of Mussolini's inner circle, the minister of post and telegraph. He had been a naval captain in the First World War, and in 1925 the king, bowing to Mussolini's desire to create a new, Fascist aristocracy, had made him a count. Widely suspected of taking kickbacks for the huge contracts he dispensed, Ciano became wealthy, and his son, Galeazzo, grew up in luxury. Suave, a ladies' man—or so he fancied himself—the younger Ciano had well-tended, slicked-back dark hair. "I don't like him," muttered Rachele, "he's not one of ours. He's a *signore*."

Galeazzo came to the Mussolini home to formally ask for Edda's hand, whereupon Mussolini escorted him from his study and announced the news to the family. Rachele did what she could to discourage Galeazzo. "You should know," she told him, "that Edda doesn't know how to do anything. She doesn't know how to cook, not even an egg, nor take care of a house. As for character, it's best not even to talk about it. I'm her mother, and I must warn you."[13]

Their wedding, in April 1930, was held in a nearby parish church. Afterward hundreds of guests—women in fur-collared coats and men in dark suits—gathered on the grounds of Villa Torlonia for the reception. Before a broad, long stairway leading up to the large gleaming white columns fronting the white villa, a newsreel captured the papal nuncio, Borgongini, chatting with Fascist bigwig Dino Grandi. The papal nuncio would later have the honor of sitting for the meal in the garden at a small round table with the hatless, balding Mussolini. Roman schoolgirls in long white dresses, each with a big white bow at her neck, sang in a chorus. Edda's little brothers were there as well, dressed in dark shorts and white open-necked shirts, hair slicked back. Following their concert, the schoolgirls paraded past the newlyweds. While Edda kept her right arm up in the Fascist salute, Galeazzo kept his hands clasped together behind his back, clutching his black top hat.

The young couple and their parents then went to St. Peter's. Galeazzo and Edda, in her white wedding dress, white lace cap wrapped around her head in a style recalling a twenties flapper, climbed the imposing stairs of the basilica, two small children carrying the end of her long, flowing trellis. Mussolini, like his new son-in-law, was dressed in tails and top hat. An enthusiastic crowd raised their arms in Fascist salute. Inside the basilica, Borgongini offered the couple Pius XI's benediction and gave Edda a present from the pope, a stunning rosary made of gold and malachite.[14] The newlyweds moved into Galeazzo's parents' home, but only briefly, for the free-spirited Edda could not stand her rather large mother-in-law, whom she took to calling "*la bertuccia*," the ape.[15]

AS AUTUMN 1930 APPROACHED, the pope, through his nuncio, repeatedly reminded Mussolini of his promise to end Italy's patriotic holiday. But the Duce was having second thoughts, worried that abolishing it would make him look weak. The pope would give no ground. Should September 20 be celebrated again, he warned, he would make his protest public.[16]

The threat got the Duce's attention. He summoned the nuncio to Palazzo Venezia, the massive medieval palace where he had moved his office into a year earlier. Built by Pope Paul II in the fifteenth century, it stood on a large piazza catercorner to the Victor Emmanuel II Monument (ridiculed by its critics as resembling a monstrous white wedding cake). In 1924 Mussolini had kicked off his program of resurrecting ancient Rome by demolishing the houses and churches—some from Renaissance times—that covered the nearby Trajan Market and Roman Forum. He would soon destroy more buildings to create an imposing avenue, its road and sidewalks thirty meters wide, running from Piazza Venezia past these ancient ruins to the Colosseum.[17]

As the bespectacled nuncio, a bit of a paunch extending his black cassock, entered Mussolini's office on the first day of September, the Duce greeted him with his usual air of gruff beneficence. He had made his new office in the cavernous Hall of the Map of the World. The room was sixty feet long and fifty feet wide, with a frescoed ceiling forty feet above. The whole western wall was covered with a huge mosaic of the world map. Mussolini was in a good mood and looked well, his sun-tanned skin set off against his white woolen suit.

Asked about the tan, Mussolini said he had been going to the beach every day, swimming and taking what he called *la cura dell'uva,* the grape cure. "The grape," Mussolini explained to the mystified nuncio, "is the medicine that nature has given men, who however don't appreciate its virtue. A bunch of grapes eaten on an empty stomach stimulates the liver, has a lightly laxative effect, and makes you feel full all day long."

The dictator was plagued by a nervous stomach. At moments of great stress, excruciating pains were likely to double him over and confine him to bed. One such bout several years earlier, right after he had announced the dictatorship, had him spitting up blood. Although medical experts were called in, no one could offer a firm diagnosis. So it was that the man once known for his love of double espressos had moved to a diet heavy on chamomile tea, fruit, and vegetables. At late-night meetings of the Grand Council, as members downed one espresso after another to stay awake, the Duce drank glasses of freshly squeezed orange juice. He avoided all coffee and alcohol.[18]

"You know why I am here," Borgongini said. Mussolini then pulled out the nuncio's recent letter, with the pope's threat, and pointed to the passages that he had underlined with his blue pencil. Mussolini was tireless in scribbling marginal notes in the documents he pored through, using a thick red or blue pencil, replacing them only when they had become small stubs.[19]

The Duce shook his head. The September 20 holiday was fixed by law, he said, and could be changed only by a vote of parliament. "So for this year let's minimize the festivities even more," he proposed by way of compromise. "We'll get rid of the lights, the flags—other than on the public buildings that is. At the next cabinet meeting we'll decide on ending it, and I will support it in parliament."[20]

"No, Your Excellency," replied the tenacious Borgongini, "these are not solutions. The holiday must be suppressed, and before next September 20. Otherwise the Holy Father's conscience will force him to make a public protest. . . . And the whole world will laugh at us, saying: 'What a great conciliation this is!'" Article six of the treaty in the Lateran Accords, he observed, abrogated all previous government acts that were inconsistent with it, and so Mussolini could simply announce that the holiday was being abolished as part of its provisions.

Mussolini thought a bit and then agreed that perhaps this offered a way out. He would talk to his legal advisers and get back to the nuncio soon.

As Borgongini got up to leave, he expressed his condolences on the recent death of Mussolini's young nephew, son of Arnaldo. This put the Duce in a pensive mood, as he reflected about the boy's final days of suffering and his brother's deep Catholic faith.

"I'm a believer too," the Duce assured the nuncio. "As if I weren't!

"But," he added, "men have made me bad."[21]

THE DUCE SOON SUMMONED the nuncio back. Although it would take a law to formally abolish the September 20 holiday, such a proposal would be on the agenda of the next cabinet meeting. It would be replaced with a new holiday on October 28, the anniversary of the March on Rome.

The pope, replied Borgongini, might find the compromise acceptable. But he would not be happy with the proposal to replace the old holiday with one commemorating October 28, rather than February 11, the date of Conciliation.

"Let's not get into this," said Mussolini, his voice rising. "You wanted me to abolish the September 20 holiday, let's content ourselves with that. Enough! I wouldn't want you now to start asking me to change the name of via 20 settembre or have you complain because the elementary school textbooks talk about Italians' entry into Rome on September 20."

Mussolini got up. "I have more important things to worry about," he said, dismissing the nuncio.[22]

Not one to be intimidated, the pope pressed for more. Although Borgongini had told him what Mussolini had said about changing street names, he insisted that Mussolini must now rename via 20 settembre, one of Rome's major roads. It should be called, the pope proposed, via 11 febbraio, honoring the date of the Lateran Accords.

When Mussolini learned of the pope's latest demand, he summoned the nuncio. "You must want to unleash a ferocious anticlerical reaction," the furious Duce told him. "I regret what I've done with September 20. . . . I no sooner conceded one thing when you demanded another, even before the cabinet met, before the law could be approved, despite the fact I specifically told you that the name of that street was not to be spoken of."

There was a reason he had brought up the name of the street at their last meeting, said the Duce. "I know you and I expected that, having gotten me to abolish the holiday, you would ask for the abolition of the street, and after getting rid of the street, who knows what other things?" What would come next? he asked. Italy had nine thousand towns, and who knew how many had streets with names that offended the pope?

Walking the nuncio to the door, Mussolini calmed down. "We are making policy like you eat an artichoke, one leaf at a time," he explained. "Because this is my strength. I do things in my own way, without any unnecessary steps. I have to respect the letter of the law. I don't want to be the elephant in the china shop."[23]

IN THE AFTERMATH of the Lateran Accords, Mussolini entered what historians portray as an era of consensus. Facing no significant opposition, his craving for adulation grew.[24] Not only did he now require newspapers to refer to him as the Duce, but he insisted that they print DUCE in capital letters.[25] Images of him were everywhere, in public buildings, homes, and shops. Newspapers and magazines ran heroic photographs of him, which he carefully reviewed before publication. He excluded any that showed him with nuns, monks, or priests, convinced they brought bad luck.[26]

Mussolini cultivated his cinematic image as well. Rome was filled with movie theaters—one of them even had a retractable roof to allow in fresh air—and people flocked to the latest offerings.[27] The Duce worked closely with the new national film agency, and a 1927 law required that all of Italy's movie theaters show its news clips.

An endless spate of news films recorded the dictator's dedications of new projects, addresses to Fascist youth groups, laying of wreaths to Fascist martyrs, and awarding of medals to brightly clad peasant women. Other clips showed him dressed in a white suit inspecting public works projects, or in open-necked shirt saddled atop a brown horse jumping over hastily placed steeple-jumps on the grounds of Villa Torlonia. Some news films offered lighter fare, a look at popular life. Some chronicled the triumphs of famous Italian boxers and cyclists. One recorded a popular festival in Rome's Trastevere, not far from the Vatican. Cinemagoers got to see men clutching the tops of large burlap bags around their chests, hopping down the street toward the finish line. An egg race followed, as each contestant (not a woman among them) struggled to keep an egg balanced atop a spoon as he scooted down the street. A playful shot of the egg-splattered cobblestones after the race's end testified to those who never made it to the finish line. The laughter in the theater quickly subsided when Mussolini appeared on-screen—people rose to their feet.

Not everyone was happy with this forced homage to the dictator. A story made the rounds that one day Mussolini decided to go to a theater, wearing a disguise. When everyone stood up as his image came on the screen, he remained seated. A man standing behind him in the darkened theater tapped him on the shoulder and whispered in his ear: "*Signore,* I feel the same way you do, but I would advise you to stand up if you don't want one of these goons to crack your head open."[28]

At public appearances, the Duce's aides made sure he was surrounded by adoring crowds, even if it meant recruiting police agents dressed in civilian clothes. Navarra, Mussolini's personal assistant, recalled that once when a picture was published of the Duce waltzing with a peasant woman, a rumor circulated that his dancing partner was really a policeman in disguise.

Mussolini sometimes forgot that the workers, peasants, and artisans with whom he was photographed were his own police agents. But at one dedication ceremony for a new building, the thought did occur to him. Turning to the "bricklayer" who was standing beside him, he asked, in a whisper, if he was a policeman.

"No, Duce!" the man replied.

"Ah, bravo!" the delighted Mussolini replied. "So what are you then, the master mason?"

"No, Duce," he responded, "I am an army sergeant."[29]

THE RETURN OF THE NATIVE SON

B Y THE TIME THE LATERAN ACCORDS WERE RATIFIED, SEVENTY-seven-year-old Cardinal Gasparri had been secretary of state for fifteen years under two popes. In 1922, after helping secure Ratti's election, he could count on having the pope's support, and Pius valued his secretary of state's experience. But as the years passed, conflict between the two was bound to emerge, for the pontiff would tolerate no separate pocket of power in the Vatican.[1]

Gasparri rarely left Rome, except to spend the summer vacation in his mountain hometown, northeast of the capital. There his extended family treated him like a celebrity, the local boy made good. When Gasparri was in Rome, his staff members came by his office each morning. He sat at a large round table, covered with piles of documents and correspondence. As each staff member entered, Gasparri gave him his own little stack. When he was at his summer retreat, his aides took turns bringing him papers. There they found the short, rotund cardinal, dressed in a simple clerical black gown, his large black, round-brim cloth hat nestled beside him, sitting underneath a large tree enjoying the shade, the fresh air, and the view.[2]

Gasparri's down-home sense of humor put others at ease, but ambassadors to the Holy See did not find him completely forthcoming. As the British envoy reported, he was "far from candid . . . or put more bluntly, he can lie well." When the French ambassador accused him one day of not telling the truth, Gasparri replied that he was simply doing what was required of all diplomats, adding, with a sparkle in his eye, that if necessary the pope would give him absolution.[3]

Thomas Morgan, an American reporter, tells of visiting Gasparri's office during the height of a crisis with the Mexican government that, in the 1920s and beyond, shut down large numbers of churches and seminaries. Morgan found Gasparri remarkably calm, talking "like a great sage." The Church, he said, had survived for many centuries and had endured much worse. It would continue to outlast its foes.

"*Non prevalebunt,*" he repeated, in Latin. "They shall not prevail."

As the cardinal ushered the reporter to the door, the parrots that Gasparri kept in his rooms began squawking. "*Non prevalebunt! Non prevalebunt!*" Apparently the secretary of state had taken the time to teach them this lesson in Church history.[4]

As early as 1926, however, rumors spread that the pope was unhappy with his secretary of state. In an effort to get him to resign, the pope was said to be humiliating him, making him wait in the anteroom before seeing him, and mortifying him in ways, as one police informant put it, that not even a servant would tolerate.[5]

The signing of the Lateran Accords in 1929 proved to be Gasparri's greatest public triumph. Few photographs were more familiar than the one showing him with pen in hand sitting alongside Mussolini. But the agreement turned out to be a mixed blessing. Pius, angered by Mussolini's parliamentary speeches and worried that the dictator was not going to cooperate as he had hoped in establishing a Catholic state, decided he needed a new secretary of state. He first informed Gasparri in July that he thought it was time for a change and told him to think the matter over. From his summer mountain retreat, Gasparri responded in a letter to the pope: "I have not forgotten (and how could I forget it) what Your Holiness told me last July, which, if I am not mistaken, is that, especially in view of the likely struggles with the Fascist Government in defense of Catholic Action, Your Holiness thought it opportune that someone else take my place." He added that he too had been thinking of leaving the position he had held so many years, "although for different reasons than the one Your Holiness cited." At his age, he said, he no longer had either the memory or the energy he once did.[6]

The pope waited another several months before making the change. He saw Gasparri less and less often, relying on others, especially his undersecretary, Monsignor Pizzardo.[7] The strain of waiting to be dismissed eroded what diplomatic reserve the secretary of state had left. "It's a difficult life," Gasparri sighed after one meeting with the pope. Pius XI, he told the Italian ambassador, had many merits, but he was often "as cold as marble."[8]

The secretary of state's replacement became a topic of intense speculation.[9] Gasparri hoped the pope would appoint his disciple, Cardinal Bonaventura Cerretti, and had reason to believe that the pope might follow this advice. In 1925, shortly after Cerretti returned from his post as nuncio to Paris and was named a cardinal, the pope had hinted that he might want him to succeed Gasparri one day. One of the Vatican's leading diplomats, Cerretti had served in Mexico, the United States, and Australia and had represented Pope Benedict XV at the postwar peace negotiations in Paris. But in the fall of 1929, Cerretti told a journalist he did not want the post. "With Pius XI," he explained, "the secretary of state has little to do. He's more of a decorative figure than someone with any power or independence. He can't assume any direct, serious responsibilities, nor give his personal stamp to the Church government. You could say, in other words, that he is simply an executor of orders from above."[10]

Cerretti's comments are a bit suspect, for while many saw him as the obvious choice, he had reason to fear that the pope would pass him over. Cerretti's sympathies for the democratic countries, and for the Popular Party in Italy, were well known, and as the pope was aware, he opposed the deal Pius had struck with Mussolini.[11] In December the pope chose instead his nuncio to Germany, Eugenio Pacelli, to be the new secretary of state. Cerretti was indignant. He was certain that Francesco Pacelli, a mere layman, had used his frequent meetings with Pius XI to build up his brother in the pope's eyes.

"That Pius XI will prefer Pacelli over me, to everything I have done for him, to my tenacious loyalty, to my diplomatic experience of over thirty years . . . it makes me furious to think of it, I can't accept it," Cerretti fumed. "Pacelli and his brother, servants and slaves of Fascism, accomplices bought by Mussolini, bring discredit on the Holy See. They humiliate the papacy, weaken its power, and lower its moral and educational authority in the eyes of all the Catholic powers."[12]

Mussolini's ambassador to Germany, Luigi Aldrovandi, viewed the appointment much more sympathetically. Eugenio Pacelli was a person of stature, he said, combining deep intelligence with the ability to stay calm. He projected both dignity and a deep religious faith. Perhaps most important, thought the ambassador, he would be a friend of the Fascist government. "Monsignor Pacelli," he reported, "had expressed his admiration for His Excellency Mussolini even before the Lateran Accords."[13]

In many ways, Pacelli was Gasparri's opposite. His father's father had served as a minister in the papal government of Pius IX, fled with the pope in 1848 when the revolution in Rome drove him into exile, and on their return helped found *L'Osservatore romano*. Pacelli's father was the dean of the Vatican lawyers and had served from 1886 to 1905 on Rome's city council. Eugenio, born in Rome in 1876, was a shy, frail child who wore spectacles from an early age and enjoyed playing the violin. He showed no interest in sports or children's games.[14]

At age eighteen, Pacelli entered the Almo Collegio Capranica, Rome's oldest seminary and, over the centuries, the launch pad for many high Vatican diplomatic careers. Although he did well in his studies, he craved solitude and missed home. Given his family's clout, he won a rare dispensation and was allowed to live at home through the rest of his studies.[15]

In 1901, two years after his ordination, Pacelli received a doctorate in civil and canon law and took a position in the Congregation for Extraordinary Ecclesiastical Affairs in the Vatican secretary of state office. He could not have risen so rapidly over the next years without participating in the antimodernist campaign, a prerequisite for advancement under Pope Pius X.[16] But Pacelli was cautious and measured in his speech and befriended Giacomo Della Chiesa while they were both in the secretary of state office. In 1914, when Della Chiesa became Pope Benedict XV, he promoted Pacelli to undersecretary of state.

Three years later the pope appointed Pacelli to be nuncio to Bavaria. For the first time, the forty-one-year-old left his mother and his parental home. A few years later he would be named nuncio to Germany and move from Munich to Berlin.

When he first departed for Munich, Pacelli took up two compartments in the train, one for himself and a second for the sixty cases of food he brought with him.[17] Once there, he asked to have nuns take care of his household. One, the twenty-four-year-old Pascalina Lehnert, was destined to play an important role in his life. She was smitten by the nuncio. "Tall and slender, his face extremely thin and pallid," she wrote, recalling her first impression, "he had eyes that reflected his soul and gave him a particular beauty." She came to think he would be helpless in handling the daily necessities without her.

In 1919 Pacelli suffered a trauma that would stay with him all his life. In April of that year, amid the postwar chaos, a Soviet Republic was briefly proclaimed in Munich. A Communist commandant, leading a squad of hastily formed militia armed with rifles, revolvers, and hand grenades, banged on the door of the nunciature. When the frightened staff opened the door, the commandant said he had come to requisition the nuncio's limousine. Pacelli was called down to confront the intruders. Horrified by the invasion, he was especially pained by their demand for the car, since he had a soft spot for his Mercedes-Benz, describing it fondly as a "splendid carriage, with pontifical coat of arms." Rejecting the demand as a flagrant violation of international law, he tried to show them the certificate of extraterritoriality protecting the nunciature. The commandant, described by Pacelli as "a horrible type of delinquent," was unimpressed, and one of the men put a rifle to his chest. The invaders pushed past the nuncio and went to the garage, but the chauffeur had disabled the car. Frustrated, they told Pacelli that if he did not have the limousine ready for them the next day, they would arrest them all and blow up the building.

Accounts of the next twenty-four hours differ sharply. In his report to Gasparri, Pacelli said that immediately following the men's departure, he was struck by a bad bout of the flu, made worse by "a bad stomach," and left Munich to recuperate in a rest home. But it appears that as soon as the squad left, Pacelli had collapsed, unnerved. He hastily left Munich, recuperating in a nursing home a hundred miles away. When the squad returned the next day, he was not there.[18]

While in Germany, Pacelli did his best to enforce top-down rule from the Vatican—no simple matter in a country where bishops had long valued their own authority. Father Hubert Wolf, one of the foremost authorities on Pacelli's years in Germany, describes his time there:

"For Pacelli, the bishops were little more than papal head altar boys, called on to act only on the instructions of the pope. . . . Rome wanted yes-men with childlike devotion to the Holy Father. This was Pacelli's crucial criterion for a good bishop, and he bent every effort to install just such men and to stamp out the independence of the German Church."[19]

Pacelli was impressed by the Germans' punctuality, their reliability, and their work ethic. Although he never overcame his fear of flying, he was smitten by German technology.

Among the experiences in Germany that would most affect him was the rising wave of hostility toward the Jews. In his early days in Munich, he wrote of a "grim Russian-Jewish-Revolutionary tyranny" and during the dozen years he spent in Germany, he made constant mention of the Jewish backgrounds of Socialists and Communists.[20] In one 1919 report he described the Communist head of Munich's short-lived revolutionary council: a "young man, also Russian and Jewish. . . . Pale, dirty, with expressionless eyes, and a hoarse and vulgar voice: a truly repugnant type, yet with an intelligent and sly face."[21]

RECALLED FROM BERLIN AND made a cardinal in December 1929, Eugenio Pacelli became secretary of state two months later. "Tall, thin, dark complexion, graying hair, ascetic face, a lively look, a benevolent expression, a red skullcap atop his small, aristocratic head, the purple satin cape upon his shoulders, a belt of the same color over his black soutane with braids and gleaming buttons, a gold cross hanging by a chain upon his chest": this is how the French ambassador described him. The short, stout self-described "sheep herder" was replaced by a tall, slender, bespectacled Roman of aristocratic bearing. It was hard to imagine Pacelli sitting in the shade of a tree on a hillside.[22] A favorite of Roman society, he won praise among the Vatican diplomatic corps for his considerate manner. They also appreciated his ability to speak with many of them in their own language, conversant as he was in French, German, English, and Spanish.[23]

In contrast to Gasparri, who rarely spoke publicly, Pacelli was a skilled orator and would represent Pius XI at several high-profile international Church gatherings. His memory was prodigious. "When I have written or typed a sermon or a talk," he once said, "I see the text roll by in front of my eyes as I speak the words, as if I were reading it."[24] He insisted that he be informed of everything and was meticulous in reviewing even the smallest details, down to the address on each envelope to be mailed. Every night his undersecretaries prepared a file of papers and letters for his signature, sometimes as many as a hundred. The next morning he would return them in one of two folders. One contained the documents he had signed, and the other those in which he had detected an error. They would all have to be retyped. His assistants took to calling the latter folder "the infirmary" and prayed each morning that it would have few patients.[25]

Pope Pius XI, a *New York Times* Vatican correspondent wrote, was "not so much austere as habitually serious . . . he seldom smiles or relaxes."[26] Others described the pope as "melancholy." In selecting Pacelli, he chose a man who was similarly reserved and someone who, like him, felt the heavy weight of his office. But Pacelli was very much in control of himself. He did not share the pope's temper or his excitability. He was also a man of his habits, and he brought Sister Pascalina with him to Rome to set up his Vatican apartment. This raised some eyebrows, given her young age, but she would remain with him until the day he died. Suspicions that they had an inappropriate relationship seem misplaced. Closer to the mark are speculations that she replaced his mother in taking care of him. She was certainly as protective as any mother, and many in the Vatican would resent her influence.[27]

Up by 6:15 A.M., the new secretary of state celebrated mass with a group of nuns and priests before taking a quick breakfast. He then waited for the pope's summons to their early morning meeting. A close, although formal, relationship developed between the scholarly, undiplomatic pope—a man from a modest small-town family—and the worldly, politically well-connected Roman Pacelli. At their early morning meetings, the new secretary of state brought an agenda and carried a stack of nuncio reports and other materials for the pope to review.

The cardinal returned from these meetings with thick, square pieces of paper in which he recorded the pope's instructions in his tiny, neat handwriting.[28] The secretary of state's spacious offices were on the second floor of the Apostolic Palace. Pacelli passed the gendarme who guarded the outside entry. His colorful uniform and tall dark fur hat made it seem that Napoleon had left him behind. As he approached his own office, he would nod to his private secretary, in black clerical gown, and the uniformed Noble Guard of Honor who stood at his door. Pacelli then called in his two undersecretaries to review the pope's instructions and plan their work for the day.

The cardinal reserved two mornings a week to meet individually with the thirty ambassadors accredited to the Holy See. They awaited their turn in a large room of noble appearance, its walls damask red. On a typical morning, in a nearby ornate room, a papal nuncio visiting Rome might be found, along with a bearded apostolic delegate from the Orient, in a monk's habit, and other ecclesiastical dignitaries. They sat in one of eleven gold-inlaid armchairs at a heavy table covered with a rich red cloth. Less high-ranking prelates—priests, monks, and nuns—sat in the simpler armchairs that lined the entryway to the secretary of state's office. At any moment during their conversations with the secretary of state, visitors risked being ejected if a cardinal heading one of the Curia departments arrived unexpectedly.[29]

After a half-hour break for lunch at one P.M., Pacelli took an hour off for a walk, sometimes in the gardens of the Villa Borghese, on the other side of the Tiber. An assistant carrying papers for review often accompanied him, as a policeman walked behind at a respectful distance.[30] Back in the Vatican, the secretary of state had more appointments before taking time alone to go over the day's documents. At 8:30 he stopped for supper, went to the chapel to recite the rosary, and returned to work until well after midnight.[31]

The general sentiment among Vatican diplomats when Pacelli first became secretary of state was that, in contrast to the genial and self-confident Gasparri, he was rather stiff and reluctant to express any ideas of his own. He was always gracious, but whenever a difficult question came up, he responded by saying he would need to consult the pope.[32] "The secretary of state," wrote the British envoy in his annual report for 1930, "was in practice reduced to the position of a clerk."[33]

The French scholar and bishop Alfred Baudrillart recorded a similar impression, describing Cardinal Pacelli as "sickly and not very influential." Baudrillart recalled an embarrassing meeting between Pacelli and the pope in April 1931, at a time when Pius XI was upset with Mussolini for his attacks on Catholic Action. An Italian cardinal, he had recently learned, had publicly blessed a Fascist banner. Pius, angry, asked Pacelli if he had known about it. When the uneasy Pacelli answered that he had, the pope asked him indignantly whether he had approved the cardinal's gesture in advance. Stricken, Pacelli admitted he had, then added, "I told you, Holy Father, that I would be incapable of carrying out the functions of the Secretary of State."[34]

But the pope had a high opinion of Pacelli's intelligence and diplomatic skills and, in these early years, no doubts as to his loyalty. "Our secretary of state," the pope once said, "works well, works hard, and works quickly."[35] Temperamentally, Pacelli balanced the impulsive pope, putting a brake on his penchant for lashing out when he thought Church principles were under attack.[36]

Gasparri, for his part, was not making Pacelli's transition easy. "You have come to take my place!" he growled shortly after Pacelli arrived in Rome. "You should not have accepted! They have exploited me, and now they send me away! You will see what kind of man the pope is!" A distraught Pacelli did his best to calm him down, but the encounter left its mark.[37]

"They have chased me out like a dog," the former secretary of state kept repeating, complaining to a fellow cardinal that in their final meeting the pope had not offered him a word of appreciation.[38] Talking to another friend, he indignantly asked how the pope could treat him so poorly. "I am the one who made the librarian a pope and a sovereign, and he chased me out worse than a mangy dog! He will pay me for it! Believe me, he will pay me for it!"[39]

Gasparri aimed much of his fire at Monsignor Pizzardo, his old undersecretary, charging him with building up his friend Eugenio Pacelli in the pope's eyes at Gasparri's expense. The passed-over Cardinal Cerretti likewise blamed Pizzardo, dismissing Pacelli as weak-kneed and indecisive, a "slave in the hands of Pizzardo, who moves him like a puppet."[40]

TAKING UP HIS NEW POST on the first anniversary of the Lateran Accords, Pacelli was immediately swept up in the celebrations. The tensions over Mussolini's speeches to parliament dissipated as the Duce showered gifts and honors on the pope and those around him. On the anniversary itself, the Italian ambassador presented the pope with a beautiful surplice made of Burano lace. Delighted, the pope told De Vecchi that he would wear it the next day in the Sistine Chapel for the ceremonies marking his eighth anniversary as pontiff. At the same time, the king awarded Gasparri Italy's highest decoration, the Supreme Order of the Most Holy Annunciation.[41]

Italy's ambassador to the Vatican, Cesare De Vecchi, thought Pacelli was a man with whom he could work well. "This Cardinal secretary of state," De Vecchi recorded in his diary, "seems to me to be basically a good person with whom as time goes on we will find complete harmony, that of a true conciliation. If the pope weren't so agitated, things would truly go much more smoothly."[42] A week and a half later De Vecchi was lamenting how difficult it was to deal with the pope and found that Cardinal Pompili agreed with him: "I don't know if he knows books," Rome's cardinal vicar said of the former librarian, "but he certainly does not understand men." In recording these remarks, De Vecchi added, "I see every day that this pope is little loved even by those who are closest to him."[43]

A month later, at their regular Friday meeting, De Vecchi and Pacelli discussed the current tensions in Europe. "I saw yet again that he clearly favors the Germans and doesn't love the French," De Vecchi observed. Aware of Pacelli's close ties to conservative circles in Germany, the ambassador suggested that he help the Fascist government establish better links with right-wing forces there. "I am certainly convinced," De Vecchi wrote, "that Cardinal Pacelli can be very useful to us in this area and I hope to convince him by appealing to his patriotism on the one hand and his affection for Germany on the other, an affection that runs very deep in him."[44]

Germany would soon be on everyone's mind, for in national elections in September 1930, Hitler's National Socialist Party received more than six million votes, becoming the second-largest party in the country. Amid Germany's severe economic depression, with widespread unemployment, government paralysis, and powerful Socialist and Communist movements, what had formerly seemed inconceivable—that the Nazis could come to power—was no longer a laughing matter. Viewing the Nazi movement as a pagan threat to the Catholic Church in Germany, the pope looked on with concern.

Signs soon appeared of the catastrophe that was about to befall Europe. But what would sour the pope's view of Mussolini had nothing to do with Hitler but with matters closer to home. De Vecchi's faith that the new Vatican secretary of state would be able to keep the emotional pope in line was about to be dramatically tested. It would suddenly seem possible, even likely, that stricken by remorse at the deal he had made with Italy's dictator, the pope would denounce both Mussolini and his Fascist regime.

CARDINAL PACELLI
HANGS ON

"FASCISTS TRAMPLE PORTRAIT OF POPE," READ THE FRONT-PAGE *New York Times* headline in late May 1931. "Mob calls Pontiff traitor and burns books—Osservatore Romano's sale banned."[1]

Tensions had been building for months over Catholic Action, the linchpin of the pope's efforts to re-Christianize Italian society. Catholic Action had a national office, its lay president appointed by the pope. Monsignor Pizzardo was technically the organization's "ecclesiastical assistant," but as one of the men closest to the pope, he allowed Pius XI to keep tight control over it. National directives went out to each diocese, where Catholic Action came under the authority of the local bishop and had a board that included laypeople. In areas where the Church was strongest—generally in the center and north of the country—each parish also had its own set of Catholic Action organizations, for men, women, girls, and boys.

Mussolini knew how dear Catholic Action was to Pius XI, but he decided it was time to put the pope in his place. Riled by newspaper stories charging Catholic Action with harboring old Popular Party activists and other enemies of the regime, hundreds of Fascist college students smashed the windows of the University of Rome's Catholic Action center. Others threw rocks through the windows of *La Civiltà cattolica*'s building and then rushed in, tossing books out the broken windows. To chants of "Down with the priests! Down with the pope," they heaved a painting of Pius XI onto the street.[2]

Furious, the pope told Pacelli to suspend his regular meetings with the Italian ambassador.[3] But Mussolini, whose ego and temper were more than equal to the pontiff's, decided he had had enough of the pope's pressures. He ordered all Catholic Action youth groups in Italy closed.[4]

Romania's ambassador, in an appointment with Pius XI, made the mistake of suggesting that the pope could give the world a lesson in peaceful dispute resolution by offering to have a trusted mediator work out his differences with Mussolini. The pope snapped back: his rights were given by God and could not be compared to those of a temporal ruler. "I am ready for anything," he said. "I will never abandon what I believe to be my mission, never, never, never!"

Pius XI, recalled the ambassador, "became more heated, striking the table with both hands. Finally he rose and continued his protests while standing, shouting almost as loud as he could. He was panting and bursting with indignation until suddenly, probably becoming aware of the impression his excited speech was making on me, he tried to control himself, sat down again and, still panting, added, 'But as you see, Minister, I remain calm.'"[5]

The *New York Times* lead story on June 1, reporting Mussolini's decision to close the Catholic Action youth clubs, described relations between Mussolini and the pope as at the breaking point. The fifteen thousand local clubs, with their membership of over half a million, would all be shut down by the next day.[6] In protest, Pius XI forbade Italy's churches from holding their traditional—and popular—Corpus Christi processions, scheduled for June 4.[7]

Worried that the conflict was spiraling out of control, and convinced that the new secretary of state was too weak to avert disaster, a group of cardinals contacted Pietro Gasparri and proposed that he meet with Mussolini. Unhappiness in the Curia had been building since the crisis began, fueled by the cardinals' anger that the pope did not consult them and their belief that Pacelli was in over his head. The pope, Gasparri was convinced, lacked any diplomatic sense—he thought he could treat Mussolini as he would an archbishop, "with whom a reprimand is more useful than a debate."[8] Still upset about his dismissal, Gasparri would have loved to play the role of peacemaker, but he told the cardinals he could do so only with the pope's approval. The pope refused.[9]

In April rumors spread that Pacelli was about to resign.[10] In late May the Fascist daily *Il Popolo di Roma* reported that the pope was planning to fire him.[11] In early June Cardinal Sbaretti, the secretary of the Holy Office of the Inquisition, told the pope that it was the unanimous opinion of the cardinals of that office that Gasparri, not Pacelli, should spearhead negotiations with the government. Pacelli was isolated. The pro-Fascist cardinals thought him too weak to get the stubborn pope to back down; the anti-Fascists thought him too eager to protect the Vatican's alliance with Mussolini.[12]

On June 9 Cesare De Vecchi went to see Pacelli and was pleased to discover that he "was completely on our side."[13] The pope had told Pacelli not to discuss the crisis with the Italian ambassador, but Pacelli ruefully shared the pope's instructions, and his disappointment at the pope's lack of confidence in him, with the French ambassador to the Holy See. The ambassador marveled at how thoroughly the pope was excluding his secretary of state from handling the crisis. Pacelli, realizing he should not have said so much, begged the French diplomat not to tell anyone.[14]

Seizing on the divisions in the Vatican, Dino Grandi, Italy's foreign minister, urged Mussolini to increase the pressure. He recommended recalling the Italian ambassador and threatening to abandon the concordat. "I am convinced," he wrote, "that if we focus only on the pope, declaring ourselves at the same time to be the most fervent supporters of the Church and of Religion, and at the same time showing the pope to be failing in his duties as head of the Catholic religion, we will truly be able to put the Holy See in serious difficulty."[15]

Later that month Giuseppe Talamo, chargé d'affaires and De Vecchi's number two, met with Pacelli at his Vatican office. "Combining unctuousness and embarrassment," as Talamo described it, the secretary of state told him the pope was preparing a statement on the conflict. Pacelli added that he hoped it would not make the situation any worse.[16]

In fact, the pope had decided to escalate his assault and was preparing a lengthy encyclical aimed directly at the Duce. Worried that Fascist censors would prevent its distribution, he gave copies to the American prelate, Francis Spellman, to smuggle across the French border. The encyclical, *Non abbiamo bisogno* ("We Have No Need"), appeared in foreign newspapers before being published in *L'Osservatore romano* in early July.[17]

In the encyclical the pope denied that Italy's Catholic Action was involved in anti-Fascist activities, and he rejected the claim that the Church's only proper role in educating young people was to provide religious instruction. "For a Catholic, it is not in keeping with Catholic doctrine to pretend that the Church, the Pope, should limit themselves to the external practices of religion (Mass and Sacraments) and that the rest of education belongs totally to the State."

But even as he lashed out, the pope was careful to distinguish between good Fascism—that which recognized the Church's rights and followed its precepts—and bad Fascism, which did not. By protesting the harm that was being done to the Church in Italy, the pope argued, "We believe that we have at the same time done good work for the [Fascist] party itself and for the regime."[18] While condemning those who would turn Fascism into pagan worship of the state, he concluded with conciliatory words: "In everything that We have said up to the present, We have not said that We wished to condemn the party and the regime as such. Our aim has been to point out and to condemn all those things in the program and in the activities of the party which have been found to be contrary to Catholic doctrine and Catholic practice."[19]

The pope had other levers to use in pressuring Mussolini. A grand ceremony inaugurating Milan's new train station was scheduled for July 1, to feature the king himself. Because of the dispute, Milan's archbishop let it be known he would not attend. The king, rather than face the embarrassment of standing alongside a lower-ranking clergyman, bowed out. For years, no major Fascist ceremony had taken place without a high prelate there to bless it.[20]

Surprisingly, rather than trigger a worsening of the conflict, the encyclical marked the beginning of its end. With the encyclical, the pope gave voice to his anger. Now, it seems, he was ready to get all the unpleasantness behind him. Perhaps his advisers had finally persuaded him of the need to make peace with Mussolini, or perhaps they had simply worn him down. Too much was at stake to let the conflict continue.[21]

At a mid-July ceremony, the pope prayed for a miracle to "help the blind see."[22] He asked Tacchi Venturi to help them out of the impasse. Mussolini let the Jesuit envoy know that he too was eager to end the conflict.[23] Tacchi Venturi rushed to report these encouraging words to the Vatican. "If I am not mistaken," he wrote to Pacelli, "the Holy Father's prayer of last Sunday is beginning to be answered. Let the Lord kindle his holy light so that the blind can see!"[24]

The pope relied on his Jesuit emissary to work out a deal with the dictator. On July 25 he spelled out his two conditions for settling the dispute.[25] First, he wanted Mussolini to acknowledge that the Church had a role to play in educating children and that it had the right to organize Catholic Action groups within "its proper religious and supernatural ends." When, later that day, the Jesuit met with the Duce, he said he would have no trouble agreeing to this request. It was the pope's second condition that posed the problem. Pius XI wanted Mussolini not only to reopen the Catholic Action youth groups but to acknowledge that his order shutting them down had been illegal. On this point, the Duce would not budge. To demand an apology, he said, was to seek to humiliate him.

Convinced that the crisis would not end unless the pope backed down, Tacchi Venturi went to Gasparri to enlist his help. The two had never been close, but they now had a common mission.

Following the meeting, Gasparri sent a letter to Pacelli. "I write with an extremely worried soul," he told him, underlining his words for emphasis. What Mussolini had already conceded to the pope, Gasparri argued, was "enormous." It was stupefying that over a matter of "procedure"—namely, requiring an apology from the Duce—the pope "would go to a condemnation of Fascism, and with it a renunciation of the concordat." It was up to Pacelli, as secretary of state, to get the pope to change his mind.[26]

"According to the rumors that have been racing around for many weeks," reported the French chargé d'affaires to the Vatican, "Cardinal Pacelli himself is being kept at a distance from the preparatory work for the resumption of talks with Italy. . . . It is the pope and the pope alone who continues to impose his will and he does not take advice from anyone."[27]

In the end, it was the pope who backed down. In mid-August, after running back and forth several times between the pope and Mussolini, Tacchi Venturi drafted their agreement, which they signed on September 2.[28] It specified that Catholic Action was to be organized on a diocesan basis, under the authority of the local bishop. No one known to have been critical of the regime could be chosen for a leadership position, and Catholic Action would confine its activities entirely to the religious sphere.[29]

The pope had bowed to the pressure. He had issued a dramatic encyclical, hoping to rally Italy's Catholics. But the Catholic faithful, having for years heard everyone from the pope to their parish priest praise Mussolini as heaven-sent, were disoriented by the dispute and wanted it settled. The pope found himself alone, and now he drew back.[30]

Not all of Italy's priests and bishops were delighted by the agreement. From exile in London, Popular Party founder Don Luigi Sturzo observed that while he was not surprised that the pope wanted to preserve his alliance with the regime, it was sad to see him agree to a deal that represented a complete victory for Mussolini. Another former Popular Party leader, also in exile, was more cutting: "The pope gave in, he retreated, he was frightened. He bowed down before the altar of the Fascist Moloch. . . . This is what they are saying in Italy and abroad after the conclusion of the ill-omened agreement of September 2."[31]

Some of the cardinals likewise grumbled at the further limits put on the Church. They thought, according to the French chargé d'affaires, "that it was Cardinal Pacelli's desire for appeasement that prevailed in the course of negotiations." The French diplomat speculated that the pope was getting old and, having spent his initial anger, he had been worn down by Pacelli and others around him.[32] There was certainly much truth to this view, although Tacchi Venturi, rather than Pacelli, seems to have played the more influential role.

Foreign ambassadors to the Holy See expressed surprise that the principled and stubborn pope had capitulated so abruptly. It had been barely two months since his encyclical had denounced the Fascist regime's claim to have a monopoly on the education of youth and warned about the worship of the state. The agreement said nothing about any of this; nor did it contain what the pope had long demanded from Mussolini, an apology for the violence against the Catholic organizations and the insults aimed at him.[33]

THE DAY AFTER MUSSOLINI and Tacchi Venturi signed the final agreement, Pius XI called in his nuncio and apologized for having excluded him from the negotiations. He instructed Borgongini to make an appointment to see the Duce. It was time to restore relations to their proper channels.

"How are you?" a smiling Mussolini greeted him a few days later. "After the storm comes the calm."

"That's why I've come," replied the nuncio. "I thought that, with calm restored, it was a good idea to reestablish contact with Your Excellency."

"You will see," said the dictator, pressing his point, "a long period of calm will begin now."

"God be praised!"

"Come and we'll take care of everything." The Duce pointed to a series of notes that Tacchi Venturi had sent him with the familiar list of papal requests. There were books to ban and Protestant proselytizing to stamp out. "I will issue orders immediately to have everything you want done."

The nuncio had one other request: although the Duce had been government head for almost a decade, he had never come to see the pope. "The pope," said Borgongini, "told me to let you know that you will be the most welcome among the welcome." Ever since the signing of the Lateran Accords, the pope had expected the Duce to visit, but the dictator had dragged his feet, finding one excuse after another for the delay—he would never be comfortable in the Vatican, surrounded by priests, and even less comfortable in a setting of such splendor that he would look insignificant in comparison. But after his latest victory, he felt more secure, less likely to be seen to be prostrating himself before the pontiff. Now that the crisis had passed, great things, he was convinced, lay ahead.[34]

MUSSOLINI IS ALWAYS RIGHT

W ITH THE RESOLUTION OF THE CATHOLIC ACTION CRISIS, THE links binding the Church to the Fascist regime became ever stronger, the collaboration deep and wide-ranging. Mussolini, now enjoying the enthusiastic support of Italy's Catholic clergy, was acquiring an image of almost godlike proportions.

Many historians have identified the pope's 1931 battle with the Duce over Catholic Action as a papal struggle against Fascism. But a look at what the organization actually did during the 1930s shows just how mistaken they are. The pope, far from seeing the Fascist regime as an obstacle in his efforts to use Catholic Action to Christianize Italian society, viewed it as an indispensable ally. Without close working relations between Catholic Action and Fascist authorities, the organization could not succeed. Its lay national head, Augusto Ciriaci, was an ardent admirer of the Duce; he was, De Vecchi told Mussolini, "not far from acting as my man and therefore also Yours" in the Vatican.[1]

Pius XI viewed Catholic Action's members as soldiers in his "battle for morality." In each diocese, a Catholic Action "Secretariat for Morality" was established to identify and report any sign of immoral activity. It put out lists of plays and films to be boycotted, and members badgered the police to shut them down. Catholic Action members were told to scour their villages and towns to identify anything the Church found offensive and report it to the authorities.[2]

Among the signs of moral decline that most upset the pope were reports of immodestly dressed women. Since 1926 Tacchi Venturi had been in constant contact with the regime's highest police authorities in an effort to get them to crack down on the bare legs, bare backs, and partially uncovered bosoms of Italian women.[3] In June of that year, in reaction to this pressure, the minister of internal affairs ordered prefects to clamp down on scantily clad bathers. The minister also ordered that dancing while wearing a bathing suit—a particular irritant to the pope—be banned.[4]

So great was the pope's interest in prohibiting the public exposure of women's bodies that even in the intense final days leading to the Lateran Accords, when he heard that barely dressed dancers were to be seen in Rome, he dispatched Tacchi Venturi to get the Duce to do something about it.

Eight days before the historic signing, they met. Tacchi Venturi began by letting Mussolini know how pleased the pope was that he had banned burlesque performances in Rome. But what had been chased out the front door was coming back in through the window. Cinema owners had discovered they could attract more patrons by having dancing girls perform during intermissions. These young women, the Jesuit told Mussolini, were "dressed as their mother Eve was before the fall, save for a thin strip or sash across their private parts, more an incentive than an impediment to the impure yearnings of concupiscence." He looked forward to the day when he could give the pope the happy news that the government had ordered a stop to the appalling spectacle.[5]

Among the public displays of female flesh to which the pope objected was a particular bugaboo, the participation of girls in gymnastics competitions. In 1928, when he learned that the Fascist Party planned to hold such an event in Rome, both the Vatican daily and *La Civiltà cattolica* published his letter denouncing it. Not even in pagan Rome, he complained, had such a travesty of female delicacy been seen.[6]

In early 1930, in response to such pressure, the president of the national Fascist youth organization released new guidelines governing girls' physical education. The groups were to aim not at developing girls' athletic skills but rather at ensuring that "the future mothers learned the necessity of seeing to the physical education of their children." *La Civiltà cattolica* praised the instruction as an example of how effectively the Fascist government was collaborating with the Vatican to improve the nation's spiritual welfare.[7]

But the pope remained vigilant, and the following year was disturbed to learn of plans for an international girls' gymnastics competition in Venice. This time he sent Borgongini to persuade Mussolini to stop it.

Mussolini was unsympathetic, explaining that international athletic groups, not the government, organized such events. In an attempt to show that he personally had little use for girls' athletic competitions (or perhaps because he always enjoyed seeing the prim nuncio squirm), the dictator added: "Women are good for two things: to have children and to be beaten." Egged on by Borgongini's discomfort, he warmed to his subject. "Women are like fur coats," he explained, "every once in a while you need to knock the dust off them."[8]

Similar pleas from local Catholic Action groups to local government officials often met an unsympathetic response as well. In such cases, frustrated bishops turned to the Vatican for help.

A letter the pope received in August 1932 was unusual only in being accompanied by a number of blurry snapshots. The bishop wrote to denounce the flaunting of women's flesh on the island of Capri. Many women could be seen there "with their backs practically entirely uncovered, often with their breasts poorly covered, and sometimes wearing a bathing top made of transparent fabric." Most of the good people of the island, he added, were nauseated by the spectacle, which he blamed on outsiders. He urged the Vatican to get the police to act. The four photographs he enclosed, all taken from behind, showed the naked backs of women wearing stylish evening gowns.[9]

Eugenio Pacelli responded on behalf of the pope. The campaign for female modesty, he assured the bishop, was one of the centerpieces of the Catholic Action program. The organization "does not let any appropriate occasion go by when it can influence the authorities to exercise greater vigilance and a severe application of the law."[10]

It is worth pausing a moment to consider the date of Pacelli's letter—September 16, 1932. Barely one year earlier Tacchi Venturi and Mussolini had initialed the agreement ending the Catholic Action dispute.[11] Throughout the country, local Catholic Action groups were now collaborating with the Fascist police.[12]

The pope continued to complain about the exhibition of female bodies on Italy's beaches. Church attempts to push Mussolini into action sometimes went too far, as happened in March 1934. That month the archbishop of Florence, Cardinal Elia Dalla Costa, lambasted the Fascist youth groups for sponsoring beach outings for their members. Mussolini was so incensed by the complaint that he wrote Pacelli a letter.

"The well known—perhaps too well known—Monsignor Elia Dalla Costa addressed the attached pastoral letter to his flock," said the Duce. "He graciously describes us as pagan and savage. Let those above him know that we are neither pagan nor savage and we don't want to become either, notwithstanding the pastoral letter of Dalla Costa."

De Vecchi, the Italian ambassador, hand-delivered the Duce's letter to Pacelli. Such attacks, he told Pacelli, were counterproductive. It took a lot of nerve, De Vecchi added—broaching a taboo topic—for the archbishop to accuse the Fascists of being savages when at the same time the Vatican expected the government to keep silent about widespread cases of priestly immorality. One of these days, the ambassador warned, the pope would go too far. He would not be happy with the result.[13]

The pope also pressed the authorities to ban books that the Church deemed offensive, like a European best seller offering advice on sex. *Ideal Marriage,* written by a Dutch gynecologist, described the biology of reproduction, advocated the pleasures of sexuality, and offered information helpful to controlling fertility. In 1930 the Vatican placed it on the Index of Prohibited Books. Sometime later, apparently prompted by the imminent appearance of an Italian edition, the pope called on Mussolini to outlaw its sale. The Duce assured him he would.[14]

Pius also pressed Mussolini to ban objectionable films and plays. Even before the signing of the Lateran Accords, the pope sent Tacchi Venturi to talk with Mussolini about how they might best collaborate in this effort. In a January 1929 meeting, the two men discussed American films. Tacchi Venturi branded them a cesspool of sin and obscenity; Mussolini voiced agreement, calling American cinema a "school of corruption that will end up ruining the Nation if it isn't stopped." Pleased, Tacchi Venturi asked the dictator to "study how the censorship system could be made most effective."[15]

"Italy Bans Sex Appeal in Pictures . . . Film Censorship Rules Ordered Tightened Due to Pope's Protests." So read the headline in the March 20, 1931, *Los Angeles Times,* reporting Mussolini's response to the pope's complaints.[16]

The pope's demands on Mussolini at times seemed overwhelming. He hectored the Duce on objectionable women's dress, books, Protestant proselytizing, films, and plays. He also regularly asked Mussolini to take action against ex-priests. Until the fall of the Papal States, the Church had been able to isolate such miscreants from the public. But following Italian unification, it lost all power over them. What especially incensed the Vatican was ex-priests teaching in public schools, which the pope thought scandalous.[17]

Pius had begun urging the Duce to act well before the concordat was signed. In January 1925 he asked Mussolini to fire the prominent church historian and ex-priest Ernesto Buonaiuti from his professorship at the University of Rome. Buonaiuti had long been a thorn in the Vatican's side. A modernist who argued for separation of church and state, he had earlier been relieved of his teaching position at one of Rome's most prestigious seminaries. In 1921 the Church had excommunicated him after he questioned whether the body of Christ was literally present in the Eucharist.[18]

In response to the pope's 1925 plea, Mussolini ordered the ex-priest suspended for the year from his teaching position, but Buonaiuti's faculty colleagues lobbied for his reinstatement.[19] In early 1927 the pope again, through Tacchi Venturi, urged the dictator to fire him. Mussolini replied that, while he wanted to keep the pope happy, he did not want to be accused of ignoring the law in order to please the pope. He suggested instead that he find other ways to prevent Buonaiuti from teaching.[20] Three days later Tacchi Venturi paid a visit on the minister of education, Pietro Fedele, to try his luck. Fedele was not happy to see the pope's emissary but was well aware of his special ties to the Duce. "I think it opportune from now on," he wrote the next day to Mussolini, "that each time Father Tacchi Venturi comes to see me or someone in my cabinet, I send you a report of the conversation."

Fedele assured the emissary that the ministry would again suspend Buonaiuti from teaching. Tacchi Venturi expressed satisfaction but added a papal warning. Should the government ever allow the ex-priest back in the classroom, Pius would forbid Catholics from attending the University of Rome.[21]

Buonaiuti remained on the University of Rome faculty until 1931 when, ironically, he ran afoul not of the pope but of Mussolini. A new law mandated that all Italian university professors swear allegiance to the Fascist regime. Of Italy's twelve hundred faculty members, no more than a dozen or so refused. One of them was the ex-priest Ernesto Buonaiuti. He, along with the others, was dismissed.[22]

In another case, erupting shortly after the concordat was signed, the pope demanded that the ex-priest Giuseppe Saitta be fired from his position as professor of medieval philosophy at the University of Pisa. This case was especially ticklish for Mussolini because, in leaving the priesthood, Saitta had become an ardent Fascist. He edited *Vita Nuova,* a publication of the Fascist Federation of Bologna, and was a follower of Mussolini's court philosopher, Giovanni Gentile. Indeed, he had been a student of Gentile in Palermo.

On June 2, 1930, the nuncio Borgongini met with Mussolini to present the pope's request. He based his demand on article 5 of the concordat, which was clear enough: "apostate priests . . . cannot be appointed or retained as teachers, or hold office or be employed where they may be in direct contact with the public."

"It would not be difficult for you to transfer Saitta to some museum," suggested the nuncio.

"Why not paleontology!" the dictator responded mischievously. When he was in a good mood, the Duce rarely missed a chance to tease the ever-earnest nuncio. But Mussolini was not enthusiastic about the request. "*Vedremo*"—"we'll see," he said.

Months went by, and Saitta remained at his post. In April 1931 the pope sent a reminder to Mussolini, but still nothing was done. Saitta had been appointed to his university post before the signing of the concordat, Mussolini argued, and the provisions of the agreement were not retroactive. Two years later Saitta, far from being consigned to a remote paleontology museum, was given the plum position of professor of philosophy at the University of Bologna. This was one battle that the pope would not win.[23]

WHEN THE POPE'S EMISSARIES complained to Mussolini about American films, Mussolini had told them he shared their view. But in fact he was a big fan of American movies, although his tastes ran to Charlie Chaplin, Laurel and Hardy, and Buster Keaton, not to Jean Harlow or Mae West. The dictator even set up a special projection room at Villa Torlonia so that, after dinner, his whole family could gather in front of the screen. "It frees my mind," he explained. Whatever relief it provided, it was brief: while the rest of the family watched the movies to the end, the paterfamilias rarely stayed more than twenty minutes.[24]

Those evenings in their private cinema were the happiest time for the Mussolini family. The dictator disliked sitting down to a family meal, and on the rare times he did, a deep silence enveloped the table as he nervously played with his fork and reduced the bread crumbs to powder in his fingers.[25] Rachele ruled not only the kitchen but the table as well. Children who failed to eat all their food incurred her wrath.

Although Rachele could stand up to her husband at home, outside the villa's walls, Mussolini stood apart from other mortal men. *Mussolini ha sempre ragione* ("Mussolini is always right") was the endlessly repeated slogan. Painted in huge letters on the sides of buildings throughout the country, the phrase was used to teach children to read.[26]

To burnish his image abroad, Mussolini somehow found time to meet with an endless parade of foreign correspondents. Rare was the reporter who interviewed the Duce in these years and failed to succumb to his rough charm. At rest, gushed one French interviewer, Mussolini resembled a marble statue sculpted by Michelangelo. His black, piercing eyes were hypnotic, his large mouth graced with beautiful teeth.[27] No one who has had the Duce's eyes fixed on him, remarked another French interviewer, could ever forget the feeling: "two eyes that see, that judge, seeing from on high, judging from afar." And like so many others, the Frenchman was struck by the sharp contrast between the Mussolini of the public piazza, haranguing the adulatory crowds, and the pensive Mussolini of the interview, seeming so alone, so reflective, lacing his remarks with historical and philosophical references.[28]

A prominent German Jewish journalist published the longest and most widely read interview with the Italian dictator.[29] Emil Ludwig met with Mussolini in his cavernous office several times in 1933. While considering one of his questions, Mussolini would put his fingertips together or rest his chin in his hands, his elbows on the table. He would look down at his desk and then raise his eyes to look straight at Ludwig as he replied. He took particular delight in citing statistics, preferably to the third decimal place. Ludwig also noticed that the dictator did not like to see anything wasted and, rather than use a notepad, took notes on the backs of the cards that contained his daily schedule.

Ludwig had heard the Duce address rallies in a military voice that brought to his mind the Russian revolutionary Leon Trotsky exhorting a crowd. But in the interviews, Mussolini never spoke loudly. Although he seemed not to understand jokes, observed Ludwig, he did have a kind of grim humor. He had only one ancestor in whom he took any pride, he said. One of his forefathers had lived in Venice and killed his wife because she was unfaithful. What recommended him to Mussolini was his élan in pausing, before fleeing the city, to place two Venetian coins on his wife's chest to pay for her burial.

Despite himself, Ludwig, a man of the left, was being won over. When Mussolini went on to express his admiration for Caesar, Ludwig asked if a dictator could ever be loved.

"Yes," replied Mussolini, "provided that the masses fear him at the same time. The crowd loves strong men. The crowd is like a woman."[30]

Later the Duce elaborated. "For me the masses are nothing but a herd of sheep, so long as they are unorganized." They were incapable of ruling themselves. Creatures of feeling and emotion, not intellect, they could not be won over by rational arguments. "It is faith that moves mountains, not reason. Reason . . . can never be the motive force of the crowd. . . . The capacity of the modern man for faith is illimitable. When the masses are like wax in my hands, when I stir their faith, or when I mingle with them and am almost crushed by them, I feel myself to be a part of them."

Here Mussolini paused. Sometimes, he told Ludwig, the crowd that he had excited disgusted him. "Does not the sculptor sometimes smash his block of marble into fragments because he cannot shape it to represent the vision he has conceived?" It all came down to this: "Everything turns upon one's ability to control the masses like an artist."[31]

But by this time Mussolini had lost his major link to the world of high culture, having increasingly pushed Margherita Sarfatti away. He no longer felt the need for her political advice or encouragement, and now that she was over fifty, putting on weight, and suffering from gout, she no longer stirred his passion.[32] Americans, slow to get the word, still viewed her as one of the people closest to the Duce. During a 1934 visit, Franklin and Eleanor Roosevelt received Sarfatti in the White

House, even as back home her star was fading. Galeazzo Ciano, then undersecretary for press and propaganda, had her biography of Mussolini, *Dux,* pulled from circulation. Perhaps Ciano's wife, Edda Mussolini, had pressured him. She despised her father's former mistress. In any case, in the wake of the Lateran Accords, and later, as Mussolini sought to make a good impression on Hitler, the aging Jew had become an embarrassment. In 1935 he ordered the Italian press to ignore her. Following the anti-Semitic racial laws three years later, she would flee Italy, making her way to South America. She would return to Italy only after the war.[33]

Mussolini was increasingly isolated. "Fundamentally," he told Ludwig, "I have always been alone. Besides, to-day, though not in prison, I am all the more a prisoner."[34] Around the same time, he explained to an admirer, "One must accept solitude. . . . A chief cannot have equals. Nor friends. The humble solace gained from exchanging confidences is denied him. He cannot open his heart. Never."[35]

The year 1932, wrote one of Mussolini's early biographers, marked the completion of the transition from the man to the mask, the reality to the legend. He had learned how to appear taller than his five-foot-six-inch frame, affecting the look of the medieval condottiere, a Renaissance warlord. His girth was expanding; despite his meager diet, he fought a constant struggle against the family tendency to fat and weighed himself every day. But his larger bulk gave new fullness to his face and helped nourish the effect of a latter-day Caesar.[36]

A vast government and Fascist Party effort went into nurturing the cult of the Duce. In 1929 a French observer in Italy marveled at how ubiquitous the Duce's resolute face was: "In the news rooms, at the pastry shop, the beauty parlor, in phone booths, in smoke shops . . . it's an obsession. You have to ask yourself if he keeps that mask on even when he is sleeping."[37]

Pius XI viewed these efforts with some alarm. One day, during an audience with Cesare De Vecchi, the pope startled the ambassador by asking if he could count on him to take Mussolini some personal advice. Nervous but curious, he agreed.

"Tell Signor Mussolini in my name," the pope began, "that I do not like his attempts at trying to become a quasi-divinity and it is not doing him any good either, quite the opposite. He should not be trying to put himself somewhere between the earth and the heavens. . . . Have him reflect, in my name, that God, Our Lord, is only one." Mussolini "could only be an idol, a fetish, or a false god, or at most a false prophet." He should realize, said the pope, that "sooner or later people end up smashing their idols. Tell him that if he doesn't change what he is doing, it will end badly for him."

De Vecchi rushed to Palazzo Venezia, where the Duce took a look at him, still in his formal morning suit, and laughed. The embarrassed ambassador explained that he had come directly from the Vatican with a personal message from the pope.

"Calm down," said the Duce, "tell me everything." As De Vecchi did his best to repeat what the pope had said, a smile—somewhere between ironic and incredulous—came over Mussolini's face.

"Are you sure these are all the pope's words?" asked the dictator. "You haven't by any chance added anything of your own?"

A flustered De Vecchi assured him he had not.

"Then tell me," said Mussolini, "what you think?"

"The same as the pope," replied De Vecchi, or at least so he claimed in his later memoir.[38]

While the pope was worried about the growing idolization of the Duce, most of Italy's clergy were not. The 1933 example of a priest from Bergamo, in northeastern Italy, may be extreme, but it gives some sense of the strength of the Mussolini cult. Having received a signed photograph of the Duce as a prize for a special act of Fascist loyalty, the priest wrote a thank-you note: "I kissed that figure of Your pensive face, and the characters that your hand wrote. . . . Your image . . . will remain sacred to me, and with the help of God I will try never to do anything to fail to deserve it. . . . Duce, every day I have prayed to the omnipotent Lord for the holy souls of Your parents and Arnaldo . . . and for You and for the Fatherland."[39]

The unctuous priest's prayers for the soul of Mussolini's brother touched an open wound for the Duce. On a foggy day in Milan in December 1931, Arnaldo, on his way home from the train station, had been felled by a heart attack. He was only forty-six years old. It was a terrible blow to Mussolini, who had shared a bed with him as a child, for there was no one he was closer to and no one he trusted nearly as much.[40]

In their phone conversations every night at ten P.M. Mussolini and Arnaldo had not only discussed what would go in their newspaper for the coming day but whatever else was on Mussolini's mind. Frequently Arnaldo came to Rome to see Benito, and it was not uncommon for the Duce to get upset and shout at his younger brother. Once, Navarra reports, Arnaldo arrived at Palazzo Chigi and, perhaps to avoid such an explosion, asked to speak only to his brother's private secretary. When Navarra mentioned to Mussolini that his brother was in the building but had not asked to see him, the Duce, annoyed, demanded that Arnaldo come immediately to his office. He complied. From outside the door, Navarra heard angry shouts aimed at the long-suffering Arnaldo. When the younger brother emerged from the office, Navarra apologized for having mentioned he was in the building.

"Don't worry," replied Arnaldo. "If everyone knew him as I do, they wouldn't get so upset. He screams but he doesn't bite."[41]

Some see Arnaldo's death as a turning point for Mussolini. The loss so suddenly and unexpectedly of the one person he could trust completely made him more closed, more suspicious of those around him. "Now," he said on the day of his brother's funeral, "I will have to rely on myself for everything." A few days later he wrote to his sister, Edvige, "The blow was so unexpected and terrible that it will take much time before my nerves are back in equilibrium. I cried and cried."[42]

Mussolini increasingly found his strength in the adulation of the crowds. A ceremony held in Rome three months after Arnaldo's death was one of scores of such rituals that fed his ever-growing sense that he was a man of destiny who would lead Italy to new greatness. It was the thirteenth anniversary of the founding of the Fascist movement. An unending stream of Blackshirts, from children to old men, marched in formation toward Piazza Venezia. A squad of airplanes flew overhead, as scores of musical bands played the Fascist hymns. Fascist cries of "alalà!" pierced the air. By six P.M. the planes were gone, but tens of thousands of delirious Fascists still filled the immense piazza, waving their banners. Veterans of the Great War, veterans of the March on Rome, members of Fascist youth groups, workers, university students, people of all ages and occupations pressed toward the balcony from which Mussolini would speak. As the joyous crowd glimpsed the dictator at his window, his right arm raised in Roman salute, the bands struck up the Fascist anthem, "*Giovinezza,*" and thousands of voices sang together in holy communion.

"Du-ce! Du-ce!" they chanted. In its glowing description, *Il Popolo d'Italia,* the Mussolinis' newspaper, remarked that the demonstration was like "an immense religious rite of faith." When the call of "attention" rang out, the thunderous noise died down, and an eerie, expectant silence fell over the piazza. Mussolini, wearing his Fascist militia uniform, his head uncovered, addressed the crowd. He ended, as he often did, with his trademark refrain, asking: "For whom is Italy?" "For us!" tens of thousands of voices responded together. After he left, two, three times the crowd got him to return to the balcony, his hand raised in Roman salute offering a kind of benediction. Finally, emotionally spent but glowing with energy and pride, the Fascists, old and young, made their way home. Italians throughout the country would endlessly repeat the rite in the coming months and years.[43]

The Catholic clergy played a crucial role in lending the Duce cult a religious flavor, promoting a heady mix of Fascist and Catholic ritual. Priests were an integral part of the Fascist youth organizations; twenty-five hundred chaplains ministered to over four million members. Appointed to oversee the chaplains' work was a bishop devoted entirely to Fascist youth. They helped ensure that Italians of the future would see their allegiance to the Catholic Church and their allegiance to Mussolini and Fascism as two sides of the same coin.[44]

In October 1933, in one of many such instances, 152 priests serving as chaplains to the Fascist militia gathered at Palazzo Venezia. As their hero looked on, they sang a musical tribute they had prepared for him, titled "Acclamation to the Duce."

> *Hail to You indomitable Duce*
> *Savior of our land*
> *In peace and in war*
> *We are ready to follow Your signals*
> *Inspiration and force, guide and light*
> *To the new heroes of Italy, you are the Leader*
> *Duce to us, Duce to us!*[45]

Major Fascist rituals typically began with a morning mass, celebrated by a priest (in a small town) or by a bishop (in a city). A parade and rally followed, and a message from the Duce was read. Churches and cathedrals were important props in these rites, adding to their emotional power. For the 1933 anniversary of the March on Rome, the stark image of Mussolini's face was projected at night halfway up Milan's Duomo; the spectral visage towered over the crowd. "The Pope," remarked European historian Piers Brendon, "gave the impression that the Catholic Church in Italy was the Fascist party at prayer; and he implied that the citizen, like the worshipper, might best do his duty on his knees."[46]

The few priests who dared say anything remotely critical of the Fascist regime were reported by local Fascists to the authorities. Many such complaints were dealt with at the local level, as bishops disciplined their wayward priests. But when a bishop balked, the matter was taken to Rome. Among the duties of Italy's ambassador to the Holy See was getting the Vatican to act when such reports came in. In a typical case, in November 1932, the Vatican received a complaint about a parish priest in the diocese of Cremona. The local bishop was told to investigate. When he tried to minimize the offense, Monsignor Pizzardo informed him that his response was inadequate. The bishop was to have the priest use the next possible opportunity "to give a speech in the opposite sense from the one he gave on November 4 that did not give a good impression."[47]

A few months later the pope acted on complaints that Giovanni Montini, the chaplain of the Catholic Action university organization, was anti-Fascist: he dismissed him from his position. Upset, Montini, whose father had been a Popular Party deputy in parliament, directed his anger not at the pontiff but at Pizzardo, who had conveyed the pope's decision. Pizzardo, he complained, had fired him without "a word of comfort, of esteem, of praise." A few years later the pope, by then less enamored of Mussolini, would rehabilitate Montini. The detour would do nothing to damage Montini's career, for three decades later he would ascend St. Peter's throne, taking the name Pope Paul VI.[48]

In 1932 Mussolini announced that the handshake—a "bourgeois" custom—was to be replaced by the more virile Roman salute. He not only required university professors to take a Fascist oath of allegiance but insisted they wear black shirts on graduation days. By the end of 1934, all elementary school teachers had to wear a black shirt and party uniform whenever they were in school.[49]

Earlier that year another plebiscite was held. Turin's diocesan weekly expressed the same sentiment that Catholics throughout the country were hearing from their priests and bishops: "Catholics of Turin! To the urns to give your consensus to the government of Benito Mussolini. . . . Anti-Fascism is finished."[50] It was the last election that Mussolini would bother holding. Ten million Italians voted yes, only fifteen thousand no.[51]

CHAPTER

FOURTEEN

THE PROTESTANT ENEMY
AND THE JEWS

O N THE MORNING OF FEBRUARY 11, 1932, THE THIRD ANNIVERSARY
of the Lateran Accords, a caravan of four black limousines made
its way to the Vatican, with festively dressed carabinieri on horseback
riding among them. Saluted at their entry into Vatican City by Swiss
Guards, the cars entered the San Damaso Courtyard. There they were
met by Papal Gendarmes, who carried a papal flag aloft, and a contingent of the Palatine Guard of Honor, in their neck ruffs, with small
curved swords in gleaming halberds strapped to their sides. Mussolini
emerged, dressed in his swallowtailed diplomatic uniform. Lavish gold
designs covered his sleeves, and a wide gold stripe ran down the sides
of his trousers. He carried his plumed hat in one hand, a ceremonial
sword strapped to his waist.[1]

The press had been speculating about the visit for months. The
previous September, three days after Mussolini and Tacchi Venturi
signed their agreement ending the battle over Catholic Action, a front-
page *New York Times* headline announced "Mussolini Will Visit the

Pope This Week."² Thereafter a steady stream of newspaper stories and diplomats' dispatches reported that the Duce's long-awaited papal visit was soon to take place, but each predicted date passed without any meeting.³ Finally Mussolini fixed the visit for February.⁴

In preparation, Pius XI awarded the dictator a special papal honor. On a January morning, Borgongini arrived at Palazzo Venezia for the presentation. A beaming Duce, formally dressed in morning coat, proudly welcomed him. The nuncio presented him with a papal brief. Mussolini studied the scroll carefully. "I am one of the few Italians who can read and understand Latin!" he boasted implausibly. The nuncio then gave the dictator the pope's gift, the Collar of the Golden Militia, a beautiful golden collar with a gold cross. The former anticlerical rabble-rouser was now a knight of the papal court.⁵

On the day of the historic meeting with the pope, Mussolini arrived with the papal cross hanging over his chest. He was a dozen minutes early, and embarrassingly, Monsignor Pizzardo, charged with greeting him, was nowhere to be seen. The papal guards had no idea what to do other than to remain at attention and salute. Alongside the door, given the honor of being among the first to see the Duce's arrival, stood the pope's elderly sister. She was certainly not going to say anything. At last Pizzardo scurried down the stairs, running late because the pope had kept him in his library giving last-minute instructions. Accompanied by various gendarmes, Swiss Guards, and papal chamberlains, they climbed the stairs.

Mussolini made his way up the broad winding staircase toward the Clementine Hall. The top two-thirds of the towering walls of the ornate hall and all of its ceiling were covered in Renaissance frescoes. On one wall, a frieze depicted the cardinal virtues, while a frieze on the facing wall depicted the theological virtues. Alberti's fresco *The Apotheosis of St. Clement* adorned the ceiling. Colorful mosaics covered the lower portion of the walls and the whole floor of the large rectangular room. The twenty people who had been invited to witness the Duce's historic arrival there seemed lost amid its grandeur.

Mussolini greeted by Monsignor Pizzardo on his arrival
at the Vatican to meet with the pope, February 11, 1932

But when Monsignor Caccia Dominioni, master of ceremonies and in charge of accompanying Mussolini to the pope's library, entered the hall to greet the Duce, he was taken aback. There amid the formally dressed men stood a woman, a foreign journalist. This was impossible. No woman was allowed to be present for such an occasion. And Mussolini was already halfway up the stairs.

"Signorina," Caccia pleaded, "I beg you to leave immediately."

The blond woman's face reddened with embarrassment, but she stood her ground. "I have a perfect right to be here, Monsignor," she replied.

"Rights here are decided by me," he responded. "You have no right to be here. I am acting under the orders of the Holy Father."

The woman waved her invitation in reproach. Caccia, hearing Mussolini's party ascend the stairs, grew frantic. "Signorina, I do not want to adopt anything but kind words." He glanced at a couple of the imposing gendarmes standing nearby. "But if you do not leave immediately you will force me to act."

Angry and humiliated, the woman relented, and a prelate guided her to a back exit. Just then Mussolini entered, and Caccia greeted him effusively. The Swiss Guards presented their arms, their swords aloft.

Caccia led Mussolini through a series of grand halls, each with a contingent of papal troops, Noble Guards, and high Church officials. They reached the Small Throne Room, and from there the Duce entered the pope's library, where Pius awaited him.[6] As had been previously arranged at the Duce's insistence, Mussolini neither bowed nor kissed the pope's ring, obeisances that were customarily expected of a Catholic head of government. The pope would allow no photograph to be taken, but an artist for a popular newsweekly captured the scene for the public. It showed the pope, wearing his white robe, white papal cap, and red shoes, sitting in one of his richly upholstered red armchairs in front of his desk facing Mussolini, who sat wearing his em-

LA DOMENICA DEL CORRIERE

Lo storico colloquio dell'11 febbraio tra Pio XI e Mussolini

Mussolini and the pope, in the pope's library, February 11, 1932

broidered diplomatic jacket and yellow-striped pants, the pope's cross around his neck.[7]

The historic meeting generated worldwide press coverage. "Pope and Duce Clasp Hands in Friendship Pact," read the *Chicago Daily Tribune* headline. The front-page *New York Times* headline declared "Pope and Mussolini Show Warm Feeling in Vatican Meeting."[8] But the best description we have of their encounter—the only time the two men would ever meet—comes from Mussolini himself, who wrote an account by hand to send to the king.

The pope invited him to sit, asking how his daughter, Edda, was doing in Shanghai, where her husband was serving as Italian consul.

After a minimum of such pleasantries, Pius brought up the subject he thought most pressing. Protestant proselytizing, he told a surprised Mussolini—who was not expecting this to be at the top of the agenda for the meeting—"is making progress in almost all of Italy's dioceses, as shown in a study that I had the bishops do. The Protestants are becoming ever bolder, and they speak of 'missions' they want to organize in Italy." They were taking advantage of the concordat's unfortunate language, which referred to non-Catholic religions as "admitted" cults. The pope had opposed that phrase, preferring that they be described as "tolerated."

Mussolini pointed out that only 135,000 Protestants lived in Italy, 37,000 of them foreigners—a mere speck amid 42 million Catholics.

The pope acknowledged that the Protestants were few but argued that the threat was nonetheless great. He handed the Duce a lengthy report on the question. Over the next years he would bombard the dictator with requests to keep the Protestants in check.

The conversation then turned to the recent conflict over Catholic Action, and here we must treat Mussolini's account of the pope's words with caution. After expressing his pleasure that the dispute had been settled amicably, the pope added—according to the Duce—"I do not see, in the complex of Fascist doctrines—which tend to affirm the principles of order, authority, and discipline—anything that is contrary to Catholic teachings."

The pope added that he could understand the principle of "totalitarian fascism," but this could refer only to the material realm. There were also spiritual needs, he said, and for these what was needed was "Catholic totalitarianism."

"I agreed with the Holy Father's opinion," commented Mussolini. "State and Church operate on two different 'planes' and therefore—once their reciprocal spheres are delimited—they can collaborate together."

Finally the pope expressed his distress at what was going on in Russia where, he said, the Bolsheviks were intent on destroying Christianity. "Beneath this," said Pius, "there is also the anti-Christian loathing of Judaism." When he was nuncio in Poland, he recalled, "I saw that in all the Bolshevik regiments the civilian commissars were Jews." The pope thought Italy's Jews an exception. He fondly told the Duce of a Jew in Milan who had made a major gift to the church, and of the help that Milan's rabbi had given him in deciphering "certain nuances of the Hebrew language."

At the end of the meeting, the pontiff presented the Duce with three more papal medals.[9] Mussolini then made his way to the secretary of state's office, where he spent twenty minutes with Cardinal Pacelli. Then he was escorted down into St. Peter's to kneel before the Altar of the Madonna. When newspaper photographers tried to take a photo of him in prayer, he abruptly got up and shooed them away. "No. No. When one is praying," he said, "one should not be photographed."[10] No one would photograph the dictator on his knees.

Mussolini arrived home in an ebullient mood. Eager to hear details of the visit, his children gathered around him. Rachele was less impressed, interrupting his glowing account by asking acidly: "Did you also kiss his feet?" On this note, his narration came to an abrupt end.[11]

The next month, in an orgy of honorifics, Mussolini and the king reciprocated the honors. They bestowed on Cardinal Pacelli the Supreme Order of the Most Holy Annunciation—Italy's highest decoration, making him a "cousin" of the king—and awarded the Grand Cross of Saints Maurice and Lazarus to Pacelli's two undersecretaries of state,

Mussolini at the Vatican following his meeting with the pope, February 11, 1932;
from front left: Monsignor Caccia Dominioni, Cesare De Vecchi, Mussolini

Monsignors Pizzardo and Ottaviani. But what most caught the attention of the clergy was the honor given to someone who had no official Vatican position at all: Father Pietro Tacchi Venturi, too, received a Grand Cross.[12]

The pope now settled into a period of collaboration with the Italian dictator. To the bishop of Nice, who happened to be in Rome, the pope explained that it was thanks to Mussolini that the Catholic Church once again occupied a powerful position in Italy. When the bishop reminded him of the recent bruising battle over Catholic Action, the pope blamed it on the anticlerics who surrounded Mussolini. "I can still see him," said the pope, "sitting in the same seat where you are sitting, telling me, 'I recognize that we made some mistakes, but I had to battle against my entire staff.'"[13]

—

THAT SAME YEAR THE pope celebrated his seventy-fifth birthday, triggering an outpouring of admiration in the world's press. In a lengthy article, *The New York Times Magazine* gushed about the "surprising discovery" that behind the "quiet scholarliness of the Prefect of the Vatican Library were the traits of a born ruler of men." (The *Times* portrait unknowingly echoed a comment Cesare De Vecchi had made after a meeting with the pope three years earlier: "Every other will gives way before that of the Holy Father," he said, adding that he could easily imagine Pius XI at the head of a government or an army. "Every possible intrigue crumbles on contact with this block of granite.")[14] Pius still had the vigorous step of a younger man, the *Times* article affirmed, and spent virtually all his waking hours at work.[15]

The pope certainly kept a crushing schedule. During the 1933–34 Holy Year, two million pilgrims would come to Rome, and he met with many of them, making innumerable speeches and celebrating countless masses. Marking the nineteen hundredth anniversary of the crucifixion, the Holy Year ran from Easter to Easter.[16]

Pius XI was no orator. At public audiences, he made up his remarks as he went along, delivering them in a slow staccato, pausing as he considered each new thought. He often spoke of "the House of the Father" or "the Common Father of the faithful." Other times he took advantage of a saint's day or seized on some characteristic—national or occupational—of the visiting group to develop his theme. He had a well-deserved reputation for long-windedness, and given the length of his speeches, the size of the crowds he drew, and the often-stifling heat, it was not unusual for someone in the audience to faint before he finished. During Lent in 1934 he lectured a group of preachers on the virtue of keeping sermons brief—speaking for forty-five minutes to make his point.[17]

Cardinals of the Curia and other Vatican prelates continued to live in fear of him. The pope, observed the archbishop of Paris, would never admit to being wrong and had a habit of uttering pithy phrases that he took to be unquestioned truths. Gaetano Bisleti, the venerable cardinal who had crowned Ratti with the papal tiara in 1922, prepared for his audiences by going to his favorite Vatican chapel, getting down on his knees on the marble floor, and praying that the pope would find no fault with what he had to say. Monsignor Alberto Mella, who following Caccia's appointment as cardinal became master of ceremonies, prayed to all the saints in heaven before entering the pope's study, hoping that the pope would not find him wanting. A number of cardinals, afraid to approach the pope and risk incurring his wrath, confided in Pacelli, hoping he would use his diplomatic skills to get the pope to do what they wanted.[18]

But especially when dealing with laymen, the pope knew the value of a soft word. A visitor who entered the pope's presence in the Apostolic Palace genuflected three times. Non-Catholics were supposed to bow as well as Catholics, but this did not come easily to some. One day a group of Protestants visited the pope. All dropped to one knee, except for one man who, ill at ease, remained defiantly—if a bit unsteadily—on his feet. The pope's aides tensed, exchanging furtive glances to see who would deal with the problem. But while they dithered, the pope walked up to the holdout and asked, "Won't you receive a simple old man's blessing?" This was too much for the recalcitrant Protestant, and he too got down on bended knee.[19]

In the tradition of European monarchs, the pope kept bags of money in his library drawers to dispense to deserving petitioners. Domenico Tardini, Pizzardo's undersecretary in the Congregation for Extraordinary Ecclesiastical Affairs, was in charge of coordinating aid for Russian relief and often had to ask for funds. A short Roman prelate with a square face and thick dark woolly hair, Tardini was highly sensitive to the pope's moods. "At nine with the pope, another hour of audience," he wrote in his diary on April 9, 1934. "Today too he is in excellent spirit: the infallible thermometer measured by the size of his donations." As Tardini detailed his request, the pope, his attention drifting, rearranged the gold coins he had extracted from his drawer, sorting them by size into neat piles atop his desk.

When he was in a good mood, the pope, not known for his sense of humor, was capable of a witty remark. Earlier that year he had urgently summoned the French ambassador to discuss something that was on his mind. Upon his arrival, the ambassador apologized for not wearing his usual formal dress. The pope smiled. "Yes, I know," he said. "Ordinarily you come in leatherbound edition. Today you come as a paperback."[20]

Other times the pope was more irritable. "Today," Tardini wrote on October 5, "the pope is readier than ever to contradict and oppose. It all depends on his mood, on some painful experience in the past, on . . . his bad digestion, I don't know. But what is certain is that the pope is always ready to be suspicious and to do the exact opposite of whatever someone suggests he do." Tardini, who knew him well, came up with a solution. When the pope was in a bad mood, he could be counted on to deny any request. So on such days, Tardini would propose the opposite of what he wanted and could be sure he would succeed, or so he claimed. "That's what I did today," wrote Tardini in his diary one day, "and with excellent results."[21]

Although working a punishing schedule, the pope did have his modest diversions. Loving order, he carefully kept every item in his desk in its proper place and wasted nothing. He even kept a neat pile of ribbons removed from packages he opened. The son of a textile factory manager, he took pleasure in little mechanical projects. For many years, he kept a tiny screwdriver in his desk so he could tinker with clocks. When a spray of oil or a drip of ink stained his white vest, he would, when he was sure no one was looking, do his best to scrub it off.[22]

Now that he no longer had to cast himself as a "prisoner of the Vatican," the pope could enjoy a new diversion. On July 10, 1933, in a carriage with blinds drawn, he left Rome for the first time, bound for the papal estate at Castel Gandolfo in the Alban Hills. The area's cool, crisp air, famed wines, and natural beauty had drawn distinguished Romans since ancient times. The papal estate there had been unused since 1869. On his first visit, Pius XI inspected the repair work under way. The next year he began spending his summers there, two months in 1934 and 1935 and longer periods later. Each day he spent at the summer palace, his assistants brought papers for him to review, and he held audiences. But his pace was much reduced. While strolling through the extensive gardens, the pope could glance down a hundred meters at the lake below, formed by the mouth of an extinct volcano. Breathing the fresh air and feeling closer to nature gave him great pleasure, bringing back memories of the small-town life he had left behind.[23]

MUSSOLINI SHOULD NOT HAVE been surprised that Pius wanted his help in combating the Protestant threat.[24] In the wake of the concordat, the pope had been unhappy about the new instructions the government had put out, specifying how non-Catholic religions were to be treated. "I told the head of government," recalled the nuncio, who brought Mussolini the pope's complaint, "that the desire to equate the Catholic Religion with the Protestant cults, which are parasites that live by damaging the true religion, was not only entirely unjust but offensive to us."[25] The following year, 1931, the pope sent his nuncio back to renew his pleas. Protestant propaganda, he told Mussolini, posed the greatest danger the country faced. The government had to act more aggressively against it.[26]

In trying to get the government to repress the Protestants, the pope looked for arguments he thought would appeal to Mussolini. None seemed more promising than the claim that loyalty to the Catholic Church and to the Fascist regime were one and the same. Protestantism, the pope insisted, was anti-Italian, a foreign force that posed as much a danger to Mussolini as it did to the Church.

Catholic Action members were ever on the lookout for signs of Protestant activity. In a typical case, in May 1931, the Catholic Action heads in one central Italian town wrote to Mussolini denouncing a man who was distributing Protestant literature there. They asked the Duce to ensure that "Protestant propaganda be forbidden in any form."[27]

For his part, Mussolini was reluctant to break up Protestant meetings and confiscate their literature. In November 1932, when the pope once again sent his nuncio to demand action, the Duce cut him off. "It's better not to exaggerate," replied the impatient dictator. The campaign was making a bad impression on leaders in Protestant countries, he added—they were appalled by the Vatican newspaper's hysterical anti-Protestant screeds.[28]

Undaunted, a few months later the pope repeated his conviction that Italy's Protestants were "the greatest cross" he had to bear. On hearing this from the nuncio, Mussolini again pointed out how few Protestants resided in Italy. Again, this made no impression on the pope.[29]

While the nuncio Borgongini was the pope's main emissary in these efforts, Tacchi Venturi played a part as well. He would spend years trying to convince Mussolini that a vast, evil conspiracy, led by Protestants and Jews, was at work, aimed as much at the Fascist dictator as at the Catholic Church.[30] He relied on a network of informants to feed him the latest news on the occult conspiracy. In June 1933 he sent Cardinal Pacelli a copy of one such report.

"I believe that in communicating the attached information I am not doing something unwelcome," Tacchi Venturi wrote in his cover note. Of the report's accuracy, he told Pacelli, "I do not believe it is possible to harbor any doubts, as its author is not only as honest as they come, but in an especially well placed position to know what he is speaking about."

Tacchi Venturi's secret informer recounted that he had recently seen a ministry of internal affairs circular addressed to all of Italy's prefects, telling them to keep an eye out for political activity by priests. This seemed odd, he thought, for "the whole world knows with what great enthusiasm all the clergy, all the Italian Catholic associations, all the Italian Catholics love the Duce and the Regime."

There was but one explanation for why the government would waste its resources on such surveillance: "at the center of the government, that is, in the ministries, there are high bureaucratic officials who are either Jews or Masons who want the Prefects to think that the clergy and the Catholics should always be considered . . . as enemies!!"[31] Instead of wasting their time investigating priests, he said, government authorities should be looking into "the formidable, underhanded, subversive activities of the Jews, the Masons, and the Protestants who, disguised as admirers of Fascism, have become practically the feudal lords of Italy, as they never were in the past." Mussolini had to be warned.[32]

THE CHARGE THAT JEWS were the evil force behind a worldwide conspiracy against Christianity and European civilization had long been heard in the Vatican; the Jesuits of *La Civiltà cattolica* were among its most avid proponents.

A feature article, titled "The World Revolution and the Jews," had appeared in the Vatican-supervised journal in late October 1922, as the Fascists were marching on Rome. It described a world in chaos, where secret forces orchestrated labor strikes and unrest in pursuit of the goal of Communist revolution. The credulous masses participating in the revolts were mere stooges, manipulated by an occult power that showed telltale signs of coming from "the ghetto."

The world's future, the article warned, would be determined by the battle then being waged in Russia. The leaders of the Bolshevik reign of terror were not "indigenous Russians" but rather "Jewish intruders" who slyly masked their true identity behind Slavic-sounding pseudonyms. A list of the 545 highest officials of the Bolshevik regime revealed, the author claimed, that true Russians numbered no more than thirty. "Those of the Jewish race comprise a full 447"; the rest were a hodgepodge of other nationalities. In short, although Jews comprised less than five percent of Russia's population, "this tiny minority today has invaded all the avenues of power and imposes its dictatorship on the nation."[33]

The 1922 article has great significance, for its argument would be used by the Nazis as a central justification for their anti-Semitic campaign. Taken up by Church publications throughout Italy and beyond, the myth that the Russian revolutionary leaders were virtually all

Jewish—and not "real Russians"—became one of the most important, and deadly, rationales for government action against Europe's Jews.[34]

The next issue of *La Civiltà cattolica,* the first to appear after Mussolini came to power, carried news from Austria under the headline "Jewish-Masonic Socialism Tyrannizes Austria." Following the Great War, the journal reported, Vienna's nineteen Masonic lodges had formed a Grand Lodge. "All of its high functionaries, without exception, were Jews." Their goal was to rule the world "under the domination of the Masons, themselves under the Jews' power." If the Jews in Vienna got their way, the journal warned, "Vienna will be nothing but a Jewish city, houses and belongings will all be theirs, the Jews will be the bosses and lords, the Christians their servants." Austria, *La Civiltà cattolica* concluded, "will be absolutely the subject, tributary and slave of the Jews, this in short is the guiding idea of our socialist Jewish-Masonic leaders."[35]

This belief in a worldwide conspiracy of Jews, Masons, and Protestants was not one that Mussolini shared at the time, but in the next years the pope's Jesuit emissary Tacchi Venturi would employ all his powers to persuade him to see the world in these terms.[36]

In 1925, in Mussolini's home region of Romagna, the official magazine of Catholic Action, *La Risveglia,* carried a long series of articles warning of the Jewish threat. Jews and Masons, the journal warned, secretly controlled international finance and were "trying with satanic greed to suck all energy from the Christian spirit." Until Christians rebelled against these agents of Satan, they would continue to be exploited. In another article, most likely drawing on the 1922 *Civiltà cattolica* piece, the Catholic Action journal blamed Jews for the Russian revolution and for Communism. "The Jews," it warned, "adorers of gold, dream of crushing the indomitable spirit of Christ." Embracing the medieval charge of ritual murder, *La Risveglia* branded Jews "insatiable suckers of Christian blood."[37] Other articles published that year repeated the bogus charge that the great majority of "commissars" of the Russian government were Jews, described as a parasitical "race" whose object was to torment Christians and reduce them to slaves.[38]

For decades, the Vatican had demonized those it saw as the beneficiaries of the much-vilified Enlightenment: liberals, Masons, Jews, and Protestants. It cast all as doing the devil's work, seeking to undermine people's faith in the one true religion. Throughout Italy, the Catholic press stoked this fear.[39] Pius XI largely shared in this worldview. In his 1928 encyclical *Mortalium animos,* he forbade Catholics to take part in groups that encouraged interfaith dialogue.

In March 1928 the Holy Office of the Inquisition—headed by the pope—ordered the dissolution of the international Catholic organization called Friends of Israel. Begun two years earlier, the group followed the accepted Church goal of seeking to convert the Jews. Its membership included not only thousands of priests but 278 bishops and 19 cardinals as well.

But its leaders soon crossed the border of what the Vatican considered acceptable. To persuade the Jews to convert, they believed it was important to treat them with respect. They criticized both the traditional Church teaching that the Jews were Christ-killers cursed by God, and the folk belief that Jews were commanded to drink the blood of Christian children as part of their Passover rites.

Cardinal Merry del Val, former secretary of state and now secretary of the Holy Office, led the Vatican attack on the Friends of Israel. He expressed outrage at their request that the phrase "perfidious Jews" be eliminated from Good Friday prayers. In February 1928 he notified its officers that the organization could continue only if it confined its activities to praying for the Jews' conversion. They had become dupes of the Jews, he warned, unwitting tools in the Jews' evil plot to "penetrate everywhere in modern society" and attempt "to reconstitute the reign of Israel in opposition to the Christ and his Church." Meeting with the pope in early March, Merry del Val found that Pius shared his view that "behind the Friends of Israel one finds the hand and the inspiration of the Jews themselves."[40]

The pope agreed that it was important to act but worried that banning a Church organization called Friends of Israel might expose him to charges of anti-Semitism. He insisted that to the decree dissolving the group, a passage be added stating that the Church opposed anti-Semitism.[41] To ensure that the faithful understood what the decree meant, he asked Enrico Rosa, his close adviser and former head of *La Civiltà cattolica,* to explain its rationale in the pages of the journal.

The dissolution decree, Rosa wrote in "The Judaic Danger and the 'Friends of Israel,'" condemned anti-Semitism "in its anti-Christian form and spirit." He explained that "in the painful struggle against the Jewish danger," *La Civiltà cattolica* had "always taken care to balance charity and justice, avoiding and . . . explicitly combating the excesses of anti-Semitism." But the Church also had to protect itself "with equal diligence from the other, no less dangerous extreme." Catholics could not ignore the great peril that the Jews posed. In the nineteenth century, the Jews had been given equal rights—something the Church had long opposed; since then they had become "bold and powerful, making them, under the pretext of equality, ever more predominant, and privileged, especially in the economic sphere."

Rosa went on to blame the Jews for both the French and the Russian revolutions. Today, in the face of the Jewish threat, he warned, Europe's governments were being inexplicably lax. As a result, Jews had established their "hegemony in many sectors of public life, especially in the economy and industry, as well as in high finance, where they are indeed said to have dictatorial power. They can dictate laws to states and governments, in political as well as in financial matters, without fear of having any rivals." Throughout Europe, he concluded, Jews were at work, "scheming to achieve their world hegemony."[42]

ITALY'S JEWS AND PROTESTANTS were feeling increasingly marginalized. The situation of Mussolini's lover, Margherita Sarfatti, was a good barometer: sensing the regime's now-tight identification with Catholicism, she decided to be baptized. Tacchi Venturi performed the ceremony in 1928, and her two children soon followed.[43]

By 1933 the Fascist press was taking up the Catholic press's warnings of a Jewish conspiracy aimed jointly at the Catholic Church and the Fascist state. A Genoese newspaper, after making the obligatory denial that it had anything against Jews as individuals, proclaimed the need "to combat Jewish-Zionist-Masonic-Bolshevik-international sectarianism, which constitutes a huge and powerful reality, operating to the detriment of Christian civilization."[44]

While Tacchi Venturi was fixated on the Jewish danger, the pope was more focused on the threat posed by the spread of Communism.[45] In 1932 the new French ambassador, François Charles-Roux, reporting to the French foreign minister, wrote of the pope's "mania" in continually warning of the Communist danger. Rattled by the Nazis' dramatic success in the recent election in Germany—they had become the nation's largest party—the French were most eager to discuss the menace posed by Hitler. But Pius insisted that it was the Communist threat, not the rise of the Nazis, that France should be worrying about.[46]

Later that year, after Franklin Roosevelt was elected president of the United States, the pope heard a rumor that the new president might offer diplomatic recognition to the Soviet Union. Giving Moscow such recognition, he feared, would provide a huge boost to Communist propaganda in the United States. He told Pacelli to contact the apostolic delegate in Washington. Pressure might better come from the American Church than from the Vatican, he said, suggesting that Cardinal Patrick Joseph Hayes, archbishop of New York, approach Roosevelt on behalf of the American hierarchy.[47]

Meanwhile the pope kept pushing the Fascist government to restrict Protestants' rights in Italy. Hitherto police had permitted Protestants to meet privately, most often in their homes, forbidding only public meetings. But in 1934, in response to the pope's continuing pressure, the government agreed to forbid private meetings of Protestants as well, if they aimed at attracting converts.

Unhappily for the pope, judges balked at enforcing the new ban. It conflicted, they argued, both with the Italian constitution and with the "admitted cults" language of the concordat. The pope sent his nuncio to complain to the minister of justice. The minister offered his sympathies but said that there was little he could do. Unfortunately, he explained, the judges sometimes decided cases on their own.[48]

PIUS WAS MORE SUCCESSFUL on another front. Shortly after coming to power, as we have seen, Mussolini had decided to require Catholic religious instruction in the elementary schools; the 1929 concordat extended this requirement to secondary schools. But the pope was not happy when he learned that the government planned to allow high schools having a sufficient number of non-Catholic children to offer them instruction in their own religion. In March 1933 Turin's superintendent of schools was about to authorize the city's chief rabbi to offer religious lessons to Jewish high school students. The pope let Mussolini know of his displeasure. Tellingly, he focused not on the Jews but on the Protestants. "Your Excellency will not fail to see the gravity of the matter," Cardinal Pacelli wrote the Italian ambassador at the pope's behest, "once you reflect on the fact that, should this precedent be allowed, there is the danger of an identical request on the part of the Protestants."[49]

Following this protest, the government revoked authorization for the rabbi in Turin and terminated a similar authorization already in place for the rabbi in Milan.[50] The pope told Mussolini of his "great pleasure" on hearing the news.[51]

HITLER, MUSSOLINI, AND THE POPE

W HILE MUSSOLINI KEPT A BUST OF NAPOLEON IN HIS STUDY, Adolf Hitler, who became chancellor of Germany in January 1933, had long kept a bust of Benito Mussolini in his.[1] The Duce was his role model. Shortly after his swearing-in ceremony, Hitler sent Mussolini a message: Fascism and Nazism had much in common. He hoped to strengthen the ties between the two countries.[2]

Mussolini basked in the flattery but had doubts about his acolyte. Hitler was "a dreamer," better suited to fiery speechifying than to governing. As for Hermann Göring, he was an "ex-inmate of a lunatic asylum." Both, Mussolini believed, suffered from inferiority complexes.[3]

"Hitler is a brilliant agitator," said Cardinal Pacelli, "but it is too early to tell if he is a man of government."[4]

German Church leaders had long been wary of Hitler's extreme nationalism, which they thought bordered on paganism.[5] But the Nazi leader, aware that one out of three Germans was Catholic, was eager to win Vatican support. Just as Italy's Catholic Popular Party had stood in

Mussolini's way, Germany's Catholic Center Party stood in Hitler's. Less than a month after Hitler came to power, the German ambassador assured Pacelli that the new chancellor wanted good relations with the Holy See. After all, the ambassador pointed out, Hitler was a Catholic.[6]

The pope too had doubts about the Nazis. "With the Hitlerites in power," asked Pius XI the previous spring, "what could one hope for?"[7] But within weeks of Hitler's appointment, he began to have a more positive view. "I have changed my opinion about Hitler," he told the surprised French ambassador in early March. "It is the first time that such a government voice has been raised to denounce bolshevism in such categorical terms, joining with the voice of the pope."

"These words," French ambassador Charles-Roux recalled, "pronounced with a firm voice and with a kind of recklessness, proved to me how much the new German chancellor had gained in Pius XI's eyes by launching a declaration of war to the death against Communism."[8] Britain's envoy to the Vatican similarly noted how obsessed the pope seemed to be with the Communist threat. It was impossible to understand Pius's actions, he argued, without realizing this.[9]

The pope's surprisingly positive view of Hitler produced consternation and confusion among Germany's Church leaders. In the campaign for the March 1933 elections, the German Catholic bishops had unanimously denounced the Nazis and strongly supported the Center Party. On March 12 the pope met with Cardinal Michael von Faulhaber, archbishop of Munich, to tell him of the need to change course. On his return to Germany, the archbishop informed his colleagues. "Let us meditate on the words of the Holy Father," Faulhaber reported, "who, in a consistory, without mentioning his name, indicated Adolf Hitler before the whole world as the statesman who first, after the pope himself, has raised his voice against Bolshevism." On March 23 Hitler reciprocated by declaring that the Christian churches were "the most important factors in the maintenance of our national identity." He pledged to protect "the influence to which the Christian confessions are entitled in school and education." Two days later, speaking with

Cardinal Pacelli, the pope expressed his appreciation of what Hitler had said, praising his "good intentions." By the end of the month, the German bishops announced that they would no longer oppose the Nazi leader.[10]

In May Charles-Roux again remarked on the pope's positive view of Hitler. "The pontiff, impulsive by nature and obsessed with his phobia for Communism," the French ambassador observed, "has allowed himself a moment of enthusiasm" for the Nazi leader. Conscious of the value of Church support, Italian government officials shared their own successful "recipes" for winning Church approval with their Nazi counterparts.[11]

The pope was eager to reach an understanding with the Nazi government that would protect the Church's influence in Germany. Cardinal Pacelli, an able negotiator, saw the Center Party as one of the Holy See's major bargaining chips. By offering to end Church support for the party, he believed, the Vatican could extract guarantees protecting the rights of Catholic associations in Germany. But he did not reckon on the precipitous effect that the withdrawal of the bishops' support would have on the Center Party itself. Before he could reach a deal with Hitler, the party announced its own dissolution.[12]

In July, Cardinal Pacelli escorted the German vice chancellor Franz von Papen into his Vatican apartment. The concordat they signed there guaranteed the German Church the right to manage its own affairs and offered various protections for priests, religious orders, and Church property. But much of its language, particularly that dealing with Catholic associations and schools, was vague.[13]

Heinrich Brüning, the Center Party leader who had served as Germany's chancellor from 1930 to 1932, was irate. The Vatican, he fumed, had sold out the Catholic party and cast its lot with Hitler. He blamed Cardinal Pacelli, who, he charged, misunderstood the nature of Nazism. Pacelli's faith in the "system of concordats," Brüning later wrote in his memoir, "led him and the Vatican to despise democracy and the parliamentary system."[14]

THE POPE SOON REALIZED that his "pact with the devil"—as the Church historian Hubert Wolf has described it—was not going to turn out the way he hoped.[15] At the same time they signed the concordat, the Nazis introduced their Law for the Prevention of Hereditarily Diseased Offspring, which mandated the forced sterilization of those deemed defective—in clear contrast with Church doctrine. Hitler also began moving against the Church's dense network of parochial schools. The Nazis wanted a church they could fully control. In early fall the Vatican secretary of state office produced an alarming analysis of these efforts; it included the text of a song popular in the Hitler Youth, calling Hitler their "redeemer."[16] In October the editor of Italy's most prominent Catholic newspaper, *L'Avvenire d'Italia,* warned that the Nazis were working toward "a German national church in which Protestants and Catholics are to be mixed together."[17] In December, in his annual Christmas address to the cardinals, Pius XI voiced his disappointment with the Nazi government. Pacelli and von Papen had signed the concordat only five months earlier.[18]

While the pope's doubts about Hitler were growing, those closest to him were trying to keep relations as harmonious as possible. In early 1934 both Cardinal Pacelli and the papal nuncio in Germany, Monsignor Cesare Orsenigo, cautioned the pope against saying anything that would anger Hitler, lest it further undermine the Church's position.[19] In Berlin, Orsenigo had help in his efforts, having retained Pacelli's personal assistant from his time as nuncio, the German Father Eduard Gehrmann. As one Vatican observer put it, Father Gehrmann "believed more in Hitler than in Christ."[20]

The fact that Pius XI chose Cesare Orsenigo as nuncio to Nazi Germany reveals much about the pope. Other than the nuncio to Italy, there was no more crucial, or complex, diplomatic assignment in the Vatican, yet Orsenigo was a man of limited intelligence and even more limited worldview. Born near the pope's hometown, in the Lake Como region north of Milan, Orsenigo like the pope had a father who was a silk factory supervisor. His father's two brothers married his mother's two sisters, daughters of a silk factory supervisor in a nearby town. Each of the three couples produced a son who would become a priest. Ordained in 1896, Orsenigo served in a Milan parish, and in 1912 he added the title of canon at Milan's Duomo.

Orsenigo had hitherto lived solely in the confines of the Church in and around Milan; he had neither diplomatic experience nor any evident interest in international affairs. Yet barely four months after Pius became pope, he appointed Orsenigo nuncio to Holland, with the title of archbishop. The appointment triggered considerable muttering among the upper clergy, who saw it as but the latest example of the pope choosing his friends from Milan rather than the men of the hierarchy with the most expertise. Cardinal Gasparri presided over Orsenigo's episcopal consecration ceremony; the Milanese priest proudly wore the cross that Pius had given him to honor the occasion, but aside from some students from the Lombard seminary in Rome, who served as altar attendants, the church was empty.

After spending two years in Holland, Orsenigo became nuncio to Hungary. In 1928, while Orsenigo was back in Rome for a visit, one of Mussolini's informers speculated that the pope might choose him to replace Cardinal Gasparri as secretary of state. The pope valued above all, thought the informer, men of unquestionable loyalty. Such a move would be a boon to the regime, the informer added, for Orsenigo was less astute and more pliable than the wily Gasparri.[21]

Although the pope passed over Orsenigo for his new secretary of state, he chose him to replace Pacelli as nuncio to Germany. Both Hitler and Cardinal Pacelli would come to view Orsenigo as a lightweight. Certainly Pacelli, himself a former nuncio to Germany, never felt the need to ask for advice about how to deal with Berlin. Cautious and conscientious, Orsenigo worried continually about offending Hitler. Later, when relations with Nazi Germany became Pius's central concern, he would not replace Orsenigo. The pope wanted neither an independent thinker nor a saber-rattler as his ambassador to Hitler. The mediocre Orsenigo would remain in his post under the next pope throughout the dramatic years of the world war.[22]

Worried about anti-Catholic elements in the Nazi movement, the pope was especially upset about *The Myth of the Twentieth Century*, written by Alfred Rosenberg, the Nazis' foremost theoretician. Rosenberg argued that God created humans as separate races; the superior Aryan race was destined to rule over the others. Jesus was an Aryan, he explained, but his Jewish apostles had polluted his teachings. Catholicism was the bastardized product of this Jewish influence. In early 1934 the Holy Office placed this German best seller on the Index of Prohibited Books.[23] Hitler himself kept some distance from it, and so for a time some in the Vatican could attribute the Nazis' anti-Catholic bent not to Hitler but to the party's anticlerical wing. It was a familiar story in the Vatican, where anti-Church actions in Italy were commonly blamed not on Mussolini but on the anticlerics around him.

In his efforts to persuade Hitler to honor the concordat, Pius turned repeatedly to Mussolini for help.[24] In the spring of 1934, when the Duce was preparing for his first encounter with Hitler, the pope sent him instructions.[25] He wanted Mussolini to extract assurances from Hitler that he would observe the concordat. Although it had been in force for less than a year, the Nazis were already ignoring it. Mussolini was also to convey a warning: Hitler would be wise not to harass Germany's bishops, for while "they can do him a great deal of good, they could also—albeit not wanting to have to—do him a great deal of harm as the Catholics will side with them."

Pius also asked Mussolini to persuade Hitler "to free himself from certain acolytes who are making him look bad," notably Alfred Rosenberg and Joseph Goebbels, the minister of propaganda. The pope thought both were encouraging attacks on the Catholic Church. The archbishop of Munich, Cardinal Faulhaber, had recently prepared a troubling report on Goebbels, whose writings, including a popular novel he wrote in the 1920s, combined a strong belief in God and Jesus Christ with disdain for the Church and the clergy. "I converse with

Christ," wrote Goebbels in his book. "I believed I had overcome him, but I have only overcome his idolatrous priests and false servants. Christ is harsh and relentless." To make matters worse, Goebbels, a Catholic, had recently married a Protestant divorcée and was, reported the archbishop, a "notorious homosexual." Receiving the pope's request, the Duce was more than happy to play the role of wise statesman and promised to do everything the pontiff asked.[26]

Mussolini was not looking forward to the meeting. The Nazis' goal of creating a greater Germany, uniting all ethnic Germans, inevitably meant they would try to annex Austria. This went directly against Italy's foreign policy, which regarded Austria as part of an Italian sphere of influence and a buffer against an overly aggressive Germany.[27] Mussolini was a strong supporter of Engelbert Dollfuss, the Christian Social head of the Austrian government, who had suspended parliamentary government in March 1933 in response to Nazi-provoked unrest. That same summer Dollfuss, with his wife and children in tow, had visited Mussolini at his summer retreat at Riccione, on Romagna's Adriatic coast, to seek his help.[28] Shortly after Dollfuss returned to Vienna, an Austrian Nazi shot him, wounding him in the arm and ribs.[29]

The Führer landed at Venice's airport on the morning of June 14, 1934, where the well-tanned Duce greeted him. Mussolini wore a magnificent uniform with rows of medals adorning his chest, a black Fascist fez, a dagger wedged in his belt, and knee-high black boots. Hitler wore a yellow trench coat, a floppy brown velvet hat, a dark suit, and simple black shoes. He looked, observed one witness, like "a laborer dressed in his Sunday best." The pasty German would long suffer by comparison with the virile Mussolini, who delighted in baring his chest in an unending variety of poses. Hitler would never let himself be seen less than fully clothed, and even during his stint in prison in the 1920s he had insisted on wearing a tie every day. While Mussolini reveled in driving fast cars and piloting planes, Hitler preferred to sit in the back of his oversize Mercedes, surrounded by bodyguards, looking, in the words of biographer Ian Kershaw, like "an eccentric gangster."[30]

As he emerged from the plane, the Führer was clearly embarrassed.

The confident Mussolini strode up to him and raised his arm in Fascist salute. Word would later spread that, as Hitler raised his arm in response, Mussolini murmured "*Ave imitatore!*" ("Hail, imitator!"). The impression Hitler made would feed Mussolini's feeling that he was dealing with a poor copy of the original, a sense that would later prove dangerous.[31]

Proud of his fluent German, the Duce insisted on meeting with Hitler alone. He had even taken lessons to improve his German in the weeks leading up to the meeting. But Mussolini found it difficult to follow Hitler's long rants, as much due to the boredom they induced as to any linguistic limitations.[32] His belief that Hitler was a bit crazed only grew over the next two days. Their meeting was not helped by an infestation of mosquitoes, described as "big as quail," nor by Hitler's vaunting of the superiority of the Nordic race compared to the partially "negroid" origins of southern Europeans. The biggest source of tension continued to be Austria, for Hitler made no secret of his goal of uniting it with Germany.

"What a clown!" quipped Mussolini as Hitler's plane took off.[33] The man boasted of the superiority of the German race. But as Mussolini delighted in telling Italian audiences, when the likes of Caesar, Cicero, Virgil, and Augustus were gracing Rome's magnificent palaces, the illiterate savages who were the Nazis' ancestors lived in filthy hovels in the forest.[34]

Following the Venice meeting, Mussolini wrote to his ambassador to the Holy See, Cesare De Vecchi, to fill him in. "I will spare you all the idiotic things that Hitler said about Jesus Christ being of the Jewish race, etc."[35] When Hitler talked about the Catholic Church, Mussolini told De Vecchi a few days later, "it was as if he had prepared a phonograph record on the subject and proceeded to play it for ten minutes until the end." Hitler had ranted that the Church was nothing but one of the Jews' mystifications. "This Jew," said Hitler, meaning Jesus Christ, had found a way to fool the entire Western world. "Thank goodness," he told Mussolini, "that you [Italians] succeeded in injecting more than a little paganism [into the Catholic Church], making its center in Rome and using it for your own ends." While he was himself Catholic, Hitler added, he could see no good purpose that Catholicism served in Germany.[36]

Mussolini told the pope none of this, other than vaguely alluding to Hitler's *sciocchezze,* nonsense, about Jesus being a Jew. Worried that if the pope learned what Hitler had said, it would only make matters worse, Mussolini offered De Vecchi an expurgated account of his conversation to use with the Vatican. He should let the pope know that he had done his best and that it might be possible in the future for him to get the Nazi leader to take a more conciliatory view.[37]

A month later armed Nazis, disguised in Austrian army uniforms, burst into Chancellor Dollfuss's office and shot him dead. Earlier that day his wife and children had arrived at Mussolini's summer home on the Adriatic, where Dollfuss was scheduled to join them. It fell to the Duce to tell them the news.[38]

Pius was despondent. Only the previous year, Dollfuss had come to Rome to sign a concordat between Austria and the Holy See. The pope knew him and regarded him as a loyal Catholic. "It's horrible! It's horrible!" he kept repeating. Sitting at his desk, he looked down, his head in his hands. When he finally looked up, he asked, "What can we do? What can we do?"[39]

Cardinal Pacelli had had a less enthusiastic view of the Austrian leader. In July 1933, when Dollfuss had learned that the Vatican was about to sign a concordat with Hitler, he became angry, convinced it would undermine Austrian resistance to a Nazi takeover. Knowing that Dollfuss had written a document expressing this view, Pacelli asked the Austrian ambassador to the Holy See for a favor. It would be good, said Pacelli, if Dollfuss's account could be removed from the Austrian diplomatic archives.[40]

THROUGHOUT THESE MONTHS, the pope received frequent reports detailing the Nazis' campaign against the Jews. In early March 1933, just before the German elections, Hitler had assured a group of bishops that he would protect the Church's rights, its schools, and its organizations. In an apparent effort to win their support, he added that they were all allies in the same struggle, the battle against the Jews. "I have been attacked for my way of dealing with the Jewish question," Hitler told them. "For 1500 years the Church has considered the Jews to be harmful, exiling them to the ghetto. . . . I am furnishing Christianity with the greatest service."[41]

In April the pope received a letter from Edith Stein, a forty-one-year-old German philosopher in Munich who had converted from Judaism eleven years earlier. Stein begged him to speak out against the Nazis' campaign against the Jews—a campaign waged by a government that called itself "Christian" and was using Christian images to support its efforts. "For weeks," she wrote, "not only Jews but also thousands of faithful Catholics in Germany and, I believe, in the whole world, have been waiting and hoping for the Church of Christ to raise its voice to put a stop to this misuse of Christ's name. What is this idolatry of race and state power which the radio hammers into the masses day by day if not in fact sheer heresy?" She concluded with a prescient plea: "All of us who are truthful children of the Church and who are observing conditions in Germany closely fear the worst for the reputation of the Church if the silence goes on any longer."

Cardinal Pacelli, replying on the pope's behalf, wrote not to Stein but to the arch-abbot who had forwarded her letter to the Vatican. Pacelli told him to let Stein know that he had shown her letter to the pope. He added a prayer that God might protect His Church in these difficult times. That was it.[42]

Perhaps surprisingly, Edith Stein's faith remained strong. Before the year was out, she took vows to become a Carmelite nun. In the late 1930s, she would seek refuge in the Netherlands. On August 2, 1942, the Nazis seized her and her sister Rosa, both Jews in their eyes, and shipped them to Auschwitz. With their last breaths, they inhaled the gas chamber's fumes.[43]

Around the time when Stein wrote her plea to the pope, Orsenigo sent Cardinal Pacelli a telegram. The Nazis had proclaimed anti-

Semitism to be official government policy. A boycott had been called of all Jewish-owned stores and businesses, as well as of Jewish doctors, lawyers, and professionals. On April 7 a law was passed dismissing Jews from the civil service. In reporting all this, Orsenigo cautioned the pope not to interfere. "Intervention by the Holy See's representative," the nuncio warned, "would be equivalent to a protest against the government."

The pope followed his nuncio's advice and remained silent.[44] Strikingly, it was Mussolini, not Pius XI, who in these early months of Nazi rule was urging Hitler to stop persecuting the Jews. On March 30 Mussolini sent a confidential note to his ambassador in Berlin instructing him to meet with Hitler immediately and advise him that his anti-Semitic campaign was a mistake: it would "increase moral pressure and economic reprisals on the part of international Judaism." He wanted to be sure that Hitler understood he was offering this advice in an effort to be helpful. "Every regime has not only the right but the duty to eliminate from positions of influence those elements that are not completely trustworthy," he argued, "but doing this on the basis of Semitic vs. Aryan race can be damaging." It was not only Jews who would turn against the Nazi regime, Mussolini warned, if he went ahead with his campaign: "The anti-Semitism question can serve as an anti-Hitler rallying point by enemies who are Christians as well." The next day the Italian ambassador met with the Führer to pass on the Duce's advice.[45] The pope was aware of it. A note in the Vatican secretary of state files reports that Mussolini's plea to Hitler "was taken and read to Hitler and Goebbels a half hour before the Ministers' meeting that approved the law that dismisses the state employees of Semitic race."[46]

Rejecting Mussolini's advice, Hitler continued on his murderous path. In 1935 the Nuremberg Laws prohibited marriages between Jews and non-Jews and stripped Jews of their German citizenship. Reporting on the national congress of the Nazi Party that year, Orsenigo informed the Vatican that the Nazis were justifying their persecution by blaming the Jews for Communism. "I don't know if all of Russian Bolshevism has been the exclusive work of the Jews," the nuncio reported, "but here they have found a way to make people believe it and to act accordingly against Judaism." He concluded ominously, "If, as seems likely, the Nazi government is going to last a long time, the Jews are destined to disappear from this nation."[47]

That Germany's Catholic population would find the notion of a Jewish conspiracy wholly believable should hardly be a surprise. For years, the Vatican-vetted *La Civiltà cattolica*—among many other Church publications—had warned that Jews were the evil force behind a dangerous conspiracy. They were said to be the secret masters of both Communism and capitalism, all aimed at enslaving Christians.[48] The only notable difference in the Nazi version—other than the additional layer of pseudobiology—was the omission of the Protestants.

Among the most influential Vatican figures pushing this conspiracy theory was Włodzimierz Ledóchowski, head of the Jesuit order. In a handwritten letter in 1936, Ledóchowski urged the pope to issue a worldwide warning about the "terrible danger that grows more menacing each day." The danger came from Moscow's atheistic Communist propaganda—all the product of Jews, he said—while "the great world press, it too under Jewish control, barely speaks of it. . . . An encyclical on this argument," he advised, would, "lead not only the Catholics but others as well to a more energetic and better organized resistance."[49]

Sharing Ledóchowski's belief that Communism posed a grave danger, Pius XI agreed to have a special encyclical prepared and, over the following months, frequently sent him drafts for his comments and suggestions. Unhappy that they said nothing about the Jews, Ledóchowski kept pushing the pope to add language linking them to the Communist danger. "It seems necessary to us in such an encyclical," he advised, in reaction to one such draft, "to at least make an allusion to the Jewish influence, being certain that not only were the intellectual authors of communism (Marx, Lassalle,[50] etc.) all Jews, but also that the communist movement in Russia was staged by Jews. And now, too, although not always openly in every region, if you look more deeply into it, it is the Jews who are the primary champions and promoters of communist propaganda."

Next to Ledóchowski's line about the Jews being responsible for Communism in Russia, the pope scribbled a single word, *Verificare*—Verify. He would issue his encyclical denouncing Communism a month later under the name *Divini redemptoris,* but much to the disappointment of the Jesuit head, it would say nothing about Jews.[51]

La Civiltà cattolica showed no such scruples, doing all it could to frighten Catholics about the dangerous Jewish conspiracy. A few months after the pope issued his anti-Communist encyclical, the journal published yet another warning, titled "The Jewish Question." It got to the point with its first sentence: "Two facts, which seem contradictory, are established among the Jews spread around the modern world: their domination over money and their preponderance in socialism and communism." Not only were the founders of Communism Jews, according to the Jesuit journal, but "the most recent revolutionary leaders of modern socialism and bolshevism are all Jews."[52]

While Hitler was developing his own plan for dealing with the Jewish threat, the Jesuit journal considered the proper Christian response. It listed three possibilities. Best would be to convert all Jews to Christianity, but clearly this was not going to happen, for Jews stubbornly insisted on remaining Jews. The second possibility was to relocate Europe's Jews to Palestine. But the land could not support all sixteen million of them, and even if it could, the Jews would never do the necessary work, for they were "uniquely endowed with the faculty of being parasites, and destroyers have no aptitude and no taste for manual labor."

There remained only the third option, the approach that the Church had used so successfully for centuries: strip Jews of their rights as citizens.[53]

Later in the same issue, *La Civiltà cattolica* reported on the recent Nazi congress in Nuremberg, held in September 1936. "With indefatigable tenacity," Hitler told the crowd, "the Jewish revolutionary headquarters prepares world revolution." After citing these remarks, the journal quoted, without comment, Hitler's assertion that 98 percent of the top positions in Russia were "in the hands of the Jews." In the years leading up to the Holocaust, both the Nazis and the Jesuit journal would keep hammering on this claim.[54] Yet of 417 members of the highest leadership bodies in the Soviet Union in the mid-1920s, only 6 percent came from Jewish backgrounds, and this figure dropped sharply in the 1930s, not least because Stalin's purge trials had strong anti-Semitic undertones. In 1938, while *La Civiltà cattolica* and the Nazi government continued to warn that almost all the leaders of the USSR were Jewish, the most powerful body in the Soviet government, the nine-man Politburo, had only one member of Jewish origin. Of the thirty-seven members of the USSR Presidium, one came from a Jewish background.[55]

In his 1932 meeting with Mussolini, the pope had expressed his own preoccupation with the Russian Communist threat and had linked it to the "anti-Christian loathing of Judaism." But much had happened since then. Hitler had come to power and was not only undermining the influence of the Church in Germany but spreading a pagan ideology antithetical to the Christian message. It was becoming ever clearer to Pius XI that the greatest danger facing Christianity came from the Nazis. But his advisers disagreed, viewing Hitler as the Church's best hope for stopping the Communist advance. They urged the pope not to offend him.

CHAPTER

SIXTEEN

CROSSING THE BORDER

MUSSOLINI'S AMBITIONS—AND EGO—WERE GROWING EVER LARGER.
He wanted to be seen as the man who restored Rome to its ancient grandeur. For this a new empire was needed. His sights turned to
Ethiopia, which, aside from Liberia, was the only part of Africa not already in European hands. It also had the advantage of having two Italian colonies, Italian Somaliland and Eritrea, on its borders.

The Duce had already hinted at his intentions. In late 1934, Ethiopian forces had fired on a group of Italian soldiers at Wal Wal, well
across the Ethiopian border from Italian Somaliland. Italy's press cast
the incident as an assault on the nation's honor. Mussolini threatened
war unless Ethiopia apologized and offered compensation.[1] With
much fanfare, he sent several army divisions to Somalia and a fleet of
ships to the Red Sea, telling them to await further instructions.[2] Pius
XI, far from happy, worried that an Italian invasion of Ethiopia would
put Catholic missionaries throughout Africa at risk.

The pope was meanwhile becoming ever more conscious of his age.
The exertions of the latest Holy Year, which had ended at Easter 1934,
had left him exhausted. He had given up his brisk strolls through the
Vatican gardens and found that even walking down the hall left him out

of breath. The heat was also bothering him.[3] In the poorer parts of the old city and in the rapidly expanding shantytowns on the outskirts, electricity and running water were rare, and tuberculosis and trachoma all too common.[4] The previous year Rome had been struck by a typhus epidemic. In the summer of 1934, the elderly pope looked forward to returning to his summer palace in the Alban Hills. "You can see how happy he is," observed Domenico Tardini, Pizzardo's assistant, on the day of the pope's departure. "He seems to be just like a schoolboy about to go on a vacation." Tardini took advantage of the pope's unusually jolly mood to get 34,000 lire from him for Russian relief. "Ah," wrote Tardini, "if the pope would only leave more often!"[5]

As one informant reported, the pope was now, "if possible, even more irascible, surly, and suspicious."[6] At public functions, dressed in his elaborate white robes, he projected a sense of regal immobility that made everyone around him seem fidgety and nervous. His fringe of hair was sprinkled with gray, but his voice was still firm and resonant, and his eyes, behind his thick spectacles, were ever vigilant. And while he had slowed down physically, he insisted on being informed of everything and deciding everything.[7]

While the pope was fretting about Mussolini's threatened invasion, others in the Church took a very different view. Bologna's *L'Avvenire d'Italia,* Italy's most influential Catholic newspaper, echoed the Fascist press. Ethiopians were pagan barbarians. War would bring civilization—and Christianity—to the savages.[8]

The looming war put the pope in an impossible position. It could have disastrous consequences not only for Italy and Ethiopia but for Europe as a whole. Only the pope—so many thought—could prevent it, and calls from abroad urged him to publicly warn Mussolini to stand down. But Pius knew that defying Italy's dictator in a matter so important to him would put their alliance at risk.

On August 27, 1935, two thousand Catholic nurses from twenty countries climbed into buses at the Vatican. They were on their way to the finale of their conference, an audience with the pope at Castel Gandolfo. Pius addressed them, praising their work, speaking for over an hour. He then offered a concluding benediction. Pizzardo, who had helped organize the meeting, stood beaming alongside him. But unexpectedly, rather than leave at that point, the pontiff began reflecting on an entirely different subject. A war of conquest, he told the nurses, could never be tolerated. It would be "an unjust war, something beyond all imagination . . . it would be unspeakably horrible."[9] Pizzardo's smile melted.

"The nurses, primarily foreigners," Monsignor Tardini wrote in his diary, "listened with interest and pleasure. Listening with even greater interest, but without any pleasure, was Monsignor Pizzardo. What a disaster!" On the nurses' return bus ride, to keep them from talking about the pope's remarks, he insisted they spend the whole trip reciting the rosary. Back at the Vatican, practically in tears, Pizzardo looked "discouraged, undone, pallid, desperate." He kept murmuring the pope's words, "an 'unjust war,' an 'unjust war.'"[10]

The next morning, when news of the pope's speech reached Giuseppe Talamo, Italy's acting ambassador to the Vatican, he rushed to the Vatican.[11] "Mons. Pizzardo showed his consternation," the Italian diplomat recalled, "telling me that nothing had suggested the Pontiff's impromptu decision to address such a sensitive subject, without first in any way asking the secretary of state's office for advice."

Talamo urged Pizzardo to water down the text of the pope's speech for publication in the Vatican newspaper. Pizzardo assured him that he and his colleagues were already doing "everything possible to mitigate and attenuate" the pope's remarks. That evening the *Osservatore romano* journalist who had recorded the speech delivered a typescript of the pope's text and, with Tardini, undertook a "surgical operation." "Here I cut a word, there I add another," recalled Tardini. "Here I modify a sentence, there I erase another. In short, with a subtle and methodical effort we succeed in greatly softening the rawness of the papal thought."[12] The text they produced was far from the clear denunciation of an invasion that the nurses had heard; it was instead a murky series of propositions open to varying interpretations.

The next morning came the ticklish part. Tardini had to get the pope's approval for the butchered text. As he handed Pius the typed pages, he tried to be nonchalant. His square face assumed a look of great sincerity. The *Osservatore romano* reporter, he explained, begged the pope's forgiveness if he had not succeeded in accurately capturing the pope's every word. The pope had spoken an hour and twenty minutes, and by the end of the speech the reporter had been worn out. He had also been distracted by a terrible toothache. And by the end of the speech, the evening light—for the audience had been held outside in a courtyard—had been fading, making it especially difficult to record the pope's last words accurately.

As the pope started to read, Tardini tried to go, but Pius raised a hand and stopped him. He put aside all but the last pages and went directly to his final remarks. As he read, he grunted. Each time the pontiff raised his eyes to look at him, Tardini tried to conceal his nervousness. The pope read his mangled remarks on the war aloud. Still Tardini feigned ignorance of any problem: "I adopted the pose of one who wants to pay attention to that which he doesn't know," he later wrote, adding parenthetically, "I know that part of his speech by heart!" The pope kept looking down at the text and then up at Tardini. Every time he read a line that Tardini had altered, he repeated, "I truly did not say it that way." Every time the pope objected, Tardini meekly offered to correct any error. But in the end the pope simply said, "No, let's leave it alone." It was just what Tardini and his superiors, Pizzardo and Pacelli, had been hoping for.[13]

But even the greatly weakened text displeased the acting ambassador. While the Fascist press selectively quoted it to demonstrate the pope's support for the war, outside Italy the remarks, even in expurgated form, were being used to argue that the pope opposed it.[14] Upset that the Fascist press was claiming his speech had offered clear support for the war, the pope ordered the Vatican daily to print a front-page column expressing his displeasure at the misuse of his words. Talamo was not pleased. "To speak at this point of the well known stubbornness and senile insistence of the Pontiff," he told Mussolini, "would not be very respectful, but it would be no less true."

At his regular Friday meeting with Pacelli that week, Talamo found a sympathetic ear. "The cardinal secretary," he reported to Mussolini, "let me know his consternation."[15]

In fact, although Eugenio Pacelli had been secretary of state for several years, his relationship with Pius continued to be marked by formality and emotional distance. Earlier in the year, hearing that Jean Verdier, archbishop of Paris, was in Rome for a visit, Pacelli had asked to see him. A major ceremony was planned for April at the French pilgrimage site of Lourdes, and Pacelli was eager to take part. But he could only go if Pius asked him, and he was afraid to broach the subject himself. A bit abashed, he pleaded with Verdier to bring the matter up with the pontiff. It was through that indirect route that he won the pope's blessing for his trip.[16] Verdier described Pacelli's relationship with the pope in these years as "cordial, at least insofar as the temperament of the old pope allowed for cordiality."[17]

IN EARLY SEPTEMBER, the League of Nations met to discuss the possibility that Italy would invade Ethiopia, a member state. Should Mussolini do so, the league threatened, it would impose severe economic sanctions.[18]

Since the settlement of the Catholic Action controversy four years earlier, the pope had been increasingly public in his support for the regime. In September 1932 he celebrated a special mass at St. Peter's for thousands of youths enrolled in the Organizations of Fascists abroad who had made a pilgrimage to Rome. That same month tens of thousands of Italian Fascist youth group members spent two weeks in exercises around Rome, accompanied by a large number of priests, their hats bearing a cross lying atop the Fascist emblem. The pope received hundreds of these priests at the Vatican and blessed them for their important work.[19]

The Vatican's enthusiasm for the Duce was again on display on the tenth anniversary of the March on Rome. *L'Osservatore romano*'s support for the dictator could scarcely have been more enthusiastic. Mussolini had worked "vast, profound, colossal changes in all branches of public administration," the Vatican daily reported. Ever since his first address in parliament in 1921, he had "exalted the incomparable beauty of the Catholic idea and the Church's mission in the world." The paper reminded readers that it was Mussolini who had placed the crucifix in the nation's schoolrooms and courtrooms. It was he who had introduced religious education in the schools and brought amity between church and state through the Lateran Accords.[20]

IN THE WEEKS FOLLOWING Pius XI's unscripted remarks to the nurses, Cardinal Pacelli and Monsignor Pizzardo tried to persuade the pope to keep his opposition to Mussolini's war to himself. On September 13 Pacelli sent word to Mussolini that the pope would not stand in the way of an invasion.[21]

But the pontiff still held out hope that he could dissuade Mussolini. On September 20 he dictated a letter to him setting out the reasons why the war would be a mistake. Although Italy had by far the greater military force, the Ethiopians would take advantage of the difficult terrain, which they knew better. Even if Italy were to conquer the country, the pope predicted—presciently as it turned out—Italian forces would face unending guerrilla attacks, not to mention the difficulties brought by high temperature and disease.[22]

Worried that a formal letter from the pope opposing the war would anger Mussolini, Pacelli persuaded him to have Tacchi Venturi convey his thoughts informally instead. Pius called in the Jesuit and gave him a text to use but cautioned him not to let Mussolini have a copy. The typescript, prepared by Pacelli, began by expressing sympathy for the Duce's stated aims of giving Italy space for expansion and exercising its right of defense. It then listed the pope's concerns, stressing the one thought most likely to sway the Duce: the likelihood that if things went badly, Mussolini would be blamed.[23]

None of this made any impression on the dictator. On the evening of October 2, he strode onto the balcony of Palazzo Venezia and electrified the crowd with the news that he had ordered Italian troops to march into Ethiopia. Buildings shook as tens of thousands took up the rhythmic chant: "Duce! Duce! Duce!"

From a large window on the opposite side of the piazza, Margherita Sarfatti gazed out at the scene. Although her allure as a lover had passed, and in recent years he had pushed her away, she had remained a faithful and effective propagandist for Mussolini, especially abroad. But the recent rise of the Nazis in Germany had filled her with increasing horror. Launching a war in defiance of the League of Nations and risking war with Britain and France, she knew, would mean driving Italy into Hitler's hands. Something was going terribly wrong.

Sarfatti turned to a friend standing next to her and remarked: "It is the beginning of the end."

"Why do you say that?" he asked. "Do you think we will lose this war?"

"No . . . I say it because unfortunately we will win it . . . and he will lose his head."[24]

The next day Tacchi Venturi, ever eager to promote goodwill between the Duce and Pius, assured Mussolini that the pope would not get in the way of his war plans. "In this most serious time," he wrote, "the Holy Father was satisfied with what he learned through me, and he told me not to fail to use the first possible occasion to tell you of his pleasure."[25]

Worried that the invasion would isolate Italy, the pope took the extraordinary step of sending a plea to Britain's King George V. It was not his first attempt—back in August he had tried to send a message to the king via the archbishop of Westminster, but learning what lay behind the archbishop's request for a meeting, the king invented a pretext not to see him.[26]

Cardinal Pacelli prepared a new letter to the king in English. "Your Majesty," it began, "the Holy Father has entrusted to me the special and personal charge of laying before Your Majesty the following matter in a very confidential manner." The pope "does not see how it will be possible to avoid the conflict with Ethiopia because Italy has been refused the minimum which he believes it has a right to claim in virtue of the accords, that is to say, a simple Mandate (not indeed a Protectorate) over the peripheral regions of the Ethiopian Empire." Mussolini's demands were reasonable, Pacelli said, explaining that the parts of Ethiopia involved were areas where "slavery and disorder" reigned, and where the Negus—Ethiopia's ruler, Haile Selassie—had little influence.

The astonished British envoy took the envelope from Pacelli and cabled London for instructions. The British foreign minister refused to accept the letter. The pope's plea was returned unopened.[27]

AT DAWN ON OCTOBER 3, 110,000 men, under the command of General Emilio De Bono, the goateed leader of the March on Rome, crossed south from Eritrea into Ethiopia. The troops included not only Italian soldiers but Eritreans and Somalis under Italian command. Joining in the invasion were assorted partially trained groups of Fascist militia, proud and excited to finally get their chance to do something tangible for the Duce and the Fatherland. The forces stretched across a front seventy kilometers wide, with 2,300 machine guns, 230 cannons, and 156 tanks. One hundred twenty-six planes stood ready in Eritrean airports to provide air cover. Within a few hours one unit came across a small fort, and the first Italian soldier was killed. The Italians, who until then had happily occupied themselves by singing patriotic songs, looked on with horror as a medic covered their comrade's bloody body with a sheet. "No one thought that you could die so quickly," commented one of them. Soon Italian planes were dropping their incendiary bombs on the nearby town of Adua. Mussolini's sons, Bruno and Vittorio, each piloted a Caproni 101 in the raid; Italian forces reduced much of the town, including its hospital, to a heap of ashes. Hundreds of residents died. The Italians pushed on.[28]

A few days after the invasion, in a 54 to 4 vote, the League of Nations imposed sanctions on Italy, applying them to all Italian imports and to those exports deemed useful to the war effort, although excluding oil.[29]

Later the same week Count Bonifacio Pignatti, the new Italian ambassador to the Holy See, presented his credentials to the pope. The announcement earlier in the year that Cesare De Vecchi was leaving the ambassadorship to become minister of education had been greeted with concern in the Vatican, where he had come to be viewed as a friend.[30]

The fifty-seven-year-old Pignatti, ambassador to France and a thirty-year veteran of the Italian diplomatic corps, offered a striking contrast with his predecessor. De Vecchi had come to his post with no diplomatic experience, his claim to fame stemming from his days as Fascist boss of Turin and one of the leaders of the March on Rome. Pignatti, by contrast, had served in Italian embassies all across Europe and South America. Of average height, his hair largely turned gray, he fit comfortably into his formal ambassador's suits. In short, unlike the outrageous De Vecchi, he looked very much like a diplomat.[31]

At the new ambassador's first meeting with Pius XI, the pontiff appeared tired and listless, although as they talked about the war, he became more animated. While the pope expressed optimism that French efforts at mediation might work, Pignatti was dubious. The pope raised no word of protest about the recently launched invasion and further pleased Pignatti by expressing his poor opinion of the League of Nations.[32]

The British envoy to the Holy See, who also noted the change in the pope's attitude, offered an explanation. The pope had strongly disapproved of the impending war and had tried to dissuade Mussolini from going ahead with it. But once the Duce launched it, he did not want to undermine the war effort, "being afraid that the fall of fascism might result from an unsuccessful war, and that a Communist or anti-clerical régime might seize power, with disastrous results for the Papacy." The French ambassador, for his part, saw some pathos in the pope's plight: the imperious pope felt powerless in the face of the pro-war zealotry of his own Italian clergy, yet he was pained by the poor impression his silence was making abroad.[33]

Italy's Catholic clergy did all they could to whip up popular enthusiasm for the war. On October 28, in a ceremony in Milan's beautiful cathedral, marking the thirteenth anniversary of the March on Rome, Cardinal Ildefonso Schuster gave a stirring homily that attracted international attention. A Benedictine monk known for his ascetic severity, Schuster had become archbishop of Milan in 1929. Like the pope, he thought Western civilization was locked in an epic battle between good and evil, a struggle of the godly against the demonic. He saw Mussolini and the Fascist regime as crucial Church allies. "Cardinal Schuster," remarked Cesare De Vecchi, "lacked only a black shirt, as for the rest he was as closely in tune with the party line as the most diligent party member."[34]

A few months before the mass commemorating the March on Rome, Cardinal Schuster had deposited a bouquet of flowers at the altar to the fallen Fascists and stopped to pray for their souls. "The cardinal's act," wrote an informant in Milan, "was very favorably remarked upon in the various circles where one sees the ever increasing fascistization of the clergy."[35] At the celebratory mass in the Duomo, Fascist government authorities, militiamen, and party bigwigs surrounded the cardinal as he explained that the commemoration of the March on Rome was not simply a political celebration "but an essentially Catholic holiday." Fascism had brought about the restoration of Catholic Italy, and the war in Ethiopia should be seen in this light. Together the Church and the Fascist state had a holy "national and Catholic mission" to perform at a time when "in the fields of Ethiopia Italy's flag triumphantly brings the Cross of Christ, smashes the chains of the slaves, and prepares the way for the Missionaries of the Gospel."[36]

Mussolini had the speech rebroadcast on Italian radio, and the cardinal's picture decorated the cover of a popular newsweekly.[37] His colleagues in France, however, were less pleased. "Cardinal Schuster," wrote Alfred Baudrillart—a cardinal as of late 1935—"is a convinced fascist."[38]

During the tense months of the war, the Duce looked to the Church not only for domestic support but for international help as well. He was especially eager to enlist the pope's aid in preventing the League of Nations' economic sanctions from spreading.[39]

In a number of long conversations with Cardinal Pacelli in mid-November, Pignatti urged the Vatican to enlist its nuncios' help for the war effort. Convincing bishops and other influential Catholics around the world of the justness of Italy's war aims would be crucial. The cardinal replied that such efforts were well under way—and that the Vatican had already accomplished quite a bit. Pacelli went so far as to add some advice of his own. It was critical, he told Mussolini, to win American support. The Duce should launch "an intense and intelligent Italian propaganda in the United States in the newspapers, in the universities, in the magazines, with means and forms best suited to the North American mentality."[40]

As Pacelli knew, Mussolini was worried that the United States—not a League of Nations member—might join the international boycott. Previously, both Republican and Democratic administrations had taken a benevolent view of the dictator, thinking that he offered the strong leadership that the rather aimless and undisciplined Italians needed. President Roosevelt, although having little personal sympathy for Mussolini, had expressed his belief that the Duce had accomplished a good deal for Italy. America's press had also been supportive. But the war triggered a precipitous change. American newspapers increasingly noted similarities between Fascist Italy and Nazi Germany. "A tyrant remains a tyrant no matter how benevolently he may philosophize and smile," editorialized *The New York Times*. Roosevelt took a much dimmer view as well, and in early 1936 he would publicly denounce Italian Fascism.[41]

The coordinated campaign by the Italian government and the Vatican, aimed largely at the Italian American community, proved successful. The Italian American press continued to support Mussolini. In Philadelphia, two hundred thousand Italian Americans marched to protest the League sanctions.[42] In other cities with large Italian immigrant populations, similar rallies were held, and petitions flooded Congress. Most influential of all, radio priest Charles Coughlin, who broadcast to tens of millions of Americans every Sunday, blasted the sanctions week after week.[43]

Born to Irish immigrant parents in 1891 in Hamilton, Ontario, and ordained in Toronto, Coughlin had moved to Detroit in the early 1920s, preaching at a simple frame church he built there. He soon started a modest radio program devoted to religious topics. By 1930 the young priest was broadening his scope, focusing on the plight of the poor. He supported Roosevelt during his first bid for the presidency in 1932 but soon turned against him and in 1934 founded his own political party, the National Union of Social Justice. Around this time he began to denounce "Jewish bankers" and to embrace Mussolini. As contributions poured in, Coughlin—now the most popular religious figure in the country—replaced his modest wood frame church with an ultramodern sanctuary. Its most striking feature was the large stone tower that rose above it, topped by a powerful radio transmitter. His fulminations alarmed many in the Church hierarchy.[44]

The Pittman-McReynolds Bill, calling on the United States to join in the sanctions, triggered an outpouring of protest from the Italian American community. Overwhelmed by thousands of letters and countless Italian American delegations, the congressmen, in the words of the head of the American arms control agency, "trembled openly in their boots." The bill was defeated.[45]

Every Italian soldier bound for Ethiopia was given a copy of a new collection of prayers, *Soldier, Pray!* In his introduction to the booklet, Augusto Gemelli, the indefatigable rector of the Catholic University of Milan, urged the young Italians to battle:

> Go where the Fatherland sends you and God calls you, ready for everything. . . .
> Trust, even if God asks you to sacrifice your life. . . .
> Soldier of Italy, your sacrifice, united with the sacrifice of Our Lord Jesus Christ, God among men, will achieve the salvation and greatness of the Fatherland.[46]

Over the next months, Italy's bishops outdid one another in their fervent professions of Fascist faith and in their proclamations of divine backing for the war. Monsignor Navarra, bishop of Terracina, near Rome, captured the mood: "O Duce! . . . Today Italy is fascist and the hearts of all Italians beat as one with yours. . . . God bless you o Duce! Let Him sustain You in your daily, titanic work, and ensure . . . victory to the Italian armies."[47]

AS ITALY BECAME INCREASINGLY ISOLATED, conspiracy theories gained new momentum. Not least among them was the Protestant-Jewish-Masonic-Communist plot that many in the Church had long decried. In early November the archbishop of Amalfi sent a circular to his priests, with a message to share with parishioners in their Sunday sermons: "The League of Nations is acting under the influence of occult forces." He went on to list them: "Freemasonry, Bolshevism, Anglicanism." They were fighting Italy because they could not tolerate the sight of the Fascist regime living "in perfect collaboration with the Catholic Church."[48]

British and French denunciations of the war angered the Duce, and he feared the impact that economic sanctions might yet have. This offered a new opening for Tacchi Venturi, who had been pushing his conspiracy theories on the Duce for years.

On November 30 the Jesuit arrived at Palazzo Venezia, sent by Pius to discuss hopes for an early end to the war. He quickly turned to the subject most on his mind.

"Has Your Excellency read the articles 'Who wants the war? Behind the Ethiopian affair?' in the November 16 and 30 issues of the [French] journal *La Revue hebdomadaire*?"

"Yes, I am familiar with them."

"Then you've seen how the anonymous author clearly demonstrates that Freemasonry, tied to the Communists and Bolsheviks, has constructed a unified front with the goal of trying to bring about the end of Fascism, of Mussolini, and bringing about revolution in Italy. It is a revolution that it considers—not wrongly—the indispensable means of installing a Bolshevik empire in Italy."

Before Mussolini could reply, Tacchi Venturi completed the picture:

"Believe me, Excellency, we are dealing with a terrible trap plotted with the complicity of the League of Nations, which is under the domination of the Jews and the Masons."

Mussolini listened as the pope's emissary spun this tale of a Jewish-Masonic-Bolshevik conspiracy aimed at destroying him. By the time he finished, the dictator, agitated, shouted that Britain and France were leading much of the rest of the world against him. They were eager, he asserted, to start a European war.[49]

Mussolini said little about the Jews, but increasingly he saw opposition to the war in conspiratorial terms. When he met with Tacchi Venturi two weeks later, it was he who raised the specter of an international plot. The Third Socialist International, Freemasonry, and the Liberals had formed a common front against Italy, the Duce told the Jesuit. Their goal was "to destroy the Regime that governs it at any cost."

"No one has any doubt about this or can doubt it," the pope's envoy replied.[50]

ENEMIES IN COMMON

S PEAKING IN EARLY NOVEMBER TO A GROUP OF WOMEN IN BOLO-
gna's massive central basilica, the city's archbishop sang Mussolini's praises: "The providential Leader of our Italian people, people of
the saints—as he put it so well—of heroes, of geniuses, of colonizers,
with that intuition that is truly unique to him and who thus towers over
all in the current historical moment, has wanted to summons you Catholic, Italian women to a great mission." The archbishop of Amalfi,
echoing themes being expressed by bishops throughout the country,
blasted the evils of the sanctions as the work of Freemasons and Angli-
cans and heralded the Duce as the new Moses: "I rejoice in the future
greatness which is Italy's destiny in the world. Italy, fatherland of saints
and heroes. Italy reconciled with the Church and blessed by the Pope.
Italy placed by the Fascist Government in a moral, Christian legislative
design."[1]

The pontiff was left to deal with the foreign reaction to the Italian
clergy's unseemly war fever. Britain's emissary to the Vatican, Hugh
Montgomery, peppered the Vatican with published extracts from the
bishops' incendiary speeches and implored Pius to put an end to them.
The pope replied that he had dispatched envoys to the offenders to

encourage them to tone down their rhetoric.[2] But the speeches, and Britain's protests, continued.

Britain and France had been putting together a proposal to end the crisis, and the pope had placed great hopes in it. The plan would partition Ethiopia, giving Italy some of its most desirable land. In mid-December the deal fell through when its terms were leaked to the press and political pressures in both Britain and France blocked it. The British foreign minister resigned in disgrace.[3]

Mussolini insisted that he would make no concessions. Nothing would stop him from conquering all of Ethiopia.[4]

In late November the Duce decided to organize a Giornata della Fede, literally a Day of Faith or Day of the Wedding Ring (*fede* meaning both "faith" and "wedding ring"). It was a brilliant propaganda idea that would further tie Italians—and especially women—to the war effort. To show their love for their country and their support for the war, all good Italians were to donate their gold wedding rings to the Fatherland.

Italy's bishops were to urge Catholics to hand over their gold bands, and they were to bless the substitute steel rings the donors would get in exchange. When the bishops learned of the role they were to play, they bombarded the Vatican with requests for guidance. The pope was not eager for Italy's high clergy to take such a public part in the war effort, not least because angry letters from Catholics abroad were denouncing the Vatican's apparent embrace of the Fascist slaughter in Ethiopia. But he did not want to provoke Mussolini. Worried that a written circular to the bishops might leak out, he decided to send an emissary to pass his message on orally: "Be cautious. . . . Do not express judgment as to the right and justice of the Abyssinian campaign, and above all avoid using any words that can offend or be found displeasing to the other side."[5]

While some of the high clergy shared the pope's discomfort, the great majority found it impossible to restrain themselves.[6] If they actually got the pope's message, they ignored it. The Catholic press had been full of articles praising the holy war to bring Christianity and civilization to the savages; prominent churchmen—such as the archbishop of Milan and the rector of the Catholic University—had embraced the war; and the pope himself had never directly expressed his misgivings about it to the clergy. So bishops in their diocesan bulletins and their homilies urged all good Catholics to offer their wedding rings to the holy cause. Priests established parish committees to ensure maximum local participation and, when the day came, donated their own gold pectoral crosses.[7]

In Milan, Cardinal Schuster personally blessed 25,000 steel rings—to be given as replacements—in his private chapel.[8] The archbishop of Messina, an impoverished diocese in Sicily, informed his priests that he expected loyal Catholics to give at least thirty kilograms of gold. On the other side of the island, the bishop of Monreale required his priests to melt down the votive offerings that the faithful had donated over the years. In the Tuscan province of Grosseto, a parish priest asked permission from his bishop to melt the bells atop the church to support the Duce and the war.[9]

December 18, the Day of Faith, found the country in a patriotic frenzy.[10] Mussolini was outside Rome dedicating the new town of Pontinia, one of his creations in the former marshlands. The local archbishop kicked off the ceremony. "Oh Duce! Those who think that they can get our people to bend are deceiving themselves. . . . Today Italy is fascist, the hearts of all Italians beat in unison with yours, and the entire Nation is ready for whatever sacrifice is necessary for the triumph of peace and of Roman, Christian civilization." At the end of his remarks, the archbishop removed his pectoral cross and pastoral ring, adding them to the day's haul.[11]

Not since the days when popes ruled the Papal States had the Catholic Church been so closely identified with the government. Not since the time of the Crusades had it played such a central role in urging Catholics to foreign conquest.

War fever nourished the darkest conspiracy theories, as priests and bishops warned the faithful that countries opposing the invasion did so because of their joint hatred of both Fascist Italy and the Roman Catholic Church.[12]

The Vatican encouraged these views. The day after Christmas Monsignor Pizzardo told the Vatican's emissary to Canada that he was to counteract opposition to the Ethiopian war.[13] The opposition, he explained, took aim jointly at both Fascism and the Church. It was "an aversion that comes naturally," he added, "against a great Catholic state like Italy, which maintains good relations with the Holy See." The attacks were motivated by "the hatred of the Church's enemies who, by striking at Italy, would like to strike a blow against the Catholic Church and the Holy See."

In his reply, the Vatican envoy noted that opposition to the Ethiopian war was widespread in Canada. Unfortunately, he wrote, Protestants, Communists, and "those who are very attached to democratic principles" had long opposed Fascism. But "the good people, as well as the more dispassionate politicians, have had to admit what marvelous work Fascism had done." As for Pizzardo's warning about the Church's occult enemies, he added, he would do his best to spread the word.[14]

IN THE SAME MONTH as Mussolini held his Day of Faith, Pius XI announced the appointment of twenty new cardinals. Fourteen were Italian. Much was made of this fact: as a number of observers noted, virtually everyone in the Vatican secretary of state office was Italian, and all the nuncios were Italian. In Germany, newspaper articles and political circles linked the pope's choice of new cardinals to the Fascist regime's growing influence in the Vatican. One German newspaper ruefully noted the contrast between Italy's bishops' enthusiastic support for Mussolini's war in Ethiopia and the failure of Germany's bishops to show similar enthusiasm for the Nazi regime.[15]

Defying expectations, the new archbishop of Westminster, Arthur Hinsley, was not among those given the cardinal's hat. Two months earlier the archbishop had defended the pope by saying there was little he could do to prevent the war. "He is a poor helpless old man," he explained, "with a small police force to guard himself, to guard the priceless treasures of the Vatican, and to protect the diminutive State which ensures his due independence." The archbishop's line of defense had not pleased the pope, and his denunciation of the Fascist regime as tyrannical—a "present day deification of Caesarism"—had angered Mussolini. The pope's decision to pass over Hinsley was widely attributed to his wish not to offend the Duce.[16]

The Italian government greeted the pontiff's choices for the Sacred College warmly. Not only had he returned Italians to a clear majority but, as one police informant put it, "one can with all confidence state that of the fourteen [Italians] nominated, almost all are—more or less—friends of the Regime."[17]

Westminster's archbishop was not the only churchman slighted. On January 9 the pope called in Tacchi Venturi to tell him that, although he had wanted to name him a cardinal, he had decided the time was not right. "Poor Father," said the pope to his crestfallen envoy, "the cardinal's hat was going to go to you! But what was one to do?" Given the delicate moment internationally, making his private emissary to Mussolini a cardinal might be misinterpreted. What, asked the pope, would the English have thought? In any case, he told the Jesuit, it was too important to keep him in his current role, something that would be impossible should he become a cardinal.[18]

Among the twenty men who were given the cardinal's hat that December was the oft-accused pederast Camillo Caccia. The pope's master of ceremonies thought the promotion was long overdue. When the list of new cardinals in 1929 had come out and his name was not on it, Caccia was furious.[19] In October 1930 Turin's newspapers reported rumors that he was about to be named the city's archbishop. The stories, according to a police informant in the Vatican, prompted "rather salacious comments."[20] Another informant, in March 1931, relayed that Caccia was furious with the commander of the Papal Gendarmes for reporting on Caccia's recent intimate relationship with a young priest. The pope had learned the news and was not pleased. Earlier, the informant recalled, only his old ties with the pope had saved Caccia from the fate that Pius had meted out to Monsignor De Samper under similar circumstances.[21]

Despite the stories surrounding Caccia, rumors that the pope was about to name him a cardinal had gathered force. This led to a new burst of allegations in 1933, as others in the Vatican came forward claiming to have seen Caccia with boys and young men in compromising situations. Among them, a count from the black aristocracy—those elite Rome families who had stuck with the popes in their decades-old battle against the new Italian state—told of the time Caccia, in his apartment at the Vatican, had been caught in the act of fondling two students while plying them with wine and liquor. Interrogated, the boys, still drunk, said that Caccia had lured them to his rooms by promising them a large sum of money. Rome's clergy, claimed the informant, disliked the pope, viewing him as an ill-tempered despot. Should he go ahead, despite Caccia's predatory reputation, to name him a cardinal, his popularity, or so the informant argued, would reach a new low.[22]

Caccia got a clear sign of papal favor, and a presumption that he would at last be named a cardinal, when Pius asked him in August 1934 to be part of the papal delegation at the Eucharistic congress in Buenos Aires.[23] But around the same time, another police informant raised doubts as to the pope's intentions. One of Caccia's supporters, during an audience with the pope, had put in a good word for him, praising the hard work Caccia had done on the pope's behalf. Given his increasing girth, the friend argued, Caccia was encountering difficulty in maintaining his frenetic pace, so perhaps the time was right to reward him. The pope, irritated by the request, turned his back on his visitor. "Have him eat less!" he muttered.[24]

Yet Pius retained an affection for Caccia, whom he had known since he was a boy in Milan, and so in the end, he added him to the list of new cardinals in 1935. If the allegations against him were well known within the Vatican, they seem not to have diminished the enthusiasm of his reception among his new colleagues. "Stout, jovial and humorous," the

British ambassador to the Holy See observed in mid-1938, "Cardinal Caccia is perhaps the most popular member of the Sacred College."[25]

THE POPE CONTINUED TO worry about the impact the Ethiopian war was having on American attitudes. On January 4, echoing Pacelli's earlier suggestion, he advised the Duce to strengthen his pro-war propaganda in the United States.[26] Mussolini told the pope not to worry, for the situation was now much improved, thanks especially to that "Irish priest"—the radio preacher Father Charles Coughlin—"who has set out to combat the offensive with quintessentially American methods which are extremely efficient with Americans."[27] Ever since the sanctions were announced, Coughlin had used his half-hour national radio broadcast every Sunday to denounce them. "The League of Nations and its sanctions," he had told his millions of listeners in late November, "exist for but one single purpose—to act only when British interests are at stake."[28]

When a problem did arise in the United States, Mussolini knew he could count on those around the Vatican to help him. In early 1936 the influential U.S. Jesuit magazine *America* published an article critical of the war.[29] The Duce sent his ambassador to speak to the head of the Jesuit order to enlist his help.

Founded in the mid-sixteenth century, the Jesuits had a reputation as intellectuals of the Church, and Pius XI had continued the tradition of relying on them for advice. Elected in 1915 to be Jesuit superior general—a position he held until his death over a quarter century later—Włodzimierz Ledóchowski had come from an aristocratic Polish family. As a boy, he had served as a page in the Austrian imperial court. His father, a count, had been a cavalry officer in the Austrian army. His uncle, a cardinal, had been prominent in the Curia, serving as prefect of the Congregation for the Propagation of the Faith.[30] Ledóchowski's office, in the Jesuits' world headquarters, was but a stone's throw from the Vatican.

Prince Bernhard von Bülow, who served as chancellor of the German Empire in the first decade of the century, described Ledóchowski in his memoirs: "The General is a man of middle height with unusually intelligent eyes, the wrinkled and moulded features of a savant, and the certainty of manner of a born aristocrat." When the prince visited the Jesuit leader in Rome in 1924, he was struck by the simplicity of his room, bare except for a statue of the Virgin and a few portraits of popes. He could easily understand why Jesuit generals had always refrained from accepting appointments as cardinals: their own position was more influential.[31]

Ledóchowski had presided over a rapid expansion of the Jesuit order, bolstering its presence in the Americas while multiplying its missions in Asia. Although in some ways tyrannical and certainly austere, he was not without a sense of humor. When one of his close collaborators came to his office to see him one day, he noticed a very large fellow

**Włodzimierz Ledóchowski, superior general
of the Society of Jesus**

member of the order leaving. "Don't you know him?" asked the Jesuit general. "That is Father B, one of our best. Did you see how fat he is? When he sits down he takes up at least three seats. That's why I always send him to official ceremonies. Because the press can say: there was a large representation of the Society of Jesus."[32]

The Jesuit leader had made no secret of his enthusiasm for the Fascist regime. From the time when Mussolini came to power, he had done what he could to stamp out Church opposition to the Duce.[33]

At their meeting in early 1936, the Italian ambassador told Ledóchowski that Mussolini wanted *America*'s anti-Fascist editor fired and a pro-Fascist editor put in his place. Ledóchowski accommodated him readily. "The Father General immediately, without any hesitation," Pignatti wrote, "gave me the head of the director of the North American Jesuit magazine." Soon a new editor was in place, suitably enthusiastic about the Fascist cause.[34]

Gratified by this support, Pignatti remarked that Italy's enemies were the Church's enemies. Ledóchowski agreed. The attacks on Mussolini for waging his war in Ethiopia, he replied, were simply "a pretext from which international Judaism is profiting in order to advance its attack on western civilization."[35]

THE DUCE WAS UNDER enormous pressure. "If the League of Nations," he later told Hitler, "had followed [British foreign secretary Anthony] Eden's advice and extended the sanctions against Italy to include oil, I would have had to beat a retreat from Abyssinia within a week. It would have been an unspeakable catastrophe for me."[36] The Italian economy was suffering from the costs of the war and the sanctions. Mussolini's calm public appearance, the pope's top financial adviser told the pontiff, masked his "state of physical depression."[37]

Fascist propaganda had imagined the war would be a brief, triumphal march of a modern European army through a barren countryside defended by spear-bearing savages, but instead the Italian troops suffered one embarrassment after another. On December 6, two months after the initial invasion, when Italians began bombing the town of Dessie, a photographer snapped a picture of the emperor, Haile Selassie, personally machine-gunning Italian planes as they passed overhead. Worse, the photographer also recorded Italian planes bombing the American hospital there, its Red Cross units clearly in view. Later that month the Ethiopians massed tens of thousands of men and briefly stopped the Italian army's advance. In early January, Italians marched on Tembien, unaware that an army of more than one hundred thousand Ethiopians awaited them. Units of Blackshirts, the Fascist militia, led the attack. Half the militia's officers were killed in one day. The panicked survivors were saved from an unceremonious retreat only by the last-minute arrival of Italian airplanes that dropped deadly payloads of poison gas.[38]

The stalled Italian invasion got back on track in February 1936, thanks in good part to the use of weapons banned by international treaties. The Ethiopians had no air force, and as the Italian planes dropped incendiary bombs on villages and poison gas on their fleeing inhabitants, they were helpless. "It's very entertaining work, tragic but beautiful," wrote Mussolini's son Vittorio of the air attacks, in which he, along with his brother Bruno and Edda's husband, Galeazzo Ciano, took part. When victims of the poison gas attacks were displayed to the world press, Italian newspapers claimed that the Ethiopians' deformities had been caused by leprosy.[39]

"Mussolini has had a lot of luck, a lot of luck," observed Pius XI. It was mid-March 1936, and a week earlier Hitler had sent German troops into the Rhineland, diverting international attention from the war in Ethiopia.[40] Newly emboldened by a string of military victories, the Duce made clear the war would end on the battlefield. In the weeks leading up to the occupation of Addis Ababa in early May, the rout turned into something approaching genocide. The Fascist Party head Achille Starace, given command of a motorized unit, oversaw the torching of the villages they passed. The parched wounded staggered to the lakes to drink but found the water saturated with mustard gas, consigning them to agonizing deaths. Tens if not hundreds of thousands died.[41]

As the Italian army approached Addis Ababa, Haile Selassie realized that all was lost. On May 2, in a move that outraged some of his proud countrymen, he and his entourage fled the city aboard a train. In the capital he left behind, the leaderless warriors, searching for guns and money, ransacked homes, stores, and offices. Some tried to burn the city down rather than have the Italians take it over. Europeans huddled in their embassies, which came under attack. The chaos was terrifying but brief, as on May 5 General Badoglio led a column of two thousand Italian vehicles into the city, preceded by cars filled with Italian journalists there to record the triumph.[42]

The next day Tacchi Venturi sent Mussolini a congratulatory letter.[43] "Excellency," he wrote, "after having thanked God for the victory and the Roman peace, allow me to address a word of sincere, fervent joy to Your Excellency! The Lord has assisted You in a wonderful way in not giving up during the most difficult, uncertain hours. The hearts of all good Italian Catholics beg God to continue to give you his divine aid to ensure that the fruits of victory are truly those that one has the right to expect of a victorious apostolic Roman Catholic nation."[44]

On May 9 a hundred thousand Romans crowded into Piazza Venezia. Raising their Fascist banners high and waving their handkerchiefs, they fixed their eyes on Mussolini's balcony. Thousands more clogged the surrounding streets. Rhythmic, thundering chants of "Du-ce! Du-ce!" shook the ancient walls.

Throughout the country, in towns and villages, no matter how small or remote, church bells beckoned all to the central piazza. Loudspeakers sputtered to life, ready to broadcast Mussolini's speech. In Rome three trumpet blasts sounded from the Duce's palazzo, but few could hear; anticipation of his imminent appearance created excitement almost too great to bear. At last the great man strode onto the balcony, standing straight, immobile, his hands on the marble railing, his broad shoulders stretched wide, the expression on his square face set, as if he too were made of marble. The Duce knitted his brow in Fascist concentration, tilting his torso back as he raised his right hand in Roman salute. Roars from the crowd bathed the piazza. Only then did his face soften into a benevolent smile, as if offering some repayment to the multitudes for their adoration and their faith.

"Italy," proclaimed the Duce, "finally has her empire."

The crowd erupted. The piazza, wrote one witness, was like a temple under a heavenly cupola. Mussolini waved in acknowledgment but then hushed the crowd. He had more to say.

Ethiopians were to become subjects of the Kingdom of Italy, he explained. Italy's king would now bear an additional title: Emperor of Ethiopia. "Raise on high your emblems, your arms and your hearts," the Duce called out, "to salute, after fifteen centuries, the reappearance of the Empire on the fateful hills of Rome.

"Will you be worthy of it?" he asked the crowd.

"Yes!" they bellowed.

"Your cries," Mussolini told them, "are like a sacred oath, which binds you before God and before men, for life and death. Salute the king!" Here he lifted his right arm in Fascist salute, and the multitudes in Piazza Venezia, and in the central squares of cities and towns throughout Italy, extended their arms and cried for joy.

The next day, in cathedrals and churches throughout the country, millions of Italians celebrated special masses of thanksgiving.[45]

THE END OF THE WAR came as a great relief for Pius XI. He had never wanted it, and it had put the Vatican under great stress. But the international situation continued to weigh heavily on him. He worried that the war had driven Mussolini further into Hitler's arms. He worried, too, that with his head swollen by his African conquest, Mussolini would turn his attention to the Adriatic. Albania, the pope told the French chargé d'affaires in early June, was likely to be next on the Duce's list.[46]

The pope was feeling ever feebler. In April he had failed to appear in St. Peter's to celebrate Easter Sunday mass. He had given up his daily walks, limiting himself to an occasional ride around the Vatican gardens in his big American sedan. An elevator had been installed in the Apostolic Palace, so that he no longer had to walk up and down the stairs from his private rooms to his study.[47]

Mussolini was triumphant, bothered only by the fact that at war's end the League of Nations sanctions still remained in effect. Again he turned to the Vatican for help.[48] Cardinal Pacelli did what he could to oblige. Meeting with the British ambassador, he insisted that there would be no peace in Europe until the sanctions were lifted.[49] Pacelli repeated the same message at his other weekly meetings with Europe's ambassadors. The pope did his part as well, telling the French ambassador that the sanctions no longer served any useful purpose.[50] On July 7 the League of Nations voted to lift them.[51]

Curiously, Italy's ambassador to the Holy See, Bonifacio Pignatti, thought Mussolini was being overly appreciative of the pope's support. The pontiff, he told the Duce, had acted only out of self-interest. A day did not go by without one Vatican emissary or another prowling the halls of government ministries, leaning on officials to do their bidding. The pope had too much to lose if anything happened to the Fascist regime.

Granted, Pignatti added, the virtually universal, enthusiastic support that the Italian clergy and the Vatican hierarchy had given the war effort had been valuable. But "don't forget, in the Italian-Ethiopian conflict the papacy found itself facing a Jewish-Masonic-Bolshevik coalition," one heavily supported by Protestantism. If the Vatican had backed Mussolini's war, he said, it was because the Church was waging its own holy battle, aimed at the same enemies.[52] Tacchi Venturi's conspiracy theory, it seems, had made another convert.

Ethiopia was Mussolini's great triumph, or so it seemed to him. Every day during the war, he had eagerly followed Italian troop movements by moving little Italian flags on the giant map he kept in his office.[53] Before him, no one had paid any attention to Italy. Now the world's leaders talked incessantly of what the Duce would do. Bishops and priests had showered their gold crosses and sacred valuables on him. Victor Emmanuel III had awarded him the state's highest military honor, the Grand Cross of the Order of Savoy. The king had also offered to make him a prince, but he had refused. "Majesty, I have been and am only Mussolini," he told the monarch. "The generations of Mussolinis were always generations of peasants and it is something I have been rather proud of."[54]

Margherita Sarfatti's prophecy a year earlier, from the window overlooking Piazza Venezia, would prove all too true. Her former lover's feeling of self-importance now knew no bounds. His trust in his instincts had grown to the point where he seemed to believe the pope was not the only one in the Eternal City who was infallible. With the help of the sycophantic Starace, he would soon take his cult of personality to a frightening new level, with statues, portraits, photographs of himself everywhere. Painted in huge letters, his slogans—"Believe, obey, fight," "Mussolini is always right," "Many enemies, much honor"—covered the sides of homes and barns.[55] Secondary school students were already reciting a "prayer to the duce," thanking God for Mussolini, "whom I love more than anything else in the world." They ended with a pledge: "I humbly offer my life to you, o Duce!"[56]

Hundreds of thousands of Fascist youth and militiamen would start spending every Saturday afternoon—dubbed "Fascist Saturday"—practicing the new *passo romano,* the Roman step. While Mussolini insisted that it was based on the ancient Roman legions' military march, its similarity to the Nazi goose step did not go unnoticed. In this respect, too, Sarfatti would not be wrong. Mussolini was leading Italy into the arms of Nazi Germany, a disaster foretold.

DREAMS OF GLORY

WHEN GERMANY'S AMBASSADOR, DIEGO VON BERGEN, ENTERED the pope's library in early 1936, he feared the encounter would be uncomfortable. It was Pius XI's custom to meet with every ambassador at the new year. In the ten minutes allocated to each, he offered his blessing and briefly bestowed praise or blame for the government's recent actions. As it happened, Bergen's meeting would turn out to be even more unpleasant than he had expected.

The pope had much to complain about. In 1933, when Hitler came to power, two-thirds of all schoolchildren in Munich, capital of Germany's largest Catholic region, Bavaria, had been attending Catholic parochial schools. By 1935, this number had been cut in half. In another two years, it would shrink to three percent.[1]

These "so-called conversations," Bergen recalled, "are monologues by the Pope, who takes it for granted that his words will be heard without demur and received with deference."

Shouting and waving his arms and becoming ever more agitated, Pius bemoaned all the ways the Third Reich was persecuting the Church. When Bergen attempted to get a word in, the indignant pope simply raised his voice further. The allotted ten minutes had long since gone by, yet the pope railed on. "There have always been those who have said that the Church is destined to disappear," he warned the ambassador. "But it is they who have always disappeared, not the Church." Then the pope pressed the electric buzzer he had had installed on his desk, beckoning the attendant outside to open the door for his departing visitor.[2]

Upset, Bergen went directly to Cardinal Pacelli's office to complain. He regarded the former German nuncio as an old friend. How much of what Pius said, he asked, should he pass on to his superiors? The pope's harsh words, he pointed out, would anger them. Pacelli recommended that he report only the gist of the pope's comments, leaving out his more inflammatory remarks.

"This episode has shown yet again," Bergen would tell the German foreign minister, "how Cardinal Pacelli constantly strives to pacify, and to exert a moderating influence on the Pope, who is difficult to manage and to influence." It was best, he added, not to take the pope's outbursts too seriously. Mussolini, on the basis of his experience with the pope's tirades, was said to have advised, "Don't get excited about it. The best thing to do is just to let the old gentleman have his say."[3]

The Duce's increasing embrace of the Führer angered the pope. Nor was he happy that Britain and France were doing so little to stop Germany's military buildup. On March 7, 1936, Hitler sent German military forces into the Rhineland, the strip of land at the border of France, Belgium, and the Netherlands that, according to the 1919 Versailles Treaty, was to remain demilitarized. The German troops had orders to retreat at the first sign of counterattack by the French, but the French did nothing. "If you had sent in 200,000 men," the pope told the French ambassador the following week, "you would have rendered an immense service to the whole world."[4] Europe moved one step closer to war.

Events in Spain were also leading to greater collaboration between the Duce and Hitler. An electoral victory by Spain's leftist Popular Front in the spring of 1936 triggered a military rebellion. The Church, long identified with the old elites and now with the rebellious officers, quickly became a target of popular anger at the revolt.[5]

Spain had worried the pope ever since the king's abdication five years earlier. In 1933 the pope issued an encyclical criticizing the Spanish government's efforts to curb Church influence.[6] Yet Pius was inclined to work with the more moderate government elements to find a solution. His efforts were thwarted both by anticlerical extremists in the government and by the hostility of many in the Spanish Church hierarchy who were opposed to any compromise with the leftists.[7]

The outbreak of the civil war in July 1936 brought unspeakable horrors. Seven hundred priests, monks, and nuns were killed. Priests' ears were cut off and passed around as if they were trophies from a bullring. Nuns' rotting remains were dug up from their graves and left exposed—French newspapers published photographs. Monasteries were transformed into socialist headquarters, religious services were banned, and almost all of Barcelona's churches were set ablaze. On August 12 Cardinal Pacelli went to the Spanish embassy to protest.[8]

Although Francisco Franco, leader of the Spanish military revolt, has sometimes been compared with Mussolini, the Duce had no particular affection for him. Franco wasn't much of a general, he thought, cowardly keeping far from the front. And the sadism of the Spanish forces was appalling. "For them," Mussolini remarked, "executing a thousand men is like eating a plate of macaroni."[9]

Motivated less by ideological camaraderie with Franco than by a desire to limit the international influence of the leftist government in France, Mussolini soon found himself conferring with the Nazis on how best to help the insurrection. In October the first Russian airplanes, tanks, and other supplies began arriving to shore up the Spanish government. The Italian Catholic press urged Mussolini to send Italian troops to aid the rebels.[10] By year's end, he had dispatched thousands of blackshirted militia and soldiers to help Franco.[11]

The pope did not share in the enthusiasm for the war. He was horrified by the bloodcurdling accounts of anti-Catholic atrocities but balked at endorsing an armed revolt against an elected government.

Nor was he eager to see Mussolini embroiled in a war that would push him further into Hitler's arms.[12]

JUST AS HE WAS GETTING the first reports of civil war in Spain, the pope received more disturbing news from Germany: the Nazis were planning to put hundreds of German monks and nuns on trial on charges of sexual perversion. Over the next year, the highly publicized trials would receive front-page coverage in the German press. "Corrupters of Youth Clad in Cassocks" screamed one headline. "Bottomless Depravity in the Monastery" declared another. The priests were accused of luring children in their charge into sexual acts and seducing vulnerable young women as well. To make matters worse, German authorities had renewed their case against the Jesuits, accused of illegally exporting funds.[13]

Then came the upsetting news that Mussolini was sending his son-in-law, Galeazzo Ciano, to Berlin for talks on strengthening the links between the two countries. Ciano had risen through government ranks at dizzying speed. By age thirty-two, in 1935, he had become minister of press and propaganda. The following year Mussolini shocked the diplomatic world by appointing him to the government's most prestigious post after his own: minister of foreign affairs. Increasingly, if unconsciously, Ciano tried to imitate his father-in-law's mannerisms. But his high-pitched, nasal voice could not reproduce the Duce's booming, staccato speech. Romans took to calling him derisively *il Ducellino*, "the little Duce," or *generissimo*, a playful combination of *genero*, "son-in-law," and *generalissimo*, the military's highest rank. "The son-in-law also rises," quipped an American diplomat. Easily impressed with power, in over his head, and a sucker for flattery, Ciano was putty in Hitler's hands.[14] That October, three months after the outbreak of the Spanish civil war, Ciano signed a secret cooperation agreement with the Third Reich. Thus the Rome-Berlin "axis" was born.[15]

A new American ambassador to Italy, William Phillips, arrived in Rome around the same time. At their first meeting, Ciano made a good impression on him—he was affable, laughed a good deal, and spoke excellent English. But Phillips soon began to have doubts about Italy's youthful foreign minister. "In appearance," he wrote, "he looked astonishingly boyish, although inclined to be plump."[16] Of medium height, Ciano had a round face and "well-oiled black hair," slicked back "in typical Italian fashion." He was clearly ambitious but had "no standards morally or politically." Ciano reveled in his position as Fascist potentate and the Duce's son-in-law. But the other Fascist leaders detested him, resenting his unmerited rise to power and his love of *la dolce vita*. Most of all, they were angry that Mussolini had apparently chosen him—without bothering to consult them—as his political heir.[17]

Ambassador Phillips had a very different impression of Mussolini. Upon entering the "vast, empty hall with polished floor" for their first meeting, he spied a figure at the far end, sitting at a desk. "A short, thick-set and powerfully built man came forward to meet me," he recalled. "Complete baldness seemed to exaggerate the size of his head." What most struck the ambassador were the Duce's eyes, which, when he wanted to make a point, "suddenly seemed to expand and the whites to protrude." They spoke in English, Mussolini's recent private lessons having served him well. Phillips would later observe that when wearing his Fascist uniform, the Duce seemed a commanding figure, but on those rare occasions when he saw him in civilian dress, he looked like a "sturdy peasant" and "a very rough customer."[18]

Roberto Cantalupo, Mussolini's ambassador to Spain, meeting with him for the first time in many months, saw a man who, in the wake of his Ethiopian victory, seemed dramatically changed. Heavier, his neck thickened, and his face enlarged, his skin was bright red from the summer days he spent on the beach. With Ciano at his side, his every word seemed false, as if meant for a large audience. The Duce's distance from Cantalupo, who had known him for years, appeared immense. After a few uncomfortable minutes, Cantalupo departed, but Ciano caught up with him before he left the building.

"How did you find him?" asked Ciano.

"I didn't find him. I found someone else," Cantalupo replied.

Ciano smiled. "You know, he has tasted great glory and sees the rest of us from on high as little, little. He lives in a world of his own. . . . Perhaps it's for the best that we leave him up there on Olympus, where he can do great things. As for the rest of us . . . we'll take care of the things of this world."[19]

Giovanni Bottai, one of the Fascist leaders closest to Mussolini, had a similar experience on his return from Ethiopia. "Not the man, but the statue, stood before me," he wrote in his diary. A "hard, stony statue, from which a cold voice emerged."[20]

The Duce's composure cracked briefly when he suffered an unexpected blow: his youngest child, seven-year-old Anna Maria, contracted polio. She struggled between life and death as the Duce looked on helplessly. Finally she recovered, although the signs of the disease remained with her. At a press conference during her illness, when foreign journalists presented Mussolini with a doll to give her, tears rolled down his famously masklike face.[21]

But his daughter's illness did nothing to soften him. He had little use for advice. He insisted that when his ministers and other officials came to see him, they speed-walk across his immense office to his desk, give a Roman salute, and hand him the papers he had requested. After answering his questions, and without offering any unsolicited comments, they would salute again, turn around, and hustle out.[22] They were lucky if they escaped without triggering his wrath. Navarra, Mussolini's assistant, who waited outside the room, regularly heard the Duce's thundering denunciations. When angry, he banged his fists on his table and convulsively spread and closed his legs, scraping his heels against a footrest under his table. Before long, Navarra reported, the footrest was completely worn down.[23]

Mussolini felt that nothing was impossible if he willed it.[24] Italy could become one of the world's great nations, if Italians followed his orders. But amid all his dreams of conquest and glory, he worried that Italians were by nature a weak people, ill suited for his martial designs. At a Grand Council meeting in December, he mused that one day he would have to "march the troops into Naples to sweep aside all the guitars, the mandolins, the violins, the organ grinders."[25]

Mussolini was increasingly leaving day-to-day matters to his associates, but not only because he had to deal with more consequential matters. He also had a new mistress. Clara Petacci was twenty-four years old when their affair began in earnest in 1936; Mussolini was fifty-three. Her family lived in a large apartment close to Mussolini's Villa Torlonia. Her father was a Vatican physician, caring for assorted monsignors, functionaries, and papal guards. Less than two years earlier, she had married, in a wedding graced by many Vatican dignitaries and presided over by Cardinal Gasparri himself. The marriage did not last long.

A buxom, vivacious young woman, with green eyes and curly hair—the product of dozens of curlers applied each night—Clara had small teeth and a low, warm, husky voice. She lived for the afternoon calls that summoned her to Palazzo Venezia. To minimize gossip, she would take a taxi to an agreed-upon spot, where she met a motorcycle policeman and hopped into his covered sidecar. At the service entrance of Palazzo Venezia, she was met by Mussolini's trusted assistant, Quinto Navarra, and escorted to the special apartment Mussolini had reserved for her. There she would lie on a sofa in the Zodiac room—so called because of the gold-painted image on the sky-blue vaulted ceiling. As she waited for the Duce—who typically arrived after six P.M.—she passed the hours reading, listening to records, drawing designs for her clothes, and filling up voluminous notebooks with her daily diary, recounting in loving detail her every encounter with the great man.[26] In the closet she kept a dozen bright-colored, frilly dresses and an assortment of gaudy hats. Navarra, who brought her tea, occasionally stopped by to chat.[27]

Although Mussolini had had a long trail of lovers, Clara Petacci represented something new. It was not so much that his former lovers were closer to his own age and were plain as often as they were pretty; rather, he developed an unusual emotional dependency on Petacci. Not that he in any way regarded her as an equal—he showed not the least inter-

Clara Petacci

est in her views. The hundreds of pages of her published diaries give no indication that he cared about her opinion on anything but her total devotion to him. But he found that he could not live without this attractive young woman, without her doting devotion and sexual availability. At a time when his horror at the prospect of getting older was growing, she provided him with a feeling of youth regained; and in the wake of his daughter's brush with death, and his sense of isolation during the Ethiopian war, she offered him freedom from the pressures of constantly having to pose as the Italian superman.[28]

THE FRONT PAGE OF THE OCTOBER 1, 1936, *New York Times* carried surprising news: Eugenio Pacelli was to sail the next day from Naples to New York for an extended American visit. Never before had anyone so high up in the Vatican visited the United States.[29] Speculation swirled in the world's capitals about why the pope would be dispatching his secretary of state to America. None took seriously the Vatican's claim that the visit was purely "personal."

Much attention focused on the radio priest Charles Coughlin, whose increasingly vicious attacks on Franklin Roosevelt, in the midst of his 1936 reelection campaign, had divided America's Catholic community and proven an embarrassment for the Vatican. The reason for Pacelli's surprising visit, *The New York Times* speculated, was the pope's desire to assure President Roosevelt that he had had nothing to do with Coughlin's assault. Other papers predicted that Pacelli would shut down the fiery radio priest's operation. Back in Rome, Italy's ambassador to the Holy See had another explanation for the trip: Pacelli was campaigning to succeed Pius XI and was courting the favor of America's four cardinals.[30]

Boston's Bishop Spellman took charge of the visit. The two men would fly from one end of the United States to the other, logging over eight thousand miles, making countless stops. Pacelli collected honorary degrees at several Catholic colleges, met with almost all of America's bishops, and spoke to large gatherings of priests and the faithful from Boston to California.[31]

From the moment his visit was announced, press speculation focused on whether the cardinal would meet with the American president. Father Coughlin used his radio program to warn the Vatican secretary of state against such a meeting, since it would suggest Vatican support for Roosevelt's reelection.[32] His listeners responded with a flood of angry letters to the papal delegate in Washington adding their own words of warning. (Lacking formal diplomatic relations with the United States, the Vatican kept a delegate, not a nuncio, in the capital.)[33] Bowing to the pressure, Pacelli waited until two days after the election to see Roosevelt.

Their meeting took place at the president's family home in Hyde Park, New York. The only record of their conversation comes from Roosevelt's recollections several years later. What most impressed him,

Cardinal Pacelli during his visit to New York City, October 1936

he said, was Pacelli's seeming obsession with the threat of a Communist takeover in the United States. He sounded, thought the president, much like Father Coughlin. The cardinal kept repeating, "The great danger in America is that it will go communist." Roosevelt countered that the real danger was that the United States might become fascist.

"Mr. President," replied Cardinal Pacelli, "you simply do not understand the terrible importance of the communist movement."

"You just don't understand the American people," responded Roosevelt.[34]

Two days later Pacelli boarded the ocean liner *Count of Savoy* in New York harbor, bound for home.[35]

ONE NIGHT IN OCTOBER, while Cardinal Pacelli was still in America, the pope fainted, banging his head against a wooden bedpost as he fell. It was a hint of what was to come. By November, the once-vigorous pope had to be carried to his public audiences in a chair borne aloft by attendants. In early December, with his heart showing signs of frightening weakness, the seventy-nine-year-old pope was confined to bed.[36]

The pope's varicose veins caused him terrible pain, eased a bit by his attendants, who massaged his legs for an hour each day. He spent most of the time in bed, and his doctor visited four times a day.[37] At night the pope's two old clerical assistants from Milan took turns sitting by his bedside, for he was too uncomfortable to get much sleep. The only regular appointment he still kept was with Cardinal Pacelli, who came by daily as the pope struggled to keep up with all that was going on.[38]

The pope was in such agony that Pacelli could barely contain his tears. Pius kept pressing his doctor to tell him how long it would take to get better. "I don't want you to hide the truth," he told the tongue-tied physician, who sputtered that he could not say. The pope drank a little milk in the morning, then some clear soup in the afternoon, listening to classical music on his radio. As Christmas approached, he insisted on giving the cardinals their traditional blessing, offered at his bedside. Meanwhile they began to talk, discreetly, about a successor. At a certain point the pope stopped asking his doctor when his health would improve. He asked only that God grant him a dignified death.[39]

The Vatican put out a series of misleading stories to explain why Pius was bedridden. But when the new year came and he still did not reappear, rumors of his declining health could no longer be brushed off. In early January 1937 *L'Osservatore romano* reported that the pontiff suffered from arteriosclerosis and weak blood circulation. There was some hope, according to the Vatican newspaper, that the pope's condition might improve, but given the nature of the disease and the pope's age, a "certain prudence" was called for.[40]

The pope was less sanguine. Every night, at his request, his secretary read him historical accounts of the final days of previous popes.

"It's time to go home," he said wearily. "We need to prepare the bags."[41] As he rested, he gazed at the painting across from his bed. It showed Andrea Avellino, patron saint of the good death. In pain and weakened by age, Pius chafed at his helplessness. The strong, self-assured, demanding pope who had so terrorized those around him seemed to be rapidly receding. But as Pius XI might have said, God works in strange ways. The pope's greatest battle was yet to come.

PART THREE

MUSSOLINI, HITLER, AND THE JEWS

ATTACKING HITLER

N O ONE THOUGHT A CONCLAVE COULD BE FAR OFF. CARDINALS SIZED one another up. American journalists snooped around the Vatican with wads of cash, eager to find someone to tip them off the moment the pope died.[1]

Mussolini's ambassador, Bonifacio Pignatti, kept him abreast of the behind-the-scenes maneuvering. In Italy, he reported, "faith in the Duce is absolute and beyond discussion in all of the Episcopal hierarchy and clergy"; Pius XI's successor "would have to be crazy" to upset the Church's good relations with the Fascist government. But outside Italy things were different, he warned: the Third Reich's "immorality trials" of Catholic clergy had united cardinals worldwide against the Nazis. Nor were they pleased by the assault on Catholic parochial schools and the recent closing of the Catholic daily press. The deification of Hitler and German blood, along with the growth of Hitler Youth at the expense of Catholic youth groups, only made matters worse. Pignatti worried that the cardinals' hostility toward Hitler was affecting their attitude to Mussolini. While Italy's cardinals would surely want a pope who would support the Vatican's alliance with Mussolini, the non-Italians might try to elect someone less enamored of Fascism.[2]

Surprisingly, the pope began to get better. Those cardinals who had begun packing their bags for a trip to Rome found themselves unpacking. Pius would never again enjoy good health, but he would recover enough to resume his most important duties, meeting with the heads of the Curia congregations and eventually even resuming his public audiences, albeit at a reduced rate. In late March 1937 Cardinal Baudrillart, seeing the pope for the first time in months, observed that he "seems very much changed to me, much thinner, his face emaciated and wrinkled. The expression on his face is softer."

On Easter Sunday, the pontiff made a dramatic return to public view, borne aloft in his *sedia gestatoria* in a cortege that snaked through a packed St. Peter's Basilica. He looked weak, his face ashen. Many cried with joy, having thought they would never see him again. The pope's eyes, too, were moist as he traversed the cavernous basilica. After the mass, his attendants carried him to the external balcony, where he looked out at the crowd that filled St. Peter's Square, awaiting his blessing. "The hour came," recalled Baudrillart. "The pope's voice remains strong and clear. The world, this sad world, is blessed!"³

A few days later, when the pope entered his library for the first time since his illness, he could barely contain his tears. Many nights as he lay awake he had wondered if he would ever see it again. In the weeks ahead, as the pains in his legs were partly relieved by elastic stockings and regular massages, the pope arrived for his public audiences in a chair borne aloft on two poles. Inside his apartment, he used a wheelchair. In those brief but precious moments when he got out into the gardens, he walked haltingly with a cane. He now held his first appointment of the day at ten A.M. and took a long nap after lunch. On Mondays he stayed in bed all day. At night he relaxed by listening to music on the radio.⁴

THE VATICAN'S RELATIONS WITH Hitler were only getting worse. The show trials of German priests were generating sensational press coverage, and the number of children in Catholic schools was diminishing to the vanishing point. Yet the Vatican's alliance with Mussolini remained strong. Months after Italian troops marched into Addis Ababa, Italians still swelled with patriotic pride. "Mussolini's smile is like a flash of the Sun god," wrote one fawning Italian journalist, "expected and craved because it brings health and life."[5] Italy's most prominent Catholic newspaper, *L'Avvenire d'Italia,* and the Vatican's *L'Osservatore romano* both expressed enthusiastic support for the regime.[6]

Mussolini's ties with Hitler had done little to lessen the Vatican's support for him, but outside Italy the dictator's luster was fading. In February, Italy's ambassador to the United States worriedly reported the change: Americans were coming to see Fascism and Nazism as two faces of the same totalitarian coin, and Americans despised the Nazis.[7]

But Mussolini still enjoyed Italian Americans' enthusiastic support. As a result, politicians in areas with large Italian American populations were reluctant to criticize him. In 1937 New York's mayor, Fiorello La Guardia, told a Jewish group that Hitler's effigy should be put in a chamber of horrors at the World's Fair, and a year later he branded the Führer a "contemptible coward." But even though Italy's anti-Semitic laws were instituted in 1938, La Guardia—whose Italian mother came from a Jewish family—dared say nothing critical of the Duce until 1940, when Italy invaded France and entered World War II on the Nazis' side.[8]

In early 1937 a German reporter arrived at the Palazzo Venezia to interview Mussolini. At the far end of the Hall of the Map of the World, framed by the enormous marble fireplace, sat his host. The Duce sprang to his feet, standing ramrod straight, and extended his right arm in Roman salute. He asked his German visitor how the Führer was. "Very well," replied the reporter, who was struck by Mussolini's vigor. His "Caesarean face" appeared to have gotten younger, and the wrinkles around his eyes had disappeared.

An epic battle was about to begin, the Duce told him. Communism was threatening to destroy Europe. The democracies had become the centers of infection, "propagators of the communist bacillus." Europe was at a turning point. "This is the age of strong individualities and predominant personalities," Mussolini explained. "Democracies are sand, shifting sand. Our political ideal of the State is a rock, a granite peak." Only Fascist Italy and Nazi Germany could save Europe.[9]

AS THE POPE REGAINED some of his strength, he again asked Mussolini to help him with Hitler, but his hopes were in vain. Mussolini told Tacchi Venturi there was little he or anyone else could do to influence the Führer when it came to questions of religion. In relaying this message to the pope, Tacchi Venturi pointed out that the Duce had tried his best. Lest the pope's enthusiasm for Mussolini diminish, he quickly added that, "with the same kindness," the dictator had agreed to all the pope's other requests. He would censor a newspaper that the pope had objected to and confiscate all copies of a pamphlet that American Protestants had recently sent their brethren in Italy.[10]

In the summer of 1936, the German bishops had asked the pope to prepare an encyclical urging the Nazi government to respect the terms of its 1933 concordat with the Church. In early 1937, in his sickbed, the pope met with three German cardinals and two bishops who had come to discuss the proposal. Pacelli, not wanting to antagonize Hitler, advised the pontiff against issuing his criticism in the form of an encyclical: he should simply send Hitler a pastoral letter, to be shared only with the German bishops. But Pius XI spurned Pacelli's advice. He wanted to issue an encyclical that all Germans—and all the world— would read. The result was dramatic. On Palm Sunday, March 21, 1937, bishops and priests throughout Germany read the encyclical, *Mit brennender Sorge* ("With Deep Anxiety"), from the pulpit to people unaccustomed to any public criticism of the Nazi regime.[11]

"It is with deep anxiety and growing surprise that We have long been following the painful trials of the [German] Church and the increasing vexations which afflict those who have remained loyal in heart and action." Thus began the encyclical. While the Church had entered into the concordat with the German government in good faith, said the pope, "anyone must acknowledge, not without surprise and reprobation, how the other contracting party emasculated the terms of the treaty, distorted their meaning, and eventually considered its more or less official violation as a normal policy." He lamented the destruction of Catholic parochial schools, despite the concordat's provision protecting them. He castigated those who idolized race and nation, deeming them guilty of distorting and perverting "an order of the world planned and created by God." He took aim at efforts to blend Christianity with race worship: "None but superficial minds could stumble into concepts of a national God, of a national religion; or attempt to lock within the frontiers of a single people, within the narrow limits of a single race, God, the Creator of the universe." Although he never mentioned Nazism by name, he thanked those priests and laypeople "who have persisted in their Christian duty and in the defense of God's rights in the teeth of an aggressive paganism." The reference was clear.

While the encyclical was hard-hitting, it could have been harsher. For months, the Holy Office of the Inquisition had been working on a separate document, offering a list of fundamental tenets of Nazism that the Church deemed to be grave errors. Among them were passages clearly taken from Hitler's *Mein Kampf.*

Worried that branding Nazi ideology un-Christian might lead Hitler to renounce the concordat altogether, the pope had decided on a less direct attack. He was supported not only by Pacelli but by Cardinal Michael von Faulhaber, archbishop of Munich, Germany's most important archdiocese. Throughout the drafting project, the Jesuit general Ledóchowski did all he could to prevent the pope from denouncing Hitler, urging the pope to "avoid going into questions that are very difficult and subtle." The term *Nazi* was deleted from the draft; nor was any mention made of the persecution of the Jews. The encyclical was to have been accompanied by a list of errors condemned by the Church, including basic tenets of Nazism, but it never made it out of the Vatican.[12]

Diluted though the encyclical was, Hitler was furious, outraged not only by the unprecedented public attack but by the pope's ability to have the message distributed so widely without his knowledge. He ordered the police to close down Catholic publishing houses and sent agents to diocesan headquarters and monasteries throughout the country to seize their files. "I will heap disgrace and shame on the Catholic Church," he told one visitor, "opening unknown monastic archives and having the filth contained in them published!"[13] Convinced that he knew the Church's weak point, he threatened to reveal graphic tales of sexual abuse by the Catholic clergy and moved quickly to gather incriminating evidence. When word of the police raids got out, the bishop of Berlin and the archbishop of Breslau ordered all files dealing with complaints against priests burned. The pope urged all of Germany's bishops to follow their example.[14]

Worried that Italian newspapers might portray the encyclical as a denunciation of Nazism rather than a plea that the terms of the concordat with Germany be respected, the pope let the Duce know that this was not his intention.[15] Pacelli, for his part, was eager to avoid a break with the Nazi government, afraid it would leave the Church there defenseless.[16]

In May, Mussolini took up the pope's cause with the German foreign minister, Konstantin von Neurath. The dispute with the Church, Mussolini told him, was harming the Third Reich's reputation. Based on his own experience, he advised the Nazis to allow religious instruction in the public schools, something he had done to great profit in Italy. By doing "small favors to the higher clergy," Mussolini suggested—he gave as examples providing free railway tickets and tax concessions—he had won them over, "so that they even declared the war in Abyssinia a holy war."[17]

It was advice that, in one form or another, the Duce was regularly giving the top Nazi leaders. The previous fall Germany's justice minister, visiting Rome, had asked him how he had succeeded in nourishing such good relations with the Church in Italy. Mussolini boasted that after a brief period of difficulty in 1931, he had brought the Vatican in line. But he advised: Never let your guard down. The Catholic Church, he explained, is like a rubber ball. If you don't keep up the pressure, it will return to its original shape.[18]

IN LATE MAY 1937 five hundred Chicago priests gathered at a local seminary, as they did four times a year, to attend their diocesan conference.[19] When Archbishop George Mundelein rose to speak, there was no indication that what he would say would be of any interest outside Chicago. But his remarks would trigger an international cause célèbre.[20] Lashing out at the Nazi regime for its persecution of the Church, he told his priests, "Perhaps you will ask how it is that a nation of sixty million intelligent people will submit in fear and servitude to an alien, an Austrian paper hanger, and a poor one at that, and a few associates like Goebbels and Goring, who dictate every move of the people's lives."[21]

The outraged German government demanded an apology from the Vatican. Cardinal Pacelli, replying on behalf of the pope, refused. No such apology could be considered, he said, unless the German government first ordered a stop to the constant stream of attacks on the Church in Germany's newspapers.

Berlin recalled Diego von Bergen, Germany's ambassador to the Holy See. "The Holy See will realize," he warned, "that its unexpected and incomprehensible conduct in this matter, as long as it is not remedied, has eliminated the conditions necessary for a normal state of relations between the German Government and the Curia. The full responsibility for this development rests solely with the Curia." [22]

If Cardinal Pacelli took the lead in this crisis, it was partly because the pope was still in such bad shape. Weakened by his failing heart and short of breath from his asthma, the pope had little of his old energy. One visitor said the pope looked as though he had "a ray of eternity on his face." Pius XI's illness, Pacelli observed, had left him "extremely emotional." He could not see the frail pope, he told a fellow cardinal in April, without crying. Ever more frequently, when asked to act, the pope responded, "That will be for our successor to do."[23]

By May the pope had retreated to Castel Gandolfo, where loudspeakers were installed for his public audiences to amplify his thin voice. On his eightieth birthday, he was supposed to inaugurate the new Pontifical Academy of Sciences, but he had to cancel at the last minute.[24]

Tensions between the Holy See and Germany triggered speculation that the ailing pope might soon excommunicate Hitler.[25] The pope's disgust with the Nazis was also having an impact on his attitude to the Spanish civil war, as he was suspicious of Franco's close ties with Hitler. Mussolini was sending men and munitions to support Franco's struggle against "communism," but the pope, he complained, while denouncing Communism in an encyclical, was doing nothing to support the revolt.[26] Meeting in May with the primate of Spain, Cardinal Isdro Gomá, Franco told him how important it would be to have the pope's public backing. Gomá agreed and informed the Vatican secretary of state office that a letter signed by the Spanish bishops would be published announcing their support for Franco. Pacelli urged the pope to have the document published as part of the Vatican's official acts—the *Acta Apostolicae Sedis*—but the ailing pope refused. "This, cardinal," he said simply, "no."[27]

For Catholics outside Italy, the Holy See's support of the Italian Fascist regime was becoming ever more uncomfortable. The Vatican's latest embarrassment came on June 9, when French fascist thugs murdered Carlo Rosselli, a founder of the most important Italian anti-Fascist organization in exile. Matteotti, Amendola, now Rosselli—Mussolini's minions had murdered three prominent leaders of the opposition, men of great moral stature.[28]

Tacchi Venturi was meanwhile working tirelessly to stamp out Catholic criticism of the Italian dictatorship. On July 12 Dino Alfieri, minister of popular culture, asked him to handle the latest incident. England's most important Catholic magazine had recently published a letter blasting Nazi Germany and Fascist Italy. Its author, a Dominican, was upset that British fascists were claiming to have Vatican support. He cited Pius XI's 1931 encyclical, *Non abbiamo bisogno,* to argue that the pope opposed Fascism.

Informed of the matter, Monsignor Pizzardo, the Vatican undersecretary of state, drafted a letter to the archbishop of Westminster, leader of the Catholic Church in England and Wales.[29] The offending piece in the British magazine, complained Pizzardo, "places Italian fascism and German racism on the same level with regard to the Catholic Church as if the former merited the same reproval and the same condemnation as the latter." Its author should have distinguished more clearly between the two regimes. While the Church had condemned "the excesses of National Socialism," the controversy over Italian Catholic Action in 1931 had quickly been settled. "Since that time," Pizzardo concluded, "it is true that not only have there been no noteworthy cases of friction between the Ecclesiastical Authority and the Italian Government, but there has often been even a fruitful collaboration between them."

Pizzardo sent the draft to Tacchi Venturi, who returned it with suggestions for strengthening its praise of the Fascist regime.[30] He also advised that a copy be sent to the master general of the Dominican order, so that he could add his own "just warning." Pizzardo made all the suggested changes and sent the letter. The chastised offender duly published a humiliating retraction in the magazine.[31]

THE SPANISH CIVIL WAR threatened to drag Europe into a larger conflagration. In August, Italian submarines began sinking ships bound for Republican-controlled Spanish ports, while Hitler accelerated Germany's rearmament. Despite the rising world tensions, Mussolini still found time for his daily visits with his young mistress, Clara Petacci, and for sporadic flings with other women.

Mussolini had hitherto been able to keep details of his many affairs out of the world press. This changed in early 1937, thanks to a seductive twenty-nine-year-old French reporter. Magda Fontanges gained worldwide notoriety when she shot and wounded the French ambassador to Italy. She had tried to kill him, she said, because she blamed him for ending her affair with Mussolini. Her trial filled the world's press with steamy stories describing their trysts. Fontanges later published her own bodice-ripping account in an American magazine under the title "I Was Mussolini's Mistress."[32] In three lurid installments, Magda described in breathless detail how Mussolini had seduced her. The second installment opened with a full-page illustration of Fontanges in Mussolini's arms as they kissed. Its inscription read: "Holding me tightly, he gives me his first kiss. I feel a sensation of intoxication." Later in the piece she described the dictator's love nest in Palazzo Venezia as he guided her toward the sofa in the darkened room.

"He has embraced me again, growing very tender," she recalled. "Then a sort of frenzy sweeps him, he becomes brutal, and he says, 'You have known Il Duce—now you shall know the man!'

"He has taken off his coat, and in his sports shirt he appears astonishingly young. Heeding nothing but his instinct, he leaps at me. Before I have time to utter so much as an exclamation, I am caught up in strong arms."[33]

The French scandal led to a raft of foreign news reports about the Duce's voracious sexual appetite. The reports, said Mussolini, were greatly exaggerated. "If I had had to couple with all those women that they claim I have," he told an interviewer, "I would frankly have had to have been not a man, but a stallion." Two years later, as he bantered with a woman acquaintance, he quipped that his flesh did not allow him to be a saint. While few things tempted him—he ate mostly fruit and vegetables and had no interest in money—he had one weakness, he acknowledged, that would always stand in the way of any saintly aspirations.

"You aren't the only one in the world," she pointed out. "I've always wondered what use having been virtuous is when one is old."

"In Romagna," replied Mussolini, "we have a proverb. . . . In youth, give your flesh to the devil, in old age, give your bones to the Lord."[34]

Being a ladies' man had always played a part in the Mussolini cult, and the Fontanges affair did nothing to change this. In early September, as a band played at a festival on a Sicilian beach, Mussolini danced with the local women, some young, some old, some thin, some fat, some attractive, others not. "Dancing is a religion in Romagna," he said. "It takes the place of Catholicism."

As Mussolini swayed to the music, his secretary rushed onto the dance floor clutching a telegram. An Italian submarine, off the Sicilian coast, had just torpedoed a Russian cargo ship bringing provisions to Republican Spain. The attack was part of a recently imposed blockade that risked triggering a larger European war. After pausing a moment to read the message, the Duce chose another partner. When the song ended, he asked, "Are there other telegrams? If every turn around the floor they announce another torpedoing, I'll never stop dancing."[35]

VIVA IL DUCE!

————

IN AUGUST 1937 NEWSPAPERS BEGAN REPORTING MUSSOLINI'S PLAN
to visit Germany.[1] It would be a fateful trip. For five days, in late
September, Hitler stood at the Duce's side, carefully choreographing a
series of processions, marches, and inspections to impress Mussolini
with the power of the Nazi regime and the Germans' devotion to their
Führer. The culmination came in Berlin on September 28 when eight
hundred thousand people filled a field near the new Olympic stadium.
Along the route leading there, nearly three million Germans cheered
the dictators, having been brought in by bus and train from throughout
the Reich. When the two leaders emerged onto the field the crowd
roared. Hitler spared no praise, hailing Mussolini as "one of those rare
solitary geniuses who are not created by history but who make history
themselves." Hitler later called him "the leading statesman in the world,
to whom none may even remotely compare himself."[2]

Mussolini had carefully prepared his text in German and, after Hitler's effusive introduction, rose to speak. When Fascist Italy had a
friend, he proclaimed, it marched alongside him "right to the end." But
a sudden downpour spoiled the desired effect, as the master of bom-

bast struggled to make out the blurry words on his rain-soaked sheets. The crowd had no idea what he was saying.[3]

"Compared to Hitler's demonstrations," observed an Italian witness to the event, "those of the Italian Fascist seem like just a bunch of people running around shouting. In his speeches, Mussolini rambles, expressing commonplaces in dramatic fashion and self-evident truths with great solemnity. He addresses the ignorant masses, and speaks for them, gesticulating with his face, his body, his eyes, with the moves of a charlatan. Hitler is always composed. When Mussolini appears . . . hands on his hips, he seems like a circus ring master. Hitler by contrast seems like an apostle, a political, religious leader."[4]

Mussolini and Hitler in Munich, September 1937

The Duce was deeply impressed. "What I saw here," he told his wife, Rachele, by telephone as he prepared to leave, "is unimaginable."[5]

Although he had promised he would convey the pope's complaints, Mussolini never did mention them to Hitler.[6] Amid the huge adulatory crowds and the imposing displays of military strength, he could not bring himself to raise such an unpleasant subject.[7]

Mussolini vowed to host Hitler for a visit in the Eternal City that would outshine his own reception in Germany. Cardinal Baudrillart, writing in his diary, wondered whether the weakened Pius XI could survive such a painful sight.[8]

For the Vatican, it was becoming increasingly important to differentiate between the two totalitarian states. Immediately following Mussolini's visit to Germany, *La Civiltà cattolica* published a piece making just this distinction. People who equated Nazi Germany with Fascist Italy, the journal argued, "do a great injustice to the Fascist Regime." Hitler was seeking to unify the German people under a new, pagan religion, its slogan the divinity of the blood and the soil. Mussolini was doing the opposite, unifying Italians under the Catholic religion. The two could scarcely be more different.[9]

On Mussolini's return from Germany the pope, although upset that the Duce had not raised the issue of the Church with Hitler, again asked his help with the Führer. It was in Mussolini's own interest, he argued, to get Hitler to stop persecuting the Church. Given Italy's links to the Third Reich, the Nazis' anti-Church campaign was harming Italian Fascism's good name.[10]

In another sign of his embrace of Nazi Germany, Mussolini announced in December that Italy was withdrawing from the League of Nations. Hitler had removed Germany from the League shortly after coming to power in 1933. The pope looked on with increasing unease. He was also embarrassed that so many non-Italian cardinals thought him naïve in expecting Mussolini to be a moderating influence on Hitler.[11] "It is not the Duce who exercises any influence on the Führer," remarked the French Cardinal Eugène Tisserant, "but rather the Füh-

L'ILLUSTRAZIONE
ITALIANA

Anno LXIV - N. 45   7 Novembre 1937-XVI

Mussolini dedicates the new town of Guidonia, as the local bishop
joins in the Fascist salute, November 1937

rer who exercises it over the Duce."[12] In the pope's Christmas speech
to the cardinals, he again lamented the persecution of the Church in
Germany.[13] It was a message he was sharing with all who would listen.

Convinced he had little time to live, Pius XI believed God was keeping him alive for a reason. "His fragile state of health," observed the
French ambassador, "is unfortunately weakening, not his intellectual
capacities, but his physical strength." Cardinal Jean Verdier, arch-

bishop of Paris, saw the pope twice around Christmas. At their first meeting, the cardinal was delighted to find him lively and attentive, but the next time the pontiff was feeble, barely able to speak, and unable to read the papers he had in front of him. Sometimes the pope was alert and articulate. Other times he was frail and frustrated. Yet, during his sleepless nights, he felt God's presence, imparting a divine message it was his duty to pass on before he died.[14]

Cardinal Baudrillart noted the change in his diary. "The pope remains very lucid, but his willpower is becoming more hesitant." Nor did the French cardinal think the secretary of state offered an adequate substitute. "Despite all of his eminent qualities," he observed, "Cardinal Pacelli does not seem to have a very firm mind, nor a very strong will."[15] Later in the month, Baudrillart observed, telegraphically: "Now atmosphere of the end of regime: secret intrigues."

Mussolini was irritated. Whipping up Italian enthusiasm for Germany was a challenge, even with his massive propaganda machine. Only two decades earlier, the Italians had fought a war against the Ger-

Mussolini, from Palazzo Venezia, announces Italy's withdrawal from the League of Nations, December 1937

mans, and all the Nazi talk of the superiority of the Nordic race was not making his task any easier. The last thing Mussolini needed was for the pope to convince Italians that Hitler was an enemy of the Church.

It was time, thought Mussolini, to apply some pressure. He delivered his message through Guido Buffarini. Elected mayor of Pisa in 1923 at age twenty-eight, Buffarini became Mussolini's undersecretary for internal affairs ten years later. Ruddy complexioned, sad-eyed, and fat, intelligent and shrewd, devoid of any moral principles, Buffarini was a blowhard with a talent for intimidation and a penchant for feathering his own nest.[16]

On December 30, Buffarini summoned the papal nuncio. He had evidence, he said, that Catholic Action groups were again mixing in politics. If this continued, he warned, a violent popular reaction was sure to follow. The dumbstruck nuncio denied the charge, but to no avail.[17]

Told of Mussolini's new threats, Pius XI sent his nuncio to appeal to the Duce's son-in-law. Ciano was brusque with him. If Mussolini was unhappy with the Vatican, he said, the pope had only himself to blame. He knew that his constant criticisms of Germany were upsetting the Duce, yet still he kept up his attacks.[18]

FEW IN ITALY WERE aware of these tensions. The vast majority of Catholic clergymen still considered Mussolini to be the man God had sent to save the nation, a message priests regularly shared with their parishioners.

Eager to highlight this support, Mussolini decided to organize a huge gathering of bishops and priests at Palazzo Venezia. The occasion was billed as a celebration honoring the clergy who had distinguished themselves in the "battle for grain," the campaign for agricultural self-sufficiency that he had been pushing for over a decade. Invitations, signed by a Catholic Fascist journal editor, went out in mid-December. By attending the January 9 event, these priests and bishops would offer "the most solemn honor to the Duce, Founder of the Empire, thus increasing its Christian significance." The archbishop of Udine, Monsignor Giuseppe Nogara, would address the Duce on their behalf.[19]

Bishops flooded the Vatican secretary of state office with letters asking what to do. "It seems to me," wrote one Tuscan bishop, "that it takes a lot of nerve for a journal editor to mobilize bishops and priests to give solemn homage to the Duce Founder of the Empire." But "I wouldn't want to be the only one absent."[20]

Cardinal Raffaele Rossi, secretary of the Curia office responsible for issues affecting the clergy, sought advice from the secretary of state. Pacelli informed him he saw no objection to having the clergymen take part in the event. But before he received Pacelli's reply, Cardinal Rossi forwarded yet another bishop's question about the Fascist fête—and offered his opinion that the invitations should not be accepted.

The cardinal had put Pacelli in an awkward position, for allowing a journalist to convene Italy's bishops was undeniably unseemly. Pacelli consulted the pope, who agreed that such an invitation "did not merit being accepted." Yet neither the pope nor Pacelli was eager to offend the Duce.[21]

Confusion reigned in the secretary of state office over the next two weeks.[22] Monsignor Tardini, who had replaced the newly elevated Pizzardo as undersecretary of state for extraordinary ecclesiastical affairs, engaged in a curious dance with the Italian ambassador. On December 30 he told Pignatti that he felt uncomfortable with such a massive political demonstration by the clergy, especially by the bishops. Pignatti responded that if he wanted him to take the matter up with Mussolini, he would need to set down the Vatican's objections in writing. A few days later, meeting with Pignatti, Tardini repeated his plea. Pignatti responded the same way. But no formal request ever came. Tardini drafted the letter, but in the end the pope decided not to send it.[23]

On Sunday morning, January 9, 1938, two thousand priests and sixty bishops marched in solemn procession through Rome's streets as the curious and the Fascist diehards lined their route to applaud. Preceding them were carabinieri in dress uniform, a military band, and a color guard of black-cassocked priests holding Italian flags aloft. Await-

Clergy at Mussolini's celebration of the Battle for Grain, January 1938

ing them at the Victor Emmanuel monument in Piazza Venezia was
Achille Starace, head of the national Fascist Party. He stood alongside
Rome's party chief. Both men accompanied the bishops up the marble
stairs, where they deposited their laurel wreaths at the tombs of the
Unknown Soldier and the heroes of the Fascist Revolution.

The procession then re-formed for the short march into Palazzo
Venezia, passing by the balcony outside Mussolini's office, where a
beaming Duce responded to their Fascist salutes. At noon, they over-
flowed the Royal Hall. After the enormous group recited another
prayer, they cheered as the Duce made his entrance. Archbishop Nogara rose to ask God's blessing on the man who had done so much for
Christianity. A parish priest then strode to the front to recite the motion
that the two thousand priests had unanimously approved: "The priests
of Italy invoke and continue to invoke the Lord's blessing on Your person, on Your work of restorer of Italy and founder of the Empire, on the
Fascist Government." He ended, "Viva il Duce!" The room shook as
the assembled priests and bishops roared "Duce! Duce!"[24]

Italian newspapers gave prominent coverage to the event. Turin's

La Stampa trumpeted the clergy's demonstration of enthusiasm for the Fascist regime: "The enemies of Fascism are also the Church's enemies. The ideals for which Fascism fights are the ideals that Catholic civilization has exalted for centuries." The German press contrasted the patriotic support that Italy's priests and bishops were giving to their Fascist regime with "the bitter experience that we in Germany have had with the German clergy."[25]

EVER EAGER TO DEMONSTRATE Italy's greatness, and having lost all sense of proportion, Mussolini had been putting in place a series of measures aimed at showing the world the nation's Fascist zeal. These ranged from the goose-step march to the prohibition on shaking hands in greeting. The primary architect of these much-ridiculed changes was Achille Starace, head of the Fascist Party since 1931. A master of bad taste,[26] with the mentality of an army drill sergeant, and devoid of either common sense or political sophistication, Starace offered Mus-

Mussolini speaks, with Achille Starace, PNF head (on far right)

solini complete devotion. For years the dutiful, uniformed Starace, gobs of brilliantine plastering his black hair to his head, walked one step behind Mussolini in practically all the Duce's public appearances. At one point, in explaining why he put up with him, Mussolini said with a smile, "Starace is truly my pit bull." When Starace heard this remark, he beamed.[27]

Through it all, the pope continued to press Mussolini to help him with Hitler. The Duce's interest in dampening tensions between the pope and the German dictator was clear: were the pope to denounce the Nazis and excommunicate Hitler, it would be impossible to persuade Italians to tie their fate to the Third Reich.

In March 1938 Mussolini reported to the pope on his latest efforts, taking credit for the Nazis' recent suspension of the embarrassing show trials of the Catholic clergy. Over the previous two years, hundreds of priests and monks had been jailed, many charged with committing sex crimes against young boys. These "immorality trials" generated huge press coverage. Goebbels, in a nationwide radio speech, charged that the "sacristy has become a bordello, while the monasteries are breeding places of vile homosexuality."[28] The pope thanked Mussolini for this help but added that if normal relations were to be restored between the Vatican and the Third Reich, he would have to persuade Hitler to allow Catholic schools and Catholic Action groups to function freely again.[29]

Italy's clergy had no more love for Hitler than the pope did, but their attitude toward Mussolini was very different. Their greatest worry was that, in an increasingly uncertain world, something might happen to threaten Mussolini's rule. While strolling through St. Peter's Square one day, Marchetti Selvaggiani, the cardinal vicar of Rome, shared this thought with Cardinal Pizzardo. "If Mussolini were to go," he said, pointing to a nearby streetlight, "you would see me hanging from that lamppost."[30]

HITLER IN ROME

E ARLY IN THE MORNING OF MARCH 12, 1938, THE GERMAN ARMY crossed into Austria. The next day a triumphant Hitler declared the country a province of the German Reich. On March 14 he arrived in Vienna to widespread rejoicing and the ringing of church bells.[1] "Jews Humiliated by Vienna Crowds: Families Compelled to Scrub Streets," read a *New York Times* headline. "A small State which has fought a battle against fate," its editorial observed, "ceased yesterday to exist." The headline in the London *Times* was more graphic: "The Rape of Austria."[2]

The next day Hitler met with Cardinal Theodor Innitzer, archbishop of Vienna and leader of the Catholic Church in Austria. "Those who are entrusted with souls and the faithful," proclaimed the cardinal, "will unconditionally support the great German State and the Führer, because the historical struggle against the criminal illusion of Bolshevism and for the security of German life, for work and bread, for the power and honor of the Reich and for the unity of the German nation, is obviously accompanied by the blessing of Providence." Innitzer ordered his priests to read his statement in every church. A facsimile of his declaration—complete with his handwritten final words: "And Heil

Hitler!"—was plastered on the walls of Vienna and throughout Austria.[3]

The Nazis scheduled a plebiscite for the following month to legitimate their rule, and Austria's bishops joined the cardinal in issuing a statement to be read from all Austrian pulpits. "We are pleased to recognize," they told Austria's Catholics, "that the National Socialist movement has done and is doing excellent things in the area of national and economic reconstruction, as in the area of social policy." They went on: "We are also convinced that, through the action of the Nazi movement, the danger of atheistic, destructive bolshevism was averted." They urged the faithful to vote yes, joining Austria to the Third Reich.[4]

Hitler's takeover of Austria struck a blow to Mussolini's prestige, for the Duce had long championed an independent Austria under Italian influence. Nor was he, like many Italians, happy about the sudden appearance of a powerful and aggressive Germany on their northern border.[5] When he had visited Germany a few months earlier, the Nazi leaders had promised him that they would not move into Austria without consulting him first.[6] But the consultation had consisted of a letter from Hitler, two days before the invasion, informing him of the imminent action.[7]

Pius XI was surprised, appalled, and embarrassed by Mussolini's meek acceptance of the Nazi takeover of Austria. "I am saddened as Pope," he said, "but I am even more saddened as an Italian." As for Vienna's archbishop, the pope was furious at him. "He signed everything they put in front of him, everything they wanted. . . . And then he added, without any prompting, 'Heil Hitler!'" The archbishops of Salzburg and of Graz had quickly followed Innitzer's lead. The pontiff offered some choice words about the character defects of the Austrian people, which, he lamented, were unfortunately shared by the clergy there as well.[8]

On the evening of April 1, a Vatican radio broadcast skewered the Austrian bishops for supporting the Nazi conquest. The following day the Vatican daily added to the criticism, noting that the bishops had prepared their statement without the Vatican's approval. Pacelli, meeting with the Italian ambassador, called Cardinal Innitzer's behavior an embarrassment for the Church. The normally unflappable if high-strung Pacelli was visibly angry. Unfortunately, he said, in his job he sometimes had to deal with "people lacking character."[9]

But later, when Pacelli spoke with Germany's ambassador, he was much more circumspect. Bergen complained about Vatican radio's "inopportune utterances." Pacelli tried to persuade him that the radio story was "neither official, nor semiofficial, nor inspired by the Vatican, and that the Pope also had nothing to do with it." Pacelli here was stretching the cherished principle of deniability to its extreme limits, and the German ambassador had good reason to realize he was lying. The radio station was a project of the pope, who had enlisted the Nobel Prize–winning Guglielmo Marconi to help design it. With Marconi at his side, the pope had inaugurated it in 1931, his half-hour address—in Latin—reaching both sides of the Atlantic.[10]

In Pacelli, the German ambassador thought, he had an ally. "The Cardinal added in confidence," Bergen reported back to Berlin, "that after this unpleasant surprise he would try to institute some control over the Vatican station. The Cardinal repeatedly protested his fervent wish for peace with Germany."[11]

The pope summoned Innitzer to the Vatican. Vienna's archbishop said he would arrive on the afternoon of April 5 but would need to leave the next morning as he had an appointment with Hitler that he did not want to miss.[12] Indignant, the pope sent word that he was not in the habit of having a cardinal dictate his schedule. Innitzer would return to Austria only when he chose to let him.[13]

At their meeting, Pius told Innitzer that his behavior was disgraceful and instructed him to sign a retraction of his statement praising the new regime. "The solemn declaration of the Austrian bishops of March 18," the statement began, "was clearly not intended to express approval of that which was not and is not in keeping with God's law, with the freedom and rights of the Catholic Church." It stressed that Austria's concordat with the Vatican had to be respected, and that Austria's children should be free to receive a Catholic education. The text, the German ambassador reported, was "wrested from Cardinal Innitzer with pressure that can only be termed extortion." Innitzer, wrote Bergen, "resisted to the utmost, but was able to effect only a few concessions." The next day the archbishop's statement was published in the pages of *L'Osservatore romano*.[14]

Pius was also upset with Mussolini, who had promised to protect Austria's independence but then did nothing to stop the Nazi takeover. "The Duce," remarked the pope to his old friend Eugène Tisserant, "lost his head some time ago."

"Most Holy Father," responded the French cardinal, "he lost it, I believe, during his trip to Berlin."

"He lost it a long time before that," replied the pontiff.[15]

Cardinal Theodor Innitzer, archbishop of Vienna,
casts his ballot in the Nazi plebiscite, April 10, 1938

The French increasingly viewed Mussolini and Hitler as kindred spirits, part of the same totalitarian threat to world peace. As French anger mounted at the pope's support for the Italian dictator, Pius XI became the object of withering criticism. "On one side," wrote Cardinal Baudrillart in his diary, "in the extremist newspapers, they accuse him of not fulfilling his moral mission and capitulating. On the other, some have mused that he should be offered a temporal state elsewhere (not Avignon) so that he is no longer at the mercy of (or an accomplice of) Italy." He concluded, "How embarrassed Cardinal Pacelli must be! What an end for Pius XI's reign!"[16]

IN THE WAKE OF the Nazi takeover of Austria, Mussolini was feeling ill used. Humiliated by the invasion that he had long vowed to prevent, he summoned Tacchi Venturi and told him it was time to put an end to Hitler's dreams of world domination. Half measures would be of no use, he warned, and hopes that Nazism would somehow simply peaceably fade away were naïve. Something dramatic was required, and it would have to come soon.

Who was in a position to take such action? The one man who could stop Hitler, the Duce told the flabbergasted Jesuit, was the pope. By excommunicating Hitler, he could isolate the Führer and cripple the Nazis.[17]

What he proposed was so explosive that Tacchi Venturi would not put it in writing. He requested an urgent meeting with the pope, where he told Pius what Mussolini had said.[18] Knowing how temperamental Mussolini could be, and in any case not inclined to take such draconian action, the pope never seriously considered following the suggestion.

Curiously, Hitler's excommunication may once have been officially considered at the Vatican, although there is no evidence that the pope knew anything about it. It was in January 1932, a year before Hitler came to power. The ground for excommunication was neither Hitler's pagan ideology nor his campaign of race hatred but the fact that he had acted as a witness in a wedding of which the Church disapproved. That month a high German Church official told Italy's ambassador to Germany that Hitler was in serious trouble with the Vatican. Joseph Goebbels, his acolyte, had gotten married, with Hitler serving as a witness. Goebbels, like Hitler, was Catholic, but the woman he married was not only a divorcée but a Protestant, and the ceremony had been performed by a Protestant pastor. For such a sin, excommunication, reported the high German prelate, was being discussed. If excommunication was in fact considered, the Vatican finally decided against it.[19]

MUSSOLINI SOON CALMED DOWN, telling himself that the German take-over of Austria had been inevitable. On reflection, Hitler's display of strength only furthered his resolve to remain the Nazi's ally. Now, far from wanting Pius to strike against Hitler, he again worried that the pope would turn Italians against the German alliance. With the Führer scheduled to visit Rome in the near future, he feared a fiasco.

As news of the Führer's upcoming visit to Rome appeared more frequently in the press, much attention was devoted to the question of whether Hitler would visit the pope.[20] Although he despised Hitler, Pius would not, in principle, refuse to meet him. Hitler was the leader of a country with a huge Catholic population, a government with which the Vatican had full diplomatic relations. But the pope knew that many outside Italy would be unhappy at the sight of Hitler in the Vatican. It would certainly anger the French, and a report from the United States warned him that Americans would be outraged as well.[21]

The Duce initially hoped that a historic visit between Hitler and

Mussolini dedicates the new Luce building with
Father Pietro Tacchi Venturi and Achille Starace, November 10, 1937

Pius XI would be one of the highlights of the Führer's triumphal tour of the Eternal City.[22] If Hitler came to Rome and shunned the Vatican, he worried, millions of Italians would be offended. No head of a state having relations with the Holy See, who had come to Rome in recent years, had failed to see the pope.[23]

Although Pius was unhappy about the upcoming visit, Mussolini could still count on him to help with some of the arrangements. He worried about the sympathies of the foreigners who lived in Rome's religious institutions that, under terms of the Lateran Accords, enjoyed the status of extraterritoriality. On March 26 Ciano contacted Cardinal Pacelli to ask for the pope's assistance. In order to identify all foreigners suspected of anti-Nazi sympathies and place them under surveillance for the visit, papal police cooperation was crucial. A week later came the reply: "The secretariat of state is honored to communicate with all solicitude to the [Italian] Embassy that His Holiness has deigned to concede the desired authorization." The Italian police were to contact their Vatican counterparts to arrange for the surveillance.[24]

Although the pope wanted to maintain his close ties with Mussolini, he was upset at the monumental scale of festivities planned for the Führer's arrival. A low-key visit would be understandable, he told the Italian ambassador. But how could the government prepare "the apotheosis of Signor Hitler, the greatest enemy that Christ and the Church have had in modern times?" He had prayed to God to take his soul back to Him before he had to suffer such a painful sight. As the pope contemplated the prospect, while talking with Pignatti, he choked up. The disgrace to the nation he loved was almost too much to bear.[25]

Three days before the Führer's arrival, the pope left the Vatican for his summer palace in Castel Gandolfo. He ordered the Vatican museums closed for the duration of Hitler's visit and instructed the bishops in the cities along Hitler's route not to attend receptions given in his honor. In the face of papal protests, the government abandoned its plans to set up giant spotlights to illuminate St. Peter's.[26] *L'Osservatore romano* published news of the pope's departure, but denied it had anything to do with the Führer's arrival.[27]

For the pope, the drive to Castel Gandolfo was a bittersweet affair. It was a trying time for him, physically and spiritually, and he sensed this would be his last summer at his retreat in the Alban Hills. Some hint of these thoughts might be read into the unusual reception he hosted on his arrival. After blessing the crowd that gathered in the piazza to welcome him, he invited his staff to a little celebration. In the hall of the frescoes, as the monsignors joined him in conversation, he ordered vermouth brought in and served to all.[28]

ON THE EVENING OF MAY 3, Hitler arrived at Rome's train station, accompanied by Ribbentrop, Goebbels, Hess, Himmler, other Nazi leaders and diplomats, a gaggle of German journalists in uniform, and hidden from public view, his lover, Eva Braun.[29] Because he was head of the German state, protocol dictated that Hitler be met by the king and not by Mussolini. As the Führer stepped off his train, the Duce stood to the side fuming, forced to occupy a supporting role at a moment that he had been eagerly imagining for months. Hitler was surprised to be greeted not by the man he had hailed as a Roman emperor but by the little king with the big white mustache.

Together the king and the Führer rode in a magnificent horse-drawn carriage through the crowd-lined streets, Italian soldiers in double file facing the throngs, kept behind wooden barriers. Searchlights illuminated Rome's ancient monuments. Smoke rising from huge Roman vases filled with burning magnesium powder lent an unearthly quality to the ruins of the Forum and the Palatine Hill.

The guest and his host made their way to the royal residence, the vast Quirinal Palace. They were not a happy couple. The king confided to his inner circle that he thought Hitler was a mental degenerate and drug addict. Hitler, in turn, wondered why he was not being hosted by his fascist ally, and he described the royal palace as "melancholy, uncomfortable, and resembling an antique shop." The Führer's sidekick, Joseph Goebbels, when shown the royal throne, remarked that it should properly be the Duce's seat. That one, he muttered, pointing to the king, is too small for it.[30]

The next day in Castel Gandolfo, in remarks to hundreds of newly-weds, the pope lamented the "sad things" taking place in Rome, the appearance of "another cross that is not the Cross of Christ." "Evidently," Pignatti observed, "the Pope felt the need to let off steam and, given his temperament, you could say he did so in a relatively bland way. But will he stop there?" He answered his own question: "I doubt it."[31]

Mussolini, Hitler, King Victor Emmanuel III, May 1938

Mussolini had worked for months to ensure that Hitler would be impressed by Fascist Italy. In addition to Rome, they would visit Naples and Florence. In every city, the day of their arrival would be proclaimed a holiday. Triumphal arches were built and special lighting mounted. Banners and flags hung everywhere.[32]

After various ceremonies held at Rome's sacred places, the party moved to Naples. Escorted by the king, the procession marched with great pomp to the port, where Mussolini awaited them at the battleship *Cavour* for a day of naval maneuvers, followed by an evening at the opera. The low point of the trip for the Führer came that evening when, following the opera, he found himself outside, in his evening dress, standing next to the king, who wore his full royal uniform, as they inspected an honor guard. As he raised his right arm in Nazi salute, Hitler frantically clutched his waistcoat with his left hand in an attempt to quell his flapping coattails. He looked, observed his aide, like a flustered headwaiter in a restaurant.[33]

After returning to Rome for another three days of military maneuvers, opera, receptions, and speechifying, the party left for Florence for the final day of the visit. More than one hundred thousand banners and flags—Italian and Nazi—hung from windows and were draped over the tops of buildings for the occasion; floral festoons were everywhere. New lights tripled the city's illumination. Lining the streets were eighteen thousand Fascist militiamen, three infantry regiments, hundreds of police from both Florence and Rome, and fifteen hundred carabinieri brought in from around the country. For three weeks police had checked the papers of all who came into the city by car. Preventive arrests were made of any of doubtful loyalty. According to the U.S. consul general, "many Jews were either forced or 'advised' or thought it wise to go away from Florence during the visit."[34]

First Hitler and then Mussolini processed triumphantly in their cars through the streets of the swastika-adorned city. In the majestic Piazza della Signoria, a huge crowd acclaimed the two dictators; then Hitler forced the reluctant Duce to take him for a tour of the Uffizi art galleries.[35] At the train station, as Hitler prepared to leave, the two men warmly bade each other farewell. "Now no force," proclaimed the Duce, "can ever separate us." The Führer's eyes filled with tears.[36]

Just how enthusiastic Italians were about the Führer's visit is a matter of dispute. William Phillips, the American ambassador in Rome, contrasted their enthusiastic cheers for Mussolini with "the apathetic greetings given Hitler." But he concluded that Mussolini had achieved his goal, for Hitler was delighted with his visit, especially impressed by Rome's ancient ruins.[37]

While Mussolini and Hitler proclaimed their mutual admiration in front of hundreds of thousands of cheering Italians, the pope seethed. A few days after the visit, he told French ambassador Charles-Roux that what bothered him most was the colossal scale of the tribute to Hitler—it was the latest sign of Italy's servility to the Führer.[38] *L'Osservatore romano* did its best to ignore the visit. *La Civiltà cattolica* concluded its dry account on a somber note: the grandiosity of the official festivities could not hide the disappointment of the Catholic faithful: the head of a nation that counted twenty-seven million Catholics had traveled to Rome but had failed "to pay his respects to the One who is loved by those millions of Catholics as father and Supreme Pastor of their souls and venerated as the Vicar of Jesus Christ on earth." The result, in *La Civiltà cattolica*'s view, was "a grave, gaping absence" that had greatly diminished the visit.[39]

This view was not universal among the Catholic clergy. Heedless of the pope's warning, many found themselves unable to contain their enthusiasm for the dictators' triumphal procession. In the diocese of Orte, on the train line between Rome and Florence, parish priests joined in the celebrations, adorning their black robes with military medals that they had acquired in the Great War. Knowing that the local Franciscans' Fascist faith ran deep, the Orte bishop had warned them not to participate. But on the day Hitler passed by, they completely covered their monastery with Italian and Nazi flags and even decorated their bell tower with swastikas. Worse, the friars positioned the hundred children enrolled in their school along the train line. When the train passed, the friars led their little charges in chanting: "Viva Mussolini! Viva Hitler!"[40]

A SURPRISING MISSION

WHILE VISITING ROME IN JUNE 1938, JOHN LAFARGE, A FIFTY-eight-year-old American Jesuit priest, was surprised to receive a message that Pius XI wanted to see him at Castel Gandolfo.

On his arrival at the pope's summer residence, LaFarge was escorted to a patio, where the pope had just returned from a walk. His white cane lay on a ledge behind him. The pope told LaFarge he wanted to talk to him about the problem of racism. He had sought him out because his recent book, *Interracial Justice*, was the best one on the subject he had ever read.

Although largely unknown in Vatican circles, LaFarge was an intellectual presence in the American Church. He was born in Newport, Rhode Island, his father a prominent artist, his mother a descendant of Benjamin Franklin. LaFarge graduated from Harvard in 1901 and was ordained four years later. He then spent fifteen years in Maryland ministering primarily to African-American congregations. In 1926 he joined the editorial staff of *America,* and in 1934 he founded the Catholic Interracial Council, aimed at promoting interracial understanding. Three years later he published the book that brought him to the pope's attention.[1]

As they sat together, Pius XI entrusted the American priest with a shocking mission. He was to secretly draft an encyclical on what the pope considered to be the most burning questions of the day: racism and anti-Semitism. Hitler's visit to Rome the previous month was still on his mind, and he no longer felt that his words condemning the glorification of race in his 1937 encyclical were enough. He had been mulling over the idea of a new encyclical when he learned that just the right person was visiting Rome. God, Pius told the flummoxed American, had sent him.

LaFarge expressed doubt that he was up to the task. But the pope persisted: "Say simply what you would say if you yourself were pope." He went on to outline the topics he wanted addressed and the principles that should guide LaFarge.

"Properly," the pope added, "I should have first taken this up with Father Ledóchowski before speaking to you; but I imagine it will be all right."

The pope was being less than forthright here, for he knew the Jesuit general would not be sympathetic. Even more telling was the fact that the pope had kept the matter secret from Cardinal Pacelli and the entire secretary of state office. Nor did he consult the various Vatican offices whose experts normally drafted papal encyclicals.

"The Pope is mad," Ledóchowski remarked, in English, after meeting with Pius that Sunday and learning of the task he had given the American Jesuit.[2]

The next day Ledóchowski met with LaFarge. Taking advantage of the American's anxiety—"I am simply stunned . . . the Rock of Peter has fallen on my head," LaFarge confided to a friend—Ledóchowski suggested that two more experienced Jesuits help him.

When LaFarge arrived in Paris a few days later, these colleagues joined him. Over the summer they worked on the encyclical, to be known as *Humani generis unitas*, "On the Unity of Humankind." If the pope had chosen LaFarge due to his work against racism in the United States, Ledóchowski had chosen his two colleagues—the forty-six-year-old German Gustav Gundlach and the sixty-nine-year-old

French Jesuit Gustave Desbuquois—for very different reasons. Ledóchowski viewed the Jews as enemies of the Church and of European civilization, and he would do all he could to prevent the pope from slowing the anti-Semitic wave that was sweeping Europe. Gundlach and Desbuquois had previous experience working on papal encyclicals and closer ties with the Vatican. They would help constrain LaFarge, who keenly felt his utter lack of experience.

Gustav Gundlach, professor of moral philosophy at the Gregorian University in Rome, was one of the foremost Jesuit experts on the Jews. In 1930 he had authored the entry on anti-Semitism in the authoritative German Catholic theological encyclopedia *Lexikon für Theologie und Kirche*. There Gundlach differentiated between two kinds of anti-Semitism. The first, which went against Church teachings, fought Jews "simply because of their racial and national foreignness." The second, embraced by the Church, combated the Jews "because of the excessive and deleterious influence of the Jewish segment of the population."[3]

In September the three men completed their draft and sent it to Ledóchowski, assuming he would send it immediately to the pope. Instead, he sent an "abridged version" to Enrico Rosa. It was Rosa, then *La Civiltà cattolica* director, whom the pope had turned to a decade earlier to explain the dissolution of the Friends of Israel. But Pius's attitudes toward the Jews were now evolving away from Rosa's. In turning to LaFarge, the pope had kept clear of him. Yet the draft encyclical now lay on his desk.

Despite the pope's apparent change of heart on the Jewish question, he had done nothing to rein in the stream of anti-Semitic venom that was being published in Rosa's journal. As Hitler was terrorizing the Jews of Germany, and while Austria, Hungary, Poland, and other European countries were introducing laws to restrict Jews' rights, the journal—its pages approved in advance by the Vatican secretary of state office—was urging them on. In May 1937 *La Civiltà cattolica* published an article on "The Jewish Question and Zionism," praising the work of "the illustrious English Catholic author, Hilaire Belloc," a notorious anti-Semite. The article got to the point with its opening: "It is an evident fact that the Jews are a disruptive element due to their spirit of domination and their preponderance in revolutionary movements." Belloc, the journal reported approvingly, compared Judaism "to a foreign body that produces irritation and reaction in the organism in which it has penetrated." Giovanni Preziosi—a former priest and noted Fascist—was delighted by the Jesuit journal's screed. He had long been pushing Mussolini to launch a campaign to protect Catholic Italy from the Jewish threat. The *Civiltà cattolica* article, he gushed, was "so perfect that I would wish to present it to those Italians who, for love of Jewish gold, deny the existence of the Jewish peril."[4]

The journal offered its enthusiastic support to Belloc's proposal to have governments segregate the Jews from the larger Christian population.[5] Jews, it charged, controlled both high finance and Communism, in Jewry's "double game" of fomenting revolution to "extend its dominion over the world." Because Jews by their nature sought to rule the world, they could never be loyal to the country in which they lived. This was why they were the most enthusiastic supporters of both Freemasonry and the League of Nations. In short, the Vatican-vetted text reported, Jews sought to reduce Christians to their slaves.[6]

In the months leading up to Mussolini's assault on Italy's Jews, which would be kicked off in July, *La Civiltà cattolica* helped prepare the way by warning of the Jewish threat and the need to act against it. The journal heralded the importance of a spate of recently published anti-Semitic books. In February 1938 a review of Gino Sottochiesa's *Under Israel's Mask* corrected the author—described as a man of "secure Catholic faith"—for his mistaken impression that *La Civiltà cattolica* called only for "charity and conversions" in dealing with the Jewish threat; it had long urged governments to adopt protective measures against Jewry.[7]

Nor was *La Civiltà cattolica* alone. In the months before the anti-Semitic campaign began, much of the Italian Catholic press was urging the government to take action. Especially influential was *L'Amico del clero* (The Clergy's Friend), the official publication of the Italian national association of Roman Catholic clergy, which counted twenty thousand priests as members.

A spring 1938 article by Monsignor Nazareno Orlandi titled "The Jewish Invasion in Italy Too" began with the usual disclaimer: "We are not, nor can we as Christians be, anti-Semitic." The monsignor went on to explain that while the "racist" anti-Semitism of the Nazis, based on a belief in the purity of blood, had to be rejected, "defensive anti-Semitism" was not only legitimate but necessary in the battle against "the Jewish invasion in politics, the economy, journalism, cinema, morals, and in all public life." While thanks to the government's vigilance, things were not as bad in Italy as elsewhere, "it is certain that many of the positions of command among us are also in the hands of the Jews who would, given the opportunity, probably do to us what they have succeeded so well in doing in other nations." While our records are limited as to what millions of Italians who attended Sunday mass in those months heard from the pulpit, and studies are almost nonexistent, it would be surprising if they did not hear repackaged versions of these dire warnings.[8]

In mid-July, while LaFarge and his colleagues were secretly drafting their encyclical in Paris, *La Civiltà cattolica* published a long, enthusiastic article on the recently introduced anti-Semitic legislation in Hungary. "In Hungary," the journal explained, "the Jews have no single organization engaged in any systematic common action. The instinctive and irrepressible solidarity of their nation is enough to have them make common cause in putting into action their messianic craving for world domination." Hungarian Catholics' anti-Semitism was not of the "vulgar, fanatic" kind, much less "racist," but "a movement of defense of national traditions and of true freedom and independence of the Hungarian people."[9]

ON JULY 14 MUSSOLINI kicked off the Fascist campaign against Italy's Jews with a statement on race, published in *Giornale d'Italia,* one of

Italy's leading newspapers. The Manifesto of Racial Scientists, prepared at Mussolini's direction, was a set of propositions drafted by an unknown twenty-five-year-old anthropologist, Guido Landra, and signed by a mix of prominent and obscure Italian academics.[10] It set out the Fascist regime's new racial theory. Italy's population, it stated, was "of Aryan origin and its civilization is Aryan," and indeed "a pure Italian race exists." Ominously, it announced that the time had come for Italians to "proclaim themselves to be frankly racist. All of the work that the regime has done thus far is, in essence, racism." Explaining that "the question of racism in Italy ought to be treated from a purely biological point of view," it incoherently added, "This does not mean however introducing into Italy theories of German racism."[11]

Historians have debated why Mussolini chose to mount a campaign against Italy's Jews. For years the Jewish Margherita Sarfatti had been both his lover and his trusted adviser.[12] Several of Mussolini's family doctors were Jewish, and after announcing the "racial" campaign, he would also have to find a new dentist.[13] Nor had he previously taken seriously Nazi claims of racial superiority. In his 1932 interview with the Jewish Emil Ludwig, he had famously said, "Nothing will ever make me believe that biologically pure races can be shown to exist today."[14]

For many historians, the timing of Mussolini's campaign—its kickoff coming just two months after Hitler's visit to Rome—was no coincidence. Hitler, they argue, told Mussolini during his visit that if he truly wanted to cement their alliance, he would have to eliminate the most obvious difference between the two regimes and declare war on the Jews. Dino Grandi, then Italian ambassador to Great Britain, gave this account. In this reconstruction, Hitler tried to induce Mussolini to join his battle against the Catholic Church as well. The Duce refused but agreed to join the Nazis' anti-Semitic campaign.[15]

There are reasons to doubt Grandi's account, not least the fact that it was written after the war, when Grandi—who had never supported the Nazi alliance—was eager to blame all that was wrong with Fascism on the Nazis. But this does not mean the timing of Mussolini's anti-

Semitic campaign was unrelated to Hitler's visit. He was eager to impress the Nazi leadership and undoubtedly thought nothing would please it more than taking aim at Italy's Jews.[16]

La Civiltà cattolica, which published the manifesto at the end of July, greeted with relief its statement that Italy's racism should be "essentially Italian." The journal worried, however, that its propositions were not clear enough. Some might interpret them as supporting the worship of blood, a Nazi concept that ran counter to Catholic teachings on the universality of humankind. The journal made no comment on the manifesto's proposition that "Jews do not belong to the Italian race."[17] *L'Osservatore romano,* in reporting the news, quoted this sentence but offered not a word of criticism. Meanwhile many papers republished part or all of a July 17 article by a member of the *Civiltà cattolica* collective commenting favorably on the manifesto.[18] Italy's major Catholic daily, *L'Avvenire d'Italia,* was one of them; four days later its editor, Raimondo Manzini, expressed his support for an "Italian racism" in its pages. Manzini would later serve for eighteen years as the editor of *L'Osservatore romano.*[19]

At 7:15 P.M. on July 14, only hours after publication of the manifesto, the Rome correspondent for the Nazi Party newspaper, *Völkischer Beobachter,* relayed the exciting news to Germany. "Following the statement on the problem of racism, National Socialism and Fascism show that in this area too they are united. From today on," the German journalist gushed, "140 million men profess the same *Weltanschauung* [worldview]."[20] The following day German newspapers reported the news glowingly, expressing the belief that Italy would soon announce its own anti-Semitic legislation, following the Nazi example.[21]

After considerable work behind the scenes, the anti-Semitic campaign got off to a strong start. Mussolini followed it closely, assigning the task to the ministry of popular culture, which had responsibility for the regime's propaganda. Professors of known Fascist sympathies were solicited to add their names as supporters of the campaign, libraries devoted to racist literature were organized, and an archive of twenty thousand racist photographs was planned. A group of Fascist academics was enlisted to write about the reality of races, aimed at a broad audience. Of special importance was the launching of a new illustrated popular magazine promulgating the racial theories, to be called *La Difesa della razza* (The Defense of the Race).[22]

In taking action against the supposedly dangerous Jewish threat, Mussolini was finally heeding the warnings that the pope's emissaries, especially Father Tacchi Venturi, had been giving him. But the pope himself showed no sign of concern about any Jewish threat in Italy. What was most exercising him was the threat posed by the Nazis.

The Duce had reason to worry that the pope would oppose his embrace of German racism. But he also had reason to believe he could keep the pope from speaking out against it. If he stood firm and distinguished his brand of racism from the Nazis', he thought, the pope would ultimately back off. The effort to differentiate Fascist racism from Nazi racism helps explain the verbal gymnastics in the racial manifesto. The distinction was also important to Mussolini because nothing angered him more than being accused of imitating Hitler.

Mussolini also knew that while the pope opposed German racial ideology, his views on state policy aimed at limiting Jews' rights were much less clear. Indeed, the Duce was counting on using the Church's own warnings about the Jewish threat to generate popular support for his anti-Semitic campaign.

Most of all, Mussolini knew how much the pope depended on him for favors that benefited the Church. Some of them, including trying to influence Hitler on the Church's behalf, involved major matters. Others, such as relying on the regime to prevent publication of books Pius XI found offensive, were more minor but nonetheless important to him. One such instance was certainly fresh in the pope's mind at the time.

In late May, Pius had learned that a new biography of Cesare Borgia was about to go on sale at newsstands in inexpensive, illustrated installments. Borgia was not a topic the Vatican was eager to have explored. Born in 1475, he was made a cardinal at age eighteen. Borgia's father was Pope Alexander VI. Renouncing his cardinal's hat in his early twenties, Borgia went on to become a military leader, fathering two children by his wife and many more with other women.[23] The pope got word to Ciano that he wanted all copies of the biography destroyed.[24]

Mussolini's son-in-law ordered a halt to the newsstand publication. The government would permit the biography to be published only as a single, weighty volume, which would cut down dramatically on its readership.[25] But the Vatican soon learned that, despite Ciano's order, the popular installments were still on sale. On instructions from the pope, the nuncio Borgongini met with Ciano on June 13.

Galeazzo Ciano

Indignant that his order had not been followed, Ciano picked up the phone and called the second-in-command of the popular culture ministry, the minister being out of town.

"Rizzoli [Angelo Rizzoli, the publisher]," Ciano told him, "is the most anti-Italian, anti-fascist, anti-Catholic person imaginable." The book, he charged, was "a lurid speculation, prepared by the Jews." Borgongini had pointed out to Ciano earlier that the author of the biography, Gustav Sacerdote, was Jewish. Rizzoli had to be taught a lesson. "Put your knee on his throat," instructed Ciano, "and slap him around so that he never forgets it."[26]

A week after that meeting Ciano let the nuncio know that not only had the popular installments of the Cesare Borgia biography been banned, but so had the book itself. The following week Cardinal Pacelli wrote a note of thanks.[27]

UNDER ACHILLE STARACE'S HEAVY HAND, Mussolini's campaign to demonstrate the regime's virility was in full swing. From June 30 through July 2, the dictator presided over highly publicized athletic events aimed at showing the intrepid spirit and toughness of the Fascist Party leadership. Summoned to Rome, the provincial party heads took part in a series of "tests." These ranged from the ridiculous (as Fascism's portly potentates attempted to vault over fake wooden horses) to the dangerous (as they leaped over upright rows of bayonets). The American ambassador described the bizarre event, noting that as Mussolini looked on, "two competitors fail[ed] to clear the bayonet hedge with somewhat uncomfortable results." Italian newspapers featured a photograph of the valiant Achille Starace jumping headfirst through a flaming hoop.[28]

At the time, Mussolini's focus on his plans for Italian greatness was diminished by an unpleasant personal matter. Clara Petacci was growing increasingly prone to fits of jealousy. She had good reason for her suspicions, for even as she camped out in her Palazzo Venezia suite, the Duce continued to have brief trysts with some of his older lovers. Clara lashed out; to calm her down, Mussolini phoned her many times a day. Almost daily through much of July, he sneaked off with her to the beach at Ostia, leaving in mid-morning and returning in mid-afternoon.[29]

The Duce's son-in-law was left to manage the fallout from the newly announced racial campaign. On July 20 he sent the Italian ambassador, Pignatti, to the Vatican to learn the pope's reaction. Two days earlier, speaking to a group of nuns, the pope had again lamented "exaggerated nationalism."

"Is it true," Pignatti asked Cardinal Pacelli, "that the pope is thinking of adopting countermeasures in opposition to the anti-Israelite campaign planned by the royal government?"

Pacelli was noncommittal: the pope had told him of no plans to speak out on the issue, he said. Pacelli expressed no opposition to the anti-Semitic campaign.

What had the pope been referring to with the phrase "exaggerated nationalism"? Pignatti asked. Such comments, he pointed out, could be interpreted as criticizing the new racial policy.

Pacelli hastened to assure him that the pope had no such intention, that his remarks were aimed primarily at Catholics in other countries to warn them not to become too identified with nationalist ideologies there.

Catholic doctrine, argued Pignatti, had to recognize the existence of races.

Cardinal Pacelli responded indirectly. Canon law, he said, was very clear: people who were baptized were to be considered Catholic. Whatever anti-Semitic policies Mussolini planned, it was crucial that he confine them to those who were truly Jewish.[30]

Six days later Pignatti met Pius at Castel Gandolfo to discuss the racial campaign directly with him. The pope appeared thinner but had regained a good deal of his strength. He still wore elastic stockings to help with the pain in his legs, but he no longer needed daily massages. His personal physician drove up from Rome each morning to check on him but no longer felt the need to spend nights there, as he had the previous summer. The pope had no illusions that he would live very long, but he wanted to die at his desk.[31]

Pignatti was pleased with the meeting. He gently scolded the pope for condemning "exaggerated nationalism," telling him his remark was open to misinterpretation. In response, the pope echoed Pacelli's explanation: he had not been referring to Italy.

Then the pontiff raised a complaint of his own. He had been getting disturbing reports that the Italian government was giving privileged treatment to Protestants in the Italian areas in East Africa. Not only was this bad for Catholicism, it was bad for Italy, he told Pignatti, as the Protestants were acting as British agents in Africa.[32] The pope also expressed concerns about the latest accusations that Catholic Action was involving itself in politics. "I pray to the Lord every day," said the pope, "that Signor Mussolini not touch Catholic Action." He added, "you can obtain anything from the pope just as long as you don't attack Catholic Action."[33]

A week after the meeting, the pope, ignoring Pignatti's warning, resumed his attacks on "exaggerated nationalism." In remarks to two hundred students at Rome's College for the Propagation of the Faith, he took his criticism a step further. There was but one, big human race, he told the students; and in a comment that would infuriate Mussolini, he added, "One can ask how it is that Italy, unfortunately, felt the need to go and imitate Germany."[34]

The pope reserved his strongest words for his defense of his beloved Catholic Action. "I warn you," he said, clearly addressing Mussolini, "not to strike Catholic Action, and I beg you for your own good, for he who strikes Catholic Action strikes the pope, and he who strikes the pope dies."

Angered above all by the charge that he was imitating Hitler, Mussolini ordered that no Italian paper publish the pope's speech.[35] Ciano told the nuncio Borgongini that if the pope continued such attacks, he would provoke a major rift. "I spoke very clearly to Borgongini," Ciano recalled. "I explained the promises and the aims of our racism." The nuncio again tried to minimize the pope's remarks. Pius had only wanted to be sure that Italian racism remained within proper bounds. Ciano was pleased: Borgongini "appeared to me to be very convinced. And he revealed himself to be very anti-Semitic."[36]

On July 31 the Italian ambassador went to see Cardinal Pacelli to complain about the pope's latest remarks. The pope could not continue his criticisms and expect to maintain the Church's productive collaboration with the regime. Pacelli promised to convey Mussolini's concerns to the pope. Pignatti thought he had Pacelli on his side but doubted the pope would pay any attention to his advice.[37]

Ambassador Bonifacio Pignatti (right), with Galeazzo Ciano, May 1939

"Collaboration was sometimes hard," Pacelli would later tell Cardinal Verdier, the Paris archbishop, in explaining his relationship with Pius XI. The pope would listen to no one, not even his secretary of state, or so it seemed to him. "My affectionate nature suffered," Pacelli confided, "but I knew that he loved me, and this thought consoled me." Later, he offered Verdier another example of this sometimes-tense relationship. Once he had felt so overwhelmed that without realizing it, he "almost violently" banged his fists on the pope's desk. He could not continue as secretary of state, he told the pontiff. "It does not fulfill me, and I am suffering."

"The pope looked at me coldly and slowly said these words that I will never forget," Pacelli recalled. " 'We have only one task, you and I, that is to do the politics of good!' " Pacelli was touched: "What a magnificent response! Humiliated by the weakness my nerves had caused me, I fell down on my knees at the pope's feet and begged his pardon.

The Holy Father lifted me up affectionately and hugged me." "*Quelle tableau!*" observed Verdier, conjuring up the image, "What a picture!"[38]

Worried about the damage the pope could do to the anti-Semitic campaign, Pignatti turned to a man who could help. On August 4 he traveled south to the Sorrento peninsula, where Father Ledóchowski was staying in a Jesuit residence recovering from a recent illness. "I went to see the general of the Jesuits," Pignatti later explained, "because in the past . . . he did not hide from me his implacable loathing for the Jews, whom he believes are the origin of all the ills that afflict Europe."

The ambassador found Ledóchowski well informed about the problem and highly sympathetic to Pignatti's cause. "Father Rosa," he said, "told me that the pope did not understand." His illness was robbing him of his mental abilities: "It is terrible, but that's the way it is." During the pope's illness, Pius had prayed to God to take his soul to Him, but "the Lord did not grant the pope's prayer, and as a result the Church today is going through a serious crisis." Pius "does not reason and does not want to hear reason." Cardinal Pacelli was at his wit's end: "The pope no longer listens to him as he once did. He carefully hides his plans from him and does not tell him about the speeches he will give."

Those around the pope, reported Ledóchowski, were terrified by what would happen if his condition deteriorated further.[39] He urged the ambassador not to let the pope's rants compromise the Church's good relations with the Fascist regime.

Pignatti replied that they could not ignore the pope's rants, for the foreign press—especially in France—was exploiting his words, and Catholics throughout the world were heeding them, "ignorant of the fact that the common Father of all the faithful was mentally debilitated." The pope's remarks "were causing a tide of hatred against Italy that was compromising it both morally and materially."

Ledóchowski agreed. A crisis loomed. After pledging the ambassador to secrecy, he confided: "The danger is too great not to do whatever is necessary to find a remedy."[40]

Just what "remedy" the Jesuit general had in mind is far from clear. But he would spend the next months doing all he could to prevent the pope from denouncing Fascist racial policy, offending the Nazis, or offering any hope for the Jews.

CHAPTER TWENTY-THREE

THE SECRET DEAL

I N JULY 1938 FORTY THOUSAND JEWS IN AUSTRIA WERE ROUNDED UP and placed in "protective custody." France reaffirmed its commitment to defend Czechoslovakia against Germany. The Germans responded by moving troops to their border with France, soon to be followed by a full military mobilization.

In early August, amid this frightening march toward war, the Italian government followed up on its racial manifesto by issuing a series of anti-Semitic laws. The first banished all foreign-born Jews from attending Italian schools. *La Civiltà cattolica* informed its readers of the measure and published the government's rationale—which was remarkably similar to the journal's own previous warnings about the Jewish threat: Jews could never be loyal to the country they lived in, since their real allegiance was to other Jews; Judaism was behind both Bolshevism and Freemasonry; and although only one Italian in a thousand was Jewish, Jews held many high-level positions. The situation was intolerable.[1]

On August 4, 1938, the pope summoned Giovanni Montini. A few years earlier, in an effort to keep Mussolini happy, he had dismissed Montini as national Catholic Action university chaplain. But late in

1937 he had decided to rehabilitate Montini and made him one of Pacelli's two undersecretaries. The decision put Montini on a path that, a quarter century later, would take him to St. Peter's throne. Now Pius wanted him to draft a letter to Mussolini setting out the pope's position on the Jews and on Catholic Action.

The next day Montini delivered the draft to Pius, and he reviewed it carefully. As far as the Jews were concerned, it said, the pope had no intention of interfering with the state's "responsibility for taking the opportune measures in defense of legitimate interests"; but he hoped Mussolini would not go beyond what Christian charity allowed. On the question of Catholic Action, the pontiff objected to threats to exclude its members from the Fascist Party. Catholic Action, he insisted, had only religious goals and so did not conflict with Fascist Party membership.

Once again Cardinal Pacelli dissuaded the pope from sending the letter, lest it anger Mussolini. Instead, Tacchi Venturi communicated the pope's thoughts to the dictator in person.[2]

The pope's latest concern about Catholic Action stemmed from a report he received from the northeastern city of Bergamo: local Fascists had attacked a Catholic Action club. When Cardinal Pacelli passed this complaint on to Pignatti, the ambassador was indignant. What did the Vatican expect? Fascist activists were outraged by the pope's criticisms of the racial campaign. Worse violence might follow.[3]

Two days later Cardinal Pizzardo, upset by Fascist press allegations that it was he who had persuaded the pope to denounce racism, met with the ambassador. Pizzardo assured Pignatti that he had never spoken to the pope about the matter. Their conversation then turned to the tensions over Catholic Action, where Pignatti proposed a solution. If the organization gave up the practice of having formal membership, it would go a long way to easing tensions. Pizzardo was noncommittal, saying this would be for the pope to decide. The ambassador suspected Pizzardo of encouraging the pope's defense of the organization. He knew where to look for help. "Since Cardinal Pacelli, who notoriously has poor relations with Cardinal Pizzardo, is not especially fond of Catholic Action the way it is organized today," observed Pignatti in his report on their meeting, "I will try to gain him as an ally in this matter."[4]

Further evidence of the pope's isolation came that week, when *La Civiltà cattolica* published a flattering piece about the regime.[5] Pignatti was delighted. When it came to the campaign against the Jews, he told Ciano, the Jesuits' sympathies were clearly with Mussolini. But he added a caution: Italy's newspapers should stop trumpeting this fact. The Jesuits could not let themselves be portrayed as opposing the pontiff.[6]

When Ciano told Mussolini he could not predict what the pope might say next, the Duce's mood darkened. "I do not underestimate his powers," he said, "but he must not underestimate mine." Had the pope not learned his lesson seven years earlier in the battle over Catholic Action? "A signal from me," warned the Duce, "would be enough to unleash all the anticlericalism of this nation."[7]

As in the past, Roberto Farinacci, the most fascist of Fascists, was more than eager to help Mussolini pressure the pope. In the pages of his Cremona-based newspaper *Il Regime fascista*, he denounced Pius XI for criticizing the racial campaign.[8]

Rushing to the pope's defense, Cremona's bishop sent Farinacci a long letter. The pontiff, he explained, had had no intention of criticizing the Fascist racial program. In objecting to "racism," he had meant only to condemn the pagan ideology that the Nazis had embraced. "And when some Catholic writer claimed that Italian Catholic Action could not, on principle, accept racism, he was speaking only of German racism. He was not speaking of an Italian racism." The pope was certainly not condemning a healthy defense of the Italian race against the danger posed by Italy's Jews. If people had been misled into thinking the pope and Church had opposed the racial campaign, it was no doubt because "the anti-Fascists and the Jews have an interest in twisting the meaning of the pope's words to benefit their anti-Fascism."[9]

Farinacci responded in his newspaper. In launching the anti-Semitic campaign, he explained, Mussolini was simply following Church teachings: "The Jews, tied to a well-organized International, have throughout the world declared themselves anti-Fascist and therefore both anti-Italian and anti-Catholic. If this pontiff has some philo-Semitic weaknesses, we cannot deny that other popes were the precursors of Fascism in dealing with the racial problem. Even today I can assure you that on this question many cardinals do not share the attitude of the pope and of *L'Osservatore romano*."[10]

While Farinacci fanned the flames, the pope turned once again to Tacchi Venturi to broker a deal, just as he had in the earlier crisis over Catholic Action. The Jesuit met with the Duce on August 8, bringing with him a memo recording the pope's thoughts. He read it aloud and, after discussing the pope's views with the dictator, left the memo with him.

Two "very grave" matters had upset the pope, said the memo. The first was the "painful" situation in which Catholic Action found itself. The Italian press was filled with calumnies aimed at the organization, and in some areas not only its leaders but even its members were at risk of being harassed. In many parts of the country, Fascist Party members were being told they had to give up their Catholic Action membership if they wanted to remain in the party. Tell Mussolini, instructed the pope, "that as in the anxious days of July 1931, now again, after seven years, We send you [Tacchi Venturi] back to him as our trusted representative with full confidence that he will know how to understand you and He who sends you." If Mussolini thought it helpful, added the pope, he would meet with him personally to find a solution.

The second of the two "painful" matters set out in the memo concerned the "Jewish question." "We recognize," said Pius, "that it is up to the nation's government to take those opportune measures in this matter in defense of its legitimate interests and it is Our intention not to interfere with them." But the pope felt duty-bound to appeal to Mussolini's "Christian sense" and warn him "against any type of measures that were inhumane and unchristian." He then turned to the question of Jewish converts and the Jews who, with Church dispensation, married Catholics. He reminded Mussolini that under the concordat it was canon law alone that determined if these marriages were valid, and he must do nothing to infringe on this right.

Pius concluded by recalling that while the Church, and the popes in the domains over which they ruled, "took care to rein in the children of Israel, and took protective measures against their evil-doing," they never mistreated them. Even though the powerful liturgy of Easter Friday called the Jews "perfidious," he observed, the popes had never forgotten that it was the Jews from whom Jesus Christ, the world's Redeemer, came.[11]

Tacchi Venturi discussed all this with Mussolini at their meeting and then filled the pope in on the Duce's reactions to his pleas. Pius sent him back to the Duce the evening of Friday, August 12, bearing another memo. This time Tacchi Venturi handed the pope's text to Mussolini to read before they began their discussion. The pope had been pleased to hear that Mussolini had no intention of moving against Catholic Action, as long as it remained within its agreed-upon limits, and he was heartened by "the moderation and the spirit of reasonableness with which you say you wish to proceed with the Israelites." His text made no further mention of the Jews, focusing entirely on his remaining concerns about Catholic Action. The pope hoped that a new accord could be reached to bring the Catholic Action dispute to a peaceful conclusion, but this could happen only if Mussolini first took three actions: remove the anticlerical Fascist Party head of Bergamo; reinstate Catholic Action members who had been stripped of their Fascist Party membership; and reinstate those who had lost their government jobs because of their Catholic Action activities.

"Without these preliminaries," Tacchi Venturi, speaking on the pope's behalf, told him, "I believe, O Duce, that our calm discussions will—to my great pain—not easily have the same happy result as those of August 1931." He ended by reminding Mussolini how valuable Church backing had been to the dictator, "not the least important reason for the Italian victory in Ethiopia." So crucial was the Vatican's support of the Fascist regime, argued the pope's emissary, that "all the earthly and infernal forces of cosmopolitan anti-fascism" would do anything they could to end it.[12]

Almost a month had now passed since the announcement of the new racial doctrine. While Jews worldwide were very nervous about what would come next, they still hoped that Italy's anti-Semitic posturing would remain without much practical effect. Italy's 46,000 Jews lived largely in cities of the north and center. The largest community by far was in Rome, with 11,000, followed by Milan with almost 7,000, and Trieste, the northeastern port city, with nearly 5,000. Jews were much more literate than the general population, and while practically half the Italian population were farmers, it was rare to find a Jew tending the soil. But Italy's Jews were far from uniformly well off. While the census listed their largest occupational category as "commerce," this covered everyone from impecunious street vendors to prosperous merchants. Rome's Jewish community was not wealthy. Many of its members depended on Jewish charity to survive.[13]

Unfortunately for Italy's Jews—both rich and poor—Mussolini was all too serious about translating his racial rhetoric into action. But he knew it would not be easy to generate popular enthusiasm for an anti-Semitic crusade that came as a complete surprise to most Italians. If the pope were to publicly oppose him, it might seriously undermine the campaign.

"Three Points of an Agreement Happily Reached the Evening of August 16, 1938, Between His Excellency the Honorable Mussolini and Father Tacchi Venturi, S.J., in order to Restore Good Harmony between the Holy See and the Italian Government that was Disturbed in Recent Weeks." This was the title of the three-page typed document that the pope's Jesuit envoy sent the next day to Cardinal Pacelli. Mussolini had dictated the text, and Tacchi Venturi had written it down. Its terms closely reflected the points that the pope had proposed to the Duce over the previous week.

Of the agreement's three points, the first dealt with the Jews, and the second two with Catholic Action. Point two pledged that Catholic

Action would be allowed to continue its activities in full, unmolested, and that those Catholic Action members who lost their Fascist Party membership would have it restored. In point three Mussolini agreed to the pope's demand that he dismiss Bergamo's party head.

Father Tacchi Venturi's agreement with Mussolini on the treatment of the Jews was spelled out in point one under the heading "The Problem of Racism and Judaism." Mussolini pledged that the new anti-Jewish laws would be no harsher than those that the popes themselves had imposed for centuries on the Jews. In fact, some of the restrictions the popes had enforced in the Papal States were specifically to be excluded. The text read:

> As for the Jews, the distinctive caps—of whatever color—will not be brought back, nor the ghettoes, much less will their belongings be confiscated. The Jews, in a word, can be sure that they will not be subjected to treatment worse than that which was accorded them for centuries and centuries by the popes who hosted them in the Eternal City and in the lands of their temporal domain.

This was the dream of the Jesuits of *La Civiltà cattolica,* one shared by Tacchi Venturi and by the Jesuit superior general. The Jews would at last be subject to restrictions aimed at protecting Christian society from their noxious influence. The Vatican's unofficial journal had been urging these measures on Europe's governments for decades.

In exchange for Mussolini's promise to remain within the bounds of Church-supported restrictions on the Jews, the Holy See would agree not to criticize the upcoming anti-Semitic laws, as the third and final paragraph of the section stated:

"Having said that [i.e., that the restrictions on the Jews would not be worse than those imposed in the Papal States], it is the strong wish of the Honorable Head of the Government that the Catholic press, the preachers, Catholic speakers, and the like abstain from discussing this topic in public. The Holy See, and the Holy Pontiff himself, do not lack the means to come to an understanding directly with Mussolini via private means and to offer him those observations believed to be opportune for the best solution of the delicate problem."[14]

Tacchi Venturi was pleased. The agreement recalled the last time the pope and Mussolini had hurled threats at each other, in 1931. Then, too, a break had seemed perilously near. After others had failed, he had been called in and negotiated an amicable settlement with Mussolini, signing on the pope's behalf. This time, too, the Fascist threat against Catholic Action was averted.

That same week the Vatican daily newspaper weighed in on the need for government action against the Jews. *L'Osservatore romano* recalled that over the centuries the popes had restricted Jews' rights in order to protect Christians. In a passage that would be quickly picked up in newspapers throughout Italy, the paper explained that while the popes had always shown compassion in dealing with the Jews, this should not be misunderstood:

> But—to put things straight—this does not mean that the Jews might abuse the hospitality of Christian countries. Along with protective measures there were decrees of restriction and persecution in their regard. The civil ruler was in agreement with the Church in this. . . . While the Christians were forbidden to force the Jews to embrace the Catholic religion, to disturb their synagogues, their Sabbaths, and their feast days, Jews, on the other hand, were forbidden to hold any public office, civil or military, and this debarment was extended to the sons of converted Jews. These precautions related to professional activities, teaching and even trade.[15]

The Vatican newspaper thus offered a blueprint of the anti-Semitic laws that Mussolini would begin enacting less than three weeks later.

On Thursday morning, August 18, Tacchi Venturi went to Castel Gandolfo to show the agreement to the pope. He knew he would have to handle the pontiff carefully—the pope's anger could explode at any moment. But the Jesuit knew that with enough time, a way could usually be found to win him over or at least ensure that he went along.

As it turned out, he had good reason to fear the pope's wrath. Tardini, who joined them in the pope's study a few minutes after eleven, noticed the tension. Something was wrong, but he did not know what it was.

On their way back to the Vatican, Tacchi Venturi showed Tardini the agreement and told him the pope was upset about the first of the three points, the one dealing with the Jews. "*Quidquid recipitur pro modum recipientis recipitur,*" said Tacchi Venturi. The phrase, identified with medieval Christian philosophy, translates as "One perceives according to one's mode of perception." The pope, the Jesuit complained, insisted on seeing things through dark lenses. He had apparently been especially upset by the agreement's explicit reference to the way the popes had treated the Jews in the past. Although he had made the same point in his earlier communication with the Duce on the Jews, he would not want to identify what Mussolini was about to do with the actions of his predecessors.[16]

Despite Pius XI's outburst, Tacchi Venturi told Tardini he hoped the pope would calm down and realize that the agreement was good for the Church. He had shown the draft to Cardinal Pizzardo, in the waiting room outside the pope's office; he hoped Pizzardo would help persuade the pontiff to accept the deal.[17]

Both Mussolini and those around the pope were eager to see an agreement reached. In letters to his prime minister, the French ambassador Charles-Roux reported that the polemics over the racial campaign were dying down; Catholic Action was the one remaining bone of contention. "As for anti-Semitism," wrote the ambassador, "the tactic employed by the Italian government is skillful, and can only leave the Vatican to stay silent." The Italian papers were filled with articles detailing how, when the popes had held temporal power, they had discriminated against the Jews. On August 17 several newspapers ran articles under the title "How the Popes Treated the Jews," citing

L'Osservatore romano's story earlier in the week.[18] The day Mussolini and Tacchi Venturi drafted their agreement, Dino Alfieri, minister of popular culture, called in the directors of Rome's newspapers and the Rome-based correspondents of other Italian papers. His message: tone down the polemics against the Vatican, because "it looks like everything is being taken care of."[19]

Word spread among journalists close to the Vatican that Tacchi Venturi and Mussolini were far along in reaching a deal. Achille Starace, head of the Fascist Party, and Lamberto Vignoli, head of Catholic Action, meanwhile met to follow up on points two and three of the agreement.[20]

On August 20 *The New York Times* featured news of the bargain on its front page. "Tensions between the Vatican and the Fascist party over Catholic Action associations, which in recent weeks the Italian press has accused of being hostile to Italy's racial doctrines, was eased today by the announcement that Achille Starace, Fascist party secretary, and Lamberto Vignoli, president of the Italian Catholic Action, had reached an understanding that places their relations on the basis of the accords of September, 1931." The *Times* reporter had learned, albeit in a vague way, of the secret deal at the heart of the agreement. In exchange for Mussolini's offer to leave Catholic Action alone, the Vatican would go along with the regime's forthcoming anti-Semitic drive: "as a result of the conversations between Mussolini and Father Tacchi Venturi Catholic Action pledged itself not to undertake any activity that could be interpreted as hostile to Italy's racial policy. In return the Fascist party gave guarantees that no retaliatory measures would be taken against party members who also belonged to Catholic Action."[21]

On August 21, Rome's *Il Messaggero* ran its own account of the agreement under the title "Accords Confirmed Between Party and Catholic Action." It reported the meeting of Starace and Vignoli and the resulting accord. It accurately described the understanding that Mussolini had reached with Tacchi Venturi on Catholic Action: as long as it abided by the terms of the 1931 accord and confined its activities to the religious sphere, it would be free to operate unmolested. But unlike the American newspaper, the Italian papers made no mention of what Mussolini expected from the pope in exchange.

The pope held up the Vatican announcement of the deal, seeking further guarantees that Catholic Action members who had lost their Fascist Party membership would indeed get it back. After more meetings between Tacchi Venturi and Mussolini, the pope was finally satisfied. The Vatican daily published news of the agreement on August 25. The dispute over Catholic Action was settled. Again, no mention was made of any quid pro quo involving Vatican support of Mussolini's anti-Semitic campaign.[22]

Encouraged by his advisers, the pope was gradually making peace with the deal that Tacchi Venturi had worked out with Mussolini. But he remained unhappy about Mussolini's embrace of Hitler and a racial ideology that struck him as anti-Christian. While the world's press was publishing news of the agreement, the pope privately expressed his anger. Have Tacchi Venturi tell Mussolini, the pope told his secretary of state, that if he wants to kill the Holy Father, the methods that he is using are effective. And he again added a threat. Before he died, he would "let the whole world know how the Catholic religion and the Holy Father are being treated in Italy."[23]

In public the pope was now more circumspect, but some hint of his continuing unease crept into his remarks. In a talk to students at the College for the Propagation of the Faith building in Castel Gandolfo, the pope returned to the topic of "exaggerated nationalism." Pignatti's number two, Carlo Fecia di Cossato, who reported the news (Pignatti was presumably off for his August vacation), thought it no coincidence that the pope returned to speak to the same audience as he had in his controversial July 28 remarks on Mussolini's new racial policy. But this time, the pope's words were more prudent. As a result of all the criticism he had received, said the diplomat, the pope "put a little water in his wine." While there was a place for "a just, moderate temperate nationalism, associated with all the virtues," the pope said, there was also an unhealthy form, an "exaggerated nationalism," which he deemed "a real curse." Cossato was pleased by the tenor of the pope's remarks: "The concern to soften the bad impression produced by the July 28 speech seems clear to me."[24]

Mussolini, sensitive to any hint of criticism, was less pleased.[25] "Contrary to what is believed," he told Ciano, "I am a patient man. It is necessary though, that I not be forced to lose this patience, otherwise I will react, destroying everything in sight. If the pope continues to talk, I will scrape off the layer of clericalism from the Italians, and before you can say it, I'll make them become anticlerical." The pope was mistaken if he believed Italians were more devoted to him than they were to their Duce. "The men in the Vatican," he told his son-in-law, "are insensitive and mummified. Religious faith is on the decline: no one believes in a God who takes care of our suffering." And with a dose of blasphemy, he added, "I would hold in contempt a God who takes an interest in the private life of the corner cop on the via del Corso."

While those around the pope were trying to bring him around, across the Tiber Ciano was trying to calm down his father-in-law. "In the difficult international situation," he wrote in his diary on August 22, "a conflict with the Church would not benefit anyone."[26]

Applying further pressure on the pope, Italian newspapers continued to cast the new Fascist campaign as simply putting long-standing Church teachings on the Jews into effect. An August 24 story in *Giornale d'Italia*—the paper that had first published the racial manifesto— recalled Pius XI's decision, ten years earlier, to suppress the Friends of Israel for opposing the Church teaching that Jews were "perfidious." The notoriously anti-Semitic newspaper *Il Tevere* ran a story that day under the identical title, "The Church and the Jews"; the use of the same title in several newspapers was a sure sign the government had planted the stories. "In every era," the paper reported, "the popes have sought to erect barriers around the Jews' activities, to isolate them as one does for an epidemic." The popes had taken harsher measures against the Jews than the ones the Fascist regime was contemplating, as the popes sought "to protect their subjects from the Jews' diabolical moral influence." After listing dozens of Church canons warning of the

Jewish threat, the article concluded: "The Italian race wants to purify itself from this perfidious, foreign people forever."[27]

The pope sent his nuncio to talk to Ciano about the continuing tensions. Ciano described their meeting, held in late August, in his diary:

Borgongini Duca, on the Pope's orders, comes to discuss the announcement which, at least for the moment, will end the dispute between the Party and Catholic Action. I nudged him a bit and he opens up about the Pope. He says that he has an awful personality, is authoritarian and almost insolent. At the Vatican they are all terrified of him. Even Borgongini himself trembles when he is about to enter the Pontiff's room. He treats everyone arrogantly: even the most distinguished cardinals. Cardinal Pacelli, for example, when he is called by the Pope must, like a petty secretary, take notes by dictation of all his instructions. He is again in good health. He eats cooked fruit and a little meat. He drinks red wine in limited quantities, and does sufficient exercise in the garden. He is 82 years old and still runs the government of the Church down to the smallest details.[28]

The government was ramping up a massive anti-Semitic propaganda campaign, relying heavily on its new popular biweekly, *La Difesa della razza*.[29] Doctored photographs and grotesque illustrations filled its pages, chronicling the degeneracy of Jews and Africans. The first issue published an image of a man's face, in profile, his enormous nose hooking down to rest against his fat lips. It bore the label "Typical photograph of a Jew, clearly showing the characteristics of his race."[30] The magazine's portrayal of the Jewish threat mirrored that of the Vatican-approved pages of *La Civiltà cattolica*, with the addition of pseudoscientific claptrap given a patina of respectability by its authors' academic titles.[31] The Jews were behind Communism and capitalism; they were taught by the Talmud to hate all Christians and to rule over them; they had no allegiance to the country in which they lived; they conspired secretly against both the Church and Fascism. One of the feature stories in the first issue of *La Difesa della razza* was titled "Fifty Years of Polemics in *La Civiltà cattolica*," concluding that "there is no incompatibility between the doctrine of the Church and racism, as it has been expressed in Italy."[32]

Pignatti, upon returning from his summer vacation in late August, was relieved to learn that the pope's remarks to his most recent audiences were harmless. Although Pius XI had briefly raised the question of racism, he had not said anything that the Italian ambassador found objectionable. But Pignatti remained nervous. "One can only hope," he told Ciano, "that the pope stops talking. With his mania for speaking . . . one always fears the worst."[33]

THE RACIAL LAWS

O N SEPTEMBER 1 THE ITALIAN GOVERNMENT REVOKED THE CITI-
zenship of foreign-born Jews who had become citizens after
1919. It ordered all Jews who were not citizens to leave the country
within six months. The following day all Jewish teachers—from elementary school through university—were fired. Christian children
could not be taught by Jews. Nor would Jewish children be allowed to
attend public schools at any level. Jewish members of honorary societies of arts, letters, and sciences were ejected. For the purposes of these
"racial laws," Jews were defined as those born of parents of the "Jewish
race," even if they might "profess a religion different from Judaism."

In announcing the new laws, *La Civiltà cattolica* expressed no
opposition—hardly surprising since it had been calling for just such
measures since 1880. But the journal was eager to distinguish the basis
of its own anti-Jewish campaign from one based on purity of blood.
Jews, in its view, were a threat to Italians not because of their biology
but because of their behavior.[1] The journal's own call for government
action against the Jewish threat had been "inspired solely by the legitimate defense of the Christian people against"—and here it quoted ap-

provingly from an earlier article—"'a foreign nation among the nations in which it lives and sworn enemy of their well-being.'"[2]

In the early days of the anti-Semitic campaign, the Fascist press made heavy use of the unofficial Vatican journal to generate popular support for the racial laws. The Vatican turned to the journal's éminence grise, Enrico Rosa, to clarify the matter. His article, "The Jewish Question and *Civiltà cattolica*," expressed no opposition to the new anti-Semitic laws but did take issue with those who, in supporting them, mischaracterized the journal's rationale for recommending that governments restrict Jews' rights.

Events had shown the wisdom, Father Rosa declared, of the journal's prophecy that granting Jews legal equality would prove catastrophic not only for Christian society but for the Jews themselves. Giving them equal rights had unleashed widespread hatred against them, since they had used their newfound freedom to accumulate occult power and wealth and to persecute the Catholic Church and oppress Christians.[3]

Near panic, many Italian Jews sought out parish priests to baptize them. Over the next three years, one out of ten Italian Jews would renounce their faith. Almost fifty of Bologna's one thousand Jews were baptized in August and September 1938, in a desperate effort to escape persecution.[4]

As the Fascist anti-Semitic campaign took its fateful turn from theory to active persecution, the country's Roman Catholic clergy voiced few objections. In those rare cases where a priest did express criticism, Mussolini had only to get word to Cardinal Pacelli, and the priest was disciplined. Such was the case on September 1, when Pacelli received a report of critical remarks from a priest in a remote village north of Milan, near Lake Como. Don Abramo Mauri lived at a Church rest home, recuperating from nervous exhaustion. The local nuns had invited him to conduct a mass in their little chapel. There, one Sunday, he complained that "they are already starting to inculcate a sense of false pride in these snot-nosed kids of only three years old." The local

Mussolini with children in a Fascist youth group, 1938

Fascist Party leader, who was present, was outraged, sure the priest was referring to Fascist youth groups. To make matters worse, the priest had gone on to criticize the new racial campaign, predicting that it would lead to war.[5]

Cardinal Pacelli asked the bishop of Como to investigate.[6] After looking into the matter, the bishop assured Pacelli that the priest's comments about the "snot-nosed kids" had been misinterpreted. They referred, he said, to overindulgent mothers who spoiled their children. But the bishop found no way to explain away the priest's criticism of the racial campaign. As a result, he ordered Don Mauri never to give another sermon in the church.[7]

EUROPE, MEANWHILE, WAS MOVING ever closer to war. On September 1 Hitler demanded that Czechoslovakia cede its German-speaking Sudetenland region to the Third Reich. France began to mobilize its troops.

In Rome, William Phillips, the U.S. ambassador, looked on with growing concern. Mussolini's racial manifesto in July had produced shock in the United States and alarm in the U.S. State Department, the latest sign that Mussolini intended to tie Italy's fate to Nazi Germany. Phillips could see few levers that might prevent this catastrophe, and none more promising than the pope. He had excitedly reported to Washington on the pope's July 20 speech and his criticism of the Duce's eagerness to imitate Hitler. A month later his hopes had been dampened when he read the *Osservatore romano* article supporting restrictions on Jews. Still he had not entirely given up. Perhaps the pope might yet be swayed.

As soon as the latest racial laws were announced in early September, evicting Jewish children and teachers from Italy's schools, Phillips asked to see Joseph Hurley, the one American prelate in the Vatican secretary of state office. The two men had met several times in the past, and in the absence of an American ambassador to the Holy See, Hurley kept Phillips informed on what was going on in the Vatican.[8]

When the two men met that evening in the U.S. embassy, the ambassador got right to the point. Both he and the American government were horrified by the new anti-Semitic laws. Not only were they outrageous in themselves; they would turn Americans sharply against the Italian government. Phillips saw the racial campaign as part of a larger, worrisome picture. Mussolini was losing his sense of reality, surrounded by sycophants and refusing to meet with foreign ambassadors who might offer a different view. Should things get worse, Phillips told Hurley, "perhaps the Vatican will be able, through its prudent intervention with the Italian Government, to ward off the catastrophe of a general war."[9]

As an incentive, Phillips suggested that should the pope denounce the new racial laws, the American public would be so pleased that it would "disarm the Protestant opposition." This would allow the American government to establish formal diplomatic relations with the Vatican. The Holy See had sought such recognition for decades, but the American political situation had so far made it impossible. The anti-Catholic prejudices of the Protestant majority, together with the belief that the Vatican was a religious organization and not a sovereign state, had stymied efforts in the past.[10] The next day Hurley passed Phillips's message on to Pacelli.

Three days later Pius XI held an audience for the staff of Belgian Catholic radio. With the American ambassador's message fresh in his mind, he spurned his counselors' advice and let his heart guide him. His voice became laden with emotion and tears came to his eyes as he began to discuss the new racial campaign. "Every time I read the words 'the sacrifice of our father Abraham,'" said the pope, referring to a phrase in the priestly blessing during mass, "I cannot help but be deeply moved." His voice trembled. "It is impossible for Christians to participate in anti-Semitism. We recognize that everyone has the right to self-defense and can undertake those necessary actions to safeguard his legitimate interests. But anti-Semitism is inadmissible. Spiritually we are all Semites."[11]

This was just what Ledóchowski, Tacchi Venturi, Borgongini, and Pacelli had feared. But they found a way to limit the damage. When *L'Osservatore romano* published an account of the pope's remarks, no mention was made of his anguished words about the Jews.[12] That some Catholics noticed the Vatican newspaper's silence is clear from a police intelligence report filed the day after the pope's comment. "Many Catholics who had fully approved of what the pontiff recently said in defense of the Jews," it read, "now do not know how to explain why the Vatican newspaper, the only one not subject to Italian government censorship, has not returned to the subject following the decisions taken by the Council of Ministers. They find this silence to be strange."[13]

How exactly Pacelli and his undersecretary, Domenico Tardini, had ensured that the Vatican newspaper ignored the pope's explosive remarks remains a mystery. Most of the pages from Pacelli's log of his meetings with the pope in these months are, curiously, missing from those open to researchers at the Vatican Secret Archives.

ITALIANS, THOUGHT MUSSOLINI, WERE a weak people. He needed to toughen them up. At an early October Grand Council meeting where additional racial laws were approved, he explained, "It is my task to bust the Italians' balls. I understand that there are, at the margins, those who love the comfortable life. But they are just the fringes of the nation. We will cut them out."[14]

In the eyes of many Italians, Mussolini had assumed godlike qualities, but along with the adulation came a dash of fear. As two members of the Institute of Fascist Culture were leaving the institute's headquarters, they ran into the elderly caretaker. One of them jokingly pointed to the other and told the befuddled custodian, "Do you see that man? He's an immortal."

"What do you mean?" replied the old man. "All men are mortal!"

"Ah! I see! So you think Mussolini too is a mortal!"

"I didn't say that!" insisted the frightened custodian.[15]

Around the same time, Foreign Minister Ciano had a visitor, Prince Philipp of Hesse, a man Hitler often used to send messages to Mussolini. It was Hesse who, earlier that year, had hand-carried Hitler's letter to Mussolini informing him of the imminent invasion of Austria. Grandson of a German emperor and great-grandson of Britain's Queen Victoria, Hesse had been a Nazi Party member since 1930. He had done much to win the German aristocracy over to the Nazi cause. When he arrived at Ciano's office that day, he was clearly embarrassed. He had come, he explained, to see Ciano about a private family matter. In 1925 Hesse had married Victor Emmanuel's daughter, and his mother-in-law, Queen Elena, had asked him to intercede on their behalf with the Duce. They wanted an exception to the racial laws to be made for their Jewish doctor. "It seems," Ciano wrote in his diary, "that the Queen is very angry about the expulsion, and also the King, who trusts this doctor very much, but does not dare to speak to the Duce. And both of them count on my friendly mediation." Delighted to have the upper hand with the nervous German aristocrat, Ciano smiled. What would the Führer say, should he mention Hesse's request to him? he wondered aloud. At this the blood drained from Hesse's face.[16]

In early September Pius XI told Tacchi Venturi to draft a message for Mussolini, on the need to exempt baptized Jews from the racial laws. The pope approved the draft, then added something else. Tell Mussolini, he instructed his Jesuit envoy, that Italy's racial laws might well "provoke reprisals on the part of Jews throughout the world."[17] A few days later Tacchi Venturi brought Mussolini a more pointed papal message. As an Italian, the pope said he was truly saddened to see "a whole history of Italian good sense forgotten, to open the door or the window to a wave of German anti-Semitism."[18]

But as the first racial laws were made known, what most upset the pope, and certainly what most bothered those around him, was not their impact on Italy's Jews but the fact that they were to apply to Catholic converts from Judaism as well.

After meeting with the pope on September 20, Tacchi Venturi prepared a memo, as he often did, to convey the pope's wishes to Mussolini. Jews who had shown special merit—especially in military service in the Great War—had, he noted, been exempted from the new laws. The pope was pleased to learn of this exception but wondered why no similar provision had been made for Jews who had "separated themselves from the Synagogue, asking for and receiving baptism." The Church "wants each of them to abhor Judaic perfidy and reject Jewish superstition, [and so] cannot forget these, its children." These converts were especially at risk, added the pope's envoy, because their own families shunned them, regarding them as traitors.

It made no sense, argued Tacchi Venturi, for Mussolini to exempt Jews who had served in the war and not those who had embraced Catholicism. The merit of the former was "certainly inferior to that much larger one that is the renunciation of the blindness and obstinacy of their error without which a Jew could not become a true Christian."[19]

In the wake of the racial laws, a parade of Jews and former Jews sought help from Italy's bishops. Uncertain what the pope expected of them, the bishops bombarded the Vatican with requests for guidance. In a typical letter, in late September, the archbishop of Turin told of all the Jews who had come to ask for his aid. If they thought they would get it, they were mistaken. "I must ordinarily limit myself," he reported, "to suggest they remain calm, that they wait for further regulations, and they have faith in the government, etc." But while he could dismiss the Jews, he did not feel he could do the same for those Catholics who had converted from Judaism and were being treated as if they were Jews. It was for this reason that he wrote.

Tardini, saying that he had shared the archbishop's letter with the pope, replied with a promise to bring the Turin cases, mentioned by the archbishop, to the government's attention. He asked Tacchi Venturi to take up the matter.[20]

Italy's Jews were feeling increasingly isolated. Primo Levi, then a nineteen-year-old student at the University of Turin, recalled those first months of the racial laws. "My Christian classmates were civil people. None of them or my professors directed a hostile word or gesture toward me, but I felt myself being distanced from them. . . . Every glance exchanged between them and me was accompanied by a small but perceptible glimmer of diffidence and suspicion. What do you think of me? What am I for you? The same as six months ago—one of your equals who does not go to mass—or the Jew?"[21]

In a September diary entry, a Jewish woman described her family's plight. Her husband, a scientist, was despondent: he had recently received a letter containing an article he had written and submitted to a journal. " 'The editor returns it herewith,'" his wife noted; "a few embarrassed words, 'no longer able to proceed with publication, most regretful,' etc. He opened the next letter. 'The president of the Academy of Science wishes to advise that, following instructions received to that effect, he is removing his name from the membership list.' . . . The fearful sense of emptiness invaded him again, sweeping over his heart. He saw, suddenly and for the first time how his one true reason for living had been torn from him."[22]

In another Jewish household, a young girl refused to come out of her room and would not eat. It was to have been her first day of school, but she would not get to share in the excitement with the other girls, for she was Jewish. Distraught, her mother entered her room "with my heart in my throat," as she recalled in her diary. She described the scene: "Young people's tears are so difficult to dry. . . . The room was quiet, looked empty. Then I saw her, stretched across the bed, asleep. Her cheeks were still wet and her hand still clutched her handkerchief, and her 'why' still echoed in the quiet room."[23]

HAVING GOBBLED UP AUSTRIA in March, the Nazis were now threatening to annex Czechoslovakia's Sudetenland. In a September 12 speech at Nuremberg, Hitler vowed that should the territory not be given to them, the Germans would take it by force.[24] Panic spread through Europe. By late September, six hundred thousand people had fled Paris, worried that a German attack was near.

In the midst of this frenzy, the Duce seized an unusual opportunity. Neville Chamberlain, the British prime minister, invited him to mediate the Sudetenland dispute at a peace conference to be held in Munich.

The French, British, German, and Italian leaders arrived at the conference site on September 29. The thickset Mussolini, dressed in his tight-fitting uniform, his chin jutted forward, and his face set in his best Caesar-like pose, acted as though he—rather than Hitler—were the host. Ciano, also in uniform, hovered around his father-in-law. Chamberlain, with his fancy suit, his abundant eyebrows, lined face, and hands bent by rheumatism, was the picture of the aristocratic diplomat of English stamp. Hitler, in business suit, was ill at ease, constantly in motion, his face pallid. Knowing only German, he clung to Mussolini, the sole German-speaker among the other government heads.[25]

A photo from the meeting shows Mussolini in his light-colored military uniform, his head shaved bald, staring somewhat menacingly as Chamberlain, in dark suit and high collar, appears to be struggling to convince him of something. For Mussolini, the umbrella-carrying British prime minister was the embodiment of the effete values his Fascist regime was battling. "I never want to see umbrellas around me," he once said. "The umbrella is a bourgeois relic, it is the arm used by the pope's soldiers. A people who carry umbrellas cannot found an empire."[26]

While the Duce was in Munich, the pope went to the Vatican radio station to broadcast a plea for peace. He spoke not in Latin but in Italian, eager that his message be heard. Tears reddened his eyes as he addressed "all Catholics and the entire universe." "While millions of men live in fear of the impending danger of war and of the threat of unprecedented massacres and ruin," he said, "We share in Our paternal heart the trepidation of so many of Our children and We invite the bishops, clergy, members of religious orders, and all the faithful to join Us in the most insistent, hopeful prayer for preserving peace with justice and charity."[27]

Back at the Munich conference, Mussolini offered his peace plan—or perhaps more accurately, he presented Hitler's peace plan and called it his own. Germany was to be allowed to seize the Sudetenland. The British and French government heads agreed to this humiliating capitulation in exchange for Hitler's promise to stop there. No representative of Czechoslovakia was invited to the meeting that dismembered the country.

Mussolini returned to Italy to a hero's welcome. In fields alongside the train tracks, farmers got down on their knees to greet the man who had brought peace to Europe. This was only one of many signs that, a month after the racial laws were first announced, his popularity remained high.[28] For his part, Hitler would have to wait until the following year to see his war begin in earnest, but he drew an important lesson from the peace conference. In August 1939, as he was about to send German troops into Poland, he told his generals: "Our enemies are small worms. I saw them in Munich."[29]

Among those singing Mussolini's praises was Milan's Cardinal Schuster. In a gushing public letter, he proclaimed that "Italy is proud because its Duce made such a precious contribution to peace." He suggested that a new church dedicated to peace be constructed to mark Mussolini's triumph. Hearing of the archbishop's proposal, the pope exploded. "What a disaster!" he exclaimed to Tardini. "I would never have believed it! I thought he was more intelligent than that!"[30]

At a Grand Council meeting a few days after his return, Mussolini

Cardinal Ildefonso Schuster, archbishop of Milan, with Mussolini

took aim at the handful of holdouts against the racial laws. He insisted that the Jews were behind what remained of antifascism in the country. Stung by the pope's criticisms, he branded Pius XI "the most harmful pope ever for the future of the Catholic Church"[31]

The pope is a "calamity," the Duce, in a pontificating mood, told Clara Petacci shortly after the meeting. "Today we are the only ones, I am the only one, supporting this religion. . . . And he does shameful things, like saying that we are all like Semites." He worked himself into a fury. "You don't know the trouble they are causing," he told Clara, whose interest in such matters was limited. "He has upset all the Catholics, he gives nasty, shocking speeches. In a word, he is evil." The Duce went on to muse that there was something unlucky about popes named Pius—they all brought disaster. Pius VI and Pius VII were both thrown out of Rome by Napoleon; Pius IX lost Rome and the Papal States; and Pius X saw all Europe erupt in war. "He is losing the whole world and now he risks destroying everything here as well. Ah, it's a true calamity." As a Catholic, he concluded, "I have to say that it would be hard to imagine a worse pope than this one."[32]

The Grand Council approved the new racial laws; *La Civiltà cattolica* published them, along with the official justification, all without comment. "Jewish elements lead all anti-Fascist forces," the government proclaimed, and so further measures against them were urgently needed. Italian Jews were to be thrown out of the Fascist Party; they could not own or direct businesses having more than a hundred employees, own more than fifty hectares of land, or remain in the Italian military. Restrictions on their ability to exercise professions would soon be announced. Special secondary schools for Jews were to be established, joining the Jewish elementary schools that had already been authorized.[33]

Ciano worried about the pope's reaction to the latest round of racial laws, but he was relieved to learn that all might work out well after all. The Holy See would offer no objection, his chargé d'affaires at the Vatican told him, as long as the new laws did not treat Catholics who had converted from Judaism as if they were Jews. Most important, the Vatican insisted that nothing be done to violate the terms of the concordat: its language clearly guaranteed state recognition of all Church-sanctioned marriages. "This is the only point in the racist proclamation of the Grand Council," the Italian diplomat told Ciano, "about which the Church would object."[34]

This reading of the pope's position is confirmed by a note Domenico Tardini made on the day the new racial laws were announced. "This evening, at the request of the Holy Father," he wrote, "*L'Osservatore romano* will publish a brief article, mentioning some concern and expressing the hope that the future law may remove every reason for reserve."[35]

The pope viewed the new racial laws as part of a larger, troubling pattern. Mussolini, rather than working with the Vatican to bring about a confessional state in which Catholicism infused Fascism with its values, seemed bent on creating a separate Fascist religion. In mid-September, Pius XI addressed this concern in remarks to a group of French union members. Some argue, said the pope, that everything should belong to the state, making it totalitarian. But such a claim was absurd. "If there is a totalitarian regime," he told them, "totalitarian in fact and by right—it is the regime of the Church, because man belongs totally to the Church."[36]

The pope was beginning to question whether he could continue to support Mussolini and his Fascist regime. But although his unscripted remarks continued to make both Fascist officials and his own advisers nervous, his opposition to specific anti-Semitic measures remained limited. Clearly those around the pope did not oppose them. Italy's chargé d'affaires, Carlo Fecia di Cossato, informed Mussolini and Ciano that according to top Vatican officials, the recent racial laws "have not, as a whole, found an unfavorable reaction in the Vatican." The only objection raised there regarded the violation of the Church's right to define what constituted a legal marriage. "I had confirmation of these impressions from Monsignor Montini, substitute for ordinary affairs at the secretary of state office, especially that the major, not to say the only, concern for the Holy See regards the case of marriages with converted Jews."

Cossato added a note about the Jesuits, echoing Pignatti's earlier advice. "The Jesuits," he explained, "have always been convinced anti-Semites—albeit for doctrinal reasons different from ours." But they could not let themselves be portrayed as opposing the pope. Better, he advised, to let the Jesuits demonize the Jews without calling attention to it, for "in the shadows and on the practical level they have been and they may still be our best allies."[37]

That same evening Cossato got to meet with Father Rosa, whose latest article on "the Jewish question" had recently been published in *La Civiltà cattolica*. Rosa told him he had written it on orders from the Vatican, "to dissipate the impression that readers might have of the total support for the racist measures adopted by the Fascist Government by the organ of the Society of Jesus." But after speaking with Rosa, the envoy felt reassured. "The Jesuits," he told Ciano, "are still today clearly and fundamentally anti-Jewish."[38]

SHORTLY BEFORE GOING TO the early October Grand Council meeting, Ciano summoned the papal nuncio and showed him reports he had received from a recent Eucharistic Congress. Borgongini saw the telltale markings of Mussolini's colored pencil on the sheets. The dictator had been upset to learn of critical remarks made by priests at the congress. One in particular had angered him. "God," the priest had warned, "will certainly punish the German people and all those who set out on their path." The Duce did not want any conflict with the Church, said Ciano, but the pope must be told that unless he prevented priests from voicing such criticism, the government would be forced to act.

"If there has been any intemperance of language," the nuncio assured Ciano, "certainly we will be the first to remind the sacred orators of their duty." But the pope did not share the nuncio's craven view. When, some days later, Pius learned of the priests' "intemperate" words, he exclaimed, "*Benissimo! Giustissimo!*" ("Excellent! Just right!") He added, "Someone needs to be saying these things!"

At the same meeting with Ciano, Borgongini again conveyed the pope's plea that Mussolini intervene with Hitler on his behalf. The pope had been upset to learn that the Nazis' persecution of the Church was now extending to Austria and the Sudetenland. "Since it is clear that no one is able to influence Hitler aside from His Excellency the Head of the Government," the nuncio told Ciano, "I beg you to tell His Excellence Mussolini that only he can get the Führer to stop his persecution."

Borgongini then turned to the question of the Fascist Party head in Bergamo. Here his words are of special interest, for they refer to the secret deal with Mussolini in mid-August, granting papal approval for the racial laws in exchange for concessions to benefit Catholic Action.

"I asked the minister [Ciano] to take care of Bergamo," the nuncio reported afterward to Pacelli, "for it was authoritatively promised that that federal secretary would be fired by the end of September, and yet he was still in his job."[39]

Reminded that he had not yet fulfilled his end of the bargain, Mussolini summoned Tacchi Venturi. The Bergamo question, he said, had gone on too long, or as he put it in his more colorful language, it had grown *"la barba troppo lunga,"* too long a beard.[40] He would remove the party head there immediately. At the same time, he asked the pope to dismiss four members of the Bergamo Catholic Action board who had once been Popular Party activists.[41]

When Pius heard what the Duce wanted, he expressed surprise that men with such a past could still be found in Catholic Action leadership positions. He had thought they had all been pruned out.[42] Tardini was startled at how readily the pope ordered the four men dismissed. On October 14, the Bergamo newspaper reported the resignation of the four board members and the removal of Bergamo's Fascist Party head.[43]

The pope's moods continued to swing sharply, linked in part to his health. His periods of depression and lashing out were followed by days when he seemed much mellower. In early October, while asking Tardini to send a letter dealing with a Milanese monastery, he joked, "Friars' stuff! It really is true what they say, 'Those who wear surplice and hood, never mutter a word to the good!'"[44] A few days later he asked his staff to find a young priest in Vienna who could send secret reports on what was going on there. He quipped, "If I were younger, I would be very happy to get an assignment like that!"[45]

But the pope's mood could change quickly. When Tardini reported that a new Fascist Party head had been appointed in Bergamo, he added his hope that the situation there would improve. "If they take away another [Fascist Party] membership card," replied the pope, in a flash of his old temper, "I will intervene energetically! I will make a scandal! I will let the world know! Taking away a person's membership means taking away his bread." He grew more agitated: "Fascism will look really good! One doesn't become old for nothing! Old folks have a certain immunity, and I intend to take advantage of it!"[46]

If the ailing pope was upset with Mussolini, he also was developing a dim view of his countrymen. "The Italians," the pope told Tardini, when the subject of the new racial laws came up in their conversation in mid-October, "are a bunch of sheep." Then he added, "For this we certainly don't need to be grateful to Mussolini."[47]

THE FINAL BATTLE

————

G USTAV GUNDLACH, WHO HAD HELPED DRAFT THE POPE'S SECRET encyclical on racism, was back in Rome, and he was not happy. In September he and his two colleagues had given their text to Ledóchowski, thinking the Jesuit general would send it on to the pope. The appearance of the Manifesto of Racial Scientists and the announcement of the first racial laws had fortified their belief that the pope wanted to see their work quickly. But Gundlach, informed that the Jesuit general had sent an "abridged version" of their draft to Father Enrico Rosa, urged his American collaborator to tell the pope what had happened. "Your intention not to let the document pass through other hands has not been realized," he told LaFarge. "Your loyalty to the Boss"—their code for Ledóchowski—"has not been rewarded. Indeed, you might be subject to the reproach that your loyalty toward Mr. Fischer"—their rather curious code name for Pius XI—"has suffered from your loyalty to the Boss." He concluded, "A person unconnected with the affair might see in all this an attempt to sabotage, through dilatory action, and for tactical and diplomatic reasons, the mission with which you were directly entrusted by Mr. Fischer."[1]

HITLER'S TRIUMPHAL TOUR THROUGH Italy had soured many Americans on the Duce. Now, with the imposition of the racial laws, Mussolini's popularity in the United States was plummeting. The Italian embassy in Washington sent a long report to Rome chronicling the decline. "As is known, American Catholics—beginning with the Church upper hierarchy, with Cardinal Mundelein of Chicago foremost among them—have from the very beginning reacted with hostility and with growing anger to the officially anti-Catholic and in part anti-Christian attitude of the Nazi authorities." Imposition of the racial laws and the latest battle over Italian Catholic Action "have led," the embassy reported, "to the rise here of further worries for the future of the Church in Italy, identifying Fascism with Nazism in the not too discerning eyes of the general public . . . who view them together as the not overly loved so-called authoritarian regimes."[2]

Relations between the Fascist regime and the American government were rapidly cooling. Italian newspapers did nothing to help, charging that Jews ruled the United States. They offered a list of the all-Jewish makeup of what was said to be the likely next American cabinet, headed by President Bernard Baruch and Vice President Albert Einstein.[3] Leon Trotsky was slated to be secretary of war; the fact that he was neither American nor lived in the country was apparently no impediment.[4]

PIUS WAS UPSET OVER MUSSOLINI'S planned new marriage law, which threatened to forbid baptized Jews from marrying other Catholics. He asked his nuncio to prepare a formal position paper.[5] The pope had in mind a statement of Catholic principle, but Borgongini thought it important that it contain something more. The Vatican needed to offer guidance for drafting racial laws that would not run afoul of Church teachings. "We must," the nuncio said, "suggest a way out. Otherwise the government . . . won't know how to find it by themselves. And then without a doubt there will be a rift."[6] It was a rift that the nuncio would spend the next weeks doing everything he could to avoid.

Borgongini's draft urged the government not to ignore the "religious element" in formulating its new laws. "It is therefore necessary that Jews not be confused with converts to Catholicism, for these have had the courage and the heroism to tear themselves once and for all from their nation of origin."[7]

In an effort to make his proposal more palatable to Mussolini, he added an aside expressing the Vatican's sympathy for the goals of the racial laws. "Certainly, for both moral and health reasons, [the Church] uses all the arguments at its disposal to try to discourage unions between whites and blacks and any union that is heterogeneous.[8] In this way it tries to avoid producing half-breeds, who combine the defects of both races." But "it cannot push its efforts of dissuasion to the point of an absolute ban."

Borgongini offered two possible compromises. The marriages in question could be allowed under the king's already existing authority to grant royal dispensations. Alternatively, language could be added to the new law stating that marriages that conflicted with its provisions but fell under article 34 of the concordat—recognizing the civil effects of religious marriages—would be recognized if the pope reviewed and approved them.[9]

The pope met with Tardini and Tacchi Venturi to discuss next steps. Tardini mentioned that the government had banned publication of articles critical of racism, even if they only criticized the German variety. "But all this is a disgrace!" said the pope. "I am ashamed, not as pope, but as an Italian! The Italian people have become a flock of stupid sheep. I will speak up, have no fear of that. The concordat means a lot to me, but my conscience means more. . . . Here they have become like so many Farinaccis. I am truly upset, as a pope and as an Italian!"

Once the storm—as Tardini described the pope's outburst—passed, Tacchi Venturi, not one to be easily thrown off course, incongruously took out a photograph of the pontiff and asked him to sign it, with a dedication to Mussolini's son Bruno, who was to get married a few days later. "I have little taste for putting my signature under the name of Mussolini!" said the pope. But he signed the photo anyway, as Tacchi Venturi had known he would.[10]

Their business over, Pius XI and the Jesuit began to reminisce. "They are two old men," reflected Tardini, recalling the scene, "one eighty-two and the other seventy-seven, sprightly and intelligent." They traded references to the Old and New Testaments and chuckled over stories of the men they had known, some long gone.[11] It was the kind of easy banter that the pope would have with few others.

Later that day Tardini, Tacchi Venturi, and Borgongini gathered in the apartment of Cardinal Domenico Jorio.[12] As prefect of the Congregation for the Discipline of the Sacraments, Jorio oversaw marriage regulations. The pope had asked the men to find a way out of the impasse. They came up with a plan, which the pope approved. The nuncio and Tacchi Venturi would try to convince government officials that it was not in their interest to cause a rupture in relations with the Holy See "for the few, rare cases [of mixed marriages], when it is possible to find a way out." They would try to get a copy of the proposed law, "to be in a position to advise on appropriate modifications."[13]

But when Tacchi Venturi asked Mussolini for a meeting, the Duce refused, telling him to put what he wanted to say in writing.[14] So the Jesuit subsequently sent the Duce a letter, in which he claimed that the Catholic Church had long opposed mixed marriages. They were "extremely rare and only tolerated for serious reasons of conscience." The pope, he assured Mussolini, was willing to go even further to reach an understanding: "The Holy Father is ready to see to it that they are even rarer and can never take place without being directly subject to the Holy Pontiff's direct review."

In his desperation to reach a deal, Tacchi Venturi was not only willing to make the pope a direct participant in the racial campaign, he was concealing a distinction that was crucial to the Church and central to the Vatican's problem with the racial laws. The pope's principal objection involved not the ban on what the Church considered to be "mixed marriages"—that is, marriages between Jews and Catholics—but rather those uniting two Catholics, one of whom had once been Jewish or who had a Jewish parent.

The Jesuit devoted the final page of his letter to singing the Duce's praises. He concluded by describing himself as "one who loves You and the Fatherland, one who—and I say it without a shadow of boasting—feels incapable of betraying You and Fascism."[15]

But the proposal failed to move Mussolini. Guido Buffarini, the intimidating undersecretary for internal affairs, told them the news: the Duce would never allow the pope to grant exceptions for mixed marriages; nor would he want to have the king review such requests.[16]

IN LATE OCTOBER THE DUCE met in Rome with Joachim von Ribbentrop, the Nazis' foreign minister. Ribbentrop had come to persuade Mussolini that it was time for a military pact binding Italy with Germany and Japan.[17] Sensing that, despite all his bombast, Mussolini still had qualms about signing a formal military alliance, Ribbentrop promised him that, with German support, the whole Mediterranean would one day become an Italian sea. Curiously, the main sour note that Mussolini sounded in the meeting regarded the Church and the pope. The Nazis' continued battle against the Catholic Church, he told the German foreign minister, remained a major impediment to a military alliance, for it undermined Italian popular support. He suggested that before such a pact be signed, the German government find a way to make peace with the Church. Should the Germans reach such an agreement, said Mussolini, alliance with the Nazis "would become very popular." Nor were all the problems with the Church on the German side. His own relations with the pope had lately become strained, he said. Having the pope denounce the pact would, he worried, place Italy's Catholics "in a difficult position."[18]

In his diary, Ciano painted a chilling picture of his own meeting with Ribbentrop at Rome's Grand Hotel. "He has a fixation about war on his mind," he wrote. "He wants war, his war. He doesn't have or doesn't say what his general marching plan is. He doesn't single out his enemies, nor does he indicate the objectives. But he wants war within three or four years." When Ciano discussed Ribbentrop's proposed military alliance with his father-in-law, Mussolini told him that the announcement of such an alliance should be put off, "above all because of the anti-German bitterness dominant in the great Catholic masses."[19]

Italy's anti-Semitic campaign was drawing a great deal of negative attention outside Italy, and given the Vatican's close ties to the Fascist regime, the pope found himself in an uncomfortable position. Tardini warned him against collaborating with Mussolini to produce a mutually acceptable text of the new racial law. Such a deal would leave the Vatican open to the accusation of collusion in the anti-Semitic campaign. Better simply to let the government do what it was going to do, he advised; assuming Mussolini went ahead with his plan, the Vatican could then condemn the provision that undercut article 34 of the concordat but take comfort from the fact that few marriages would be affected. Most important, he told the pope, the rest of the concordat would remain in effect.[20]

At first the pope agreed. But under pressure from his other advisers to work out a deal with the dictator, he would find it impossible to follow Tardini's advice.[21]

On October 29 a crowd gathered in the piazza in front of the pope's summer palace, hoping to get his blessing as he departed. It was a cold, windy day. A miserable mixture of hail, snow, and icy rain drove the faithful to seek cover in nearby shops. When it let up, the pope appeared at the small balcony of the palace, and people rushed back into the piazza. It was the last time he would ever be seen in Castel Gandolfo.[22]

A month earlier, much to the surprise of the Vatican diplomatic corps, Cardinal Pacelli had left for his regular vacation in Switzerland.[23] He arrived back in Rome on the overnight train, Sunday morning, October 30, and went directly from the station to the pope's office.[24] Tacchi Venturi, who was already there, reported the latest developments. The pope agreed to let him make one last attempt to speak with Mussolini and find an amicable solution.[25]

In an attempt to get through to the Duce, the Jesuit gave Buffarini a note. The Holy Father, it said, was distressed to think of all the damage that would be done to Catholic support for the regime if the government went ahead with the new racial law without coming to an understanding with the Vatican. It would bring "immense joy to the anti-Fascists of every language and nation." The pope believed there was still time to find wording for a new marriage law that would be "to the mutual satisfaction of both parties."[26]

Although Pius was ailing, over the next weeks he met repeatedly with Tacchi Venturi, Pacelli, and Tardini to direct the frenetic, last-minute negotiations. On November 2, when they finally procured a copy of the proposed new law, the pope asked the group that had been meeting at Cardinal Jorio's apartment to convene again.

Article 1 of the draft law stated, "Marriage between an Italian citizen of the Aryan race with a person belonging to another race is prohibited." It excepted only those marriages provided for in article 7, which Mussolini had added as a sop to the Vatican: it allowed exceptions for a person who was dying or to legitimize children.[27]

Tardini repeated the advice he had earlier given the pope: the Vatican should officially oppose the racist principle behind the new law and let the world know it had not had a hand in its drafting.

But the others rejected Tardini's pleas. Terrified of opening a rift with the regime, Borgongini, the nuncio, proposed that they threaten to announce that the new law conflicted with the concordat but, should it go into effect, not actually make any public protest. This would allow them to continue to lobby behind the scenes for the changes they sought.[28]

"It is obvious," wrote Tardini, in later reporting that day's developments, "that the nuncio's great concern was to avoid a conflict between the Holy See and the Italian government. And since any declaration or protest by the Holy See (no matter how attenuated) might have been exploited by Fascism's enemies both internally and especially abroad to provoke a conflict, the nuncio sought to find a way—with some opportune modification of the law—to avoid any protest at all by the Holy See."

Borgongini recalled that in its October 6 statement, the Fascist Grand Council declared that the children of a mixed marriage who professed another religion (namely, Catholicism) would not be considered Jews under the law. If the Vatican could get the regime to agree to insert this language in the new law, it would substantially reduce the number of marriages between Catholics that would be affected. That would be enough, thought the nuncio, to allow the Holy See to permit the new law to go into effect without protest.

But the pope did not agree, for under such terms Catholic converts from Judaism would still be considered Jewish. He insisted that the new law contain an exception permitting marriages of former Jews with other Catholics.[29]

Tacchi Venturi took the suggested revisions to Buffarini, although he knew the pope's proposal had no chance of winning the dictator's approval. Reading the suggested text as Tacchi Venturi looked on, Buffarini shook his head. He would not show it to the Duce, he said. It would only make matters worse.

That same evening Tacchi Venturi received the final text of the marriage law. Even the few exceptions contained in the earlier version, he saw, had been deleted.[30] Mussolini was willing to bet that, despite all his threats, the pope would not in the end break with the Fascist regime.

CHAPTER TWENTY-SIX

FAITH IN THE KING

NCREDULOUS THAT MUSSOLINI WOULD SO BRAZENLY VIOLATE THE
concordat that had served them both so well, Pius XI wrote to the
Duce to warn him of his folly.

"To Our Dearest Son," the pope began. He made no mention of the
first article of the new law, which established that "marriage between an
Italian citizen of the Aryan race with a person belonging to another race
is prohibited." Rather he objected to article 7, which clearly violated
the concordat's provision that Church-approved marriages be civilly
recognized. "Such a *vulnus* [wound] can easily be avoided," the pope
told the Duce, "if instead of the text of the above-mentioned article . . .
one substituted the version that we provided to your collaborators, but
that unfortunately we do not see accepted here." The pope appended
his recommended text, the revision of article 7 that Buffarini had so
angrily rejected a day earlier. It would permit marriage between two
Catholics, regardless of their "race."[1]

In a last desperate effort to sway the dictator, Tacchi Venturi sent
him a personal appeal. As someone who served the Duce for so many
years and who had constantly proved his faithfulness and his love, he
begged him to accept the pope's request.[2]

Mussolini rejected the pontiff's last-minute appeal out of hand, letting him know the next morning that he would make no change in the law. Furious at the brush-off, the pope decided to appeal to the king. Never had Pius written to Victor Emmanuel other than for ceremonial purposes. Now he asked him "to intervene with Your supreme authority to obtain that which we were not able to accomplish . . . with Your Prime Minister." The pope reminded the king of the treaty that had been solemnly signed in his name in 1929, and the fact that the proposed marriage law ran directly contrary to its provisions. He attached his proposed alternative version of article 7.[3]

Several years later, in the aftermath of a disastrous war, Italians would hold a referendum on whether to keep the monarchy. They turned on the king, blaming him for not standing up to the dictator. Nowhere was Victor Emmanuel's cowardice clearer—or in retrospect, more humiliating—than in his approval of every racial law that Mussolini proposed. As Jews were thrown out of schools and jobs, vilified by the state and robbed of their livelihood, the king continued to sign all the bills that Mussolini, at their twice-a-week meetings at the Quirinal Palace, brought him. In some ways making matters worse, the king had no sympathy for the Nazis' deification of the Aryan race or for Mussolini's attempts to craft an Italian variant; he simply did not have the courage to stand up to the Duce.

The king's reply to the pope on November 7 reflected this same cowardice.[4] Victor Emmanuel thanked the pontiff for his letter and said he had sent a copy of it to Mussolini, hoping a solution could be found that "conciliates the two points of view." That was it.[5] For his part, Mussolini again let the pope know he could not agree to his request, for doing so would mean undermining the whole intent of the new marriage law.[6]

Earlier in the week Ciano met with Hermann Göring, head of the German air force and Hitler's minister of planning. Despite his infatuation with the Nazis, Mussolini's dandified son-in-law found many of their leaders rather boorish. He left a vivid image of Göring in his diary: "Dressed in civilian clothes, with an expensive and loud gray suit. His tie, knotted in an old fashioned style, has a ruby ring pinned on it. Other large rubies on his fingers. On his lapel, a large Nazi eagle with diamonds. He vaguely resembles 'Al Capone.'"

Afterward Ciano filled his father-in-law in on his discussions with Göring. He then brought up the pope's appeal to the king. "I cannot say," observed Ciano, "that the Duce is very shaken."[7]

Ciano was part of a lunch party that day, held at the American embassy in Rome. The guest of honor was none other than the archbishop of Chicago, Cardinal Mundelein, on a visit to the Vatican. President Roosevelt, to show solidarity with Mundelein in the wake of the storm that his denunciation of Hitler had stirred up the previous year, had hosted him at the White House before his departure. The president instructed Ambassador Phillips to do everything he could to show American support for the archbishop during his time in Italy.[8]

The papal nuncio was also present at the lunch party and, spotting Ciano, made his way through the crowd to reach him. The new marriage law was on the Council of Ministers agenda the next day, and Ciano was worried. Mussolini had gotten so worked up about the matter that the text was now much more drastic than the earlier version. If the law were to end Vatican support for the Fascist regime, thought Ciano, it would be a disaster.

"What will the pope do?" Ciano asked Borgongini.

"I don't know, because the pope doesn't tell anyone what he will do," the nuncio responded. "But you can be certain he will do something big."

"Will it be a diplomatic protest, or a public protest?" asked Ciano nervously.

Borgongini replied that he didn't know, but suggested that Ciano, as foreign minister, could still intervene to save the Lateran Accords.

"And what can we propose now? Both the Holy Father and the Head of the Government have been dealing with it. So I, as minister of foreign affairs, and you, as nuncio, can't do anything."

Borgongini argued that it wasn't too late, that Ciano could propose a bilateral commission to study the matter. When Ciano asked what he could say to persuade the Duce, the nuncio again stressed how few marriages would be involved. By the end of their conversation, Borgongini was convinced that if Ciano could do anything to prevent a crisis with the Vatican, he would.[9]

That night, November 9, 1938, remains etched in historical memory as *Kristallnacht,* a night of horrors in Germany. Using as a pretext the assassination in France of a German diplomat by a teenaged Jewish refugee from Poland, marauding Nazis burned synagogues to the ground, sacked Jewish-owned stores, and hunted down and beat terrified Jews. Scores of Jews were murdered, tens of thousands arrested, and many sent to concentration camps. Hundreds of synagogues were burned to the ground, and thousands of Jewish-owned businesses were plundered. In the aftermath of the violence, the German government announced that Jews would no longer be allowed to own stores or other businesses, practice trades, or enter theaters or concert halls, and that what remained of their property would be seized and turned over to Christians. Hundreds of Jews committed suicide. Ciano received a long report from the Italian ambassador in Germany giving the grisly details. Pacelli received a lengthy report from the nuncio in Berlin.[10]

Italy's Catholic press had little to say about the horrors visited on Germany's Jews. Venice's diocesan weekly aimed all its scorn at the Jewish teenager who shot the Nazi diplomat, the "Jew who coldly aimed his revolver . . . armed in his heart by a deep sense of hatred, vendetta, and rancor." It added, "We confess we cannot understand how a man's hand can, with calculated premeditation, strike a pacific and unknown functionary." Of the government-sponsored mass murder and destruction of the Jews in Germany, the diocesan weekly said nothing.[11]

As German synagogues were being torched and German Jews hunted down, Father Tacchi Venturi was in bed, unable to sleep. Knowing that Mussolini's Council of Ministers would be meeting the next day, he cast about for a way to prevent a break between his two patrons. He rose from bed, turned on the light, and drafted a letter to the Duce.

"The change that I am proposing," he wrote, "saves the basic principle of the law"—the proposition that Italians are Aryans and Jews are not. "It simply allows for an exception." Again Tacchi Venturi pleaded how rare such cases would be. "If one takes into account the small number of Italian citizens of Jewish race, the aversion that almost all Israelites have for marrying Christians, and the Christians for Jews, even if converted, I am not afraid of saying that there would be fewer than a hundred such marriages between spouses of different race, but both professing the Catholic religion." That the normally astute Jesuit would get up in the middle of the night simply to repeat arguments he had already made many times to the Duce shows how desperate he was.[12]

Meanwhile Roberto Farinacci, delighted to play his part in needling the Vatican, was helping the Duce whip up popular support for the anti-Semitic laws. He cast the new measures as rooted in the teachings of the Roman Catholic Church. The previous summer he had run a series of anti-Semitic articles in his newspaper, citing *La Civiltà cattolica* to justify the campaign. He titled one "A Lesson in Catholicism for Catholics." On November 7, in a widely publicized lecture given in Milan, billed as "The Church and the Jews," he quoted extensively from the New Testament to argue that the Catholic Church was the original source of the Fascist anti-Semitic measures. Unfortunately, he lamented, the pope had recently shown signs of straying from this core Church teaching. "What has happened," he asked, "to make the official Church today become philo-Semitic rather than anti-Semitic? ... Why," he asked, "do Communists, Freemasons, democrats, all the avowed enemies of the Church, praise her today and offer to help her?" His answer was simple: "To use her against Fascism."

Il Regime fascista gave Farinacci's speech full-page coverage, adding a three-column historical insert with the title "The Dispositions of the Councils and the Popes Against the Jews Through the Centuries."[13] Many papers picked up the story. *Il Giornale d'Italia,* which had first published the Manifesto of Racial Scientists, captured the central message in a few words: "The Honorable Farinacci concludes, amid fervid applause, by stating that it is impossible for the Catholic Fascist to renounce that anti-Semitic conscience which the Church had formed through the millennia."[14]

At its November 10 meeting, the government's Council of Ministers approved the new racial laws. The Duce waited anxiously to see if the pope would follow through on his threats. Despite all his bluster, he was not eager to see the Vatican turn against him. The support of the Church hierarchy, from the pope down to the parish priests, had proven too valuable, and he now had greater ambitions for his regime. Losing Church backing could be costly.[15]

If the Duce was not more worried, it was because in all the weeks of frenetic negotiations and brinksmanship, in all the weeks of the pope's lamentations, neither Pius XI, nor his Jesuit emissary, nor his secretary of state, nor his nuncio had ever voiced any opposition to the great bulk of the racial laws, aimed at stripping Jews of their rights as Italian citizens. The Vatican had not protested the ejection of Jewish children or Jewish teachers from the schools, nor that of Jewish professors from the universities. Neither Pacelli nor the pope's two emissaries—the official nuncio and the unofficial Jesuit—had ever uttered a word to challenge the government's decision to treat Jews as a danger to healthy Italian society. For anyone eager for a sign of the Vatican view of the new campaign of persecution, including parish priests and bishops seeking guidance on how to respond to it, the message was clear. The state was finally heeding the warnings that had been appearing in the Vatican daily newspaper and that had been regularly repeated in the Vatican-supervised *La Civiltà cattolica* and in much of the Italian Catholic press, from weekly diocesan bulletins to major daily newspapers.

The recent opening of the Vatican Secret Archives has brought to light a report that makes clear that, as far as the Vatican was concerned, the August 16 agreement Tacchi Venturi negotiated with Mussolini, promising not to criticize the racial laws in exchange for favorable treatment of Catholic Action, remained in effect. Prepared in early November in the secretary of state office, it chronicles the Vatican's dealings with the Fascist government over the anti-Semitic campaign. Following a description of Pius XI's July 28 remarks denouncing "exaggerated nationalism" comes a long section titled "Mussolini-Tacchi Venturi Agreement (August 16, 1938)." The entry reads "Meanwhile the Holy See directed Father Tacchi Venturi to reach an agreement. And Father Tacchi Venturi succeeded. The August 16, 1938, agreement consists of three points" and went on to summarize each of them.[16]

Mussolini thought the Holy See was profiting too much from its alliance with the Fascist state to want to jeopardize it. For years the Vatican had been counting on its privileged relations with the regime to have books and magazines that it found offensive confiscated, Protestants kept from proselytizing, and Church standards of women's modesty enforced. Mussolini was, after all, the "man from Providence" who had ensured that every Fascist youth group had a priest attached to it, that Italian taxes were used to pay for Church expenses, and that Catholic clergy were given positions of honor at all state functions.

Had Mussolini seen the confidential telegram that Cardinal Pacelli sent to the papal nuncios around the world the day after the marriage

The racial laws, displayed in *La Difesa della razza*, November 20, 1938

law was approved, he would have realized his gamble had paid off. By forbidding marriage between two Catholics of different races, Pacelli informed them, the new law clearly violated the concordat. What lesson were the nuncios to take from this, and what should they be telling those who asked? Pacelli did all he could to minimize the dispute: "It should be noted that the violation of the concordat is limited to a small number of cases . . . A few dozen, while each year in Italy more than 300,000 religious marriages are celebrated and will continue to be celebrated, all regularly recorded."[17]

The Vatican's official letter of protest to the Italian government could not have been meeker. The pope himself decided to say nothing. After all his threats, in the end he was still unwilling to let the dispute disrupt the mutually beneficial relationship between the Church and the Fascist regime. The pope told Pacelli to prepare the letter. He was to send it not to the king, nor even to Mussolini or Ciano, but to Pignatti, the Italian ambassador.

The letter began by noting that the new marriage law conflicted with article 34 of the concordat. After observing that the Church welcomed people of any race, Pacelli again tried to minimize the Church's objections to the regime's new racial theory. The Church, too, he wrote, had long been concerned about race mixing. "The Church, always the loving mother," explained the future pope, "generally advises its children against contracting marriages that present the risk of defective offspring, and in this sense is disposed, within the limits of divine right, to support the civil authorities' efforts to achieve this very virtuous goal." But when, despite the Church's discouragement, two Catholics of different races insisted on being married, it could not deny them that sacrament.

Pacelli's note adopted the Fascists'—and Nazis'—view that the Jews were a separate race. He made no effort to disabuse the government of the notion of the possible noxious physical effects of "race mixing" between Italian Catholics and Jews, and he minimized the impact the new law would have. Marriages between Catholics and Jewish converts to

Catholicism were extremely rare, he wrote, "a rarity also favored by the aversion common to both Catholics and Israelites of uniting with a person of another race."

The secretary of state concluded his letter by expressing regret that it had become necessary for him to protest the wound inflicted on the concordat, but he ended on a positive note. He voiced the hope that the government might still make the modest changes needed to restore harmony with the Church.[18]

The public protest, such as it was, came in the November 15 issue of *L'Osservatore romano,* in a front-page article titled rather blandly "Regarding a New Decree-Law." Pacelli carefully reviewed the text before publication. "He wanted to give it," Tardini noted, "a calm, serene tone, among other reasons so as not to prejudice the possibility of future improvements in the laws and an end to the conflict."[19] The article reflected the language used in Pacelli's formal protest letter. It concluded by expressing the hope that an agreement might still be found to deal with the "exiguous number of cases affected."[20]

But a dramatic story lay behind the bland protest published in the November 15 issue of the Vatican daily. At 10:20 that morning, Monsignor Tardini, the square-faced secretary for Extraordinary Ecclesiastical Affairs, got an urgent message: Pius XI wanted to see him immediately. He was to bring the material prepared for the *Osservatore romano* article with him. Fearing what lay ahead, Tardini picked up the file and rushed to the pope's quarters. "I found the pope red-faced and excited," he recalled. The pope held a copy of the newspaper in his hands.

Why, asked the pope, was the most important part of the article missing, the one he had reviewed and approved the previous day? The pope had wanted the article to include the text of his letters to Mussolini and the king. Most of all, he had wanted to feature the king's reply. Victor Emmanuel's letter, Pius XI insisted, had told Mussolini to alter the marriage law to accommodate the pope's concerns. The pope wanted the world to know Mussolini had ignored the royal request.

Tardini tried to calm him down. Yes, he said, the pope had told them to publish the text of the letters, but he must have forgotten that Cardinal Pacelli had convinced him the previous evening not to do so. Not only was it not customary to publish diplomatic correspondence without the consent of the other party, Pacelli had argued, but the king's response, which the pope had put so much stock in, was actually embarrassingly vague and, in the end, totally ineffective. The effect of publishing it would have been to let the world know that the king "counted for nothing." Pacelli had not wanted to publish the king's reply for another reason as well: it would have called attention to the fact that Mussolini had not bothered to respond, which would put Mussolini in a bad light. When Pacelli raised this point, the pope had interrupted him: "Sovereign courtesy opposed to supreme villainy!" Undaunted, Pacelli had held his ground. Highlighting Mussolini's failure to respond, he insisted, could lead to government reprisals.

Tardini's attempt to remind Pius XI of that conversation did nothing to stem the pope's anger. In an aside, Tardini observed that the pontiff—famous for his attention to detail—was lately becoming increasingly forgetful. It was because he had entirely forgotten his conversation with his secretary of state the previous evening that he was so upset by the *Osservatore romano* story. When Tardini mentioned Pacelli's hope that Mussolini might still do something to lessen the impact of the new law, the pope again grew agitated. "But who gave you these hopes?" If there was any basis for hope, thought the pontiff, it was because the king had asked Mussolini to act, and it was exactly this request that they had excised from the article.

At this point, Cardinal Pacelli joined them, and the pope tore into him. It had made him sick, he said, to see what they had done to the story. Pacelli expressed concern for the pope's health, for he had not been well and was not sleeping. But these attempts to distract the pope were in vain.

"Who wrote the article?" asked the pope.

"I did, Holiness," Tardini replied.

"I don't like it at all," he responded.

Cardinal Pacelli, unwilling to stand by while Tardini took the blame, interrupted: "Holiness, I reviewed the article, and I take all responsibility."

Calming down a bit, the pope insisted they rectify the problem by publishing the king's reply in the next issue of the Vatican newspaper. Neither Pacelli nor Tardini wanted to allow this. Tardini went to find Tacchi Venturi, who might persuade the pope to change his mind. The Jesuit rushed to the Vatican.

He had been speaking with people close to Mussolini, Tacchi Venturi told Pius, and was delighted to report that the measured tone of that day's *Osservatore romano* article had made a very good impression. If he hoped this news would please the pope, he was mistaken. The pope interrupted: "No wonder I'm upset! But this evening I am having them publish a new press release!" Tacchi Venturi was alarmed, but his pleadings failed to change the pontiff's mind.[21] Once again Cardinal Pacelli and his colleagues, by allowing the pope to vent his anger, were able to prevail. *L'Osservatore romano* never did publish the king's letter.[22]

While Italians could be forgiven if they believed that the Fascist campaign against the Jews found favor in the Vatican, at least one influential Italian prelate sounded a dissonant note. His objection was surprising: Cardinal Ildefonso Schuster, archbishop of Milan, had been one of Mussolini's most vocal and enthusiastic supporters. Only the previous year the French ambassador to the Holy See had reported that Schuster, "known for his very Fascist sentiments," had given a lecture to the School of Fascist Mysticism praising Mussolini for establishing a new Catholic Roman empire.[23] In 1930 the archbishop had received a letter from three hundred Catholics in Milan berating him for his uncritical embrace of the Fascists, leading to a request from the government authorities to hand over the list of signatories.[24] In September 1937 a police informant recounted that Schuster's prospects for succeeding the sickly Pius XI were meeting strong resistance from cardinals outside Italy, who thought he was too closely linked to the Fascist regime.[25]

But on Sunday, November 13, speaking in Milan's Duomo, Schuster did what no one in the Vatican would do: he denounced Italy's racial laws as a product of neopagan ideology, and argued that the Church could never accept them. "It is useless to want to establish a bilateral harmony between Religion and Fatherland. The Fascist State is creating its own ethic which has absolutely nothing in common with the religious idea." He went on to accuse Mussolini of slavishly following Hitler, embracing a racist ideology of Nordic, pagan origin.

With this one speech, Schuster fell from being darling of Milan's Fascists to being enemy number one in the eyes of the party leadership. Only in 1951 would the text of his remarks finally appear in Milan's diocesan journal, but the Catholic newspaper *L'Italia* reported it on November 15, generating excited discussion and amazement. As a secret police informer in Milan reported, people were especially chilled by the archbishop's warning that the Nazis' racist ideology would one day be turned against the Italians themselves. "On this point," the informer wrote, "Cardinal Schuster expressed a fear that is extraordinarily widespread in northern Italy."[26]

The government did not respond to Pacelli's letter protesting the marriage law. On November 22, three days after the law was officially published, Pacelli sent a brief new note to Pignatti expressing regret that the exceptions requested by the Vatican were not included.[27] A week later Pignatti replied that while the government had tried to resolve the differences over the text of the new law and had been willing to make some exceptions, the Vatican would settle for nothing less than to have all marriages between two Catholics recognized, regardless of their race. The Fascist state could not accept this. Pignatti pointed out that the Vatican had recognized the "good ethical basis" of the state's concerns and had advised "against marriages that raise the danger of producing defective children."[28]

If the Vatican protests of the racial laws were limited and muted, the chorus of denunciation coming from the United States was anything but. Given the Italians' close ties to America, Mussolini worried they might be swayed. The Fascist press soon counterattacked. The reason the United States was being so critical, the newspapers explained, was that Jews there ran the government and controlled the press.

A Roman newspaper charged that Jews had a "strangle-hold" on the country. It claimed that Jews occupied fifty-two of the seventy-five most important government positions in the United States and controlled 75 percent of American industry. The "same occult force which prevails in England, France, and Russia," the paper reported, "is absolutely dominant in Washington. It is in Washington that anti-fascist activity and the plans of the democracies, which are a synonym for Jewry and Free Masonry, are coordinated." Charging that President Roosevelt, "a Jew by race," was the "Pope of World Jewry," it asked when Italians would finally realize this awful truth.[29]

The atmosphere in the Vatican was meanwhile becoming increasingly uncertain. As the international situation rapidly deteriorated, the pope was growing ever weaker. On November 25, Pius XI suffered a heart attack. Although once again he recovered, no one thought he could last long.[30]

CARDINAL PACELLI REMAINED MUSSOLINI'S most powerful ally in the Vatican. Following Archbishop Schuster's unexpected attack, Pignatti, worried that others might follow his lead, went to see the secretary of state to ask him to send written instructions to all of Italy's bishops telling them not to criticize the anti-Semitic campaign.

The Italian ambassador found Pacelli supportive but not eager to expose himself. "The Cardinal," Pignatti wrote, "observed that it would be easy to give the advice that I was suggesting orally, but that, having to put it in writing it would become more difficult." The ambassador knew Pacelli could be pressured and kept pushing. "In the end," Pignatti told Ciano, "the secretary of state told me that something had already been done as far as the diocese of Rome went. In addition, he made a written note of my request, promising to study the best way to take care of Italy's other dioceses."[31]

Mussolini was worried by signs that the racial laws might be erod-ing Italians' enthusiasm for the regime. Police reports from cities with significant numbers of Jews told of widespread unhappiness. A police informant from Milan observed that while some people were being won over by the anti-Semitic propaganda, "a strong majority still find many of its measures exaggerated and condemn the head of the govern-ment and the Grand Council for having reached these decisions only after Germany imposed it as one of the necessary conditions for the Rome-Berlin axis." People were also upset that the Fascists who were charged with implementing the policy were giving the jobs vacated by Jews to their own clients. They were also buying up Jewish properties at a small fraction of their value.[32]

Italy's Jews were desperate, having lost their jobs and property, their children thrown out of school. Formerly friendly Catholic neigh-bors now nervously crossed the street to avoid having to greet them. Rumors spread about Nazi plans to set up concentration camps. Jewish suicides multiplied. Angelo Formiggini, a well-known editor and poet, wrote to his colleagues that while he was a good Italian, he could not face the unending persecution. In a letter to his non-Jewish wife, he explained that only his death could free her from abuse. After mailing the letters, he climbed the 190 stairs to the top of the medieval tower that loomed over Modena's central piazza and leaped out. A pool of blood dampened the cobblestones around his broken body.

"He died just like a Jew," quipped party head Achille Starace on hearing the news. "He threw himself from a tower to save the cost of a bullet."[33]

A CONVENIENT DEATH

AFTER SIXTEEN YEARS OF NURTURING HIS PARTNERSHIP WITH THE Vatican, Mussolini was allowing his megalomania, his infatuation with the Third Reich, and his sense of invincibility to get in the way of his political judgment. The pope felt poorly used. Increasingly frail, he knew his own death could not be far off.

The assault on the concordat in Italy and the persecution of the Church in Germany had produced unhappiness among the cardinals. "Our attitude on the racial question and especially toward the Jews," Pignatti told Ciano in mid-December, "has had strong repercussions on the Sacred College, a majority of whom must now be considered not well disposed toward Fascism." The cardinals worried that Mussolini might imitate Hitler and launch a campaign against the Church's influence in Italy.

The Italian dictator remained defiant and, as Pius saw it, wholly lacking in the respect due the pontiff. Disillusioned and despondent, the pope worried he had not been true to the sacred trust placed in him. He had let his patriotic sentiments as an Italian color his judgment. He vowed to do all he could in the little time he had left to make amends.

Hearing of the pope's new resolve, Pignatti became alarmed. "The pontiff threatened to do something before dying that would be remembered in Italy for a long time," he told Ciano, underlining his words. Pius XI, he warned, might use the upcoming celebrations marking the tenth anniversary of the Lateran Accords to pronounce a wholesale "condemnation of Fascism."[1]

Told of this latest warning, Mussolini erupted. Pius could not die soon enough. Didn't the pope realize all he had done for him? Italians had long resented the Church's power. He, Mussolini, was the one who had kept the Church's critics in check. If the pope wanted to play this game, he would play as well, for he knew how to "stimulate the people's anti-clerical sensibilities." The Church had long been in decline, stopped only because of his own efforts to shore it up. If Italians still attended mass, it was only because they knew that their Duce wanted them to go. After a stream of such fulminations, the dictator eventually calmed down and, no doubt encouraged by Ciano, grudgingly acknowledged that this was no time to have the pope call on Catholics to abandon him. He needed to find a way to prevent a break.[2]

A French bishop visiting Rome in mid-December found the sickly pope restless, sad, discouraged, and still complaining about Mussolini's failure to reply to his personal letter on the marriage law. "You are young," Pius told the French prelate. "You will live to see more horrible things than the Church has seen for centuries."[3]

On the day before Christmas, the cardinals gathered around the pope at the Vatican to receive his annual blessing. Pacelli, Tardini, and the others of Pius's entourage were nervous. Normally, he sent a copy of his text in advance to the secretary of state office, but not this time.

Seated in his throne, the pope held his handwritten notes in his trembling hands. He began warmly enough. February 11 would mark the tenth anniversary of the concordat, he reminded the cardinals. Thanks should be offered to "the most noble sovereign and his incomparable minister, to whom credit is due if such an important and beneficial work was crowned by a good result and gratifying success."

But after praising Mussolini, he repeated the words that had so enraged the Duce a few months earlier: he lamented "the recent apotheosis in Rome prepared for a cross that is the enemy of the Cross of
Christ." He went on to link the swastika's appearance in the Eternal
City to the wound recently inflicted on the concordat and the persecution of members of Catholic Action.[4]

Upset, Cardinal Pacelli tried to persuade the pope to delete the offending phrase about the swastika from the published version of his
talk. It was irrelevant to the pope's main point, he argued, since he had
been focusing on Italy and not Germany. But Pius knew exactly what
he was saying. He needed to warn Italians against the Nazis. Pacelli's
pleas, recalled Tardini, were all in vain: "The pope held firm."
L'Osservatore romano published his full text the next day.[5]

Mussolini was again angry, viewing the pope's remarks as yet another attack on the Rome-Berlin axis.[6] The upcoming anniversary of
the Lateran Accords was taking on all the appearance of a dramatic
showdown. The pope believed Mussolini had a choice: he could use
the day to show the world he still stood by the agreements; or by snub-
bing the pope, he could declare war on the Vatican. The nuncio, eager
to ease tensions, proposed that the Duce visit Pius XI on the anniversary, but the dictator dismissed the suggestion. He had gone once to
pay tribute to the pope. He would not go again.[7]

The men of the Duce's inner circle worried that he was losing touch
with reality. At times Mussolini clearly recognized the importance of
Vatican support and even criticized Hitler for antagonizing the Church.
But he was getting ever more reckless. At year's end, at his coastal retreat in Romagna, he brooded over the fateful decisions to be made in
the next months. The French ambassador to Italy captured the scene:
"The dictator's friends, his intimates are . . . the first to confirm that he
is surrounding himself with an ever more impenetrable secrecy, that
he is no longer the person he once was, that he is much changed, that
he no longer receives anyone and that no one, today, except perhaps
Ciano, would know what he is preparing to do and toward what end he
is moving."[8]

THE DUCE'S AFFAIR WITH Clara Petacci was increasingly the subject of snide remarks, but he was unwilling to give her up. Two months earlier one of his former maids had come to ask for help. He gave her some money, but before leaving, she timorously asked if he realized what people all over Rome were saying. He reluctantly urged her to speak up. "They say," she told him, "that you have a young lover who is the daughter of a big shot in the Vatican."

"The usual gossip, *fantasie*," replied the Duce, who was not pleased. He had had many lovers over the past years and had not been overly concerned about word of them hurting his reputation. In fact, he rather thought they helped his image. But to be linked to the Vatican in this way was distasteful to him.[9]

Back in his office on New Year's Day, Mussolini phoned Clara at 9:15 A.M., then three times more before, at 2:15 P.M., calling to say he was ready to have her join him. When she arrived, he was sitting in an armchair in the dark, with only a little light on by his side. He fell asleep. When he awoke, he asked her to sit on his lap, and then they made love. He ate a tangerine as he dressed, then returned to his office, coming back at 7:30 P.M. Sitting with a stack of papers, he muttered various deprecations as he read: "These French pigs! Listen to this. . . . What idiots!" He paced, working himself into a foul mood, and told Clara he hated her, as he often did before showering her with protestations of his love. "I never loved anyone," he said. "I have had many women, but it's been a revolving door." He was now much less wild, he told her, and kept up relations with only the two women she knew about—Romilda Ruspi and Alice Pallottelli—and only because they had given birth to his children. He had once loved Margherita Sarfatti, he admitted, but only for a couple of years, and he had constantly betrayed her as well. They turned on the phonograph and listened to Beethoven's Fifth, cuddling up with Clara's fur coat stretched over them. "He holds me with my head on his chest and caresses me every so often," Clara wrote in her diary, "but he is always a little distracted."[10]

The next day the Duce summoned both Ciano and Pignatti to discuss the latest developments. He was still mulling over the phrase "incomparable minister" that the pope had used in referring to him in his Christmas address. He was sure the pope was being sarcastic, taking him for a fool. "We do not want a conflict," Mussolini told the two men, "but we will not shy away from one, and in that case we shall arouse all the dormant anticlerical rancor." Fearful of where Mussolini's temper might lead, Pignatti tried to defend the pontiff, and Ciano too thought it madness to risk alienating the Church. But Mussolini wanted to apply pressure and prepared a sharp note of warning for his ambassador to deliver to the Vatican secretary of state.[11]

Pignatti presented the Duce's note to Pacelli the next day. The cardinal insisted that the phrase that had so upset Mussolini—"incomparable minister"—had been sincere. The pope had intended to express his appreciation for all that Mussolini had done for Italy and the Church. Pignatti replied that relations with the Holy See were at a dangerous juncture. If the Church were not careful, he warned, it would find itself in trouble.[12]

What made the past months so painful to the pope was his realization that his dreams of turning Italy into a confessional state—one where the machinery of the authoritarian regime would be at the service of the Church—had been so naïve. True, he had been able to do what no modern pope before him had done: get the government to impose the Church's will on the Italian population. Catholic clergy now played active roles in many state institutions—from schools to government-sponsored youth groups—where before they had been absent. But the battle over the marriage law had made it clear that for any matter that Mussolini deemed crucial to his regime, it was he who would decide, not the pope.

The London *Daily Mail* published a story by its Rome correspondent claiming that Pius XI was planning a secret gathering of the cardinals to draft a ringing denunciation of racism. Rumors spread that the pope was preparing a secret encyclical with the same aim. Cardinal Pacelli denied the reports but told the Italian ambassador that the pope had warned that he "would have more to say and that at his age he had no fear." In conveying these remarks to Ciano, Pignatti nervously recalled the pope's comment that "before dying, he might do something that Italy would remember for a long time."[13]

THE POPE'S CRITICAL REMARKS about racism had left Italy's Church leaders some room to voice criticisms of their own. Cardinal Schuster of Milan had been the most clamorous case. The possibility that other high prelates might follow his example had Mussolini and his acolytes worried.[14]

Roberto Farinacci led the attack on Schuster, asking in *Il Regime fascista* how someone who had been a "super-Fascist" could so suddenly go to the other extreme. It could certainly have nothing to do with the Catholic religion, Farinacci argued, for in battling the Jews, Fascism was fighting "the enemies of Christianity, who offend and insult Christ."[15] Farinacci turned to the influential head of the Catholic University of Milan for help. Father Gemelli, the rector, was scheduled to give a major public lecture in Bologna.

Two days before it was to take place, Farinacci sent Mussolini a letter, telling the Duce how he had recently gotten Giovanni Cazzani, the bishop of Cremona, to give a sermon supporting the anti-Semitic campaign. Then he added, "I hope to have persuaded Father Gemelli to give one of the same kind in Bologna."

A week later *L'Osservatore romano,* the Vatican daily, would publish the Cremona bishop's sermon, which had all the appearance of offering a Vatican endorsement of the anti-Semitic laws. All of Italy's bishops were in agreement on the treatment of the Jews, the paper's editor explained in his preface, and their views were in perfect harmony with the pope's.

"Germanic exaggerated racism," warned Bishop Cazzani, was a "doctrine contrary to the revealed truth." But the fact that the Nazis had gone about their anti-Jewish campaign for the wrong reasons did not mean that Italy's racial laws were unjustified. The problem with the

Nazis' exaggerated racism was that it extended its reach to Catholics. "The Church," said the bishop, "has always judged living together with the Jews—as long as they remain Jews—to be dangerous to the faith and to the tranquility of Christian peoples. It is for this reason that you find an ancient and long tradition of ecclesiastical legislation and discipline, directed to stopping and limiting the action and influence of the Jews in the midst of the Christians and the contacts of Christians with them, isolating the Jews and not permitting them to exercise those offices and those professions by which they could dominate or influence the spirit, the education, the custom of Christians." The Church, he insisted, had been unfairly accused of opposing the laws aimed against the Jews. What the Church had condemned was "exaggerated Germanic racism." It "has not and does not condemn any political defense of the integrity and the prosperity of the race, and any legal precaution taken against an excessive and damaging Judaic influence in the life of the Nation."[16]

Father Gemelli was in Bologna on January 9 to take part in a high-profile tribute to a fourteenth-century surgeon who had lived there. Jarringly—for the surgeon was not Jewish—at the end of his remarks, he turned his attention to the Jews. Italians today, Gemelli told his illustrious audience, "have suffered most of all from that conflict between church and state that, as a result of the efforts of the Judaic-Masonic cabals, sought to reduce Religion to a private affair." Thanks to the resolution of the Roman question, he said, Italians had become "one in blood, religion, language, custom, hopes, ideals." Meanwhile, "that terrible sentence that the deicide people brought on themselves and for which they go wandering through the world, is fulfilled. They are incapable of finding the peace of a homeland, while the consequences of that horrible crime follow them everywhere and in every time."[17]

Bologna's *L'Avvenire d'Italia,* Italy's most influential Catholic newspaper, gave Gemelli's remarks heavy coverage. The lesson to be drawn from the talk was "that the cardinals and the bishops have always and everywhere combated foreign racism, but that that has nothing to do with Italy's racial policy." Returning to the speech a week later, the paper informed its readers that "Father Gemelli's speech and Monsignor Cazzani's sermon . . . are an authorized and solemn illustration of this Catholic doctrine that is professed and taught by all in the Church hierarchy from top to bottom and by the sovereign pontiff in the infallibility of his magisterium."[18]

THE AILING POPE WAS SHOWING signs of losing control of the Church he had long ruled with an iron hand. Those around him were frustrating his every attempt to prevent Italy from joining the Nazi cause. When Pius read Gemelli's text, he broke down and cried, sending Pacelli out of his room so that he could be alone.[19] But that same week the Vatican newspaper had approvingly published the Cremona bishop's justification of the racial laws.[20] And if Pius was upset with Gemelli for his remarks, it seemed to do nothing to affect their close relationship. The pope continued to give him unusual access, receiving Gemelli again on January 22.[21] For those Italians who perceived any dispute between the Fascist state and the Vatican over the racial laws, what was at issue was not laws aimed against the Jews, for these the Vatican embraced, but Mussolini's flirtation with Nazi racial ideology, which conflicted with the Church's doctrine and its universal ambitions.

Convinced he hadn't much longer to live, the pope saw the upcoming tenth anniversary of the Lateran Accords as his final chance to address Italy's bishops, two-thirds of whom he had named.[22] He felt responsible for them, and amid all the dangers the world faced, and all the threats to Christian values, he believed he had a sacred duty to convey God's will.

The pope was eager to learn if Mussolini would be in St. Peter's for his speech. Cardinal Pacelli told him he didn't know but thought it unlikely. "If he does not want to celebrate the tenth anniversary," replied the pope, "I will do it by myself."[23]

There was no escaping the sensation in the Vatican that an era was ending. After almost seventeen years, there would soon be a new pope. Rumors rocketed around Europe. French papers reported that the ailing pope, angry at Mussolini, wanted to leave Italy and move to France and was weighing the relative merits of Avignon and Fontainebleau. The London *Daily Mail* and various radio broadcasts announced that, as he prepared the Catholic world for his successor, the pope was planning to move to Castel Gandolfo in midwinter, to prepare a final testament denouncing all the errors of the time. *L'Osservatore romano* ridiculed the stories, in an article under the heading "Cronache della Befana" (Fairy Tales). The pope, reported the Vatican paper, was in "excellent health."[24]

Mussolini was still fuming over the pope's complaints about the persecution of Italian Catholic Action in his Christmas remarks to the cardinals, which the foreign press had quoted to trumpet the pope's unhappiness with the regime.[25] The Italian ambassador reported the Duce's displeasure to Cardinal Pacelli. No one, replied Pacelli, could prevent such papal outbursts. "The Holy Father's irritability gets more pronounced every day," the ambassador reported to Ciano, "and makes his collaborators' work extremely difficult."

According to Pignatti, the pontiff was fixated on the idea that the government was persecuting Catholic Action groups. The pope was taking minor incidents and turning them into major problems. At a recent meeting, Pius had asked Tardini for the latest news of Catholic Action. When he responded that there were no significant incidents to report, the pope blew up. Thrusting a stack of letters in front of the hapless Tardini, he shouted, "You never know anything. Read what they are writing me."

"I fear," Pignatti told Ciano, "that there isn't much to be hoped for as long as the present pontificate endures." Pius XI, he added, suffered from "pathological cerebral irritation," a condition that worsened as he aged.

Things were likely to improve when the pope died, but nothing should be left to chance. The government needed to work discreetly with Italy's cardinals. "It is necessary," he advised, ". . . that there be a good group of cardinals in the future conclave that can authoritatively affirm that the Fascist government has remained faithful to its agreements and to the spirit behind them. The decree on mixed marriages is a minor matter, blown up by the pope's irritability."[26]

Mussolini faced a dilemma. He dreaded participating in a Vatican extravaganza in which all attention would focus on the pontiff. Yet not to take part in commemorating what the world saw as one of his greatest triumphs could be seen as a sign of weakness, as if he felt he no longer had the Church behind him.[27]

Mussolini got word to Cardinal Pacelli that he was willing to discuss how best to organize the festivities. He proposed a series of events in which he was at the center, the kinds of Fascist celebrations that he presided over regularly. He and the pope would give separate speeches, exchange messages of congratulations, and hold a mass. Mussolini wanted to hold his mass at the huge Roman sports field that had been built in his honor. He would not step foot in St. Peter's. He also wanted to host a reception for Italy's bishops while they were in Rome.

Pacelli conveyed the Duce's proposals to the pope the next day, hoping to find a way to present the event as a joint celebration by the Holy See and the Italian state. But the pope again went off on a tangent, tearing into Mussolini for not responding to the letter he had sent him on the marriage law. Then, turning to Mussolini's suggestions for the celebration, the pope said he could accept the exchange of messages but would not allow the bishops to attend a reception at Palazzo Venezia. He was the one who had invited them to Rome, not Mussolini. And if Mussolini wanted to hold a mass somewhere else in Rome, the pope would certainly not have anything to do with it.

The more the pope mulled over Mussolini's proposals, the more upset he got. Two days later he told Pacelli he had changed his mind and would not exchange messages of congratulation with Mussolini. The Lateran Accords had been signed in the king's name, he said, and any such exchange should be with the monarch, not with the Duce.[28]

IT WAS NOW SEVEN MONTHS since the pope had secretly summoned Father LaFarge to Castel Gandolfo to prepare a draft encyclical on racism and anti-Semitism. But he had received nothing. Unable to keep the secret from his advisers any longer, he told Tardini about the project and asked him to find out from Ledóchowski what had become of the American Jesuit's work.

When, months earlier, Ledóchowski had sent the draft encyclical to Rosa, he had enclosed a cover note: "I send Your Reverence a copy of Father LaFarge's work with the prayer that you look through it and tell me . . . if it can be presented in this form to the Holy Father as a first draft." Ledóchowski quickly answered his own question: "I very much doubt it!" Rosa never got to finish his revisions.[29] On Saturday evening, November 26, while sitting at his desk, the sixty-eight-year-old former *Civiltà cattolica* editor suffered a heart attack and died.[30]

Still Ledóchowski kept the draft encyclical from the pope. In reluctantly forwarding it to the pope in January, he attached a letter of his own. Tellingly, he referred to the encyclical's subject as "nationalism," not racism, much less anti-Semitism. "It seemed to both Father Rosa and me," Ledóchowski told the pope, "that the outline does not correspond to what Your Holiness had desired." Rosa had been working on a new outline but died before he could complete it. Ledóchowski gave no explanation for what he had been doing with the material since Rosa's death, but he offered to assist the pope in any way he could in preparing a more acceptable version.[31]

Rumors of the secret encyclical against racism had somehow leaked out, and Mussolini and his entourage were worried. In late January a police informer sent in a long report on the latest high prelate to criticize Nazi racism and its Italian echoes. The archbishop—or patriarch as he was called—of Venice had recently given a sermon for Epiphany, which *L'Osservatore romano* had published. Nothing, Cardinal Piazza had said, justified the "excessive exaltations of races," which had no scientific basis and went against basic Church teachings.[32]

The informant warned that the increasing flow of antiracist pronouncements by high churchmen "represents a steady stream that has a substantial effect on public opinion, given the authoritative nature of the persons from whom it is coming, the wide Catholic sentiment in the masses, the potent means of publicity constituted by the Catholic press, its circulation continually growing and much read by vast social strata."[33]

Pignatti, commenting on the episode, argued that the problem was partly of their own creation. Cardinal Piazza would never have made his recent remarks against racism if the Fascist press hadn't been so effusive in its praise of his earlier, more accommodating comments on the anti-Semitic laws. The patriarch had felt compelled to "clarify" his views. "No prelate," argued Pignatti, "no matter how high-ranking he is, will dare oppose the pontiff, knowing he would be crushed if he tried." There was only one hope: "Only a new pontificate—I have already written this repeatedly in the past—will be able to adopt a different, conciliatory approach to the racial question."[34]

The pope began work on his speech, or rather his speeches, as he had decided to extend the celebration to two days, February 11–12. On Saturday the eleventh, he would mark the tenth anniversary of the Lateran Accords with the bishops in the presence of government and diplomatic dignitaries. On the following morning, he would speak to the bishops and other high clergy alone.[35]

Ciano was nervous, fearing what the pope might say. "The atmosphere for the celebration of the tenth anniversary is becoming murky," he wrote in his diary.[36]

Mussolini was playing tough. No government official, he informed Pacelli, would take part in the celebration unless he received assurances that the pope would not use the occasion to criticize the regime.[37]

The pope was also keeping up the pressure. He told Pacelli to pass on a warning to the Duce: Italians would be shocked if the country's leaders boycotted the anniversary event. He warned Mussolini that if the government were not represented at the highest level, he would feel compelled to comment on its absence in his address.

Cardinal Pacelli passed the pope's new threat on to Pignatti, adding that the pope was still angry at the Duce for not responding to his letter on the marriage law. Exasperated, Pignatti reminded him that it was Mussolini who had dictated the king's reply to the pope, and so the

Duce believed that he had already responded. He warned Pacelli that should the pope use the anniversary ceremonies to criticize the regime, "a situation in Italy similar to the one the Church faces in Germany could result."[38]

Pignatti sought a compromise. He knew he would never get Mussolini to attend the pope's speech in St. Peter's, but if Ciano attended, that might be enough to keep the pope from saying anything truly damaging.[39]

The Duce was growing more and more bellicose, believing war was near and that Italy's greatness—and his own—were soon to be proven on the bloody fields of battle. At a Grand Council meeting, held on the same day Pacelli and Pignatti were discussing who from the government would take part in the anniversary ceremonies, Mussolini unveiled his new watchword: "March to the Ocean!" Italy, he told his colleagues, was trapped in a Mediterranean "prison." It had to gain access to the open seas. Among his first targets would be Corsica, and if it took a war with France to acquire the island, he was ready. Only a week earlier Franco's forces, with Italian help, had taken Barcelona, the last major Spanish city not in their hands. Europe's map was about to be redrawn.[40]

The Duce agreed to let Ciano represent him at the anniversary celebration at St. Peter's. The Prince of Piedmont, the king's son and heir, would represent the monarch.[41] By midweek all of Italy's newspapers were reporting on the magnificent celebration to take place during the upcoming weekend, trumpeting the participation of both the Italian foreign minister and the prince.

As the big event approached, the pope's health worsened. His heartbeat became irregular, his blood circulation, weak to begin with, grew even weaker, and he became feverish. He had begun drafting his remarks for the Saturday address late at night on January 30. On the thirty-first Cardinal Jean Verdier, archbishop of Paris, came to see him and was shocked by how frail he looked. "A truly painful impression," he recalled. "Physically this old pope is but a ruin. He was much thinner, his face shrunken and wrinkled." But the pope's mind was lucid, and his voice still clear. He spoke rapidly, as if he knew he had little time left and much to say.[42]

Early the next morning, Pius, the former librarian, carefully went through the papers in his desk drawers, making sure they were all in order. After his morning audiences, he reread the text of his speech. He was so engrossed that his assistants had to beg him to stop and take his lunch break, for it was already three P.M. But he found it difficult to tear himself away from his text, reading it aloud with tears in his eyes. At last he relinquished the pages and gave them to Monsignor Confalonieri to type. At the elevator to go up to his apartment, he was met by his nurse, Father Faustino, who was alarmed by his pallor and weakness. Faustino felt the pope's pulse, which he was shocked to discover had fallen to forty.[43]

It was Pacelli who brought the bedridden pope the welcome news that Ciano and the prince would attend the ceremony. In recent weeks, the pope's constant refrain had been "What a boor and a traitor Mussolini has been with me!"[44] Now he began to feel some peace.

Cardinal Pacelli urged the pope to put off the celebration until he recovered his strength, but the pontiff knew he had little time left. On February 7 he dictated a message for *L'Osservatore romano,* beginning, "The Holy Father is well." When later that day Pacelli again urged the grievously ill pope to postpone the celebration, he replied, "But didn't we announce this morning that the pope is well?"[45]

The next day it looked as if the end could come at any moment. The pope's breathing was labored, he was heavily medicated, his heartbeat irregular. But he did not forget the speech that meant so much to him and asked Pacelli to read it. The cardinal made some small suggestions. The sheets were sent to the Vatican printer to make copies for the bishops.[46]

Monsignor De Romanis normally came to take the pope's confession every Friday. When the timid monsignor appeared at his bedside that Wednesday, the pope first told him he must have made a mistake. When the tongue-tied monsignor sputtered, too embarrassed to explain why he had been called in two days early, the reason for his visit dawned on the pope. "We understand," said the pope, weakly. "Confess me."

On Thursday, February 9, feeling a little better, Pius XI again asked to be sure that his text for the big event was printed and ready to give the bishops.[47] Together with his two loyal assistants, who had served him since his days in Milan, he recited the rosary as he lay in bed. He then asked them to say the prayer he had learned as a child:

Jesus, Joseph, and Mary, I give you my heart and my soul,
Jesus, Joseph, and Mary, be with me in my final moments,
Jesus, Joseph, and Mary, may my soul go forth in peace with you.

That evening Pignatti reached Ciano with word that the pope was gravely ill. He passed the news on to Mussolini, who simply shrugged. Ciano was worried. Should the pope die before the anniversary celebration, the result could be "a conclave quite hostile to our purposes." After weeks of worry, he had finally been convinced that the Vatican's spectacular ritual at St. Peter's would help heal the tension; it would impress on Italian Catholics how solid the link between the Holy See and the Fascist regime still was. Should the ceremony be canceled, "we might have to expect unpleasant surprises."[48]

That night, as the pope lay in bed, his condition worsened and last rites were again given. In the early hours of Friday morning, February 10, it was only with the help of an oxygen mask that he could breathe. Around four A.M. Cardinal Pacelli and others nearby were alerted and joined the sorrowful scene. Weeping, they asked for the pope's blessing. With great effort, Pius opened his eyes and, too weak to speak clearly, mumbled a few words, stopped, then mumbled something else. Most could not make out what he said, but those closest to him later reported his words as "God bless you, my children," followed by an even weaker "Let there be peace."[49]

At 5:31 A.M., the long-suffering Pius XI died. Following tradition, the chamberlain, Cardinal Pacelli, was charged with officially verifying the death. He knelt beside the bed, drew back the veil that had been placed over the pope's face, and in a loud voice addressed him using his baptismal name, Achille, while tapping his forehead gently with a silver mallet. There being no movement from the pope, Pacelli uttered the ritual declaration: "The Pope is truly dead." He pulled the Fisherman's Ring from the pope's cold finger.[50]

The bishops had already arrived in Rome for the celebration that had meant so much to the pope, a celebration for which Ciano had his hopes and Mussolini his fears. On the pope's desk was the folder of *Humani generis unitas,* the encyclical prepared by Father LaFarge. Rejecting the idea that a good Christian could embrace racism, it demanded an end to the persecution of the Jews. It was Pius XI's fervent hope that such a statement be issued, but among those who survived him, many were eager to see it buried along with the pope.[51]

A DARK CLOUD LIFTS

A LTHOUGH HE HAD MET WITH PIUS XI MANY TIMES, THE FRENCH
ambassador had never seen his private quarters. Now, a few hours
after the pope's death, he joined the macabre scene on the top floor of
the papal palace. He entered a large, high-ceilinged room, its majestic
appearance ruined, he thought, by the jumble of mismatched, amateur-
ish artwork that littered its walls. One displayed "an exotic embroidery
of mediocre taste," an offering of the nuns who had woven it. Assorted
other objects decorated the rest of the room, gifts to the pope from missions around the world.

After signing his name in the guest book, Charles-Roux made his
way through the narrow hallway that led into the pope's bedroom.
There the pope's body lay on his iron-frame bed, dressed in a white
soutane, a red, ermine-edged papal cap pulled down to his ears. His
head rested on a simple pillow. In his hands, which lay together on his
chest, were a crucifix and a rosary. "Life," observed the French ambassador, "had abandoned his body in a pitiful state." His face was completely changed, "defeated, ravaged." A large candle burned at each
corner of the bed. A Noble Guard stood at attention on each side,
clutching his saber.

As he passed back into the reception hall, Charles-Roux was appalled. Other members of the Noble Guard, awaiting their turn, were biding their time chatting in small groups with an assortment of high prelates and lay functionaries. The men talked loudly, showing no trace of sorrow or respect.[1]

"The Pope is dead," Ciano wrote in his diary on February 10. "The news leaves the Duce completely indifferent." That afternoon Ciano went to the Vatican to pay his respects. Cardinal Pacelli met him and escorted him up to the Sistine Chapel. The pope's emaciated body had just arrived. It lay on a high platform beneath the vaulted ceiling, frescoed by Michelangelo. From below, Ciano could only see the pope's white sandals and the hem of his robe. As they walked back down to the courtyard, Ciano recalled, Pacelli "spoke to me about the relationship between State and Church with very agreeable and hopeful expressions."[2]

Mussolini still felt aggrieved, and in any case he had become so enamored with himself that his aides had to massage him before he could bring himself to display any sign of mourning. The Vatican expected the Duce to join the wake that day at the Sistine Chapel, but he did not come. One mourner noted his absence: "Today the king went at about seven P.M. to visit the body," he observed in his diary. "Mussolini did not go, perhaps because he did not deign to; perhaps because he did not want to displease Hitler."[3]

Pignatti and Ciano had given a great deal of thought to this moment. Despite Mussolini's occasional claim that he didn't care what happened in the upcoming conclave, they knew how important it was that the next pope be someone with whom they could work. Their constant worry that the pope might do something to turn Italy's Catholics against them had been a nightmare.[4]

And although the Duce professed little interest in the conclave, he heard something that worried him. In cleaning out the pope's room, Vatican officials had apparently discovered a secret document on his desk. They promptly gave it to Cardinal Pacelli. On February 12, Mussolini asked Ciano to find out what it was. Ciano passed the order on to

Cardinal Pacelli accompanies Galeazzo Ciano
in viewing the body of Pius XI, February 10, 1939

Pignatti, leaving himself free to spend the unusually warm, sunny February day at his golf club.[5] Mussolini, too, had other plans. When, at four-thirty that afternoon, Clara Petacci arrived at their apartment in Palazzo Venezia, carrying sandwiches and a bouquet of violets, she was surprised to find her lover already there, sitting in an armchair, reading some papers. She suspected he had gotten there first to be sure nothing incriminating remained from his latest tryst. "Give me a kiss," said the Duce, "sit on my lap." Over the next hours, as the faithful filed by the pope's body in the Vatican, they made love twice.[6]

While the Duce was thus occupied, Pignatti was on his way to see the nuncio Borgongini to ask about the rumored secret document left behind by the pope, and about another disturbing report he had heard. A foreign newspaper reported that when Italy's bishops had gathered at the Vatican Saturday morning, the day after the pope's death, they were each given a copy of a secret document denouncing Fascism. It had been the pope's last wish that they receive this message, should he not live long enough to give it to them himself. Borgongini assured the ambassador there could be no truth to the story, as he himself had been with the bishops that morning. Perhaps, he speculated, the rumors had started because, as the bishops emerged from the Vatican, each carried a large envelope in hand. In one of his last moments, the pope had decided to give each of the bishops a thousand lire to pay their travel expenses and sponsor a mass back home in honor of the occasion. These were the contents of the envelopes the reporter had seen.[7]

It is not clear whether the rumors that the pope was about to deliver a denunciation of Fascism drew on leaks about the pope's plans for a secret encyclical against racism. There is every indication that Fathers LaFarge and Gundlach, although unhappy that their efforts had been sabotaged, kept their vow of secrecy, and neither Ledóchowski nor Rosa had any interest in letting anyone outside know of the pope's plan. Pius XI, having received the text only three weeks before his death, never had a chance to do anything with it.

Learning of Mussolini's concern, Pacelli moved quickly. On February 15 he ordered the pope's secretary to gather up all written material the pope had produced in preparing his address. He also told the Vatican printing office to destroy all copies of the speech it had printed, copies that Pius had intended to give the bishops. The vice director of the office gave his assurance that he would personally destroy them, so that "not a comma" remained. Pacelli acted two days after learning of Ciano's worries that the text of the pope's speech might get out. Pacelli also took the material that Ledóchowski had sent the pope three weeks earlier—what has since come to be known as the "secret encyclical" against racism—eager to ensure that no one else would see it.

The words the pope had so painstakingly prepared in the last days of his life would never be seen as long as Pacelli lived. Only twenty years later, four months after Pacelli died, would Pope John XXIII, in one of his first acts, release excerpts of the speech. But he excised those passages that were most critical of the Fascist regime, presumably to protect Pacelli, suspected of having buried the speech in order not to offend Mussolini or Hitler. Only with the opening of the Vatican archives for the papacy of Pius XI in 2006 has the world seen the full text.

The speech was far from the ringing denunciation of the Fascist regime that Mussolini had feared, but the Duce would not have been pleased to have it heard by Italy's bishops and then read by millions around the world. The pope complained about efforts to conceal and misrepresent his speeches, and warned the bishops to be on their guard when they spoke with "the so-called hierarchs" of the government. "Be careful, dearest Brothers in Christ, and do not forget that often there are observers and informers (you would do well to call them spies) who, of their own initiative or because charged to do so, listen to you in order to condemn you, after, it is understood, having understood nothing at all and if necessary just the opposite." He went on to bewail "these pseudo-Catholics who seem happy when they believe they have identified a disagreement or discrepancy between one Bishop and another, or even better between a Bishop and a Pope." He then urged the bishops never to use a telephone when saying words they did not want known, for their lines were likely tapped. ("We have never once in all these years used the telephone," the pope proudly noted.)

Pius XI briefly lamented the persecution of the Church in Germany and castigated those who denied it. His concluding remarks hit the note he was most eager to impart to the bishops: he looked forward to the day when "all peoples, all the nations, all the races, all joined together and all of the same blood in the common link of the great human family" would unite in the one "true Faith."[8]

Along with the text of the pope's Saturday speech, Pacelli took the notes the pope had prepared for his Sunday address to the bishops. Although these notes have not been found, Tardini saw the materials and left behind a description. Among the major points the pope planned to address were three that would have not pleased the Duce: Catholic Action; the religious situation in Germany; and the "wound inflicted to the concordat by the prohibition of marriages between Aryans and non-Aryans."[9]

Mussolini would never learn that it was Pacelli who had ordered the suppression of the pope's last projects. What he heard instead was that a special gathering of the Sacred College of Cardinals had decided to bury the speech, judging it too hostile to Mussolini. The cardinals, or at least the Italian majority, Pignatti reported to him, were now eager to concentrate their votes on a person who would take a more conciliatory view toward the Fascist regime.[10]

Mussolini hoped that Pignatti was right, but he had reason to worry.

Speculation regarding the most likely choice ranged dizzyingly from Jean Villeneuve, archbishop of Quebec—said to be the most likely non-Italian—to Mussolini's recent antagonist, Cardinal Schuster. *The Boston Globe* published pictures of Cardinal Schuster and Cardinal Giovanni Piazza, patriarch of Venice, reporting them to be the leading candidates.[11] *The New York Times* reported Piazza as the favorite, followed by eight other cardinals in the order of their presumed chances. Eugenio Pacelli was at the bottom of the list. He had no pastoral experience—all the others presided over archdioceses—and there was a long tradition against choosing either a secretary of state or a chamberlain; Pacelli was both.[12]

Even though many outsiders thought Pacelli had little chance, Mussolini had long been getting reports from police informants identifying him as the front-runner. Pius XI was said to have regarded his secretary of state as his most qualified successor. Indeed, Mussolini was told, the pope had sent Pacelli on so many missions abroad—to France, to South America, to the United States, and elsewhere—to help him win over the foreign cardinals. All this was good news for the Duce. A secret police report a year earlier described Pacelli as a "man of great intrinsic merit, an excellent Italian, a great and sincere friend of our regime." It added a bit of advice: for this reason, "the good Vatican circles fervently hope in the wisdom of our government, which—especially in this moment—they say, should completely avoid showing—even remotely—the least sympathy for Cardinal Pacelli."[13]

In the wake of the pope's death, similar reports kept coming in. One police informant spoke with Cardinal Angelo Dolci, a former papal nuncio, who also thought Pacelli the most likely choice. "Dolci, who is a good Italian and very sympathetic to Fascism and an admirer of the Duce," reported the informant, "continues to be convinced that Pacelli would be a true friend of the regime as pontiff." Cardinal Dalla Costa of Florence—a man seen as so holy that he could work miracles—was also said to have a good chance. If one of these two were elected, the conclave would be very short; if not, it could last weeks.[14]

The government proclaimed the day of the pope's funeral a holiday, closing schools, offices, and theaters. Reluctantly, Mussolini attended the memorial requiem, held in the Church of Sant'Andrea della Valle in Rome, as did other high government officials, along with the king and queen.[15]

Mussolini and the other Fascist leaders felt as if they had woken up to find that an irritating sore that had long plagued them was miraculously gone. Pacelli's firm hand could be seen in a dozen ways. In the oceans of ink that the Vatican and Italian Catholic press devoted to Pius XI's papacy, the subject of his conflict with the regime was not mentioned; nor was his conflict with Hitler and the Nazis. The Italian newspapers quickly got the message. In their prodigious coverage of Pius XI's papacy, they gave great play to the Conciliation. If the pope had ever had anything negative to say about Mussolini or Fascism, it was all forgotten.[16]

On the day of the pope's death, Pignatti provided the Foreign Ministry with a list of all the conclavists and their ages, from the eighty-eight-year-old Cardinal Pignatelli di Belmonte to the fifty-five-year-old Cardinal Tisserant. Of the sixty-two members of the Sacred College, thirty-five were Italian.[17]

On the eighteenth, as the cardinals gathered in Rome, Diego von Bergen, Germany's ambassador to the Holy See, came to talk to his Italian counterpart. Bergen was eager to tell Pignatti of his recent conversation with Cardinal Pacelli: the cardinal had been moved by Hitler's message of condolence and asked to have his own personal thanks, and that of the Sacred College, communicated to the Führer. Pacelli also wanted to let Hitler know that he hoped conciliation between the Reich and the Holy See would now be possible. The message had greatly pleased the Nazi government.

"The ambassador told me," recounted Pignatti, "that if the conclave's choice should fall on Cardinal Pacelli, Pacelli would do everything he could to reconcile with Germany, and probably he would succeed."

The Italian ambassador offered Bergen some advice, in the spirit of helping both their causes. The Reich's relations with the Vatican could be repaired, he said, only if the German government took steps to improve the atmosphere. First, the German newspapers needed to tone down their criticism of the Vatican. The cardinals paid close attention to what was said in the foreign press, and recent hostile articles from Germany were not helping.[18]

Pignatti also urged the German ambassador to do everything possible to get the four German cardinals to take a conciliatory attitude at the upcoming conclave. Should they preach a holy war against the Nazi regime, he warned, "all will be lost." It was crucial they convince the other cardinals that an understanding with the Nazis was still in reach. Bergen said he would telegraph Berlin immediately to ask for an end to the polemics in the press. As for the German cardinals, he said, he was optimistic.[19]

For the Italian ambassador, the question of how the German cardinals would behave at the conclave was too important to leave entirely to Bergen. On February 21 he visited Ledóchowski to enlist his aid; the Jesuit general said he would do all he could to help.[20]

As the conclave neared, Pignatti checked back in with the German embassy, speaking to Bergen's number two, Fritz Menshausen. The Nazi envoy, Pignatti reported, "repeatedly insisted on the candidacy of Pacelli as pope and Tedeschini"—former nuncio to Spain—"as secretary of state. This would represent the best solution for Germany and would make possible an easing in relations between the Holy See and the Reich."[21]

Pignatti rushed from one Italian cardinal to another, trying to convince them of the wisdom of choosing a pope who was favorably disposed toward the Fascist regime and would not publicly criticize the Nazis. With the German cardinals supporting Pacelli, if the French cardinals fell in line, he believed the rest of the non-Italians would as well. The Italian cardinals were a different story. They faulted Pacelli "for a weakness of character, for being easily influenced, and sometimes stumbling, as happens to people who are weak." Pignatti related all this to Ciano, adding, "These points are, in my opinion, quite well founded."[22]

Cardinal Baudrillart's train from Paris arrived in Rome on February 20. Deeply devoted to Pius XI, he was disturbed to hear many of his colleagues be so critical of him. "One quickly stops being a great man in this country," the French cardinal observed. Two days after his arrival, he went to see Cardinal Pacelli, who, after a moment of hesitation, was willing to reflect on his chances at the upcoming conclave. "In the end," Baudrillart predicted, "he will be a conciliator."[23]

The main holdout among the French cardinals was Eugène Tisserant, who thought Pacelli too eager to please the Germans; he preferred the former nuncio to France, Luigi Maglione. The French cardinals discussed the matter and came up with a compromise: Pacelli as pope and Maglione as secretary of state. Tisserant went to see Pacelli, who, apparently unaware that Tisserant had reservations about him, confided his nervousness. The Italian cardinals of the Curia, he was convinced, did not like him and would not vote for him. "I may as well get my passport to go to Switzerland right after the conclave," said Pacelli, referring to his regular vacation spot.

"The French cardinals will hold firm," replied Tisserant reassuringly. "However, their decision will be unanimous and more solid if they learn that you plan to choose Cardinal Maglione as secretary of state."

"You can give them my assurance," Pacelli replied, and the deal was struck.[24]

"THE GREAT DAY HAS ARRIVED." It was Wednesday, March 1, and the conclave was about to begin. Baudrillart was up at five-thirty A.M. and, after celebrating mass, left for the Vatican. He dressed with the other cardinals, and they then processed to the Pauline Chapel, where a mass was said, followed by a "glacial, monotonous" sermon in Latin that few of them could make any sense of. By evening the last three cardinals arrived—William O'Connell, archbishop of Boston; Sebastião Leme, archbishop of Rio de Janeiro; and Santiago Copello, archbishop of Buenos Aires—their ship having docked that morning in Naples.[25]

While the other cardinals were crammed into small rooms in the Apostolic Palace, Cardinal Pacelli, as chamberlain, was granted the special privilege of staying in his own apartment, technically within the conclave's restricted area. The other cardinals dined together. Pacelli dined alone.[26]

The next morning the cardinals filed into the Sistine Chapel, some of the older ones walking only with difficulty. Each found his assigned seat with its little canopied table, forming two lines along the length of the chapel, facing each other. By now it was clear that either Pius XI's heir apparent, Eugenio Pacelli, would win in an early vote, or if his detractors succeeded in blocking his election, the conclave would go on for many days.

The names of three cardinals were drawn by lot, to serve as the ballot counters. Silence then filled the chapel as each cardinal dipped his pen into ink and scrawled his choice on a paper slip. One by one they rose from their seats and formed a line. As each cardinal approached the altar, he got down on his knees, offered a prayer, and recited the required vow, in Latin, then deposited the folded piece of paper with his vote.

On the first ballot, Pacelli received thirty-two votes, a bare majority of the sixty-two cardinals present. Nine had voted for Dalla Costa, Florence's archbishop, and seven for Maglione, the former papal nuncio to France. Pacelli needed ten more votes to reach the required two-thirds. Other favorites in the past had attained a majority but then faded when they failed to attract other support. "He who comes in the conclave as a pope leaves as a cardinal" went the old adage, not without some historical basis.

For a second time, the cardinals sat at their tables, wrote the name of their choice on the paper, and folded it. Again they formed a line and, following the old rite, brought their ballots to the altar. This time Pacelli picked up eight more votes, but still he fell short. Again, wet straw was added to the paper slips in the fireplace so that black smoke would bellow above the Apostolic Palace. The two morning ballots were now complete. No pope had been elected. The cardinals broke for lunch.

If some had been hoping Pacelli could be blocked, they were disappointed when the cardinals convened after lunch to hold their third ballot. Only fourteen cardinals held out against what seemed to many to be inevitable. Eugenio Pacelli, who for nine years had served Pius XI as secretary of state, received forty-eight votes. He had exceeded the required two-thirds with half a dozen votes to spare. It was his sixty-third birthday.[27]

Before they could announce the new pope to the world, he would need to formally state his acceptance. The tall, gaunt Pacelli—serious, dignified, and pious—was trembling, but, Baudrillart observed, "he was not able to pretend he would turn down the position that he had desired for such a long time." The cardinal deacon, Camillo Caccia Dominioni, strode outside on the loggia of St. Peter's to address the excited crowd, their eyes glued on its door ever since they had seen the white smoke rise. "*Habemus papam,*" he intoned. Fifteen minutes later the new pope appeared on the balcony to bless the enthusiastic throng. He took the name Pius XII, honoring not only the man at whose side he had stood for so long but both Pius IX and Pius X, heroes of Church traditionalists.[28]

The newly elected Pope Pius XII blesses throngs in St. Peter's Square, March 1939. Cardinal Caccia Dominioni is in front, at the pope's right side.

That evening Pignatti sent the news to Ciano, attributing Pacelli's success to his having made it clear to his colleagues that while, as secretary of state, he had faithfully executed the pope's orders, he preferred a much more accommodating approach to Italy and Germany.[29]

Ciano received the good news while returning from a trip to Warsaw. In his diary, he recalled the conversation he had had with Pacelli the day of the pope's death: "He was very conciliatory, and it seems also that in the meantime he has improved relations with Germany. In fact, Pignatti said only yesterday that he is the cardinal preferred by the Germans." Back in Rome the following afternoon, Ciano went to see Mussolini, who was pleased by Pacelli's election. He told Ciano he would help the new pope by sending him advice on how to effectively govern the Church. Mussolini ordered the press to praise the new pope: "Comment sympathetically on the election of the new pontiff," the instructions read, "recalling his piety, his culture, and his vast political experience."[30]

Barely forty-eight hours after his election, Pope Pacelli summoned the German ambassador, meeting with him the morning of March 5. Pius XII was eager to assure the Nazi government that he sought a new era of understanding. After telling Bergen how close he felt to the German people as a result of his many years in Munich and Berlin, he came to his main point. He understood that different countries adopted different forms of government, and it was not the pope's role to judge what system other countries chose. He reminded Bergen that the two of them had had a good relationship for thirty years. He expressed his wish that this not change.[31]

Bergen was pleased, but found himself in the unusual position of warning the Nazi government about unrealistically rosy expectations. "The attitude of our press toward the new pope," he wrote to the German Foreign Office three days later, "has been observed very closely, not only in Vatican but also in Italian circles, and has been received with satisfaction." He had sent Pius XII copies of several positive articles from the German press on his election, hoping they would help persuade him to end the anti-Nazi tone of *L'Osservatore romano*. But he added a caution: "The unmistakable relaxation of tensions which has set in here since the death of the pope has aroused very strong hopes in some quarters for the early removal of differences between Germany and the Vatican." In order to prevent "over optimistic expectations" and "overcome the considerable difficulties," he advised, "patience and time are required, besides good will."[32]

A week later, on March 12, forty thousand people crowded into St. Peter's to witness the new pope's coronation. A procession of two thousand prelates in rich robes, and distinguished guests, many in diplomatic or military uniform, solemnly marched in. A platoon of Swiss Guards in full dress with glittering halberd at their side led the way, followed by a long line of representatives of all the religious orders, then hundreds of bishops, and cardinals in their scarlet robes, covered with white and gold vestments. Finally came the somber figure of the new pontiff, wearing a miter studded with radiant jewels, carried aloft on a throne by ushers in livery of red velvet. Behind him walked two prelates carrying huge ostrich-feather fans that they waved gently, followed by yet more Noble Guards and Swiss Guards, their commander wearing gleaming silver armor and a plumed helmet.[33]

The man who would have the honor of placing the papal tiara on Pacelli's head was none other than Cardinal Caccia Dominioni. Somehow the Vatican and the Fascist police had been able to conceal the cardinal's trail of pederasty accusations. The latest episode in the Italian police files had come only recently. While riding on a bus in Rome the previous August, a policeman had found his attention drawn to the cartons of foreign cigarettes that a young messenger boy was carrying. Suspicious, he discovered that they lacked the required Italian tax stamp. When he asked the lad where he had gotten the contraband cigarettes, the boy replied that someone high up in the Vatican had given them to him. Pressed further, the boy identified Cardinal Caccia. When the police phoned the cardinal to check the boy's story, he confirmed the account and asked that the boy be left alone. "As Caccia Dominioni enjoys the reputation of pederasty," the police informant concluded, "they are saying that the reason for the offer of these ciga-rettes was easily explained."[34]

Joseph Kennedy, President Roosevelt's personal emissary to the coronation ceremony, had another kind of sexual interest in mind as he found himself walking down the aisle alongside the uniformed Gale-azzo Ciano. "I have never met a more pompous ass in my life," Ken-nedy remarked afterward. As Ciano processed through the basilica, he kept giving the Fascist salute, strutting in such a way as to make it seem he was "trying to share honors with the Pope." At a tea in honor of the occasion, Ciano spent all his time trying to corner attractive women. And at the dinner, "he could not talk seriously for five minutes for fear that the two or three girls, who were invited in order to get him to come, might get out of sight." Given what he had observed of Ciano and what he had heard about Mussolini, Kennedy "came away with the belief that we could accomplish much more by sending a dozen beautiful chorus girls to Rome than a flock of diplomats and a fleet of airplanes."[35]

ON MARCH 15, THREE DAYS after the papal coronation, the German army seized the rest of Czechoslovakia. In Prague the next day, Hitler proclaimed the country a protectorate of Germany.[36] Few could deny that Europe was about to endure another terrible war.

The day after the Führer's triumphant speech from Prague, Ciano had his first meeting with the new pope and was pleased to find him unchanged, "benevolent, courteous, and human." Pius XII expressed his concern about the German situation but told Ciano he planned to take a more conciliatory approach to the Reich and hoped to see an improvement in the Vatican's relationship with Berlin. If these efforts were to be successful, he observed, the Nazi government would have to do its part. Ciano, happy to hear all this, expressed his belief that Mus-solini could help persuade Hitler to cooperate. As for the Vatican's re-cent dispute with the Italian government, the new pope "declared himself optimistic," wrote Ciano. He promised to remove Cardinal Pizzardo as head of Catholic Action and entrust its direction to a committee of diocesan archbishops. Mussolini had long wanted Pizzardo dismissed, but Pius XI would never agree to it.

The Vatican had recently asked Italy's bishops if any tensions remained between Catholic Action groups in their diocese and local government or Fascist Party officials. The replies came in during the weeks after Pius XI's death. With the notable exception of Milan, where Cardinal Schuster reported difficulties, the picture was hopeful. Virtually all reported excellent relations. The new pope did his part, instructing Dalla Torre to avoid publishing anything in *L'Osservatore romano* that either the Italian or the German government would find "irritating." For Mussolini and all those who sought a return to the happy days of collaboration between the Vatican and the Fascist regime, it was as if a dark cloud had lifted.[37]

HEADING TOWARD DISASTER

O N GOOD FRIDAY, APRIL 7, MUSSOLINI SENT ITALIAN TROOPS INTO Albania. The new pope, under international pressure to denounce the invasion, said nothing. "Not a word from his mouth about this bloody Good Friday," complained one prominent French Catholic intellectual.[1] Italy's ambassador to the Holy See was much relieved by the new atmosphere in the Vatican. "It is now clear," Pignatti told Ciano two weeks later, "what peace it is that Pius XII is invoking for humanity. It is not the peace of Roosevelt, but rather that of the Duce."[2]

The contrast between the two popes was clear to all who knew them. The American reporter Thomas Morgan, who spent years in Rome and had often met both men, described the two as opposite in temperament. While Pius XI was "gladiatorial, defiant, commanding and uncompromising," his successor was "persuasive, consoling, appealing and conciliatory." Or as the French ambassador Charles-Roux put it, a mountaineer from Milan was succeeded by a Roman bourgeois; a man quick to speak his mind was succeeded by a cautious diplomat.[3]

The Nazi government, too, was pleased by the new pope's attempts to repair the damage done by Pius XI. In his memoirs, Ernst von

Weizsäcker, the head of the German Foreign Office who would soon succeed Bergen as German ambassador to the Holy See, wrote, "If Pius XI, so impulsive and energetic, had lived a little longer, there would in all likelihood have been a break in relations between the Reich and the Curia."[4] But as it was, for Hitler's birthday, on April 20, the papal nuncio in Berlin personally gave the Führer the new pope's best wishes. Throughout Germany church bells rang in celebration. The German newspapers were full of praise for Pope Pacelli, lauding him for warmly congratulating Franco and his compatriots on their conquest of Spain. The papers drew special attention to the pope's remarks equating Communism with democracy. In reporting all this to Ciano, the Italian ambassador in Berlin remarked that the new pope had come at an op-

Pope Pius XII, March 1939

portune time. As the world was condemning the Nazis' invasion of Czechoslovakia, the Reich needed, "perhaps for the first time, to have the Church with it and not against it."[5]

In May the pope met with Giuseppe Bottai, Italy's minister of education and one of the men closest to Mussolini. Although the room was the same that Pius XI had used, Bottai was struck by how different it seemed. Early in his papacy, Pius XI had kept a spartan office, but as he aged he increasingly accumulated mementoes as well as oft-consulted tomes. As Bottai described it, the elderly Pius XI had been surrounded by a "picturesque disorder of furniture, ornaments, knick-knacks, papers, newspapers, books." In contrast, Pius XII sat amid a "meticulous order." His desk held only a few indispensable objects. Most of all, compared to the voluble, excitable Pius XI—certain that God was guiding him, apt to go off on tangents—his successor exuded a sense of calm and the air of someone who knew his job.[6]

Over the next months, Mussolini became more confident that a new, happier era had arrived. Among the various bits of good news he received was the pope's decision, in July, to reestablish relations with the right-wing Action Française. In response to a request from its leader, Charles Maurras—protofascist and France's foremost anti-Semite—the pope reversed Pius XI's 1926 ban on Catholic participation in the organization. The move angered not only the French government but also many of France's most influential clergymen.[7]

Pius XII, Pignatti reported, was not only a conservative but "has a clear sympathy, I would almost say a weakness, for the nobility, which is in his blood." Roman nobles were delighted. His predecessor, coming from a modest social background, had shown little deference to them and over the years cut back on their privileges. Pius XII, a product of the black aristocracy, moved quickly to reintroduce their old prerogatives.[8]

Mussolini got another encouraging report about the new pope, this one from Switzerland. His ambassador there had spoken at length with the papal nuncio, recently returned from Rome. The atmosphere in the Vatican, the nuncio reported, was "completely changed," like a "breath of fresh air." The Holy Father spoke "with much sympathy for Fascism and with sincere admiration for the Duce." He was convinced that his reorganization of Catholic Action in Italy would remove a major source of tension with the regime. As for Germany, the new pope could not be more eager to come to an agreement.[9]

Many in the Church were also pleased by the change. After years of the stubborn, combative Pius XI, they found audiences with Pius XII a relief. In contrast to Pius XI's long-winded monologues, the new pope listened carefully to his visitors and never seemed to forget anything they told him. Like Pius XI, the new pope followed the tradition of taking his meals alone. They were if anything even simpler than his predecessor's, and as he ate, he enjoyed watching his canaries flutter in the birdcage he kept in the dining room. But Pius XII readily agreed to pose for photographs with small visiting groups, something Pius XI thought beneath his dignity, and unlike Pius XI he was happy to use the telephone. "Pacelli here," Francis Spellman was startled to hear when the new pope decided to call his old friend, recently appointed archbishop of New York.[10]

After the tensions of the last months of Pope Ratti's life, all the elements of the clerico-Fascist regime soon returned. Emblematic was a ceremony held at one of Rome's major churches in April 1940. The national Fascist girls' association had long been campaigning, under the guidance of the priests attached to their local groups, to make Saint Catherine Italy's female patron saint. The girls got their way shortly after Pacelli became pope, and to mark the first celebration of the new national holiday, the bishop overseeing the Fascist girls' association presided over a special mass. Each of the two thousand girls there carried a white rose that, one after another, they deposited at the church altar.[11]

But the normal pleasures of life in Rome were about to give way to the realities of war. Early on the morning of September 1, 1939, German troops invaded Poland. They imprisoned or murdered many Catholic priests, but the pope confined his remarks to a generic appeal for peace and brotherhood. He did not want to take sides, not least because of a belief that the Nazis were likely to win.[12] Two days later Britain and France declared war on Germany. The next month, under the supervision of Adolf Eichmann, German forces began to deport Jews from Austria and Czechoslovakia to camps in Poland. The Second World War, and the Holocaust, were under way.

In the spring of 1940, German armies were marching from conquest to conquest. Eager to share in the spoils, on June 10 Mussolini declared war on France and Britain. He rushed Italian forces into southern France to grab territory before Nazi troops seized everything for themselves. In their enthusiasm, many Italians thought the war would be short. Tacchi Venturi predicted it would be over by Christmas.[13]

Italy's Jews lived lives of desperation, vilified as enemies of the state, thousands out of work, their children forced from the schools. To build support for its anti-Semitic campaign, the government continued to rely heavily on Catholic imagery, citing Church texts. The government's main vehicle for spreading its anti-Semitic bile remained the twice-monthly, color, glossy *La Difesa della razza*. Much of its content was cannibalized from Catholic anti-Semitic materials. A typical issue, in April 1939, published an article titled "Christ and Christians in the Talmud," and another "Catholics and Jews in France." Articles such as "The Eternal Enemies of Rome" told readers that the Church had always treated Jews as second-class citizens in order to protect Catholics from their predation. The enemy for *La Difesa della razza,* as for the Holy See, was the French Revolution, cast as the work of a liberal, Masonic, Jewish conspiracy.[14]

Mussolini again began to make use of Father Tacchi Venturi. Two weeks after the new pope's coronation, the Duce summoned the Jesuit to convey the message that he wanted the pontiff to direct Spain's Catholic clergy to support Franco even more strongly than before.[15] He also wanted the pope's help in getting priests in Croatia to encourage the faithful to support Italy rather than Germany; and he asked the pope to mobilize the Catholic clergy in Latin America to combat pro-United States sentiment there.[16]

Meanwhile, the Vatican-supervised *La Civiltà cattolica* was drumming up Catholic support for the racial laws. In November 1940 the journal praised a new government-published book that explained Italy's brand of racism and compared its racial campaign favorably to Germany's. Italy's campaign loyally followed Catholic teachings, while Germany's relied on specious biological theories. When the former head of the University of Rome, a Jew who had converted to Catholicism, wrote to the Vatican secretary of state to complain about the article, Monsignor Tardini wrote back defending it.[17]

THE FATE OF ITALY'S troops soon showed the hollowness of Mussolini's saber rattling. Poorly equipped, poorly led, and poorly trained, Italian soldiers proved incompetent. Emblematically, within three weeks of Italy's declaration of war, Italo Balbo, Fascist aviator extraordinaire, died when an Italian antiartillery unit mistakenly shot down his plane as he was landing at an Italian airfield in Libya.

Invading Albania, then Greece, then joining forces with the Germans in North Africa and on the eastern front in Russia, the Italians depended time and again on the Germans to come to their rescue. In the fall of 1942, Italian troops and their German allies retreated before advancing allied forces in North Africa. That winter two hundred thousand Italian troops fought alongside the Germans on the eastern front in the disastrous Battle of Stalingrad. Nearly half were killed or captured. The tide had turned, and it was becoming clear that the Axis powers were headed for defeat. Initial Italian enthusiasm for the war evaporated. In early July 1943 Allied troops landed in Sicily, meeting little Italian resistance. On July 19 hundreds of Allied planes dropped bombs on Rome, aiming at military targets but causing thousands of civilian casualties.

On Saturday, July 24, the Grand Council of Fascism met for the last time. As usual, Mussolini sat at his desk at one end of the vast Hall of the Map of the World. Seated at two long tables that stretched at either side of him were the bigwigs of Italian Fascism. The meeting began in mid-afternoon, when a cocky Mussolini unleashed a tirade, blaming the recent military disasters on incompetent generals. He heaped special scorn on Sicilians, who had greeted the Allied troops as liberators.

Dino Grandi, dapper and goateed, one of the regime's luminaries, sitting near the Duce, rose and delivered a speech such as the dictator had never heard. Mussolini alone, Grandi proclaimed, was to blame for the disastrous situation the country now faced. "The Italian people were betrayed by Mussolini," said Grandi, who had served as Mussolini's foreign minister and then ambassador to Great Britain, "the day that Italy began to be Germanized." Mussolini, he charged, "engulfed us in a war that is against honor, and against the interests and the sentiments of the Italian people."

Dumbfounded, his confidence shaken, Mussolini's attempts to interrupt became progressively weaker, as Grandi called for deposing him and bringing back parliamentary democracy. Then Grandi turned left to face Mussolini: "You believe you still have the devotion of the Italian people? You lost it the day that you consigned Italy to Germany. You think you are a soldier: Italy was ruined the day you put on your commander's stripes. There are hundreds of thousands of mothers who cry out: Mussolini killed my son!"

Seated at the long tables, some Grand Council members, astonished and furious, swore at Grandi. "You will pay with your head for this treachery!" shouted one. Those who agreed with Grandi considered whether to support his motion, which called for deposing the dictator, returning control of Italy's military from Mussolini to the king, and restoring the constitutional order. They nervously wondered what fate would befall those who dared vote in its favor.

It was now well past midnight, July 25, 1943. Following hours of heated argument, the fateful vote was taken. Nineteen of the twenty-seven men—while fearful they might not survive the night—voted for the motion. They were relieved, perhaps even a bit surprised, when no Fascist militiamen stopped them as they left the room.

Mussolini headed home, angry but confident that the king would support him. Later that day, as he set out to inform Victor Emmanuel what had happened, his wife, Rachele, tried to stop him. She did not trust the king. Now that it was clear that Mussolini was on the losing side of the war, the cowardly king would be eager to cast all the blame on him and find a way to escape responsibility for the disaster he had played such an important part in creating. Rachele's intuition proved right. The king had Mussolini arrested and appointed General Pietro Badoglio, hero of the Ethiopian war, to head an emergency government.

The following weeks were chaotic. The regime that had ruled Italy for two decades had fallen, but it was unclear what could take its place. The king and other Italian leaders were eager to remove themselves from Hitler's grip. But with thousands of Italian troops fighting alongside Nazis in eastern Europe, and Nazi troops fighting alongside Italian troops in Sicily and stationed elsewhere in the peninsula, disentangling themselves from the Germans was far from simple.

Tacchi Venturi saw his chance. On August 10, amid the pandemonium gripping Rome, he wrote Cardinal Maglione to remind him of all the efforts made by the Vatican on behalf of Catholics who continued to be considered Jews by the state. Amazingly he was still trying to burnish Mussolini's image with the Holy See. Mussolini, he wrote, had considered the situation of the Catholics treated as Jews by the racial laws to be "painful." As far back as July 1941, he claimed, the Duce had prepared a new law to alleviate the problem. Had the war not gotten in the way, it would have been enacted.

The Jesuit envoy had excellent relations with many in the Ministry of Internal Affairs and, he told Maglione, thought they would be open to the changes the Vatican had been urging. He asked for permission to make three requests. The first was to have mixed families—meaning those that contained a converted Jew—deemed "fully Aryan." The second was to ensure that Jews who were in the process of conversion before October 1, 1938, and only baptized later, be considered Christians and not Jews. The third was to permit state recognition of marriages between two Catholics, one of whom had been born Jewish.[18]

On August 18 Maglione wrote back, saying Pius XII had given his approval.[19]

Tacchi Venturi then met with the minister of internal affairs to make his request.[20] According to his subsequent, highly revealing report to Maglione, he confined them to the three changes approved by the pope. He was very careful not to ask for an end to the racial laws, which, he wrote to the cardinal secretary of state, "according to the principles and the tradition of the Catholic Church, have some provisions that should be abrogated, but certainly contain others worthy of confirmation."[21]

Although the political situation in Rome was chaotic following Mussolini's arrest, it is astounding that neither the wily Tacchi Venturi nor the politically experienced Cardinal Maglione nor Pius XII himself realized that the anti-Semitic laws they had so long supported could not be propped up any longer.

On September 8 the king announced he had signed an armistice with the Allies. Fearing the advance of German troops, he and Badoglio ignominiously fled south to the Adriatic city of Brindisi, which was under Allied control, leaving the Italian military without any orders. Hitler, who had been preparing for this moment since Mussolini was deposed, sent troops flooding through the Italian peninsula. In a dramatic rescue, German forces plucked Mussolini from his captivity and established him as the puppet head of the Italian Social Republic, based in Salò, far in the north. A bloody civil war began, as Allied soldiers pushed northward through the killing fields.

On September 10 Nazi troops reached Rome and seized the city. Among their highest priorities was to hunt down Italy's Jews and send them north to the death camps. Later that month, aboard a British naval ship near Malta, Marshal Badoglio, representing Italy, and General Dwight D. Eisenhower, for the Allies, signed a pact committing Italy to the Allied cause. Among the provisions that Eisenhower insisted on was one nullifying all the racial laws and freeing the Jews still imprisoned in Italian-run concentration camps.[22]

On the morning of October 16, the Nazis surrounded Rome's old ghetto and went house to house hunting for Jews. While most of the roughly seven thousand Jews still living in Rome succeeded in fleeing, some hiding in the city's monasteries and convents, 1,015 were captured and imprisoned in a building near the Vatican. There they awaited their fate.

Cardinal Maglione, alarmed, called in the German ambassador, Ernst von Weizsäcker, to plead on behalf of the captives. The Holy Father, said the secretary of state, was pained to see such suffering for a people simply because they belonged to a particular stock.

The German ambassador asked him, "What would the Holy See do if things were to continue?"

Maglione replied, "The Holy See would not want to be put in the position of having to say a word of disapproval."

For the past four years, said Weizsäcker, he had admired the Vatican's attitude, its willingness to "maintain a perfect equilibrium" in dealing with the two sides in the war. After having done this so well, he asked, was this really the time to place the Vatican's relations with Germany in danger? The order, the ambassador made clear, had come from Hitler himself. Did the secretary of state really want him to tell his government that the Vatican was considering a protest over the deportation of Rome's Jews?

"I observed," wrote Maglione of the unsettling conversation, "that I had begged him to intervene by appealing to his humanitarian instincts. I left to his judgment whether or not to mention our conversation, which was such a friendly one." He then told the Nazi envoy "that the Holy See had been, as he himself had recognized, extremely prudent so as not to give the German people the impression of having done or wished for anything against Germany during a terrible war.

"Meanwhile, I repeat," Cardinal Maglione told the German ambassador, "Your Excellency has told me he will try to do something for the poor Jews. I thank you for it. As for the rest, I defer to your judgment. If you think it more opportune not to mention our conversation, so be it."[23]

At the nearby building where the Jews were being held, frightened mothers tried to comfort their sobbing children. Two days later Germans herded them into trains bound for Auschwitz. Of the thousand, only sixteen would survive. Over the next two months, seven thousand more Jews were seized in Nazi-occupied Italy, many with the help of Italians loyal to Mussolini's Republic of Salò. From the time the first racial laws were proclaimed in 1938 to the end of the war seven years later, six thousand Jews in Italy converted to Christianity in the hope of gaining Church protection and avoiding the fate of their brethren. In all, Nazi forces and their Italian cronies sent 7,500 of Italy's Jews to Auschwitz. Few would leave alive.[24]

EPILOGUE

WHILE THE JEWS WERE BEING TAKEN TO THEIR DEATHS IN POLAND, Cesare De Vecchi, Mussolini's first ambassador to the Vatican, was being hidden by Salesian priests. They had taken him in following the regime's demise in 1943. Having voted against Mussolini at the last Grand Council meeting, De Vecchi lived in fear not only of the approaching Allies but of the Nazis as well. Later, at the war's end, when Italy's surviving Fascist leaders were put on trial, he escaped capture, still hidden by the Salesians. Worried that their fugitive might be discovered, the priests managed to get him a Paraguayan passport and onto a ship bound for Argentina. There local Salesians protected him until a 1949 amnesty allowed him to return home. He died in Rome a decade later.[1]

With Mussolini's arrest in July 1943, Galeazzo Ciano also found himself in an untenable position. Jubilant crowds celebrating the end of the regime filled Rome's streets, embracing one another and tearing pictures of the Duce to pieces. They blamed Ciano, as much as Mussolini, for the disastrous decision to go to war. But because he had voted to depose his father-in-law, he was not at all certain that the Germans, should they arrive in time, would treat him any better than the Allies, marching northward from Sicily.

Ciano and his wife, Edda Mussolini, sought refuge in the Vatican, but their request was denied. Whether it was ever seriously considered we do not know, as the Vatican archives for these years are not yet open.[2] On August 27 Ciano and his family evaded the Italian police detail outside their home and boarded a flight that they thought was bound for safety in Spain but that took them to Germany. A few weeks later Ciano was sent to Verona, in northern Italy, under the control of the Republic of Salò, the Nazi-installed puppet government led by Mussolini. He was not entirely surprised when members of the Fascist militia met him at the airport. They put him in a car headed for the nearby prison, where he joined other members of the Grand Council who had voted against Mussolini at that fateful meeting.

On the morning of January 11, 1944, following a brief trial, Ciano and his codefendants were driven to a military firing range near Verona. Two days earlier his wife, Mussolini's daughter Edda, had crossed the Swiss border. Before leaving, she had sent letters to both her father and to Hitler with a last-minute threat. If they did not spare her husband, she would have his secret diary published. Its revelations, she said, would embarrass both the Duce and the Führer. As she walked through the open field leading to the Swiss border, expecting to be seized by German troops at any moment, she had the diary strapped to her waist.

Edda's threat failed to save her husband. At the firing range, Ciano and those condemned with him trod across ground white with frost, then were forced to sit backward in a line of rickety wooden folding chairs facing a wall. Seventy-seven-year-old General Emilio De Bono, marshal of the Italian armed forces, with his trademark white goatee, sat alongside him. He wore a dark suit and a black hat, sitting with legs splayed apart, hands tied behind his back. Both men asked to face their executioners but were refused. Ciano was hit in the back five times but still breathed. Lying on the ground, legs still awkwardly straddling his chair, he cried for help. The commander of the firing squad rushed to his side. Extracting his pistol from its holster, he fired a shot into the *ducellino*'s head. "It was like the slaughtering of pigs," said a German diplomat who witnessed the scene.[3]

Unlike his wife, who had always disliked her son-in-law and thought he got just what he deserved, Mussolini took no comfort in Ciano's death. Perhaps he had a presentiment that his own was not far off and would be no less sordid. In mid-April 1945 the Allied army broke through the mountains south of Bologna. It advanced northward as the remaining German forces retreated. On April 24, with the Allied army approaching, popular insurrections erupted in Venice, Genoa, and Milan. Mussolini had spent the previous week in Milan where, on April 25, Cardinal Schuster hosted a meeting between the Duce and a delegation from the central resistance committee, hoping to avoid a final bloodbath. Mussolini, learning that the Germans had begun talks with the resistance forces without telling him, remarked, "They've always treated us like servants." Looking pallid, shrunken, like a man who could foresee his own death, he asked for guarantees for his Fascist compatriots and their families, but the resistance leaders said they would accept nothing other than unconditional surrender. Mussolini asked for an hour to decide. Faced with the prospect of being taken before a "people's tribunal," he decided to escape.

Reaching the town of Como, on the southwestern tip of the lake of the same name, Mussolini, in Rachele's account, stopped to write her a letter. He had one of his fat blue pencils with him. "Dear Rachele. Here I am, having arrived at the last phase of my life, the last page of my book. Perhaps we two will never see each other again. . . . I ask your forgiveness for all the bad things that, without meaning to, I did to you. But you know that you were for me the only woman whom I truly loved."

At three A.M. the next morning, along with other Fascist leaders, he got in a convoy of cars going north, undecided whether to try to escape over the Swiss border or to seek a hideout in the Italian Alps. The weather was terrible, and they were hoping for reinforcements, so they stopped at a town along the lake, where Mussolini went for a walk in the rain with his daughter Elena Curti, who had come to be with him. Clara Petacci, chasing after her lover, found him strolling along the lakefront with the attractive young redhead. Furious, she threw a tantrum so violent, she injured her own knee.

Early on the morning of the twenty-seventh, a detachment of two hundred German soldiers passed by. Mussolini and his SS guard decided their best chance lay in joining them. Putting on a German uniform, Mussolini, accompanied both by his daughter and by Clara Petacci, got into an armored car bound for the border. They did not go far before a squad of partisans intercepted them. The Germans, although greatly outnumbering their foe, had lost their stomach for fighting and offered to talk. After six hours they reached an agreement. The partisans would let the Germans cross the border unmolested on the condition they be allowed to inspect the vehicles for any hidden Italians. Despite his German uniform and dark glasses, Mussolini was recognized and seized, along with his fellow Fascists.

The local partisan chief, astonished by the prisoner he had taken, sent word to the resistance headquarters in Milan, requesting instructions. For his part, the diminished Duce asked only to be able to say good-bye to Clara. Until then the partisans had not realized she was among their captives. Clara insisted on staying by her lover's side and sharing his fate, and the two spent a final sleepless night together in a nearby farmhouse. In the meantime, instructions had come from Milan. In the morning, the two prisoners were put in a car for the short drive to Mezzegra, along Lake Como. There, as they approached a modest villa, they were told to get out and stand in front of a wall. It was raining. Clara, still wearing her fur coat, was crying. "Are you happy that I have followed you to the end?" she asked. Mussolini, impassive and resigned to his fate, perhaps unaware she had even spoken, did not respond. As the partisan took aim, Clara struggled to put herself in front of Mussolini in a final, futile effort to protect him.

The next morning the partisans placed the two bodies in a truck and carted them off to Milan. In Piazza Loreto the Duce and his mistress were dumped alongside the cadavers of fifteen other Fascist leaders who had met similar fates. The previous August the Germans had shot fifteen imprisoned partisans, in reprisal for Allied bombings and resistance raids, and had exhibited their bodies in that same piazza. Such was popular justice. Twenty-three years of Fascist rule had suddenly ended—the city was freed from the German army and SS. In their delirium and anger, the growing crowd took their revenge on the bodies, spitting on them, cursing them, kicking them, striking the corpses with sticks and their bare hands. A woman fired five shots into Mussolini's corpse, to avenge her five sons, she said, who were dead because of him.

To shield the bodies from the crazed crowd, some of the partisans hoisted them up, one after another, hanging them by their feet from scaffolding at a gas station on one side of the piazza. From the wounds in Mussolini's head, brain matter seeped out and dripped onto the ground. Next to him swung Clara Petacci, who had always called him "Ben." Someone with a sense of propriety had fastened her skirt to her legs with a piece of rope, so that as she hung upside down, it did not fall over her head.[4]

Achille Starace, longtime stage manager for the Mussolini cult, swung alongside the Duce. It was the closest he had gotten to him in years. Mussolini had stripped Starace of his position as party head in the fall of 1939, thinking the Fascists needed a different approach for the oncoming war. By the spring of 1945, the Duce's once proud pit bull had been living penniless and abandoned in Milan, spending his days wandering the streets in a sweat suit and torn sneakers. When Milan was liberated, a group of partisans recognized him, although his unintended disguise was, in its own way, more complete than Mussolini's had been. His trial that day lasted only twenty minutes before he was shot, his body hauled up at the gas station scaffolding in Piazza Loreto.[5]

Rachele, Mussolini's long-suffering but ever-feisty wife, was taken by Allied forces and, along with her two youngest children, confined to the island of Ischia in the gulf of Naples. She would later return to the small village of Predappio, where she had first met Benito as a school-girl. In 1957, after years of effort, she finally succeeded in getting his body back so that it could be buried where he had been born. Unlike her husband, she lived to old age, dying in 1979.

Loyal Fascist to the last, Roberto Farinacci had fled Rome the day after Mussolini was deposed in July 1943, flying to Munich. He was taken directly to Hitler's headquarters where, after first meeting with Ribbentrop, he saw the Führer. Once Mussolini was installed to lead the Republic of Salò in the north, Farinacci returned to his old fiefdom in Cremona, still predicting a Nazi victory. In late April 1945, with Allied troops poised to enter the city, he and a small group of followers hurried into their cars and drove off. Attempting to run a roadblock north of Milan, they came under fire. Their driver was killed, and Farinacci was seized. The partisans marched their captive to a nearby town, where a "people's tribunal" was quickly assembled. Following a trial that lasted only an hour, he was condemned to die.

At the town plaza where he was to be executed, Farinacci asked for a priest, who took his confession and offered absolution. Blindfolded and told to stand facing the wall so he could be shot in the back, Farinacci resisted. His captors did their best to beat him into submission. But just as the men of the firing squad began to squeeze their triggers, Farinacci turned around and raised his arm in Fascist salute. The bullets hit his chest as he shouted *"Viva l'Italia!"* His body remained where he fell for several hours, giving passersby ample time to add their kicks and spittle. Those with guns fired gratuitous bullets into the lifeless body of the most fascist of Fascists.[6]

Guido Buffarini, with whom the papal nuncio and Tacchi Venturi had met so frequently, had enjoyed the Duce's confidence to the end. One of the minority who had voted in Mussolini's favor at the fateful Grand Council meeting, he had been arrested by the new Badoglio government but then freed by the Germans. Making his way to Salò, he became minister of internal affairs in the puppet Italian government, doing Hitler's bidding in rounding up the Jews. On April 25, 1945, he was with Mussolini in Milan, and he, too, tried to make it to the Swiss border. The partisans who seized him sent him to Milan for trial, where he outlived the Duce by several weeks, a firing squad putting an end to him on July 10.[7]

Eighty-three years old when Mussolini was shot, Father Pietro Tacchi Venturi returned to his books. In 1951, forty-one years after the first volume of his classic history of the Jesuits was published, the final tome appeared. When he died, in March 1956, *The New York Times* and *The Washington Post* published brief obituaries. Both credited him for brokering the Lateran Accords, the one significant negotiation between Pius XI and Mussolini in which he had played only a secondary role.[8]

On ascending St. Peter's throne, Pius XII decided to keep the devout, unworldly Francesco Borgongini on as his nuncio. Through the war years and beyond, he remained in that post. In 1953, a year before his death, the pope named him a cardinal.

Father Agostino Gemelli, founder and rector of the Catholic University of Milan, who had won such applause from Farinacci with his anti-Semitic lecture in Bologna in 1939, continued to curry the favor of whoever was in power.[9] At the war's end, Italian authorities established a commission aimed at removing the most important Fascists from positions of public influence.[10] Confronted with the fact that in 1933 he had denounced two of his own students to the police for engaging in anti-Fascist activities, and in the face of other accusations, Gemelli was suspended from his position as rector, pending further hearings.

The following year, a second commission continued the work of the first, presided over by Ezio Franceschini, professor of literature at Gemelli's own Catholic University. The new commission absolved Gemelli and allowed him to return as rector. Gemelli then appointed Franceschini to be dean of the Faculty of Letters, eventually to become rector of the university himself.[11] Today Gemelli enjoys a place of special honor in Rome, where the city's most important Catholic hospital and a train station bear his name.

The king fared less well. In late August 1939 the American ambassador in Rome received urgent instructions from President Roosevelt: he was to carry the president's personal appeal to the king, urging him to do all he could to prevent Italy from going to war. As Victor Emmanuel was then at his mountain retreat in Piedmont, Phillips boarded a train bound for Turin. When the ambassador's car reached the remote camp, the king stood awaiting him, dressed in ordinary country clothes and a soft brown hat. He walked the ambassador to a small wooden cabin, where Phillips delivered Roosevelt's last-minute appeal.

Victor Emmanuel remained silent as the ambassador read. When he finished, the king spoke. He was simply a constitutional monarch, he explained. "All I can do, in the circumstances, is to refer the message to my government." Phillips was deflated. A thick silence fell between them. Not knowing what else to say, the American ambassador asked him how the fishing was going. The king's face lit up. He had already caught seven hundred trout, he said proudly, but would remain at his camp until he had caught his customary thousand. Asked if he would then return to Rome, as the world was descending into a horrific war, he answered that no, he planned to go to his farm near Pisa, adding, "You know, I hate palaces."[12]

Having added King of the Albanians to his proliferating titles, following Italy's invasion of that defenseless country in April 1939, Victor Emmanuel did his best to avoid blame as Italian troops suffered one disaster after another. At the war's end, disgraced by his close association with the Fascist regime, the king abdicated, in the vain hope that the monarchy could survive under his son, Umberto. In a 1946 plebiscite, Italians voted to send the royal family into exile. Postwar Italy would be a republic.

Unlike the king, Pius XII escaped any blame for the disaster that had befallen Italy. Indeed, many have portrayed him as a heroic opponent of the Fascist regime. The "Pius war,"[13] as they have been called—the heated debates over Pius XII—have focused not on his relations with Mussolini but on those with Hitler. Did he bear responsibility for not condemning the Holocaust when Nazis and their collaborators—many of whom considered themselves Catholics—were murdering Europe's Jews? Was he "Hitler's pope," as the provocative, if misleading, title of John Cornwell's controversial book suggested?[14] His critics accuse him of cowardice and betrayal of the pope's prophetic mission. His defenders argue that he was the best friend that the Jews had.

To date, rather little attention has been paid to Eugenio Pacelli's role in Italy in the years leading up to the war. His relations with the

Fascist regime, and his role in preventing the elderly and irascible Pius XI from doing anything to upset the Vatican's collaboration with it, have remained curiously out of the limelight.

Pius XII, Pope Pacelli, died in 1958. His successor, John XXIII, convened a Second Vatican Council and dramatically changed the Church's direction. No longer would Jews be demonized. Interreligious understanding would be prized, not scorned. Freedom of religion and speech were to be applauded, not attacked.

Since those heady years of the Second Vatican Council, both Pope John XXIII and the Council itself have become controversial among those in the Church who yearn for the old days. Pius XII has become their hero, defender of the Church's eternal verities. Meanwhile, his predecessor, Pius XI, remains all but forgotten.

AUTHOR'S NOTE

THE ROMAN CATHOLIC CHURCH, OR SO THE COMMON NARRATIVE GOES, fought heroically against Italian Fascism. The popes opposed the dictatorship, angry that it had deprived people of their civil rights. Italian Catholic Action, the Church's organization of the laity, stood as one of the most potent forces opposing the regime. The Fascist "racial laws" in 1938, in this comforting narrative, sparked indignant protests from the Vatican, which denounced their harsh treatment of the Jews.

Unfortunately, as readers have seen in these pages, this story bears little relation to what actually happened. The Vatican played a central role both in making the Fascist regime possible and in keeping it in power. Italian Catholic Action worked closely with the Fascist authorities to increase the repressive reach of the police. Far from opposing the treatment of Jews as second-class citizens, the Church provided Mussolini with his most potent arguments for adopting just such harsh measures against them. As shown here, the Vatican made a secret deal with Mussolini to refrain from any criticism of Italy's infamous anti-Semitic "racial laws" in exchange for better treatment of Catholic organizations. This fact is largely unknown in Italy, and despite all the evidence presented in this book, I have no doubt many will deny it. That the Duce and his minions counted on the men around the pope to keep Pius XI's increasing doubts about Mussolini and Hitler under control is a story embarrassing for a multitude of reasons, not least the fact that the central player in these efforts was Cardinal Eugenio Pacelli, the man who would succeed Pius XI. There is no cause dearer to Church traditionalists today than seeing Pacelli—Pope Pius XII—proclaimed a saint.

With the opening in 2006 of the Vatican archives covering this dramatic period, the full story of these years, in all its richness, emotional highs and lows, and surprises can finally be told. Cardinal Pacelli's daily logs of his meetings with the pope, along with tens of thousands of other documents that shed light on this history, are now available in the Vatican Secret Archive. Precious documents are also found in other newly opened Church archives for the period, including those at Rome's Jesuit headquarters. There we find the copious papers of the pope's shadowy private emissary to Mussolini, Father Pietro Tacchi Venturi.

While Church documents offer precious new insight, they do not tell the full story. Much is to be learned from the records of the Fascist regime itself. Thanks to its files, no other period of history offers such vivid descriptions of Vatican intrigue or such graphic accounts of its scandals. Among those whose exploits are mercilessly chronicled in one such thick Fascist police file is the papal protégé who became a cardinal in these years despite a long trail of pederasty accusations. It is in such police files, as well, that we learn of the strange assassination attempt against Father Tacchi Venturi, and the secret he so desperately sought to conceal. We have all this thanks to the regime's extensive spy network in the Vatican, whose reports fill scores of boxes in the state archives. They tell tales of prelates' jostling for power that no Vatican document would record. They describe papal investigations whose embarrassing revelations remain today safely ensconced in Vatican "personnel" files hidden from view.

Over the course of the seven years of archival research that went into this book, I compiled digitized copies of twenty-five thousand pages of documents from these different archives. I also pored through thousands of pages of published Italian, French, British, American, and German diplomatic correspondence, diaries, and memoirs. The work was rarely tedious, for the surprises kept coming. The challenge of piecing together documents from different archives to solve long-standing puzzles was intoxicating.

The relationship of the two larger-than-life figures at the center of this book turned out to be even more intriguing than I suspected. This was not because Mussolini and the pope were so different—although of course in many ways they could scarcely have been more different—but rather because of all they had in common. Both had explosive tempers. Each bristled at the charge of being the patsy of the other. Both demanded unquestioned obedience from their subordinates, whose knees literally quaked in fear of provoking their wrath. Each came to be disillusioned by the other, yet dreaded what would happen if their alliance were to end.

These pages, then, recount the story of two men who came to power in Rome in the same year and together changed the course of twentieth-century history. Scholarly, proper, and devout, Pius XI had spent much of his adult life poring over old manuscripts. He longed for the medieval times when the Church's verities went unquestioned. Mussolini, apostle of the new, was a rabble-rouser, a violent bully, and a visceral anticleric. As readers of this book have seen, their relationship did not end well. Pius XI, who had earlier hailed Mussolini as the Man sent by Providence, ended his life feeling ill-used. Mussolini was no happier. As he told the members of the Fascist General Council, the pope was a disaster.

ACKNOWLEDGMENTS

I T WAS IN 2002, WHEN POPE JOHN PAUL II AUTHORIZED THE OPEN-
ing of the archives of the papacy of Pius XI, that I decided to write
this book. In 2003 materials related to the Vatican's relations with Germany were made available to scholars, followed three years later by the
general opening of the archives for the Pius XI years. The period was
such a dramatic one, and the controversies over the role of the Vatican
in the major events of the time so heated, that I found the challenge irresistible.

My work began in earnest during a sabbatical year I spent in Italy in
2004–5. Although the main Church archives dealing with the pope's
relations with the Fascist regime were not yet open, the archives on the
other side—the Italian Fascist government—were, and I spent many
months working in Italian archives, primarily the Central State Archive
and the archives of the Italian Foreign Ministry. Three years later, with
the opening of the Church archives at the Vatican and elsewhere, a
bounty of new sources, and new insights, became available.

Having worked on this book now for nearly a decade, I have accumulated many debts. None is greater than to Alessandro Visani, who
worked alongside me from practically the start of the project, as we
pored over correspondence and memos shoulder to shoulder in the
Italian archives and then in the various Church archives. Visani, who

has a doctorate in the history of this period, brought not only his outstanding archival research skills but an infectious enthusiasm and prodigious energy to the project, in work done on both sides of the Atlantic.

I have also been fortunate that a number of talented research assistants at Brown—both doctoral students and undergraduates—have helped with the work for this book. Among them I would like to thank Stephen Marth, Simone Poliandri, Harry Kasdan, Andy Newton, and Monica Facchini. I would also like to thank Anne-Claire Ignace, who helped me with the work in the French Foreign Ministry archives in Paris. Thanks as well to various staff members at Brown who helped support my labors: Matilde Andrade, Catherine Hanni, Katherine Grimaldi, and Marjorie Sugrue. I also acknowledge with gratitude research funding provided by the Paul Dupee University Professorship at Brown University.

My ability to write the book was facilitated in various ways—and certainly made more pleasant—by the hospitality of colleagues and institutions in Italy and France during my 2011–12 sabbatical year. Special thanks to the Foundation for Religious Sciences, John XXIII, in Bologna, and its director, Alberto Melloni; to the Rockefeller Foundation Study Center and its resident director, Pilar Palaciá; to the American Academy in Rome, its director, Chris Celenza, and its president, Adele Chatfield-Taylor; and to Gilles Pécout, at the École Normale Supérieure in Paris.

Many colleagues have been kind enough to answer my questions and provide help in various ways. Among them I would especially like to thank my colleague in Italian studies at Brown, Massimo Riva, for my frequent pestering about questions of Italian literary history, English renderings of various Italian dialect and literary materials, and an assortment of other issues. Among the other friends and colleagues whose help I would like to acknowledge are Alberto Melloni, Emilio Gentile, Evelyn Lincoln, Lesley Riva, Ronald Martinez, Charles Gallagher, S.J., Robert Maryks, John A. Davis, Giovanni Pizzorusso, Matteo San Filippo, Reda Bensmaia, Dagmar Herzog, Lucia Pozzi, and Alberto Guasco.

Special thanks are due to Mauro Canali, one of the world's foremost experts on the history of the Italian Fascist regime, for his help in the state archives and for our discussions of this period of Italian history. Thanks as well to Bonifacio Pignatti, grandson of the eponymous Italian ambassador to the Holy See of the late 1930s, for allowing me to use a photograph of the ambassador from the family archives.

Wendy Strothman, my friend and literary agent, deserves special credit. Her deep knowledge of books and publishing, her literary judgment, and her strong support have meant much to me. I am also fortunate to have had David Ebershoff, of Random House, as my editor. It is rare to have an editor who is also such a talented and accomplished writer himself, and I feel deeply grateful to have had the benefit of David's keen literary eye and his belief in the importance of this book. He has made this a much better book. Thanks as well to David's talented assistant, Caitlin McKenna, for all her editorial efforts. I am grateful as well for all the other support I received at Random House and would like to thank especially Dennis Ambrose, Michelle Jasmine, Susan Kamil, Michael Gentile, and Lani Kaneta for all they have done.

Finally, to my wife, Susan Dana Kertzer, who has lived with this book for many years, sharing in the pleasures of life in Italy. She has never let me forget the goal of writing a book that not only the experts but people who know little of this history will want to read. If I am lucky, one of her book groups may even read it.

NOTES

ARCHIVAL SOURCES AND ABBREVIATIONS

The following abbreviations are used in the endnotes.

ARCHIVAL SOURCES

ACDF: Archivio della Congregazione per la Dottrina della Fede, Vatican

     S.O.   Sant'Offizio

ACS: Archivio Centrale dello Stato, Rome

    MCPG   Ministero della Cultura Popolare, Gabinetto
    MCPR   Ministero della Cultura Popolare, Reports
    MI   Ministero dell'Interno, Direzione Generale della Pubblica Sicurezza

       DAGR   Direzione Generale Pubblica Sicurezza, Divisione Affari Generali e Riservati

       DAGRA   Direzione Generale Pubblica Sicurezza, Divisione Affari Generali e Riservati-annuali

         FP   Direzione Generale della Pubblica Sicurezza, Divisione Polizia Politica, fascicoli personali

         PS   Direzione Generale della Pubblica Sicurezza

         PP   Direzione Generale della Pubblica Sicurezza, Divisione Polizia Politica, "materia"

    SPD   Segreteria Particolare Duce

        CO   Segreteria Particolare Duce, Carteggio Ordinario
        CR   Segreteria Particolare Duce, Carteggio Riservato
        CV   Segreteria Particolare Duce, "carte della valigia"

ARSI: Archivium Romanum Societatis Iesu, Rome

    TV   Fondo Tacchi Venturi

ASMAE: Archivio Storico, Ministero degli Affari Esteri, Rome

    APG   Affari Politici, 1931–45, Germania
    APIN   Affari Politici, 1919–30, Italia
    APSS   Affari Politici, 1931–45, Santa Sede
  APNSS   Affari Politici, 1919–30, Santa Sede
    AISS   Ambasciata Italiana presso la Santa Sede
    Gab.   Gabinetto

ASV: Archivio Segreto Vaticano, Vatican City

    ANI   Archivio Nunziatura Italia
   AESE   Segreteria di Stato, Affari Ecclesiastici Straordinari, Spagna
   AESG   Segreteria di Stato, Affari Ecclesiastici Straordinari, Germania
   AESI   Segreteria di Stato, Affari Ecclesiastici Straordinari, Italia
   AESS   Segreteria di Stato, Affari Ecclesiastici Straordinari
            Stati Ecclesiastici
   AESU   Segreteria di Stato, Affari Ecclesiastici Straordinari, Ungaria

MINISTÈRE DES AFFAIRES ÉTRANGÈRES, PARIS

MAEI   Ministère des Affaires Étrangères, Direction des Affaires Politiques et Commerciales, Italie

MAESS   Ministère des Affaires Étrangères, Direction des Affaires Politiques et Commerciales, Saint-Siège

NARA: U.S. NATIONAL ARCHIVE AND RECORDS ADMINISTRATION, COLLEGE PARK, MARYLAND

All are found in the National Archives Microfilm Publications series

LM142   Confidential U.S. State Department Central Files, Italy, Foreign Affairs, 1940–44

LM192   Confidential U.S. State Department Central Files, Germany, Foreign Affairs, 1930–39

M530   Records of the Department of State Relating to Political Relations between Italy and Other States, 1910–29

M561   Records of the Department of State Relating to Internal Affairs of the Papal States, 1910–29

M563   Records of the Department of State Relating to Political Relations between the Papal States and Other States, 1910–29

M1423   Records of the Department of State Relating to Internal Affairs of Italy, 1930–39

PUBLISHED DIPLOMATIC DOCUMENTS

DBFP	Documents of British Foreign Policy
DDF	Documents Diplomatiques Français
DDI	Documenti Diplomatici Italiani
DGFP	Documents on German Foreign Policy
FCRSE	Further Correspondence Respecting Southern Europe, Great Britain Foreign Office

OTHER ABBREVIATIONS

ADSS	Actes et documents du Saint Siège relatives à la seconde guerre mondiale
BG	*Boston Globe*
CC	*La Civiltà cattolica*
CDT	*Chicago Daily Tribune*
LAT	*Los Angeles Times*
NYT	*New York Times*
OR	*L'Osservatore romano*
PNF	Partito Nazionale Fascista
PPI	Partito Popolare Italiano
WP	*Washington Post*

NOTES

CHAPTER 1: A NEW POPE

1. Salvatorelli 1939, p. 9; Pizzuti 1992, p. 99; Pollard 1999, p. 14.
2. Pollard 1999, p. 16. The American journalist Anne McCormick (1957, p. 17) offered similar observations of Della Chiesa as pope: "Benedict XV seemed one of the negative Popes, dwarfed by his position and overpowered by the events of his time. One saw him at public functions in the Vatican, drooping under his tiara, dwindling within his embroidered state, plainly bored and burdened by his augustness."
3. ASV, AESS, pos. 515, fasc. 529, ff. 59r–94r.
4. At the first meeting of the new session of parliament on December 1, 1919, as King Victor Emmanuel III stood to give the ceremonial opening, the Socialist deputies rose and walked out, shouting "Long live the socialist republic!" Milza 2000, pp. 284–85.
5. Fornari 1971, p. 50.
6. On the proviso that it be made clear to the public that the Vatican had no authority over the party. For Carlo Sforza's account of this meeting, see Scoppola 1976, pp. 22–23. See also De Rosa 1958; De Rosa 1959; Molony 1977. For the rest of his long life, Sturzo would say a mass in honor of Benedict XV every year on the anniversary of his death. Pollard 1999, pp. 172–74.
7. The Italian Foreign Ministry archive has a folder filled with encrypted telegrams from its

embassies abroad reporting the voting intentions of cardinals from these countries. They contain several different names. ASMAE, APIN, b. 1268.

8. The latter remarks were made by the Belgian ambassador. Beyens 1934, pp. 102–3. The remarks about the pope's indifference to dress were made by the British envoy, Sir Alec Randall, quoted in Pollard 1999, p. 70. My description also relies on later British envoy reports found in C. Wingfield, *Annual Report 1934*. January 12, 1935, R 402/402/22, in Hachey 1972, pp. 285–87, sections 126–36, as well as on Roberti 1960, pp. 6–7; Morgan 1944, pp. 15, 136–37; and De Vecchi 1983, p. 143.

9. Aubert 2000, p. 230 (based on the diary of Cardinal Mercier); Lazzarini 1937, pp. 160–61; Beyens 1934, pp. 83–84.

10. Vavasseur-Desperriers 1996, p. 141.

11. Venini 2004, p. 128.

12. Chiron 2006, pp. 20–25.

13. Puricelli 1996, pp. 28, 36; Durand 2010, p. 4; Aradi 1958, p. 21.

14. Aradi 1958, p. 43. Manzoni, the pope was convinced, would one day be recognized as a writer as great as Dante; Venini 2004, p. 181.

15. Aradi 1958, pp. 65–66.

16. After he was elected pope, the Alpine Club put together a number of Ratti's own descriptions of his climbs in a little book (Ratti 1923). An English version of the book was published in March 1923, in the form of a three-part series in the daily newspaper *Atlantic Constitution* under the title "The Mountaineer Priest" (March 4, 11, and 18). Lazzarini (1937, pp. 69–71) provides a long list of his climbs.

17. The French ambassador to the Holy See, François Charles-Roux (1947, pp. 21–22), reported his conversations with Pope Ratti about his Alpine past.

18. Tisserant 1939, pp. 393–94; Chiron 2006, p. 86.

19. Domenico Tardini recounted this misapprehension in a letter to Confalonieri on the publication of his memoirs about Pius XI. Confalonieri 1993, p. 276.

20. Lazzarini 1937, pp. 35–36

21. I tell this story in Kertzer 2001.

22. CC 1880 IV, pp. 108–12.

23. "La rivoluzione mondiale e gli ebrei," CC 1922 IV, pp. 111–21; "Il socialismo giudeo-massonico tiranneggia l'Austria," CC 1922 IV, pp. 369–71.

24. Morozzo della Rocca 1996, p. 108; see also Kertzer 2001, pp. 247–49.

25. ASV, ANI, b. 192, ff. 534r–38r, Achille Ratti a Pietro Gasparri, 24 ottobre 1918.

26. Achille Ratti to Pietro Gasparri, January 9, 1919, in Wilk 1997, pp. 3:250–61. For a fuller presentation of Ratti's views of the Jews while he was in Poland, see Kertzer 2001, pp. 245–62.

27. Pizzuti 1992, p. 110; Chiron 2006, pp. 111–12.

28. As Levillain (1996, p. 8) described it, "Mons. Ratti's nomination to the see of Saint Ambrosio is a kind of response by Rome to an insurrectional climate."

29. For a fuller account of the circumstances that led to Ratti's departure from Poland, see Morozzo della Rocco 1996. Gasparri's own typescript account of this episode is found at ASV, AESS, pos. 515, fasc. 530, ff. 35r–36r. For a good look at Ratti's experience in Poland, see Pease 2009, chap. 2.

30. Gasparri's memoir account of this conversation is found in Spadolini 1972, pp. 259–60. Gasparri writes that it was Pope Ratti himself who told him what had happened.

31. Pizzuti 1992, pp. 12–13.

32. Sources report somewhat different numbers for the various papal ballots. I use the most complete set we have, found in Aradi 1958, p. 127. For an account of Gasparri's behind-the-scenes role in getting Ratti elected, see Falconi 1967, pp. 152–54. Falconi, along with other sources, also details the passage of *zelanti* support from Merry del Val to Cardinal

Pietro La Fontaine, conservative patriarch of Venice, who on the eleventh ballot reached twenty-three votes, to Ratti's twenty-four. Also useful is Cardinal Mercier's diary entries, found in Aubert 2000, as well as Lazzarini 1937, pp. 160–63.

33. Fogarty 1996, p. 549. As a result of this experience, Pius XI would change the rules governing the conclave to give more time for non-European cardinals to participate, as they would on his death in 1939.

34. Aubert 2000, p. 200.

35. News of Benedict XV's illness had produced a wave of worry around the Catholic world. In New York City, the 96,000 children attending Catholic parochial schools were shepherded into their local churches on January 20 to pray for his health. That they had not been entirely optimistic was evident from the fact that many added to their prayer for a speedy recovery the additional caveat "or the grace of a happy death." "96,803 Children Pray for the Pope," NYT, January 21, 1922, p. 1. The next day a premature report of the pope's demise reached the president of Germany's Reichstag, resulting in a halt in the proceedings as members rose while the president improvised a eulogy. "Reichstag President Eulogizes the Pope," NYT, January 22, 1922, p. 2.

36. Among those watching for the smoke in St. Peter's Square on February 5, the day before Pius XI was chosen, was Benito Mussolini. Gentile 2010, p. 95.

37. Aradi 1958, p. 128.

38. There is some controversy about whether the idea of imparting this initial benediction from the outside loggia was Ratti's idea or was suggested to him by the worldly Cardinal Gasparri. Cardinal Mario Nasali Rocca, archbishop of Bologna, reported that it was Gasparri's idea (Chiron 2006, p. 138n), but Confalonieri (1957, p. 24) insists it was Ratti's own. A description of these events can be found in Aradi 1958, pp. 146–47, and in CC 1922 I, pp. 371–72.

CHAPTER 2: THE MARCH ON ROME

1. E. Mussolini 1957, p. 135.

2. Altogether, the report concluded, somewhat surprisingly, he had a *fisionomia simpatico*, a friendly face. Baima Bollone 2007, p. 22; see also Ludwig 1933, p. 37.

3. Bosworth 2002, p. 62. An English translation of Mussolini's first publication, "*Dieu n'existe pas*," is found in Seldes 1935, pp. 387–90. The 1908 articles are quoted by Gentile 2010, p. 84.

4. Rhodes 1974, p. 27.

5. Baima Bollone 2007, pp. 23, 27.

6. For this piece in *Avanti!* he was indicted and later brought to trial for incitement to violence. Cannistraro and Sullivan 1993, pp. 96–97.

7. E. Mussolini 1957, pp. 31–32.

8. Motti 2003, p. 198.

9. Cannistraro and Sullivan 1993, p. 97. This is not one of Mussolini's better-documented children. At some point, the line between the tales of affairs and children out of wedlock and the reality becomes blurred, although I have no reason to believe Cannistraro and Sullivan fell on the wrong side of that line here. They also discuss a son Mussolini sired in 1918 by yet another woman, Bianca Veneziana, with whom he would sporadically continue an affair for many years (1993, p. 275).

10. Rafanelli 1975.

11. Cannistraro and Sullivan 1993, p. 137. Rachele Mussolini (1974, pp. 74–75) provided her own account of the wedding in her memoir. Later, amid Dalser's very public calls on Mussolini to recognize her as his wife, and her attempts to let the world know that little Benito was his son, the embarrassment proved too much for him. Once he came to power,

he had Irene removed to an insane asylum, where she died in 1937. Little Benito's fate remains somewhat more obscure. Placed under surveillance from the time his mother was taken away, he eventually became too great a liability for Mussolini. He, too, was placed in an asylum, dying there in 1942, at twenty-six. Ibid.; Festorazzi 2010, p. 49.

12. Much controversy has surrounded the question of how Mussolini found the funds to mount the ambitious paper. Part of the funding appears to have come from Mussolini's lovers, including Ida Dalser, who apparently sold her beauty salon to come up with cash for it. In addition, while proclaiming his opposition to the money-grubbing bourgeoisie, he was taking money from those who stood to make a profit from Italy's entrance into the war. He received secret payments from both French and British government sources as well, eager as they were to encourage Italy's war effort. Bosworth 2002, pp. 105–7.

13. Ibid., pp. 106–7.

14. "Un Appello ai lavoratori d'Italia dei fasci d'azione rivoluzionaria. Statuto-programma," *Il Popolo d'Italia,* 6 gennaio 1916, p. 1.

15. Festorazzi 2010, p. 37; Cannistraro and Sullivan 1993, p. 96.

16. Milza 2000, p. 257. But in February 1918 Margherita suffered a tragedy when her first-born child, Roberto, who had insisted on enlisting in the army at only seventeen, was killed at the front. As Mussolini was turning away from the Socialists, castigating them for undermining the war effort and disrespecting Italy's soldiers, Margherita had a deep wound that propelled her along with him. Urso 2003, p. 119. Together they would build a new myth around the sacrifice and heroism of the Italian troops.

17. Cannistraro and Sullivan 1993, p. 178.

18. Margiotta Broglio 1966, pp. 79–81; Gentile 2010, p. 87.

19. In Milan, Mussolini succeeded in convincing two well-known cultural figures to run with him on the Fascist ticket, Arturo Toscanini, famed conductor of La Scala—who would before long regret his choice—and Filippo Marinetti, leading light of the Futurist movement.

20. Cannistraro and Sullivan 1993, pp. 215–16.

21. Galeotti 2000, pp. 20–23.

22. De Felice 1966, pp. 115–16.

23. Lyttleton 1987, p. 53; Ebner 2011, pp. 23, 30–31.

24. De Felice 1966, pp. 87, 92.

25. De Felice 1966, p. 128; Scoppola 1996, p. 186; Kent 1981, pp. 5–6.

26. Gentile 2010, p. 92.

27. Venini 2004, p. 22.

28. CC 1922 I, p. 558; CC 1922 II, pp. 178, 372. Examples in this period of *L'Osservatore romano* stories of violent attacks on priests, PPI headquarters, and Catholic groups include: "Popolari bastonati dai fascisti," 29 marzo 1922, p. 4; "Un parroco e un avvocato aggrediti dai fascisti," 27 aprile 1922, p. 4; "Dopo l'aggressione fascista al sacerdote Gregori," 6 giugno 1922, p. 4; "Conflitto tra fascisti e popolari," 21 giugno 1922, p. 4; "Esplosione di odio," 26 luglio 1922, p. 4; "Circoli cattolici devastati," 20 agosto 1922, p. 4; "Le aggressioni dei fascisti contro i Parroci," 22 agosto 1922, p. 2; "Il circolo cattolico di Milzano incendiato dai fascisti," 2 settembre 1922, p. 4; "Cattolici assaliti dai fascisti a Catania," 12 settembre 1922, p. 4; "Cattolici aggrediti dai fascisti," 14 settembre 1922, p. 4; "I fascisti contro i cattolici veronesi," 23 settembre 1922, p. 4; "Nuove aggressioni fasciste contro cattolici a Verona," 24 settembre 1922, p. 4; "La sede nel Partito Popolare di Nocera devastata dai fascisti," 4 ottobre 1922, p. 4; "I fascisti diffidano un parroco a buttare la veste entro 48 ore," 8 ottobre 1922, p. 4; "Due sacerdoti insultati dai fascisti," 10 ottobre 1922, p. 4; "L'adunata fascista a Firenze s'inizia con atti ostili contro la G. Diocesana e il Partito Popolare," 14 ottobre 1922, p. 4; "Una protesta della Federazione Giovanile Dio-

cesana di Firenze," 17 ottobre 1922, p. 4; "I fascisti contro le associazioni cattoliche," 18 ottobre 1922, p. 4.

29. Among the many biographies of Farinacci are Fornari 1971, Festorazzi 2004, and Pardini 2007. Innocenti (1992, pp. 147–50) provides a popular but colorful portrait that captures him well.
30. Milza 2000, p. 326; De Felice 1966, pp. 222–23.
31. Chiron 2006, pp. 256–57.
32. The latter account, of a fearful Mussolini hiding out with his mistress near the Swiss border, is given by Festorazzi (2010, pp. 69–70). De Felice (1966, pp. 373–74), in his authoritative multivolume biography of Mussolini, places him at the theater in Milan with his wife.
33. Cannistraro and Sullivan 1993, p. 276; Festorazzi 2010, p. 78.
34. Pietro Badoglio quoted in Milza 2000, p. 332.
35. Milza 2000, pp. 332–33.
36. Lyttleton 1987, p. 89.
37. De Felice 1966, p. 359.
38. McCormick 1957, pp. 7–9.
39. CC 1922 IV, pp. 354–55.
40. Bosworth 2002, p. 172.
41. De Felice 1966, p. 311.
42. Their conversation took place in early November 1922. Beyens 1934, pp. 136–37.
43. Navarra 2004, p. 15.
44. From Salandra's *Memorie politiche,* quoted by De Felice 1966, p. 462.
45. Lamb 1997, pp. 59–60.
46. This account comes from Morgan (1941, pp. 81–85), who attended the dinner.

CHAPTER 3: THE FATAL EMBRACE

1. Tisserant 1939, pp. 389, 397; Chiron 2006, p. 151.
2. Beyens 1934, p. 102.
3. Confalonieri 1957, pp. 116–17. On Pius X, see Pollard 1999, p. 78.
4. Quoted in Rhodes 1974, p. 19; Biffi 1997, p. 74.
5. Aradi 1958, pp. 65–66; Venini 2004, p. 23.
6. Chiron 2006, p. 126.
7. Ibid., p. 141.
8. What Italians would call the third floor.
9. Dante and Manzoni held pride of place. Confalonieri 1957, pp. 173, 270–71.
10. Confalonieri 1969, p. 36; Charles-Roux 1947, p. 10.
11. Aradi 1958, p. 138.
12. Lazzarini 1937, p. 319.
13. Confalonieri 1957, pp. 71–2; Chiron 2006, pp. 141–46. Photographs of the pope during his garden walk, and aside his carriage, are found in *Illustrazione italiana,* 8 ottobre 1922, pp. 2–3.
14. Potter 1925, pp. 9, 242–47, 254–55; MacKinnon 1927, pp. 44–45, 189–90.
15. Potter 1925, p. 164.
16. E. Rosa, "L'unità d'Italia e la disunione degli italiani," CC 1922 IV, p. 106.
17. De Rosa 1999.
18. Sale 2007, p. 26. Ledóchowski's letter to Rosa, dated October 31, 1922, is found in the *Civiltà cattolica* archives, to which Sale as part of the *Civiltà cattolica* collective has access.

19. In his annual report to London, prepared on October 25, 1922, the British envoy at the Vatican wrote, "Everything in the Vatican is dominated by the Pope's fear of Russian Communism." Rhodes 1974, p. 18.

20. Quoted in Sale 2007, p. 25.

21. Sale, who examined Rosa's archive at *Civiltà cattolica* headquarters, concludes that the pope seems to have been the one to direct Rosa to prepare the friendlier editorial, although he does not provide details. Ibid., p. 27.

22. E. Rosa, "Crisi di stato e crisi di autorità," CC 1922 IV, p. 204.

23. This is the conclusion reached as well by Sale 2007, pp. 27–28.

24. Beyens 1934, pp. 136–39. Just days after the March on Rome, Secretary of State Gasparri explained to a French diplomat that the king had made the right choice in refusing to call out the army. Fascism, he said, "has become a necessity." Sale 2007, p. 10.

25. Encyclicals are generally high-profile messages on issues the pope deems significant, often addressed to the bishops of a particular country or, as in this case, to all the bishops of the world.

26. *Ubi arcano*, English translation at the Vatican website: http://www.vatican.va/holy_father /pius_xi/encyclicals/documents/hf_p-xi_enc_23121922_ubi-arcano-dei-consilio_en.html.

27. Milza 2000, p. 343.

28. Ibid., pp. 345–46.

29. Motti 2003; Falconi 1967, p. 185; Sale 2007, p. 37; Milza 2000, pp. 354, 401. For the requirement that religious textbooks receive Church approval, see DDI, series 7, vol. 2, n. 155, 1 agosto 1923. On Mussolini's visits and disbursement of funds to local clergy, see Morgan 1941, p. 239.

30. Quoted in Molony 1977, p. 152. The cardinal made the remarks at a wedding where Mussolini was present. So pleased was Mussolini with his words that he sent a copy of them to all Italy's foreign embassies. The next day the Italian ambassador to Great Britain telegraphed back, reporting coverage of Vannutelli's remarks in many British papers. The London *Times* declared that the cardinal's remarks were not simply his personal opinion but faithfully represented the Holy See's view. DDI, series 7, vol. 1, n. 535, 22 febbraio 1923; DDI, series 7, vol. 1, n. 544, 23 febbraio 1923.

31. ASV, AESS, pos. 515, fasc. 523, ff. 8r–9r.

32. Molony 1977, pp. 190–1; Falconi 1967, p. 187.

33. The Santucci and Acerbo accounts are reproduced in Pirri 1960.

34. Sale (2007, pp. 36, 54–55) points out that while a number of historians have identified the January secret meeting between Mussolini and Gasparri as the moment when the decision was made to have Tacchi Venturi become the secret intermediary, there is no clear documentary evidence for this. But by early February Tacchi Venturi was already acting in this role.

35. Scaduto 1956, p. 47; Maryks 2012, pp. 302–5; Martina 2003, pp. 234–35; Tramontin 1982, p. 631. During the war, Tacchi Venturi regularly contacted police officials to get permission to travel to Switzerland, where Ledóchowski had set up his office. Immediately after the war, he repeatedly contacted Italian government authorities to get permission for Ledóchowski and other Jesuits in exile to return to Rome. Tacchi Venturi's correspondence with the police officials during and after the war is found in ACS, MI, PS, 1919, b. 1, "Curia Generalizia della Compagnia di Gesù."

36. A later briefing by a Fascist police informant inside the Vatican described him as having always been a reactionary, but one whose main aim was to promote the Jesuits' interests. ACS, MI, DAGR, b. 1320, informatore, Città del Vaticano, 23 aprile 1930.

37. Amid the huge pile of materials in the papers that Tacchi Venturi left behind at his death is a small postcard. On one side is a picture of the Madonna and baby Jesus. On the other, written in pen, is the date, October 28, 1919, and a short note from Ratti, then in Warsaw,

thanking him for the congratulations he had sent on his elevation to the rank of bishop. ARSI, TV, b. 29. On the 1899 meeting, see Maryks 2012, p. 305.

38. Arnaldo's wife, according to Mussolini, had gone to Tacchi Venturi for confession. De Begnac 1990, p. 591.

39. Tisserant 1939, pp. 398–99; Martina 2003, p. 236.

40. "Comunicazione del Vescovo di Vicenza sulle violenze al clero," OR, 21 novembre 1922, p. 4. It does not appear that any Fascist was ever excommunicated in these years for violence against the Church.

41. "Contro un sacerdote giornalista." OR, 24 novembre 1922, p. 4.

42. "Partiti e fazioni—Circolo cattolico devastato ad Aosta," OR, 13 dicembre 1922, p. 4.

43. "Violenze contro giovani cattolici," OR, 15 dicembre 1922, p. 4.

44. "Le violenze contro il clero nel Vicentino," OR, 20 dicembre 1922, p. 4.

45. Some examples: "Violenze fasciste a Fabriano," OR, 10 aprile 1923, p. 4; "Festa missionaria di Piacentino turbata dai fascisti," OR, 19 aprile 1923, p. 2; "Protesta della Giunta Diocesana di Piacenza," OR, 20 aprile 1923, p. 2; "Minaccie fasciste contro un Congresso eucaristico," OR, 16 maggio 1923, p. 4; "I fascisti di Secondigliano distruggono un Circolo cattolico," OR, 26 maggio 1923, p. 4. In Perin's (2011, p. 183) analysis of the weekly diocesan press in Veneto, she finds that the papers did not hold Mussolini responsible for the violence. Following the Vatican's legitimization of Mussolini after his coming to power, this pattern would grow more pronounced.

46. Sale 2007, pp. 92–94; Pollard 1985, p. 24.

47. Poggi 1967, p. 21; Casella 1996, pp. 606–7, 620. The pope's remarks were made in September 1922. The new national Catholic Action president, Luigi Colombo, was just as clear about his job: "I did not follow my personal view," he recalled later, "but obeyed . . . the august directives of the Holy Father"; Zambarbieri 1982b, p. 114.

CHAPTER 4: BORN TO COMMAND

1. OR, 17 marzo 1923, cited in Coppa 1999, p. 89; "Liberalismo in pena," CC 1923 II pp. 209–18.

2. "Liberalismo in pena," CC 1923 II pp. 209–18. Evidence that *L'Osservatore romano* acted only following the pope's wishes is indirect, but in the context of the dramatic change of Vatican position, any other explanation seems implausible.

3. Although the Vatican publicly denied that the prelate in question, Monsignor Enrico Pucci, was speaking for anyone other than himself, a later secret briefing for the Fascist police reported that Pucci was at the time "following the precise instruction of the Secretary of State" in publishing the piece. ACS, MI, FP "Pucci," f. 19, n.d. For a semiofficial denial that the Vatican had any hand in Pucci's call for Sturzo to resign, see CC 1923 III, p. 184.

4. The pope made his new request through Gasparri, whose July 5 letter to Tacchi Venturi began: "For reasons that it is unnecessary to enumerate, the Holy Father allowed Don Sturzo to delay his response. . . . Now, having thought long and hard before God, the Holy Father believes that in Italy's current circumstances a priest cannot, without causing serious damage to the Church, remain at the direction of a party—indeed directing the opposition of all the parties against the government—to the delight of the masonry as is well known." ASV, AESI, pos. 617, fasc. 50, f. 5, Gasparri a Tacchi Venturi, 5 luglio 1923. These documents have been discussed and quoted extensively in Sale 2007, pp. 80–84.

5. Quoted in Sale 2007, p. 82.

6. On receiving the pope's orders, Sturzo had called an emergency meeting of the PPI directorate, scheduled for July 10, and he did not want word of his decision to get out before he could inform its members.

7. Down to arranging the exact hour when news of Sturzo's resignation would be made public. ASV, AESI, pos. 617, fasc. 50, ff. 14–15. Tacchi Venturi was also eager to get a promise from Mussolini that Don Sturzo would not be harmed.

8. Sale 2007, pp. 69–70.

9. Molony 1977, pp. 172–73; Bedeschi 1973.

10. Sale 2007, pp. 74–75.

11. Beyens 1934, pp. 167–69.

12. Navarra 2004, p. 42.

13. Baima Bollone 2007, pp. 24–26.

14. E. Mussolini 1957, p. 121.

15. R. Mussolini 1974, p. 96.

16. Ibid.

17. Milza 2000, pp. 354–55.

18. Festorazzi 2010, pp. 74–77.

19. Cannistraro and Sullivan 1993, pp. 273–74; E. Mussolini 1957, p. 32; Navarra 2004, p. 48.

20. Quoted in De Felice 1966, pp. 472–73.

21. Monelli (1953, p. 102) describes the Cremona rally. Gentile (1993, pp. 160–72; 2001) is the most influential scholar examining the use of symbol, ritual, and myth by the Fascist regime. For more on how and why ritual is so important to political movements, see Kertzer 1988.

22. Gentile 1993, pp. 281–82.

23. Beyens 1934, p. 245.

24. DDI, series 7, vol. 2, n. 155, Mussolini a Gentile, 1 agosto 1923; Talbot 2007, p. 27; Sale 2007, pp. 37, 96; Gentile 2010, p. 107; Milza 2000, p. 432.

25. ASV, AESI, pos. 573, fasc. 22, 15, 25 settembre 1923, quoted in Sale 2007, pp. 320–22.

26. CC 1924 I, p. 175, which also contains the excerpt from *Il Popolo d'Italia*.

27. Sale 2007, p. 333; CC 1924 I, p. 80.

28. Including raising the annual government payments to bishops from 6,000 to 12,000 lire per year and raising the payments to parish priests from 1,500 to 2,500 lire. CC 1924 II, p. 82.

29. Ebner 2011, p. 38.

30. Quoted in Sale 2007, p. 130.

31. Ibid., pp. 134–37. The printed circular is found at ASV, AESI, pos. 617, fasc. 50, ff. 30r, 30v; the handwritten note not to send is at f. 47r.

32. Chiron 2006, p. 152; Confalonieri 1957, p. 172.

33. Lazzarini 1937, pp. 309–10. Lazzarini does not give the date of Carrère's visit but says he came shortly after publication of *Le Pape,* which was published in 1924.

34. Confalonieri 1957, p. 172; Charles-Roux 1947, p. 14.

35. Chiron 2006, p. 151.

36. Durand 2010. Merry del Val's comment, made in 1927, was reported back to the pope, who summoned him for a humiliating dressing down. "The pope," he wrote in his account of the meeting, "treated me as if I were a little schoolboy." Durand 2010, pp. 48–49.

CHAPTER 5: RISING FROM THE TOMB

1. Giacomo Matteotti, "Discorso alla Camera dei Deputati di denuncia di brogli elettorali" (1924), http://it.wikisource.org/wiki/Italia_-_30_maggio_1924,_Discorso_alla_Camera_dei_Deputati_di_denuncia_di_brogli_elettorali.

2. Milza 2000, pp. 365–7; De Felice 1966, p. 620. For a thorough consideration of the Matteotti murder and its aftermath, see Canali 2004b.

3. Milza 2000, p. 370; CC 1924 III, pp. 80–89.
4. De Felice 1966, p. 630.
5. Milza 2000, p. 378.
6. De Felice 1966, p. 644. Later, thinking back to those weeks after the killing, Mussolini recalled "I had the sense in those days, the sense of isolation, because the halls of Palazzo Chigi, normally so crowded, were deserted as if a blast, a storm had passed through it."
7. Navarra 2004, pp. 25–27.
8. Cannistraro and Sullivan 1993, p. 295.
9. CC 1924 III, pp. 85–87.
10. ASMAE, Gab., b. 32, Tacchi-Venturi a Mussolini, 27 giugno 1924.
11. Baima Bollone 2007, p. 96.
12. Sale 2007, p. 162.
13. Ibid., pp. 162–68.
14. In late June, speaking on behalf of the opposition, a Popular Party deputy called on the king to name a new prime minister to restore democratic freedoms and put an end to private armed groups; CC 1924 III, pp. 179–80. In mid-July the party's provincial leaders met in Rome, where they agreed on a plan. The alternative to the Fascists, they insisted, was not the traumatic government paralysis and chaos of 1922, as Mussolini's supporters were arguing, but a solid coalition of *popolari*, disaffected liberals, and democratic socialists. See Ferrari 1957, p. 70; Sale 2007, pp. 169–71.
15. ASMAE, Gab., b. 32, Tacchi Venturi a Mussolini, 20 luglio, 1924; ibid., Paulucci de' Calboli a Tacchi Venturi, 22 luglio 1924. Mussolini's handwritten note was scrawled atop Tacchi Venturi's cover letter to his secretary, Baron Paulucci de' Calboli. Ibid., Tacchi Venturi a Paulucci de' Calboli, 20 luglio 1924.
16. The detailed and unusual account of the close control that the pope exercised is found in a document in Felice Rinaldi, S.J., "Resoconto della stesura dell'articolo 'La parte dei cattolici nelle presenti lotte dei partiti politici in Italia,'" 11 agosto 1924, in the *Civiltà cattolica* archives, published in Sale 2007, pp. 477–78. See also Sale's discussion at pp. 172–82.
17. "La parte dei cattolici nelle presenti lotte dei partiti politici in Italia," CC 1924 III, pp. 297–306.
18. Gasparri did, later confiding to the Belgian ambassador that he had no idea what use the women made of them. Beyens 1934, pp. 235–36.
19. Quoted in Sale 2007, p. 182–83. The pope's remarks provoked outrage from anti-Fascists, both in Italy and abroad. Some argued that in opining on such political matters, he spoke not with the infallibility of a pontiff, but only as a man offering a personal opinion. A week later *L'Osservatore romano* struck back. The pope's words, the Vatican daily informed the Catholic world, constituted a "categorical directive." Those who claimed that Catholics were free to follow their conscience in the matter were gravely mistaken; quoted in Sale 2007, p. 184.
20. As it happened, the lessons were conducted at a Calmodese abbey across the Tuscan border from the Mussolinis' summer house in Romagna, where the elderly Cardinal Vannutelli was spending his summer vacation. Before long, Mussolini arrived for a family visit and sought out Vannutelli. He asked the cardinal if, immediately after the abbey's Father Major administered first communion to the children, he would personally preside over their confirmation. And so it was that on September 8 the Mussolini children took first communion in the morning and the cardinal administered confirmation around noon. Vannutelli's letter, from the Vatican Secret Archives, is reproduced in Sale 2007, pp. 345–46.
21. Curiously, rather than communicate the decision to Sturzo directly, on September 16 Gasparri wrote to Sturzo's brother, a bishop in Sicily, telling him what was "the desire, nay the

command of the Holy Father," and asking him to let Don Sturzo know the pope's decision. This the indignant brother refused to do, leaving Gasparri to find another way to inform the former PPI head.

22. The Vatican Secretary of State archives have a handwritten receipt dated October 17 from Sturzo's lawyer, acknowledging the ten thousand lire that Monsignor Pizzardo had given him to cover the expenses of Sturzo's trip abroad. While grateful for the funds, Sturzo thought it would be more useful to have the money in British pounds, and a second hand-written note, this from Sturzo himself, dated October 20, informed Pizzardo that he would send his same emissary back the next day to exchange the currency. ASV, AESI, pos. 617, fasc. 50, ff. 26r, 27r; Molony 1977, p. 192.

23. Cannistraro and Sullivan 1993, p. 296; Monelli 1953, p. 109; De Felice 1966, p. 716.

24. Here I build on De Felice's (1966, p. 717; 1968, pp. 50–51) interpretation.

CHAPTER 6: THE DICTATORSHIP

1. Exact numbers for membership in the Fascist militia, known as the Milizia Volontaria per la Sicurezza Nazionale (Voluntary Militia for National Security, or MVSN), are not available, given the difference between those who were effectively organized in the militia and those enrolled on paper, but it would seem that there were well over one hundred thousand effective members and perhaps two or three times that number.

2. Milza 2000, pp. 386–87.

3. Fornari 1971, pp. 101–11.

4. Tacchi Venturi's draft letter to Mussolini, dated September 18, 1925, is found in an uninventoried series of documents in the CC archives and published in Sale 2007, pp. 364–65. I did not find the original or any copy of this letter in Mussolini's own archives at the Central State Archives, so there is no proof I am aware of that it was sent. Franzinelli (1998, p. 45) reports the wedding date. Milza (2000, p. 401) reports on Rachele Mussolini's lack of enthusiasm at being belatedly baptized. The account of the wedding is from R. Mussolini 1974, pp. 123–24.

5. Typical was his June 21, 1925, speech to the national congress of the PNF: "Those who have the responsibility for leading a revolution are like the generals responsible for conducting a war"; Discorsi di Benito Mussolini, "Discorso del 21 giugno 1925," http://www .dittatori.it/discorso21giugno1925.htm.

6. Quoted in Baima Bollone 2007, p. 28.

7. That the powerful Duce did not intimidate Farinacci is clear from the *ras*'s reply the next day. "This morning your messenger brought me one of your usual 'epistolary tantrums,'" wrote Farinacci. "I have fulfilled the engagements made at Rome, and you amaze me by saying I did not keep my promises. . . . The trial has become political? But this was known long ago; otherwise I would not be at Chieti."

8. Fornari 1971, pp. 119–25, 135. The U.S. State Department files in the National Archives contain an intriguing series of documents from 1934 that offer a curious epilogue to the trial of Matteotti's murderers. Amerigo Dumini, the ringleader of the murder, had sent a sealed package to a San Antonio lawyer, telling him that his life was in danger from certain enemies, naming Arturo Bocchini, national head of the Italian police, as principal among them. Dumini said that the ability to let it be known that the documents in the packet would be opened in case of his death could save him from assassination. The lawyer, not knowing who Dumini was, asked his friend, a Texas U.S. senator, to find out. In response to the senator's request, the U.S. consul in Florence sent back a report to the State Department, informing it of Dumini's role in the Matteotti murder. The State Department regarded the consul's letter as too sensitive to send on to the Texas lawyer. Instead, it briefed the senator on the report and had him discreetly let the lawyer know what he was dealing

with. NARA, M1423, reel 1, Arnold Cozey, San Antonio, to Joseph Haven, U.S. Consul in Florence, March 1, 1934; et seq.

9. Urso (2003, pp. 160–65) discusses Sarfatti's role in introducing the theme of *romanità* and in crafting the cult of the Duce. The book had been first published outside Italy the previous year with a different title.

10. Duce is pronounced *DOO-chay.*

11. Quoted in Falasca-Zamponi 1997, pp. 64–65.

12. Quoted in Baima Bollone 2007, p. 78.

13. O. Russell, *Annual Report 1925,* April 21, 1926, C 5004/5004/22, in Hachey 1972, pp. 74, 77–78, sections 3, 14–18; Chaline 1996, p. 162; Agostino 1991, pp. 44–45; Morgan 1939, p. 205.

14. ACS, MI, DAGRA, b. 129, Vice Questore, Borgo, al Signor Questore, 21 gennaio 1925; Venini 2004, pp. 24–25.

15. "You are not fully Christian," the pope pronounced on April 21, the birthday of Rome, "unless you are Catholic, and you are not fully Catholic unless you are Roman." See Baxa 2006, p. 116.

16. In the middle of the Holy Year, Cardinal Merry del Val, fearful that Pius XI was being infected by the thousands of pilgrims who got the privilege of kissing his hand, reportedly proposed, and the pope agreed, that he wear gloves in the future. A. C. Jacobson, M.D., "To Guard the Hands that Pious Pilgrims Kiss," WP, November 15, 1925, p. SM8.

17. The Pontifical Gendarmes consisted of a hundred men, with five officers, who with the Swiss Guards policed the Vatican.

18. Bosworth 2011, p. 180.

19. Father Martina (1978, pp. 226–27), one of the Church's foremost historians, characterizes the pope's vision, as expressed in *Quas primas,* as anachronistic. See also Bouthillon 1996; Verucci 1988, pp. 35–37; Chiron 2006, pp. 233–34.

20. *Quas primas,* English translation at http://www.vatican.va/holy_father/pius_xi/encyclicals /documents/hf_p-xi_enc_11121925_quas-primas_en.html. The quote is from paragraph 33. (There are 34 paragraphs in all.)

21. "Lutherans to Fight Papal Feast Edict," NYT, March 21, 1926, p. 12.

22. Seldes (1934, p. 128) reports this as fact, although it admittedly has the ring of the apocryphal.

23. Beatrice Baskerville, "How the Pope Spends His 24 Hours," BG, November 1, 1925, p. C5.

24. This episode is reported by the "noted Vatican informer," who added that the pope was an "insensitive egoist." ACS, MCPG, b. 155, 20 marzo 1926. In an otherwise admiring profile in the *Boston Globe,* the author similarly reported that "Prelates who were attached to Benedict XV think Pius XI somewhat cold." Baskerville, "How the Pope Spends," p. C5.

25. These reports, written by Mussolini's informants, can now be found in the Central State Archives in Rome. The informants were not above peddling unconfirmed gossip or trying to besmirch the reputation of those they disliked. But as a result of the Fascist spy network that they constituted, we have a picture of the power struggles, backbiting, personality conflicts, and scandals in the Vatican that is richer than for any other period in history. Among the new police agencies that were added, the most feared was the Organization for Vigilance and Repression of Anti-Fascism (OVRA), a kind of elite political spy force. Fiorentino 1999; Canali 2004a. For more on the repressive measures introduced in 1925–26, see among many other sources Milza 2000, pp. 394–96; Gentile 2002, p. 153–54; CC 1926 IV, pp. 459–65, 560.

26. ACS, MCPG, b. 155, n.d. [1926]. The "noted Vatican informer" filled his reports with accounts of prelates' complaints about the pope's imperious personality and his rude treatment of them. Typical is one from October 28, 1927: "A Monsignor who often has

occasion to talk with the Pope told me that, as time goes on, the Pope becomes increasingly frightful and authoritarian, and therefore one is afraid to speak with him." ACS, MCPG, b. 156.

27. Ambassador Eugène Beyens, 10 février 1925, quoted in Ruysschaert 1996, pp. 252–53; Beyens 1934, pp. 286–87.

28. Cesare Pasini, "Il bibliotecario con la pistola," OR, 19–20 novembre 2007, p. 5.

29. De Felice 1968, pp. 200–1; Cannistraro and Sullivan 1993, pp. 326–27. Gibson apparently intended to kill the pope after she had shot Mussolini.

30. Baima Bollone 2007, p. 53.

31. "Mussolini si è salvato per un vero miracolo!" Il Regime fascista, 9 aprile 1926, p. 1.

32. Within hours of the attack, Tacchi Venturi was at Palazzo Chigi, carrying the pope's personal expression of gratitude. ARSI, TV, b. 7, fasc. 431, Tacchi Venturi a Monsignor Pizzardo, 11 settembre 1926; De Felice 1968, p. 202.

33. De Felice 1968, pp. 204–8.

34. The message was delivered through Tacchi Venturi. DDI, series 1, vol. 4, n. 473, Grandi, Roma, a Mussolini, a Forlì, 1 novembre 1926.

35. Censorship had begun before this, but was less repressive. A July 15, 1923, law gave police the authority to fire newspaper editors and sequester copies of their newspapers if they published anything deemed injurious to Italy's reputation or offensive to the king, pope, or Catholic Church. See Talbot 2007, p. 27.

36. La Civiltà cattolica expressed its approval, while without comment, the Vatican daily reported the minister of justice's speech to parliament, including his words affirming the support of the Catholic Church for the measure. CC 1926 IV, pp. 459–62; Rogari 1977, p. 174.

CHAPTER 7: ASSASSINS, PEDERASTS, AND SPIES

1. One of the more notable of these requests came in July 1928. Alcide De Gasperi—who had replaced Don Sturzo as head of the PPI and would become Italy's prime minister following the Second World War—was arrested in 1927 for attempting to leave the country without permission and was jailed. Released in an amnesty the following year, he was told not to leave Rome. Eager to join his wife and children in their family home in northeastern Italy, he prepared an appeal to Mussolini. As De Gasperi was a well-known anti-Fascist, his friends convinced him that Mussolini would reject his plea unless he could get Tacchi Venturi to deliver it personally. Reluctantly, De Gasperi asked for the Jesuit's assistance, but the pope's emissary refused to help him. As De Gasperi explained in a handwritten note scribbled in the margin of his typed appeal to the Duce: "Not accepted by Father Tacchi because it contains no thanks for the amnesty and lacks any words of homage!" See De Gasperi 2004, p. 94.

2. ACS, MI, DAGR, b. 1320, informatore n. 204, Roma, 28 ottobre 1928.

3. Maryks 2012, p. 308.

4. Alongside the threat of what he termed "internal disintegration."

5. ARSI, TV, b. 7, fasc. 430a, no date.

6. The booklet was Filippo Maria Tinti, Sionismo e Cattolicismo (Bari, 1926). ASMAE, Gab., b. 32, Tacchi Venturi a Marchese Giacomo Balucci, capo di gabinetto, 6 settembre 1926. Balucci replied that Mussolini appreciated receiving it. ASMAE, Gab., b. 32. Tacchi Venturi saw a link between the danger posed by the Jews and their various co-conspirators and the difficulty that the Church was having in enforcing its norms of morality. In a memo to Gasparri on December 1, he recommended ways of dealing with what he called the threat posed by the "antireligious" campaign in Italy. Every Catholic, he told Gasparri,

rejoiced in seeing the Fascist government work ever harder in the interests of the Catholic Church, as it tied church and state together ever more firmly. But Mussolini's efforts were encountering resistance in the provinces, where officials often ignored his orders. Standing in the way of the renaissance of religious sentiment, the Jesuit advised, were "the Jews, the Protestants, the Masons and the Bolsheviks, all constantly and powerfully allied against religion, against the Church, and against the National Government itself." Here again Tacchi Venturi identified the conspiracy as aimed not at the Vatican alone but at Mussolini and the Fascist government as well. Aware of Mussolini's sensitivity about Britain's power, he added that the Jews and their allies, in so mercilessly seeking to weaken the Catholic Church, were working on behalf of "Anglo-Saxon hegemony." This, he warned, "is putting in place a vast plan of conquest of Italy that is today religious, but tomorrow political." ARSI, TV, b. 8, fasc. 446, Tacchi Venturi a Gasparri, 1 dicembre 1926, lettera con allegati.

7. The informant said he couldn't vouch firsthand for the accuracy of the verse, or even if the whole story was made up, but it was making the rounds. In fact, other versions of the story cropped up elsewhere, each with a slightly different wording of the verse. ACS, MI, DAGRA, b. 1320, 1927.

8. "Stabs Jesuit Agent in Vatican Issue," NYT, February 29, 1928.

9. "Anti-Mussolini Plot Seen in Rome Stabbing," WP, March 1, 1928, p. 3.

10. "Father Tacchi Venturi," one police informant's report read, "is convinced that the aggression against him was related to the listing of his name some months ago right after that of the Duce in a list of people to eliminate. It is said that the list was compiled in France among circles composed of Freemasons and Italian exiles. They blame him, as a member of the Jesuit order, for having suggested to the Duce that he take repressive measures against the masonry and for this they had presumably ordered his death." ACS, MI, DAGR, b. 1320, informatore, Roma, n.d.

11. The police chief also found it curious that after the police had expressed disbelief at finding the Jesuit's name second on the list of targets, Tacchi Venturi's secret report offered an explanation: Salvemini told the informant that "the Jesuit Order is completely fascist and they are the great pillar on which fascism rests."

12. "The document," wrote the police chief, "was clearly a fantastic and crude tissue of facts and news that reveals paradoxically an ignorance of the most basic political circumstances." ACS, MI, DAGR, b. 59, pp. 15–16. Salvemini would later make his way to the United States, where in 1934 he would be given a chair at Harvard.

13. Two years earlier, when Violet Gibson had tried to assassinate Mussolini, the man had attempted to convince the police that the Irish woman was part of a plot that he knew all about. He had been in jail in Florence at the time, serving time for fraud, and the police undoubtedly suspected him of inventing the story to win his release. But no lead could be ignored in a case like this. Interviewed by police, he claimed that the assassination attempt was plotted by a previously unknown Irish women's secret political society, in league with Italian anti-Fascist exiles in France. The police were not impressed. He got into trouble again trying to sell a secret weapon to the French military. It would, he claimed, stop the engines of enemy airplanes in midflight. It didn't.

14. ACS, MI, DAGR, b. 1320, Roma, 20 marzo 1928.

15. Ibid., Roma, dal direttore, Capo Divisione Polizia Politica, 30 marzo 1928, p. 29.

16. The police chief also observed that, in trying to prevent the police from identifying his attacker, Tacchi Venturi had given a description of him very different from that provided by the doorman. The Jesuit had attributed the discrepancy to the fact that the doorman was becoming old and demented. But in the police chief's view, the man was "not that poor muddle-headed scatterbrain that Father Tacchi would have us believe." ACS, MI, DAGR, b. 1320, informatore, n.d.

17. "Naturally," the police chief wrote in his final report, he had refused "to credit other absurd, not to say outrageous voices given the respectability of the Man, namely, of immoral relations between the victim and the aggressor." ACS, MI, DAGR, b. 59, p. 13.

18. Whether Tacchi Venturi had actually had an affair or a sexual liaison, or had sexually abused a boy or a young man, remains in the realm of speculation. The evidence, while tantalizing, is far from conclusive. Several years later a report from a regular police informant related that Tacchi Venturi "has great affection for a young man who is not his relative. It may be his young secretary . . . I had it confirmed that this is his only true love." ACS, MI, DAGR, b. 1320, informatore n. 590 (=Eduardo Drago), Roma, maggio 1936. For the identification of police informants by their coded number, I rely on Canali 2004a.

19. ACS, CR, b. 68, 4 maggio 1928.

20. In the usage at the time, *pederast* referred to a man having sexual relations either with boys or with young men.

21. Both men thought they were due a cardinal's hat, and according to Mussolini's "noted Vatican informer," both were using their position at the pope's side to poison him against Cardinal Gasparri, whom they blamed for turning the pope against them. If the pope was gradually excluding his old secretary of state from the most important decisions he was making, it was in part due to the influence that Samper and Caccia enjoyed. ACS, MCPG, b. 155, noto informatore vaticano, 1926. The note was most likely written in late June, as it references Samper's disappointment at not being in the most recent list of newly appointed cardinals, and the consistory took place on June 21, 1926.

22. ACS, MCPG, b. 157, noto informatore vaticano, 23 luglio 1928. Indeed, Samper was not even Italian but Colombian. The informant had previously referred to the secret papal inquiry in his reports of 22 and 30 giugno. Samper's mysterious suspension is mentioned in *The Cardinals of the Holy Roman Church, Biographical Dictionary (1902–2012)*, online at http://www2.fiu.edu/~mirandas/bios-s.htm. In his memoir of his years as unofficial French emissary to the Vatican, in 1914–18, Charles Loiseau (1960, p. 102) recalls Samper, then Benedict XV's majordomo, fondly as "a young, wealthy prelate of handsome presence who then enjoyed the intimate favor of Benedict XV." He learned only much later that Samper "had fallen into disgrace and that they had driven him from the Vatican for rather delicate reasons. . . . Whatever they might have been," Loiseau added, "I retain a good memory of him." The French ambassador, Fontenay, also discussed the mysterious dismissal in a report to Paris on December 17, 1928, cited in Chiron 2006, p. 152n57.

23. The "noted Vatican informer" also reported that Caccia employed the pope's negotiator, Francesco Pacelli, to defend him. ACS, MCPG, b. 157, noto informatore vaticano, 30 giugno 1928.

24. Canali 2004a, p. 288.

25. De Felice (1968, p. 464) makes this point, noting that in this way Bocchini contrasted with his Nazi counterparts, Heydrich and Himmler, who were sadistic. Both of them, however, thought highly of Bocchini and sought his technical advice. According to the American journalist Thomas Morgan, who knew him, Bocchini was unhappy about Mussolini's increasing embrace of the Nazis, and when he died in November 1940, still chief of police and in excellent health until then, suspicions of foul play fell on the Germans. Morgan 1941, p. 236.

26. De Felice 1968, p. 465.

27. Canali 2004a, pp. 283–84.

28. Ibid., p. 766n840. Much of the information Pucci sent in got reported through Pupeschi, who appears as informant no. 35 in the secret reports. In 1929 Pupeschi would report that when a cardinal pleaded with the pope to send Pucci away from the Vatican, the pope replied that he was too valuable in handling the press but would not be given any confiden-

tial missions—"and we," the pope added, "will know how to keep an eye on him." ACS, MI, FP "Cerretti," informatore n. 35 (=Bice Pupeschi), Roma, 25 ottobre 1929.

29. The large, good-looking prelate, whose dignity was magnified by his colorful monsignor robes and his mellifluous voice, was also well known to the foreign correspondents covering the Vatican, offering them information for a price as well, and entertaining them with an inexhaustible stock of stories. See Alvarez 2002, pp. 156–57; Canali 2004a, p. 195; Franzinelli 2000, pp. 259–60, 701–3. Morgan (1944, pp. 31–36) offers a lengthy portrait of a good-natured and popular Pucci, continually playing one U.S. news organization against another in an effort to jack up his earnings.

30. Copious grains of salt are required in interpreting these fascinating, newsy, gossipy, and unreliable reports, for its author had many axes to grind. As I mentioned, the identity of the "noted Vatican informer" remains a mystery. There has been some speculation that he was Monsignor Enrico Pucci himself, the Vatican's unofficial press agent, who had the run of the Vatican and was friendly with many of the Vatican's highest officials. But I have my doubts. The first report identified as coming from him predates Bocchini's appointment to police chief, and until 1934 the informer provided a huge stream of often-lengthy reports on the highest levels of the Vatican. He sometimes describes Pucci in ways that make it seem odd that he would be referring to himself; e.g., ACS, MCPG, b. 155, 20 marzo 1926, and ibid., ca. aprile 1926, reporting on the Knights of Columbus. The "noted Vatican informer" constantly sought to discredit Cardinal Gasparri. In an April 1927 report, he colorfully quotes Gasparri as railing against Mussolini, continually saying he "should go take a shit." ACS, MCPG, b. 156, 12 aprile 1927. But Gasparri in his memoirs expresses fondness for Pucci, so it seems odd that Pucci would have been so intent on undermining Mussolini's view of him.

31. ACS, MCPG, b. 157, noto informatore vaticano, 22 e 30 giugno 1928. To get Caccia away until the scandal died down, the pope sent him as a papal representative to the Eucharistic Congress in Australia. But following the monsignor's return, months later, the rumors began again; ACS, MI, PS, Polizia Politica, b. 210, informatore n. 35, Roma, 27 settembre 1929. A handwritten note on this report records that a copy was sent to Dino Grandi, then minister of foreign affairs.

CHAPTER 8: THE PACT

1. I tell the story of the popes' efforts to retake Rome in Kertzer 2004. After World War I, Benedict XV tried to reach an agreement with the Italian government but had no luck. The Italian prime minister involved in the Paris negotiations wrote an account; see Orlando 1937, pp. 140–46. So did the papal representative; ibid., pp. 177 86. Victor Emmanuel III's negative reaction to the agreement is recorded in Margiotta 1966, pp. 56–58.

2. When newspaper stories about the commission later appeared, the pope had *L'Osservatore romano,* the Vatican newspaper, claim that "the Ecclesiastical Authority has had nothing to do either with the naming or choice of the three ecclesiastical legal consultants, or with the work of the Commission." A copy of a memo signed by Mussolini, addressed to his minister of justice, tells the story: "In relation to previous agreements," Mussolini begins, "I inform your Excellency that the Holy See has designated the following people to take part in the Commission for the Reform of Ecclesiastical Legislation." The names and positions of two high Vatican officials and a professor of law at the Roman Pontifical Seminary followed: "The same Holy See has provided me with the enclosed memo in which are noted the main points that it would like to see incorporated in the reform." Mussolini appended a memo that Tacchi Venturi had given him on behalf of the pope listing six measures that the pope wanted to see adopted. ASV, AESI, pos. 628, fasc. 56, ff. 91r–93r, 3

agosto 1924. De Felice (1995, pp. 106–10) wrote an account of these events before the documents in the Vatican archives became available; it largely agrees with what we now know. See also Margiotta 1966, pp. 131–33.

3. The pope's handwritten letter is found at ASV, AESI, pos. 702, vol. 1, ff. 14r–16v.

4. DDI, series 7, vol. 4, n. 308. On May 16, 1926, Tacchi Venturi wrote Mussolini with news that following his meeting with the Duce a few days earlier, he had spoken to Gasparri and learned that the Vatican was now ready to enter into direct talks with him to settle the Roman question; DDI, series 7, vol. 4, n. 312.

5. NARA, M530, reel 2, U.S. ambassador Henry F. Fletcher, Rome, to secretary of state, October 4, 1927, n. 1410.

6. No opportunity was too small to exploit. Following a prominent priest's funeral, family members visited Mussolini and presented him the monsignor's pectoral cross, explaining that it contained a relic of the Holy Cross. Mussolini kissed it—an effort that for the famously anticlerical rabble-rouser from Romagna must have been difficult—and told them he would always keep it with him. The pope, hearing the story, was pleased. "*Bene, bene*," good, good, he said. ACS, MCPG, b. 155, 5 luglio 1926.

7. "La parola di Merry del Val," *Il Regime fascista*, 7 ottobre 1926, p. 1; Franzinelli 1998, p. 54.

8. Franzinelli 1998, p. 68.

9. "Aristocrazia nera," *Il Secolo XX*, 20 febbraio 1929, p. 11, has a photo of Francesco Pacelli as an exemplar of the category. Bosworth 2011, p. 26.

10. The Chicago paper was the *Chicago Daily News*. A secret police report in November 1926 reported that the American Knights of Columbus were coming up with the funds for the land; ACS, MI, DAGRA, b. 113, n. 52199.

11. The Jesuit contacted the minister of internal affairs, Luigi Federzoni. The police report revealed that the headquarters of both organizations were in the same building and that the longtime local Popular Party head was a priest.

12. It was especially outrageous, he added, that the Popular Party would oppose the Fascists while being open to the possibility of allying with the Socialists, "sworn enemies of every Christian principle." Tacchi Venturi to Gasparri, AESI, pos. 611, fasc. 46, ff. 23r–23v; the police reports are at ff. 25r–30r.

13. ASV, AESI, pos. 734, fasc. 241, ff. 4r–5v, Tacchi Venturi a Gasparri, 8 gennaio 1926. The Jesuit added a note on Federzoni's view of the bishop of Brescia: "While he respects the pastoral virtues of Monsignor Gaggia, as well as his religious learning and culture, nonetheless he thought that because of his venerable age, he does not realize that, hiding themselves behind the mask or name of Catholic Action, quite a number of its members were leading a secret campaign against the government, seeking by hook or crook to involve the ecclesiastical authority in this struggle."

14. *Balilla* is the surname of a youth who was said to have triggered a popular revolt against Austrian troops in Genoa in 1746. Gibelli 2003, p. 267.

15. ASV, AESI, pos. 667, fasc. 129, ff. 68r–69r.

16. ACS, MCPG, b. 157, noto informatore vaticano, 29 aprile 1928.

17. Coco 2009, pp. 164–65.

18. Rhodes 1974, p. 41. This account is based on the testimony of the German ambassador in Rome.

19. Pacelli 1959, p. 99, emphasis in the original. Just a few months earlier, on March 1, the pope had been indignant when Francesco Pacelli relayed the suggestion that he abandon his desire to have Villa Doria Pamphili considered part of Vatican lands. Pius XI insisted at the time that he would rather remain without an accord than have the property excluded. Ibid., p. 82.

20. "Not accepting," Barone added, "would be tantamount to saying that . . . they didn't want

to end the conflict, but I can assure you that Mussolini thinks differently." Ibid., p. 100. "Barone also tells me confidentially," Pacelli reported in his diary, "that on various occasions the king had shown a lack of enthusiasm for the resolution of the Roman question."

21. R. Mussolini 1974, p. 154; Bosworth 2002, pp. 347–49; Milza 2000, p. 537.

22. Navarra 2004, p. 16.

23. The pope's failure to appear at Gasparri's jubilee, and its impact, are discussed in a series of reports in 1926 from the "noted Vatican informer." ACS, MCPG, b. 155.

24. ACS, MCPG, b. 157, noto informatore vaticano, 1 gennaio 1928; ibid., 5 gennaio 1928; ibid., 12 gennaio 1928;

25. DDI, series 7, vol. 7, n. 240; Arnaldo Cortesi, "Only 9 to see pact signed in Rome tomorrow," NYT, February 11, 1929, p. 3.

26. Quoted in Gannon 1962, p. 62. Two days later, Monsignor Spellman would describe the pope as "delighted with everything." Ibid., p. 63. Borgongini, one of Gasparri's two undersecretaries, had brought Spellman in three years earlier to help with English-language materials and with the American Church. Mussolini's main Vatican informant at the time, no fan of Borgongini, claimed that the nuncio had wanted to ingratiate himself with the Knights of Columbus in the United States, a group that had become an important source of funds for the Vatican. In late 1926 the pope, having heard so much about the young American priest, not least his seemingly inexhaustible ability to come up with funds from the United States, asked to meet Spellman in a private audience. Before long, the pope began referring to him as "Monsignor Prezioso," Monsignor Valuable. ACS, MCPG, b. 155, noto informatore vaticano, 1926 (no more specific date given); and MCPG, b. 155, noto informatore vaticano, 5 gennaio 1927. Spellman told his mother of the pope's nickname for him with great pleasure. Gannon 1962, pp. 57–59.

27. The last dispute involved the status of the Palace of the Holy Office of the Inquisition. The imposing sixteenth-century building lies along the wall of the Vatican, to the left as one faces St. Peter's, but its front door opens onto a public street. The pope had wanted both the building and the street in front of it to be considered part of the new Vatican City. But the king had opposed giving the Church any more territory, and in the end the pope had been willing to compromise. The street would remain outside papal control, and while the palace itself would not technically be on Vatican land, it would, like a number of other Church buildings in Rome, be granted special legal status. ASMAE, Gab., b. 718, Roma, 10 febbraio 1929.

28. While this provision was found in the 1848 statute of the Savoyard state that was subsequently adopted by the fledgling Italian state in 1861, it was there viewed in the context of the doctrine of "a free Church in a free State."

29. Toschi 1931.

30. Bosworth 2011, p. 171.

31. Based on the 1929 Italian lira/U.S. dollar exchange value found in Nenovsky et al. 2007.

32. Grandi 1985, pp. 254–55.

33. Martini 1960b, p. 113. Gasparri later told Charles-Roux that he had cried five times that day: both in entering and leaving the pope's study, when arriving at the Lateran Palace for the signing, during the act of signing itself, and in reporting on the day to the pope. Charles-Roux 1947, p. 48.

34. Reese 1996, p. 11.

35. Spellman to his mother, February 10, 1929, in Gannon 1962, p. 63.

36. A photo of Mussolini getting out of his car is found in *Il Secolo XX,* 20 febbraio 1929, p. 7.

37. "Signing in Constantine's Palace," NYT, February 11, 1929, p. 2.

38. "Informazioni Stefani sul Trattato e Concordato," OR, 13 febbraio 1929, p. 2.

39. Arnaldo Cortesi, "Vatican and Italy Sign Pact Recreating a Papal State; 60 Years of Enmity Ended," NYT, February 12, 1929, p. 1; Casella 2005, p. 24. Pizzardo's salute was chroni-

cled in NARA, M530, reel 2, n. 2140, February 15, 1929, Alexander Kirk, chargé d'affaires ad interim of the U.S. embassy in Rome, report to the U.S. secretary of state in Washington, p. 5.

40. Grandi 1985, p. 255.

41. The various actions that Mussolini had taken to benefit the Church over the previous few years were not all that gave the pope this hope; so did, Moro argues, Mussolini's view of using the Church as an *instrumentum regni,* an instrument of his rule. It would be a return—or at least so the pope hoped—to the cozy arrangement that the Church had enjoyed with a number of absolute rulers in the ancien régime, before ideas of democracy and separation of church and state had transformed western Europe. No less important was the fact that the basic principles Mussolini embraced and the principles championed by the pope were in such broad agreement on the need for order, discipline, and top-down authority, and in their rejection of the idea that people should decide for themselves what is best based on their own conscience. Virtue lay in people acting not in their own personal interest but for the larger good, and that larger good was to be determined by a higher authority. Moro 1981, pp. 192–93. Moro here builds on the work of Giovanni Miccoli (1973, 1988). De Felice (1995, pp. 382–83), author of the definitive biography of Mussolini, argues that only with the signing of the Lateran Accords was the Fascist regime fully established.

42. Quoted in Confalonieri 1957, p. 215.

43. Prefect reports are found in ACS, MI, DAGRA, b. 187, 11 febbraio 1929.

44. As one celebratory magazine account put it, the agreement was a miracle, "produced by the perfect coincidence . . . between the policies of the Church and the Fascist State in raising the moral and spiritual level of the people. That would have certainly failed in a parliamentary regime." Giuseppe Bevione, "La portata dell'accordo fra l'Italia e il Vaticano," *XX Secolo,* 15 febbraio 1929, p. 7. *L'Osservatore romano,* the Vatican daily, quoted at length coverage of the event in *La Gazzetta del popolo,* heralding the fact that "the Fascist Regime was able to resolve the 'Roman question' because it had liberated Italy from all the democratic lies of anticlericalism and parliamentarianism." "Dopo la firma dei trattati fra la Santa Sede e l'Italia," OR, 15 febbraio 1929, p. 1.

45. Arnaldo Cortesi, "280,000 Cheer Pope," NYT, February 13, 1929, p. 1; H. G. Chilton, *Annual Report 1929,* March 27, 1930, C 2470/2470/22, in Hachey 1972, p. 165, section 99; "La dimostrazione al Quirinale," OR, 14 febbraio 1929, p. 1. Reports of other such celebrations outside Rome are found in "L'esultanza delle città italiane per il fausto evento della conciliazione," *L'Avvenire d'Italia* [Bologna's Catholic newspaper], 12 febbraio 1929, p. 4, and all the issues of *L'Osservatore romano* over the next several days.

46. The *New York Times* front-page headline was typical: "60 Years of Enmity Ended. . . . Throngs Cheer in the Streets." Arnaldo Cortesi, "Vatican and Italy Sign Pact Recreating a Papal State," NYT, February 12, 1929, p. 1.

47. The words are those of Domenico Tardini (1988, p. 294), who was then under Francesco Borgongini in the Vatican secretary of state office.

48. NARA, M530, reel 2, n. 2140, February 15, 1929, p. 8; Caviglia 2009, p. 94.

49. ACS, CR, b. 6, 13 febbraio VII [1929]. The three-page report bears the handwritten penciled notation "da Rosati."

CHAPTER 9: THE SAVIOR

1. Morgan 1939, p. 174.

2. Arnaldo Cortesi, "Mussolini Cheered by Papal Audience," NYT, February 18, 1920, p. 5. Rome's aristocracy made the transition to Fascist rule without any notable difficulty. Tellingly, from 1926 to Mussolini's fall in 1943, the Duce appointed a succession of four

princes to serve as Rome's governor, the aristocratic line broken for only a brief period in 1935–36, when Giuseppe Bottai served in that role. Insolera 1976, p. 119.

3. Parliament had approved the new electoral system in 1928; Milza 2000, p. 415. The procedure included a first step in which the Grand Council received one thousand nominations from "a list of people of unquestioned fascist faith" provided by various government-controlled groups; the final decision on candidates was to be made by the Grand Council, which also had the ability to add candidates not found among the nominees. De Felice (1995, p. 437) discusses the "plebiscite" terminology used by the regime.

4. The appeal published in the Vatican daily was signed by the national executive board of Catholic Action and is quoted in Scoppola 1976, pp. 195–96. See also De Felice 1995, p. 445.

5. On February 17 Mussolini got a surprising ultimatum in a letter from Cardinal Gasparri, sent via Francesco Pacelli: "The Holy See, while admiring and praising with great satisfaction the work accomplished by the Honorable Mussolini to the immense advantage to religion, keenly feels the desire for the upcoming political elections to have a great value, as it is said, of a plebiscite, a value of praise and support for the Duce and the Regime that he created and which is embodied in him." The Holy See was eager for the elections to furnish "truly eloquent and solemn proof of the full consensus of Italian Catholics with the Government of the Honorable Mussolini." Pacelli sent the letter in with a cover note, representing it as a letter from Gasparri, although offered in Pacelli's own "faithful" transcription. ACS, CR, b. 68, Roma, 17 febbraio 1929.

6. The Pope gave his instructions to Cardinal Gasparri, who then dictated the letter to Francesco Pacelli. It was Pacelli who conveyed it to Mussolini. ACS, CR, b. 68.

7. The quote is from Tacchi Venturi's account. ASV, AESI, pos. 630a, fasc. 63, ff. 88r–89v, Tacchi Venturi a Gasparri, Roma, 21 febbraio 1929. Apparently word had gotten out that the pope's Jesuit emissary had the power to get loyal Catholics added to Mussolini's list of candidates. His files contain letters from various people vaunting their credential of being a "good Catholic" and asking to be put on the list. Gasparri sent Tacchi Venturi other names for the list. ARSI, TV, fasc. 1037.

8. In February 1923 the Fascist Grand Council identified Freemasonry as a threat to Fascism and declared membership incompatible with membership in the Fascist Party. *Squadristi* sacked and burned Masonic lodges throughout the country. *La Civiltà cattolica* praised the Fascist Grand Council for its action, while warning that the Jewish-Masonic plot that it had long railed against was now aimed not only at the Church but at Mussolini as well. The government should also act against Italy's Jews, it added, charging them with exercising influence greater than their minuscule numbers justified. CC 1923 I p. 464, quoted in Sale 2007, pp. 42–43. See also Molony 1977, p. 152.

9. Some flavor of the mobilization by the Italian Church hierarchy is offered by a circular that one central Italian bishop sent to all his parish priests. It was the "sacred duty for all Catholics, without exception," he instructed, to cast their vote for "the providential Man," who had worked so closely with the pope, "to give God back to Italy and Italy back to God." The priests were to do all they could, wrote the bishop, to persuade their parishioners to go to the polls and vote. Monsignor Alberto Romita, bishop of Campobasso, quoted in Piccardi 1995, p. 50. Luigi Colombo, national president of Catholic Action, similarly issued a public call for all members of the organization to vote yes. "Un discorso del Comm. Colombo," OR, 13 marzo 1929, p. 4.

10. Binchy 1970, p. 199.

11. CC 1929 II, pp. 184–85.

12. This appears to be based on the *Confessions* of St. Augustine, chap. 11.

13. Jacini's account of his visit with the pope is reproduced in Fonzi 1979, pp. 676–78. For more on Jacini, see Ignesti 2004.

14. In its brief comment on the speech, *La Civiltà cattolica* (1929 II, p. 473) quoted this passage disapprovingly.

15. The texts of Mussolini's addresses to both houses of parliament were printed as a book (Mussolini 1929).

16. Following the signing, Gasparri read the text of a telegram from the pope, addressed to Victor Emmanuel III: "The first telegram that we send from the Vatican City is to tell You that the exchange of ratifications of the Lateran Accords has just been, thanks to God, completed. . . . It is also to offer a heartfelt, deep paternal apostolic blessing to Your Majesty, to your August Consort, to all the Royal Family, to Italy, to the World. Pius XI." History had been made. Pius IX had excommunicated King Victor Emmanuel II; in the years since, no pope had sent a blessing—or even a letter—to an Italian king. Pacelli 1959, pp. 144–54; "Gli accordi lateranensi tra la S. Sede e l'Italia," CC 1929 II, pp. 544–45.

17. ACS, CR, b. 4, Roma, 1 maggio 1923, Mussolini a De Vecchi. In Mussolini's private secretary files are copies of De Vecchi's military records. Throughout the war, his superiors gave him their highest praise for his military spirit and skills as an artillery officer. ACS, CR, b. 4.

18. Grandi 1985, p. 175 (25 ottobre 1922).

19. "It isn't true that De Vecchi is a fool," began one such joke. "On the contrary, he was a precocious child. At age five he thought just as he did at fifty." A decade after De Vecchi's appointment to the Vatican post, General Enrico Caviglia, holder of Italy's highest military rank, Marshal of Italy, and a longtime member of the Senate, put it pithily. De Vecchi, he observed, was a "conceited weirdo." De Begnac 1990, pp. 232, 469; Bosworth 2002, pp. 182–83; Innocenti 1992, p. 154; Caviglia 2009, p. 301; Romersa 1983, p. 5.

20. NARA, M530, reel 2, n. 2362, Rome, June 27, 1929, Henry P. Fletcher, U.S. Embassy, to secretary of state, Washington; CC 1929 III, pp. 170–72; De Vecchi 1983, pp. 136–37.

21. De Vecchi 1998, p. 141.

22. Quoted in Casella 2009, pp. 74–75.

23. De Vecchi 1998, pp. 23–25.

24. The actual Italian expression was more colorful: the pope *aveva un diavolo per capello*, literally, the pope "had a devil in his hair"; Casella 2009, p. 82.

25. The audience was held on November 15, 1929. ASMAE, APNSS, b. 7, De Vecchi a Dino Grandi, Minstro per gli Affari Esteri, 22 novembre 1929. See also the account in De Vecchi 1983, pp. 162–64.

26. De Vecchi 1983, p. 141. The pope had informed the cardinals of the Curia of the talks around the time they were initiated but then not again until they were virtually concluded. Showing more nerve—and less prudence—than his other colleagues, Monsignor Giuseppe Bruno, secretary of the Pontifical Commission in charge of interpreting canon law, decided to take his complaints to Pius XI himself. At a private audience, he told the pope that if he had only asked his advice in negotiating the concordat, he would have been sure to include a number of important guarantees that had gone unmentioned. The pope responded curtly, saying it had been necessary to pass over many things in order to settle the Roman question. Still upset, Bruno went to see Cardinal Sbarretti, one of the Curia's most influential members, hoping to enlist his support. But Sbarretti knew better than to get on the wrong side of the pope and advised Bruno to let the matter go. There was nothing anyone could do. As the informant who reported all this to the police put it, "No one dares to mount any real opposition for fear of falling out of the good graces of Pope Ratti." ASMAE, AISS, b. 2, fasc. 6, Roma, 14 luglio 1929.

27. Police informant report cited by Coco (2009, p. 168). The term Cardinal Cerretti used is not easily translated: "*il papa si è fatto mangare da Mussolini la pappa in testa.*"

28. ASMAE, AISS, b. 2, fasc. 6, Roma, 14 luglio 1929. On Pompili and this dispute, see Fiorentino 1999, pp. 131–33.

29. De Vecchi 1983, p. 141.

30. ASMAE, AISS, b. 2, fasc. 6, Roma, 10 agosto 1929. A copy is found at ACS, MI, FP "Pompili." It identifies the informant as n. 39 and bears the note "Copy for His Excellency Grandi for the Ambassador." ASMAE, AISS, b. 2, f. 6, Roma, 12 novembre 1929.

31. ACS, MI, FP "Pompili," Città del Vaticano, 19 novembre 1929. The source for this account, according to the police informant, is Monsignor Pascucci, personal secretary of Pompili.

32. ACS, MI, FP "Pompili," informatore n. 35, Città del Vaticano, 30 marzo 1930.

33. Just before Pompili's death, while the Roman clergy, who had long served under the irascible cardinal, worried about his health, the pope, according to an informant, expressed gratitude that he would soon be freed from a bad nightmare. ACS, MI, FP "Pompili," informatore n. 40 (=Virginio Troiani di Merfa), Città del Vaticano, 25 aprile 1931. See also Fiorentino 1999, pp. 131–38.

34. ACS, MI, FP "Pizzardo," informatore n. 40, Città del Vaticano, 9 luglio 1931.

35. Four years later another informant reported that Pizzardo was widely known in the Vatican by the nickname "Rasputin." ACS, MI, FP "Pizzardo," informatore n. 35, Roma, 13 agosto 1929; ACS, MI, FP "Pizzardo," informatore n. 390, Milano, 6 giugno 1933. As I've previously noted, these police informants' reports need to be treated with care.

36. ACS, MI, FP "Pizzardo," informatore n. 52 (=Filippo Tagliavacche), Roma, 21 luglio 1933; Casella 2000, pp. 176–77.

37. O. Russell, *Annual Report 1924,* February 28, 1925, C 3342/3342/22, in Hachey 1972, p. 71, section 60. Britain at the time had only two cardinals. Pollard (2012) details the importance of U.S. funding of the Vatican in these years. For the reasons for and significance of Mundelein's appointment as cardinal, the first in the United States outside the east coast, see Kantowicz 1983, pp. 165–66.

38. Fogarty 1996, p. 556.

39. ACS, MI, FP "Pizzardo," informatore n. 40, Roma 14 novembre 1929. Over the next several years, constant rumors would swirl around the Vatican that Pizzardo was about to be appointed to a nunciature abroad. Germany, the United States, and Poland were all mentioned as destinations at one time or another. See ACS, MI, FP "Pizzardo." But each time Pizzardo pesuaded the pope to let him stay in the Vatican.

40. Borgongini's own description of his new job is telling: "Here one writes everything by dictation. The Holy Father dictates to the Cardinal [secretary of state]; the Cardinal to me and I dictate to my assistant." Quoted in Guasco 2012. Father Martina (2003, p. 237) similarly describes Borgongini's abilities as "modest" and points out that when the pope needed a more "authoritative" intermediary with Mussolini, he turned to Tacchi Venturi.

41. FCRSE, part XIV, p. 72, Perth to Halifax, April 26, 1938, R 4359/280/22.

42. ACS, MI, PP, b. 154, informatore n. 40, Città del Vaticano, 20 ottobre 1930. In a meeting with Monsignor Pizzardo in June 1930, De Vecchi complained that he had been in office practically a whole year, but the pope had not yet seen fit to give him any papal honorific. He recorded in his diary that he would take up the question the next day with Borgongini; see De Vecchi 1998, pp. 216–17.

43. But Borgongini would not be put off, mentioning the pope's further unhappiness about the recent government seizure of a number of Catholic newspapers. The argument he adopted with Mussolini was one that Tacchi Venturi had long been using with him. Indeed, it was an argument that, as the nuncio told the Duce, he had "heard many times from the Holy Father, that is, that the Church's enemies are Fascism's enemies, and that those who fight the Church cannot be friends of Fascism." ASV, ANI, pos. 23, fasc. 1, ff. 8r–18r. Soon after the announcement of the Lateran Accords, senior figures in the Church warned all who would listen that various nefarious "sects" were devoted to destroying both the Roman Catholic Church and the Fascist regime. Within two weeks of the February 11

signing, for example, the bishop of Padua, Elia Dalla Costa (who two years later would be made a cardinal by Pius XI), thanked God for giving Mussolini "great intelligence and great courage." In his sermon at Padua's cathedral on February 24, he told his flock that Mussolini had needed all his strength "to confront the fury of the conspiracy of all the sects that are both enemies of God and enemies of Italy." Quoted in Perin 2010, p. 152.

CHAPTER 10: EATING AN ARTICHOKE

1. ASV, ANI, pos. 22, fasc. 10, ff. 2r–3r, Borgongini a Mussolini, 12 settembre 1929.
2. ASMAE, AISS, b. 2, Mussolini a Borgongini, 15 settembre 1929.
3. While Mussolini claimed that September 20 proved to be a good thing for all, argued Borgongini, "all of the popes, from Pius IX to Pius XI, have always believed the opposite, and so have all Catholics." ASMAE, AISS, b. 2, Borgongini a Mussolini, 18 settembre 1929.
4. Cannistraro and Sullivan 1993, p. 328.
5. E. Mussolini 1957, pp. 40–50, 103; De Felice 1974, pp. 19–20; De Felice 1981, p. 274n38; Morgan 1941, pp. 109–11, 138–39; Festorazzi 2010, pp. 80–81; Motti 2003, pp. 198–99; E. Mussolini 1957, p. 39.
6. CC 1929 IV, pp. 548–52; "La solenne visita dei Sovrani d'Italia al Santo Padre," OR, 6 dicembre 1929, p. 1. Cardinal Merry del Val was afraid that Borgongini—"who is capable of anything"—might bow to the government pressure and get the pope to reciprocate the royal visit, something the former secretary of state thought beneath the pope's dignity. Tardini 1988, p. 450n32. The following week, marking the first anniversary of the Lateran Accords, OR recalled the event as the product of "the charity of a Father, the wisdom of a King, and the genius of a Statesman"; "XI Febbraio," OR, 11 dicembre 1929, p. 1.
7. E. Mussolini 1957, p. 135.
8. Confalonieri 1957, p. 160; CC 1930 I, pp. 80–81. Although a number of cardinals had come to Rome for the final celebrations of the Holy Year, including two from the United States, none were told of the visit and so none got to witness it. NARA, M561, reel 1, John W. Garrett, U.S. embassy in Rome, to secretary of state, December 20, 1929; "475,000 Visit in Rome for Pope's Jubilee," CDT, December 19, 1929, p. 35.
9. Baudrillart 2003, pp. 381–83 (6 décembre 1929), quoted in Durand 2010, p. 44.
10. R. Mussolini 2006, p. 97.
11. Moseley 1999, p. 5.
12. E. Mussolini 1957, pp. 122–24.
13. Thomas à Kempis's Caracciolo 1982, pp. 102–5; Innocenti 1992, p. 14; Moseley 1999, pp. 4, 7, 11; Morgan 1941, p. 114.
14. CC, 1930 II, p. 284. "This business of the pope's gift to the newlyweds," De Vecchi (1998, pp. 147–48) wrote in his diary that day, "is terrific for public opinion not only in Italy but throughout the world." Later that year, just before Ciano and Edda left for China, where Ciano would take up a new diplomatic post, the pope gave them a private audience and presented them with leather-bound editions of Thomas à Kempis's *Imitation of Christ,* bearing the pope's autograph. "Son-in-law and Daughter of Il Duce Chat with the Pope," CDT, September 9, 1930, p. 31.
15. Moseley 1999, p. 15.
16. DDI, series 7, vol. 9, n. 231, 26 agosto 1930. Borgongini's draft of the letter, with corrections, is found in ASV, ANI, pos. 23, fasc. 2, ff. 165r–169r.
17. The Duce ordered the destruction of historic palaces and churches, in the words of one historian, "as if they were a sterile lava flow that had descended on Rome rather than on Pompey in the days of its glory." De Felice 1974, pp. 52–53; Insolera 1976, pp. 128, 132–33; Painter 2005, pp. 22–23.

18. Navarra 2004, pp. 17, 44; De Felice 1968, pp. 55–56; Festorazzi 2010, p. 94; Cannistraro and Sullivan 1993, p. 298; ASV, ANI, pos. 22, fasc. 10, ff. 23r–34r, 4 settembre 1930.

19. R. Mussolini 1974, p. 97.

20. "You are perfectly correct from a logical point of view," Mussolini told the nuncio, referring to his argument that with Conciliation it made sense to drop the contested holiday. "But I am not entirely wrong from the viewpoint of *opportunità*."

21. "No, you are a believer," replied the nuncio, "and the Lord is clearly helping Your Excellency." See Borgongini's lengthy account of the meeting in his letter to the new secretary of state, Eugenio Pacelli. ASV, ANI, pos. 22, fasc. 10, ff. 23r–34r, 4 settembre 1930.

22. ASV, ANI, pos. 23, fasc. 10, ff. 53r–62r, Borgongini a Pacelli, 15 settembre 1930.

23. Both meetings between Borgongini and Mussolini are described in ASV, ANI, pos. 23, fasc. 2, ff. 204r–213r, Borgongini a Eugenio Pacelli, segretario di stato, 15 settembre 1930.

24. A number of historians maintain that Mussolini was constructing a civil religion in Italy. The Fascists themselves used that term: in 1930, one of the men closest to Mussolini described Fascism as "a civil and political religion . . . the religion of Italy." By the late 1920s, Augusto Turati, head of the Fascist Party, was devising a system of ritual and myth modeled on the Catholic Church. He called on all Italians to believe in the Duce and Fascism without question, "as one believes in the divinity." After the Lateran Accords, Turati published a Fascist catechism; one of its primary items of faith was "the subordination of everyone to the Head's will." Mussolini, like the pope, was said to be infallible in matters of faith, and his judgment, like the pope's, was not to be questioned. The "man of Providence" knew what was best for his flock. Gentile 1995, pp. 144–45; Gentile 1993, pp. 124, 293–94.

25. Mack Smith 1982, p. 168. In February 1933 the head of the PNF, Achille Starace, announced that henceforth all official government acts would contain the name DUCE only in capital letters. Falasca-Zamponi 1997, p. 61.

26. Gentile 1995, pp. 144–45; Gentile 1993, pp. 124, 293–94. A reporter for Mussolini's newspaper, *Il Popolo d'Italia,* stationed in China, passed on a special request. The Catholic missionaries in Wei Chou wanted a photograph of the Duce, hoping especially to get one he himself had signed. The journalist explained, "These are people who are facing unheard of difficulties and dangers, but are raising the voice of Italy by speaking to the Chinese of Mussolini as a God." Later, upon receiving a signed photograph, the deeply appreciative head of the mission expressed his thanks for "our Duce, whom God has chosen to guide the great destiny of our Fatherland." Franzinelli and Marino, 2003, p. *xii.*

27. MacKinnon 1927, p. 81.

28. Ibid., p. xv.

29. Navarra 2004, p. 65.

CHAPTER 11: THE RETURN OF THE NATIVE SON

1. A British envoy, looking back on these years, would later express surprise that the much more experienced Gasparri had adapted so well to the pope's "autocratic ways." C. Wingfield, *Annual Report 1934,* January 12, 1935, R 402/402/22, in Hachey 1972, p. 286, section 133.

2. Ottaviani 1969, pp. 502–3.

3. Rhodes 1974, p. 40.

4. Morgan 1944, p. 137. The famous phrase—also found on the masthead of *L'Osservatore romano,* derives from Matthew 16:18, where Jesus says "and upon this rock I will build my church. And the gates of hell shall not prevail against it."

5. ACS, MI, DAGRA, b. 113, 8 novembre 1926; ACS, MCPG, b. 155. These reports should be read with some caution, for the "noted Vatican informer" clearly had it in for Gasparri.

According to a December 1927 secret police report, Gasparri also distrusted Tacchi Venturi, whom he accused of playing a double game, sharing confidential Vatican information with the Duce; ACS, MI, DAGR, b. 1320. At the time of the commotion over the presumed assassination attempt against Tacchi Venturi, Gasparri had tried to turn the pope against him by suggesting that the episode had been concocted by the Jesuit for some obscure purpose. ACS, MI, DAGR, b. 1320, 5 settembre 1928. Further evidence of Gasparri's efforts to displace Tacchi Venturi comes from a police report to Mussolini in 1928, informing him of Gasparri's opposition to the Jesuit's involvement in the negotiations over the Roman question; ACS, CR, "Appunto," undated report on Principe Pignatelli. The police informant also reported that Monsignors Caccia and De Samper, the pope's master of ceremonies and his majordomo, blamed Gasparri for their failure to be named cardinals and were poisoning the pontiff against him.

6. The letter is published in Martini 1960b, pp. 129–30.

7. ACS, MI, FP "Pietro Gasparri," Città del Vaticano, 8 ottobre 1929. Recently, with Borgongini's appointment as nuncio to Italy, Pizzardo had been named to replace him as secretary of the Congregation of Extraordinary Ecclesiastical Affairs.

8. De Vecchi 1983, p. 144. When the Portuguese ambassador to the Vatican came to see him in October, Gasparri confided that he had offered his resignation, but the pope had not yet accepted it. He added that Mussolini had become a "fearful nightmare" for the pope, who, angered at pressures on Catholic Action youth groups, called him a "persecutor of young Catholics." ACS, MI, FP "Pietro Gasparri," Città del Vaticano, 23 ottobre 1929.

9. As early as November 1928, *The New York Times* was already reporting not only the rumor that Gasparri would be replaced but also that he would be replaced by Eugenio Pacelli. "Say Nuncio Will Be Raised," NYT, November 19, 1928, p. 2.

10. Informatore n. 35, Rome, 2 ottobre 1929, in Fiorentino 1999, p. 238.

11. Coco 2009, pp. 176–77. The pope may have considered another factor in his decision as well: rumor had it that Cerretti, while in Paris, had often been seen in the company of women.

12. ACS, MI, FP "Cerretti," informatore n. 35, Roma, 14 dicembre 1929.

13. It was not going to be easy, the ambassador concluded, to find a person of his quality to replace him in Berlin. ASMAE, AISS, b. 4, n. 6361, Berlino, 10 dicembre 1929.

14. Coppa 2011, pp. 20–21; O'Shea 2011, p. 81.

15. Coppa 2011, p. 1; O'Shea 2011, pp. 74–80.

16. Wolf (2010, p. 36) finds strong evidence that in these years Pacelli was linked to Umberto Benigni's notorious network of informants but was savvy enough to avoid becoming "discredited by too open an association with Benigni and his 'secret service.'"

17. Coppa 2011, p. 30.

18. Noel 2008, pp. 38–39.

19. Wolf 2010, p. 74. Among the unorthodox practices in the German Church that Pacelli worked to stamp out was allowing women to sing in church choirs during High Mass; ibid., p. 61.

20. Ibid., pp. 75–79.

21. Ventresca 2013, p. 55. In September 1929 Monsignor Spellman visited Berlin; Eugenio Pacelli met him at the train station and hosted him during his stay. The American priest was impressed with his charm. "Seven out of ten people," Spellman wrote to his mother on September 8, "consider him the most likely next Holy Father." This prescience was especially impressive as the fifty-two-year-old Pacelli was not yet a cardinal. Gannon 1962, pp. 66–67.

22. Papin 1977, p. 42.

23. Charles-Roux 1947, pp. 74–77.

24. Ibid., p. 77.

25. Papin 1977, pp. 42–43.

26. McCormick 1957, p. 75.

27. Pacelli asked Pascalina to do her best to duplicate the congenial living quarters he had grown accustomed to in Germany. When he heard that the German bishops, in honor of his appointment as secretary of state, were planning to give him a new pectoral cross, he let them know that he would prefer German furniture. Pascalina then arranged for the furniture to be selected and sent from Germany. On the new secretary of state's desk, visitors could see a little silver plaque containing the names of all the German bishops who had paid for it; Schad 2008, pp. 53, 62–65.

28. For more on Pacelli's "fogli di udienza," see Pagano 2010.

29. Charles-Roux 1947, pp. 74–75, 197; Ottaviani 1969, pp. 502–4.

30. Tornielli 2007, p. 164.

31. Ibid., pp. 164–65.

32. ACS, MI, PP, b. 154, informatore n. 35 (=Bice Pupeschi), Città del Vaticano, 5 marzo 1930.

33. O. Forbes, *Annual Report 1930,* February 13, 1931, C 1077/1077/22, in Hachey 1972, p. 196, section 147.

34. Quoted in Ventresca 2012, p. 288.

35. Martin 1996, pp. 18–19.

36. As Wolf (2010, p. 138) put it, "The pope tended to be impulsive and effervescent, and sometimes not the least shy about making injurious statements; his secretary of state, the consummate diplomat, was always restrained and balanced, intent on avoiding anything that might feed the flames."

37. ACS, MI, FP "Gasparri," informatore n. 42 (=Bianca D'Ambrosio), Roma, 21 gennaio 1930.

38. ACS, MI, FP "Gasparri," informatore n. 35, Città del Vaticano, 15 febbraio 1930.

39. ACS, MI, FP "Gasparri," informatore n. 35, Città del Vaticano, 4 marzo 1930.

40. ACS, MI, FP "Cerretti," informatore n. 35, Città del Vaticano, 29 maggio 1930. Monsignor Spellman, in a letter to his mother from Berlin in the fall of 1929, remarked that Pacelli and Pizzardo were good friends; see Gannon 1962, pp. 66–67. "Taking advantage of the pontiff's personal benevolence toward him, Pizzardo, with an ability that recalls that of Cardinal Richelieu, has insinuated himself into the good graces of the pontiff in such a way that he is free to maneuver in any way he likes." So reported a Vatican police informant in the fall of 1929. A creature of the Vatican, Pizzardo, according to the informant, had won the protection of key cardinals by "his ingratiating manner and Jesuitical unctuousness"; see Fiorentino 1999, pp. 89, 224–25. His staff was not entirely enamored of him. In 1934 all the major figures in the Vatican secretary of state office were invited to Rome's Grand Hotel for a lunch in honor of a visiting American bishop. Monsignor Domenico Tardini, Pizzardo's chief assistant, was there, as were Ottaviani and Borgongini. But Pizzardo was missing, busy giving a speech to the ecclesiastical assistants of Catholic Action. "If instead of going to give the talk," noted Tardini, "he had come to the luncheon, it would have been better for him and . . . for the assistants of Catholic Action." Tardini, diary entry, ca. 1934, quoted in Casula 1988, p. 87; the ellipsis is in the original.

41. "Italian State Gives Supplice to Pope," NYT, February 12, 1930, p. 5.

42. De Vecchi 1998, pp. 182–83 (30–31 maggio 1930).

43. Ibid., pp. 194–95 (11 giugno 1930). On Tuesday, June 24, while attending a senate session, Mussolini spotted De Vecchi and asked how everything was going at the Vatican. The ambassador replied that on balance things were going well, but "the pope continued to be that very difficult person he has always been." Mussolini asked about the pope's health, and De Vecchi replied that the French ambassador had told him that the pope's prostate was giving him problems, but that the doctors did not think an operation would

help. When Mussolini replied that he was sorry to hear it, De Vecchi told him that should it come to it, a change in pope might not be a bad thing. Mussolini, having apparently already heard the reports of the problematic papal prostate, ignored De Vecchi's comment and asked if it was true that the pope had requested an apparatus for his use during the long ceremonies in the Sistine Chapel so that he could relieve himself there. Ibid., pp. 209–10.

44. Ibid., pp. 212–14 (27 giugno 1930).

CHAPTER 12: CARDINAL PACELLI HANGS ON

1. "Fascists Trample Portrait of Pope; Vatican Is Guarded," NYT, May 28, 1931, p. 1. The following day, *The New York Times* published yet another front-page story on the crisis: "Mussolini Checks Anti-Catholic Riots."

2. Arnaldo Cortesi, "Catholic Meddling Charged by Fascisti," NYT, May 27, 1931, p. 1; Casella 2009, p. 137.

3. ASV, AESS, b. 430a, fasc. 342, ff. 37, 23 maggio 1931. The pope had another problem on his mind as well. In early May, Pacelli told the pope that Hermann Göring wanted to meet with him during his upcoming visit to Rome. Göring at the time was leader of the Nazi parliamentary delegation. The pope refused and told Pacelli he should not meet with him either, but Pacelli did arrange for Göring to meet with his undersecretary, Pizzardo. Wolf 2010, pp. 148–49.

4. De Vecchi 1998, p. 225. Reports from the prefects over the next few days chronicle the shutdown of the Catholic Action youth groups and the protests lodged by the local bishops. ACS, CR, b. 33.

5. Falconi 1967, pp. 201–2.

6. Arnaldo Cortesi, "Pius XI Charges Fascisti with Hate and Violence; Four Bombings in Bologna," NYT, June 1, 1931, p. 1. Later, the Vatican daily reported that more than 5,000 local male Catholic Action youth groups and about 10,000 female groups were shut down, affecting 800,000 members: "In margine alle polemiche," OR, 10 luglio 1931, p. 1.

7. When a number of southern Italian parishes went ahead with the holiday celebrations anyway, the pope ordered their priests to suspend all church public functions until further notice. Arnaldo Cortesi, "Pope Shifts Leader of Catholic Action: Punishes Parishes," NYT, June 11, 1931, p. 1.

8. ASMAE, AISS, b. 2, fasc. 6, Il segretario particolare di S.E. Il Capo del Governo a De Vecchi, 13 aprile 1931. The accompanying "pro-memoria" is dated 9 aprile 1931.

9. Martini 1960a, pp. 578–79.

10. Coco 2009, pp. 214–15.

11. It also claimed that many cardinals objected to the pope's recent actions, naming four in particular, among them Pietro Gasparri. The pope was furious. He told Monsignor Tardini to get in a car immediately and visit the four cardinals. Each would be required to issue a formal denial, to be published in the Vatican newspaper. "I have always been, and I will always be with the pope," wrote Cardinal Gasparri. Coco 2009, pp. 217–18.

12. Ibid., pp. 222, 242–43.

13. He added, "and it was clear that Monsignor Borgongini"—also present at the meeting— "was on the other."

14. MAESI, vol. 266, 80–81, 10 juillet 1931.

15. Coco 2009, pp. 241–42.

16. DDI, series 7, vol. 10, n. 322. "I didn't want it," De Vecchi (1998, pp. 267–68) would later quote Pacelli as saying of the escalation of the conflict with Mussolini. "It is the wish of my superior" (diary entry for July 11, 1931). The account of Pacelli's meeting with Talamo comes from Dino Grandi's diary. Coco 2009, p. 239.

17. The issue was put out five hours earlier than normal that day and was practically sold out before government agents realized what had happened and seized the remaining copies; Binchy 1970, pp. 522–23. Binchy reports that several hundred copies of the encyclical were smuggled out of Rome in a plane piloted by the future cardinal archbishop of New York, Francis Spellman, bound for Paris. It is not clear where Binchy gets the idea that Spellman piloted a plane, which seems improbable. Morgan (1939, pp. 186–87) interviewed Spellman about the episode. His account confirms that the pope called Spellman to his library and handed him the copies of the encyclical with instructions to ensure they were published abroad, and that Spellman then did get them across the French border and to Paris, where he gave the copies to various American news services. De Vecchi's diary (1998, p. 257) reports that, according to Monsignor Pizzardo, "the Pope is suffering greatly, he is not eating and he sleeps very little; he lives in anxiety and angst."

18. Quoted from the text of the encyclical as published in CC, 9 luglio 1931 III, pp. 97–122.

19. *Non abbiamo bisogno,* encyclical of Pope Pius XI, English translation, http://www.vatican.va /holy_father/pius_xi/encyclicals/documents/hf_p-xi_enc_29061931_non-abbiamo-bisogno _en.html. This translation omits the phrase "and regime," found in the original Italian text, which I have restored. The parenthetical clarification of "Fascist" Party appears in the official Vatican translation. On the pope's effort to make clear he was not opposing the Fascist regime as such, see also Moro 2008, p. 423.

20. Garzonio 1996, pp. 58–59.

21. Mussolini, too, was eager to put the battle behind him. With a few exceptions, the Fascist newspapers greeted the encyclical with moderate and respectful tones. *Il Lavoro fascista,* identified with the extreme anticlerical wing of the PNF, was among the exceptions, accusing the pope of serving the interests of the international anti-Fascist movement. It also repeated widespread rumors that saw the origin of the crisis in Monsignor Pizzardo's ambitions to take Cardinal Pacelli's place as secretary of state. In this view, Pizzardo—the Vatican official responsible for overseeing Catholic Action—was working in league with *L'Osservatore romano* editor Giuseppe Dalla Torre on behalf of anti-Fascist forces, while Pacelli supported collaboration between the pope and the Fascist regime; MAESI, vol. 266, ff. 64–66.

22. Gentil, the French chargé d'affaires to the Vatican, who was present, reported on this to the French foreign minister, in MAEI, vol. 266, 110–112, 20 juillet 1931.

23. ASV, AESI, pos. 849, vol. 3, fasc. 519, f. 79r. By mid-July both sides were working to put the battle behind them. At two A.M. on July 17, a bomb went off in the Vatican. The explosion woke up many in the city—although the pope slept through it—and thousands in nearby areas of Rome. Pacelli was said to have heard it go off while he was still at work in his office. A Vatican attendant had found the homemade bomb the previous evening inside St. Peter's Basilica, hidden under a portable pulpit. Papal Gendarmes had inspected the metal cylinder and, hearing no ticking, concluded it was likely a hoax. To be on the safe side, they had left it in the middle of a field on Vatican grounds for the night, before deciding what to do. It was there it exploded, leaving a big hole and uprooting trees twenty yards away. The Fascist press attributed the bomb to anti-Fascists eager to worsen the conflict between the regime and the Vatican, and the Vatican did nothing to contradict this view. Arnaldo Cortesi, "Bomb Roar at Night Alarms the Vatican," NYT, July 18, 1931, p. 1.

24. ASV, AESI, pos. 849, vol. 3, fasc. 519, ff. 80r–80v.

25. ACS, CR, b. 68, Tacchi Venturi a Mussolini, 25 luglio 1931. The previous day the pope had told Pacelli about the message he was sending to Mussolini via Tacchi Venturi, reminding the Duce that the pope had refrained from condemning him or Fascism as such, but only wanted a satisfactory way out of the impasse. Even in Masonic France, the pope told Pacelli, Catholic associations enjoyed more freedom than they did in Italy. ASV, APAC, b. 430a, fasc. 343, ff. 21.

26. Far from convinced that his successor was up to the task, Gasparri included a script for him to use in talking to the pope. It read: "Most Blessed Father, I come as your most humble son to let Your Holiness know what I feel from my conscience. I am extremely upset at the impasse that the negotiations with Mussolini have reached. It seems to me that Your Holiness, who has said he does not want to humiliate anyone, would do a fatherly act by giving Father Tacchi Venturi the order not to insist on the *conditio sine qua non* and go right ahead with the note that would bring the conflict to an end forever." ASV, AESI, pos. 849, vol. 3, fasc. 519, ff. 91r–92v.

    Even as he was trying to get the pope to let up, Gasparri was also peppering Mussolini with unsolicited advice. On July 14, professing to be the Duce's "friend and admirer" (a phrase he repeated before his signature), Gasparri pleaded with him not to do anything to worsen the conflict. ASV, AESS, pos. 515, fasc. 530, p. 83r, Gasparri a Mussolini, 14 luglio 1931. Then in a letter apparently sent after his meeting with Tacchi Venturi, Gasparri told the Duce that he had just been briefed on the Jesuit's mission. Proclaiming himself an "admirer and friend of Your Excellency," he begged Mussolini to take this new opportunity to end the conflict between church and state. ASV, AESS, pos. 515, fasc. 530, pp. 80r–80v, Gasparri a Mussolini, n.d. An annotation by Domenico Tardini explains that the letter dated from late July or the first days of August, but there is no proof that it was sent.

27. Curiously, the French diplomat attributed Pacelli's lack of influence to the pope's anger at his brother. The pope blamed Francesco Pacelli for not foreseeing the regime's move against Catholic Action and not ensuring that the concordat had clearer language protecting it. MAEI, vol. 266, 122–24, 6 août 1931, Gentil au Ministre des Affaires Étrangères. Rumors were circulating that Pacelli would be replaced as secretary of state as soon as the Catholic Action crisis was resolved. "Pacelli to Quit Soon, the Vatican Indicates," NYT, August 13, 1931, p. 8.

28. The typed version of this in Mussolini's private papers refers to "Pio IX" rather than Pio XI; perhaps it was a Freudian slip. ACS, CR, b. 68, Roma, 2 settembre 1931.

29. "L'Accordo fra la Santa Sede e il governo italiano per l'Azione cattolica," CC 1931 III, pp. 549–52. The second paragraph dealt with Mussolini's objection to the existence of separate Catholic Action groups linked to particular professions: they risked competing with the Fascist professional societies, which had a monopoly on the organization of labor. Professional Catholic Action groups were to limit their scope to religious activities and give their full support to the Fascist regime's professional organizations. The final point specified that local Catholic Action groups were not to engage in any athletic activity, as all organized sports were to come under the authority of the Fascist sports groups. This was no small matter, since sports had been one of the most important attractions in recruiting boys to local Catholic Action chapters; see De Felice 1974, p. 275.

30. De Felice 1974, p. 263.

31. Francesco Ferrari quoted in Malgeri 1994, p. 57. Italy's foremost historian of Fascism came to the same conclusion. "It seems to us," wrote Renzo De Felice (1974, pp. 270–71), "to be beyond debate that at the time the agreement represented a defeat for the Church."

32. MAEI, vol. 266, 153–55, Gentil au Ministre des Affaires Étrangères, 8 septembre 1931. However, on his return from his summer holiday, Fontenay reported that on September 3 the pope convened a secret meeting of eleven cardinals, summoning Gasparri back to Rome from his summer mountain retreat, and of the eleven, ten expressed support for the deal he had struck. MAEI, vol. 266, 174–80, Fontenay au Ministre des Affaires Étrangères, 29 septembre 1931. Given the pope's forceful personality and the consequences that a cardinal would suffer for incurring the pope's wrath, it is not clear how revealing this "vote" is.

33. MAEI, vol. 266, 167–69, Gentil au Ministre des Affaires Étrangères, 17 septembre 1931.
34. ASV, ANI , pos. 23, fasc. 3, ff. 46r–48r, Borgongini-Duca, handwritten memorandum, "Dopo il conflitto," n.d.

CHAPTER 13: MUSSOLINI IS ALWAYS RIGHT

1. De Vecchi to Mussolini, January 18, 1933, quoted in De Vecchi 1998, p. 53n60. An informant described Ciriaci as "an intelligent, able man, accommodating and compliant in the relations between the highest Catholic organization in the Kingdom over which he presides and the organs of the Fascist State." ACS, MI, FP "Ciriaci," informatore no. 390, "Orientamento in senso nazionale e verso il Regime da parte del Comm. Ciriaci," 18 gennaio 1933.
2. Moro 1981, pp. 289–91. The Fascist regime, Moro writes, encouraged this moralizing campaign, but as I will argue in this chapter, this is only partly true. In many cases the Church's moralizing campaign pushed the regime further than it wanted to go. The campaign, calling on local Catholic Action members to report offending behavior to the local police authorities, began in the 1920s. A seventy-two-page booklet, *Per la difesa della moralità*, was already in its fourth edition in 1928, published by the Central Secretariat for Morality of national Catholic Action. Praising the Fascist government's efforts to combat "the disastrous effects of freedom that has degenerated into license," it offered boilerplate language for local groups to use in sending denunciations in to the local authorities. ASV, AESI, pos. 929, vol. 1, fasc. 615, f. 35.
3. The Fascist press, taking note, reported what it called Pius XI's "holy struggle against the immorality of female fashion." "Il papa contro la moda femminile," *Il Regime fascista*, 22 giugno 1926, p. 2.
4. These controls were to be enforced through the licenses granted to beachfront establishments. ARSI, TV, b. 7, fasc. 393, "Circolare per tutti i prefetti dal Ministero dell'Interno, 18 giugno 1926; Oggetto: bagni." On June 27, 1926, the minister sent a copy of the order to Tacchi Venturi along with a letter showing how seriously the government was taking the papal concern. In an audience with a Catholic girls' group that month, the pope called for a national crusade against women's immoral dress. In audiences with women's groups, he regularly denounced current female fashions. The outside world, he warned one such group in June, did all it could to seduce them into forgetting even the most elementary sense of female dignity. "Il papa contro la moda femminile," *Il Regime fascista*, 22 giugno 1926, p. 2. By 1928 Tacchi Venturi, following the pope's instructions, was lobbying with government ministers to extend the government's repressive action against girls' dress both in school and in public. Immodest female clothing, he argued, was a great source of corruption. If the government made it a crime for a woman to wear a dress that failed to go well below her knees, it "would be of huge consolation to the Vicar of Christ." ARSI, TV, b. 15, fasc. 1067, 26 novembre 1928. Tacchi Venturi's note bears his annotation "presentato a S.E. il 26 novembre 1928." S.E., or "Sua Eccellenza" (His Excellency), could refer to Mussolini but could also refer to one of the government ministers. Bressan (1980, pp. 106–8) recounts the lavish attention that the pages of *L'Osservatore romano* devoted to questions of "immorality" and to pressuring the government authorities to take more aggressive action.
5. ACS, CR, b. 68, Tacchi Venturi a Mussolini, 3 febbraio 1929. A copy of Tacchi Venturi's letter is found in his own archive: ARSI, TV, b. 16, fasc. 1133.
6. In order to raise healthy women, *La Civiltà cattolica* (1928 II, pp. 367–72) explained, it was "not necessary to train them to jump four meters." Both the American embassy in Rome and the British embassy to the Holy See felt the pope's protest over the girls' gym-

nastics event to be worth reporting to their governments. NARA, M530, reel 2, Henry Fletcher to secretary of state, n. 1691, May 11, 1928; H. G. Chilton, *Annual Report 1928,* May 9, 1929, C 3397/3397/22, in Hachey 1972, p. 142, section 55.

7. CC 1930 I, pp. 460–61. In a late 1932 meeting, when Borgongini handed Mussolini a copy of the latest issue of *La Civiltà cattolica,* the Duce waved it away, saying he already knew what it said, adding, "it's a journal that I always read very carefully." ASV, ANI, pos. 23, fasc. 4, ff. 47r–48r, Borgongini a Pacelli, 22 novembre 1932.

8. "If I were to prohibit the competition," said Mussolini, returning to the subject at hand, "and people discovered that I had done it on orders from the Holy Father, all hell would break loose." ASV, ANI, pos. 23, fasc. 3, ff. 28r–34r, Borgongini to Pacelli, 14 febbraio 1931. This was one papal request he rejected. On earlier papal protests over girls' gymnastics and athletic events, see CC 1928 II, pp. 367–72; ASV, AESI, pos. 773, fasc. 317, ff. 77r–85r, 28 settembre 1929; CC 1930 I, p. 460. In fact, the Fascist regime's policies regarding women were mixed; some were much in harmony with Church teachings, like opposition to birth control and measures to discourage women from working outside the home; others supported girls' and women's recreational activities that the Church disapproved of. See among other works on Fascism and women, De Grazia 1992.

9. ASV, AESI, pos. 902, fasc. 596, ff. 49r–50r.

10. Ibid., f. 51r, 16 settembre 1932.

11. The next time the bishop wrote to call for state action, he wrote directly to Monsignor Giuseppe Pizzardo, one of the men closest to the pope and the Vatican official then responsible for Catholic Action: "This year is worse. From morning to evening in every street and in the little piazza many women (especially foreigners and those from northern Italy) are seen dressed in such an indecent manner that it is a nauseating spectacle. . . . Could not the Central Authority at the Head of the Government be made to take an interest in this?" ASV, AESI, pos. 902, fasc. 596, f. 52r, 20 agosto 1933.

12. On February 23, 1933, Augusto Ciriaci, national president of Catholic Action, wrote directly to Mussolini to praise him for all he had done to date and to indicate the areas where greater enforcement efforts were necessary. Catholic Action would continue to collaborate with the regime, wrote Ciriaci, to contribute to the greatness of the Fatherland. The government should ban objectionable movies and plays, seize immoral magazines and books, and require women to wear modest dress. "We do not ask for new laws," concluded Ciriaci. "We ask only that the excellent existing laws—existing in fact in large part due to Your Excellency's wisdom and strength—be respected and applied with great vigor." ASV, AESI pos. 929, vol. 1, fasc. 616, ff. 31r–36r. By the 1930s, the pope's battle against revealing clothing dovetailed to some extent with Mussolini's pro-fertility campaign, which saw the liberation of women from their traditional domestic role as a cause of declining fertility. On July 11, 1933, for example, the government told newspaper editors not to publish pictures of naked women "because they constitute an anti-demographic element." Two years later Ciano complained about magazines publishing pictures of women in revealing bathing suits, again on grounds that they were "anti-demographic." Tranfaglia 2005, pp. 171, 177.

The pope's battle for public decency also took aim at the "scandal" of public dancing, in which men's and women's bodies touched. In June 1933, at the pope's request, Pacelli wrote to all the bishops in northern Italy, where the problem was thought to be particularly acute, asking them to report back on conditions in their dioceses. In response, the archbishop of Milan expressed the hope that the minister of internal affairs could be prevailed upon "to heed the voice of the Episcopate of northern Italy in this matter." To illustrate the seriousness of the problem, he included a recent letter he had received from the bishop of Cremona, reporting that the local Fascist organizations, most notably the *dopolavoro* ("after work") social groups, had made public dances "an organized industry." The police, the bishop complained, took little action. One of his parish priests had tried to persuade the head of one such group to hold dances less often, but he was told that many men joined precisely because of the dances. ASV, AESI, b. 935, fasc. 628, ff. 2r–3v. The Vatican's battle against public dancing continued through the end of Pius XI's papacy, much to the dismay of the Fascist hierarchy. Typical was the lament of Bonificio Pignatti, who in 1935 replaced Cesare De Vecchi as Mussolini's ambassador to the Holy See: "Unfortunately, as far as popular dances are concerned, the Holy See's attitude, from the Pope on down, is unshakeable and there is no hope of obtaining any change." ASMAE, APSS, b. 42, Pignatti a Starace, 10 settembre 1938.

13. ASV, AESS, pos. 430b, fasc. 360, f. 115, 14 marzo 1934. De Vecchi's reference to the government's silence regarding cases of clerical immorality may have in part been inspired by his spies' reports about cardinals said to be having relations with young boys, men, and girls. The skin on display did not have to be actual flesh to attract the pope's attention or induce him to act. In October 1937 the pope learned that nude statues had recently been put on display in a museum, so he sent Tacchi Venturi to have something done about it. The curator, who had heard of the pope's objection, assured Tacchi Venturi that the "four or five male statues that you deplored were immediately removed so that an abundant foliage of figs could be applied." ASV, AESI, pos. 985, fasc. 669, ff. 4r–5r.

14. The pope made his request through Tacchi Venturi. ACDF, S.O., 1930, 1413/30i, Tacchi Venturi a Cardinale Donato Sbarretti, S.O., 13 aprile 1933. Later that same year Tacchi Venturi presented the police head, Arturo Bocchini, with a list of foreign magazines, prepared by the central office of Catholic Action, that he wanted banned. After going through the list, Bocchini explained that he could not confiscate all the titles but promised to ban many of them. In reporting the matter to Pizzardo, Tacchi Venturi especially called his attention to the police chief's promise: if Tacchi Venturi were to bring other titles to his attention, his office would give his censorship requests very careful consideration. "Occasions to take advantage of his offer will, unfortunately, not be lacking!" Tacchi Venturi concluded, in his enthusiasm allowing himself an uncharacteristic exclamation point. AESI, pos. 929, vol. I, fasc. 617, ff. 2r–3r. For Tacchi Venturi's role in ensuring that articles dealing with subjects of interest to the Church in the influential *Enciclopedia italiana* met with Church approval, see Turi 2002.

15. ASV, AESI, pos. 669, fasc. 132, ff. 34r–35r, Tacchi Venturi a Gasparri, 23 gennaio 1929. The Vatican also exerted pressure on the government to prevent sex education in the public schools, as can be seen in an intercepted telephone call made by Pizzardo to the Italian embassy to the Holy See on April 25, 1935. ACS, MCPG, b. 165, n. 3093. A theatrical work could now be banned for offending the pope or stirring up disdain for "religious sentiment." Talbot 2007, pp. 148–49.

16. "Italy Bans Sex Appeal in Pictures," LAT, March 20, 1931, p. 4. Borgongini had urged Mussolini on January 19 to introduce stricter censorship over film and theater; he had found Mussolini not particularly sympathetic. ASV, ANI, b. 23, fasc. 3, Borgongini a Pacelli, 20 gennaio 1931.

17. Although the cases I discuss below focus on university professors, the great majority of the papal complaints to Mussolini regarded ex-priests who found jobs teaching in public schools, most commonly elementary schools. The pope insisted they be fired.

18. After a brief rehabilitation, his definitive excommunication came in January 1926. Leading up to the decision, the Holy Office asked Father Gemelli to examine Buonaiuti and offer his opinion; see Martina 2003, p. 238; Zambarbieri 1982a. The modernist professor, Gemelli reported back to the Vatican, was in need of treatment "not from the priesthood, but from professionals who assist unhappy psychic deviants." Quoted in Luzzatto 2010, p. 142.

19. In April 1924 Tacchi Venturi had met with then minister of education Giovanni Gentile to get him to remove Buonaiuti. Sale 2007, p. 335.

20. ARSI, TV, b. 9, fasc. 527, Tacchi Venturi a Gasparri.

21. In reporting this to Mussolini, Fedele advised Mussolini that bowing to papal pressure and subjecting university faculty appointments to the pope's approval would be a disaster. DDI, series 7, vol. 5, n. 11, Fedele a Mussolini, 11 febbraio 1927. As the pope kept up the pressure via Tacchi Venturi over the course of the year, Fedele finally called Buonaiuti in, explained the situation, and asked him to accept a research leave from his teaching post. Bonaiuti, upset, pointed out that there was no legal basis for keeping him from teaching but reluctantly agreed. "It is a huge concession made by the Government to the Holy See!" Fedele wrote to Mussolini in reporting the news. ACS, CR, b. 68, Fedele a Mussolini, 17 ottobre 1927.

22. Buonaiuti had lambasted Fascism as promoting the pagan worship of the state. Zambarbieri 1982a, p. 64; Goetz 2000.

23. The 1931 negotiations were handled by Borgongini and Dino Grandi, then Mussolini's foreign minister. ASV, ANI, pos. 23, fasc. 2, ff. 99r–101r, Borgongini a Pacelli, 4 giugno 1930; ASMAE, APSS, b. 6, Borgongini a Grandi, 17 aprile 1931; Grandi's undated reply is also found there. The minister of national education's advice to Grandi on the Saitta case is found in a memo published in DDI, series 7, vol. 10, n. 342, 19 giugno 1931.

24. Petacci 2010, pp. 129–30; R. Mussolini 2006, p. 88–89.

25. Navarra 2004, p. 52.

26. Mack Smith 1983, p. 6.

27. C. Drexel interview, December 1934, in De Felice 1974, p. 866.

28. H. Massis interview, September 1933, ibid., p. 854.

29. Fifty-one years old when he got to conduct a series of interviews with the Duce in March 1932, Ludwig was already famous for interviewing other world leaders, from modern Turkey's founder, Mustafa Atatürk, to Joseph Stalin.

30. Ludwig 1933, p. 62.

31. Ibid., pp. 126–27.

32. Cannistraro and Sullivan 1993, pp. 383–84; Urso 2003, pp. 193–94.

33. Cannistraro and Sullivan 1993.

34. Ludwig 1933, pp. 222–23.

35. Bosworth 2002, p. 243.

36. Monelli 1953, pp. 119–26. Such was the sacred power that now emanated from the dictator that his assistant, Navarra, was finding it difficult to recruit a barber willing to give him a shave. A policeman from Mussolini's security detail who had once been a barber finally agreed to do it, but as soon as he held the razor near the Duce's face, he began to shake uncontrollably. Navarra 2004, pp. 39–40.

37. Quoted in Franzinelli and Marino 2003, p. xi.

38. De Vecchi 1983, pp. 223–24.

39. Quoted in Franzinelli and Marino 2003, p. xii.

40. Bosworth 2002, pp. 44–46.

41. Quoted in Navarra 2004, p. 21.

42. De Felice 1974, pp. 174, 300–3.

43. Gentile (1993, pp. 283–85) reproduces extensive excerpts from the March 24, 1932, piece in *Il Popolo d'Italia*. For an analysis of the ritual aspects of Mussolini's speeches and their impact, see Galeotti 2000, pp. 49–50.

44. Franzinelli 1995, pp. 171–72. The membership number is from 1934. In April 1928 Tacchi Venturi congratulated the national head of the PNF on the recent promulgation of eight commandments to guide all Fascist female youth groups (commandment three: Love the Duce). But he noted a glaring omission—there was no mention of God—and to repair it proposed the addition of a ninth commandment: "Fear and love God, origin and source of all good." ARSI, TV, b. 13, fasc. 878, Tacchi Venturi a Augusto Turati, 28 aprile 1928.

Turati replied that the proposed addition was unnecessary, as it was already implied "in that all of the spirit that permeates these norms is the Christian and Catholic spirit." Ibid., Turati a Tacchi Venturi, 2 maggio 1928.

45. Franzinelli (1995, p. 140) remarks that the priests' behavior would be comic if it did not illustrate the appalling degree of servility that many clergy displayed toward their "holy Duce."

46. Brendon 2000, p. 133. The Duomo image is reproduced in Gentile 1993, p. 173.

47. ASV, AESI, pos. 812, fasc. 444, ff. 7r–13r, Pizzardo a Cazzani, 21 novembre 1932. In this case the bishop, Giovanni Cazzani, stood his ground, writing that it would be humiliating for a priest to do what was being suggested.

48. See Wolff 1985, pp. 239, 245; Bendiscioli 1982.

49. Goetz 2000; Falasca-Zamponi 1997, pp. 110, 203–4.

50. Quoted in Reineri 1978, p. 183.

51. Ninety-six percent of all eligible voters voted. See De Felice 1974, p. 313.

CHAPTER 14: THE PROTESTANT ENEMY AND THE JEWS

1. According to De Vecchi, the visit had nearly been canceled at the last minute, as the previous day Mussolini had been angered by the fact that *L'Osservatore romano* made no mention of the upcoming event. Only by intervening with Monsignor Pizzardo, and having the Vatican newspaper come out with a special afternoon edition that day with the news, did De Vecchi persuade Mussolini to relent and go through with the visit. De Vecchi 1983, pp. 219–21.

2. The next week a story announced that the visit would "almost certainly" take place that week. Arnaldo Cortesi, "Mussolini's Visit to Pope Arranged . . . Event May Occur Today," NYT, September 17, 1931, p. 13. The French ambassador reported that the visit had been fixed for September 19, but that Mussolini had backed out at the last minute, since such a visit, on the eve of the recently abolished September 20 holiday, "could be interpreted as a capitulation." MAEI, vol. 266, 178, Fontenay au Ministre des Affaires Étrangères, 29 septembre 1931.

3. MAEI, vol. 266, 209–11, Fontenay au Président du Conseil, Ministre des Affaires Étrangères, 17 janvier 1932.

4. Cardinal Pacelli reports this in his notes of November 27, based on a conversation with Tacchi Venturi. ASV, AESS, pos. 430b, fasc. 357, f. 68. On December 19, 1931, a note labeled "dictated by the Holy Father to the Most Eminent Pacelli," directed Tacchi Venturi to inform Mussolini that the pope had decided—"after some reflexion"—to accept the proposed February 11 date for the meeting. He was also to tell Mussolini that the pope would interpret it as an expression of Mussolini's atonement for infringing on the concordat by his recent treatment of Catholic Action. "I must say this because if Mussolini comes that day the Holy Father will receive him, will have him sit down, and then will speak and will tell him, perhaps while smiling, that he gladly accepted the proposed date . . . because he believes that [Mussolini] wished, with praiseworthy aim, to honorably make amends for the violation of articles 43 and 44 [the articles of the concordat allowing Catholic Action to function freely]." ARSI, TV, b. 20, fasc. 1524, Pacelli a Tacchi Venturi, 19 dicembre 1931.

5. A few days earlier Borgongini had gone to the Quirinal Palace at the pope's request to award King Victor Emmanuel III the Collar of the Supreme Order of Christ. "Dopo il conferimento dell'Ordine Supremo di Cristo a S.M. il Re d'Italia," OR, 7–8 gennaio 1932, p. 1. Then to complete the medley, the nuncio conferred the Great Cross of the Piano Order both on Cesare De Vecchi and on Foreign Minister Dino Grandi. "La Gran Croce dell'Ordine Piano al Ministro italiano Grandi e all'Ambasciatore De Vecchi," OR, 12 gen-

naio 1932, p. 2. The French ambassador to the Holy See was told in advance about the planned papal honors for the king, Mussolini, and the others. He was led to believe that the pope had decided to give them out in reaction to expressions of government displeasure that the honors that Mussolini had given Pacelli, Borgongini, and Tacchi Venturi had not been reciprocated. MAEI, vol. 266, 202–4, Fontenay au ministre des affaires étrangères, 8 janvier 1932.

6. "Nostre informazioni," OR, 12 febbraio 1932, p. 1. The incident of the ejected woman was described by Morgan (1939, pp. 190–97), who was present as an invited guest when it happened. It was not reported in the Vatican or Italian press.

7. The illustration appeared on the cover of *La Domenica del Corriere*, February 21, 1932. When the Italian edition of Emil Ludwig's book-length interviews with Mussolini was published, one of the paragraphs that most offended the pope was the Duce's description of how he had refused to bow or kiss the pope's ring. This paragraph and others that the pope found objectionable—including one where Mussolini said he thought people should be left to decide themselves how to worship God—were purged from the Italian edition after its first printing. MAEI, vol. 266, 255, Charles-Roux à président du conseil, 29 juillet 1932; ibid., 291–92, 27 ottobre 1932; Chiron 2006, p. 293. In July, according to De Vecchi's second-in-command at the Italian embassy, Mussolini said that in publishing his comments on the Church, "that big Jew betrayed me." ASV, AESI, pos. 887, fasc. 593, f. 42r, 15 luglio 1932. On November 10, Tacchi Venturi happily reported that a new edition of the Ludwig interview was just then being published—it had shrunk by five pages, all the objectionable passages in the section "Rome and the Church" having been deleted. ASV, AESI, pos. 667, fasc. 128, f. 48r.

8. David Darrah, "Pope and Duce Clasp Hands in Friendship Pact," CDT, February 12, 1932, p. 10; Arnaldo Cortesi, "Pope and Mussolini Show Warm Feeling in Vatican Meeting," NYT, February 12, 1932, p. 1.

9. Mussolini's handwritten report of his meeting with the pope addressed to the king can be found in ACS, CV, b. 1, fasc. 34; a published copy is available in DDI, series 7, vol. 11, n. 205. The pomp around the visit is described in CC 1932 I, pp. 480–81.

10. "Sgr. Mussolini and the Pope" [London] *Times,* February 12, 1932, p. 11.

11. E. Mussolini 1957, p. 135.

12. But Fontenay, the French ambassador to the Holy See, worried that the exchange of honors had given Italian Catholics the impression of "a sort of recognition of fascism by the Holy See." MAEI, vol. 266, 229–31, Fontenay à président du conseil, ministre des affaires étrangères, 4 mars 1932; and vol. 232–33, 10 mars 1932. Tacchi Venturi's letter to Mussolini thanking him for the honor is found in ACS, CR, b. 68, 7 marzo 1932. In a letter to the General of the Jesuit order, Tacchi Venturi also reported that De Vecchi had told him that Mussolini wanted to honor the Jesuits for all they had done to promote understanding between the Italian government and the Church. ARSI, TV, b. 20, fasc. 1534, Tacchi Venturi a Ledóchowski, 3 marzo 1932.

13. These comments were made in late 1932. MAEI, vol. 266, 298–99, Charles-Roux à président du conseil, 15 decembre 1932.

14. ASMAE, AISS, b. 4, protocollo 24, De Vecchi a Mussolini, Roma, 21 luglio 1929; De Vecchi 1998, pp. 15–16.

15. Arnaldo Cortesi, "Pope Pius at 75: Scholar and Leader," NYT *Magazine,* May 29, 1932, p. 3.

16. C. Wingfield, *Annual Report 1934,* January 12, 1935, R 402/402/22, in Hachey 1972, pp. 287–88, sections 138–40.

17. Tardini 1988, p. 296 (entry for 13 febbraio 1934); Charles-Roux 1947, p. 62.

18. Papin 1977, pp. 56, 62; Confalonieri 1957, p. 188; Ottaviani 1969, pp. 504–5.

19. Pierre van Paassen, "A Day with the Pope," BG, February 11, 1934, p. C5.

20. Tardini 1988, p. 313; Charles-Roux 1947, p. 23. On Tardini, see Riccardi 1982 and Casula 1988.

21. Tardini 1988, p. 355.

22. Confalonieri 1969, pp. 42–43.

23. R. H. Clive, *Annual Report 1933,* January 1, 1934, R 153/153/22, in Hachey 1972, p. 259, sections 117, 118; Agostino 1991, p. 19.

24. ARSI, TV, b. 8, fasc. 442, 446. In the months following the signing of the accords, Tacchi Venturi continued his pressure on the pope's behalf. In May 1930 he sent Mussolini a list of locations of Protestant churches in Italy. ARSI, TV, b. 19, fasc. 1408, "Protestanti. La situazione in Italia nel 1930," with draft of Tacchi Venturi a Mussolini, 3 maggio 1930.

25. ASV, ANI, pos. 23, fasc. 2, ff. 129r–130r, 4 giugno 1930.

26. "The Holy Father," Monsignor Pizzardo reported to the nuncio in February 1931, "has revealed that the true and serious danger that threatens the religious and national unity of Italians is to be found in the growing Protestant propaganda, about which the government does not seem to adequately concern itself." Mussolini's zeal "for a praiseworthy defense of the spiritual unity of the Nation" should, the pope argued, "be directed with sufficient energy against the above-mentioned heretical, foreign propaganda." Borgongini passed this papal request on at his next meeting with De Vecchi. ASV, ANI, pos. 49, fasc. 2, f. 21r, 15 febbraio 1931.

   Between the two world wars, the Vatican launched an aggressive anti-Protestant campaign. Moro 2003, p. 317. The pope helped set the tone in his Epiphany encyclical in 1928, *Mortalium animos,* forbidding Catholics to participate in organizations or meetings that encouraged dialogue among different Christian groups: "So, Venerable Brethren, it is clear why this Apostolic See has never allowed its subjects to take part in the assemblies of non-Catholics: for the union of Christians can only be promoted by promoting the return to the one true Church of Christ of those who are separated from it, for in the past they have unhappily left it. To the one true Church of Christ, we say, which is visible to all, and which is to remain, according to the will of its Author, exactly the same as He instituted it." The English text of the encyclical is at http://www.papalencyclicals.net/Pius11/P11MORTA.HTM. See also Perin 2011, p. 151.

27. ASV, ANI, pos. 49, fasc. 2, ff. 122r–122v, 14 maggio 1931, Alanna. The Church loudly protested attempts by Protestants to establish churches in Italy and pressured government officials to prevent them from being built. Some of these are discussed in Rochat 1990, pp. 218–22. On April 8, 1931, just as the Catholic Action crisis was heating up, Borgongini told De Vecchi that the pope wanted the government to act "energetically to stop this insane propaganda." De Vecchi tried to calm the nuncio, reminding him that the concordat allowed members of other religions to conduct their religious activities in peace. But mindful of the pope's increasing irritation over the treatment of Catholic Action, the ambassador saw a new way to get the pope to back down. Once the relations between the two parties were placed back "on the right track," he told the nuncio, the government would find a way to satisfy the pope's desire to prevent Protestant proselytizing. ASV, AESI, pos. 794, fasc. 389, f. 55r, 9 aprile 1931. Some months later *La Civiltà cattolica* followed up with an article titled "The Duty of Catholics in the Face of the Protestant Propaganda in Italy." It began by asking whether Italy truly did face a "Protestant danger," responding with a resounding yes. Protestantism, the Vatican-supervised journal informed its readers, meant "de-Christianization." And it linked the Protestant enemy to another enemy, liberalism, described as of "pure Protestant origin." The journal then issued a call for action. In a section headed "Unmask the Enemy!" it warned of a vast Protestant conspiracy. Fortunately, the journal informed its readers, the Roman Catholic Church had the Duce on its side, for he, too, realized the danger to national unity should Italians turn away from the Rome-based Church. "Il dovere dei cattolici di fronte alla propaganda protestante in Ita-

lia," CC 1932 IV pp. 328–43. In an article in 1932, *L'Osservatore romano* had described the Valdese church, the largest Italian Protestant community, centered in the northwest, as *"un'associazione a delinquere,"* a criminal organization, a term associated with the mafia today. Spini 2007, p. 133.

28. ASV, ANI pos. 23, fasc. 4, ff. 47r–47v, Borgongini, "Udienza del Capo del Governo," 22 novembre 1932.

29. ASV, ANI, pos. 23, fasc. 5, ff. 15r–19r, Borgongini a Pacelli, 18 marzo 1933. The meeting with Mussolini was on March 14.

30. The Church was widely pushing this conspiracy theory in these years. In May 1931, in response to a Vatican request to Italy's bishops to report on local Protestant activity, the bishop of Monopoli, near Bari (in southern Italy), lamented the existence of a group of Protestants in his diocese. They were led, he reported, by immigrants returned from the United States. Embracing the view that the Protestants sought to subvert both the Catholic Church and the Fascist regime, he called on the authorities to put a stop to it. But he feared the government would not take the needed action lest it offend the United States, which was under the thumb of Jews and Masons, who were behind the Protestant attempts to undermine the Catholic Church. Perin 2010, pp. 147–48.

31. The ellipsis is in the original.

32. ASV, AESI, pos. 855, fasc. 548, ff. 38r–39r.

33. "La rivoluzione mondiale e gli ebrei," CC 1922 IV, pp. 111–21.

34. In Part III, I will discuss the Vatican's role in preparing the ground for the introduction of Italy's anti-Semitic "racial laws."

35. "Il socialismo giudeo-massonico tiranneggia l'Austria," CC 1922 IV, pp. 369–71.

36. The Vatican had long viewed Freemasonry as one of its most dangerous enemies. The first group appeared in Rome in 1724, seven years after the organization got its start in London. Beginning with Pope Clement XII in 1738, pope after pope had excommunicated those who joined the Masons, vilifying them for bringing Catholics together with Protestants, Jews, and nonbelievers. The Masons, seen as the source of secularization and an alternative to a Church-centered society, would later be blamed for the French Revolution, as well as for Italian unification and the demise of the Papal States.

   In his 1884 encyclical, *Humanum genus,* Pope Leo XIII launched a new anti-Masonic campaign, branding Freemasonry a "synagogue of Satan." In the last two decades of the nineteenth century, *La Civiltà cattolica* and other Catholic publications continually warned of a Jewish-Masonic conspiracy. They would soon add a third enemy, Socialism, to the evil plot. A vast Jewish-Masonic-Socialist conspiracy, they said, aimed at overthrowing all that was good and Christian in Europe and replacing it with a world order run by Jews. The new code of canon law of 1917 confirmed the Masons' excommunication. Vian 2011, pp. 106–16. The first Italian national Masonic association arose with Italian unification in 1859 and quickly established lodges through much of the country. Seeing the Church as the main bulwark of reactionary regimes rooted in the Middle Ages, the Masons were firm supporters of the new Italian government that had displaced the Papal States. Calling for equality of all religions, they campaigned to keep priests out of the public schools. Emblematic was the Masons' most prominent member, Giuseppe Garibaldi, hero of Italian unification and caustic critic of the Vatican and of clerical power. Conti 2006. Adriano Lemmi, national head of the main Italian Masonic order in the late nineteenth century, famously called the ending of the pope's temporal power "the most memorable event in world history." Populated in large part by the middle classes, the organization counted some of Italy's most important late-nineteenth-century politicians among its members. At the time of the First World War, the main national Masonic organization had about twenty thousand members in 486 lodges. Although the great majority of the members came from Catholic families, Italy's tiny Protestant and Jewish populations were overrepresented. Conti 2005.

37. The most common variant of the ritual murder libel held that the Talmud required Jews to murder Christian children in order to use their blood to make Passover matzos.

38. Romagna's Catholic Action magazine is examined by Nardelli (1996, pp. 40–50), on which my description is based.

39. One such article in 1927, in Padua's diocesan weekly, dismissed American Protestants as no longer having a real religion, adding that Protestant ministers "would be more sincere if, like the Jews, they worshipped the golden calf." Perin 2011, p. 185.

40. Cardinal Merry del Val's account of the pope's words at their meeting, quoted in Deffayet 2010, p. 97.

41. Here the pope proved prescient, for papal defenders subsequently did cite the decree dissolving the Friends of Israel as demonstrating that the popes opposed anti-Semitism. Wolf (2010, p. 121) characterized Pius XI's tactic as "a sort of prophylactic defense in the form of a condemnation of modern anti-Semitism." which Wolf termed "a mark of moral impoverishment because it is easy to condemn hatred of Jews in others while not changing one's own anti-Semitic conduct."

42. "Il pericolo giudaico e gli 'Amici d'Israele,'" CC 1928 II, pp. 335–44.

43. Among the last letters the Jesuit received was one that Sarfatti wrote him a month before his death in 1956, which she signed, "Most devoted in Christ, Margherita Sarfatti." Maryks (2011, pp. 309–10) found it in Tacchi Venturi's archive, along with a note written by one of the Jesuit archivists, which identified Sarfatti as "Lover of Mussolini: A Jew converted and baptized by T[acchi] V[enturi], as were, too, her son [Amedeo] and daughter [Fiametta]." See also Cannistraro and Sullivan 1993, pp. 344–45.

44. *Liguria del Popolo,* 1 luglio 1933, quoted in Starr 1939, p. 113.

45. Kent 1981, pp. 128–29.

46. The term *mania* is found in MAESS, vol. 37, 36–38, Charles-Roux à Monsieur le Président du Conseil, 16 octobre 1932. Other references to the pope's obsession with the Bolshevik danger are found in Charles-Roux's reports of July 19 (MAESS, vol. 37, 12–13) and July 23 (MAESS, vol. 36, 14–15).

47. ASV, AESS, pos. 474, fasc. 476, ff. 58r–58v, Pacelli a Monsignor Pietro Fumasoni-Biondi, 2 gennaio 1933.

48. In an effort to convince the minister of the seriousness and scope of the problem, Borgongini handed him a booklet he had prepared, titled *Protestant Proselytism in Italy.* It explained why Protestantism was the joint enemy of both the Catholic Church and the Fascist state. "The Protestant sects," it began, "are anti-hierarchical. Their principle is that each individual is the interpreter of divine revelation and therefore free to form his own interpretation through reading the Bible. This principle is the basis of every democratic error, from liberalism to socialism to anarchism." ASV, ANI, pos. 49, fasc. 2, ff. 281r–282r, Borgongini a Pacelli, 22 marzo 1935. The booklet is available at ibid., 284r; the quote is from p. 25. The booklet devoted twenty pages to listing every Protestant church in Italy.

49. Pacelli added, "I have full faith however that your good offices will want to ward off this evil." ASMAE, AISS, b. 21, Pacelli a De Vecchi, 22 marzo 1933.

50. ASMAE, AISS, b. 21, De Vecchi a Pacelli, 7 aprile 1933.

51. Let De Vecchi know, the pope told Pacelli, "that the Holy Father has viewed this news with great pleasure." ASV, AESS, pos. 430a, fasc. 348, f. 25, 8 aprile 1933.

CHAPTER 15: HITLER, MUSSOLINI, AND THE POPE

1. E. Mussolini 1957, p. 143; Kershaw 1999, p. 343. A few days after the March on Rome, Hermann Esser, one of Hitler's main lieutenants, told a packed rally, "Germany's Mussolini is called Adolf Hitler." Kershaw 1999, p. 180.

2. DDI, series 7, vol. 13, n. 61, Renzetti a Chiavolini, 31 gennaio 1933.

3. DBFP, 1919–39, series 2, vol. 5, n. 444, Graham to Wellesley, October 11, 1933; DDF, series 1, vol. 4, n. 293, Chambrun à Paul-Boncour, 11 octobre 1933.

4. Pacelli's notes of his conversation with French ambassador Charles-Roux are at ASV, AESS, pos. 430b, fasc. 359, f. 35, "L'Ambasciatore di Francia.," 1 febbraio 1933. Mussolini's chief of cabinet reported secondhand on a conversation in which Pacelli said that Hitler "had performed a great service for Germany because he has permitted a strong government," but added that he thought Hitler himself would not last. DDI, series 7, vol. 13, n. 13.

5. In 1931 *La Civiltà cattolica* reported the concerns voiced by many German bishops about ultra-nationalist Nazi ideology: "Il 'Nazionalsocialismo' in Germania," CC 1931, II, pp. 309–27.

6. ASV, AESS, pos. 430b, fasc. 359, f. 55, "L'Ambasciatore di Germania," 24 febbraio 1933.

7. The pope spoke these words to Fontenay on his final visit as French ambassador. MAESS, vol. 37, 3–4, Fontenay à président du conseil, 14 juin 1932.

8. MAESS, vol. 37, 63–66, Charles-Roux à ministre des affaires étrangères, 7 mars 1933.

9. "The present Pope takes the view that the most serious and immediate danger to the Church is the spread of Communism. His first concern is to combat this menace and he is doing so in every country with all his strength." FCRSE, C2887/2887/22, Mr. Kirkpatrick, British legation to the Holy See, to Sir John Simon, London, March 20, 1933.

10. Kent 1981, pp. 154–55. Wolf (2010, pp. 155–68) reviews the evidence behind the pope's decision to get the German bishops to support Hitler in March 1933.

11. MAESS, vol. 37, 70–77, Charles-Roux à ministre des affaires étrangères, 20 mai 1933.

12. Wolf 2010, pp. 174–75.

13. A proud Catholic, von Papen had befriended Pacelli years earlier in Germany. He had often hosted him at the Guards Cavalry Club, where he introduced him to many of Germany's leading conservatives. CC 1933 IV, p. 89; Wolf 2010, pp. 174–75; Ventresca 2013, p. 62.

14. Ventresca 2013, pp. 75–79.

15. Wolf 2010, p. 178.

16. Ibid., pp. 227–28.

17. ASMAE, AISS, b. 77, "Il punto di vista cattolico di fronte al sistema Tedesco di concepire la Chiesa," 19 ottobre 1933.

18. As recorded in Pacelli's notes. ASV, AESS, fasc. 430a, fasc. 349, ff. 27r–27v, 30 dicembre 1933. The Italian ambassador to Germany was also reporting in December the growing conflict between the Catholic Church and the German government, especially in dealing with youths. ASMAE, APG, b. 13, "S. Sede e Governo germanico," 27 dicembre 1933.

19. According Italy's ambassador in Berlin, Monsignor Orsenigo had reached an understanding with the Nazi leaders. He was doing all he could to thwart the opponents of the Vatican-Nazi collaboration, both those within the Nazi hierarchy and those in the Vatican. ASMAE, AISS, b. 35, ff. 70–71, ministero degli affari esteri a De Vecchi, 25 gennaio 1934.

20. Giorgio Angelozzi Gariboldi quoted in Biffi 1997, p. 99.

21. ACS, MCPG, b. 157, 19 maggio 1928.

22. Biographical details on Orsenigo are taken from Biffi (1997). See also Godman 2004, pp. 30–31.

23. Pacelli had opposed the move, fearing it would do more harm than good. Wolf 2010, pp. 245–52; Godman 2004, pp. 48–50.

24. In December 1934 Mussolini, unafraid of criticizing the Nazis, boasted to the French magazine *Le Figaro* of his close relations with the Vatican and faulted the Nazi regime for its misguided religious policies. MAESI, vol. 267, 49–53, Charles-Roux au ministère des affaires étrangères, 26 décembre 1934.

25. On May 25 the pope instructed Pacelli to tell Mussolini that he prayed for him morning

and night. The pope wanted Mussolini to get Hitler to recognize the Church's right to provide the moral and spiritual education of young people. ASV, AESS, pos. 430a, fasc. 350, f. 29.

26. ASMAE, AISS, b. 35, "Udienza dal Cardinale Segretario di Stato—Venerdì 1 giugno 1934," "Udienza da S.E. il Capo del governo—Lunedì 4 giugno 1934," "Udienza dal Cardinale Pacelli—Martedì 5 giugno 1935." The Goebbels passage is taken from his novel *Michael* (Steigmann-Gall 2003, pp. 20–21). Faulhaber's report is quoted in Wolf 2010, pp. 162–63. On June 15, the day of the meeting of the two dictators, De Vecchi met with Pacelli to reassure him that Mussolini would be forcefully raising the pope's points. ASV, AESS, pos. 430b, fasc. 361, ff. 32/33, "L'Ambasciatore d'Italia," 15 giugno 1934.

27. Mussolini was also concerned about the German-speaking population of Italy's Alto Adige region, which Italy had acquired following the First World War, and whose allegiances were in doubt.

28. DDI, series 7, vol. 14, n. 112, "Colloqui fra il capo del governo,. Mussolini, e il cancelliere federale austriaco Dollfuss, Riccione," 19–20 agosto 1933; Lamb 1997, pp. 100–1.

29. DDI, series 7, vol. 14, n. 246, "Appunto," 3 ottobre 1933.

30. Kershaw 1999, p. 282. On the political uses of Mussolini's body, see Luzzatto's (1998) excellent book.

31. Rauscher 2004, pp. 193–94.

32. De Felice (1974, p. 494) disputes the common view that Mussolini's German was too weak to understand Hitler, quoting Hitler's Italian translator: "The Duce usually spoke German, with a heavy accent, very slowly, carefully articulating every syllable, and it was clear that he spoke it willingly."

33. Milza 2000, pp. 694–96.

34. De Felice 1974, p. 505.

35. ASV, AESS, pos. 430b, fasc. 361, ff.52/53, "L'Ambasciatore d'Italia," 6 luglio 1934.

36. DDI, series 7, vol. 15, n. 469, "Colloquio fra il Capo del Governo . . . e . . . De Vecchi," 2 luglio 1934.

37. ASMAE, AISS, b. 35, Mussolini a De Vecchi, 22 giugno 1934.

38. Lamb 1997, pp. 106–7.

39. ACS, MCPG, b.158, "Riservato, da fonte Vaticana," Roma, 26 luglio 1934.

40. Ventresca 2013, p. 85.

41. Quoted in Fattorini 2007, p. 110n8. According to Orsenigo, the bishops voiced no objection to Hitler's claim. Duce 2006, pp. 32–33, based on Orsenigo's March 7, 1933 report to Pacelli. The bishop of Osnabrück said that at the meeting Hitler spoke "not a word against the church, only appreciation for the bishops." The themes used by the Nazis to vilify the Jews (Herf 2006, pp. 37 41) were largely the same as those pushed by the Vatican's unofficial journal *La Civiltà cattolica*. From the 1920s, Hitler and his sidekick Joseph Goebbels had warned of a Jewish conspiracy against Western civilization and of Jewish control of high finance, the press, and Bolshevism. It was all aimed at reducing Christians to the Jews' servants.

42. ASV, AESG, pos. 643, fasc. 158, ff. 14r–19r. See also Hubert Wolf's (2010, pp. 184–90) discussion of the case.

43. Wolf 2010, p. 190.

44. "Anti-Semitic struggle has assumed an official government character. Intervention Representative of Holy See would be equivalent to a protest against a government law." ASV, AESG, pos. 643, fasc. 158, f. 5r. And a few days later: "Unfortunately the anti-Semitic principle has been accepted and sanctioned by the entire government, and this fact will unfortunately remain as an ignoble stain on the very first pages of the history that German National Socialism—not without its merits—is writing!" ASV, AESG, pos. 643, fasc. 158, 6r–6v, 11 aprile 1933.

45. The remarkable correspondence between Ambassador Vittorio Cerruti and Mussolini at the end of March and early April 1933 records these frenetic attempts. ASMAE, Gab., b. 668. The Duce's telegram to Cerruti is reproduced in DDI, series 7, vol. 13, n. 327, Mussolini a Cerruti, 30 marzo 1933. The telegram containing the Duce's message to Hitler is found in the ASMAE file, labeled "absolute precedence, personal for His Excellency Cerruti." Cerruti's wife, whom he met in Vienna, was Hungarian and, although she does not discuss it in her memoir, was apparently from a Jewish family. Cerruti 1953. Pacelli knew that the Duce was voicing this criticism, as did, most likely, the pope himself.

46. ASV, AESG, pos. 643, fasc. 158, f. 5r, Orsenigo a Pacelli, 9 aprile 1933. The (undated) note regarding Mussolini's protest is at AESG, pos. 643, fasc.158, f. 8r. Mussolini met with Chaim Weizmann, the Zionist leader, in late April. Weizmann described the campaign of Nazi persecution of the Jews in these early weeks of Hitler's rule, and told of his plan to try to get permission to have large numbers of Germany's Jews migrate to Palestine. DDI, series 7, vol. 13, n. 480, "Colloqui fra il capo del governo . . . Mussolini e Chaim Weizmann," 26 aprile 1933. The next month an Italian envoy to Germany reported back to Mussolini that the Nazi leaders were beginning to have second thoughts about their anti-Semitic campaign, given the bad publicity it was generating. "Thus," he wrote, "the Duce, whose thought I clearly laid out to Hitler both in the past and recently, is beginning to be shown to have been right." If, as he thought likely, Hitler was about to soften the restrictions on the Jews, the Jews would have Mussolini to thank. DDI, series 7, vol. 13, n. 595, Renzetti a Chiavolini, Berlino, 14 maggio 1933.

    Remarkably, in reaction to Mussolini's pleas, Franz von Papen, German vice chancellor, meeting with the Duce in Rome on April 10, assured him that he recognized "that the campaign against the Jews was an error." Mussolini also took advantage of the meeting to stress the importance for the new Nazi regime of maintaining good relations with the Holy See. DDI, series 7, vol. 13, n. 401, "Colloquio fra il Capo del Governo e Ministro degli Esteri, Mussolini, e il Vice Cancelliere del Reich, Papen," Roma, 10 aprile 1933. The next day both von Papen and Hermann Göring, Hitler's henchman and president of the Reichstag, met with the pope at the Vatican. We have no account of what was said; L'Osservatore romano simply reported that the meetings had taken place, offering no comment or explanation. "Nostre informazioni," OR, 13 aprile 1933, p. 1.

47. Neither the Vatican nor the German bishops' organization protested the Nuremberg Laws; nor did they voice any opposition to the renewed Nazi campaign to demonize the Jews. Wolf 2010, p. 217.

48. Taking up this theme at the 1935 Nuremberg Rally, Joseph Goebbels spoke of the Jews' secret plan for "international Jewish world domination." Herf 2006, pp. 41–42.

49. Ledóchowski addressed the letter to Pacelli, hoping he would convince the pope of the need for the encyclical. At the time, the Nazi government was mounting a highly publicized trial of Jesuits, charging them with illegally exporting funds abroad, but strikingly, the Jesuit leader was defending Hitler. In July, in talking to Pignatti, Ledóchowski blamed Goebbels and Rosenberg—noted enemies of the Catholic Church—for the problems, telling the Italian ambassador that he thought it very possible that Hitler did not approve of the campaign against the religious orders that was then under way. ASMAE, APG, b. 33, fasc. 1, Pignatti al ministero degli affari esteri, "Processi antireligiosi in Germania," 14 luglio 1936.

50. Ferdinand Lassalle was one of the founders of the socialist movement in mid-nineteenth-century Germany.

51. Fattorini 2007, pp. 64–69.

52. How to explain the apparent contradiction of Jews controlling both capitalism and Communism? The Jesuit journal's answer was that both grew out of "a materialistic economic conception of the world, of Jewish-Puritan origin." But something more nefarious was at

work, for despite all appearances, socialism was but a tool that the Jews used as "an arm and a means of destruction that favors the designs of international finance."

53. "La questione giudaica," CC 1936 IV, pp. 37–46.

54. CC 1936 IV, pp. 83–85.

55. Herf (2006, pp. 95–96) cites the important work of Pinkus 1988 on this topic. See also AJC 1939, pp. 56–59. Members of the USSR government organs are listed in *The States-man's Year Book* for 1935 and for 1938. As Hitler was railing against the Jewish-Communist threat in late 1936, *La Civiltà cattolica* recommended to its readers Alfredo Rosmanini's *Ebrei, cristianesimo, fascismo (Jews, Christianity, Fascism)*, praising this influential anti-Semitic, Fascist diatribe as "written with sincerity and the warmth of faith." It "can do good among the people." "A collection of articles and essays on the communist, atheist, destructive danger," its enthusiastic review began, "in which Judaism plays a large role, and on the merits of Fascism in defending religion and social order." It went on: "We note that the influence of not a few Jews, as exploiters, is well known." Here the journal added a reference to its own recent article on the subject. CC 1936 IV, p. 252. Calimani (2007, p. 235) terms the Rosmanini book the first intensely anti-Semitic book to come out of the Fascist regime's anti-Semitic campaign.

CHAPTER 16: CROSSING THE BORDER

1. The French ambassador, François Charles-Roux, reported on February 15, 1935, that Dalla Torre told him of the pope's concern about a possible invasion. Charles-Roux at the time did not think Mussolini would be so rash as to launch one. DDF, series 1, vol. 9, n. 226.

2. When Mussolini sent two army divisions to Somaliland in March, blessed by various Italian cardinals on their departure, the French chargé d'affaires to the Vatican reported that the blessings occasioned much comment. DDF, series 1, vol. 9, n. 400, Truelle à Laval. On the military buildup, see Del Boca 2010, pp. 90–92.

3. ACS, MCPG, b. 172, Zanetti, 25 giugno 1935.

4. Bosworth 2011, p. 171.

5. Tardini 1988, p. 332; C. Wingfield, *Annual Report 1934*, January 12, 1935, R 402/402/22, in Hachey 1972, pp. 287–88, sections 138–40.

6. ACS, MCPG, b. 172, Zanetti, 19 giugno 1935.

7. McCormick 1957, pp. 69–76.

8. DDF, series 1, vol. 11, n. 348, Charles-Roux à Laval, Ministre des Affaires Étrangères, 24 juillet 1935. Months earlier, in February, Dalla Torre, the editor of *L'Osservatore romano*, had been telling the French ambassador about the pope's worries concerning Mussolini's plans for a war in Ethiopia. DDF, series 1, vol. 9, n. 226, Charles-Roux à Laval, 15 février 1935. Chargé d'affaires Talamo reported in late June on the *Avvenire* article, which he said reflected Vatican attitudes toward the Ethiopian situation. DDI, series 8, vol. 1, n. 450, Talamo a Mussolini, 27 giugno 1935.

9. Ceci 2008, p. 297; Ceci 2010, p. 43. Ceci 2010 offers an excellent analysis of the evolution of the pope's position in the Ethiopian war.

10. "He is very friendly and obliging," the British envoy to the Vatican wrote some time later in a capsule description of Pizzardo, "but very much overworked and not of first class ability." R5802/5802/22, FCRSE, pt. 14, p. 155, Osborne to Halifax, June 21, 1938.

11. Talamo learned the news from Augusto Ciriaci, national Catholic Action head, who rushed to tell him early that morning, in an effort at damage control. Since Cesare De Vecchi had been appointed minister of education earlier that year, Talamo was serving as acting ambassador.

12. Tardini 1988, p. 385.

13. Ibid., pp. 385–86.

14. *The Times* of London called attention to the pope's remarks that "a war of conquest, an offensive, unjust war, [would be] unspeakably horrible." "Views of the Pope on Abyssinia," *Times,* September 2, 1935, p. 11. *The Washington Post* the same day carried a front-page article titled "Pontiff Plans Plea to Il Duce to Avert War," curiously highlighting the key role that Tacchi Venturi was to play in bringing the pope's message to Mussolini. The following day the paper devoted an editorial to the pope's plea for peace, attributing a highly dubious quote to Tacchi Venturi. "Pope to Emperor," WP, September 3, 1935, p. 8.

15. ASMAE, AISS, b. 56, fasc. 1, sf. 1b, Pignatti a Mussolini, 30 agosto 1935.

16. Verdier's account is in Papin 1977, p. 63.

17. Ibid., pp. 56, 62.

18. Bosworth 2002, pp. 304–5.

19. MAEI, vol. 266, 269–71, Charles-Roux à président du conseil, 17 septembre 1932. However, he drew the line at receiving the Fascist children in their black shirts and military uniforms, for the sight of children dressed for war repelled him. De Rossi dell'Arno 1954, p. 46.

20. "Per la celebrazione del decennale in Italia," OR, 3 novembre 1932, p. 1; discussed in MAEI, vol. 266, 294–97, Charles-Roux à président du conseil, 3 novembre 1932. The article has a curious backstory. Giuseppe Dalla Torre, the paper's editor and perhaps the only layman who felt free to visit the pope while dressed informally, apparently refused a request from the secretary of state office to write the tribute. Agostino 1991, p. 153. Mussolini was long convinced, with good reason, that Dalla Torre was hostile to him. Charles-Roux relied on Dalla Torre for inside word on the pope's views, and during the Ethiopian crisis, Dalla Torre expressed his opinion that both of the pope's emissaries to Mussolini, Borgongini and Tacchi Venturi, were in the Duce's pocket and filtering out much of the pope's criticism in attempting to win the Duce's favor. DDF, series 2, vol. 1, n. 107, Charles-Roux à Flandrin, ministre des affaires etrangères, 27 janvier 1936. Knowing of Augusto Ciriaci's enthusiasm for the regime, Pacelli turned to him to draft the piece. Ciriaci did so. Then Pius XI added much of his own, finalizing the article. ASMAE, AISS, b. 21, fasc. 8, De Vecchi a Mussolini. Not everyone in the Church appreciated the panegyric to Mussolini, including some of Dalla Torre's colleagues on the *Osservatore romano* staff. What was next? they asked. Would *L'Osservatore romano* be replacing its emblem of the papal tiara with the Fascist fasces? ASMAE, AISS, b. 21, f. 8, Città del Vaticano, 3 novembre 1932.

21. ASMAE, AISS, b. 56, fasc.1, sf. 1c, Pacelli a Mussolini, 14 settembre 1935. According to an informant's report, the pope sent Tacchi Venturi on a secret mission to England to lobby local Catholics to support the Italian government in the face of strong British opposition to Mussolini's war plans. But no evidence has yet been found to suggest that this trip ever took place. ACS, DAGR, b. 1320, informatore n. 52, Roma, 12 settembre 1935.

22. ASV, AESS, pos. 430a, fasc. 352, ff. 49, 20 settembre 1935.

23. ASV, AESI, pos. 967, vol. 1, ff. 156r–159r. At his meeting on September 27 with Charles-Roux, the pope repeated his fears that disaster could befall Italy and Mussolini if the Duce were to go ahead with his planned invasion. He had offered to meet with Mussolini secretly to discuss how he might help negotiate a way out of the war, he told the French ambassador, but Mussolini had declined. DDF, series 1, vol. 12, n. 254, Charles-Roux à Laval, 27 septembre 1935.

24. Quoted in Milza 2000, p. 724.

25. ACS, CR, b. 68, Tacchi Venturi a Mussolini, 3 ottobre 1935.

26. DDF, series 1, vol. 12, n. 412, Charles-Roux à Laval, 10 octobre 1935 (footnote 1).

27. Pacelli's original envelope and letter to the king are found not in the royal archives in Lon-

don but in the Vatican archives. That fact tells the story. A handwritten note on the Vatican file explains: "Letter signed by Cardinal Pacelli to the king of England 3 October 1931. Note: The letter was first accepted, and then sent back by the British Legation." ASV, AESI, pos. 967, vol. I, ff. 201r–208r. The British prime minister viewed the pope's attempt to communicate directly with the king on a matter of foreign policy to be a breach of diplomatic protocol.

28. Del Boca 2010, pp. 104–7.

29. Federico 2003, p. 590.

30. ACS, MCPG, b. 159, 1 febbraio 1935. On leaving his post, De Vecchi was honored by the pope, who presented him with a gold medal and rich praise. CC 1935 I, pp. 423–24, 647. According to an informant, the pope was fond of De Vecchi, and it was he who told the Vatican daily to print a laudatory article about the departing ambassador. ACS, MCPG, b. 159, informatore, Roma, 5 febbraio 1935. Back in 1932 Cardinal Pacelli was already hearing rumors that De Vecchi would be replaced and began speculating about who his replacement would be. He made clear that he thought De Vecchi a rather mediocre sort. MAEI, vol. 266, 250–54, Charles-Roux au président du conseil, 25 juillet 1932.

31. ASV, AESI, pos. 985, fasc. 658, ff. 23r–27r. On Pignatti's diplomatic experience, see Casella 2010, p. 185n1. Rumors about who De Vecchi's replacement would be had swirled around Rome. Many of the most illustrious names of the regime were mentioned, from Federzoni to Alfredo Rocco to Mussolini's son-in-law Galeazzo Ciano. Before naming Pignatti, Mussolini had sought the pope's approval. The pope in turn had contacted Monsignor Luigi Maglione, his nuncio to France, who assured him that the count was a good choice, a practicing Catholic, a fine father, intelligent, modest, and upright. ACS, MI, PP, b. 168, informatori, relazioni, 3 marzo, 22 marzo, 27 marzo.

32. In short, concluded the new ambassador, "the Holy Father spoke like a good Italian." ASMAE, APSS, b. 25, fasc. 2, 13 ottobre 1935; Casella 2010, p. 189.

33. H. Montgomery, *Annual Report 1935*, January 9, 1936, R 217/217/22, in Hachey 1927, pp. 322–23, sections 161–64; MAESS, vol. 37, 188–89, Charles-Roux, télégramme, Affaires étrangères, 17 décembre 1935.

34. Garzonio 1996; Rumi 1996, pp. 38–39; De Vecchi 1983, p. 219.

35. The informant cautioned that the archbishop's behavior was opportunistic rather than ideological, adding, "it is best not to trust too much as the priest will be fascist only as long as things go in his favor." ACS, MI, FP "Schuster," informatore n. 52, Milano, 3 gennaio 1935.

36. Saresella 1990, p. 460.

37. Ceci 2010, pp. 86–87.

38. Quoted in Baudrillart 1996, pp. 193–94 (5 mai 1936).

39. At an October 24 meeting—diplomatic efforts to prevent the economic sanctions having failed—Mussolini told Tacchi Venturi that the pope's hopes for French intercession to help mediate the dispute were misplaced. Tell the pope, said the Duce, that our friendship with France is finished. Only Nazi Germany remained Italy's friend. "Who would have thought," Mussolini added, "that our friends of twenty years ago . . . would have become our enemies, and we would have to become friends with our enemies of that time. . . . God knows what's going to happen." ASV, AESI, pos. 967, vol. 2, ff. 80r–80v, "Udienza col Capo del Governo," 24 ottobre 1935, P.T.V.

40. DDI, series 8, vol. 2, n. 664, Pignatti a Mussolini, 19 novembre 1935.

41. Diggins 1972, pp. 279–82. The *New York Times* editorial dates from October 1937. Diggins 1972, pp. 276–78, 290–91, 317.

42. The demonstration was held on November 10. Ceci 2012, p. 95; Diggins 1972, p. 107.

43. In a letter to Dino Alfieri, then undersecretary for press and propaganda, the fascist Italian American secretary of the Unione Italiana d'America in New York City stressed how im-

portant Father Coughlin's efforts were there. While most Americans opposed the war in Ethiopia, Italian Americans had given it strong support, which, along with Coughlin's efforts, had prevented Roosevelt from getting his sanctions bill passed. Much to his disgust, he said, when a newsreel on the war was shown in movie theaters, people jeered and whistled when Mussolini came on the screen but cheered images of the Ethiopians. ACS, MCPR, b. 21.

Meeting with Pacelli on November 22, Pignatti stressed how crucial it was that oil not be added to the sanctions—as some in Britain and elsewhere were proposing—and how important it was that the United States not join the sanctions. Again he asked Pacelli to activate the Holy See diplomatic network to help the war effort. In pointing out the good that the Church could do in the United States, he praised the work of Father Coughlin. Pacelli reassured the Italian ambassador that the Vatican was doing what it could but added that as Coughlin "has already spoken strongly against England and the sanctions, there was no need to incite him to do more." ASV, AESS, b.430a, fasc. 362, f. 136. The news that Coughlin played a helpful role in getting the American Catholic clergy to support the Ethiopian war was passed on to the undersecretary for press and propaganda on November 28. ACS, MCPR, b. 21, "Appunto per S.E. il Sottosegretario di stato." Meeting with Pacelli again on December 6, the Italian ambassador noted with pleasure all that Father Coughlin was doing to inspire the American movement to oppose sanctions. ASV, AESS, pos. 430b, fasc. 362, ff. 145/146. On the Coughlin story and Coughlin's relations with the Holy See, see Fogarty 2012.

44. In 1935 Cardinal Dougherty, archbishop of Philadelphia, complained that Coughlin was "now quite beyond control." He added that Coughlin had become "a hero in the minds of the proletariat and especially those members of that rabble who are of Jewish extraction or belong to the Socialists or Communists." Given Coughlin's anti-Semitic bent, this was a rather peculiar characterization. Fogarty 2012, pp. 108–10. Some of my description is based on the report sent from the Italian embassy in Washington to Rome. ASMAE, AISS, b. 33, "Oggetto: Padre Coughlin," 22 ottobre 1936.

45. Luconi 2000, pp. 11–12. Enthusiasm for the Ethiopian war was widespread in the Italian American community. In April 1936 the Italian vice consul in Providence, Rhode Island, dressed in black shirt, distributed more than seven hundred iron wedding rings. So great were the donations of gold wedding rings in that city that the vice consul had to have four hundred more iron rings delivered later. Ceci 2012, pp. 95–96.

46. Quoted in Franzinelli 1995, pp. 311–12.

47. De Felice 1974, p. 761. The bishop's remarks were printed in Il Popolo d'Italia, 19 dicembre 1935.

48. De Rossi dell'Arno 1954, pp. 69–70. The next month the bishop of Ventimiglia addressed the women of his diocese, identifying "the enemies of Italy, the enemies of its greatness and its future," as "Russian bolshevism, communism, international masonry, English Protestantism" (pp. 105–8).

49. ASV, AESI, pos. 967, vol. 2, ff. 187r–88v, Tacchi Venturi, "Relazione dell'udienza avuta col Capo del Governo," 30 novembre 1935. Renzo De Felice (1981, p. 291n85) concluded that Tacchi Venturi had likely helped lead Mussolini to subscribe to the theory of a plot of "international Judaism" against his Ethiopian war effort.

50. ASV, AESI, pos. 967, vol. 2, ff. 257r–260r, Tacchi Venturi, "Relazione dell'udienza avuta con S.E. Mussolini," 14 dicembre 1935.

CHAPTER 17: ENEMIES IN COMMON

1. Quoted in Franzinelli 1998, p. 137; Franzinelli 2008, p. 258.

2. ASV, AESI, pos. 967, vol. 5, f. 186r, "Memoria d'archivio," 28 novembre 1935.

3. Brendon 2000, p. 426.

4. ASV, ANI, pos. 23, fasc. 7, ff. 24r–27r, Borgongini a Pacelli, 18 dicembre 1935. The meeting had taken place the previous day.

5. ASV, AESI, pos. 967, vol. 5, f. 201r, "Istruzioni per Monsignor Roveda da impartire verbalmente ai vescovi d'Italia," 30 novembre 1935.

6. Cardinal Nasalli Rocca, archbishop of Bologna, was among those who were uncomfortable. "Aside from the fact that giving up my gold rings does not particularly please me," he wrote Pacelli, "the matter is apparently settled and it only remains for me to ask for instructions for the benediction." Pacelli brought Nasalli's letter to the pope, who said it was fine for the parish priests to bless the rings, but the cardinal himself should avoid it. ASV, AESI, pos. 967, vol. 5, ff. 217r–218r.

7. Ceci 2010, p. 97. In Mantua the local newspaper reported the bishop's advice: "Those who give to the Fatherland give to God!" With much fanfare, Augusto Ciriaci, national president of Catholic Action, gave Achille Starace, head of the Fascist Party, his gold watch, which the Catholic Action men's organization had given him on its tenth anniversary. Terhoeven 2006, p. 102. For more details, see Terhoeven 2006 and Ceci 2010, pp. 94–101.

8. The pope could not have been happy with Schuster, as the idea of an archbishop donating sacred symbols of holy office to the state offended his sense of the rightful position of the Church. According to a police informant, the Vatican supported the collection of gold rings and "the offerings of gold by the Bishops too are viewed positively. . . . Where the reservations begin is for the pectoral crosses, believing that . . . they constitute something sacred." ACS, MCPG, b. 172, informatore, 11 dicembre 1935.

9. Terhoeven 2006, pp. 102, 104, 105; Ceci 2012, p. 92. Nobili (2008, pp. 271, 275–76) gives other examples of the donations of golden sacred objects by bishops in Lombardy. A popular postcard commemorating the Day of Faith showed an image of a robed, bearded, and long-haired Jesus hovering in heaven over two large hands, one removing the wedding ring from the other. Above were the words, "For the sanctity of the Cause." Falasca-Zamponi 1997, fig. 20.

10. The king and queen led the way, depositing their gold ornaments at the tomb of the Unknown Soldier at Rome's Vittoriano Monument. Playwright Luigi Pirandello gave away his Nobel Prize gold medal, and other members of Italy's cultural elite followed suit. Milza 2000, p. 731.

11. Terhoeven 2006, pp. 118–19. Seeking to make a dramatic gift that day, the Duce offered the gold commemorative medal that the pope had given him when the Lateran Accords were signed. As it turned out, an examination of the papal medal revealed that it was made not of gold but a cheap metal with a thin gold coating. The news caused a crisis at the Roman PNF office, where staffers worriedly discussed whether to let Mussolini know. They decided to ask the national head of the party, Starace, who apparently did inform the Duce. Terhoeven 2006, p. 82.

12. The Turin diocesan weekly, for one, warned darkly of a Masonic conspiracy allied with Bolshevism and Protestantism, "fiercely united against Italy, wanting to strike together against Italy and also the Holy See and Catholicism." Quoted in Reineri 1978, pp. 170–71. On April 25 Pizzardo again warned Pignatti of a "Jewish-masonic campaign . . . that moves in parallel fashion against both the Church and against Fascism." ASMAE, AISS, b. 81, fasc. 1, sf. 1, Pignatti, "Congresso dei 'Senza Dio' in Praga."

13. Like the United States, and for similar reasons—the opposition of the majority Protestants—Canada had no official diplomatic tie with the Vatican and so had no nuncio.

14. ASV, AESI, pos. 967, vol. 5, ff. 129r–131r, Pizzardo a Monsignor Andrea Cassulo, delegato apostolico, Ottawa, 26 dicembre 1935; ibid., ff. 132r–134r, Cassulo a Pizzardo, 11 gennaio 1936. Pizzardo shared the Canadian envoy's report with Pignatti on February 1,

eager to show how much the Vatican was doing behind the scenes to help Mussolini's war effort. He reminded the Italian ambassador that the Vatican had earlier instructed its envoy to Canada to "support the movement in our favor among these Catholics." In his later report of the conversation, Pignatti hastened to tell Mussolini something else he thought would be of interest. The head of the Capuchin order in Ottawa had gotten a report from his fellow Capuchins in Ethiopia, complaining that their efforts to win support for the Italian invasion were being frustrated by the "anti-Italian propaganda of Jews and Masons." DDI, series 8, vol. 3, n. 158, Pignatti a Mussolini, 1 febbraio 1936. Shortly after receiving its Canadian emissary's report, the Vatican secretary of state office received another message from Ottawa about the conspiracy aimed at the Church and Italy, but this from a surprising source. Mackenzie King, Canadian prime minister, had received a letter "from a certain E. Pound from Rapallo," informing him that "the sanctions are the work of an international Jewish clique as a means they have devised to provoke a European war." Until then, the Canadian prime minister said, he hadn't given much thought to the question of Jewish influence in Canada, but given this new information, he would now study the matter carefully. He added, according to the Vatican note, his belief "that Judaism has extremely powerful elements in England and in the United States, both in government circles and in general in public opinion." ASV, AESI, pos. 967, vol. 2, f. 396r, "Appunto," Roma, 4 febbraio 1936. It is not clear from the Canadian prime minster's comments whether he was aware that "E. Pound" was the famed poet Ezra Pound.

15. As reported by Italy's ambassador in Berlin, and copied by the foreign affairs ministry to the Italian embassy to the Holy See. ASMAE, APSS, b. 27, fasc. 1, 9 dicembre 1935. Britain's envoy to the Vatican was also unhappy. "One of the results of the new cardinal selections," he reported to London, "and many will think an unfortunate one . . . is that it readjusts the balance of nationality within the Sacred College in a manner very favourable to Italy." He added: "The few lingering hopes which may have been entertained here and there of a foreign successor to the present Pope must thus be finally dismissed." H. Montgomery, *Annual Report 1935,* January 9, 1936, R 217/217/22, in Hachey 1972, p. 322–23, sections 161–64.

16. Montgomery, *Annual Report 1935,* sections 161–64, 347; MAEI, vol. 267, 61–63, Charles-Roux à Flandrin, 14 mars 1936. In his report on the naming of the twenty new cardinals, Pignatti similarly noted the glaring absence of the archbishop of Westminster, attributing it to the Vatican's displeasure at the archbishop's criticism of the Italian war effort and comments about the pope. ASMAE, APSS, b. 25, Pignatti al ministro degli affari esteri, "Concistoro," telespresso n. 7748/26, 22 novembre 1935. The Sacred College had previously been reduced to only forty-nine cardinals; with the new infusion, it would be within one of the maximum, seventy.

17. ACS, MCPG, b. 172, Roma, 21 novembre 1935. The Brazilian government sent its ambassador to complain to Pacelli about the lack of a single Brazilian cardinal, even though Brazil had twice as many Catholics as the United States, which had four cardinals. Pacelli responded that he would not accept the government's request to convey its argument to the pope, for the pope "rightly jealously guards his exclusive right and freedom in the choice of cardinals and therefore could not admit that one spoke of 'disillusion' or 'requests' in this matter, nor make comparisons to other States." ASV, AESS, pos. 430b, fasc. 363, ff. 2/3, 3 gennaio 1936. The pope had used the large number of nominations to sneak in one that he had long sought but had not wanted to bring attention to: Monsignor Caccia Dominioni, the fellow Milanese and longtime aide who had literally stood at his side for thirteen years, finally got his cardinal's hat.

18. Pius did not tell him that Ledóchowski had urged the pope not to make the appointment. The Jesuit general was upset that Tacchi Venturi's prestige in the Vatican was eclipsing his

own and could not bear to have his Jesuit colleague given such exalted status. Martina 1996, pp. 103–8; 2003, pp. 271–72.

19. ACS, MI, PS, Polizia Politica, b. 210, informatore n. 35, Città del Vaticano, 26 novembre 1929. The informant, Bice Pupeschi, claimed to have heard Caccia's complaints directly in a conversation with him the previous evening.

20. ACS, MI, PS, Polizia Politica, b. 210, informatore n. 52, Città del Vaticano, 21 ottobre 1930.

21. Ibid., informatore n. 293, Città del Vaticano, 27 marzo 1931. Caccia blamed Pizzardo for his problems, believing he was the one informing the pope. In the summer of 1931, a new round of recrimination followed Caccia's criticism of Pizzardo's leadership of Catholic Action. Striking back, Pizzardo dredged up an old story that Caccia—apparently catholic in his sexual interests, at least if this report can be believed—had had a son by a woman who owned a store in the city. As proof of the allegation, Pizzardo claimed that the boy had a nervous tic in his eyes identical to Caccia's. ACS, MI, PS, Polizia Politica, b. 210, informatore n. 40, Città del Vaticano, 30 agosto 1931.

22. ACS, MI, PS, Polizia Politica, b. 210, informatore n. 40, Roma, 12 settembre 1933. The next year, the "noted Vatican informer" would remark, as further evidence of the pope's unpopularity in Rome, that being "unsentimental," he almost never did anything to show concern for prelates he knew to be sick. ACS, MCPG, b. 158, luglio 1934.

23. According to an informant's report, it was Pacelli who had persuaded the pope to promote the wayward monsignor. ACS, MI, PS, Polizia Politica, b. 210, informatore n. 40, Città del Vaticano, 12 agosto 1934.

24. ACS, MI, PS, Polizia Politica, b. 210, informatore n. 390, Milano, 15 ottobre 1934.

25. FRSCE, n. 350, Osborne to Halifax, June 21, 1938.

26. The pope made the suggestion through his nuncio. In a December 28 letter to Mussolini, Pignatti reported that in his recent visit to the Vatican secretary of state office, he had been assured that the Vatican was doing all it could to encourage the effort by the Church in Ireland and the United States to lobby in favor of Italy in the Ethiopian war. One of the Vatican officials—most likely Pizzardo—explained that one reason most Irish supported Mussolini in the Ethiopian war was their "sense of contrast to the English Protestant propaganda" against the war. ASMAE, AISS, b. 56, Pignatti al ministro degli affari esteri, "Cattolici in Irlanda Stati Uniti e Canadà," n. 8048/126.

27. Mussolini also asked Borgongini to tell the pope that the Freemasons had become the Duce's sworn enemies, angry at him for destroying their lodges and for bringing about Conciliation with the Church. "They want revenge," said Mussolini, "first against me, so they can then turn on the Church." But "they will not win." ASV, AESI, pos. 967, vol. 2, ff. 343r–346r, Borgongini, "Relazione dell'udienza avuta con S.E. Il Capo del Governo," 3 gennaio 1936.

28. "Coughlin Berates League of Nations," *Ludington Daily News,* November 25, 1935, p. 1. Mussolini was notified of Coughlin's value and more generally of the positive role that Catholics in the United States were playing in opposing the sanctions, in mid-November 1935 by a letter from the president of the Unione Italiana d'America. ACS, MCPR, b. 21, Casagrande di Villaviera, New York, a Dino Alfieri, 15 novembre 1935.

29. In his review of George Seldes's highly critical biography of Mussolini, *Sawdust Caesar,* Gerard Francis Yates concluded: "It should be read by all those who, through mental sluggishness or disgust at the japery of our parliamentarians, sigh for a dictatorship (whether Fascist or proletarian) as a cure for our ills." *America* 54, n. 16, (January 25, 1936), p. 382.

30. "New Jesuit Head Is a Russian Pole," NYT, February 12, 1915, p. 11; Pagano 2009, pp. 401–2n.

31. Von Bülow 2007, pp. 279–80. Another indication of the general view of the great power of

the head of the Jesuit order is the fact the Jesuit superior general was commonly termed the "black pope," referring both to the simple black Jesuit habit and to the contrast—at least in the minds of those having a more conspiratorial bent—between the pure white pope with the scheming black pope.

32. Muñoz 1942, pp. 5–6.

33. Recall that Ledóchowski had made his displeasure known to the *Civiltà cattolica* editor Enrico Rosa in October 1922, when Rosa had written an article attacking Fascism. In the summer of 1929, in the immediate aftermath of the Lateran Accords, when the pope was upset with Mussolini, the Jesuit general was again angry at Rosa for encouraging the pope's criticism. According to a secret police report, he sent Rosa off to a Church congress in Spain in an effort to get him out of the way and allow time for the pope to cool down. ASMAE, AISS, b. 2, "Roma, 12 agosto 1929," and "Roma, 7 agosto 1929."

34. The man who was fired at Mussolini's request, Wilfrid Parsons, S.J., had been editor of the Jesuit weekly for eleven years. He was a bitter foe of Charles Coughlin. Parsons was replaced by Francis Talbot, S.J., a Coughlin supporter and Fascist booster. Gallagher 2012.

35. Ledóchowski went on to warn that Anthony Eden, the British foreign minister, was "in the hands of the Jews and especially in those of the Rothschilds." ASMAE, AISS, b. 102. A copy of the same report, signed by Pignatti, is found at ASMAE, APSS, b. 30. Following the opening ceremony for the world Catholic press exposition in the Vatican on May 12, 1936, Pignatti ran into Ledóchowski, who was delighted because in his remarks the pope had stressed the Communist threat. "Father Ledóchowski," reported Pignatti, "sees Judaism, allied with Bolshevism, to be the origin of all current evils and a great danger for our civilization." ASMAE, APSS, b. 33, fasc. 1, 13 maggio 1936.

36. De Felice 1974, p. 701.

37. Ventresca 2013, p. 104.

38. Mockler 2003, pp. 74–85.

39. Brendon 2000, p. 324. On February 7 Borgongini found the Duce in a "black mood," furious with France. Yes, England, too, was Italy's enemy, he said, but France was worse, for France had betrayed them. Following the left's recent electoral victory, the new French foreign ministry "was put together by the masons in the lodge of that pig Mandel, who, to avoid calling himself Jereboam de Rothschild, calls himself Mandel. But he is a Jew, sold to England, a sworn enemy of Italy." The Duce ranted on, "The government is made up of fourteen masons and three Jews. The Jewish Masonry—who, according to the Protocols of the Elders of Zion, 'corrupt even the dogs,' that is, the Catholics—have succeeded in turning the French into morons." ASV, ANI, pos. 23, fasc. 8, ff. 4r–8r.

40. DDF, series 2, vol. 1, n. 447, Charles-Roux à Flandin, 17 mars 1936.

41. Milza 2000, pp. 726–27. The most fascist of Fascists, and scourge of the Vatican, Roberto Farinacci was granted his wish of joining the Italian air forces in Ethiopia. Arriving in February, he did not last long. In April he took a break from bombing defenseless tribesmen and went fishing in a small lake. Lacking fishing gear, he and his comrades decided to use their hand grenades. Perhaps distracted by the banter with his mates, he held on to a grenade too long, and it blew up in his hand. Farinacci returned to Italy some weeks later to a hero's welcome and got a fitting for his new metal appendage. The government put out the story that the courageous leader had been wounded during a military exercise. Fornari 1971, p. 161; Bottai 2001, p. 102.

42. Mockler 2003, pp. 133–42.

43. Later that week Charles-Roux reported that Tacchi Venturi was an *"ami personnel,"* a personal friend, of the dictator. DDF, series 2, vol. 2, n. 185, Charles-Roux à Flandrin, 8 mai 1936.

44. ACS, CR, b. 68, Tacchi Venturi a Mussolini, Roma, 6 maggio 1936.

45. Ojetti 1939, pp. 116–20; Morgan 1941, pp. 188–91.
46. DDF, series 2, vol. 2, n. 287, Chambrun à Delbos, 10 juin 1936.
47. "Pope Gives Up All Exercise as 80th Year Approaches," and "Vatican Easter Quietest in Years," BG, April 13, 1936, p. 2.
48. ASMAE, APSS, b. 31, Mussolini a Ambasciata presso la Santa Sede, Roma, telegramma in partenza, 14 maggio 1936.
49. ASV, AESS, pos. 430b, fasc. 363, f. 57, "Il Ministro d'Inghilterra," 15 maggio 1936.
50. DDI, series 8, vol. 4, n. 78, Pignatti a Mussolini, 19 maggio 1936. Pignatti concludes: "I will also keep an eye on the Holy See's actions to be able, if need be, to direct them in conformity with the information and instructions of the Royal Minister." DDF, series 2, vol. 2, n. 287, Chambrun à Delbos, ministre des affaires etrangères, 10 juin 1936.
51. De Felice 1974, pp. 756–7.
52. DDI, series 8, vol. 4, n. 40, Pignatti a Mussolini, 14 maggio 1936.
53. Navarra 2004, p. 86.
54. Quoted in De Felice 1974, p. 759.
55. The dictator was also becoming ever more cynical. Anyone or anything that stood in his way had to be overcome. Italians, the Duce told a foreign interviewer in May 1936, needed music and flags to stir them. "The crowd is disorganized and dispersed like a herd of animals, until it is disciplined and guided," he said, using one of his favorite images. "It does not need to know, it needs faith, for it is faith that moves mountains. . . . The truth is, the tendency of our modern men to believe is absolutely incredible!" Quoted in De Felice 1974, p. 799.
56. Galeotti 2000, pp. 29–30.

CHAPTER 18: DREAMS OF GLORY

1. Chiron 2006, p. 371.
2. Quoted by Pacelli in his notebook, ASV, AESS, pos. 430a, fasc. 352, f. 81, 30 dicembre 1935. On the buzzer, see Charles-Roux 1947, p. 13.
3. DGFP, C 4b, n. 482, Ambassador Bergen to Foreign Minister Neurath, Rome, January 4, 1936. Because Pacelli was eager to avoid angering Hitler, he always dealt solicitously with the German ambassador. But to others, he occasionally let his anger show. In 1936 Anton Mussert, head of the Dutch Nazi party, came to see him and, in an attempt to win his favor, told him that two forces were effectively opposing the advance of Bolshevism in Europe: Mussolini and Hitler. Pacelli tore into him, saying curtly that while he shared his view of Mussolini, he did not share his admiration for Hitler. Later, simply in recounting this conversation, Pacelli became so heated that the veins bulged from his neck. DDI, series 8, vol. 4, n. 316, Pignatti a Ciano, 19 giugno 1936.
4. DDF, series 2, vol. 3, n. 114, Charles-Roux à Delbos, ministre des affaires étrangères, 9 août 1936.
5. By mid-August, in Madrid, those churches that had not been burned down or sacked were being occupied by "red militias." Canosa 2009, pp. 63–69.
6. Among other steps, the government introduced new public controls over Church property, evicted the Jesuits from the country, and ended the involvement of the religious orders in public education.
7. Kent 1981, pp. 140–41. *L'Osservatore romano* published many articles lamenting the various elements of the anticlerical campaign in Spain.
8. Acknowledging that "excesses" had occurred, the ambassador argued that in many cases rebel arms were being stored in churches and monasteries, and that the military revolt had left the government no choice but to arm the civilian population to defend itself, creating many of the conditions the cardinal was lamenting. ASV, AESS, pos. 340b, fasc. 363, f.

102, appunti di Pacelli, 12 agosto 1936. See also Brendon 2000, pp. 374–75. A few days later Pacelli received a report from the nuncio in Madrid. No church was able to operate, and Republican forces occupied the archbishop's headquarters, the seminary, and the presses of all the Catholic newspapers. The archbishop had fled to parts unknown, and priests had taken refuge in the homes of friends and relations, moving constantly "to avoid falling into the hands of the reds." Many priests, deemed enemies of the people, had been brutally killed. Others had been jailed. The famous monument to the Sacred Heart of Jesus had been profaned and then destroyed. Those few private homes where mass was still secretly celebrated did so at great risk. ASV, AESE, pos. 889, fasc. 263, ff. 30r–32r, Silvio Sericano, Madrid, 20 agosto 1936.

9. ASV, AESE, pos. 889, fasc. 264, ff. 74r–76r, Borgongini a Pacelli, 28 novembre 1936.

10. De Felice 1981, pp. 358–89.

11. De Felice 1981, pp. 390–91.

12. In October the pope, looking tired and beaten down, told Charles-Roux he thought Mussolini was playing with fire in threatening to tie Italy's fate to Germany's in his game of brinksmanship with France and Britain. MAESS, 38, 28–34, Charles-Roux à Delbos, ministre des affaires étrangères, 22 octobre 1936.

13. Micheler 2005, pp. 113–14. An angry Pacelli told the Italian ambassador that if the Jesuits were put on trial, the repercussions would be enormous and "all of Germany would be shaken." DDI, series 8, vol. 4, n. 613, Pignatti a Ciano, 24 luglio 1936. The pope wanted Mussolini to intercede on behalf of the Jesuits. The day after their meeting Cardinal Pacelli called Pignatti to relay instructions he had just gotten from the pope: Mussolini was not to mention he was acting at the pope's request. DDI, series 8, vol. 4, n. 636, Pignatti a Ciano, 27 luglio 1936. The next month, when the Italian ambassador in Berlin, on instructions from Rome, pleaded on behalf of both the Austrian nuns and the Jesuits, Pacelli expressed his thanks. DDI, series 8, vol. 5, n. 150, L'Incaricato d'affari presso la Santa Sede, Cassinis, a Ciano, 2 ottobre 1936.

14. "The Germans," wrote Grandi (1985, pp. 410–11), made Ciano "their pliable tool." See Innocenti 1992, pp. 14–16; Moseley 1999, pp. 4–9; Morgan 1941, p. 265; De Felice 1974, p. 804; Brendon 2000, p. 559. Grandi's comment should be viewed with caution, however, as he saw himself as losing influence with the Duce to Ciano. On this conflict, see also Renzo De Felice's preface to Ciano's (2002, p. xiv) diary.

15. Rauscher 2004, p. 220.

16. Later the American reporter Thomas Morgan (1941, p. 265) wrote of Ciano: "When he was getting fat—which was a dangerous omen, for his father and mother were mildly monstrous—he adopted Il Duce's diet of fruit, fish and fowl."

17. Milza 2000, p. 737. But it was hard to take Ciano seriously, observed Phillips (1952, p. 188), because "it was impossible to keep his attention for more than a few minutes"; his eye was constantly on the lookout for attractive women. Elisabetta Cerruti, wife of Italy's ambassador to Germany, captured him well: "Although he was not attractive, being too fat for his age and somehow unhealthy, he had a certain unrefined handsomeness and thought himself quite irresistible to the ladies. . . . The prettiest women blatantly pursued him, vying with one another for one of his smiles. It was painful to watch." Quoted in Moseley 1999, p. 30.

18. Phillips 1952, pp. 189–91.

19. Quoted in De Felice 1981, p. 273.

20. Bottai 2001, pp. 109–10.

21. Baratter 2008.

22. Giuseppe Bastianini's dramatic description of this rite is quoted in De Felice 1981, p. 283.

23. Navarra 2004, pp. 64–65, 97.

24. In Italy, faith in the Duce was rivaling faith in Jesus Christ. The Fascist federation of Ascoli Piceno, for example, in the August 22, 1936, issue of its periodical, *Eja,* recommended, "Always have faith. The faith that you have given to Mussolini, because it is something sacred. . . . All that the Duce affirms is true. One does not discuss the Duce's word. . . . After reciting the 'Credo' in God every morning, recite the 'Credo' in Mussolini." Quoted in Gentile 1993, p. 127.

25. Bottai 2001, p. 115; De Felice 1981, p. 267.

26. In 1938 alone she wrote 1,810 pages, scribbled on loose pieces of paper. Her accounts of her phone conversations with Mussolini were so detailed that, when the inspector general of the Italian State Archives later examined them, he suspected she had installed a recording device on her telephone. Petacci 2010, p. 5; Festorazzi 2012, p. 308.

27. Milza 2000, p. 528; Monelli 1953, pp. 153–56; Petacci 2011, p. 423.

28. Here I share a number of perspectives first articulated by De Felice (1981, p. 277).

29. The importance of the American Church was taking some getting used to in Rome, for the Holy See had long regarded the United States as something of a backwater. Only a few decades earlier Vatican relations with the Church in the United States were still being conducted not by the secretary of state office, as for all the European countries, but rather by the Congregation for the Propagation of the Faith, which dealt with those areas—Asia and Africa mostly—regarded as remote, the home of missions rather than of established churches. But by the 1930s the United States had solidified its place not only as a major, thriving center for Roman Catholics and the Church but as the single largest financial source of support for the Holy See. Pollard 2012.

30. Arnaldo Cortesi, "Papal Secretary of State Coming Here; Rome Speculates on Subject of Mission," NYT, October 1, 1936, p. 1; Cortesi, "Pacelli Reported Seeking Aid of U.S. in Anti-Red Drive," NYT, October 2, 1936, p. 1. The Italian embassy in Washington reported these rumored motives for the trip to Ciano, mentioning that the Vatican's apostolic delegate was himself surprised, perplexed, and somewhat alarmed by the visit. DDI, series 8, vol. 5, n. 151, L'Incaricato d'affari a Washington, Rossi Longhi, al ministro degli esteri, Ciano, 3 ottobre 1936; and ibid., n. 160, Rossi Longhi a Ciano, 6 ottobre 1936. For Pignatti's speculation about Pacelli's papal ambitions, see DDI, series 8, vol. 5, n. 170, Pignatti a Ciano, 7 ottobre 1936. In November 1934 Pacelli had been the pope's representative to the International Eucharistic Congress in Buenos Aires, where he had drawn large crowds. On the way home, he stopped in Brazil, where he addressed, in Portuguese, the National Assembly and Supreme Court. Blet 1996, p. 202.

31. Among the honorary degrees were those at Georgetown ("Pacelli Urges World Peace, Blesses Many," WP, October 23, 1936, p. 1), Fordham College, and Notre Dame ("Papal Aide Gets Notre Dame Honor," NYT, October 26, 1936, p. 18).

32. Coughlin's political party, the National Union of Social Justice, was running a candidate against Roosevelt—or "Franklin Double-Crossing Roosevelt," as the priest called him. Fogarty 2012, p. 110.

33. In September Coughlin called for "bullets" to be used against the president—for which he later, under pressure, apologized—and added that Roosevelt was a pro-Communist "dictator." D'Alessio (2012, pp. 133–34) quotes from two of Cicognani's letters to Pacelli, written on October 9 and 10.

34. Joseph Kennedy—a Catholic business magnate and father of a future president—helped arrange the meeting and took part in it. Pacelli's preoccupation with the Communist threat was likely heightened by his focus on the Spanish civil war. Roosevelt's account, to Florence Kerr at a dinner in Hyde Park in 1943, is quoted in Gallagher 2008, pp. 87–88.

35. Examinations of the Pacelli trip to the United States are offered by Gannon 1962, pp. 106–16; Fogarty 2012, p. 115; and D'Alessio 2012, pp. 131–35. Sister Pascalina accom-

panied Pacelli to the United States, as she had two years earlier to Buenos Aires. However, for propriety's sake she traveled on a different ship and kept in the background. Schad 2008, pp. 81–87.

36. ASMAE, APSS, b. 36, Ciano al ministero dell'interno, telespresso n. 691938, 7 dicembre 1936; Falconi 1967, p. 226; Confalonieri 1957, pp. 334–38.

37. Baudrillart 1996, p. 364 (6 décembre 1936). The pope's old friend Agostino Gemelli made frequent visits, once personally administering an electrocardiogram. Venini 2004, p. 201. According to Lazzarini (1937, pp. 142–43), on one visit Father Gemelli heard the pope complain about the food. The "magnificent terror," as Gemelli was known, asked, in his Milanese dialect, if he could prepare him a meal. The pope's eyes lit up. Gemelli, said to be an excellent cook as well as a physician, found a kitchen nearby and soon reappeared with a plate of *risotto à la Milanese,* made with saffon and cooked al dente. "The best," said the pope, as he happily devoured the risotto, "is still that which comes from home."

38. Tardini's marginal note on Pacelli's notes of his meeting with the pope tells of these sick-bed visits. ASV, AESS, b. 560, fasc. 592, f. 16r, 9 dicembre 1937.

39. Both Venini (2004, pp. 182–87) and Baudrillart (1996, pp. 364, 371, 378–79) discuss these events in their diaries.

40. CC 1937 I, pp. 182–83; OR, 4–5 gennaio 1937. The British envoy chronicled all the earlier health reports being put out by the Vatican: D. G. Osborne, *Annual Report 1936,* January 1, 1937, R 57/57/22, in Hachey 1972, p. 365, section 101.

41. Confalonieri 1957, pp. 349–50.

CHAPTER 19: ATTACKING HITLER

1. ACS, MCPG, b. 172, ff. 57–59, 28 gennaio 1937.

2. In Pignatti's words, "the German cardinals, a good part of the North American and English cardinals, and virtually all of the French cardinals will not vote for a cardinal who has shown sympathy for the fascist regimes." DDI, series 8, vol. 6, n. 456. Reporting to Paris in mid-March, Charles-Roux, the French ambassador, recalled that ever since the "brief but violent" conflict over Catholic Action in 1931, relations between the Holy See and the Fascist state had been smooth, because Vatican officials were "with very rare exceptions, entirely Italian," and the Italian clergy were virtually unanimous in their enthusiasm for Mussolini. MAEI, vol. 267, 78–79, Charles-Roux à Ministre des Affaires Étrangères, 19 mars 1937. Charles-Roux devoted the bulk of his lengthy report to urging that both the Sacred College of Cardinals and the main administrative and diplomatic staff of the Holy See be internationalized and that the Vatican move away from the Italians' overwhelming domination. On the Catholic press in Germany, see Conway 1968, p. 171.

3. As usual for the Easter mass in St. Peter's, the Vatican diplomatic corps were all there, with the notable exception of the German ambassador to the Holy See, who boycotted the ceremony. Baudrillart 1996, pp. 456, 464–65 (22 mars 1937; 28 mars 1937); "Pope in Tears at St. Peter's," BG, March 29, 1937, p. 1.

4. Confalonieri 1957, pp. 367–68; Venini 2004, pp. 203, 208–9; Chiron 2006, p. 414.

5. From Asvero Gravelli, quoted in Bosworth 2002, p. 339.

6. MAEI, vol. 70, 64–70, Charles-Roux à Delbos, ministre des affaires étrangères, 17 mars 1937.

7. In America, he wrote, "there is a diffuse strong antipathy for the Nazi regime, which the Jews—who have important positions in the press, in politics, in finance—are naturally taking advantage of." DDI, series 8, vol. 6, n. 126, Suvich a Ciano, 4 febbraio 1937.

8. Luconi 2004, p. 159. The case of Cardinal Schuster, head of Italy's most important archdiocese, Milan, was emblematic of the strong and high-level backing that the Church provided to the Fascist regime. Having done all he could to whip up support for the Ethiopian

war, Schuster continued over the following year to cultivate close relations with the Milanese Fascist Party. In January 1937 Milan's PNF head awarded him a medal in the name of Milanese Fascism, and many locals thought the city's Fascist leader consulted with the cardinal before he made any important decision. ACS, MI, FP "Schuster," Milano 7 gennaio 1937. In February, at a lecture attended by Milan's top Fascist and military leaders, Schuster praised Mussolini again as the man sent by God, comparing him to Constantine, the first Roman emperor to embrace Christianity. ACS, MI, FP "Schuster," Milano, 27 febbraio 1937.

9. The interview with Mussolini appeared on the front page of *Völkischer Beobachter,* January 17, 1937. William Dodd, U.S. ambasssador to Germany, sent an English translation of excerpts to the secretary of state, NARA, LM192, reel 6, January 23, 1937, no. 3265.

10. ASV, AESI, pos. 855, fasc. 551, ff. 38r–39v, Tacchi Venturi a Pio XI, 2 marzo 1937.

11. Godman 2004, pp. 133–54. *Mit brennender Sorge* was preceded, a week earlier, by an encyclical that denounced Communism, *Divini redemptoris.*

12. In the interest of trying to keep the peace with Hitler, writes historian Peter Godman, "the Pope decided against speaking out on racism, human rights, and allied issues in the direct and detailed form prepared by the Supreme Tribunal [of the Inquisition]. Emphasizing his desire to 're-establish true peace in Germany,' Pius XI sacrificed on the altar of the Concordat the outright attack on the Nazis that, in 1937, Rome might have launched." Godman 2004, pp. 146–47. The official English and German translations of the encyclical are available at www.vatican.va. The Italian version is found in CC 1937 II, pp. 216–30.

13. Godman 2004, p. 149; Fattorini 2007, p. 132.

14. In his letter to Pacelli reporting the decision of the bishops of Berlin and Breslau to burn the documents, Orsenigo wrote that when other bishops asked him if they should do likewise, he replied that they should use their own judgment. In the margin of Orsenigo's letter, Pacelli scribbled a note: "The Holy Father judges this a weak response. . . . He instructs that you respond instead that they burn *without question* all that which might cause problems." Quoted in Fattorini 2011, pp. 123, 236n; emphasis by Pacelli in original.

15. Pignatti conveyed the message; his memo does not directly cite Pacelli as the source but implies it: "the Holy See does not want any comments in the Italian press to emphasize that this letter reflects Vatican opposition to Nazism." ASMAE, APSS, b. 35, Ministero degli Affari Esteri, "Appunto."

16. Pignatti said that Pacelli, whom he saw often, did "not want a break in relations and has been cheered up lately, after having seen that the other side has also hesitated to push the fight to the next level." ASMAE, AISS, b. 67, fasc. 9, Pignatti a Ciano, "Le tre Encicliche Pasquali," 1 aprile 1937. The Italian chargé d'affaires analyzed the German reaction to the encyclical in a memo sent the next day to Ciano. DDI, series 8, vol. 6, n. 388, Magistrati a Ciano, Berlino, 2 aprile 1937. On April 17 Ciano reported to the Italian ambassador in Berlin on Cardinal Pacelli's comments about not wanting Hitler to see the encyclical as an attack on Nazism; he attached a copy of Pignatti's report detailing his conversation with Pacelli. Ciano remarked that the German bishops had pressured the pope into preparing the encyclical and the pope had gone ahead with it "without worrying about the consequences." Mussolini and his son-in-law were most worried about the consequences that a papal repudiation of the Nazis would have on their own plans to bring Italy ever closer to the Third Reich. But they remained convinced that the pope approved of Mussolini and could be counted on to resist those in the Church outside Italy who wanted him to denounce Fascism along with Nazism. As Pignatti put it, "I have it from an authoritative source that some advisers of the Pontiff would have liked the papal document to strike at all totalitarian regimes. Pius XI rejected these suggestions."

"The Cardinal Secretary of State," Pignatti reported in the letter that Ciano sent on to Berlin, "did not expressly ask me for an intervention in Berlin by Your Excellency, but he did not conceal from me the great wish that the Holy See be helped in this moment to avoid a rupture and facilitate an accommodation." Ciano then came to the point, telling his ambassador in Berlin: "I pray that Your Excellency will want to weigh the opportunity of taking action with this Government in the sense and within the limits suggested by the Cardinal Secretary of State." ASMAE, APG, b. 38, Ciano a Regia Ambasciata, Berlino, telegramma in partenza n. 740, 7 aprile 1937. In reporting a role for the Duce in urging Hitler not to risk a break with the Vatican in the wake of the encyclical, the *Boston Globe* strangely reported that Tacchi Venturi "carried the Italian Premier's appeal for moderation to Hitler." "Duce Aids Nazi in Vatican Row," BG, April 16, 1937, p. 11. Chenaux (2005) offers extensive evidence to show that Cardinal Pacelli in this period "never stopped hammering with the same message," namely, that *Mit brennender Sorge* did not entail a condemnation of the Nazi state or the Nazi Party as such, and that "the search for a modus vivendi with the regime remained the primary goal of the Holy See's policies toward Germany" (p. 264). On April 30 Pacelli sent a long letter to Bergen rejecting the hostile interpretation the German government had given the encyclical. DGFP, series D, vol. 1b, n. 649.

17. DGFP, series D, vol. 1b, n. 650, "Memorandum by the Foreign Minister, Baron von Neurath," Rome, May 4, 1937.

18. "Conversation between the Duce and Herr Frank, Palazzo Venezia," September 23, 1936, quoted in Muggeridge 1948, pp. 47–48.

19. "Mundelein Rips into Hitler for Church Attacks," CDT, May 19, 1937, p. 7.

20. Mundelein was born and raised in New York City, his father from a family of German origin, his mother Irish American. He had been appointed archbishop of Chicago in 1914, when he was only forty-two. He had traveled to Rome in 1924 to take his cardinal's hat and on other occasions as well. Mundelein was well known to the pope, who was pleased by the financial support he continued to bring with him from Chicago. Mundelein also had a personal relationship with Franklin Roosevelt, whom he had publicly supported from the time he became president in 1933. In 1934, on his way to Rome, Mundelein visited the president in Hyde Park. He continued to visit Roosevelt regularly over the next years. The president saw Mundelein—the only American cardinal outside the northeast—as important to his effort to attract Catholic support. Kantowicz 1983, pp. 220–36.

21. This is the version of Mundelein's remarks communicated by the German foreign ministry to the German embassy to the Holy See. DGFP, series D, vol. 1c, n. 652, 21 maggio 1937. Pacelli requested an explanation of his speech. Mundelein responded, writing to the Vatican delegate in Washington: "This time, being provoked by the daily repetitions in the press of the so-called morality trials in Germany . . . I just hurriedly wrote what was on my mind and gave it to the priests just as I wrote it." Quoted in Trisco 2012, p. 159. The trials had started in 1935 but were suspended for the 1936 Berlin Olympic Games; Hitler ordered them resumed on April 7, 1937, and by the time of Mundelein's speech, they were getting massive publicity in Germany. Hundreds of Catholic priests and members of religious orders were put on trial, accused of having "unnatural sexual relations" or luring children into sexual acts. Front-page newspaper headlines warned of "moral degeneracy" in the Catholic clergy and of "corrupters of youth clad in cassocks." The priests and monks were vilified for exploiting their priestly relationship with children to engage in "unnatural fornication." Given the German government's efforts to end the hold the Catholic Church had on education and youth activity in Catholic areas, the campaign was a propaganda bonanza for the Nazis. German foreign ministry to the German embassy to the Holy See, DGFP, series D, vol. 1b, n. 642, 7 aprile 1937; Trisco 2012, p. 153; Micheler 2005, pp. 113–14. Historians have almost uniformly presented these trials as evidence of the Nazi regime's persecution of the Catholic Church and of Nazi homophobia. Miche-

ler 2005, p. 113. They were certainly both, but the extent to which the alleged behavior had some basis in fact has not been systematically examined.

22. DGFP, series D, vol. 1c, n. 655, Bergen to the German foreign minister, Vatican, May 25, 1937; ibid., n. 657, Bergen to the German foreign minister, Vatican, May 26, 1937; ibid., n. 658, Neurath to the German embassy to the Holy See, May 27, 1937.

   Two weeks before Cardinal Mundelein's speech, Chicago's Italian consul general had visited him. In their amicable conversation, the archbishop expressed "his admiration for the Duce and for Fascism, asserting that Italy today is a country that the Church can truly count on." In response to the consul's question, Mundelein acknowledged that some American Catholic priests had succumbed to anti-Fascist propaganda, but he assured him they were not numerous. ASMAE, APSS, b. 35, "Visita del R. Console Generale in Chicago al Cardinale Mundelein," telespresso 215383, 8 maggio 1937.

23. Pacelli shared these thoughts with the French cardinal Baudrillart. Bauldrillart 1996, p. 476 (7 avril 1937).

24. "Pope's Voice Fails As Health Wanes," NYT, May 19, 1937, p. 9; "Pope Has Setback On 80th Birthday," NYT, June 1, 1937, p. 25. An informant, referring to the pope's continued ill health, characterized him as "more irritable and surly than ever." ACS, MCPG, b. 172, fasc. 23, informatore, 15 maggio 1937.

25. Baudrillart 1996 p. 536 (21 juin 1937).

26. Mussolini's remarks were made to Tacchi Venturi. ARSI, TV, b. 25, fasc. 1950, Tacchi Venturi a Pizzardo, 31 maggio 1937.

27. Fattorini 2007, p. 95. The previous December Pacelli had sent the Vatican's sympathies to Franco, expressing his hope for the Generalissimo's "rapid and total" victory. Ibid., p. 96.

28. Carlo Rosselli's brother Nello was also killed in the attack, having had the misfortune of visiting his brother at the time the assassins struck. Mussolini most likely knew and approved of the murder plan, although no proof has yet been found. In discussing the case, while admitting that the Duce probably did give his approval, De Felice (1981, pp. 420–21) raises the possibility that he may have learned about it only after the fact. This seems unlikely. On the three murders, see Mack Smith 1983, p. 8.

29. "In Rome, people are convinced that [Pizzardo's] rather predominant role will end on the pope's death. He is a prodigious worker, but he is not, they say, up to his role either by intelligence or by outlook." With the ailing pope in Castel Gandolfo, a police informant reported, Pizzardo "remains the true *padrone*" in the Vatican. ACS, MCPG, b. 172.

30. He particularly wanted the last sentence strengthened. Pizzardo should drop the word *noteworthy* in describing the absence of cases of friction over the past several years between the Vatican and the Fascist regime: there were no cases of friction at all, noteworthy or not. The second change he wanted was to replace "there has often been even a fruitful collaboration between the two [the Vatican and Mussolini]" with "it has been usual for the two authorities to proceed upon the ground of a fruitful collaboration."

31. The magazine was *The Tablet,* and its author, Father Hilary Carpenter, was the Dominican prior of Blackfriars Monastery in Oxford. ASV, AESS, pos. 555, fasc. 588, 3r, ff. 5r, 23r–43r. This file also includes the letter from Carpenter bowing to the higher ecclesiastical request and saying he would send in a retraction of his anti-Fascist views. The August 7 issue of *The Tablet* carried the abbot's retraction. "I am informed authoritatively that I have been mistaken in bracketing Fascism and Nazism with relation to the Church, as though both merited the same condemnation . . . since the Concordat of 1931 [*sic*] not only have there been no cases of friction between the ecclesiastical authority and the Italian government, but for the most part the two authorities have proceeded along the lines of a fruitful collaboration. . . . I beg to be allowed to state my unqualified acceptance of the above information." Quoted in Chadwick 1986, pp. 12–13.

32. The volcanic and not entirely stable Fontanges had followed Charles de Chambrun, the French ambassador to Italy, to the Gare du Nord in Paris. There she took out a revolver and shot at him twice. Fortunately, her skills as an assassin were inferior to her other talents, and she wounded him only lightly. Tronel 2007; De Felice 1974, p. 303n1.

33. Magda Fontanges, "My Love Affair with Mussolini," *Liberty,* August 17, 1940, part 2, p. 40. It refers to April 1936.

34. Quoted in De Felice 1981, p. 276n41. In 1927, writing to his sister, Mussolini told her he was practically on an all-liquid diet, due to his stomach problems, but added, "as I have never been one to have a weakness for the sin of gluttony, abstinence leaves me indifferent." E. Mussolini 1957, p. 121. Just how much flesh Mussolini gave to the devil is a matter of some debate among his later biographers, or at least those who speculate on a subject that the less prurient may ignore. At one extreme, Nicholas Farrell, in his 2000 biography, *Mussolini: A New Life* (cited by Baima Bollone 2007, pp. 118–19), estimated that the Duce had sex with five thousand women, which indeed seems high even for a stallion or someone not otherwise employed. Other estimates seem suspiciously precise, one by Duilio Susmel (as reported by Cannistraro and Sullivan 1993, p. 602n) totting up 169 lovers.

35. The local parish priest, having heard of the distinguished visitor's arrival, hurried to the beachfront scene. Mussolini's first thought was that the man of the cloth would disapprove of what he found, and hastened to assure him that their dancing was innocuous. But the priest had something else on his mind: he invited the Duce to visit his church, where he pointed out the sad state of the organ. The priest beamed as the generous dictator handed him a wad of cash to pay for the much-needed repairs. Bottai 2001, pp. 119–20 (4 settembre 1937).

CHAPTER 20: VIVA IL DUCE!

1. "No one gets to Rome without or against Berlin, or to Berlin against Rome!" proclaimed the Duce (Rauscher 2004, p. 224). Mussolini quoted these remarks himself during his German trip. DGFP, series C, vol. 6b, n. 568, Hassell to Weizsäcker, October 7, 1937.

2. Hitler's comments to Ciano were made on October 24. Kershaw 2000, p. 25.

3. Milza 2000, p. 754.

4. Caviglia 2009, pp. 204–5.

5. Rauscher 2004, p. 226.

6. On September 17 Pignatti met with Cardinal Pacelli, who asked him to urge Mussolini to try to persuade Hitler to improve the German government's relations with the Catholic Church. ASMAE, APG, b. 47, Pignatti a Ciano, "S. Sede e Reich," 17 settembre 1937. That word of this got out can be seen in the headline of the page-two story in the CDT on September 23, "Duce to Be Pope's Envoy to Hitler on Church Strife."

7. "If the Holy See has hoped for a result from Mussolini's trip to Germany that would be favorable to it as well, the Vatican will have to bury this hope, for Mussolini has avoided broaching the subject of our relations with the Vatican in any form." DGFP, series D, vol. 1d, n. 682.

8. Baudrillart 1996, pp. 624–5 (1 octobre 1937).

9. ASMAE, APSS, b. 34, Pignatti a regio ministero degli affari esteri, telespresso, 4 ottobre 1937. Pignatti quotes from M. Barbera's article in CC, quaderno 2095. The pope's own relations with the Duce continued to be good. Among the signs of their collaboration was the start of the huge construction project outside St. Peter's Square. Announced by Mussolini the previous year as a way of commemorating the Lateran Accords, the work would demolish the densely populated buildings, alleys, and churches that were packed between two narrow streets running from the Tiber to St. Peter's. These would be replaced with a broad boulevard, named via della Conciliazione. Work had begun on the construction

only after the pope gave his approval, and the pope went to inspect the work shortly after Mussolini's return from Germany. Insolera 1976, pp. 130–31; Painter 2005, pp. 68–70.

10. Pizzardo delivered the pope's message to the Italian chargé d'affaires, who, in relaying the message to Ciano, added another worry: "Italy runs the risk of seeing a pope elected having sentiments very different from those of Pope Ratti." DDI, series 8, vol. 7, n. 424, Venturini a Ciano, 12 ottobre 1937. Ciano had the text of this memo sent to the Italian ambassador in Germany. ASMAE, APG, "S. Sede Reich e Fascismo," 14 ottobre 1937.

11. In late December Pignatti, while waiting with Charles-Roux outside the pope's library for their annual papal New Year's audience, told him that the pope was still "furious" with Mussolini for his visit to Berlin. DDF, series 2, vol. 7, n. 393, Charles-Roux à Delbos, 29 décembre 1937.

12. Tisserant made the comments to the French ambassador. DDF, series 2, vol. 7, n. 393, Charles-Roux à Delbos, ministre des affaires étrangères, 29 décembre 1937.

13. This was reported in the Italian press as well. The Italian nuncio archives have a clipping, "Un discorso di Pio XI al Sacro Collegio," from the December 25, 1937 edition of *Il Popolo di Roma*, ASV, ANI, b. 24, fasc. 14, f. 20r. A few days later, meeting with the Italian ambassador, the pope, looking as if he had lost more weight but as mentally sharp as ever, found time in their five-minute Christmas greeting to tell him that "nothing good could be expected from Germany." ASMAE, AISS, b. 115, Pignatti a Ciano, 28 dicembre 1937.

14. DDF, series 2, vol. 7, n. 374, Charles-Roux à Delbos, 20 décembre 1937; Baudrillart 1996, p. 703 (28 décembre 1937).

15. Baudrillart 1996, p. 731 (17 janvier 1938). The Spanish ambassador shared the opinion of Ernst von Weizsäcker, head of the German foreign office: "Pacelli presents no real counterweight to Pius XI, because he is completely devoid of will and character." Rhodes 1974, pp. 222–23.

16. De Felice 1974, p. 299; De Felice 1981, p. 280; Deakin 2000; Innocenti 1992, p. 169.

17. "We are on the eve of war with France and with England," Buffarini told him. "The regime needs to ensure that the nation is united. Therefore it cannot stand by while young Catholics say that the alliance with the Germans is unnatural." ASV, ANI, pos. 24, fasc. 14, ff. 6r–11r. Borgongini a Pacelli, 31 dicembre 1937.

18. Ciano added that Mussolini was also upset about signs of a warming in relations between the Vatican and the French government, which had been under the control of a popular front of Socialists and Communists since 1936; Nazi Germany and Fascist Italy viewed it as an implacable enemy. In Spain, Ciano told the nuncio, German planes and men were fighting alongside Italians "for the cause of the Catholic religion against that of red Spain," which, he said, was being armed by the French government. Borgongini replied by reminding Ciano that the Italian government's 1929 Conciliation with the Church had benefited the government "not a little, especially in the Ethiopian war, and above all in contributing to Italian prestige abroad." Ciano did not dispute him and agreed to talk to the Duce the next day and see what could be done. Borgongini offered to see the Duce himself if it would be helpful, but Ciano dismissed the idea. Mussolini found it more profitable to deal with Tacchi Venturi, something both Ciano and Borgongini knew, but was left unsaid. ASV, ANI, pos. 24, fasc. 14, ff. 53r–58r., Borgongini a Pacelli, 4 gennaio 1938.

19. A follow-up letter, sent a week later, warned the priests that should they not attend, their absence might be "misinterpreted." The two letters of invitation, on the stationery of the "National Competition of Grain and Farms Among Priests," are found in the Vatican files at ASV, AESI, pos. 1044, fasc. 722, ff. 60r–61r and 48r–48v.

20. ASV, AESI, pos. 1044, fasc. 722, f. 45r, Francesco Niccoli, vescovo di Colle, a Mons. Domenico Tardini, Sostituito per gli Affari Ordinari, Segreteria di Stato, 16 dicembre 1937.

21. Before making a final decision, the pope wanted to check with the archbishop of Udine,

who was billed as the main speaker at the event; the pope wanted to find out how he had agreed to play such a prominent role. Pacelli relayed the pope's request to Rossi, adding that, in past years, bishops had been taking part in such patriotic demonstrations without any problem. The correspondence between Cardinal Rossi and Pacelli is found in ASV, AESI, pos. 1044, fasc. 722, ff. 52r, 56r, 57r, 63r–64r. "The news is true," replied Archbishop Nogara. But "before I agreed to participate and give the address, I contacted Mons. Pizzardo (now Cardinal)"—Pizzardo had been made a cardinal just the previous month— "who spoke of it with the Holy Father. . . . He received his consent." Nogara added, with a hint of concern, "I hope it does not cause any complications." Ibid., p. 70r. Presumably Pizzardo had asked for the pope's approval, the pope had given it, and then, such was the state of his mind on some days, he had forgotten about it.

22. On December 30, in response to a new wave of queries from nervous bishops, the pope informed Cardinal Rossi that bishops who received the invitation from a journalist "were not required to accept it." ASV, AESI, pos. 1044, fasc. 723, f. 4r.

23. Ibid., ff. 16r–17r, "Appunto," 30 dicembre 1937, with penciled comment: "prepared for the Italian ambassador, but then not given to him." The Italian ambassador was convinced that the pope overruled Cardinal Rossi, having learned that Rossi opposed the bishops' participation in the Fascist rite. In the same report to Ciano, Pignatti reiterates his belief that it was Pius XI who was the most "Italian" of anyone in the Vatican. For the Fascists and those in government being "Italian" was equated with supporting Mussolini. Not only did the pope not try to prevent the clergy from taking part in the celebration, but those who received invitations from their local prefect, as some did, were told they should not refuse it. One bishop—from Sicily—complained he had gotten an invitation despite the fact that he had had nothing to do with the battle for grain, adding, ruefully, "because I don't have even a meter of land to plant." Nonetheless, he wrote, "given the repeated invitations, I believed it my duty to accept and to come to Rome." Ibid., p. 31r., vescovo di Agrigento, 30 dicembre 1937.

24. De Rossi dell'Arno 1954, pp. 138–43. "Mussolini," the British envoy to the Holy See observed, "has taken an opportunity of nailing the Catholic flag to the Fascist flag staff." FCRSE, part XIII, p. 11, Osborne to Eden, January 12, 1938, R 495/495/2..

Three days after the Palazzo Venezia rally, the pope hosted the bishops and priests who had come to Rome for it. The pope had been put on the spot. The original invitation to the priests and bishops had stated that arrangements were being made for them to be received by the pope, yet in fact no such arrangements had at the time been made. The pope consulted with the Consistorial Congregation, which, through its secretary, Cardinal Rossi, advised him against a papal reception for the group, fearful of how such an open embrace of Mussolini's celebration would look outside of Italy. But the pope ignored this advice and instead decided to show solidarity with the clergy, something he knew would please Mussolini. ASMAE, AISS, b. 115, Pignatti al Ministero degli Affari Esteri, 15 gennaio 1938. He blessed the priests, complimented them for their good work with their rural parishioners, and praised all the good that had come out of Conciliation. CC 1938 I, pp. 277–79.

25. This quote, from the *Völkischer Beobachter,* is found in the Vatican archives, ASV, AESI, pos. 1044, fasc. 723, f. 56r; the same quote was sent by the Italian ambassador in Berlin to both the Italian ministry of foreign affairs and the ministry of popular culture. ASMAE, APG, b. 47, 11 gennaio 1938. The quote from *La Stampa* is reproduced at p. 53r.

26. The term is Innocenti's (1992, p. 93). Dino Grandi (1985, pp. 360), former foreign minister and a major figure in the Fascist regime, captured Starace well: "Lacking in intelligence and absolutely uncultured, incapable of distinguishing the things that were important from those that were superfluous or, worse, damaging, he nourished a fanatical adoration for Mussolini and listened with rapt attention to the monologues that the Duce launched into at their morning briefing."

27. De Felice 1974, pp. 216–17; Innocenti 1992, pp. 94–95; Petacci 2011, p. 37.
28. Conway 1968, pp. 158–9; Johnson 1999, pp. 212–14.
29. Three telegrams from Pignatti to Ciano, forwarded to the Italian ambassador in Berlin, chronicle this episode. ASMAE, APG, b. 46, Ciano, "Questione religiosa Germania-Vaticano," telespresso n. 210989, 26 marzo 1938.
30. DDI, series 8, vol. 8, n. 130, Pignatti a Ciano, 10 febbraio 1938.

CHAPTER 21: HITLER IN ROME

1. DDF, series 2, vol. 8, n. 422, Puaux, ministre de France à Vienne, à Paul-Boncour, ministre des affaires etrangères, 14 mars 1938.
2. NYT, March 16, 1938, p. 8; "Austria disappears," NYT, March 14, 1938, p. 14; *Times,* March 15, 1938, p. 14.
3. Charles-Roux 1947, p. 122; Passelecq and Suchecky 1997, pp. 50–51. Chiron 2006, p. 448.
4. CC 1938 II, p. 189.
5. Mussolini initially had his minister instruct the Italian press to provide minimal coverage of the invasion. "Do not dramatize," the editors were told. But the next day, March 12, as the new reality set in, Mussolini decided to make the best of it and try to soften up the Italian population to the new situation. And so the March 12 instructions read, "the news should be objective but sympathetic toward the new state of things." Tranfaglia 2005, p. 248.
6. As Mussolini reported to the king on his return from his German visit. DDI, series 8, vol. 7, n. 393, 4 ottobre 1937. In 1937 both Pacelli and Pizzardo assured the French ambassador that Mussolini would never willingly allow Hitler to take over Austria, but the ambassador was much less sure. DDF, series 2, vol. 5, n. 232, Charles-Roux à Delbos, 8 avril 1937, and ibid., n. 297, Charles-Roux à Delbos, 17 avril 1937.
7. Lamb 1997, pp. 206–7.
8. Baudrillart reported his conversation with the pope to Charles-Roux. DDF, series 2, vol. 9, n. 209, Charles-Roux à Georges Bonnet, ministre des affaires étrangères, 20 avril 1938. See also Charles-Roux 1947, p. 121.
9. DDI, series 8, vol. 8, n. 437, Pignatti a Ciano, 2 aprile 1938.
10. "Hear, O ye heavens, the things I speak," proclaimed the pope in that first Vatican radio broadcast. "Let the earth give ear to the words of my mouth. Hear these things, all ye nations; give ear, all inhabitants of the world." Confalonieri 1957, pp. 147–49; Agostino 1991, pp. 66–67.
11. DGFP, series D, vol. 1d, n. 700, Bergen to the German foreign minister, April 4, 1938.
12. That the reason for Innitzer's rush to get back to Vienna was so that he could meet Hitler was reported by the pope to Cardinal Baudrillart. DDF, series 2, vol. 9, n. 209, Charles-Roux à Georges Bonnet, ministre des affaires étrangères, 20 avril 1938.
13. As they awaited the cardinal's arrival, the pope told Pacelli that if the archbishop offered his resignation, he would accept it. Durand 2010.
14. "In this matter, too," concluded Bergen, "the pope had allowed himself to be swayed by his morbid irritation with Germany." DGFP, series D, vol. 1d, n. 702, Bergen to the German foreign minister, April 6, 1938. The statement was published in *L'Osservatore romano* on April 7 in its original German; an Italian translation was published the following day: "La dichiarazione dell'Episcopato Austriaco," OR, 8 aprile 1938, p. 1.
15. DDF, series 2, vol. 9, n. 125, Rivière, chargé d'affaires de France à Rome Saint-Siège, à Paul-Boncour, 6 avril 1938.
16. Baudrillart 1996, p. 809 (3 avril 1938). The archbishop of Vienna, following his unpleasant trip to Rome, hurried home in time for the April 10 plebiscite. Unbowed and unrepen-

tant, he led the way to the polls, raising his arm in a Nazi salute as he deposited his ballot in favor of annexing Austria to the German Reich. Whatever control the ailing pope still had over his high prelates in Nazi territory seemed to be slipping away. ASMAE, APSS, b. 39, ministero degli affari esteri a R. Ambasciata S. Sede, "Il plebiscito del 10 aprile," telespresso n. 217705, 23 maggio 1938. By the end of the month, the new regime—so enthusiastically championed by the cardinal and his bishops—ordered Austria's Jewish teachers and students thrown out of the schools, Jewish doctors removed from hospitals, Jewish lawyers dropped from the list of those able to practice law, Jewish newspaper directors fired, Jewish factory owners forced out, and Jewish theatrical directors and actors dismissed. Signs reading "Jewish store" were placed in the front windows of Jewish-owned shops. Catholic customers so bold as to ignore the warning were forced to wear a sign on their backs proclaiming: "I am an Aryan pig." The Italian consul general in Vienna reported all this to Ciano on April 26. DDI, series 8, vol. 9, n. 10.

17. Mussolini realized that the pope might balk at such a move, worried that anything that undermined the Nazi government might weaken the anti-Communist forces, and he acknowledged that some of the Church's enemies would be heartened by the excommunication. But, he added, "that does not take anything away from the need for it."

18. The only account we have of the conversation came to light when, following the opening of Pius XI's archives at the Vatican in 2006, Cardinal Pacelli's handwritten notes of his meetings with the pope were found. ASV, AESS, pos. 430a, fasc. 355, f. 41, 10 aprile 1938.

19. ASMAE, APSS, b. 39, ministero degli affari esteri, Roma, a R. Ambasciata presso S. Sede, "Contrasti fra Hitler e Vaticano," telespresso n. 200305, 5 gennaio 1932.

20. In mid-January, Cardinal Pacelli told the French ambassador that the Vatican had so far received no request from the German government for any meeting. Given the tense relations, he thought it unlikely that it would. In a separate conversation, Monsignor Tardini told Charles-Roux that should Hitler ask for an audience with the pope, he did not see any way the pontiff could refuse to see him. DDF, series 2, vol. 8a, n. 5, Charles-Roux à Delbos, ministre des affaires étrangères, 18 janvier 1938. Later in January Pignatti reiterated this impression: if Hitler asked for a visit with the pope, the Vatican would have no difficulty arranging it. ASMAE, AISS, b. 87, "Riservato," unsigned typed report, 24 gennaio 1938. Bergen, the German ambassador to the Holy See, reported that Pacelli had made feelers about Hitler visiting the pope, if Hitler would first make "an agreed statement on the treatment of the Catholics and the Catholic Church." The pope, said Bergen, "had definitely been counting on a visit of the Führer." But "to various feelers," he reported, "I expressed myself in accordance with my instructions and left no room for doubt that a visit was out of the question." DGFP, series D, vol. 1, n. 708, Bergen to Weizsäcker, May 18, 1938 He later reported that the pope had expected Hitler to visit him and "had hoped for that until the last moment." Ibid., May 23, 1938, n. 710.

21. ASMAE, AISS, b. 87, Pignatti a Regio Ministero degli Affari Esteri, "Germania e Santa Sede," 21 gennaio 1938.

22. In the weeks leading up to the visit, the pope was still regularly calling on the Duce to intercede on the Church's behalf with the Führer. On March 16, Cardinal Pacelli wrote to Mussolini to tell him of the pope's gratitude "for your moderating action with the Chancellor of the German Reich, Signor Hitler, and for your intervention against the continuation of the policy of religious persecution in Germany." The pope, added Pacelli, appreciated Mussolini's intervention even more given that it came on the eve of Hitler's visit to Rome. ASMAE, APG, b. 46, Pacelli a Mussolini, 16 marzo 1938. Pacelli's handwritten draft of this letter, with corrections, is found at ASV, AESG pos. 735, fasc. 353, f. 4r. Tacchi Venturi told Mussolini that the pope had been "*contentissimo*" to hear that Mussolini would do everything possible to ensure that religious persecution—meaning

persecution of the Catholic Church—did not begin in Austria. ACS, CR, b. 68, n. 028790, 17 marzo 1938.

23. The French ambassador was convinced that if Hitler wanted to come, the pope would receive him. "One consideration dominates all others for the Holy See," he observed, "that of not doing anything to worsen the situation by giving the National Socialist government the pretext that the extremists there seem to be seeking." DDF, series 2, vol. 8, n. 41, Charles-Roux à Delbos, ministère des affaires étrangères, 26 janvier 1938. Although Mussolini wanted to have Hitler visit Pius XI—if he could be sure it would go smoothly—the Führer found the prospect distasteful. The German foreign ministry was in an awkward spot in explaining why Hitler would not follow custom and see the pope. In mid-February, the new German foreign minister, Joachim von Ribbentrop, suggested a possible excuse to use. Hitler was going to Rome on the invitation of the King of Italy, he argued, "and has no reason for visiting other sovereigns on non-Italian territory on this occasion." He advised that, in providing this as their explanation, they not use what others were suggesting they give as a rationale: the fact that they had received no invitation from the pope. "To point out that, after all, no invitation has hitherto been forthcoming seemed to us inadvisable as it involves the risk that the Vatican might then extend such an invitation." DGFP, series D, vol. 1d, n. 691, "Memorandum," signed by Mackensen, based on his conversation with Ribbentrop, February 14, 1938.

24. ASMAE, APSS, b. 39, Ciano a Pignatti, "Viaggio in Italia di S.E. il Cancelliere Hitler," 26 marzo 1938, and Pignatti a Ciano, "Viaggio in Italia del Fuehrer," 2 aprile 1938.

25. ASMAE, APSS, b. 39, Pignatti a Ciano, telegramma n. 2022, 7 aprile 1938. The pope and his secretary of state were eager to let Italy's cardinals know that if Hitler failed to visit the pope while in Rome, it would not be because the pope had refused to see him but because Hitler had never requested the meeting. On the day of Hitler's arrival in Rome, Cardinal Pacelli sent a message to this effect to the cardinals and enclosed a copy of Borgongini's report of his early May meeting with Buffarini, reporting the pope's willingness to meet Hitler. ASV, AESG, pos. 735, fasc. 353, ff. 26r–27r, "Circa l'omissione di una visita del Cancelliere del Reich Germanico al Santo Padre," marked "Sub secreto pontificio," 3 maggio 1937. While the pope was willing to receive Hitler, he made clear he would do so only if Hitler signaled his intention to observe the terms of the concordat he had signed.

26. Pacelli notes of meeting with Pignatti, March 25, 1938, in Casella 2010, pp. 210–11.

27. ASMAE, AISS, b. 87, Pignatti a Ciano, 28 aprile 1938; CC 1938 II, p. 368.

28. Confalonieri 1957, p. 372.

29. Rauscher 2004, p. 241.

30. Milza 2000, p. 759; Gallagher 2008, p. 71; Cerruti 1953, p. 240. The American ambassador to Italy had described Victor Emmanuel III only slightly more generously, as "a thin little man with too short legs, a screwed-up face and a bristling mustache, but with a certain dignity in spite of his insignificant appearance." Phillips 1952, p. 192. It was Ciano (2002, pp. 86, 88–89) who, in his diary, related the private views of the king about Hitler. Ciano complained that the king was "useless and troublesome" during the Führer's visit. The American ambassador later repeated—and vouched for the accuracy of—the story going around Rome that when Hitler first arrived at the Quirinal Palace and saw his room, he asked if a male or female attendant had made his bed. On hearing it had been a man, he insisted that a woman be found to make it again for him. He would not sleep in a bed made by a man. Phillips 1952, p. 214.

31. DDI, series 8, vol. 9, n. 53, Pignatti a Ciano, 5 maggio 1938.

32. The triumphal mood of Hitler's visit was magnified by the recent victories of Franco's forces in Spain, which the previous month had cut Republican Spain in two. Strikingly, it was while Hitler was in Rome that the Holy See formally announced it was appointing a nuncio to the new Nationalist government in Spain, with Franco sending an ambassador

to the Vatican shortly thereafter. Kent 1986, p. 457. Mussolini's decision to send troops to fight for Franco cost Italy close to four thousand dead. De Felice 1981, p. 465.

33. Hitler took out his anger over his embarrassment on Ribbentrop, who fired the Nazi head of protocol. Kershaw 2000, p. 98.

34. The American consul added that invitations to the gala dinner were withdrawn from four women because of their "Jewish antecedents or connections." One of them however, "made such a strong protest, proving she was not a jew [sic], that the request not to attend the dinner was withdrawn in her case." NARA, LM192, reel 5, John Putnam, U.S. consul general, Florence, to William Phillips, May 21, 1938.

35. Mussolini was not much of a museumgoer, having remarked in 1922 that he had never visited a museum in his life. Boswell 2011, p. 201.

36. Ciano 2002, p. 89.

37. NARA, LM192, reel 5, William Phillips, U.S. ambassador, Rome, to U.S. secretary of state, Rome, "Hitler's Visit to Italy," 12 page report plus attachments, May 13, 1938. The Florence festivities are described in U.S. consul in Florence, "Memorandum of Visit of Their Excellencies Adolf Hitler and Benito Mussolini, May 9, 1938," May 18, 1938, appendix to report of John Putnam, consul general, cited in note 34 above. The British diplomatic assessment came to the same conclusion: FCRSE, pt. 14, R 4789/43/22, p. 93, Earl of Perth to Viscount Halifax, May 9, 1938.

38. DDF, series 2, vol. 9, n. 346, Charles-Roux à Georges Bonnet, 15 mai 1938.

39. CC 1938 II, pp. 376–77.

40. ASV, AESG, pos. 735, fasc. 353, ff. 59r–60r, Il delegato vescovile, Curia ecclesiastica generale di Orte, alla segreteria di stato, Vaticano, 15 maggio 1938.

CHAPTER 22: A SURPRISING MISSION

1. Probably through a *Civiltà cattolica* article that discussed it: M. Barbera, "Giustizia tra le 'razze,'" CC 1937 IV, pp. 531–38. LaFarge had been featured in a 1932 article published in *L'Osservatore romano,* reporting a piece he had written for *America* on Communist attempts to woo African-Americans: "Diventeranno comunisti i Negri?" OR, 5 giugno 1932, p. 4. Details on his family can be found in Eisner 2013.

2. We have learned of the superior general's reaction from a document, found in the uninventoried archives of *La Civiltà cattolica,* quoted in Sale 2009, p. 37.

3. The first type of anti-Semitism, he wrote, was not Christian, being based on ideas of racial difference. By contrast, "the second type of anti-Semitism is permissible when it combats, by moral and legal means, a truly harmful influence of the Jewish segment of the population in the areas of economy, politics, theater, cinema, the press, science, and art." Most dangerous were the liberal, more assimilated Jews, Gundlach argued, for "being for the most part given to moral nihilism and without any national or religious ties, they operate within the camp of world plutocracy as well as within that of international Bolshevism, thus unleashing the darker traits of the soul of the Jewish people expelled from its fatherland." The Church, in its charity, had always opposed the unjust persecution of Jews but had long supported measures designed to protect European society from Jews' harmful economic and intellectual influence. The English translation is in Passelecq and Suchecky 1997, pp. 47–49. My account of LaFarge's encounters with the pope and Ledóchowski is based on Passelecq and Suchecky's excellent study. See also Eisner 2013.

4. Quoted in Starr 1939, p. 118. On May 27 Turin's *La Stampa* quoted the same lines from Belloc's book, in a prominent anti-Semitic article warning of the Jewish danger. "Il numero e il denaro," *La Stampa,* 27 maggio 1937, p. 1. It was clipped and saved by the Vatican secretary of state office. ASV, AESI, b. 1031, fasc. 717, f. 88r.

5. The Jesuit journal then discussed a significant recent book, *Israel, son passé, son avenir,*

by a distinguished Dutch Catholic, Herrmann De Vries. After their exile, De Vries wrote, the Jews had historically passed through five periods that were continually repeated as they were thrown out of one country and fled to another. First the Jews were welcomed; then they were tolerated. In the third period they got richer, causing others to grow envious. This resulted in a popular reaction against them, which led to the fifth stage, an attempt to exterminate them or drive them out.

6. "La questione giudaica e il sionismo," CC 1937 II, pp. 418–31.

7. CC 1938 I, p. 460. The next month *La Civiltà cattolica* renewed its warning of the Jewish drive for world domination. It contrasted good early Judaism, which had given rise to Christianity, with current Judaism, "in reality a profoundly corrupt religion." It informed its readers that "the fatal mania for financial and political world domination . . . is the true and deep cause that makes Judaism a fount of disorder and a permanent danger to the world." Defensive action was necessary. The best path would be to follow the popes' traditional blend of charity with "prudence and opportune measures, that is, a form of segregation appropriate to our times." The next month the journal reminded its readers that "the Jews have brought on themselves in every time, and still today, people's just aversion with their all too frequent abuses of power and with their hatred toward Christ himself, his religion, and his Catholic Church." "La 'teoria moderna delle razze' impugnata da un acattolico," CC 1938 III, pp. 62–71, quote on p. 68.

8. Monsignor Orlandi's article, "L'invasione ebraica anche in Italia" (*L'Amico del Clero*, vol. 20, no. 3, 1938), is quoted extensively in Miccoli 1988, p. 866.

9. Mario Barbera, "La questione dei giudei in Ungheria," CC 1938 III, pp. 146–53. On April 12, 1938, the papal nuncio in Budapest sent Pacelli a report on the new laws, which set quotas for Jewish participation in the professions, in finance, and in business. Concerned, he noted that the new law treated as Jews all those Jewish converts to Catholicism who had been baptized after 1919, along with their children who had been baptized at birth. The University Student Association, to which most Catholic university students in Hungary belonged, had added a clause to its bylaws stating that it "does not view as unconditionally Hungarian the baptized Jew and his descendants." In early May, Cardinal Pacelli replied to the nuncio, sharing his concern: "The overly general judgment that they would like to give to the insincerity of the conversions from Judaism to Christianity that have taken place since 1919 seems strange and arbitrary and in contrast with the spirit of generosity of the Hungarian people." Pacelli concluded, "In particular, it is to be hoped that, while protecting the just interests of the Magyar nation, this Government does not stoop to measures of excessive severity against the Jews and that the Hungarian Catholics in these circumstances show reasonable moderation in this work." ASV, AESU, b. 77, fasc. 57, ff. 6r–9v, Angelo Rotta, nunzio, a Pacelli, Budapest, 12 aprile 1938; ibid., ff. 10r–10v, Pacelli a Rotta, 8 maggio 1938.

10. Maiocchi 2003; Bottai 2001, p. 125; Gillette 2001, 2002a, 2002b.

11. At a diplomatic dinner on July 18, Bottai (2001, p. 125) raised the subject of the manifesto with Mussolini, who explained with great emotion, "I've had enough of hearing people saying that a race that has given the world Dante, Machiavelli, Raffaello, Michelangelo is of African origin."

12. Cannistraro and Sullivan 1993, pp. 218–19. Mussolini's foremost French biographer portrayed Sarfatti as the single most important influence in his postwar conversion to the idea of championing a nationalist revolution led by young war veterans. When he first became prime minister, she helped convince him he could be Italy's new Caesar. Milza 2000, pp. 257, 354. On Sarfatti's influence on Mussolini, see also Urso 2003.

13. Festorazzi 2010, p. 96; Navarra 2004, p. 68.

14. Ludwig 1933, pp. 69–70. But following Mussolini's September 1937 visit to Germany and his tightening alliance with the Führer, Italian Jews began to worry that he might try to

imitate Hitler's anti-Semitic campaign. Ciano, receiving agitated requests from Italian Jews, noted that the Germans had never raised the issue with him. "Nor do I believe that it would be in our interest to unleash an anti-Semitic campaign in Italy. The problem does not exist here. They are few and, apart from some exceptions, good." Ciano 2002, p. 32. As late as February 1938, Mussolini wrote a note for the Italian foreign ministry denying that the government was planning an anti-Semitic campaign. DDI, series 8, vol. 8, n. 162, "Nota n. 14 dell'informazione diplomatica," 16 febbraio 1938.

15. Grandi 1985, pp. 443–44. But Rauscher (2004, p. 225) asserts that during Mussolini's 1937 visit to Germany, he let Hitler know he would soon be introducing anti-Semitic measures in Italy.

16. Many works discuss the question of how Mussolini's 1938 anti-Semitic campaign came about. Fabre (2005) argues that Mussolini was always anti-Semitic. But De Felice (1981, pp. 312–13) maintains that he never really was an anti-Semite; only with the Ethiopian war did he become convinced that an international Jewish conspiracy was organizing against him, whereupon he began down the path of a "political" anti-Semitism. For other perspectives, see Israel 2010, pp. 159–70; Matard Bonucci 2008; and Vivarelli 2009, p. 748.

17. CC 1938 III, pp. 275–78.

18. The *Civiltà Cattolica* writer was Father Angelo Brucculeri. Among the other Catholic publications republishing Bruccleri's praise of the new racial policy was *La Settimana religiosa,* the diocesan weekly of Venice. Perin 2011, pp. 200–1.

19. "Il fascismo e i problemi della razza," OR, 16 luglio 1938, p. 2. On the Brucculeri article, see Miccoli 1988, p. 871. Manzini was the editor of *L'Osservatore romano* from 1960 to 1978; De Cesaris 2010, p. 139. The Roman Catholic Church's embrace of anti-Semitism is heatedly debated. Many seek to draw a sharp line between the Church's religiously based "anti-Judaism" and the racially based "anti-Semitism" that led to the Holocaust; I deal with this debate in Kertzer 2001. *La Civiltà cattolica* and the rest of the Italian Catholic press in these years commonly referred to Jews as a "race." Typically, in a pastoral letter for Easter 1938, the patriarch of Venice, Cardinal Adeodato Piazza, branded the Jews as a "race" collectively responsible for having murdered Jesus. Condemned to wander the earth, he claimed, they were "implicated in the shadiest sects, from masonry to Bolshevism." Quoted in Perin 2011, pp. 216–17.

20. A government wiretap picked up the call. ACS, MCPG, b. 166, wiretap n. 5102, Roma, 14 luglio 1938. The conversation was in German.

21. Examples of German press enthusiasm for the new Italian racial campaign, reported to the Italian Holy See desk, can found at ASMAE, AISS, b. 102, "Servizio speciale," Monaco, 15 luglio 1938.

22. ACS, MCPG, b. 151, ministro di cultura popolare a Mussolini, 19 luglio 1938.

23. Curiously, in 1933 the interviewer Emil Ludwig, upon seeing Mussolini close up, thought of the resemblance he bore to Borgia: "Now he sat facing me across a table. The condottiere Cesare Borgia, whom I had once portrayed in a Roman palace, the hero of the Romagna, seems to have been resurrected, though he wore a dark lounge suit and a black necktie." Ludwig 1933, p. 23.

24. The pope's instructions were conveyed to Borgongini through Pacelli. The Borgia pope had previously been the subject of vigorous Vatican attempts at censorship. In 1934 the pope learned that the play *Caterina Sforza,* which portrayed Alexander VI in all his corruption, was to open in Rome in April. He dispatched Tacchi Venturi to stop it. The government had the playwright entirely cut the first scene and radically cut another that was deemed offensive to the Church. ASV, AESI, pos. 855, fasc. 549, ff. 4r–24r.

25. ASV, ANI, pos. 47, fasc. 2, ff. 124r–129r.

26. Ibid., ff. 132r–134r, Tacchi Venturi a Tardini, 15 giugno 1938.

27. Pacelli's letter, sent to Borgongini, expressed his pleasure at receipt of such good news.

ASV, ANI, pos. 47, fasc. 2, ff. 135r–136r, Pacelli a Borgongini, 22 giugno 1938. Catholic Action continued to play a major role in alerting police to books, magazines, plays, and films that the Church deemed objectionable. The national organization sent the diocesan morality secretariats detailed instructions on how to operate a network of informants, to ensure that no offensive work escaped police attention. ASV, AESI, pos. 773, fasc. 356, ff. 104r–115r. As for the publisher Rizzoli, he would survive and go on to create a publishing and bookstore empire—and in the postwar years would again run afoul of the Vatican. In 1960 he produced a film, *La Dolce Vita,* directed by Federico Fellini, that would be condemned by *L'Osservatore romano* and initially censored in Italy.

28. NARA, M1423, reel 1, n. 991, William Phillips to U.S. secretary of state, Washington, "Physical Fitness Tests for High Fascist Party Officials," July 7, 1938.

29. Petacci 2010, pp. 131, 370.

30. In particular, Pacelli told Pignatti, nothing should be done to prevent a marriage between a Catholic convert from Judaism and another Catholic. Pacelli had reason to worry, because the 1935 Nuremberg Laws had instituted just such a measure in Germany. Pacelli quoted the language of the concordat, which specified that Church marriages were to be regarded as civilly valid, and he reminded Ciano that "Canon Law recognizes as valid marriage between baptized individuals (Canon 1012) regardless of any other consideration." ASMAE, AISS, b. 102, Pignatti al ministro degli affari esteri, 20 luglio 1938.

31. ASMAE, APSS, b. 40, Pignatti, "Notizie sulla salute del Pontefice," telespresso n. 1818/678, 11 luglio 1938. Pucci based his description of the pope's health on his conversation with Father Gemelli, who had recently visited the pope.

32. DDI, series 8, vol. 9, n. 336, Pignatti a Ciano, 26 luglio 1938.

33. Ibid., n. 337, Pignatti a Ciano, 26 luglio 1938.

34. "La parola del Sommo Pontefice Pio XI agli alunni del Collegio di Propaganda Fide," OR, 20 luglio 1938, p. 1, republished in CC 1938 III, pp. 371–76.

35. ASV, AESI, pos. 1054, fasc. 732, f. 19r.

36. Ciano 2002, p. 113 (July 30, 1938). Borgongini told Italy's ambassador to the Holy See that the Church had always discouraged interracial marriages, recognizing that the "crossbreeds" who resulted "combine the defects of both races." As for the anti-Semitic campaign, what upset the pope was not the prospect of government action against the Jews but that Italy might follow Germany in treating Catholic converts as if they were Jews. Pignatti made no direct response, simply reassuring the nuncio that the Italian racial campaign would be different from the Nazis'. ASV, AESI, pos. 1054, fasc. 728, ff. 46r–48r, Borgongini a Pacelli, 2 agosto 1938. The next day Borgongini recounted the conversation directly to the pope.

37. ASMAE, AISS, b. 115, Pignatti a Ciano, 31 luglio 1938.

38. Quoted in Papin 1977, p. 62.

39. "In recent memory," Ledóchowski noted, "there was no case of a pope who had lost his reason." ASMAE, Gab. b. 1186, Pignatti a Ciano, 5 agosto 1938.

40. Ibid.

CHAPTER 23: THE SECRET DEAL

1. CC 1938 III, pp. 377–78.

2. ASV, AESI, pos. 1007c, fasc. 695, ff. 70r–75r, "Progetto di una lettera del S. Padre a Mussolini circa Ebrei e Azione Cattolica," agosto 1938.

3. Eager to placate Pignatti, Pacelli told him that the pope had just sent Tacchi Venturi with a message for Mussolini. While it lamented the recent violence against Catholic Action, it did so respectfully, with "expressions of great admiration and deference for the Duce." ASMAE, AISS, b. 102, Pignatti a Ciano, 6 agosto 1938.

4. From Pignatti's August 8, 1938 report, quoted by Casella 2010, pp. 268–69.

5. The piece quotes Mussolini justifying the anti-Semitic campaign at length, including his remarks that "to say that Fascism has imitated someone or something else is simply absurd. . . . No one can doubt that the time is ripe for Italian racism." The journal offered no comment on the Duce's remarks. CC 1938 III, pp. 376–78.

6. The Jesuits worked best, advised Pignatti, when they were able "to exercise that secret action of which they are masters." ASMAE, AISS, b. 102, Pignatti a Ciano, 7 agosto 1938.

7. But Ciano was more optimistic, believing that those around the pope were beginning to get through to him. "As for the matter of race, the pope, who now knows the real terms of the problem," he wrote that day in his diary, "is beginning to yield." Ciano 2002, p. 113.

8. Farinacci charged that it was Cardinal Pizzardo who had persuaded the pope to criticize the racial campaign. On August 3, Farinacci repeated the accusation in a letter to Mussolini. He concluded by asking Mussolini: "Dear President, is it true that the pope's mother is a Jew?" He added, "If it is true, what a laugh!" ACS, CR, b. 44, Roberto Farinacci, direttore, *Il Regime fascista,* Cremona, a Mussolini, 3 agosto 1938. Farinacci had likely picked up the allegation that the pope was Jewish from the German press, which was circulating such stories at the time.

9. ASV, AESI, pos. 1060, fasc. 749, ff. 14r–21r, Monsignor Giovanni Cazzani, vescovo di Cremona, a Farinacci, 17 agosto 1938.

10. ASV, AESI, pos. 1060, fasc. 749, ff. 22r–26r, Farinacci a Cazzani, 18 agosto 1938.

11. Fabre (2012, pp. 109–10) has recently published and analyzed this text, found in Tacchi Venturi's papers. ARSI, TV, f. 2143.

12. ASV, AESI, pos. 1007c, fasc. 695, ff. 37r–39r, "Nota da me presentato al Duce la sera di venerdì 12 Agosto," Tacchi Venturi, 12 agosto 1938.

13. Sarfatti 2006, pp. 19–41; Sarfatti 2005, pp. 67–68. By 1938 roughly 21 percent of the Jews living in Italy were refugees from other countries, seeking to escape persecution.

14. ASV, AESI, pos. 1054, fasc. 730, ff. 40r–41r. Years before the Vatican archives for the papacy of Pius XI were opened, Father Angelo Martini, S.J., was given access and reported the existence of this document. Although he quoted its text (Martini 1963), he gave little background and judged it "unfortunately so generic as not to inspire confidence." Miccoli (1988, pp. 847–48), in reporting Martini's finding and his comment, and not at the time having access to the archive, noted its significance and disagreed with Martini's attempt to minimize it. Only with the 2006 opening of the Vatican archives did the document, and those surrounding it, become available and its full import visible. De Cesaris (2010, pp. 160–61) argues that the document must have been drafted by Mussolini or someone close to him in the government and not by Tacchi Venturi or anyone from the Vatican. I find his attempt to distance the pope and the Vatican from the proposal to be unconvincing. The document closely reflects proposals the pope had been making to Mussolini in the days preceding it.

15. "Gli Ebrei ed il Concilio Vaticano," OR, 14 agosto 1938, p. 2. I use the English translation provided by the American ambassador, who lamented the fact that the Vatican seemed to have decided not to object to the racial campaign in Italy. NARA, M1423, reel 12, Ambassador William Phillips to U.S. secretary of state, "Progress of Racial Movement in Italy," August 19, 1938. For an examination of the correspondence between the U.S. secretary of state and the Italian ambassador regarding the pope's reaction to the Italian anti-Semitic campaign, see Kertzer and Visani 2012.

16. Fabre (2012, p. 119), who has provided the most comprehensive study of the August 16 agreement, comes to the same conclusion about the reason for the pope's outburst.

17. ASV, AESI, pos. 1007c, fasc. 695, ff. 41r–42r, handwritten unsigned three-page memo, 18 agosto 2011. Later in the month, discussing the conflict with the government over Catholic Action in a conversation with members of the French embassy, Tardini held Mussolini

blameless. The fault, he argued, lay with the "left wing" of the Fascist Party, especially Party head Achille Starace. MAEI, vol. 267, 126, Charles-Roux à Bonnet, 29 août 1938.

18. MAEI, vol. 267, 94, Charles-Roux, 17 août 1938; and ibid., 95–96, 18 août 1938.

19. MAEI, vol. 267, 97, Charles-Roux, 18 août 1938. The minister added that they should not worry about the pope's Propaganda Fide remarks, as they did not reflect the Vatican position on the racial campaign; they were simply the product of a moment when the elderly pope had happened to be in a bad mood. Tranfaglia 2005, p. 151.

20. MAEI, vol. 267, 102–3, Charles-Roux, 20 août 1938.

21. "Pope and Fascists Reach New Accord on Catholic Action," NYT, August 21, 1938, p. 1. A similar story in the *Los Angeles Times* that day began, "Through the good offices of a 77-year-old Jesuit priest, Pietro Tacchi Venturi, Premier Mussolini and Pope Pius XI have again smoothed over the differences between the Catholic Church and the Fascist party." "Pope and Duce Renew Peace," LAT, August 21, 1938, p. 2.

22. "Circa le relazioni tra l'Azione Cattolica Italiana e il Partito Nazionale Fascista," OR, 25 agosto 1938, p. 1. The *Messaggero* clipping is found at AESI, pos. 1007c, fasc. 695, f. 64r. The last-minute flurry of negotiations involving the pope and the Italian government is chronicled in the report by Cossato. ASMAE, AISS, b. 102, Cossato, 23 agosto 1938; and ibid., 24 agosto 1938.

23. ASV, AESS, pos. 430, fasc. 355, f. 70, 27 agosto 1938.

24. ASMAE, AISS, b. 102, Cossato, 22 agosto 1938.

25. He summoned Tacchi Venturi to tell the pope how angry he was. Mussolini's meeting with the Jesuit was on his calendar for seven-thirty P.M. on August 22. ACS, CO, b. 3136.

26. Ciano 2002, pp. 117–18. Mussolini, meanwhile, had recently introduced the requirement that all government employees wear their uniform to work, provoking a certain amount of grumbling. Told of the unhappiness, he responded, "Remember: the cassock makes the monk!" Bottai 1989, p. 131.

27. The clippings are found at ASV, AESI, pos. 1054, fasc. 728, ff. 19r, 20r.

28. Ciano 2002, p. 119. The pope was in fact eighty-one years old at the time.

29. Mussolini himself chose its director, Talesio Interlandi, who had been pushing him for years to follow Hitler's example and move against Italy's Jews.

30. Guido Landra, "Concetti del razzismo italiano," *La Difesa della razza* 1, n. 1 (1938), p. 10.

31. Many, I am sorry to say, including the author of the appalling piece published in the first issue, cited above, were Italian anthropologists.

32. The government required all universities to place copies of *La Difesa della razza* in their libraries and called on all professors to read it carefully and share its message with their students. Italian newspapers were likewise directed to cite its stories and use its material for their own articles. Giuseppe Pensabene, "L'evoluzione e la razza. Cinquant'anni di polemiche ne 'La Civiltà Cattolica," *La Difesa della razza* 1, n. 1, 5 agosto 1938, pp. 31–33. See also Mughini 1991, pp. 145–46. Israel 2010, pp. 203–4; Cassata 2008, p. 116; Tranfaglia 2005, p. 152.

33. ASMAE, AISS, b. 102, Pignatti a Ciano, 29 agosto 1938.

CHAPTER 24: THE RACIAL LAWS

1. "The daily newspapers are citing *Civiltà cattolica* as occupying a position of honor in today's struggle against the Jews, especially for the three articles it published in 1890," the Jesuits of the journal wrote. "To tell the truth, we must note that that vigorous campaign, inspired by the spectacle of the invasion and the arrogance of the Jews, cannot be credited with having 'known how to fascistically impose the racial problem' . . . as *Il Regime Fascista* (28 August) would have it." CC 1938 III, pp. 559–61.

2. Ibid.; emphasis in the original.

3. Enrico Rosa, "La questione giudaica e 'la Civiltà cattolica,'" CC 1938 IV, pp. 3–16.

4. Matard-Bonucci 2008, p. 309; Onofri 1989, p. 153.

5. ASV, AESI, pos. 985, fasc. 671, f. 47r, "Appunto," 1 settembre 1938.

6. Pacelli also wrote both to Cardinal Schuster—who as archbishop of Milan, had authority over the Como bishop—and to Don Mauri's own archbishop, the archbishop of Turin. ASV, AESI, pos. 985, fasc. 671, f. 49r, Pacelli al Cardinale Schuster, 2 settembre 1938.

7. ASV, AESI, pos. 985, fasc. 671, f. 53r, Alessandro Macchi, vescovo di Como, 15 settembre 1938; ibid., f. 54r, Sac. A. Negrini, Como, 15 settembre 1938. In a later report, Pacelli was told that the whole episode could be attributed to the fact that the PNF head in Aprica owned a hotel there and had a long-standing conflict with the nuns who owned a building nearby. In this account, the Fascist had exaggerated Don Mauri's remarks to embarrass the nuns. ASV, AESI, pos. 985, fasc. 671, f. 60r, "Circa l'incidente sollevato in occasione del discorso tenuto in Aprica."

8. Gallagher 2008, pp. 72–73. Recall that the United States did not recognize the Vatican as a sovereign state and so had no official diplomatic relations with it.

9. Phillips was also convinced that Mussolini had no understanding of the United States or its importance. In his memoirs, he reproduces a letter he received from President Roosevelt on September 15, 1938, in which the president shared this view. Roosevelt said that the ignorance of the United States on the part of Mussolini and those around him reminded him of a conversation that his youngest son, Johnny, had with the Italian minister of finance. When the minister suggested the president pay a visit to Mussolini, Roosevelt's son suggested the Duce might want to pay a visit to his father in Washington. When the minister seemed to find the idea odd, "Johnny told him with complete politeness that the United States had three times the population and ten times the resources of Italy, and that the whole of Italy would fit very comfortably into the State of Texas." Phillips 1952, p. 219.

10. ASV, AESI pos. 1054, fasc. 731, ff. 8r–10r, "Appunto," Hurley, 3 settembre 1938.

11. Sale 2009, pp. 88–89; Fattorini 2012, p. 390. For the implications of the pope's phrase regarding a state's legitimate right to self-defense in this context, see Kertzer 2001, pp. 279–80. The day the pope was making his plea against the racial laws, the radio priest Charles Coughlin wrote to Mussolini offering his help. Coughlin invited the Duce to write an article for his magazine, *Social Justice*, with its millions of readers, in which he could "clarify" his "attitude toward the Jews." Coughlin concluded, "Wishing Your Excellency God's blessings and good health, and praying that the Italian Empire under your leadership will crush Communism." Mussolini decided against writing the piece. ACS, MCPR, b. 3, Coughlin a Mussolini, 6 settembre 1938; ACS, MCPR, b. 3, stampa estera, telegramma n. 16848 a R. Ambasciata d'Italia, Washington, 18 ottobre 1938.

12. The Vatican daily devoted only a paragraph to the audience, making no reference at all to comments about race or anti-Semitism. "Il paterno elogio di Sua Santità ai pellegrini della Gioventù Cattolica del Belgio," OR, 9 settembre 1938, p. 1.

13. ACS, MCPG, b. 164, "Notizia fiduciaria," Roma, 7 settembre 1938.

14. Bottai 2001, p. 137 (7 ottobre 1938).

15. Ibid., p. 133 (8 settembre 1938).

16. Ciano 2002, p. 124 (September 10, 1938); Lamb 1997, pp. 206–7. Two days later the king spoke directly with Buffarini Guidi, undersecretary for internal affairs, on behalf of his doctor. The king's craven acquiescence to the racial laws was again on display. The king felt uncomfortable because a number of highly decorated Jewish military officers had contacted him to complain about the new anti-Semitic campaign. When Buffarini told him that provisions were being made to exempt such men from the laws, the king replied, "I am truly happy that the president [Mussolini] intends to make these distinctions, recognizing the merits of those Jews who are noteworthy for their loyalty to the Fatherland." He added,

"I was sure that the president's great sensibility, his profound intuition and expansive generosity would have led to such a line of conduct." Quoted in De Felice 1981, p. 492.

17. ASV, AESI, pos. 1054, fasc. 727, f. 48r, 6 settembre 1938, Consegnato dal P. Tacchi Venturi per riferire al S. Padre, 6 settembre 1938; ibid., f. 46r, 7 settembre 1938, Segreteria di Stato di Sua Santità, 7 settembre 1938.

18. The Church, the pope added, teaches that both Christians and Jews are descended from the seed of Abraham, and that Abraham was the patriarch of all. The pope gave his instructions through Cardinal Pacelli. The page is handwritten by Pacelli, of the sort found in the notes of his audiences with the pope, but it is not collected with the rest of the secretary of state's notes. ASV, AESI, pos. 1054, fasc. 727, f. 45r, "Udienza del 9 settembre 1938." The label of the Vatican folder containing the record of these talks is revealing. Although the pope may have seen the question differently, under Pacelli the secretary of state office remained clear about its focus: "Directives to Father Tacchi Venturi for Negotiations with the Head of Government About the Racist Question. Question of Jews who Converted to Catholicism." ASV, AESI, pos. 1054, fasc. 727, f. 40r, settembre 1938. On the same day as Tacchi Venturi met with Mussolini to discuss the racial laws, Pignatti met with Pacelli. They discussed the pope's continuing complaints about PNF sponsorship of public dances in which working-class girls took part. ASMAE, APSS, b. 42, Pignatti a Starace, 10 settembre 1938.

19. ASV, AESI, pos. 1054, fasc. 727, ff. 41r, 43r, 20 settembre 1938.

20. Ibid., fasc. 732, ff. 48r–48v, Cardinal Fossati, arcivescovo di Torino, a Domenico Tardini, 28 settembre 1938; ibid., f. 49r, Tardini a Fossati, 1 ottobre 1938; Tardini a Tacchi Venturi, 1 ottobre 1938.

21. Primo Levi, *The Periodic Table,* quoted by Cavarocchi and Minerbi 1999, p. 483.

22. The reference is to the diary of Sylvia Lombroso (Nidam-Orvieto 2005), p. 162.

23. Ibid., pp. 162–63.

24. Lamb 1997, p. 221.

25. André François-Poncet, the French ambassador to Berlin, left an excellent description of the meeting; quoted by De Felice (1981, p. 528). Édouard Daladier was the French representative at the conference.

26. Lamb 1997, figs. 12–13; Navarra 2004, p. 38. Navarra apparently thought it wise not to mention the fact that notwithstanding their umbrellas, the British had founded a rather substantial empire.

27. "Mentre Milioni," 29 settembre 1938, http://www.vatican.va/holy_father/pius_xi/speeches /documents/hf_p-xi_spe_19380929_mentre-milioni_it.html. Pius XI was not pleased with the Munich agreement. He complained to Charles-Roux about the lack of French support for Czechoslovakia and the shame of France and Britain agreeing to the country's dismemberment without allowing it any representation at the negotiating table. At an audience on September 30, the pope shared this view with two Italian senators, who let Mussolini know. The Duce erupted in anger. The Holy Father, he remarked, had apparently not stopped shooting himself in the foot. MAESS, vol. 38, 209–10, Charles-Roux, 5 octobre 1938.

28. Milza 2000, pp. 762–63, Rauscher 2004, pp. 261–64; Grandi 1985, pp. 452–53; De Felice 1981, p. 530. A number of recent works have challenged the notion that the racial laws were unpopular in Italy and led to a fall in support for the regime: Rigano 2008; Pavan 2010; Israel 2010. Miccoli (2004, p. 25) denies that the racial laws undermined Italian Catholic support for Mussolini and dates decline of Catholic support from 1942, when the war began to go badly.

29. Kershaw 2000, p. 123.

30. ASV, AESS, pos. 560, fasc. 592, f. 98v, Tardini, diario, 2 ottobre 1938. Schuster was but

one of many, many priests who were praising Mussolini as the man sent by God to save Italy and Europe. A particularly fulsome ode to Mussolini as the new Moses was the sermon given by the archpriest of the cathedral of Campobasso on October 7. Piccardi 1995, pp. 218–20.

31. Bottai 2001, p. 136. Bottai, whose diary records Mussolini's remarks, was an enthusiastic proponent of the racial laws.

32. Quoted in Petacci 2010, p. 421.

33. CC 1938 IV, pp. 269–71.

34. DDI, series 8, vol. 10, n. 238, l'incaricato d'affari presso la Santa Sede, Fecia di Cossato, al ministro degli affari esteri, Ciano, 7 ottobre 1938.

35. ASV, AESI, pos. 1063, fasc. 755, ff. 10r, 12r, 7 ottobre 1938.

36. Quoted in Guasco 2010, pp. 94–95.

37. DDI, series 8, vol. 10, n. 252, l'incaricato d'affari presso la Santa Sede, Fecia di Cossato, al ministro degli affari esteri, Ciano, 10 ottobre 1938.

38. ASMAE, AISS, b. 102, l'incaricato d'affari presso la Santa Sede, Fecia di Cossato, al ministro degli affari esteri, Ciano, 11 ottobre 1938. In citing his previous reports informing Ciano of the Jesuits' strong support for the government's anti-Semitic campaign, Cossato mentions his reports of August 5 and 17. These dates are significant because during those weeks Mussolini was formulating the first anti-Jewish laws and was eager to have assurance that the Church would support his anti-Jewish campaign.

39. ASV, ANI, pos. 24, fasc. 14, ff. 160r–163r, Borgongini a Pacelli, 10 ottobre 1938. A note in the files of the Vatican secretary of state, dated October 7, 1938, similarly makes reference to the August 17 agreement reached by Mussolini and Tacchi Venturi, treating it as in effect. ASV, AESI, pos. 1060, fasc. 747, f. 6r.

40. Tacchi Venturi a Monsignor A. Bernareggi, vescovo di Bergamo, 11 ottobre 1938, published in Presenti 1979, p. 562.

41. "All this," Tacchi Venturi informed the pope the next day, ever eager to build up the Duce in the pope's eyes, "he told me showing how sorry he was that the question had ended up taking so long and wanting to proceed with maximum goodwill." ASV, AESI, pos. 1060, fasc. 747, f. 4r, Tacchi Venturi a Pio XI, 11 ottobre 1938.

42. ASV, AESS, pos. 560, fasc. 592, f. 107r, 10 ottobre 1938. The pope instructed Tardini to announce the replacement of the Bergamo party head and of the Catholic Action board members quickly. When Tardini suggested Saturday the fifteenth, the pope replied, "No, that's too late! And it is a weekend. Do everything on Friday the fourteenth." ASV, AESS, pos. 560, fasc. 592, ff. 107v–108r, 11 ottobre 1938. The bishop of Bergamo was not pleased about removing four of the most valuable and respected members of his Catholic Action board. In an effort to console him, Tacchi Venturi told the bishop that as good Catholics, the men would certainly want to do whatever most benefited Catholic Action. "I also think," he added, "that a little changing of the guard (to use the Fascist terminology) never hurt any institution." Tacchi Venturi a Monsignor A. Bernareggi, vescovo di Bergamo, 11 ottobre 1938, in Presenti 1979, p. 562.

43. ASV, AESI, pos. 1060, pos. 747, f. 17r, l'incaricato d'affari presso la Santa Sede, Conte Carlo Fecia di Cossato, consigliere dell'ambasciata d'Italia presso la Santa Sede, a Domenico Tardini, 12 ottobre 1938; ibid., 18r–19r, Tardini a Fecia di Cossato, 13 ottobre 1938; ASV, AESS, pos. 560, fasc. 592, f. 108v, 12 ottobre 1938.

44. From Tardini's notes. ASV, AESS, pos. 560, fasc. 592, f. 106r, Tardini, 9 ottobre 1938. The pope's phrase is loosely translated here, with thanks to Lesley Riva. The Italian is: "*Roba da frati! È proprio vero che: cappuccio e cotta sempre borbotta!*"

45. ASV, AESS, pos. 560, fasc. 592, f. 109r, 14 ottobre 1938.

46. Ibid., f. 112r, 15 ottobre 1938.

47. Ibid., f. 114r, 16 ottobre 1938.

CHAPTER 25: THE FINAL BATTLE

1. Passelcq and Suchecky 1997, p. 69.

2. ASMAE, APSS, b. 39, fasc. 1, Cosmelli, R. Ambasciata Washington, a Ciano, "Stati Uniti e Cattolicesimo," 20 ottobre 1938. Discussed further in Kertzer and Visani 2012.

3. Baruch, a former Wall Street tycoon, was at the time a philanthropist and part of Franklin Roosevelt's "brain trust" of advisers.

4. The U.S. ambassador reported all this to Washington, adding that police officers in Trieste had prevented people there from celebrating Columbus Day. He suspected they had gotten their orders from Rome, motivated by the belief that Columbus was a Jew, and as a way of signaling Mussolini's displeasure at the U.S. government's protests over the racial laws. NARA, M1423, reel 12, Phillips to U.S. secretary of state, "Anti-Jewish measures in Italy," n. 1120, October 21, 1938.

5. ASV, AESS, pos. 560, fasc. 592, f. 117r, Tardini notes, 19 ottobre 1938. "The official memorandum is necessary," wrote Tardini, "to ensure there is evidence that the Holy See warned the Italian government of the consequences of its new laws." ASV, AESI, pos. 1063, fasc. 755, f. 15r, Tardini appunti, 19 ottobre 1938.

6. Borgongini's comments were made to Tardini. ASV, AESS pos. 560, fasc. 592, ff. 119r–119v, Tardini appunti, 20 ottobre 1938.

7. ASV, AESI, pos. 1063, fasc. 755, ff. 20r–21r, Borgongini, Nunziatura Apostolica d'Italia, "Progetto di appunto," n. 6480, n.d.

8. Here, in pencil, Tardini inserted "too" before "heterogeneous."

9. Borgongini was desperate to reach an agreement. If neither of these proposals were acceptable to the government, he added, the Vatican and the government would have to come to some other understanding before the new laws were announced. ASV, AESI, pos. 1063, fasc. 755, ff. 22r–23r, Borgongini, Nunziatura Apostolica d'Italia, "Progetto di appunto," n. 6481, undated.

10. Tardini has left two somewhat different handwritten accounts of this meeting: ASV, AESI, pos. 1063, fasc. 755, f. 36r, 23 ottobre 1938; AESS, pos. 560, fasc. 592, ff. 123v–125r, 23 ottobre 1938.

11. ASV, AESI, pos. 560, fasc. 592, f. 125v, 23 ottobre 1938.

12. Monsignor Francesco Bracci, the secretary of the Congregation of the Discipline of the Sacraments, was also present.

13. Monsignor Alfredo Ottaviani, until 1935 substitute secretary of state and then assessor for the Holy Office, was also at the meeting. The men there decided that in any discussions with the government, three points had to be communicated: (1) Mixed marriages— whether between Catholics and non-Catholics, or between two Catholics of different races—were rare "and for the future the Holy Father has arranged to have them submitted to his review." (2) The government should agree to recognize these rare marriages, if necessary using the route of royal dispensation. (3) In any case, the government should recognize that it would seriously offend religious sentiment—and here, when the pope reviewed the text, he added: "and natural law"—if it were to punish those who, for reasons of conscience, celebrated such marriages. ASV, AESI, pos. 1063, fasc.755, f. 40r, Tardini appunti, 23 ottobre 1938, followed by his minutes of the meeting on the same date: 41r–45r. On the pope's approval of the plan, see ASV, AESI, pos. 1063, fasc. 755, ff, 49r–50r, Tardini appunti, 24 ottobre 1938.

14. ASV, AESI, pos. 1063, fasc. 755, f. 53r, Tardini appunti, 25 ottobre 1938.

15. Ibid., ff. 56r–59r, Tacchi Venturi a Mussolini, 26 ottobre 1938.

16. Ibid., ff. 61r–64r, Adunanza presso l'E.mo Sig. Cardinale Jorio, 27 ottobre 1938. At his audience with the pope the next day, Tardini brought along data to show how few cases they were talking about. The previous year, he informed the pontiff, out of more than

377,000 marriages in Italy, only 61 involved a Church-approved marriage between a Catholic and a non-Catholic. Nor were there many more marriages involving converted Jews. Ibid., f. 72r, Tardini appunti, 28 ottobre 1938.

17. Previously the Nazis had worried about the negative impact that such an announcement would have in the United States, but now the German foreign minister was less concerned: the recent crisis over the Sudetenland had revealed how strong the isolationists in the United States were. His one worry was that the announcement would provoke anger among America's Jews, but "Jewish propaganda in America directed against Germany and Italy was strong only in the eastern part, while it was dwindling more and more in the western part of the United States. It was precisely this western part of the United States of America which exerted a dominating influence on foreign policy." DGFP, series D, vol. 4, n. 400, "Conversation between the Reich foreign minister, Herr von Ribbentrop, and the Italian foreign minister, Count Ciano," Rome, October 28, 1938.

18. From Ciano's diplomatic papers, "Conversation between the Duce and the foreign minister of the Reich, von Ribbentrop, in the presence of Count Ciano, Rome, 28th October 1938," in Muggeridge 1948, pp. 242–46.

19. Quoted in Ciano 2002, 148–49.

20. ASV, AESI, pos. 1063, fasc. 755, ff. 71r–83r, Tardini, "Appunto per l'Ufficio. Letto al Santo Padre," 29 ottobre 1938.

21. ASV, AESI, pos. 1063, fasc. 755, ff. 76r–76v, Tardini appunti, 29 ottobre 1938.

22. CC 1938 IV, pp. 371–72; Confalonieri 1957, p. 379.

23. MAESS, vol. 38, 196–97, Charles-Roux, 27 septembre 1938.

24. ASV, AESI, pos. 1063, fasc. 755, ff. 88r–89v, 30 ottobre 1938.

25. "Accustomed to seeing Mussolini very often," Tardini observed that day, Tacchi Venturi "was struck by his good qualities and always retained a deep affection for him." But now that Mussolini refused to see him, the Jesuit was unnerved. Although carrying that day's date, Tardini actually wrote the note later, which makes its interpretation difficult. He added, "Notwithstanding his various attempts [to see the Duce], Mussolini no longer showed confidence in P.T.V. He received him from time to time, but rarely and coldly. At the end he would not see him at all." ASV, AESI, pos. 1063, fasc. 755, ff. 129r–129v, 31 ottobre 1938.

26. ASV, AESI, pos. 1063, fasc. 755, ff. 130r–131r, 31 ottobre 1938. Tacchi Venturi's note on the meeting is found at ARSI, TV, b. 28, fasc. 2159, "Promemoria da me letto a S. E. Buffarini il 31 ottobre 1938." In the midst of Mussolini's standoff with the Vatican, a note in the German diplomatic archives reports a jarring episode. On November 1, while Mussolini and Ribbentrop were traveling on a train to Verona, the Duce made a special request. Could the foreign minister do something to improve relations with the Catholic Church in Germany? His own relations with the Vatican, he confided, had become strained as a result of his newly announced racial policy, and he was eager to see the Axis powers' relations with the Catholic Church improved. He pressed the point hard enough that Ribbentrop ordered the foreign ministry to prepare a report on what could be done to improve relations with the Vatican. Mussolini's request had another effect: Ribbentrop decided to leave Bergen in Rome as ambassador to the Holy See. Pacelli had for months been worrying that Bergen would be replaced by a Nazi hard-liner. DGFP, series D, vol. 4, n. 468, "Memorandum by the Director of the Political Department," Woermann, Vienna, November 3, 1938.

27. ASV, ANI, pos. 9, fasc. 5, ff. 139r–141r, "Provvedimenti per la tutela della razza italiana."

28. Tacchi Venturi also told them of the need to draft new language for the marriage instructions that the Congregation of the Discipline of the Sacraments gave to the Catholic Church in Italy. The new wording he proposed would forbid priests from performing religious marriages if the new racial law did not allow them, except for those cases involving

"very serious reasons of conscience." Exactly what was meant by this last phrase was left undefined. All present voiced their agreement. ASV, AESI, pos. 1063, fasc. 755, ff. 139r–141r, "Adunanza presso l'E.mo sig. Card. Jorio," 2 novembre 1938.

29. "It is obvious that with such an addition," observed Tardini, "the government would have fully accepted the Holy See's principle, that is, that the concept of religion prevails over that of race." ASV, AESI, pos. 1063, fasc. 755, ff. 149r–150v, Tardini appunti, 3 novembre 1938, emphasis in original.

30. ASV, AESI, pos. 1063, fasc. 755, ff. 162r–164r, "Relazione del colloquio avuto con S.E. Buffarini il 3 novembre 1938," Tacchi Venturi; ibid., f. 171r, Tardini appunti, 4 novembre 1938.

CHAPTER 26: FAITH IN THE KING

1. ASV, AESI, pos. 1063, fasc. 755, ff. 177r–178r, Pio XI a Mussolini, 4 novembre 1938.

2. Ibid., ff. 180r–181r, Tacchi Venturi a Mussolini, 4 novembre 1938. In an effort to endear the pope to the Duce, Tacchi Venturi added that the pope had thought first to write directly to the king, as protocol would dictate, but recognizing how much the Duce had done for the Church, he decided to give him the chance to put things right first.

3. At the pope's request, Pacelli drafted both the letter to the king and the one to Mussolini. A published version of the letter to the king is available in DDI, series 8, vol. 10, n. 360, "Sua Santità Pio XI a Re Vittorio Emanuele III," 5 novembre 1938; Pacelli's original handwritten draft, with corrections, is at ASV, AESI, pos. 1063, fasc. 755, ff. 184r–184v.

4. A few years later Dino Grandi, who had served as Mussolini's foreign minister and was then his ambassador to Britain, reflected on the king's relationship with the Duce. "For twenty years," he observed, "the King and Mussolini looked at each other over like two fencers on the mat, with their swords raised." While Grandi captures the mutual wariness of the two men, his description fails to note that the match was unequal—the king was ever fearful of displeasing the Duce. But despite their radically different backgrounds and temperaments, and the king's servility, they shared a profound solitude, an unlikely chemistry, and a dim view of their fellow human beings. De Felice 1981, pp. 14–15.

5. ASV, AESI, pos. 1063, fasc. 755, f. 186r.

6. Mussolini communicated this response through Buffarini. ASV, ANI, pos. 9, fasc. 5, f. 141r, Buffarini a Tacchi Venturi, 7 novembre 1938.

7. Ciano 2002, pp. 151–52.

8. Fogarty 1996, p. 562. Roosevelt had ordered the flagship of the American naval fleet in French waters to go to Naples to assist in ceremonies honoring Mundelein, and Phillips participated in a lunch on board hosted by the American rear admiral. "At this particular moment, when religious persecution is on the increase, even in Italy," Roosevelt told Phillips, "the significance of what I wish done will not be overlooked by the Italians and I think the effect cannot but be salutary." Phillips 1952, pp. 222–23.

9. Before they finished their conversation, the guest of honor joined them. Cardinal Mundelein told Ciano he was confident he spoke for all American Catholics—"and many non-Catholics in the United States"—in urging the government to maintain its commitments to the Holy See. ASV, AESI, pos. 1063, fasc. 755, ff. 200r–202v, Borgongini a Pacelli, 9 novembre 1938.

10. ASMAE, APG, b. 46, R. Ambasciata, Berlino, a Regio Ministero degli affari esteri, "Reazioni anti-Semite in Germania," 26 novembre 1938. The papal nuncio, Cesare Orsenigo, also sent a detailed report on the pogrom to the Vatican, but there is no record of any words uttered by the Holy See to protest. Wolf 2010, pp. 205–6. The violence was also reported in CC 1938 IV, pp. 476–78.

11. Perin 2011, p. 207.

12. ASV, AESI, pos. 1063, fasc. 755, ff. 203r–204r, Tacchi Venturi a Mussolini, 10 novembre 1938.

13. Fornari 1971, pp. 185–86; *Il Regime fascista,* 8 novembre 1938, p. 3

14. "La chiesa e gli ebrei in un discorso dell'on. Farinacci," *Il Giornale d'Italia,* 9 novembre 1938.

15. DDI, series 8, vol. 10, n. 390, Pignatti a Ciano, 12 novembre 1938.

16. The document, possibly prepared by Tardini, is titled "Action Taken by the Holy See on the Question of Racism." ASV, AESI, pos. 1054, fasc. 738, ff. 34r–39r. It is undated but refers to events on September 21, 1938, and so it could have been prepared no earlier than the end of September. However, the file is found in the Vatican archives immediately after one dated November 4, 1938, which suggests a date in the first half of November.

17. ASV, AESI, pos. 1063, fasc. 755, ff. 212r–213r, Pacelli, telegramma per Parigi, San Sabastiano, Londra, 11 novembre 1938.

18. ASV, ANI, pos. 9, fasc. 5, ff. 162r–166r, Pacelli a Pignatti, 13 novembre 1938. The following day Pacelli sent a memo to the cardinals of the Curia to brief them on the situation, appending several documents for their information, including two of Tacchi Venturi's obsequious letters to Mussolini, the text of the new law, the pope's letters to Mussolini and to the king, with his suggested changes in the wording of article 7 of the proposed new law, the king's reply, and Pacelli's letter of protest to Pignatti of November 13. ASV, ANI, pos. 9, fasc. 5, ff. 143r–161r.

19. Reproduced in Sale 2009, p. 286.

20. "A proposito di un nuovo Decreto Legge," OR, 14–15 novembre 1938, p. 1. On November 16 the British ambassador to Italy, D'Arcy Osborne, sent his analysis of the pope's protests to Viscount Halifax in London. After summarizing the *L'Osservatore romano* article and its protest of the violation of the concordat, he observed, "It will be interesting to see whether anything comes of this protest, for it will show whether Signor Mussolini attaches greater importance to the views and influence of the Fascist extremists and their Nazi confederates or to those of the Italian Catholics. I suspect that the Vatican's protests will be weighed, not on its own merits, but on a basis of pure expediency. And I shall be agreeably surprised if considerations of compliance with Fascist principle and Nazi practice do not win the day." FCRSE, pt. 16, October to December 1938, n. 58.

21. The next day, talking to Tardini, Pius XI recounted his conversation with the old Jesuit: "Yesterday Father Tacchi Venturi came here solely to tell me that the article made a good impression on the government. But I really let him have it!"

22. Whether Pacelli prevented it by waiting until the pope forgot about it, given his faltering memory, or by convincing him that it was not a good idea, is not clear from Tardini's account, which is our only glimpse into this conversation. Tardini simply wrote that Pacelli "succeeded in preventing it." Tardini's handwritten account, dated November 15, 1938, but written some time later, is found at ASV, AESI, pos. 1063, fasc. 755, ff. 321r–321v, 329r.

23. Charles-Roux, 27 février 1937, cited in LaCroix-Riz 1994, p. 55.

24. ASMAE, AISS, b. 5, fasc. 1, sf. 5, "Lettera aperta a S. E. il Cardinale Schuster Arcivescovo di Milano," marzo 1930. Further details of the episode are provided in ACS, MI, FP "Schuster."

25. ASMAE, APSS, n. 314682, Ministero degli Affari Esteri, "Appunto per la Dir. Gen. A.E.M. Uff. V," 1 settembre 1937.

26. Ferrari 1982, p. 590. ACS, MI, FP "Schuster," informatore n. 553, 27 novembre 1938. As a police informant reported, the shock in Milan occasioned by Schuster's attack came from "the common conviction that this cardinal . . . was entirely tied to the PNF and as such also disposed to follow the racial policy." Ibid., 30 novembre 1938. See also ibid., informatore n. 37, 2 dicembre 1938.

27. ASV, ANI, pos. 9, fasc. 5, ff. 168r–169r, Pacelli a Pignatti, 22 novembre 1938.

28. Ibid., ff. 170r–171r, Pignatti a Pacelli, 29 novembre 1938.
29. The paper in question was *Il Popolo d'Italia*. The same day Milan's prestigious *Corriere della Sera* claimed that Roosevelt was losing popular support in the United States and predicted that he "may soon be confronted by a violent reaction in favor of the principle of American neutrality and against the treacherous Jewish influences now dominating the White House." The newspaper articles are all cited by Reed in NARA, M1423, reel 1, Edward L. Reed, chargé d'affaires ad interim, Rome, to secretary of state, Washington, n. 1184, December 2, 1938.
30. Confalonieri 1957, p. 379.
31. DDI, series 8, vol. 10, n. 510, Pignatti a Ciano, 6 dicembre 1938.
32. ACS, MI, DAGR, b. B7-G, #81980-3, Milano, 4 dicembre 1938.
33. ACS, MI, DAGR, b. B7-G, #81984-5, Milano, 5 dicembre 1938; Israel 2011, p. 62; Matard-Bonucci 2008, p. 293.

CHAPTER 27: A CONVENIENT DEATH

1. DDI, series 8, vol. 10, n. 539, Pignatti a Ciano, 12 dicembre 1938. These last words, too, are underlined in the original.
2. Ciano 2002, pp. 165–66.
3. Baudrillart 1996, pp. 902–3.
4. "Parole di Padre," OR, 25 dicembre 1938, p. 1.
5. Pacelli enlisted Montini to help him try to convince the pope. ASV, AESI, pos. 1063, fasc. 755, ff. 479r–479v, Tardini appunti, 24 dicembre 1938.
6. At a meeting where Ciano communicated the Duce's anger, Borgongini defended the pope. He blamed the recent tensions on Mussolini's embrace of the Nazis, including the government's inexplicable drive to undermine the concordat by banning mixed marriages. The pope, with his generous remarks about the Duce in his address to the cardinals, he said, was doing his part to restore the harmonious relations they all so desired. Now it was up to Mussolini to meet him halfway. ASV, ANI, pos. 24, fasc. 5, ff. 2r–6r, Borgongini to Pacelli, 28 dicembre 1938.
7. Ciano 2002, p. 171 (January 1, 1939).
8. François-Bonnet, December 31, 1938, quoted in De Felice 1981, pp. 571–72.
9. Petacci 2010, pp. 445–46.
10. Petacci 2011, pp. 21–35.
11. Ciano 2002, p. 172 (January 2, 1939).
12. DDI, series 8, vol. 11, n. 6, Pignatti a Ciano, 3 gennaio 1939. Also on January 3, Ciano and Mussolini met with the American ambassador to receive a proposal from President Roosevelt. In a letter dated December 7, Roosevelt asked the Duce to help deal with the humanitarian crisis created by the large numbers of Jews who were forced to leave their homes in Europe but had nowhere to go. Roosevelt proposed that Italy designate a region of Ethiopia to create a Jewish refuge. *Foreign Relations of the United States,* vol. 1, pp. 858–59, "President Roosevelt to the Chief of the Italian Government (Mussolini)," December 7, 1938; and ibid., pp. 859–60, "Memorandum Elaborating the Points Referred to in President Roosevelt's Letter to the Chief of the Italian Government, December 7, 1938." Mussolini responded that the Italian government, given its position with respect to the Jews, could not contemplate such a role, but he told Ambassador Phillips, somewhat playfully, that the United States had vast territories and asked why the United States did not allocate a region of its own to Europe's Jewish refugees. DGFP, series D, vol. 4, n. 424, ambassador in Italy to foreign ministry, January 4, 1939; NARA, M1423, reel 1, Edward Reed, Rome, to secretary of state, January 6, 1939, no. 1238; DDI, series 8, vol. 11, n. 47, Vitetti ai Direttori Generali degli Affari Transoceanici, Roma, 11 gennaio 1939.

13. DDI, series 8, vol. 11, n. 26, Pignatti a Ciano, 7 gennaio 1939; ASMAE, AISS, b. 95, fasc. 1, sf. 1, Pignatti, 7 gennaio 1939.

14. Renato Moro (2005, pp. 51–55) offers an insightful analysis of how even Cardinal Schuster, the most notable critic among Italy's cardinals and bishops of the Fascist regime's embrace of the racial laws, retained his belief in the goodness of the Italian Fascist regime as such. The problem was the move by some Fascist currents to transform Italian Fascism by importing what he saw as the pagan ideology of the Nazis.

15. Charles-Roux, in his report to the French foreign minister on the December 31, 1938, quoted from the previous day's issue. MAEI, vol. 267, 152–53.

16. The bishop's sermon on the Jews was published in two parts in the Vatican daily: "Un'Omelia del vescovo di Cremona, La Chiesa e gli Ebrei," OR, 15 gennaio 1939, p. 2; "L'Omelia del vescovo di Cremona, Perchè si accusa la Chiesa," 16–17 gennaio 1939, p. 2. The version of the bishop's Lenten sermon published in *L'Osservatore romano* seems to have been toned down by deleting the bishop's phrase: "the Church has said nothing and done nothing to defend the Jews and Judaism." For a discussion of these changes, see Binchy 1970, pp. 622–23, and Bocchini Camaiani 1989, pp. 62–63. Gallina (1979, pp. 523–24) reproduces a segment of the Cremona prefect's January 8 report of the sermon to Buffarini, describing it as strongly backing the Fascist anti-Semitic campaign.

17. Bocci 2003, pp. 501–5. That Farinacci would think to call on the influential Gemelli for the task of demonstrating strong Church support for the anti-Semitic campaign was not surprising. The gist of what Gemelli said in Bologna was taken from his much-publicized recent opening address for the 1938–39 academic year at the Catholic University of Milan. Not only did he blast the "Judaic-Mason cabals" as the enemy, but his panegyric to Mussolini could scarcely have been more enthusiastic: "We must form the new Italian, the Italian of the era of Mussolini, these 'youths of Mussolini' as they have been called, capable of putting down the book to take up the rifle to serve the Fatherland as soldiers." Published in Gemelli's journal, *Vita e pensiero* 15, n.1, pp. 5–12, 1939, discussed in Bocchini Camaiani 1989, p. 48n14. Gemelli's views of the Jews were very much in line with those of the Jesuit general and *La Civiltà cattolica*. From the time he founded the Catholic University, he periodically raged against the Jews. Just a few months before his Bologna speech, he wrote to a friend that Western democracy was a smoke screen being manipulated by a "Jewish Masonic" conspiracy. Bocci 2003, p. 523n14.

    Gemelli was a holy terror, as he was the first to admit. He had willed the Catholic University into creation, fought for it, and regarded it as his own fiefdom. In doing so, he had gotten the strong support of both the pope and the Fascist authorities. "I have many defects," he told an audience in 1931. "I recognize them all. I am violent, a bully, muddleheaded." But God, he went on to say, knew how to use people's defects for His own ends. "To make a university it takes a man like me. Even a tyrant." Cosmacini 1985, p. 203.

    Gemelli's anti-Semitic rant, giving timely support to Farinacci's efforts to show that the regime's anti-Semitic laws were in keeping with Church teachings, may have been even more squalid. There is some evidence that, in doing Farinacci's wishes, he hoped to be appointed to the Italian Academy, Italy's most prestigious honorary academic society. If so, Farinacci fulfilled his part of the bargain. On March 19 he urged Mussolini to appoint Gemelli to the Academy. Farinacci was convinced that Gemelli would soon be made a cardinal, and to have someone who was "truly our man" so close to the new pontiff would, he told the Duce, be most useful. ACS, CR, b. 44, n. 033912, Farinacci a Mussolini, 19 marzo 1939. Mussolini responded that "the time is not mature" and did not make the appointment. Nor was Gemelli appointed a cardinal. For a discussion of this episode, see Bocci 2003, pp. 506–8.

18. MAEI, vol. 267, 158–59, Charles-Roux à Georges Bonnet, 19 janvier 1939.

19. ACS, MI, FP "Gemelli," informatore n. 390 (=Arrigo Pozzi), "Gli umori del nuovo papa verso padre Gemelli. Una scena pietosa con Pio XI," Milano, 10 marzo 1939.

20. In the first weeks of 1939, *La Civiltà cattolica* also ran an article renewing the charge that the Masons were the great foe of Christian civilization, allied with "cosmopolitan Judaism, which has no allegiance to any country." Antonio Messineo, "L'internazionalismo cosmopolita e l'essere nazionale," CC 1939 I, pp. 7–20, cited in Vian 2011, pp. 131–32.

21. Venini 2004, p. 251. Venini makes no mention of any friction between the pope and Gemelli.

22. Riccardi 1996, p. 536. Italy had 274 dioceses, each headed by a bishop or archbishop.

23. Pignatti, informed of this exchange by Pacelli, immediately reported it to Ciano with a request that the two meet to discuss it. ASMAE, AISS, b. 101, fasc. 1, Pignatti a Ciano, 11 gennaio 1939.

24. Monsignor Montini, knowing how sensitive Mussolini was to reports of papal unhappiness with the Italian government, sent Pignatti a copy of the Vatican newspaper. But Pignatti was not pleased and told him that the subject was not one that should be dealt with humorously. The Vatican should have issued a formal denial instead. ASMAE, APSS, b. 44, fasc. 2, Pignatti a Ciano, 11 gennaio 1939. From January 11 to 14 both Ciano and Mussolini were distracted by a visit to Rome by the British prime minister and foreign minister. DBFP, 1919–39, series 3, vol. 3, n. 500, pp. 517–30, R 431/1/22, "Conversations between British and Italian Ministers, Rome, January 11–14, 1939," and n. 502, pp. 531–540, R 546/1/22, "The Earl of Perth (Rome) to Viscount Halifax (Received January 23)," January 19, 1939. The two British visitors had a brief audience with the pope on January 13. Chamberlain described the pope as "in fairly good health." "British Statesmen Confer with Pope," NYT, January 14, 1939, p. 5.

25. In the Christmas issue of *The New York Times*, a front-page headline read, "Pius XI Deplores Fascist Hostility, Reveals Incidents" (December 25, 1938, p. 1). The article is not entirely accurate, as most papers in the United States, France, and Britain were eager to portray the pope as an implacable foe of the racial laws and of the Fascist regime, eliding the distinctions that were actually being made in the pope's protests.

26. DDI, series 8, vol. 11, n. 56, Pignatti a Ciano, 14 gennaio 1939.

27. On the nineteenth, Borgongini asked Buffarini, Mussolini's undersecretary for internal affairs, how the government planned to mark the tenth anniversary. The Fascist leader snapped, "How should we celebrate given this state of affairs?" But when the nuncio pointed out how much joy the Conciliation had produced among the Italians a decade earlier, and how they were certain to expect a major celebration, Buffarini admitted, "Yes, yes, you're right, we have to do something." ASV, ANI, pos. 24, fasc. 14, ff. 174r–177r, Borgongini a Pacelli, 19 gennaio 1939.

28. These events are recorded in Tardini's account: ASV, AESS, pos. 576, fasc. 607, ff. 15r–15v, 17r.

29. Sale 2009, p. 45.

30. How the original draft, along with the work that Rosa had done on it in the previous several weeks, got back to Ledóchowski, we do not know. Father Rosa may well have told the secret to his successor as journal editor, and in that case he would certainly have gathered up the material immediately to send to Ledóchowski. If not, the Jesuit general, on hearing of Rosa's death, must have sent word to bring it to him.

31. Sale 2009, pp. 45–47. Father Sale, who first reported the existence of this correspondence in his 2009 book, defends Ledóchowski and Rosa from the charge of trying to prevent the pope from issuing an encyclical denouncing racism and anti-Semitism. He argues (Sale 2009, p. 47) that their problem with the draft was that LaFarge, being unfamiliar with the peculiar style of papal encyclicals, had not followed the proper form. That this was their main concern is very difficult to believe.

32. "Un'Omelia dell'E.mo Patriarca di Venezia," OR, 19 gennaio 1939, p. 2.

33. ASMAE, AISS, b. 102, "Notizia fiduciaria," Roma, 19 gennaio 1939.

34. DDI, series 8, vol. 11, n. 102, Pignatti a Bastianini, 24 gennaio 1939.

35. ASV, AESS, pos. 576, fasc. 607, ff. 22r–23v, Tardini appunti, 22 gennaio and 1 febbraio 1939.

36. Ciano 2002, p. 184 (February 1, 1939).

37. Mussolini communicated this via Pignatti. ASMAE, AISS, b. 101, Pignatti a Ciano, n. 414/133, 3 febbraio 1939. Pacelli's account of the meeting is found in ASV, AESS, pos. 576, fasc. 607, f. 19r, 3 febbario 1939.

38. ASV, AESS, pos. 576, fasc. 607, f. 20r, 4 febbraio 1939.

39. "If, despite your presence in St. Peter's," Pignatti advised Ciano, "the pope still gives vent to his ill temper, the Catholic world and all right-thinking people cannot but take note of the correctness of the royal government even if the pope responded rudely." ASMAE, AISS, b. 101, Pignatti a Ciano, n. 439/144, 4 febbraio 1939.

40. Bottai 2001, p. 141.

41. ASV, AESS, pos. 576, fasc. 607, f. 21r, 6 febbario 1939. Charles-Roux provided his reflections on the decision to send Ciano in his February 8 report to Paris. MAEI, vol. 267, 165–66.

42. Papin 1977, p. 49.

43. Confalonieri 1957, pp. 385–86.

44. Tardini recorded the pope's words. ASV, AESS, pos. 576, fasc. 607, f. 102r.

45. Ibid.

46. Fattorini 2007, p. 213.

47. Venini 2004, p. 254.

48. Ciano 2002, p. 187 (February 9, 1939).

49. Camille Cianfarra, "Pope Pius Is Dead at the Age of 81; Cardinals at Bedside in the Vatican," NYT, February 10, 1939, p. 1. Such secondhand reports of a pope's last words are, of course, notoriously unreliable.

50. "Death of the Pope," The Times (London), February 11, 1939, p. 12.

51. Chiron (2006, 463–64) describes the pope's last hours.

CHAPTER 28: A DARK CLOUD LIFTS

1. Charles-Roux 1947, pp. 243–44.

2. Ciano 2002, p. 188 (February 10, 1939). The dramatic timing of the pope's death, a day before he was to give the speech to all of Italy's bishops that Mussolini feared might denounce him, has inspired a variety of conspiracy theories. The key figure in such speculation has been Clara Petacci's father, Francesco, a senior physician in the Vatican health office. For a multitude of reasons, tied not only to Clara but to her brother—he was involved in a number of questionable financial affairs, taking advantage of the family's links to Mussolini—Francesco was arguably subject to blackmail. Noting that in the pope's last days his own personal physician, Aminta Milani, was sick and bedridden, proponents of this theory argue that somehow the elder Petacci took advantage of his position to push the ailing pope over into the next life before he could give the much-feared address on the tenth anniversary of the Lateran Accords. In a front-page story in 1972, The Times of London reported that Cardinal Tisserant had told his close colleagues that he believed the pope had been murdered and that he suspected Petacci. As further evidence, it was alleged that Petacci had been placed in charge of preparing the pope's dead body for the funeral and so could have removed any signs of poisoning. "Support for Theory of 1939 killing of Pope," Times, June 23, 1972, p. 1. In 2005 the Italian historian Piero Melograni revived the theory. Antonio Carioti, "La morte sospetta di Pio XI. Stava per condannare il Duce,"

Corriere della sera, 11 luglio 2005, p. 25. Although the timing of the pope's death lends itself to suspicion, there is in fact no good evidence to suggest he died of other than natural causes. But the story is so sensational that it keeps reappearing, most recently in Mauro Suttora, "Pio XI fu assassinato dal padre di Claretta?" *Corriere della Sera,* 17 maggio 2012.

3. Caviglia 2009, p. 227 (10 febbraio 1939).

4. Over the previous weeks Pignatti had advised that the regime do nothing to strengthen the hand of the anti-Fascist forces among the cardinals. But even as the pope lay dying, Achille Starace, the PNF head, had demanded that the government lodge a new protest: certain Catholic Action groups were engaging in political activity. The day after the pope's death, Pignatti wrote to Starace, telling him he was not eager to bring the matter to the Vatican at that moment. In the absence of a pope, it would have to be referred to the Sacred College of Cardinals, the very men who would be voting on the pope's successor. Apparently even the super-Fascist Starace appreciated the ambassador's logic and that evening sent a telegram saying he understood. ASMAE, APSS, b. 42, Pignatti a Starace, 11 febbraio 1939, n. 545; ibid., Pignatti a Ciano, 12 febbraio 1939, n. 553.

5. Ciano 2002, p. 189 (February 12, 1939).

6. Petacci 2011, pp. 52–53 (12 febbraio 1939).

7. ASV, ANI, pos. 1, fasc. 7, ff. 7r–9r, Borgongini a Monsignor Vincenzo Santoro, segretario del Sacro Collegio, 13 febbraio 1939. Santoro replied two days later confirming that no such secret document had been given to the bishops. Ibid., f. 10r, Santoro a Borgongini, 15 febbraio 1939. Pignatti had asked Pacelli about the rumor as well and got the same denial. ASMAE, AISS, b. 101, Pignatti a Ciano, 13 febbraio 1939, n. 557.

8. Fattorini (2011, pp. 210–15) provides an English version of the full text, having published the original Italian version in Fattorini (2007, pp. 240–44). For her analysis of Pacelli's decision to conceal the speech, see pp. 187–93 of the English edition. The document is found in ASV, AESS, pos. 576, fasc. 606, ff. 147r–153r.

9. ASV, AESS, pos. 576, fasc. 607, f. 165r, appunto Tardini, "Materiale preparato da S.S. Pio XI per l'adunanza del 12 febbraio 1939," 12 gennaio 1941.

10. ASMAE, AISS, b. 101, Pignatti a Esteri-Gabinetto, 22 febbraio 1939, n. 23.

11. "Mentioned to Succeed Pius," BG, February 11, 1939, p. 3. The *Los Angeles Times* speculation focused on Pacelli and Schuster as the two top contenders for the papacy at the time of Pius XI's death. "Italian Seen as Successor," LAT, February 11, 1939, p. 1.

12. "Nine Leading Candidates," NYT, February 12, 1939, p. 43. The following day *The New York Times* ("5 Cardinals Lead in Vatican Contest," February 13, 1939, p. 1) amplified this theme, arguing that "the chances of the Curia putting forward a successful candidate for the papacy are slight," and adding, "If by some coincidence the next Pope should happen to be one of their number, Cardinals Massimi and Tedeschini are the most likely." For its part, *The Times* of London thought the new pope would most likely be Italian but chosen from those deemed "non-political." Further, the pope would be chosen not from the Vatican Curia but from among the residential archbishops. "Choosing a Pope," *Times,* March 1, 1939, p. 15.

13. ACS, MCPG, b. 169, Roma, 16 febbraio 1937.

14. ACS, MCPG, b. 170, Roma, 24 febbraio 1938. On Dalla Costa's powers to work miracles, see Cardinal Verdier's comments in Papin 1977, pp. 53–54.

15. ASV, ANI, pos. 1, fasc. 7, Borgongini a Santoro, 16 febbraio 1939; ibid., f. 15r, Cardinal Belmonte a Borgongini, 18 febbraio 1939.

16. Fattorini (2007, pp. 221–22) also points this out.

17. Next in number, though distant, were the six French cardinals. Germany had four; Spain and the United States each had three; no other country had more than a single cardinal, and of these only four came from outside of Europe: a Canadian, an Argentinean, a Brazil-

ian, and a Syrian. Power in the Sacred College was heavily concentrated in Rome: twenty-four of the cardinals lived there, all but one of whom—Eugène Tisserant—were Italian, most with positions in the Curia, at the center of Vatican power. ASMAE, AISS, b. 95, 10 febbraio 1939; *Annuario Pontificio* 1940, pp. 71–72. Pius XI had created seventy-seven cardinals, fourteen of whom had come from the Vatican diplomatic service, and another twenty from the Curia. Most of the rest had been residential archbishops whose archdioceses typically merited a cardinal as archbishop. Not all of them were alive at the time of the conclave. Agostino (1991, pp. 29–30) writes that twenty-seven were resident in Rome, but I here use the figure (twenty-four) drawn from examining the addresses listed in *Annuario* 1940.

18. Monsignor Montini, unhappy about a number of offensive articles in the Nazi press, had been planning to have *L'Osservatore romano* print a story criticizing them. But when Pignatti complained to Cardinal Pacelli about it, he intervened to prevent publication. That Bergen followed up on Pignatti's advice can be seen in the telegram he sent to the German foreign minister in Berlin later that day, reporting his conversation and urging that the German press tone down its criticism of the recently deceased pope and any of the cardinals whose goodwill they needed. DGFP, series D, vol. 4, n. 470, Bergen to foreign ministry, February 18, 1939.

19. One reason for Bergen's optimism was that since Pius XI's death, he had noticed a much more sympathetic atmosphere in the Vatican. A number of cardinals had made clear that they hoped they could reach an agreement with the Reich. ASMAE, AISS, b. 95, Pignatti a Ciano, 18 febbraio 1939; also published in DDI, series 8, vol. 11, n. 197. Pignatti's report to Ciano of this conversation was sent to Mussolini.

20. ASMAE, AISS, b. 95, Pignatti, 21 febbraio 1939.

21. Ibid., Pignatti a Ciano, 25 febbraio 1939.

22. Ibid., Pignatti a Ciano, 26 febbraio 1939. On February 27 Pignatti met with the German ambassador to compare notes. Two of the German cardinals had recently assured Bergen that they would take a "conciliatory attitude" at the conclave. Pacelli, speaking recently to one of the German cardinals, had expressed "unequivocal intentions in favor of conciliation" with both the German and the Italian governments. Pignatti asked again what the Nazi government's view was of Pacelli's candidacy. Bergen replied he had informed the German Foreign Office of his strong preference for Pacelli "and did not receive any contrary instructions." From this he concluded that his government took a favorable view of the former secretary of state. For his part, the Italian ambassador shared his concern about what the Italian cardinals would do at the conclave. He had met with many of them, he said, and they were not terribly fond of Pacelli. ASMAE, AISS, b. 95, Pignatti a Ciano, 27 febbraio 1939.

23. Baudrillart 1996, pp. 963–65, 968 (20 février, 22 février, 24 février 1939).

24. This is Verdier's account of the conversation, in Papin 1977, pp. 56–57.

25. Two of the cardinals were too ill to make it into the Sistine Chapel , so they cast their ballots from their Vatican bedrooms. On the arrival of the North and South American cardinals, see "Liner to Be Held," NYT, February 11, 1939, p. 1; Camille Cianfarra, "Vatican Door Shut on 62 Cardinals as Conclave Opens to Elect Pope," NYT, March 2, 1939, p. 1.

26. Ventresca 2013, p. 136.

27. A number of people close to the pope have testified that Pius XI had wanted Pacelli to succeed him. Among them was Pacelli himself, who shortly after his election confided in Cardinal Verdier: "Twice Pius XI had told me, 'You will be my successor.' I thought I should protest, but the Holy Father added drily, 'We know what we are saying.'" The new pope went on to tell Verdier that he believed Pius XI had sent him on his missions abroad in order to improve his chances of election. Papin 1977, p. 62.

28. Baudrillart 1996, pp. 973–76 (1 mars, 2 mars 1939); NARA, M1423, reel 2, Phillips to U.S. secretary of state, report n. 1316, March 3, 1939.

29. DDI, series 8, vol. 11, n. 240, Pignatti a Ciano, 2 marzo 1939.
30. Ciano 2002, pp. 195–96 (March 2 and 3, 1939); Tranfaglia 2005, p. 159.
31. Pius XII also reminded Bergen of remarks he had made the previous year at a Eucharistic Congress in Budapest: "It is not the business of the Church," Pacelli had said (in German), "to take sides in purely temporal affairs and in the accommodations between the different systems and methods which may arise for overcoming the urgent problems of the present." DGFP, series D, vol. 4, n. 472, Bergen to foreign ministry, March 5, 1939.
32. DGFP, series D, vol. 4, n. 473, Bergen to foreign ministry, March 8, 1939.
33. Morgan 1944, pp. 159–60.
34. ACS, MI, PS, Polizia Politica, b. 210, informatore n. 52, Roma, 15 agosto 1938. In a report six months later, informant n. 571 added another charge: "As for Vatican circles, the best known pederasts would be Cardinals Pizzardo and Caccia Dominioni. Pizzardo is said to have intimate relations with male youths from Trastevere." ACS, MI, FP, FP "Pizzardo," 20 febbraio 1939. As this is the only informant (of whom I am aware) who made this charge against Cardinal Pizzardo, it must be regarded as unproven.
35. NARA, M1423, reel 2, Joseph Kennedy, London, to U.S. secretary of state [Cordell Hull], March 17, 1939. William Phillips, the U.S. ambassador to Italy, recalled in his memoirs that each winter he gave a large dinner dance in honor of Ciano and his wife, Edda Mussolini. Despite the presence of the top foreign diplomats in Rome, recalled Phillips (1952, p. 218), Ciano devoted all his attention to the young attractive women who had been invited, "paying little or no attention to ambassadors and their wives or to the distinguished Italians present."
36. "Of all the 'facts' that took place in these fatal years," wrote Dino Grandi (1985, p. 459), "this was the most crucial one."
37. Ciano 2002, pp. 203–4 (March 18, 1939); Chenaux 2005, p. 273; De Cesaris 2010, pp. 251–53; Casella 2010, p. 290. The following month, reporting the new pope's decision to remove Pizzardo from the position and to create the commission of archbishops, Charles-Roux observed that the impression in Rome was that the pope had made the move to put himself "in the good graces of the Fascist regime." MAEI, vol. 267, 172–73, Charles-Roux à Bonnet, 13 avril 1939. The reports of the bishops on relations between Fascist authorities and local Catholic Action groups are found in ASV, AESS, pos. 576, fasc. 607, ff. 179r–190v.

CHAPTER 29: HEADING TOWARD DISASTER

1. Emmanuel Mounier, quoted in Ventresca 2013, p. 149.
2. ASMAE, APSS, b. 42, Pignatti a Ciano, 21 aprile 1939.
3. Morgan 1941, pp. 241–42; Chadwick 1986, p. 56.
4. Fattorini 2007, p. ix.
5. ASMAE, APSS, b. 43, Ministero degli Affari Esteri a Pignatti, 26 aprile 1939. At the same time Ciano's office received a report from the Italian consulate in Munich, telling of the dramatic change in the local press attitude toward the new pope. Previously, the consul reported, the German press had been suspicious of Pacelli, thought to be too close to the old leadership of the Center Party from his days in Munich and Berlin, and nostalgic for the days when the Church was the dominant political influence in Bavaria. But now, in light of his first actions as pope, he was being presented in a positive light. ASMAE, APSS, b. 43, "Atteggiamento nazionalsocialista nei confronti del nuovo Pontefice," Munich, 27 aprile 1939.
6. Bottai 2001, p. 148 (19 maggio 1939).
7. There is a large literature on the papal action against Action Française. Prévotat (2001) offers a thorough examination. Spadolini (1972, pp. 291–96) published Gasparri's account of the battle.

8. ASMAE, APSS, b. 44, Pignatti a Ciano, 17 luglio 1939.
9. Pius XII also let the nuncio know that, as secretary of state, he had done all he could to prevent Pius XI from protesting the appearance of the swastika during Hitler's visit to Rome, but to no avail. ASMAE, APSS, b. 43, Tamaro, R. Legazione d'Italia, Berna, al R. Ministero degli Esteri, telespresso n. 3461/1236, 21 luglio 1939.
10. Papin 1977, p. 67.
11. Parsons 2008, p. 92.
12. Ventresca 2013, pp. 153–54, 166.
13. ACS, MI, DAGRA, b. 1320, Roma, 11 novembre 1940.
14. Salvatore Costanza, "Gli eterni nemici di Roma," *La Difesa della razza* 2:16 (20 giugno 1939), p. 30; Mario de Bagni, "Cristo e i cristiani nel talmud," *La Difesa della razza* 2:14 (20 maggio 1939), pp. 8–9; Carlo Barduzzi, "Cattolici e giudei in Francia," *La Difesa della razza* 2:14 (20 maggio 1939), pp. 26–27; Cassata 2008, p. 127.
15. On April 1, four days after Mussolini made his request, Pope Pius XII addressed a congratulatory telegram to General Franco. "Raising our heart to God, We rejoice with Your Excellency for Catholic Spain's greatly desired victory." The new pope concluded by offering his blessing to Franco and the Spanish people. Franzinelli 1998, p. 173. Two weeks later the pope followed up with a radio broadcast to the Spanish people, saying, "With immense joy We address ourselves to you, most beloved children of Catholic Spain, to express our paternal congratulations for the gift of peace and the victory with which God has deigned to crown the Christian heroism of your faith and charity, shown in such great and generous suffering." Fattorini 2007, p. 104.
16. ARSI, TV, b. 28, fasc. 2228, Tacchi Venturi a Luigi Maglione, 28 marzo 1939. The Italian ambassador expressed his own delight with the new pontiff following his meeting with him in mid-November. The pope, he told Ciano, "said that our country gives him great satisfaction. He praised the Italians' spirit of religiosity, morality, and hard work, insisting on declaring himself satisfied with everything." Casella 2010, p. 343.
17. Antonio Messineo, in CC 1940 IV, pp. 216–19. The letter of complaint, from Giorgio Del Vecchio, and Tardini's reply, are discussed by Sale (2009, p. 149), based on correspondence found in the archives of the journal.
18. ADSS, vol. 9, 1974, n. 289, Tacchi Venturi au Cardinal Maglione, 10 août 1943.
19. ADSS, vol. 9, 1974, n. 296, Cardinal Maglione au Père Tacchi Venturi, 18 août 1943.
20. ARSI, TV, 36, n. 2660, Tacchi Venturi a Umberto Ricci, 24 agosto 1943. This letter is also published in ADSS vol. 9, annex to n. 317.
21. ADSS, vol. 9, 1975, n. 317, Tacchi Venturi au Cardinal Maglione, 29 août 1943.
22. Caretti 2010, pp. 148–49.
23. ADSS, vol. 9, n. 368, Cardinal Maglione, notes, Vatican, 16 octobre 1943.
24. Gilbert 1985, pp. 622–23; http://www.ushmm.org/wlc/en/article.php?ModuleId= 10005189. The Jews in Italy during the war included approximately 35,000 native Italian Jews and 10,000 recent refugees from Nazi-controlled areas. The estimate of conversions in Italy in the period 1938–43 is from "Jews in Italy 04: Holocaust Period 1938–1945," *Encyclopaedia Judiaca* online, http://www.geschichteinchronologie.ch/eu/it/EncJud _juden-in-Italien04-holocaust1938-1945-ENGL.html.

EPILOGUE

1. Santarelli 1991; Romersa 1983, pp. 269–73.
2. Ciano had spent the last months as Mussolini's ambassador to the Holy See.
3. Moseley 1999, pp. 176–247.
4. A huge literature has been spawned dealing with Mussolini's last days. My account here is based largely on Milza (2000, pp. 935–47) and Bosworth (2002, pp. 410–12). It seems

that the letter Mussolini was reported to have written from Como to his wife may have been a later invention of Rachele's. On this, see Luzzatto 1998.

5. Innocenti 1992, pp. 116–17.

6. Pardini 2007, pp. 439, 455–59; Festorazzi 2004, pp. 260–61.

7. Innocenti 1992, pp. 169–70.

8. NYT, March 19, 1956, p. 31. *The Washington Post* (March 19, 1956, p. 26) reported that, while the Jesuit died a forgotten man, it was he who had "engineered the Lateran Pact" in 1929.

9. Gemelli's eulogy for the pope, published in his journal, *Vita e pensiero,* offered the most Fascist interpretation possible of Pius XI's sympathies. The obituary ended, rather jarringly, with a paean not to the man it was supposed to be eulogizing but to Mussolini, recalling "the gratitude that Italian Catholics owe to the incomparable Man, whom Pius XI called the Man Providence had him meet." Ranfagni 1975, p. 216. Father Coughlin, for his part, engaged in a similar attempt to give the most pro-Fascist possible image to Pius XI following his death. "Pius XI Saved Western Civilization from Reds, Declares Fr. Coughlin," BG, February 12, 1939, p. 8; "Coughlin Says Pope Was Europe's Savior," NYT, February 13, 1939, p. 2. With Allied troops chasing the Germans out of Rome in June 1944 and continuing their march north, Father Gemelli, and many like him, desperately tried to convince the victors that he had never been a Fascist. In July, speaking with Don Domenico Rigoni, an old acquaintance from the days before Mussolini's rise to power, he trotted out arguments that he would soon use with anyone who would hear them: if he had done anything to please Mussolini and the other Fascist leaders, it was only because he was forced to do so to protect the Catholic University; he was really an anti-Fascist, a Christian Democrat. Don Rigoni stopped him. "No, my friend. You were a Fascist and it's useless for you to deny it." ACS, MI, FP "Gemelli," Milano, 10 luglio 1944.

10. Bocci 2003, p. 505.

11. Mysteriously, the papers of the commission dealing with Gemelli subsequently went missing. On Gemelli's struggle to keep his position following the war, and the support given him by the Vatican, see Parola 2003.

12. Phillips 1952, pp. 231–33.

13. Ventresca 2013.

14. Cornwell 1999.

REFERENCES

*Note: All references to contemporaneous newspapers, magazines,
and journals are cited in full in the endnotes.*

Agostino, Marc. 1991. *Le pape Pie XI et l'opinion (1922–1939)*. Rome: Ecole française de Rome.

Alvarez, David. 2002. *Spies in the Vatican: Espionage and Intrigue from Napoleon to the Holocaust*. Lawrence: University of Kansas Press.

Amal, Oscar L. 1985. *Ambivalent Alliance: The Catholic Church and the Action Française, 1899–1939*. Pittsburgh: University of Pittsburgh Press.

Annuario Pontificio per l'anno 1940. 1940. Vatican City: Tipografia Vaticana.

Aradi, Zsolt. 1958. *Pius XI, the Pope and the Man*. New York: Hanover House.

Aubert, Roger. 2000. "Le Cardinal Mercier aux conclaves de 1914 et de 1922." *Bulletin de la Classe des lettres et des sciences morales et politiques* 11:165–236.

Baima Bollone, Pierluigi. 2007. *La psicologia di Mussolini*. Milan: Mondadori.

Baratter, Lorenzo. 2008. *Anna Maria Mussolini: L'ultima figlia del Duce*. Milan: Mursia.

Baudrillart, Alfred. 1996. *Les carnets du cardinal Baudrillart (20 novembre 1935–11 avril 1939)*. Edited by Paul Christophe. Paris: Éditions du Cerf.

———. 2003. *Les carnets du cardinal Baudrillart (26 décembre 1928–12 février 1932)*. Edited by Paul Christophe. Paris: Éditions du Cerf.

Baxa, Paul. 2006. "A Pagan Landscape: Pope Pius XI, Fascism, and the Struggle over the Roman Cityscape." *Journal of the Canadian Historical Association* 17:107–24.

Bedeschi, Lorenzo. 1973. *Don Minzoni il prete ucciso dai fascisti*. Milan: Bompiani.

Bendiscioli, Mario. 1982. "Paolo VI (Giovanni Battista Montini)." In *Dizionario storico del movimento cattolico in Italia*, vol. 2. Edited by Francesco Tranello and Giorgio Campanini, pp. 448–53. Milan: Marietti.

Beyens, Eugène-Napoléon. 1934. *Quatre ans à Rome, 1921–1926; fin du pontificat de Benoît XV—Pie XI—les débuts du fascisme*. Paris: Plon.

Biffi, Monica. 1997. *Mons. Cesare Orsenigo nunzio apostolico in Germania (1930–1946)*. Milan: NED.

Binchy, David A. 1970. *Church and State in Fascist Italy*. London: Oxford University Press.

Biocca, Dario. 2012. "Casa Passarge: Gramsci a Roma (1924–6)." *Nuova storia contemporanea* 26 (1):17–36.

Blet, Pierre. 1996. "Le Cardinal Pacelli, secrétaire d'état de Pie XI." In *Achille Ratti pape Pie XI: Actes du colloque organisé par l'École française de Rome, Rome 15–18 mars 1989*. Edited by Philippe Levillain, pp. 197–213. Rome: École française de Rome.

Bocchini Camaiani, Bruna. 1989. "Chiesa cattolica italiana e leggi razziali." *Qualestoria* 17:1:43–66.

Bocci, Maria. 2003. *Agostino Gemelli rettore e francescano: Chiesa, regime, democrazia*. Brescia: Morcelliana.

Bosworth, R. J. B. 2002. *Mussolini*. London: Arnold.

———. 2011. *Whispering City: Modern Rome and its Histories*. New Haven, Conn.: Yale University Press.

Bottai, Giuseppe. 1949. *Vent'anni e un giorno*. Milan: Garzanti.

———. 2001. *Diario: 1935-1944*. Edited by Giordano Bruno Guerri. Milan: Biblioteca Universale Rizzoli.

Bouthillon, Fabrice. 1996. "D'une théologie à l'autre : Pie XI et le Christ-Roi." In *Achille Ratti pape Pie XI: Actes du colloque organisé par l'École française de Rome, Rome 15-18 mars 1989*. Edited by Philippe Levillain, pp. 293-303. Rome: École française de Rome.

Brendon, Piers. 2000. *The Dark Valley: A Panorama of the 1930s*. New York: Knopf.

Bressan, Edoardo. 1980. "Mito di uno stato cattolico e realtà del regime: Per una lettura dell'*Osservatore romano* alla vigilia della Conciliazione." *Nuova rivista storica* 64:81-128.

Calimani, Riccardo. 2007. *Storia del pregiudizio contro gli ebrei*. Milan: Mondadori.

Canali, Mauro. 2004a. *Le spie del regime*. Bologna: Il Mulino.

———. 2004b. *Il delitto Matteoti*. Bologna: Il Mulino.

Cannistraro, Philip V., and Brian R. Sullivan. 1993. *Il Duce's Other Woman*. New York: Morrow.

Canosa, Romano. 2009. *Pacelli: Guerra civile spagnola e nazismo*. Rome: Sapere 2000.

Caracciolo, Nicola. 1982. *Tutti gli uomini del Duce*. Milan: Mondadori.

Caretti, Paolo. 2010. "Il *corpus* delle leggi razziali." In *A settant'anni dalle leggi razziali*. Edited by Daniele Menozzi and Andrea Mariuzzo, pp. 117-57. Rome: Carocci.

Carnahan, Ann. 1949. *The Vatican: Behind the Scenes in the Holy City*. New York: Farrar, Straus.

Casella, Mario. 1996. "Pio XI e l'Azione Cattolica Italiana." In *Achille Ratti pape Pie XI: Actes du colloque organisé par l'École française de Rome, Rome 15-18 mars 1989*. Edited by Philippe Levillain, pp. 605-40. Rome: École française de Rome.

———. 2000. "La crisi del 1938 fra stato e chiesa nella documentazione dell'archivio storico diplomatico del ministero degli affari esteri." *Rivista di storia della chiesa in Italia* 54:1:91-186.

———. 2005. *Stato e chiesa in Italia dalla conciliazione alla riconciliazione (1929-1931)*. Galatina: Congedo Editore.

———. 2009. *Gli ambasciatori d'Italia presso la Santa Sede dal 1929 al 1943*. Galatina: Congedo Editore.

Cassata, Francesco. 2008. *"La Difesa della razza": Politica, ideologia e immagine del razzismo fascista*. Turin: Einaudi.

Casula, Carlo F. 1988. *Domenico Tardini (1888-1961): L'azione della Santa Sede nella crisi fra le due guerre*. Rome: Edizioni Studium.

Caviglia, Enrico. 2009. *I dittatori, le guerre e il piccolo re: Diario 1925-1945*. Edited by Pier Paolo Cervone. Milan: Mursia.

Ceci, Lucia. 2008. "'Il Fascismo manda l'Italia in rovina': Le note inedite di monsignor Domenico Tardini (23 settembre-13 dicembre 1935)." *Rivista storica italiana* 120:294-346.

———. 2010. *Il papa non deve parlare: Chiesa, fascismo e guerra d'Etiopia*. Rome: Laterza.

———. 2012. "The First Steps of 'Parallel Diplomacy': The Vatican and the U.S. in the Italo Ethiopian War (1935-1936)." In *Pius XI and America*. Edited by David Kertzer, Charles Gallagher, and Alberto Melloni, pp. 87-106. Berlin: LIT Verlag.

Centerwall, Bror. 1926. "An Audience with the Pope." *Living Age* (May 22), pp. 408-411.

Cerruti, Elisabetta. 1953. *Ambassador's Wife*. New York: Macmillan.

Chadwick, Owen. 1986. *Britain and the Vatican During the Second World War*. Cambridge: Cambridge University Press.

Chaline, Nadine-Josette. 1996. "La spiritualité de Pie XI." In *Achille Ratti pape Pie XI: Actes du colloque organisé par l'École française de Rome, Rome 15-18 mars 1989*. Edited by Philippe Levillain, pp. 159-70. Rome: École française de Rome.

Charles-Roux, François. 1947. *Huit ans au Vatican, 1932–1940*. Paris: Flammarion.

Chenaux, Philippe. 2005. "Il cardinale Pacelli e la questione del nazismo dopo l'enciclica 'Mit brennender Sorge' (1937)." *Annali del Istituto storico italo-germanico in Trento* 31:261–77.

Chiron, Yves. 2006. *Pio XI: Il papa dei patti lateranensi e dell'opposizione ai totalitarismi*. Cinisello Balsamo: Edizioni Paoline.

Ciano, Galeazzo. 1980. *Diario 1937–1943*. Edited by Renzo De Felice. Milan: Rizzoli.

———. 2002. *Diary 1937–1943*. Translated by R. L. Miller and U. Coletti-Perucca. Coedited by S. G. Pugliese. New York: Enigma Books.

Coco, Giovanni. 2009. "L'anno terribile del cardinale Pacelli *Archivum historiae pontificiae* 47:143–276.

Confalonieri, Carlo. 1957. *Pio XI visto da vicino*. 3rd ed. Milan: Edizioni Paoline.

———. 1969. "Pio XI intimo." In *Pio XI nel trentesimo della morte (1939–1969): Raccolta di studi e di memorie*. Edited by Carlo Colombo, Ernesto Basadonna, Antonio Rimoldi, and Virginio Rovera, pp. 21–58. Milan: Opera diocesana per la preservazione e diffusione della fede.

———. 1993. *Pio XI visto da vicino*. Cinisello Balsamo: Edizioni Paoline.

Conti, Fulvio. 2005. "Adriano Lemmi." *Dizionario biografico degli Italiani*, 64:345–348.

———. 2006. "Massoneria e sfera pubblica nell'Italia liberale, 1859–1914." In *Storia d'Italia, Annali 21, La Massoneria*. Edited by Gian Mario Cazzaniga, pp. 579–610. Turin: Einaudi.

Conway, John S. 1968. *The Nazi Persecution of the Churches 1933–1945*. New York: Basic.

Coppa, Frank J. 1999. "Mussolini and the Concordat of 1929." In *Controversial Concordats*. Edited by Frank J. Coppa, pp. 81–119. Washington, D.C.: Catholic University Press.

———. 2011. *The Policies and Politics of Pope Pius XII: Between Diplomacy and Morality*. New York: Peter Lang.

Cosmacini, Giorgio. 1985. *Gemelli: Il Machiavelli di Dio*. Milan: Rizzoli.

D'Alessio, Giulia. 2012. "The United States and the Vatican (1936–1939)." In *Pius XI and America*. Edited by David Kertzer, Charles Gallagher, and Alberto Melloni, pp. 129–54. Berlin: LIT Verlag.

De Begnac, Yvon. 1990. *Taccuini Mussoliniani*. Edited by Francesco Perfetti. Preface by Renzo De Felice. Bologna: Mulino.

De Cesaris, Valerio. 2010. *Vaticano, razzismo e questione razziale*. Milan: Guerini.

De Felice, Renzo. 1966. *Mussolini il fascista*. Turin: Einaudi.

———. 1968. *Mussolini il fascista: L'organizzazione dello stato fascista, 1925–1929*. Turin: Einaudi.

———. 1974. *Mussolini il duce: Gli anni del consenso, 1929–1936*. Turin: Einaudi.

———. 1981. *Mussolini il duce: Lo stato totalitario, 1936–1940*. Turin: Einaudi.

———. 1995. *Mussolini il fascista: L'organizzazione dello stato fascista, 1925 1929*, 2nd ed. Turin: Einaudi.

———. 2010. *Mussolini il rivoluzionario, 1883–1910*. Milan: Mondadori.

De Gasperi, Maria Romana. 2004. *De Gasperi: Ritratto di uno statista*. Milan: Mondadori.

De Grazia, Victoria. 1992. *How Fascism Ruled Women*. Berkeley: University of California Press.

De Rosa, Gabriele. 1958. *Storia del Partito popolare*. Bari: Laterza.

———. 1959. "Una lettera inedita di Cardinale Gasparri sul Partito Popolare." *Analisi e prospettive* 1:568–73.

De Rosa, Giuseppe. 1999. *La Civiltà Cattolica: 150 anni al servizio della Chiesa, 1850–1999*. Rome: La Civiltà Cattolica.

De Rossi dell'Arno, Giulio. 1954. *Pio XI e Mussolini*. Rome: Corso.

De Vecchi, Cesare M. 1983. *Il Quadrumviro scomodo: Il vero Mussolini nelle memorie del più monarchico dei fascisti*. Edited by L. Romersa. Milan: Mursia.

———. 1998. *Tra papa, duce e re: Il conflitto tra Chiesa cattolica e Stato fascista nel diario 1930–1931 del primo ambasciatore del Regno d'Italia presso la Santa Sede*. Rome: Jouvence.

Deakin, F. W. 2000 [1962]. *The Brutal Friendship: Mussolini, Hitler and the Fall of Italian Fascism*. London: Phoenix Press.

Deffayet, Laurence. 2010. "Pie XI et la condemnation des Amis d'Israël (1928)." In *Pie XI et la France*. Edited by Jacques Prévotat, pp. 87–102. Rome: École française de Rome.

Del Boca, Angelo. 2010. *La Guerra d'Etiopia*. Milan: Longanesi.

Diggins, John. P. 1972. *Mussolini and Fascism: The View from America*. Princeton: Princeton University Press.

Duce, Alessandro. 2006. *La Santa Sede e la questione ebraica (1933–1945)*. Rome: Edizioni Studium.

Durand, Jean-Dominique. 2010. "Lo stile di governo di Pio XI." In *La sollecitudine ecclesiale di Pio XI*. Edited by Cosimo Semararo, pp. 44–60. Vatican City: Libreria Editrice Vaticano.

Ebner, Michael R. 2011. *Ordinary Violence in Mussolini's Italy*. Cambridge: Cambridge University Press.

Eisner, Peter. 2013. *The Pope's Last Crusade*. New York: Morrow.

Fabre, Giorgio. 2005. *Mussolini razzista: Dal socialismo al fascismo: La formazione di un antisemita*. Milan: Garzanti.

———. 2012. "Un 'accordo felicemente conchiuso.'" *Quaderni di storia* 76:83–154.

Falasca-Zamponi, Simonetta. 1997. *Fascist Spectacle*. Berkeley: University of California Press.

Falconi, Carlo. 1967. *I papi del XX secolo*. Milan: Feltrinelli.

Fattorini, Emma. 2007. *Pio XI, Hitler e Mussolini, la solitudine di un papa*. Turin: Einaudi.

———. 2011. *Hitler, Mussolini and the Vatican: Pope Pius XI and the Speech that Was Never Made*. Translated by Carl Ipsen. Cambridge, UK: Polity Press.

———. 2012. "The Repudiations of Totalitarianisms by the Late Pius XI." In *Pius XI and America*. Edited by David Kertzer, Charles Gallagher, and Alberto Melloni, pp. 379–96. Berlin: LIT Verlag.

Federico, Giovanni. 2003. "Sanzioni." In *Dizionario del fascismo*. Edited by Victoria de Grazia and Sergio Luzzatto, pp. 2:590–92. Turin: Einaudi.

Ferrari, Ada. 1982. "Ildefonso Schuster." In *Dizionario storico del movimento cattolico in Italia*. Edited by Francesco Traniello and Giorgio Campanini, pp. 2:586–91. Milan: Marietti.

Ferrari, Francesco L. 1957. *L'Azione Cattolica e il "regime."* Florence: Parenti.

Festorazzi, Roberto. 2004. *Farinacci, l'antiduce*. Rome: Il Minotauro.

———. 2010. *Margherita Sarfatti*. Costabissara: Colla.

———. 2012. *Clara Petacci*. Bologna: Minerva.

Fiorentino, Carlo M. 1999. *All'ombra di Pietro: La Chiesa cattolica e lo spionaggio fascista in Vaticano, 1929–1939*. Florence: Le Lettere.

Fogarty, Gerald P. 1996. "Pius XI and the episcopate in the United States." In *Achille Ratti pape Pie XI: Actes du colloque organisé par l'École française de Rome, Rome 15–18 mars 1989*. Edited by Philippe Levillain, pp. 549–64. Rome: École française de Rome.

———. 2012. "The case of Charles Coughlin: The view from Rome." In *Pius XI and America*. Edited by David Kertzer, Charles Gallagher, and Alberto Melloni, pp. 107–28. Berlin: LIT Verlag.

Fonzi, Fausto. 1979. "Il colloquio tra Pio XI e Jacini il 25 marzo 1929." In *Chiesa e società dal IV secolo ai nostri giorni: Studi storici in onore del P. Ilarino da Milano*, pp. 2:651–79. Rome: Herder.

Fornari, Harry. 1971. *Mussolini's Gadfly: Roberto Farinacci*. Nashville, Tenn.: Vanderbilt University Press.

Franzinelli, Mimmo. 1995. *Stellette, croce e fascio littorio: L'assistenza religiosa a militari, balilla e camicie nere (1919–1939)*. Milan: F. Angeli.

———. 1998. *Il clero del duce/ il duce del clero: Il consenso ecclesiastico nelle lettere a Mussolini (1922–1945)*. Ragusa: La Fiacciola.

———. 2000. *I tentacoli dell'Ovra*. Turin: Bollati Boringhieri.

———. 2008. "Il clero italiano e la 'grande mobilitazione.'" In *L'impero fascista: Italia e Etiopia (1935-1941)*. Edited by Riccardo Bottoni, pp. 251-66. Bologna: Il Mulino.

Franzinelli, Mimmo, and Emanuele Marino. 2003. *Il duce proibito: Le fotografie di Mussolini che gli italiani non hanno mai visto*. Milan: Mondadori.

Galeotti, Carlo. 2000. *Mussolini ha sempre ragione: I decaloghi del fascismo*. Milan: Garzanti.

Gallagher, Charles R. 2008. *Vatican Secret Diplomacy: Joseph P. Hurley and Pope Pius XII*. New Haven, Conn.: Yale University Press.

Gallina, Giuseppe. 1979. "Il vescovo di Cremona Giovanni Cazzani e il suo atteggiamento di fronte al fascismo durante il pontificato di Pio XI." In *Chiesa, Azione Cattolica e Fascismo nell'Italia settentrionale durante il pontificato di Pio XI (1922-1939)*. Edited by Paolo Pecorari, pp. 505-25: Milan: Vita e Pensiero.

Gannon, Robert I. 1962. *The Cardinal Spellman Story*. Garden City, N.Y.: Doubleday.

Garzonio, Marco. 1996. *Schuster*. Casale Monferrato: Piemme.

Gentile, Emilio. 1993. *Il Culto del Littorio*. Rome: Laterza.

———. 1995. *La via italiana al totalitarismo: Il partito e lo stato nel regime fascista*. Rome: La Nuova Italia Scientifica.

———. 2002. *Fascismo, storia e interpretazione*. Rome: Laterza.

———. 2010. *Contro Cesare: Cristianesimo e totalitarianismo nell'epoca dei fascismi*. Milan: Feltrinelli.

Gibelli, Antonio. 2003. "Opera nazionale ballila." In *Dizionario del fascismo*, vol. 2. Edited by Victoria de Grazia and Sergio Luzzatto, pp. 67-71. Turin: Einaudi.

Gilbert, Martin. 1985. *The Holocaust: A History of the Jews of Europe During the Second World War*. New York: Henry Holt.

Gillette, Aaron. 2001. "The Origins of the 'Manifesto of Racial Scientists.'" *Journal of Modern Italian Studies* 6:305-23.

———. 2002a. *Racial Theories in Fascist Italy*. London: Routledge.

———. 2002b. "Guido Landra and the Office of Racial Studies in Fascist Italy." *Holocaust and Genocide Studies* 16:357-75.

Godman, Peter. 2004. *Hitler and the Vatican*. New York: Free Press.

Goetz, Helmut. 2000. (German orig., 1993). *Il giuramento rifiutato: I docenti universitari e il regime fascista*. Translated by Loredana Melissari. Milan: La Nuova Italia.

Grandi, Dino. 1985. *Il mio paese: Ricordi autobiografici*. Edited by Renzo De Felice. Bologna: Il Mulino.

Guasco, Alberto. 2010. "Un termine e le sue declinazioni: Chiesa cattolica e totalitarismi tra bibliografia e ricerca." In *Pius XI: Keywords*. Edited by Alberto Guasco and Raffaella Perin, pp. 91-106. Berlin: LIT Verlag.

———. 2013. "Tra segreteria di stato e regime fascista: Mons. Francesco Borgongini Duca e la nunziatura in Italia." In *Le gouvernement pontifical sous Pie XI: Pratiques romaines et gestion de l'universel*. Edited by Laura Pettinaroli. In preparation.

Hachey, Theodore. 1972. *Anglo-Vatican Relations, 1914-1939: Confidential Annual Reports of the British Ministers to the Holy See*. Boston: G. K. Hall.

Herf, Jeffrey. 2006. *The Jewish Enemy: Nazi Propaganda During World War II and the Holocaust*. Cambridge, Mass.: Harvard University Press.

Hermet, Guy. 1996. "Pie XI, la République espagnole e la guerre d'Espagne." In *Achille Ratti pape Pie XI: Actes du colloque organisé par l'École française de Rome, Rome 15-18 mars 1989*. Edited by Philippe Levillain, pp. 499-527. Rome: École française de Rome.

Hibbert, Christopher. 2008. *Mussolini: The Rise and Fall of Il Duce*. Basingstoke: Palgrave Macmillan.

Hilaire, Yves-Marie. 1996. "Le Saint-Siège et la France, 1923-1939: Charles-Roux, un ambassadeur de politique étrangère." In *Achille Ratti pape Pie XI: Actes du colloque organisé par l'École française de Rome, Rome 15-18 mars 1989*. Edited by Philippe Levillain, pp. 765–73. Rome: École française de Rome.

Ignesti, Giuseppe. 2004. "Jacini, Stefano." *Dizionario biografico degli italiani* 61:767–79.

Innocenti, Marco. 1992. *I gerarchi del fascismo: Storia del ventennio attraverso gli uomini del Duce*. Milan: Mursia.

Insolera, Italo. 1976. *Roma moderna*. Turin: Einaudi.

Israel, Giorgio. 2010. *Il fascismo e la razza: La scienza italiana e le politiche razziali del regime*. Bologna: Il Mulino.

Johnson, Eric A. 1999. *Nazi Terror: The Gestapo, Jews, and Ordinary Germans*. New York: Basic Books.

Kantowicz, Edward R. 1983. *Corporation Sole: Cardinal Mundelein and Chicago Catholicism*. Notre Dame: University of Notre Dame Press.

Kent, Peter C. 1981. *The Pope and the Duce: The International Impact of the Lateran Agreements*. London: Macmillan.

———. 1986. "The Vatican and the Spanish Civil War." *European History Quarterly* 16:441–64.

Kershaw, Ian. 1999. *Hitler: 1889-1936 Hubris*. New York: Norton.

———. 2000. *Hitler: 1936-1945 Nemesis*. New York: Norton.

Kertzer, David I. 1988. *Ritual, Politics, and Power*. New Haven, Conn.: Yale University Press.

———. 2001. *The Popes Against the Jews: The Vatican's Role in the Rise of Modern Anti-Semitism*. New York: Alfred A. Knopf.

———. 2004. *Prisoner of the Vatican: The Popes' Secret Plot to Capture Rome from the New Italian State*. Boston: Houghton Mifflin.

Kertzer, David I., and Alessandro Visani. 2012. "The United States, the Holy See and Italy's Racial Laws." In *Pius XI and America*. Edited by David Kertzer, Charles Gallagher, and Alberto Melloni, pp. 327–41. Berlin: LIT Verlag.

Lacroix-Riz, Annie. 1994. "Le rôle du Vatican dans la colonisation de l'Afrique (1920-1938): De la romanisation des missions à la conquête de l'Ethiopie." *Revue d'histoire moderne et contemporaine* 41:29–81.

Lamb, Richard. 1997. *Mussolini and the British*. London: John Murray.

Lazzarini, Luigi. 1937. *Pio XI*. Sesto San Giovanni: Edizioni Barion.

Ledóchowski, Włodzimierz. 1945. *Selected Writings of Father Ledochowski*. Chicago: American Assistancy of the Society of Jesus.

Levillain, Philippe. 1996. "Achille Ratti Pape Pie XI (1857-1939)." In *Achille Ratti pape Pie XI: Actes du colloque organisé par l'École française de Rome, Rome 15-18 mars 1989*. Edited by Philippe Levillain, pp. 5–13. Rome: École française de Rome.

Loiseau, Charles. 1960. "Ma mission auprès du Vatican (1914-1918)." *Revue d'histoire diplomatique* 74:2: 100–15.

Luconi, Stefano. 2000. *La "diplomazia parallela": Il regime fascista e la mobilitazione politica degli italo-americani*. Milan: Angeli.

———. 2004. "Fascist Antisemitism and Jewish-Italian Relations in the United States." *American Jewish Archives Journal* 56:151–77.

Ludwig, Emil. 1933. *Talks with Mussolini*. Boston: Little Brown.

Luzzatto, Sergio. 1998. *Il corpo del duce*. Turin: Einaudi.

———. 2010. *Padre Pio: Miracles and Politics in a Secular Age*. Translated by Frederika Randall. New York: Henry Holt.

Lyttleton, Adrian. 1987. *The Seizure of Power: Fascism in Italy 1919-1929*. 2nd ed. Princeton: Princeton University Press.

Mack Smith, Denis. 1982. *Mussolini*. New York: Vintage.

———. 1983. "Mussolini cent'anni dopo: quale eredità?" In *Mussolini, il Duce: Quattrocento immagini della vita di un uomo e di vent'anni di storia italiana.* Edited by Denis Mack Smith, pp. 5-10. Milan: Gruppo Editoriale Fabbri.

MacKinnon, Albert G. 1927. *Things Seen in Rome.* London: Seeley, Service & Co.

Maiocchi, Roberto. 2003. "Manifesto degli Scienziati razzisti." In *Dizionario del fascismo,* vol. 2. Edited by Victoria de Grazia and Sergio Luzzatto, pp. 87-88. Turin: Einaudi.

Malgeri, F. 1994. "Chiesa cattolica e regime fascista." *Italia contemporanea* 194:53-63.

Margiotta Broglio, F. 1966. *Italia e Santa Sede dalla grande guerra alla Conciliazione: Aspetti politici e giuridici.* Bari: Laterza.

Martin, Jacques. 1996. "Témoignage sur le pontificat de Pie XI." In *Achille Ratti pape Pie XI: Actes du colloque organisé par l'École française de Rome, Rome 15-18 mars 1989.* Edited by Philippe Levillain. Rome: École française de Rome.

Martina, Giacomo. 1978. *La Chiesa nell'età dell'assolutismo, del liberalismo, del totalitarismo,* vol. 4, *La chiesa nell'età del totaritarismo.* Brescia: Morcelliana.

———. 1996. "La mancata nomina cardinalizia del P. Tacchi Venturi. Relazione dell'interessato." *Archivium historicum Societatis Iesu* 129:101-9.

———. 2003. *Storia della Compagnia di Gesù in Italia (1814-1983).* Brescia: Morcelliana.

Martini, Angelo. 1960a. "Gli accordi per l'Azione Cattolica del 2 settembre 1931." *Civiltà cattolica* I, pp. 574-91.

———. 1960b. "Pietro Gasparri Cardinale della Conciliazione." *Civiltà cattolica* I, pp. 113-31.

———. 1963. "L'ultima battaglia di Pio XI." In *Studi sulla questione romana e la conciliazione.* Edited by Angelo Martini. Rome: Cinque Lune.

Maryks, Robert A. 2011. *Pouring Jewish Water into Fascist Wine.* Leiden: Brill.

———. 2012. "The Jesuit Pietro Tacchi Venturi and Mussolini's Racial Laws." In *Pius XI and America.* Edited by David Kertzer, Charles Gallagher, and Alberto Melloni. Berlin: LIT Verlag.

Matard-Bonucci, Marie-Anne. 2008. (French orig. 2007.) *L'Italia fascista e la persecuzione degli ebrei.* Translation by Andrea De Ritis. Bologna: Il Mulino.

McCormick, Anne. 1957. *Vatican Journal 1921-1954.* New York. Farrar, Straus and Cudahy.

Miccoli, Giovanni. 1973. "La Chiesa e il fascismo." In *Fascismo e società italiana.* Edited by Guido Quazza, pp. 185-208. Turin: Einaudi.

———. 1988. "Santa sede e chiesa italiana di fronte alle leggi antiebraiche del 1938." *Studi Storici* 29:821-902.

———. 2004. "Chiesa cattolica e totalitarismi." In *La Chiesa cattolica e il totalitarismo.* Edited by Vincenzo Ferrone, pp. 1-26. Florence: Olschki.

Micheler, Stefan. 2005. "Homophobic Propaganda and the Denunciation of Same-Sex-Desiring Men Under National Socialism." In *Sexuality and German Fascism.* Edited by Dagmar Herzog, pp. 95-130. New York and Oxford: Berghahn.

Milza, Pierre. 2000. (French orig. 1999.) *Mussolini.* Translated by Gian Carlo Brioschi and Filippo Scarpelli. Rome: Carocci.

Mockler, Anthony. 2003 [1984]. *Haile Selassie's War.* New York: Olive Branch Press.

Molony, John N. 1977. *The Emergence of Political Catholicism in Italy: Partito Popolare 1919-1926.* London: Croom Helm.

Monelli, Paolo. 1953. *Mussolini: An Intimate Life.* London: Thames and Hudson.

Morgan, Thomas B. 1939. *A Reporter at the Papal Court: A Narrative of the Reign of Pope Pius XI.* New York: Longmans, Green.

———. 1941. *Spurs on the Boot: Italy Under her Masters.* New York: Longmans, Green.

———. 1944. *The Listening Post: Eighteen Years on Vatican Hill.* New York: Putnam.

Moro, Renato. 1981. "Azione Cattolica, clero e laicato di fronte al fascismo." In *Storia del Movimento Cattolico in Italia,* vol. 4. Edited by Francesco Malgeri, pp. 87-378. Rome: Poligono.

——. 2003. "Cattolicesimo e italianità. Antiprotestantismo e antisemitismo nell'Italia cattolica." In *La Chiesa e l'Italia*. Edited by A. Acerbi, pp. 307–39. Milan: Vita e Pensiero.

——. 2005. "Religione del trascendente e religioni politiche: Il cattolicesimo italiano di fronte alla sacralizzazione fascista della politica." *Mondo contemporaneo* 1:9–67.

——. 2008. "Le chiese e la modernità totalitaria." In *Le religioni e il mondo moderno*, vol. 1, *Cristianesimo*. Edited by Giovanni Filoramo and Daniele Menozzi, pp. 418-51. Turin: Einaudi.

Morozzo della Rocca, Roberto. 1996. "Achille Ratti e la Polonia." In *Achille Ratti pape Pie XI: Actes du colloque organisé par l'École française de Rome, Rome 15–18 mars 1989*. Edited by Philippe Levillain, pp. 95–122. Rome: École française de Rome.

Moseley, Ray. 1999. *Mussolini's Shadow: The Double Life of Count Galeazzo Ciano*. New Haven, Conn.: Yale University Press.

Motti, Lucia. 2003. "Mussolini, Rachele." In *Dizionario del fascismo* vol. 2. Edited by Victoria de Grazia and Sergio Luzzatto, pp. 197–200. Turin: Einaudi.

Muggeridge, Malcolm, ed. 1948. *Ciano's Diplomatic Papers*. London: Odhams Press.

Mughini, Giampiero. 1991. *A Via della Mercede c'era un razzista: pittori e srittori in camicia nera . . . lo strano "caso" di Telesio Interlandi*. Milan. Rizzoli.

Muñoz, Antonio. 1942. "Ricordo del padre Ledóchowski." *L'Urbe* 7 (11–12): 2–7.

Mussolini, Benito. 1929. *Gli Accordi del Laterano*. Rome: Libreria del Littorio.

Mussolini, Edvige. 1957. *Mio fratello Benito*. Firenze: La Fenice.

Mussolini, Rachele. 1974. *Mussolini: An Intimate Biography by His Widow*, as told to Albert Zarca. New York: Morrow.

Mussolini, Romano. 2006 [2004]. *My Father, il Duce*. San Diego: Kales Press.

Nardelli, Fabio. 1996. *I periodici cattolici bolognesi e gli ebrei durante il periodo fascista*. Tesi, Università di Bologna, Facoltà di Scienze Politiche (relatore: Mauro Pesce).

Navarra, Quinto. 2004 [1946]. *Memorie del cameriere di Mussolini*. Naples: L'ancora del mediterraneo.

Nenovsky, Nikolay, Giovanni Pavanelli, and Kalina Dimitrova. 2007. "Exchange Rate Control in Italy and Bulgaria in the Interwar Period: History and Perspectives." Paper no. 13, Second Conference of the South-Eastern European Monetary History Network.

Nidam-Orvieto, Iael. 2005. "The Impact of Anti-Jewish Legislation on Everyday Life and the Response of Italian Jews, 1938–1943." In *Jews in Italy Under Fascist and Nazi Rule, 1922–1945*. Edited by Joshua D. Zimmerman, pp. 158–81. Cambridge: Cambridge University Press.

Nobili, Elena. 2008. "Vescovi lombardi e consenso alla guerra: il cardinale Schuster." In *L'impero fascista: Italia e Etiopia (1935-1941)*. Edited by Riccardo Bottoni, pp. 267–85. Bologna: Il Mulino.

Noel, Gerald. 2008. *Pius XII: The Hound of Hitler*. London: Continuum.

Onofri, Nazario Sauro. 1989. *Ebrei e fascismo a Bologna*. Crespellano (BO): Grafica Lavino.

O'Shea, Paul. 2011. *A Cross Too Heavy: Pope Pius XII and the Jews of Europe*. New York: Palgrave Macmillan.

Ojetti, Ugo. 1939. *Cose viste 1934-1938*, vol. 7. Milan: Mondadori.

Orlando, Vittorio Emanuele. 1937. *Rome v/s Rome: "A Chapter of My War Memoirs."* Translated by Clarence Beardslee. New York: Vanni.

Ottaviani, Alfredo. 1969. "Pio XI e i suoi Segretari di Stato." In *Pio XI nel trentesimo della morte (1939-1969): Raccolta di studi e di memorie*. Edited by Carlo Colombo, Ernesto Basadonna, Antonio Rimoldi, and Virginio Rovera, pp. 491–508. Milan: Opera diocesana per la preservazione e diffusione della fede.

Pacelli, Francesco. 1959. *Diario della Conciliazione: Con verbali ed appendice di documenti*. Edited by Michele Maccarrone. Vatican City: Libreria Editrice Vaticano.

Pagano, Sergio. 2009. "Dalla porpora al chiostro. L'inflessibilità di Pio XI verso il cardinale Louis Billot." In *La Papauté contemporaine, XIXe-XXe siècles—Il Papato contemporaneo, secoli XIX–XX: Hommage au chanoine Roger Aubert.* Edited by Roger Aubert, Jean-Pierre Delville, Marko Jačov, Luc Courtois, Françoise Rosart, and Guy Zelis, pp. 395–410. Louvain-la-Neuve-Leuven: Collège Érasme.

———. 2010. "Presentazione." In *I «Fogli di Udienza» del Cardinale Eugenio Pacelli Segretario di Stato.* Edited by Marcel Chappin, Giovanni Coco, and Sergio Pagano, pp. xi–xxv. Vatican City: Archivio Segreto Vaticano.

Painter, Borden. 2005. *Mussolini's Rome: Rebuilding the Eternal City.* New York: Palgrave Macmillan.

Papin, Chanoine. 1977. *Le dernier étage du Vatican: Témoignage de Pie XI à Paul VI.* Paris: Albatross.

Pardini, Giuseppe. 2007. *Roberto Farinacci ovvero della rivoluzione fascista.* Florence: Le Lettere.

Parola, Alessandro. 2003. "Epurare l'Università Cattolica? Il processo per filofascismo a carico di Agostino Gemelli." *Passato e presente* 21/60: 81–91.

Parsons, Gerald. 2008. "A National Saint in a Fascist State: Catherine of Siena ca. 1922–1943." *Journal of Religious History* 32:76–95.

Passelecq, Georges, and Bernard Suchecky. 1997. *The Hidden Encyclical of Pius XI.* Translated by Steven Rendall. New York: Harcourt Brace.

Pavan, Ilaria. 2010. "Fascismo, antisemitismo, razzismo. Un dibattito aperto." In *A settant'anni dalle leggi razziali.* Edited by Daniele Menozzi and Andrea Mariuzzo, pp. 31–52. Rome: Carocci.

Pease, Neal. 2009. *Rome's Most Faithful Daughter: The Catholic Church and Independent Poland, 1914–1939.* Athens: Ohio University Press.

Perin, Raffaella. 2010. "Pregiudizio antiebraico e antiprotestante: Alcuni riflessi sull'atteggiamento della chiesa verso il fascismo." In *Pius XI: Keywords.* Edited by Alberto Guasco and Raffaella Perin, pp. 147–62. Berlin: LIT Verlag.

———. 2011. "La Chiesa veneta e le minoranze religiose (1918–1939)." In *Chiesa cattolica e minoranze in Italia nella prima metà del Novecento.* Edited by Raffaella Perin, pp. 133–223. Rome: Viella.

Petacci, Clara. 2010. *Mussolini segreto: Diari 1932–1938.* Edited by Mauro Suttora. Milan: Biblioteca Universale Rizzoli.

———. 2011. *Verso il disastro: Mussolini in guerra: Diari 1939–1940.* Milan: Rizzoli.

Phillips, William. 1952. *Ventures in Diplomacy.* Boston: Beacon.

Picardi, Luigi. 1995. *Cattolici e fascismo nel Molise (1922–1943).* Rome: Edizioni Studium.

Pincus, Benjamin. 1988. *The Jews of the Soviet Union.* New York: Cambridge University Press.

Pirri, Pietro. 1960. "Per una storia del Card. Pietro Gasparri." In *Il cardinale Pietro Gasparri.* Edited by L. Fiorelli, pp. 31–61. Rome: Pontificia Università Lateranense.

Pizzuti, G. M. 1992. "Da Benedetto XV a Pio XI. Il Conclave del febbraio 1922 nel suo significato politico-religioso e nei suoi riflessi sulla storia d'Europa del ventesimo secolo." *Humanitas* 47:99–115.

Poggi, Gianfranco. 1967. *Catholic Action in Italy: The Sociology of a Sponsored Organization.* Stanford, Calif.: Stanford University Press.

Pollard, John F. 1985. *The Vatican and Italian Fascism, 1929–1932.* Cambridge: Cambridge University Press.

———. 1999. *The Unknown Pope: Benedict XV and the Pursuit of Peace.* London: Wellington House.

———. 2012. "American Catholics and the Financing of the Vatican in the Great Depression: Peter's Pence Payments (1935–1938)." In *Pius XI and America.* Edited by David Kertzer, Charles Gallagher, and Alberto Melloni, pp. 195–208. Berlin: LIT Verlag.

Potter, Olave. 1925. *The Colour of Rome.* With illustrations by Yoshio Markino. London: Chatto and Windus.

Presenti, Antonio. 1979. "I contrasti tra il fascismo e la Chiesa nella diocesi di Bergamo negli anni 1937–1938." In *Chiesa. Azione Cattolica e Fascismo nell'Italia settentrionale durante il pontificato di Pio Xi (1922–1939): Atti del quinto convegno di storia della chiesa, Torreglia, 25–27 marzo 1977.* Edited by Paolo Pecorari, pp. 535–63. Milan: Vita e Pensiero.

Prévotat, Jacques. 2001. *Les catholiques et l'Action Française: Histoire d'une condamnation 1899–1939.* Paris: Fayard.

Puricelli, Carlo. 1996. "Le radici brianzole di Pio XI." In *Achille Ratti pape Pie XI: Actes du colloque organisé par l'École française de Rome, Rome 15–18 mars 1989.* Edited by Philippe Levillain, pp. 25–52. Rome: École française de Rome.

Rafanelli, Leda. 1975. *Una donna e Mussolini.* Milan: Rizzoli.

Ranfagni, Paolo. 1975. *I clerico-fascisti: Le riviste dell'Università cattolica negli anni del regime.* Florence: Cooperativa editrice universitaria.

Ratti, Achille. 1923. *Climbs on Alpine Peaks.* Translated by J. Eaton. Boston: Houghton Mifflin.

Rauscher, Walter. 2004. (German orig. 2001.) *Hitler e Mussolini.* Translated by Loredana Battaglia and Maria Elena Benemerito. Rome: Newton and Compton.

Reese, Thomas J. 1996. *Inside the Vatican: The Politics and Organization of the Catholic Church.* Cambridge, Mass.: Harvard University Press.

Reineri, Mariangiola. 1978. *Cattolici e fascismo a Torino 1925–1943.* Milan: Feltrinelli.

Rhodes, Anthony. 1974. *The Vatican in the Age of the Dictators, 1922–1945.* New York: Holt, Rinehart and Winston.

Riccardi, Andrea. 1982. "Tardini, Domenico." In *Dizionario storico del movimento cattolico in Italia, 1860–1980.* Edited by Francesco Traniello and Giorgio Campani, vol. 3. Casale Monferrato: Marieti.

———. 1996. "Pio XI e l'episcopato italiano." In *Achille Ratti pape Pie XI: Actes du colloque organisé par l'École française de Rome, Rome 15–18 mars 1989.* Edited by Philippe Levillain, pp. 529–48. Rome: École française de Rome.

Rigano, Gabriele. 2008. "Note sull'antisemitismo in Italia prima del 1938." *Storiografia* 12:215–67.

Roberti, Francesco. 1960. "Il Cardinal Pietro Gasparri—L'uomo—Il sacerdote—Il diplomatico—Il giurista." In *Miscellanea in memoriam Petri Card. Gasparri.* Pp. 5–43. Rome: Pontificia Universitas Lateranensis.

Rochat, Giorgio. 1990. *Regime fascista e chiese evangeliche: Direttive e articolazioni del controllo e della repressione.* Turin: Claudiana.

Rogari, Sandro. 1977. *La Santa Sede e fascismo dall'Aventino ai Patti lateranensi.* Bologna: Forni.

Romersa, Luigi. 1983. "Premessa" and "Conclusione." In Cesare De Vecchi, *Il Quadrumviro scomodo.* Edited by Luigi Romersa, pp. 5–13, 265–73. Milan: Mursia.

Rumi, Giorgio, and Angelo Majo. 1996. *Il cardinal Schuster e il suo tempo.* 2nd ed. Milan: Massimo-NED.

Ruysschaert, José. 1996. "Pie XI, un bibliothécaire devenu pape et resté bibliothécaire." In *Achille Ratti pape Pie XI: Actes du colloque organisé par l'École française de Rome, Rome 15–18 mars 1989.* Edited by Philippe Levillain, pp. 245–53. Rome: École française de Rome.

Sale, Giovanni. 2007. *Fascismo e Vaticano prima della Conciliazione.* Milan: Jaca Books.

———. 2009. *Le leggi razziali in Italia e il Vaticano.* Milan: Jaca Books.

Salvatorelli, Luigi. 1939. *Pio XI e la sua eredità pontificale.* Turin: Einaudi.

Santarelli, Enzo. 1991. "De Vecchi, Cesare Maria." *Dizionario biografico degli italiani* 39:522–31.

Saresella, Daniela. 1990. "Le riviste cattoliche italiane di fronte alla guerra d'Etiopia." *Rivista di storia contemporanea* 19:447–464.

Sarfatti, Michele. 2005. *La Shoah in Italia: La persecuzione degli ebrei sotto il fascismo.* Turin: Einaudi.

————. 2006. *Gli ebrei nell'Italia fascista.* Turin: Einaudi.

Scaduto, Mario. 1956. "Il P. Pietro Tacchi Venturi, 1861–1956." *Civiltà cattolica* II, pp. 47–57.

Schad, Martha. 2008. *La signora del Sacro Palazzo: Suor Pascalina e Pio XII.* Cinisello Balsamo: San Paolo.

Scoppola, Pietro. 1976. *La Chiesa e il fascismo: Documenti e interpretazioni.* Bari: Editori Laterza.

————. 1966. "La Chiesa e il fascismo durante il pontificato di Pio XI." In *Coscienza religiosa e democrazia nell'Italia contemporanea.* Edited by Pietro Scoppola, pp. 362–418. Bologna: Il Mulino.

Seldes, George. 1935. *Sawdust Caesar: The Untold History of Mussolini and Fascism.* New York: Harper.

Spadolini, Giovanni, ed. 1972. *Il cardinale. Gasparri e la questione romana, con brani delle memorie inedite.* Florence: Le Monnier.

Spini, Giorgio. 2007. *Italia di Mussolini e protestanti.* Preface by Carlo Azeglio Ciampi. Edited by Stefano Gagliano. Turin: Claudiana.

Starr, Joshua. 1939. "Italy's Antisemites." *Jewish Social Studies* 1:105–24.

Steigmann-Gall, Richard. 2003. *The Holy Reich: Nazi Conceptions of Christianity, 1919–1945.* Cambridge: Cambridge University Press.

Sturzo, Luigi. 1926. *Italy and Fascism.* Translated by Barbara Carter. New York: Harcourt.

Talbot, George. 2007. *Censorship in Fascist Italy, 1922–1943.* New York: Palgrave Macmillan.

Tardini, Domenico. 1988. "Diario Inedito (1933–1936)." In *Domenico Tardini, 1888–1961: L'azione della Santa Sede nella crisi fra le due guerre.* Edited by Carlo Felice Casula, pp. 291–390. Rome: Studium.

Terhoeven, Petra. 2006. *Oro alla patria: Donne, guerra e propaganda nella giornata della fede fascista.* Bologna: Il Mulino.

Tisserant, Eugène. 1939. "Pius XI as Librarian." *Library Quarterly* 9:389–403.

Tornielli, Andrea. 2007. *Pio XII: Eugenio Pacelli, un uomo sul trono di Pietro.* Milan: Mondadori.

Toschi, Umberto. 1931. "The Vatican City State from the Standpoint of Political Geography." *Geographical Review* 21:529–38.

Tramontin, Silvio. 1982. "Pietro Tacchi-Venturi." In *Dizionario storico del movimento cattolico in Italia,* vol. 2. Edited by Francesco Tranello and Giorgio Canpanini, pp. 631–33. Milan: Marietti.

Tranfaglia, Nicola. 2005. *La stampa del regime 1932–1943: Le veline del Minculpop per orientare l'informazione.* Milan: Bompiani.

Trisco, Robert. 2012. "The Holy See and Cardinal Mundelein's Insult of Hitler (1937)." In *Pius XI and America.* Edited by David Kertzer, Charles Gallagher, and Alberto Melloni, pp. 155–94. Berlin: LIT Verlag.

Tronel, Jacky. 2007. "Magda Fontages, maîtresse du Duce, écrouée à Mauzac (Dordogne)." *Arkheia, Revue d'histoire,* pp. 17–18.

Turi, Gabriele. 2002. *Il mecenate, il filosofo e il gesuita.* Bologna: Il Mulino.

Urso, Simona. 2003. *Margherita Sarfatti: Da mito del dux al mito americano.* Venice: Marsilio.

Vavasseur-Desperriers, Jean. 1996. "La presse française à l'avant-veille du Conclave (24–28 janvier 1922)." In *Achille Ratti pape Pie XI: Actes du colloque organisé par l'École française de Rome, Rome 15–18 mars 1989.* Edited by Philippe Levillain, pp. 125–45. Rome: École française de Rome.

Vecchio, Giorgio. 1996. "Achille Ratti, il movimento cattolico, lo stato liberale." In *Achille Ratti pape Pie XI: Actes du colloque organisé par l'École française de Rome, Rome 15–18 mars 1989.* Edited by Philippe Levillain, pp. 69–88. Rome: École française de Rome.

Venini, Diego. 2004. *Venini, collaboratore di Pio il Grande: Diari 1923–1939.* Edited by Franco Cajani. Milan: GR Edizioni.

Ventresca, Robert A. 2012. "Irreconcilable Differences? Pius XI, Eugenio Pacelli, and Italian Fascism from the Ethiopian Crisis to the Racial Laws." In *Pius XI and America*. Edited by David Kertzer, Charles Gallagher, and Alberto Melloni, pp. 285–302. Berlin: LIT Verlag.

———. 2013. *Soldier of Christ: The Life of Pope Pius XII*. Cambridge, Mass.: Harvard University Press.

Verucci, Guido. 1988. *La Chiesa nella società contemporanea*. Bari: Laterza.

Vian, Giovanni. 2011. "La Santa Sede e la massoneria durante il pontificato di Pio XI." In *Chiesa cattolica e minoranze in Italia nella prima metà del Novecento*. Edited by Raffaella Perin, pp. 105–32. Rome: Viella.

Vivarelli, Roberto. 2009. "Le leggi razziali nella storia del fascismo italiano." *Rivista storica italiana* 121:738–72.

Von Bülow, Bernhard. 2007. *Memoirs of Prince Von Bulow*. Edited by Geoffrey Dunlop. Wilmington, Ohio: Frazer Press.

Wilk, Stanislaus, ed. 1995–2000. *Achille Ratti (1918–1921), Acta Nuntiaturae Polonae*. Tomus 57, vols. 1–6. Rome: Institutum Historicum Polonicum.

Wolf, Hubert. 2010. *The Pope and the Devil*. Translated by Kenneth Kronenberg. Cambridge, Mass.: Harvard University Press.

Wolff, Richard J. 1985. "Giovanni Battista Montini and Italian Politics, 1897–1933: The Early Life of Pope Paul VI." *Catholic Historical Review* 71:228–247.

Zambarbieri, Annibale. 1982a. "Buonaiuti, Ernesto." In *Dizionario storico del movimento cattolico in Italia 1860–1980*, vol. 2. Edited by Francesco Traniello and Giorgio Campanini, pp. 58–66. Milan: Marietti.

———. 1982b. "Colombo, Luigi." In *Dizionario storico del movimento cattolico in Italia 1860–1980*, vol. 2. Edited by Francesco Traniello and Giorgio Campanini, pp. 112–17. Milan: Marietti.

PHOTOGRAPH CREDITS

250   *L'Illustrazione Italiana,* March 5, 1939.

267   Su concessione del Ministero per i Beni e le attività culturali, Archivio Centrale dello Stato, Fototeca, PNF, Ufficio propaganda, Attività del Duce, 1937.

269   *L'Illustrazione Italiana,* November 7, 1937.

270   Su concessione del Ministero per i Beni e le attività culturali, Archivio Centrale dello Stato, Fototeca, PNF, Ufficio propaganda, Attività del Duce, 1937.

273   *L'Illustrazione Italiana,* March 6, 1938.

274   Su concessione del Ministero per i Beni e le attività culturali, Archivio Centrale dello Stato, Fototeca, PNF, Ufficio propaganda, Attività del Duce, 1934.

279   *L'Illustrazione Italiana,* April 17, 1938.

281   Istituto Luce, Gestione Archivi Alinari, Firenze.

284   Raccolte Museali Fratelli Alinari (RMFA), Firenze.

295   Keystone/ Hulton Archive/ Getty Images.

299   Reproduced with the permission of the Archivio Famiglia Pignatti Morano.

318   Su concessione del Ministero per i Beni e le attività culturali, Archivio Centrale dello Stato, Fototeca, PNF, Ufficio propaganda, Attività del Duce, 1938.

326   Mondadori/ Mondadori/Getty Images.

346   *La Difesa della Razza,* November 20, 1939.

372   *L'Illustrazione Italiana,* February 19, 1939.

380   Stringer/Hulton Archive/ Getty Images.

386   *L'Illustrazione Italiana,* March 12, 1939.

INDEX

DAVID I. KERTZER is the Paul Dupee, Jr. University Professor of Social Science and professor of anthropology and Italian studies at Brown University, where he served as provost from 2006 to 2011. He is the author of ten previous books, including *The Popes Against the Jews,* which was a finalist for the Mark Lynton History Prize, and *The Kidnapping of Edgardo Mortara,* which was a finalist for the National Book Award. He has twice been awarded the Marraro Prize from the Society for Italian Historical Studies for the best work on Italian history. He and his wife, Susan, live in Providence.

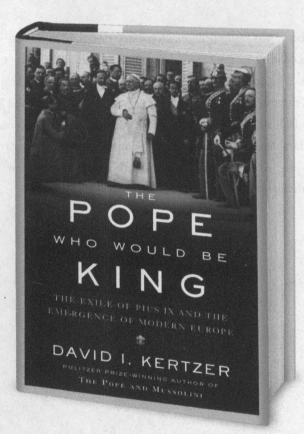